THE SWAY OF THE GRAND SALOON

BOOKS BY JOHN MALCOLM BRINNIN

POEMS

The Garden Is Political
The Lincoln Lyrics
No Arch, No Triumph
The Sorrows of Cold Stone
The Selected Poems of John Malcolm Brinnin
Skin Diving in the Virgins

BIOGRAPHY

Dylan Thomas in America
The Third Rose: Gertrude Stein and Her World

HISTORY

The Sway of the Grand Saloon

CRITICISM

Emily Dickinson, *a selection of poems*
Casebook on Dylan Thomas, *a collection of essays*
William Carlos Williams, *a critical study*
Selected Plays of Gertrude Stein

ANTHOLOGIES

Modern Poetry: American and British (*with Kimon Friar*)
The Modern Poets:
An American-British Anthology (*with Bill Read*)

FOR CHILDREN

Arthur, The Dolphin Who Didn't See Venice

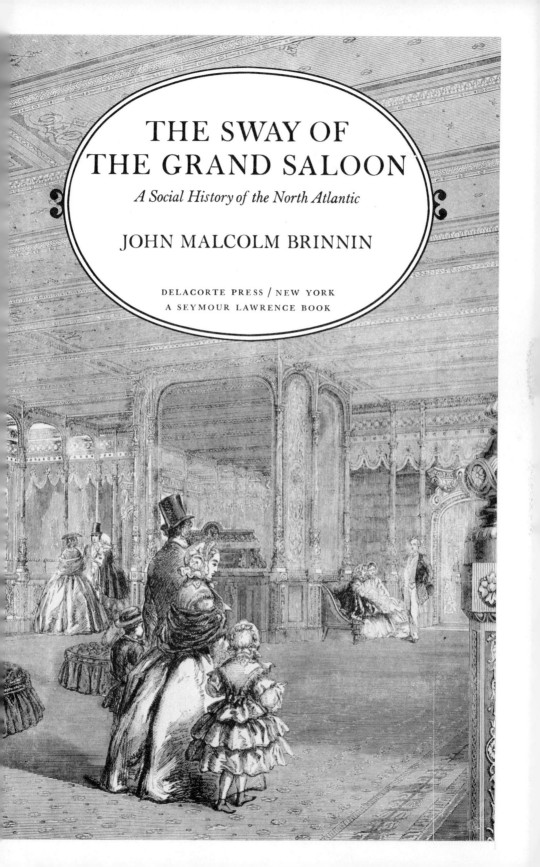

THE SWAY OF
THE GRAND SALOON

A Social History of the North Atlantic

JOHN MALCOLM BRINNIN

DELACORTE PRESS / NEW YORK
A SEYMOUR LAWRENCE BOOK

✸ ACKNOWLEDGMENTS ✸

Grateful acknowledgment is made to the following for permission to reprint from copyrighted material:

Doubleday & Company, Inc., for excerpts from THE BIG SPENDERS by Lucius Beebe; copyright © 1966 by Doubleday & Company, Inc., copyright © 1966 by Lucius Beebe, copyright © 1965 by HMH Publishing Co., Inc. Reprinted by permission.

Funk & Wagnalls, for excerpts from ETIQUETTE by Emily Post, 1922 edition; copyright © 1969 by Emily Post Institute. Reprinted by permission.

Harcourt Brace Jovanovich, Inc., for excerpts from SELECTED LETTERS OF E. E. CUMMINGS, edited by F. W. Dupee and George Stade; copyright © 1969 by Marion Morehouse Cummings. Reprinted by permission.

Harper & Row, Publishers, for excerpts from THE INNOCENTS ABROAD, Vol. II (Miss. Ed.) by Mark Twain, and Abridgement of pp. 470-472, 485-486, "The Modern Steamer and the Obsolete Steamer" from THE AMERICAN CLAIMANT AND OTHER STORIES (Author's National Ed.) by Mark Twain. Reprinted by permission.

Houghton Mifflin Company, for excerpts from TO BE YOUNG WAS VERY HEAVEN by Marion Lawrence Peabody and from "Crossing the Atlantic" from LIVE OR DIE by Anne Sexton. Reprinted by permission.

The Macmillan Company, The Macmillan Company of Canada Limited, and Macmillan & Company, Ltd., for "The Convergence of the Twain" from COLLECTED POEMS by Thomas Hardy. Reprinted by permission.

The Society of Authors as the Literary Representative of the Estate of John Masefield, and *The Times* (London), for lines from John Masefield's poem for the launching of the Queen Mary.

Wesleyan University Press, for lines from "Epigoni Go French Line" from WATCHBOY, WHAT OF THE NIGHT? by Turner Cassidy, Middletown, Conn.: Wesleyan University Press, 1966. Reprinted by permission.

The picture on the title page is from London Illustrated News, 1859.   1. Radio Times Hulton Picture Library (London)   2. Archives of the Province of Nova Scotia   5. Press Association Photos, Ltd.   6. *Illustrated London News*, 1859   9. Radio Times Hulton Picture Library (London)   10. Radio Times Hulton Picture Library (London)   11. Radio Times Hulton Picture Library (London)   12. Radio Times Hulton Picture Library (London)   13. *Illustrated London News*, 1859   15. Peabody Museum, Salem, Massachusetts; Markham W. Sexton, Staff Photographer, Margene M. Bishop, Photographer Assistant   16. Peabody Museum, Salem, Massachusetts; Markham W. Sexton, Staff Photographer, Margene M. Bishop, Photographer Assistant   17. *Illustrated London News*, 1888   18. *Illustrated London News*, 1881   19. *The Graphic Magazine*, 1850's (out of circulation)   23 (top). Radio Times Hulton Picture Library (London)   24. Peabody Museum, Salem, Massachusetts; Markham W. Sexton, Staff Photographer, Margene M. Bishop, Photographer Assistant   25. Peabody Museum, Salem, Massachusetts; Markham W. Sexton, Staff Photographer, Margene M. Bishop, Photographer Assistant   26. Cunard Lines, Ltd.   28. Radio Times Hulton Picture Library (London)   29. Cunard Lines, Ltd.   30. Radio Times Hulton Picture Library (London)   31. Radio Times Hulton Picture Library (London)   32. Frank O. Braynard   33. Peabody Museum, Salem, Massachusetts; Markham W. Sexton, Staff Photographer, Margene M. Bishop, Photographer Assistant   34. Peabody Museum, Salem, Massachusetts; Markham W. Sexton, Staff Photographer, Margene M. Bishop, Photographer Assistant   35. Peabody Museum, Salem, Massachusetts; Markham W. Sexton, Staff Photographer, Margene M. Bishop, Photographer Assistant   36. Cunard Lines, Ltd.   37. Cunard Lines, Ltd.   38. Cunard Lines, Ltd.   39. Radio Times Hulton Picture Library (London)   40. (both photos) Cunard Lines, Ltd.   41. Peabody Museum, Salem, Massachusetts; Markham W. Sexton, Staff Photographer, Margene M. Bishop, Photographer Assistant   42. Peabody Museum, Salem, Massachusetts; Markham W. Sexton, Staff Photographer, Margene M. Bishop, Photographer Assistant   43. Radio Times Hulton Picture Library (London)   44. Peabody Museum, Salem, Massachusetts; Markham W. Sexton, Staff Photographer, Margene M. Bishop, Photographer Assistant   45. Peabody Museum, Salem, Massachusetts; Markham W. Sexton, Staff Photographer, Margene M. Bishop, Photographer Assistant   46. Peabody Museum, Salem, Massachusetts; Markham W. Sexton, Staff Photographer, Margene M. Bishop, Photographer Assistant   47. Cunard Lines, Ltd.   48. Steamship Historical Society of America   49 (top). Peabody Museum, Salem, Massachusetts; Markham W. Sexton, Staff Photographer, Margene M. Bishop, Photographer Assistant   49 (bottom). Peabody Museum, Salem, Massachusetts; Markham W. Sexton, Staff Photographer, Margene M. Bishop, Photographer Assistant   50. *Illustrated London News*   51. Steamship Historical Society of America   52. Radio Times Hulton Picture Library (London)   53. Drawing by Garrett Price; Copr. 1953, The New Yorker Magazine, Inc.   54. United States Lines   55. Cunard Lines, Ltd.

FOR
JACK THOMPSON
OF COLUMBIA, MISSOURI,
WHO PIPED ME ABOARD

✂ AUTHOR'S PREFACE ✂

NOT LONG AGO I boarded the rubber duck of a ferryboat that crosses Halifax Harbor, got off on the Dartmouth side and stepped forty years back into a neighborhood I used to know. The yellow enameled mansion with its white balusters and finials that once topped our hillside like a flourish of pastry is now a lusterless gray tenement house. On the little plateau in front, where neat lawns used to be, and blazing dahlia beds, four building-block cottages are crowded together with just enough space between to allow cats' cradles of laundry to lift and sag in the brutally changeable Nova Scotia weather. But "our" modest clapboard house (it belonged to my great-uncle—an embittered, teetotalling old salt who once skippered workaday coasting schooners laden with dried cod, molasses and lumber) is still more or less as it was—except that the clapboard is now sheathed with synthetic brick—and so is the room high over the Harbor where I probably felt the first subliminal impulse leading to this book.

Nearly all of my "good" early memories are somehow involved with the sounds and smells of the Atlantic Ocean—especially with the ragged industrial margins of it. By the time I was ten, these feelings may have been sharpened by the fact that for the greater part of every year I lived on a macadam sidestreet on the treeless plains of "outer" Detroit. But my hunger for the sea—even then, it was as real as that—must have had its source in some genetic disposition, passed on to me by chance, then encouraged by everything in sight. That big gloomy oil painting of a Cunard liner of the 1870s, for instance. Its frilled black waves and clouds lined with lightning hung like a permanent storm in the entrance hall of our Dartmouth house, and fascinated me like sin. Yet the point of it was merely to remind us that another great-uncle—the one from New Brunswick—had served on that very ship as First Engineer. Then, family legend had it, there was the case of my mother's grandfather: for months from his sickroom the old man had watched his beloved brig *Belle* gradually sinking in a tidal backwater; and when she finally went under for good, within the hour so did he. Everyone we knew had something to do with the ocean. In the house behind ours sad, half-crazed "Flo" Gilson came and went in a dream of days she could neither separate nor remember; while her husband, the mild-mannered Captain Gilson, seemed like Ulysses always to be on his way home, forever returning from still another supply-ship run "up Hudson Bay." In the house across from ours lived Mr. Roue, designer of the fishing schooner *Bluenose*, the pride of the Maritimes. Time and again, this elegant little craft would outrun the swiftest racer that the fishermen of Gloucester, Massachusetts, could put into the water against her. From my window I could see the actual spot where Samuel Cunard was born, the docks from which his very first vessels had cast off for Bermuda and Newfoundland. When I awoke in the morning, just by noting which of the regular liners from Liverpool or Boston was berthed at Pier Nine I could tell what day of the week it was.

Yet, long before I realized how the trivia of circumstance had shaped my thoughts, something had caused me to be fascinated by ships and by all the meanings of what the Bible terms their "business in great waters." When I was still an infant, my greatest excitement, according to my parents, was the sight of White Star's peerless *Olympic* being pushed by tugboats toward her wartime berth. The first word I ever spoke, they told me, sounded very much like the syllables of her name— or at least the final two of them. And when I was old enough to be led by the hand down Barrington Street and alongside the little cemetery that stands at the corner of Spring Garden Road, I felt a touch of awe I can still remember as my mother told me that those "new" rows of headstones belonged to people who had drowned in the *Titanic*.

Whatever the promptings, steamships and their movements became an almost obsessive interest, endlessly open and every day renewed. Nothing ever interested me as much until I came to adolescence and discovered poems and novels that put me at once into a condition I would describe as passionate bewilderment. For the next several years, until my father died and we no longer went to Nova Scotia for the summer, I would sit in my room-with-a-view, one eye on Hart Crane and Virginia Woolf, Nathanael West and Gerard Manley Hopkins, Djuna Barnes and William Carlos Williams—the other eye on the *Berengaria*. As morning sun burned through the mist around the Ocean Terminal to reveal her three vast buff-and-black funnels, there the great ship would stand, idly smoking, imperial, remote—a whole floating city from Europe that would stay a few hours, conclude its business with a ritual of bells, sloshings and whistles, then slide, grandly impervious, back to sea.

Such are my fancies of this book's beginnings; yet I suspect I wrote it simply because I wanted to read it. Every account of the steamship era I could find dealt, ponderously, with economics and engineering or, sensationally, with Blue Ribands, shipwrecks, holocausts at sea—to the exclusion of just the factors which seemed to me to be the most significant. These factors involved, above all, the human element—the day-to-day experience of the millions of people who had crossed the ocean, along with the idea that the passenger ship on the Great Circle route between the Old World and the New was a kind of traveling metaphor reflecting society and indicating the nature of social change.

To tell my version of this story I have had to depend on everyone—historians, chroniclers, obscure letter writers, diarists, counting house clerks, biographers, retired captains, public relations officers, shipbuilders in Glasgow, shipowners in Liverpool, keepers of archives and lyricists of disaster. Through lack of care, or out of ignorance—sometimes out of an irresistible but falsifying sense of "drama"—many of these individuals have dealt in errors, errors often institutionalized and thus preserved for a hundred years. In a number of instances I have tried to locate the source of long-lived mistakes, to correct, explain, or at least to modify them. Such an undertaking has its perils. If, in the course of it, I have made new mistakes, I hope they will not stand for long. To say that I have scrutinized books, records and manuscripts in the Library of Congress and in the British Museum; in Kingston, Jamaica, and in Cardross, Scotland; in Leningrad and Paramaribo, may suggest the breadth of my inquiry. Yet nothing, alas, guarantees even the most avid and wide-ranging eye against its own kinds of waywardness.

Research into this history has for years kept me preoccupied, in a conventional way, with its "materials." Yet I have also been continually beguiled. How does one finally account for a dog-eat-dog business that has managed for more than a century to maintain itself as a public romance? Long since, the Atlantic Ocean has shrunk to the size of a pond; in the wide lens of the mind's eye, Cunard's primitive paddle-wheeled *Britannia* and Cunard's computer-guided *Queen Elizabeth 2* sit ever more closely and congenially side by side. How does one account for a phenomenon that is, at once, both a matter of living memory and of ancient history?

Now that there is nothing further to read, nowhere else to go in pursuit of still another diminutive fact or extenuating circumstance, I must finally and reluctantly give over a long labor of love. As I do, I want to cite, in gratitude and a sense almost of endearment, those marine historians, living and dead, to whom I am most beholden. Their aims were limited, their facts hard, their statistics sober. How surprised they would be to know that, to at least one of their readers, they spoke like archangels. Their names are Robert G. Albion, N. R. P. Bonsor, Frank C. Bowen, Frank O. Braynard, E. Keble Chatterton, Carl C. Cutler, R. A. Fletcher, C. R. Vernon Gibbs, George C. V. Holmes, J. H. Isherwood, G. H. Preble, H. P. Spratt, Frederick A. Talbot, Warren Tute, David Budlong Tyler.

To other individuals I am indebted for substantial help and small but useful contributions. Some of them will remember that they made me a gift of an old passenger list, a faded menu or a mildewed pamphlet; others will not even be aware that they provided me with a lucky clue, a pretty line or, on more than one occasion, an insight that would find its way into the following pages. Whether they believe it or not, I owe thanks to William Abrahams, Jon Bannenberg, Millicent Bell, Margene Bishop, Frank Bustard, Tram Combs, George Danforth, Leonard F. Dean, Patricia Dunn, Bruce Fergusson, Robert Fetridge, Gerald Fitzgerald, James Gardner, Leslie N. Gay, Victor Glasstone, Frederick Hill, Jack Jackson, Melvin R. Jackson, Tom Kameen, Donald Kelly, Dennis Lennon, Douglas Lobley, Richard Ludwig, Geoffrey Thrippleton Marr, David McKain, Rollie McKenna, David McKibbon, John McTernan, Edward Mitchell, Charles Morton, Howard Moss, Ellis Napier, Leslie Newell, Colin Norton-Smith, George O'Reilly, Fergus Pritchard, John Rannie, Basil Rauch, Bill Read, Marc Schuster, James Scully, D. H. Shimmin, John Smith, Frances Smythe, Peter Stansky, Holly Stevens, Jon Thompson, William Vance, Dan Wallace, Rex Warner, Richard Wilbur, James Wilkie, Reg Young.

❧ CONTENTS ❧

PART ONE: BEGINNINGS (1818-1838)

PART TWO: ASCENDANCY (1839-1889)

PART THREE: APOGEE (1890-1919)

PART FOUR: THE LONG WAKE (1920-1968)

Photo sections follow pages 170, 330, and 490.

PART ONE

BEGINNINGS
1818-1838

❧ SECTION I ❧

Departure of the First Scheduled Atlantic Carrier / Aristocrat and Lumpenproletariat *at Sea / The Blackballing of William Cobbett / The Yankee Skippers: Autocrats of the Groaning Board / Alexis de Tocqueville Tells His Mother / Tyrone Power Takes a Bath / Harriet Martineau Becalmed / Ralph Waldo Emerson Disoriented / The Packet* Yorkshire *Transports P. T. Barnum and General Tom Thumb / The American Mercantile Navy: "Eyewash" and Trumpery*

J ANUARY 5, 1818. A small blizzard, skittering down Broadway, suddenly envelops that "immense pile" of red brick, five stories high, known as the City Hotel, then blusters on toward the tip of Manhattan and out across the harbor. In spite of the tricky weather, people have been crowding into the hotel's Ordinary for breakfast—poached bloaters, spitchcocked eel, "Fine Green Turtle"—since well before dawn. Among the guests checking out this cold morning are two men in stovepipe hats bound for Europe—John Large from Philadelphia, Daniel Fisher from Montreal—and they are in a hurry. For the first time in history, a man who dawdles is apt to miss the boat.

Mirrors in the lobby catch their reflections, marble floors echo the click of their heels as they follow their luggage through a winter garden of potted palms and Boston ferns. When they see that their bags are firmly roped down on the roof of the waiting hackney, they get in and tell their driver to head for "Packet Row." This is the name of a stretch of docks, jutting bowsprits and bobbing masts along the waterfront between Wall Street and Maiden Lane. The cobblestones of South Street rumble as the carriage weaves through a bundled-up as-

3

sortment of orange-women, street musicians, tinkers and pedlars mill-
ing around Pier 23, East River, and pulls up at the end of a narrow
wooden gangplank. Here, taut and whistling, her black hull shining
like newly poured tar, her flush-deck superstructure studded with brass,
lies the tall packet *James Monroe*. Her house flag—a square banner of
crimson with a jet-black disc the size of a cannonball in its center—
signals the fact that she belongs to the Black Ball Line. A big black
moon inked on her fore topsail, just below the close-reef band, confirms it.

A new vessel of 424 tons, two decks and three masts, she has been
designed to make money and she is about to make history. In a new
age of ships, she will be a pioneer—the first packet to sail, sun or
snow, "full or not full," on the very day her owners have said she
would sail.

They have offered accommodations "extensive and commodious,"
and they mean it. The days of the floating dungeons—the notorious
"coffin brigs"—are numbered. The *James Monroe* is not only a trig
cargo vessel but also a sea-going hostelry. In her saloon, slabs of
Egyptian porphyry support a decoratively carved arch, chairs with
seats of black haircloth range the length of a gleaming mahogany table.
Her "sleeping closets"—or staterooms, as they are just beginning to
be called—are all of seven feet square, paneled in satinwood. Over the
entrance to each one is an arch held up by pillars of pure white Carrara marble.

As announced in the papers, the regard of the *James Monroe* for the
comfort and convenience of passengers is "studious." Although her first
voyagers will sleep in creaking boxes on hair mattresses, this is still
great improvement over the lumpish sacks filled with scratchy straw,
paillasses known as "the donkey's breakfast" which, up to now, have
served. For most of a month, her passengers will have to put up with
the dismal light of sputtering candles extinguished by a steward whenever the captain says so, with water jugs rattling and swaying, with
mere crockery birdbaths for all of their ablutions, and with triple-
duty *pots de chambres* in little closets on the floor. But at least the
essential *pots* are now rimmed with gold and printed with pretty sprawls
of forget-me-nots.

As for food, they can look forward to bread baked daily, and meat
on the hoof. Inside a housed-over longboat on deck stand shivering
sheep and pigs. On the top of this boat, egg-laying hens peek and

squawk through the slats of wooden coops. Nearby, over the main hatch, two miserable but obliging cows stare from the half-door of a rickety sea-going barn. Aiming to please, the packet ship offers a traveler the first improvements in comfort afloat since the *Mayflower*. Suggesting even greater ease and amenity, these improvements have already set up an insatiable demand. In the course of the century, this demand will be answered by brilliant mechanical innovations, whimsical experiments and sybaritic excesses. It will lead to the technological sophistication of the lean thrusting lines of the ocean greyhound; it will also produce the baronially bloated appointments of the floating palace.

At the last minute, just as the rawhide mailbags from the Tontine Coffee House at the corner of Wall and Water Streets are being handed aboard, the bells of St. Paul's, six blocks away, ring ten o'clock. Standing on his paddle box like a bridegroom on a wedding cake, Captain James Watkinson gives orders to cast off. Snow is still falling as the *James Monroe* trembles into midstream and steers for the lower harbor. To shake the canvas out of its gaskets, men in the rigging have to use their bare hands to plow away deposits of snow. Driven hard, the pioneering packet ship will take Messrs. Large and Fisher and six other gentlemen passengers—along with apples in barrels, flour, cranberries, hops, ashes, bales of cotton and wool—to Liverpool via St. Patrick's Channel and a stop to discharge a passenger at Mul Galloway, Scotland, in twenty-eight days on a "downhill' run that has often stretched out to sixty. On the way over she will pass one of her three Black Ball running mates —the *Courier*, carrying five men in her cabin "in addition to a Mrs. Tring, the first woman packet passenger," seven other passengers in steerage and hundreds of cases of British woolens. Inauspiciously out of the King's Dock, Liverpool, three days late because of a northwest wind that all but closed the port, the 380-ton *Courier* will nevertheless be doing her part to initiate the first scheduled "uphill" passage across the Atlantic.

Thus, in 1818, more than a year before even the first quasi-steamship would wallow and puff from the mouth of the Savannah River to Fastnet Rock—twenty years before full-fledged, businesslike steamers would churn their paddles across the wakes of sailing vessels and erase their proud passage records—the American packets, "the square-riggers on schedule," were off and away. Within seven years, whole fleets of schedule-keeping ships would dominate the sea lanes that ran from Sandy Hook to Cape Clear and the lighthouse on Fastnet, through St. George's Channel and around by Holyhead, where on clear days one could see the turning windmills of the Welsh peninsula, then across the bar of the Mersey into Liverpool.

Aristocratic preserves at first—holding themselves to the social code that called for scrupulous segregation of ladies and gentlemen from the clatter of the common run—the packets catered only to those who could afford their expensive amenities. But soon they had to bend to the appeals of displaced peasants and to the tug of a *lumpenproletariat*. Their satinwood staterooms were paneled to the taste of generals, admirals, performers from the London music halls, Italian coloratura soprani, authors and well-heeled drummers. But when the economics of shipping showed that the elite, after all, comprised only a very thin upper crust, they began to find vast cubic spaces of room in their steerages for "live" cargo—emigrants in the scores of thousands, each one of whose five pounds of passage money represented a clear profit of just about five pounds.

The forbidding center of this human traffic was Caleb Grimshaw & Company, 12 Gorée Plaza, Liverpool. Gorée, a tiny island off the African coast near Dakar, had been a principal port of call for slave traders until public pressure had forced shipowners to abandon the traffic, at least openly, in 1804. Now Grimshaw and his cohorts began to fit "white cargo" into the suffocating holds of packet ships with the same head-of-cattle calculation and disregard for human dignity and human suffering that had distinguished their predecessors.

What the emigrant got from the packet companies was minimal: transportation, "firing" (i.e., a place to cook), drinking water (often tasting of indigo or tobacco; the casks had already been used), a place to sleep. He had to bring his own food and prepare it; he had to provide his own bedding and make his own bed. Consequently, the grimy alleyways close to the Liverpool landing stages became one extensive gimcrack bazaar. There the departing emigrant bargained for bread and potatoes, plates, pannikins and shoddy cooking utensils. Likely as not, these would come apart the first time they were used. The experience of J. B. Howe, an impoverished actor who was determined to get to America, is probably typical. "I went about the neighbourhood of the docks," he wrote, "and purchased what I thought I should want, such as a ham, butter, a stone jar full of fresh eggs, some bacon, pickled onions, a bag of hard biscuits, and carried them . . . to the 'steerage.' The concentrated effluvia from a thousand and one charnel houses could not win the race against the stench which ascended the nostrils as you descended the steep steps of the 'companion' on your progress to the falsely styled 'berth' in the steerage." Within hours, the young actor had succumbed to a condition he described as "chronic coma," from which he did not emerge for fourteen days.

"The filthy state of these ships," wrote the marine historian W. S. Lindsay, "was worse than anything that could be imagined. It was scarcely possible to induce the passengers to sweep the decks after their meals, or to be decent with respect to the common wants of nature; in many cases, in bad weather, when they could not go on deck, their health suffered so much that their strength was gone, and they had not the power to help themselves. Hence 'between decks' was like a loath-some dungeon. When the hatchways were opened under which the people were stowed, the steam rose, and the stench was like that from a pen of pigs. The few beds they had were in a dreadful state, for the straw, once wet with sea water, soon rotted; beside which, they used the between decks for all sorts of filthy purposes."

Regarded as cargo, assigned to quarters as ready for the storage of salt and cotton as for warm bodies, the emigrant was nevertheless, by 1819, not entirely without rights. In that year, urged by shameful statis-tics that had piled up in the New York record offices (on many voyages ten percent or more of steerage passengers died at sea), the United States Congress passed a measure to reduce overcrowding and thereby to curb the spread of disease; eighteen years later a second American statute guaranteed to each passenger fourteen clear feet of deck space, with a special provision for children: two youngsters under fourteen, or three under seven, were to be "computed as one adult." About the same time the British Government clamped down on shipowners. To prevent poorly provisioned passengers from dying at sea, or from becoming sea-going beggars, they ordered the shipping companies (some of which had begun to advertise the fact that their birth rates actually *exceeded* their death rates) to supply their steerage passengers with a weekly ration as follows: 21 quarts of water, 2½ pounds of biscuits, 1 pound wheat flour, 5 pounds of oatmeal, 2 pounds of rice and 2 pounds of molasses.

"Ship fever," the common name for typhus, was the most prevalent disease and the most quickly contagious. Its causes were not known, yet the conditions which caused typhus to spread were recognized. When the disease became rampant, whole ships were decimated. When they could find no other way to check it, American authorities decided to put responsibility on ships' captains. For each corpse he delivered to the New World, a ship's master had to pay a fine of ten dollars.

Illness aside, conditions in steerage were often not much of a cut above those on the recently outlawed slave ships. One genteel cabin passenger with a lively curiosity recorded that she was intrigued to know about life below, but that the ship's surgeon frustrated all her attempts to find out. The doctor "held it not only dangerous and unwholesome, but as being a spectacle wholly unfit for the eyes of a female unaccustomed to behold the strange, and sorry, and demoralizing economy which prevails in those dens of disease and misery." Later, "when the skylight of the saloon was opened to give air below," she apparently found grounds for agreeing with the surgeon, since "the effluvia was such as to compel me in all weathers to go on deck."

The new laws provided the emigrant with at least enough space to die in properly, but no legislation as yet alleviated the mephitic aura of spoilage and excrement from which, for weeks on end, he could take but moments of respite. Every corner or pocket of empty space, said one traveler, was "filled with every sort of filth, broken biscuit, bones, rags, and refuse of every description, putrefying and filled with maggots." "If crosses and tombs could be erected on water," said an American immigration official, "the whole route of the emigrant vessels from England to America would long since have assumed the appearance of a crowded cemetery."

Yet once emigration as an alternative to grubbing for bare life in the outlying parts of Ireland and Scotland had taken hold, the way westward was endlessly open. "They call it 'America,'" wrote James Boswell in his *Journal of a Tour of the Hebrides with Samuel Johnson, LL.D.,* and he was talking about a dance "performed, with much activity. . . . Each of the couples, after the common involutions and evolutions, successively whirls around in a circle till all are in motion; and the dance seems intended to show how emigration catches, till a whole neighbourhood is set afloat. Mrs. M'Kinnon told me that last year, when a ship sailed from Portree for America, the people on shore were almost distracted when they saw their relations go off; they lay down on the ground, tumbled, and tore the grass with their teeth. This year there was not a tear shed. The people on shore seemed to think that they would soon follow. This indifference is a mortal sign for the country."

For all the degradation and mistreatment visited upon them, steerage passengers were nevertheless regarded as part of the human family. Ships' crews, in the eyes of many captains and their employers, were species of the subhuman. Driven like slaves, taught to obey commands and whips like circus animals, their working lives were briefer than those of men in any other following. From the fecal alleys of slums ashore they were trundled into the galleys of slums at sea. Without rights of any kind, they lived under the threat that they could be replaced in a moment by any one of the hundreds of indigents who continually crowded the docking areas looking for any ship that might sign them on. In the nature of the system, some captains even came to see themselves as magnanimous spirits whose benefactions were rewarded only with resentment and abuse.

"If any one imagines that this class of sailors ever felt or expressed gratitude," complained Captain Arthur Clark, "he is much mistaken. Let him picture to himself these creatures in their watch below, laying off in their frowzy berths or sitting around their dirty, unkempt forecastle on their chests smoking their filthy clay pipes, amid clouds of foul tobacco smoke, reeking in the stench of musty underclothing mouldy sea boots, and rancid oilskins, rank enough to turn the stomach of a camel . . . The noxious air is too much for the sooty slush lamp that swings uneasily against the grimy bulkhead; it burns a sickly blue ame with a halo of fetid vapor; while the big fat-witted samples of humanity in the bunks and on the sea chests cheerfully curse their captain up-hill and down dale as their natural enemy."

The way to deal with these ingrates was to see that they were kicked and beaten for all infringements of shipboard rules, any infraction of the captain's whims. "Unfortunately," said Captain Clark, "this was the only way. . . . They were amenable to discipline only in the form of force in heavy and frequent doses, the theories of those who have never commanded ships or had experience in handling degenerates at sea to the contrary notwithstanding. To talk about the exercise of kindness or moral suasion with such men, would be the limit of foolishness; one might as well propose a kindergarten for baby coyotes or young rattlesnakes." Yet, said the Captain, with a jot of manly respect, "with all their moral rottenness, these rascals were splendid fellows to make or shorten sail in heavy weather on the Western Ocean. The packet sailors showed up at their best when laying out on a topsail yardarm, passing a weather reef-earing with their Black Ball caps, red shirts, and trousers stowed in the legs of their sea boots along with their cotton hooks and sheath knives, a snow squall whistling about their ears, the rigging a mass of ice, and the old packet jumping into the big Atlantic seas up to her knightheads. These ruffians did not care much for India and China voyages, but preferred to navigate between the dance-halls of Cherry Street and the grog-shops of Waterloo Road and Ratcliffe Highway. They worked like horses at sea and spent their money like asses ashore."

The home of these men at sea was in the fo'c'sle, the eyes of the ship, damp and leaking most of the time, stifling when the weather was warm, dingy and ill-lit, inhabited by rats in all weathers. In the absence of tables or chairs, men roosted on their sea chests. Food—mostly boiled beef, salt pork, boiled rice—came in wooden tubs and pails set on the floor in the middle of the airless compartment. Without plates, the seaman carved chunks of meat with his jackknife and ate them from his hands along with hardtack and rice sometimes sweetened with molasses. The couplet from "Blow the Man Down"

> On a trim Black Ball liner I first served my time
> And in that Black Baller I wasted my prime

contained more truth than poetry.

No wonder packets could and did make money. On one fifty-eight-day round trip to England, Donald McKay's *Dreadnought* cleared a profit of forty thousand dollars. Yet the lives of many such ships were as short as they were famous. Captains drove their crews like galley slaves to post speed records, loaded their ships to the gunwales in an attempt to hasten the accumulation of fortunes. (Captains got as much as 5 percent of freight charges, 25 percent of cabin passages, 5 percent on steerage, plus mail allowances.)

Under these conditions, one out of every six packet ships was wrecked. Others, once their high-pressure days were over—as in the case of the illustrious *James Monroe*—came into more adventurous and exotic employment. "Aboard of those liners," wrote Herman Melville, "the crews have terrible hard work owing to their carrying such a press of sail in order to make as rapid passage as possible and sustain the ship's reputation for speed . . . they are the very best of sailing craft and built in the very best possible manner . . . yet a few years of sailing before the wind, as they do, seriously impairs their constitutions . . . and they are soon sold out for a song, generally to the people of Nantucket, New

Bedford and Sag Harbour who repair and fit them out for the whaling business. Thus the ship that once carried over-gay parties of ladies and gentlemen . . . to Liverpool or London now carries a crew of harpooners round Cape Horn into the Pacific. And the mahogany and bird's-eye maple cabins which once held rosewood card tables and brilliant coffee urns and in which many a bottle of champagne and many a bright eye sparkled, now accommodates a bluff Quaker from Martha's Vineyard who . . . in the Bay of Islands, New Zealand, entertains a party of naked chiefs and savages at dinner."

The *haut monde* of the early packet days not only indulged itself but took careful pains to protect itself from social contamination. When the English radical William Cobbett, who had lived for two years on a Long Island farm, applied for a cabin on the Black Ball liner *Amity*, word of his intentions got out and his prospective fellow travelers closed ranks: if that rabble-rouser Cobbett is granted passage, they informed the company, we will cancel ours. The company bowed to the pressure; for this voyage at least, Cobbett was told, he was *persona non grata*. Understandably outraged, he wrote to Isaac Wright, one of the owners of the line: "Now, Sir, this is such an insult and injury to me, on the part of those passengers, that I hope you will, this evening or in the course of tomorrow, inform me of *their names*.

"Your ships are called *packets*. It is understood that they are for the use of anyone who is ready to pay the usual price; and as I have notified my friends in England that I am going in the *Amity*, they will be much disappointed if I do not." Cobbett concluded without entreaty, telling Wright, "Please clearly to understand that I mean to claim my right, legally to go in the ship." With an ominous reference to "justice for this insult and injury," he demanded again to know by whom besides the Black Ball Line itself he had been, in the nice coincidence of the thing, blackballed. Wright remained adamant and close-mouthed; whereupon Cobbett took revenge by dispatching abroad the falsehood that an epidemic of yellow fever was raging in New York. The *Amity*, he reported to England, was caught in the plague. However, she was scheming to sneak out of port "via Amboy, New Jersey," where, by the chicanery of Isaac Wright, "a very cunning old Quaker," she hoped to get clearance that would forestall quarantine at Liverpool. Meanwhile, he said, "It would be impossible for her to be laden without taking cargo from the Store-House, the very seat of contagion." He would himself return to England, not on the pestilential *Amity*, but on "a clean ship." Neither the Black Ball Line nor its uppity clientele knew that among the trunks and parcels Mr. Cobbett was packing for transport to England was a little box containing the recently exhumed, dismantled and whistle-clean bones of Tom Paine.

Cobbett may have suffered the trials of a pariah, but these did not blind him to the excellence of American seamanship and the character of American personnel. In a book called *The Emigrant's Guide*, which he published a few years later, his advice was unequivocal: "The ship will be no other than an American one, if you wish for a *quick* and *safe* passage. The Americans sail *faster* than others, owing to the greater *skill* and greater *vigilance* of the captains, and to their great sobriety and the wise rules that they observe with regard to other men. They carry *more sail* than other ships, because the captain is everlastingly looking out. I have crossed the Atlantic three times in American ships, once in an English merchant ship, once in a king's ship, and once in a king's packet; and I declare, that the superiority of the Americans is indeed, so decisive, that, if I were going to cross again, nothing should prevail on me to go on board of any ship but an American one. I never knew an American captain to *take off his clothes to go to bed, during the whole voyage*; and I never knew any other who did not do it. The consequence of this great watchfulness is that advantage is taken of every puff of wind, while the risk from the squalls and sudden gusts is, in a great measure, obviated."

Assured that they would have to suffer neither the obtrusion of pariahs nor the sight of the rabble below decks, the fashionable and talented continued to crisscross the ocean in happy cabals with the famous autocrats who commanded the packets. Models of Yankee self-reliance, these men, nearly all of them from old Colonial strongholds in Connecticut or from farms in New York, were seldom more than thirty-five years of age. This, in the opinion of the actress Fanny Kemble, made "having the command of a ship rather an awful consideration." Their years of service were comparatively short, but within a seven- or eight-year span, they could count upon something like twenty-thousand dollars per annum—an income, in those days, large enough to make a man rich.

As a group, packet captains made up a professional elite. At sea they exercised authority under God alone; on land, they were owners of businesses and estates, speculators and investors. They moved in an aura of distinction and, in the words of Julian, son of Nathaniel Hawthorne, "with a disposition to wear a high-colored necktie and a broad, gold watch-chain, and to observe a certain smartness in their boots and general shore rigging." The careers of packet ships on the broad tracks of the ocean were as closely calibrated as those of race horses. The all-encompassing aim was speed; the lives and limbs of those who honed the edge of every speed-making device were expendable.

"They were driven to the extreme edge of safety at all times," said historian Carl Cutler. "They carried sail until it was worth a man's life to go aloft. . . . Speed meant not only money for owners and fame and future patronage for the ship, but it was the all-important factor in keeping out foreign competition." The arrivals and departures of noted captains, their record voyages and average voyages were reported with care and argued over with schoolboy passion. Their celebrity was equal to that of politicians and generals; their wealth was often considerably greater and more tangible. They represented daring and mastery— the rugged power to handle a "packet-rat" crew and the *savoir faire* to preside at the head of a table as host to the rich and eminent. Given the nature of their jobs, the packet captains earned every bit of their money and deserved their badges of singularity. They might be forbidding autocrats in the confines of their ships, but they were also men of courage who would allow no delegation of duty, countenance no relief of tasks which often found them lashed to stanchions as they guided their vessels through seas that ripped sails to ribbons. In the great age of the sailing ship, a packet, in the eyes of at least one awed correspondent, was "the noblest work of man, and her commander the noblest work of God."

But captains had to suffer the weight of their celebrity. No matter how sophisticated his navigational skills might be, the packet commander's social graces and sense of diplomacy were factors of equal account. On public show from the beginning of the voyage, his star-turn performance on the quarterdeck witnessed by passengers, crew and dock-side crowd, the successful captain had to be possessed of stentorian voice and the bearing of a monarch. At sea, personal contact with his charges was close and constant. In hours of tension, storms or fog, he was himself watched by apprehensive passengers as closely as he watched his barometer. His tart ripostes to foolish questions were well published, examples of his gruff wisdom repeated. (Passenger: "Captain, I'm afraid that cloud prevented you from making your observation." Captain: "Yes, Sir, but it did not hinder you from making yours.")

Most commanders played the host with a show of enthusiasm and some *bon vivants* among them seemed positively to enjoy the role. It was not uncommon for a captain to ensure good public relations for his ship and his company by actually paying social visits to the passengers he had recently disembarked in England or France. Some travelers felt a twinge of Puritan guilt about high life at sea. "Could our ancestors have seen our refinements and our luxuries," said one, "they would have thought us effeminate." But most of them publicly doted on being pampered. Often, at the end of a voyage, they would present their captain with lavish gifts of silver plate, scrolls of poetry, swags of hard cash and, sometimes, a "card" inserted in the newspapers testifying to his skill, charm and husbandry. Perhaps the most elaborate thanks to come to any captain were those tendered to Bailey of the Black Ball packet *Yorkshire*. When he brought over a troupe of young Viennese dancers in "sixteen days and a pirouette," reported the New York *Herald*, "those beautiful children were so delighted with him and his ship [he had broken the westward record for speed] that they danced the splendid *Pas de Fleurs* on his quarter deck in coming up the harbor, and on Saturday presented him with a magnificent silver pitcher, with their hearts engraved all over it." But such testimonials belonged to the salad days of the packets. Before their term was out, captains would be involved in circumstances where, upon arrival in New York, they would have to call upon the police to protect them from assault by emigrants who had endured a hell at sea over which, trident in hand, the figure of a horned master had presided.

As scheduled voyages multiplied, distinctions in appointments and fittings of rival ships became as much a matter of public romance as speed records. When the packet *Liverpool* came to town, "What next?" asked a writer for *The Herald*. "The length of her upper deck, almost flush from stem to stern, is 183 feet, and has a small cabin for smokers and for the men at the helm. This will be exclusive for the use of cabin passengers. The main deck is 176 feet long, and upon it are built the cabins, bathing houses, apartments for the cuisine, houses for cows, sheep, swine and poultry. The main saloon is constructed upon the most improved idea. It is large enough for forty cabin passengers and is high enough for any man under eight feet in his boots. The state rooms are fitted up somewhat like those of the Ashburton and Stephen Whitney, and connect so that families can have a suite of rooms as at the Astor House." One of the new features of the *Liverpool* was a bathing room where one could take showers with salt water hauled aboard. "But it should be recollected," warned the reporter, "that this dipping does not make it fresh water. This bathing room is a new idea and it is capital as it is new. It has heretofore been a desideratum in packet ships. Forward of all are the pantries for making pastry, and two excellent cabooses, one for the cabin and the other for the steerage passengers. These," concludes the account, "are divided by an iron partition."

On the happier side of this partition, now that ocean travelers were no longer regarded as "the cash equivalent of a hogshead of tobacco," the privileged might dine gluttonously, sleep fitfully and devise ways to punctuate the inevitable boredom of lengthening weeks on the water.

"You cannot imagine, dear Mother," wrote Alexis de Tocqueville en route to America, "what a droll life one lives in this great stagecoach called a ship. The necessity of living on top of each other and of looking each other in the eye all the time establishes an informality and a freedom of which one has no conception on terra firma. Here each one carries on in the middle of the crowd as if he were alone: some read aloud, others play, others sing; there are those who write as I do for instance at this moment, while close by a neighbor is supping. Each one drinks, laughs, eats or cries as his fancy suggests. Our cabins are so narrow that one goes outside them to dress; and but for publicly putting on one's pants, I know not what part of one's toilet doesn't take place in the face of Israel."

But whether the passenger occupied a two-berth cabin alone—thereby, at the price of an additional half-fare, "conserving" his "individuality" —or was crammed into the dank dormitories 'tween decks, he was aware of jeopardy, perhaps more acutely than he need have been. While about ninety sea-going vessels were wrecked in one way or another every year, few among them were packets in the passenger service. Within the first twenty years of such service, only three packets were known to have foundered at sea. Yet things did happen, and stories did come back. There was the flash of lightning that set the *Poland* ablaze and forced her passengers into boats towed through the fumes of smoldering bales of cotton in her hold. There was the fatal encounter of the *William*

Brown with an iceberg, after which sixteen survivors, "young girls as well as men," were systematically jettisoned from overcrowded lifeboats. There were the forty-one passengers who froze to death in the icy rigging of the *John Minturn* as, in sight of shore, she was smashed to pieces in a snowstorm off Barnegat.

Enlarged to the last gruesome detail in grainy lithographs and breathless journalism, such incidents tended to make every departing voyager somewhat histrionic. The *bon-voyage* party often had the atmosphere of a wake, as baleful family and friends inspected the casket-sized quarters of the departing soul. But this sense of the dramatic was generally counterbalanced by the passenger's dulling certainty that he would be for days immobilized, pale green and supine. Seasickness darkened or obliterated the early part of the voyage for almost everyone. Foresighted travelers bought garments advertised by a New York outfitter, somewhat mysteriously, as being specifically useful to those who knew they would succumb to *mal de mer*. Other cautious ones brought fresh lemons to suck, or a supply of Reverend B. Hibbard's Vegetable Anti-Bilious Pills. Others got drunk on Barbados rum while the ship was still in the East River and stayed that way.

"The assembling of the passengers of the large packet-ship is necessarily an affair of coldness and distrust," wrote James Fenimore Cooper, "especially with those who know the world. . . . Although necessity brings chaotic elements into something like order, the first week commonly passes in reconnoitering, cool civilities, and cautious concessions, to yield at length to the never-dying charities; unless, indeed, the latter may happen to be kept in abeyance by a downright quarrel, about midnight carousals, a squeaking fiddle, or some incorrigible snorer."

Bathtubs aboard ship were still unthinkable; running water did not exist. Fastidious passengers determined to take baths or the equivalent had to be brave. One of these offered advice to others contemplating an ocean passage. "Give directions to the steward to rouse you at deck-washing," he counseled, "that is, about six A.M.; put on drawers and jacket of fine cotton, and, sunshine or cloud, calm or squall, run on deck, leave your *robe de chambre* in the roundhouse, and slide down into the lee gangway, where, according to previous contract, you see a grim-looking seven-foot seaman waiting for you with a couple of buckets of sea-water, one held ready in the claw, with a half-grin upon his puckered phiz as he inwardly blesses the simplicity of the landsman who turns out to be soused like the captain's turtle in cold salt water."

For the reasonably doughty passenger, to live at sea was mainly to attend the groaning board. Some voyagers had little enthusiasm for this, and some were not persuaded that the so-called fresh meat offered by the packets was anything more than "pork fed in the longboat; mutton from sea-sick sheep with eyes as white as those of whitings; turkeys and fowls that are never killed until at the point of death; ducks and geese that would not die, but that will be poor as a dog-horse." But to zesty spirits like the Irish comedian Tyrone Power, a morning on a packet was a promise kept. "Pricking your ears at certain sputtering and hissing sounds," he wrote, you entered a gallery where you got a "foretaste of boiled ham, spitch-cock, eggs, frizzled bacon, and mutton cutlets. . . . If the incipient traveler will benefit by my experience he will develop his main battle against the mutton chops *au naturel*; then gossip over a slice of boiled *Virginy* ham, with an egg or twain, while his souchong is getting pleasantly cool; then, having emptied his first cup, flirt with a couple of delicate morsels raised from the thin part of a salted shad-fish, the which shad, for richness and flavor, is surpassing. To his second cup he will dedicate the upper crust of a well-baked roll with cold butter; and, after having duly paused awhile, choose between Cognac and Schieldam for a *chasse*."

After a breakfast of these proportions, said Power, you should take care not to spoil your appetite for late afternoon dinner by over-indulgence at the luncheon table. Instead, you might merely "lift a piece of pilot biscuit, request some kind soul to shave the under side of the corned round for you, then desiring the steward to follow with a tumbler of Guinness's porter, fly the place and seek the deck."

Four times every day the ladies and gentlemen of quality sat down to a table of largess sufficient to nourish an emigrant for a week. When the packet captain did not care to dine with his charges, or when he was for one reason or another indisposed, the voyagers often elected their own Emperor of the Groaning Board and expected him to make the most of the ship's larder. The position was not a sinecure. "Every-one knows the weight of obloquy," said one so chosen, "which falls upon the man in office when there is no fat on the sirloin, or the legs of the fowl may have the flavor and consistency of guitar strings. My prime minister was a black cook; my kingdom, animal and vegetable;

my subjects three or four gaunt sheep in the launch, and, under the forecastle, a couple of pigs. On the poop were several rows of coops, a sort of charitable institution for superannuated geese and ducks."

Between meals, passengers found diversions in the saloon. "There is an occasional game of chess," wrote one of them, "some playing on the flute, a great deal of shooting with the rifle, and yesterday, being the King's birthday, the Captain sported champagne, and the gentlemen fired a *feu de joie* with rifle and pistols." Whist and dominoes were popular; some emancipated boatloads even went so far as to find a fiddler and make up dancing parties in which they flung themselves into everything "from the graceful attitudes of the *catabaws* to the spread-eagle monotony of the *minuet de la coeur*." Making wagers on the ship's run developed into a kind of stock exchange as shifts in the weather raised or lowered prices on tickets designating arrival times.

In mild weather off the Grand Banks, passengers and ships' officers fished for cod and, on occasion, even did a bit of ship-to-schooner trading with the bearded crews of Nova Scotia fishing boats. Porpoises were amusing to watch; when they came close enough, they were harpooned. Sometimes, for the fun of it, passengers coaxed sharks to follow the packet by tossing them hunks of beef and mutton. On the very rare occasions when polar bears were sighted clambering about the peaks of drifting icebergs, passengers would bring out their rifles and use the animals as targets. Now and then someone would organize a rat hunt— a diversion even ladies found it quite proper to join. Rats were a major nuisance at sea, partly because they liked the taste of leather mailbags and partly because they found the corks in champagne bottles a particular delicacy. The game of hunting and killing them provided voyagers with exercise and a certain bloody joviality, the shipowners with an unpaid sanitation squad.

"We endeavored to amuse ourselves as best we could during the twenty-eight days we were on the deep," said one packet passenger, "sometimes holding mock courts, and trying some of our fellow-passengers on fictitious charges; discussing grave matters of law, life and logic; singing songs and psalm tunes; and, for the want of work, turned boys again, and went to play."

In dead calms, passengers would sometimes dive from the bowsprit and take constitutional swims clear around the ship. A long period of calm, in fact, was less bearable than an equally long period of storm.

In the beginning of such a spell, everyone busied himself with little personal tasks ordinary sea weather made difficult. "The difference after a calm is remarkable," wrote Harriet Martineau, who crossed on the Red Star packet *United States* in the summer of 1834. Characterized as "that dyspeptic Radical battle-axe" and said to be "the ugliest woman in the world," Miss Martineau was acutely observant, perhaps because, being denied the sense of smell, the sense of taste and the sense of hearing, she had refined her faculty for seeing. "The cap-borders are spruce," she wrote, "the bonnets wear a new air; the gloves are whole; the married gentlemen appear with complete sets of buttons, and rectified stocks."

But as the stillness became protracted and the sails remained slack, both men and beasts tended to take out on one another the irritations of the lolling emptiness. On such an interim in one voyage, noted a passenger, the pigs had "taken to quarrelling, the elder and stronger ones, like so many schoolboys, abusing the little ones and biting their ears off." In the pervasive ennui, even the most proper ladies and gentlemen were likely to lose their *savoir faire* and become snappish. "If there be an infirmity of temper," wrote Miss Martineau, "it is sure to come out then. At such a time, there is much playing of shuffle-board upon deck; and the matches do not always end harmoniously. 'You touched mine with your foot'—'I did not, I declare'—'Now, don't say so, etc., etc.'—'You are eight'—'No, we are ten'—'I can show you you are only eight'—and so on. After three days of calm, there may be heard a subdued tone of scolding from the whist party at the top of the table, and a stray oath from some check-mated person lower down; and while the ladies are brushing their hair in the cabin, certain items of information are apt to be given of how Mrs. A. looked when the lady's partner turned up trumps, and how shockingly Mr. B. pushed past Mr. C. in going up the cabin to dinner."

As quickly as *savoir faire* succumbed to tedium in the grand saloons, so did moral fortitude in the lower depths. So many Irish girls, en route to America, embarked as virgins and disembarked as "outcasts" that the priests of Galway were moved to make public protest against lack of adequate shipboard chaperonage. When the taxpayers of New York and Brooklyn got fed up with having to support the illegitimate children born of transatlantic dalliance, they took their case to Congress. The result was an Act providing that if any member of an American crew seduced a passenger "under promise of marriage, or by threats, or by the exercise of his authority, or by solicitation, or the making of gifts or presents," he either had to marry the girl or take the choice of a fine of one thousand dollars or a year in the jailhouse.

When the days became especially tedious on Miss Martineau's voyage, the solicitations of the captain were genteel: half an hour before dinner he sent the ladies a "whet of cherrybounce." Some flagging spirits were revived by this, but not Miss Martineau's. She who had once mesmerized Charlotte Brontë, who had deplored the coronation of Victoria, saying that the service gave the impression of "endowing the Queen with divinity and the Almighty with royalty," spent nearly all of her time ostentatiously on deck, reading Shakespeare, writing articles for magazines, and keeping a journal. She professed herself to be enchanted, at least in the early stages of the crossing; but as the trip dragged on toward becoming a passage of six weeks, not even cherrybounce could temper certain hard facts. "A sheep has jumped overboard," she wrote, "and so cheated us of some of our mutton." The vegetables were drying up. "It was found best not to look into the dishes of dried fruits which formed our dessert."

A less redoubtable Englishwoman who braved a long packet crossing was Sarah Mytton Maury. She was one of only three cabin passengers on a ship carrying nearly four hundred souls in steerage, and while she reported that she and her shipmates "had a ball every evening, which usually ended in a fight," the grander aspects of the voyage were what she was most moved to record. "Forty-three hours after departure," she wrote, "we were beyond sight of land" when "the ship gave a long heave." Captain Bursley "exclaimed with the enthusiasm of a seaman, 'Ha ha! There is the first roll of the Atlantic.' And truly it was unlike all other motion that I had ever experienced in a ship; prolonged, and breathing, and swelling, while the vessel, plunging gently onwards, seemed to recognize with joy the friendly welcome of the ocean billow. I watched and waited for the repeated greeting of the wave, and for the first time I felt and understood the *rapture of the sea*. The night was breezy, with a brilliant crescent and stars; the wind, which had been north west, suddenly became north, and grew violent; then began a gale.

"We had come down the Channel with all our studding sails set, so that we had much sail to shorten. I lay on a sofa in the cabin, and there listened to such a collection of noises as nothing on land can rival; the sea roared and the wind howled; the belaboured ship creaked and moaned, and shrieked and sighed like a living thing, for she was light upon the waters, and therefore fully at their mercy; the men were stamping and the blocks banging, and the sails flapping in the wind and dropping upon deck; above all was heard the Captain's voice of thunder, shouting his orders and cheering his men. The unhappy creatures in the steerage who had passed the day before in singing and dancing, were now screaming with fright, and sick to death; the children cried, the mothers wept, and the men uttered prayers and imprecations by turns. Soon I became sick and sore, a dead-alive wretch, neither hearing nor seeing, nor knowing anything around me. The good steward managed to drag me to my state room, and here I lay for thirty-seven hours in mortal sickness. I then recovered, and slept almost incessantly for two days, when I contrived to rise, and crawl upon deck with the Captain's aid; here I was lashed to my chair with the ship's colours, from the chair to the capstan; I sometimes fainted, from weakness, but nobody had time to watch my condition; left to myself, and sprinkled by the waves, and fanned by the winds, I soon recovered my consciousness, and, being tied fast, was never injured."

When a packet finally reached the vicinity of Sandy Hook, likely as not penultimate delays there would make for an almost intolerable new hiatus of tedium. If the ship came in at night, she would send up rockets as a signal for one or more pilot boats that might be lying in wait for a customer. Night or day, she might be boarded at once by rival pilots, who would then argue their rights to possession of her for the trip upstream. To visitors from abroad, arrival in New York was also an initiation into the colorful, sometimes rude ways of those who lived in the Home of the Free. Henry Bradshaw Fearon, who came over on the packet *Washington*—among whose other passengers were Secretary of State John Quincy Adams and his wife—tells what it was like: "Several sailing boats passed with gentlemen, many of them wearing enormously large straw hats, turned up behind. At one o'clock we anchored close to the city. A boy procured us two hackney coaches, from a distance of about a quarter of a mile. I offered him an English shilling, having no other small coin in my possession." This was refused, said Fearon, "with a tone of independence, which, although displeasing to my pride, was not so to my judgment. Mr. Adams satisfied the young republican by giving him half a dollar. There was no sense of having received a favor in the boy's countenance or manner, a trait of character which, I have since learned, is by no means confined to the youth of America. A simple, 'I thank you, Sir,' would not, however, derogate from a free man's dignity."

Widely published accounts of ships awash, afire or becalmed gave a lurid tinge to the business of travel between Europe and America. Yet lyrical flights about the joys of sea-going continued to overwhelm the sorry reports of thousands of frightened and seasick passengers. For every hundred individuals who detailed their discomfort in "the light of consumptive-looking lamps, carried about by the condemned spirits of this floating purgatory," there were a hundred who told of "riding the high billows in a brisk breeze," of the eerie beauty of the black-fringed moon in the Irish Sea, of glittering castles of ice adrift, of bearded colossi in oilskins outwitting the very gods of the air. A ship with her sails loosened and her ensign abroad was already an American image of romance as potent as an Indian on horseback acceding to the sunset.

"It was a glorious sight when we were abreast of her," said an American traveler of an encounter with an American packet en route, "and saw her swelling canvas—royals, studding sails, and all—and her bright, high sides, rising from the waves like a walled city, and plunging again into the glittering abyss of waters." Even the tempests were endurable, said another. "The dark sea, the storm, the night, all were forgotten, as in that beautiful saloon, in social converse, time flew on silken wings."

The sea brought out the poet in ordinary men. But, on one occasion at least, it brought out the ordinary man in a poet. When Ralph Waldo Emerson found himself in need of "a change and a tonic" in 1847, he thought a visit to England would do the trick, as would "the dread attraction and salutary influences of the sea." He sailed on the packet *Washington Irving* from Boston on a Tuesday in October. By noontime on Friday the ship had gone only 134 miles. "A nimble Indian would have swum as far," he noted, "but the captain affirmed that the ship would show us in time all her paces, and we crept along through the floating drift of boards, logs and chips, which the rivers of Maine and New Brunswick pour into the sea after a freshet."

Emerson was not impressed with the ship's library—Basil Hall, Dumas, Dickens, Bulwer, Balzac, Sand—and was fretful about the dimness of the light in his cabin. He eventually became resigned to many aspects of the voyage as "the costly fee we pay for entrance to Europe," but not to the constant sense of danger. "I find sea life an acquired taste," he said, "like that for tomatoes and olives. The confinement, cold, motion, noise and odor are not to be dispensed with. The floor of your room is sloped at an angle of twenty or thirty degrees, and I waked up every morning with the belief that someone was ripping up my berth. Nobody likes to be treated ignominiously, upset, shoved against the side of the house, rolled over, suffocated with bilge, mephitis and stewing oil. We get used to these annoyances at last, but the dread of the sea remains longer. Is this sad-colored circle an eternal cemetery?" In coming to his final word on the subject, he quoted the widely traveled Persian poet Saadi. "There are many advantages in sea-voyaging," said Emerson, "but security is not one of them."

Banquets, ceremonial dedications, any excuse to board a new ship brought New Yorkers out in droves. When the packet *Henry Clay* went down the ways, ten thousand people turned out to see her splash into the East River. "In a word," said *The Herald*, "she is a monster of the deep." The docking area was crammed with carriages, hansoms, cabs, carts; men hung like locusts in the rigging of ships nearby; every fence and roof in the vicinity became a grandstand.

"All went off smoothly as the ship glided into the Atlantic," continued *The Herald*. "Nothing marred the splendor of the day, the beauty of the thousand women present, the music of the band on board the packet, or the magnificence of the launch itself. Even the sailor who ascended to the bows of the ship to embrace the full-length figure of Henry Clay, went off with éclat, although efforts were made to dislodge him. The rapid progress of our shipwrights is to be seen from one launch to another. It is truly astonishing."

When the packet *Yorkshire* was fitted out and ready to begin her maiden voyage, the leading citizens of Manhattan came to a ceremony in which the ship was "presented with a splendid set of flags, signals and cabin cutlery, by the Yorkshire gentlemen of this city, in return for the compliment paid them in naming her after their birthplace." Tom Thumb, the celebrated midget, was there, sitting on a cut-glass tumbler as he listened to the speeches. When they were over he wandered off to take a look at the five staterooms he and P. T. Barnum had already engaged for themselves and their party. But he was quickly called back to the saloon and importuned to sing. To oblige the company, he hopped, according to local report, upon a piece of *boeuf à la mode* and filled the cabin with a spirited rendition of "Life on the Ocean Wave."

A life on the ocean wave, a home on the rolling deep.
Where the scattered waves rave, and the winds their revels keep.

Like an eagle caged I pine, on this dull unchanging shore,
O give me the flashing brine—the spray and the tempest roar.

The afternoon was concluded in an aura of "utmost conviviality," and soon Tom Thumb got what he pined for. With his parents and a tutor in tow, a contract in hand promising him fifty dollars per week plus all expenses, the miniature General was off "to test the curiosity of men and women on the other side of the Atlantic." *The New York Sun* covered the departure: "Several thousand persons joined in procession yesterday to escort this wonderful little man on board of the ship *Yorkshire*, by which splendid packet he has sailed for the purpose of visiting Her Majesty Queen Victoria, Louis Philippe, and the nobility of England and France. The procession passed down Fulton Street, preceded by the city brass band. The General was in an open barouche, and bowed very gracefully to the myriads of ladies who filled the windows on each side of the street, and who testified to their delight at seeing him by the waving of thousands of white silk handkerchiefs. The shipping adjacent to the *Yorkshire* was black with the multitude gathered to witness the departure of the smallest man and the finest ship the world ever produced."

Such shows of adulation had already begun to weary the midget celebrity. When the *Yorkshire* was greeted in Liverpool by a crowd calling for a sight of him, Tom Thumb arranged to be smuggled ashore by his mother, who simply carried him like a babe in arms.

Years before New England clipper ships had become the supreme artifacts of the ocean, American eminence in the building and operation of sailing ships was uncontested, even by Englishmen. "The mercantile navy of England is the least speedy and most unsafe that belongs to a civilized nation," wrote the British scientist Augustin Creuze. "America is not only in possession of a better mercantile navy, with which to compete with us, but she has also the vantage-ground of superior knowledge, and a far more extended experience, from which to start for future competition. The merchant builders of Britain are, with a few honourable exceptions, unequal to the task of competition with the more educated and more practical foreigner." This was no lesser claim than Americans made for themselves. When Philip Hone saw ships flying the Stars and Stripes at anchor in Le Havre, he recorded in his journal: "They are so neat and trim, so beautiful and yet so majestic, they hold the same station in the commercial marine which their nation is destined to hold amongst the nations of the earth. This is not bravado or prejudice, everything tends to it, and I do most potently believe it."

Others did not. To them, to take a barnacled old workhorse of the sea and deck her out with porphyry and brocade, to put lumpish, illiterate sailors in uniform and try to get them to run sailing ships as though they were men-of-war was nothing but "eyewash" and trumpery. Why should these prinked-out lackeys "enjoy a prescriptive privilege of being most noisy, of wearing tremendous boots and of trilling, like sea larks, upon little silvery whistles known indiscriminately as 'pipes' or 'calls'?" Yet the men who sat in the home offices of the packet companies obviously sensed that the right image of brass, braid and "shippiness" would impress Americans, especially those bound for England "to learn how my Lord Shuffleton waltzes, what wine Baron Hob-and-Nob patronizes, which tints predominate in Lady Highflyer's dress, and what is the probable color of the Duchess of Doublehose's garters."

⚛ SECTION II ⚛

S.S Savannah *and the Czar of All the Russias*
Robert Fulton's Compact

THE VOYAGE of a small, rickety, sail- and steam-propelled vessel from Savannah—the port whose name she bore—to Liverpool, in 1819, has found a secure spot in maritime history, but not a very comfortable one. In some accounts, her twenty-six-day ocean passage signals an American triumph—in marine architecture, engineering and in seamanship. In other accounts her trip is a farcical little misadventure on the part of some sharp Southern operators who tried to parlay a nautical stunt into a royal ransom. The career of the *Savannah* gives credence to neither, or both, of these attitudes. She made no nonsense about national glory and was in fact up for sale as soon as she got to Europe. Yet she was undoubtedly the trailblazer, the first ship with steam-powered machinery to cross from America to the Old World.

Going over, she sailed many hundreds more miles than she steamed. Coming back, she proceeded fully under steam only when, leaving Cronstadt and arriving in Savannah, she was aware of a shore-line audience to whom she could show off. Ostensibly equipped for transatlantic service in steam, she did not have enough bunker space for the fuel that might have made one steam-powered voyage possible. Yet even before she was launched, she had a knack for garnering attention. In a time when scores of steamboats from Albany to Memphis were blowing up and burning down with fearful regularity, she enticed even a President of the United States to board her for a clanking little cruise to nowhere and back. With engines, paddle wheels, three masts full-rigged and a black funnel (this was fitted with an elbow joint that could be swiveled ninety degrees when smuts and sparks threatened to set fire to the sails) almost as tall as her decks were broad, she became the ship of the hour. Yet she could not get one living soul to buy one passage ticket for the maiden voyage that, lucky or not, was bound to find its place in the chronicles of the ocean.

She was overtaken by more than one puzzled sailing ship en route to Liverpool, and when she got there crowds gawked at her in curiosity while jealous rivals studied her in suspicion. She went through her paces for the crowned heads of two great Continental nations, but no one, on or off the throne, would meet her price. She had to come home as she went—begging. Yet, against the clear report of her log book—which details the information that she raised steam only six times and used her engines for but 80 out of the 663 hours she was at sea—her reputation as the first steamship to cross the Atlantic remains, sentimentally at least, secure.

In drawings and paintings that picture her breasting the Atlantic waves, she looks unpretentiously staunch and lighthearted. Lacking paddle boxes to house her big naked wheels (at least in some illustrations: actually, each paddle wheel was equipped with a portable canvas covering stretched over an iron frame), she also gives an impression of being starkly fundamental and efficient. Yet in every assessment of pioneer steam passages across the Western Ocean, the merit of her performance is either highly qualified, summarily dismissed or patronized with the sort of smile one confers on a braggart child. Historically, she is one of the bright particular stars of American sea power. Yet she remains both a mistake and a dud. Nearly one hundred and fifty years after her famous voyage, she bequeathed her name and, sad to say, her propensity toward failure to another American ship—the world's first nuclear-powered merchant vessel. What she lacked in power, speed and market value, she has made up for in her ability to generate and sustain legend against the facts, doubts and scholastic scrutiny of a century of maritime historians.

The *Savannah* was designed and laid down as a pure and simple sailing ship in the shipyards of Crocker & Fickett at Corlaer's Hook— that particular bulge on the marshy shores of Manhattan Island that extended into the East River near the site of the present Williamsburgh Bridge. But while she was still on the stocks, she caught the attention of a man who was shopping about for a vessel sturdy enough to support the weight of engines and paddle wheels—an auxiliary steamship capable of crossing the Atlantic. He was Captain Moses Rogers and he was acting not only for himself but for the prosperous and ambitious firm of Scarborough & Isaacs in Savannah. For his purposes, Captain Rogers' eye was uniquely sophisticated. As far back as 1809 he had taken John Stevens' steamboat, the *Phoenix*, "a frail, narrow box, pointed at the bow" (and barred from the Hudson by the influence of the Fulton-Livingston monopoly), from New York to Philadelphia, the first instance of a deep-water voyage by any such craft. Although the trip took thirteen days and the *Phoenix*, escorted by a schooner, anchored at night in various coastal havens, Captain Rogers had made the first gesture toward earning his place in history as the pioneer ocean navigator under steam. Four years later he made an even longer trip when he piloted the steamboat *Eagle* from New York to Baltimore.

Rogers liked what he saw in Crocker & Fickett's establishment and told Mr. Scarborough and Mr. Isaacs that he believed the vessel would take readily to being fitted out with engines and boilers, and that they ought to buy her. The partners accepted his advice. With a sail-plus-steam transatlantic crossing in mind, they bought the little ship, so to speak, off the rack. They then had a New Jersey–made boiler and engines installed, along with wrought-iron paddle wheels of eight radii each, hinged at the axles, capable of being folded up like a fan and removed from the paddle shaft and stowed on deck in about twenty minutes.

When she was fully accoutered they sent her on speed trials in New York Harbor. "Although there was at no time more than an inch of steam upon her," reported the New York *Mercantile Advertiser*, "with a strong wind and tide ahead, she went within a mile of the anchoring ground at Staten Island and returned to Fly Market Wharf in one hour and fifty minutes. When it is considered that she is calculated to bear twenty inches of steam and that her machinery is entirely new, it may be easily imagined that she will, with ease, pass any of the steamboats upon our waters." Then she advertised for passengers and cargo for Georgia. The same reporter, impressed with the "wonderful celerity" of "this prodigy," asked, "Who would have had the courage twenty years ago to hazard a prediction that a ship of 350 tons burthen would be built in the port of New York to navigate the Atlantic propelled by steam?"

Without passengers or freight, "Fickett's steam coffin" sailed for Savannah on March 28, 1819. Until she was five days out, her wheels were kept high and dry on deck, her engines cold. But by the time she got to the Savannah River her paddles were churning and she was fully under steam. Hundreds of people had turned out to cheer her from elevated points along its banks. "The utmost confidence is placed in her security," said the Savannah *Republican*. "It redounds to the honor of Savannah . . . this first attempt to cross the Atlantic in a vessel propelled by steam. We sincerely hope the owners may reap a rich reward for their splendid and laudable undertaking."

Before she had even attempted an ocean crossing, the *Savannah*'s fame generated envy, and the threat of competition. While she was still biding her time in the bosom of her home port, a group of New York businessmen, among them the eminent old shipowner Preserved Fish, inveigled the New York state legislature into granting them a charter for a firm to be called the Ocean Steam Ship Company. They were "desirous of constructing and employing steam ships in navigating the ocean," because they were confident "that vessels may be so constructed as to unite all the safety and other advantages of common ships, to the additional velocity to be gained by the application of steam." But as the sailing-ship trade continued to do well and its profits continued to rise, this project, like a score of other early plans for ocean steamers, simply dwindled and then disappeared.

The newly constituted Savannah Ship Company was meanwhile alert to opportunity. As their ship was being made ready at her berth in Savannah, the newspapers reported that President Monroe was on his way south for a series of visits, the main purpose of which was only to show his friendly face. He had traveled from Washington to Norfolk on a steamboat, and he was looking forward to brief sojourns at Wilmington, Charleston, Augusta and Savannah. William Scarborough at once saw his chance to garner further publicity and to prove to everyone still dubious about steamships that they were safe because the President of the United States himself regarded them as safe. He proposed to the President that he make a journey from Charleston to Savannah on the new ship. The President declined, saying that the citizens of Charleston did not wish him to leave their state "in a Georgia conveyance." But he promised to visit the ship as soon as he got to Savannah. On May 11, boarding the *Savannah* at seven A.M., along with Secretary of War John C. Calhoun, five generals and two judges, the President set out on an inspection tour of Savannah River forts and defenses. "With the utmost majesty," said the local paper, "she proceeded down the sound," and noted that "the wheels were the essential powers that forced her through the water." The President was impressed. No doubt, he said, the Navy could make good use of her. As if she might already be used to back up the Monroe Doctrine, he suggested that the *Savannah* might be considered for service as a cruiser on the coast of Cuba.

All this made fine publicity as the *Savannah* approached sailing day and her moment of truth. The idea was to send her back to New York, then fill her berths with persons of substance and renown for the great trip to Liverpool and ports in the Baltic. But when advertisements for even the trip to New York brought only three responses, that leg of the voyage was canceled. Prospects for the little ship were not good, yet her owners continued to treat her with every kind of attention. In fitting out the *Savannah* they had provided two saloons—one for ladies, one for gentlemen—handsomely furnished with carpets "from the Orient," curtains and hangings of rich stuff, mirrors galore. There were thirty-two staterooms appointed with a care usually given only to pleasure yachts. When she was finally brushed and polished, advertisements were placed in the newspapers. "For Liverpool," they announced, "The Steamship *Savannah*, Captain Rogers, will without fail, proceed, direct, to-morrow, 20th instant. Passengers, if any, can well be accommodated. Apply on board."

But no one offered. Two days later, two days late, the *Savannah* cast off without cargo. Mirror reflected mirror in her empty saloons. She sailed in ballast—a portent and a humiliation. Steaming sixteen miles down the River and into the Sound on a breezy Saturday morning in May, she anchored off Tybee Light and spent most of another two days in getting ready for the trip. On Monday morning, May 24, 1819—on the very same day that Victoria, daughter of the Duke of

Kent, was born—she "put to sea with steam and sails." Approaching the Grand Banks, she was sighted by the little *Pluto* of Duxbury, Massachusetts, bound from Bremen to Baltimore. "Spoke and passed the elegant steamship eight days out of Savannah to Petersburg by way of Liverpool," said the notation in the *Pluto's* log. "She passed us at the rate of nine or ten knots, and the heartiest compliment we could bestow was to give her three cheers, as the happiest effort of mechanical genius that ever appeared on the Western Ocean."

Scudding, wallowing and, now and then, smokily puffing her way to England for still another nineteen days, the *Savannah* was experiencing difficulties that all early paddle-wheelers would have to contend with. At first, she was so heavily laden with fuel that her paddles were too deeply submerged to work efficiently. Later they were not submerged deeply enough. When her sails were set, she tended to bend toward the lee, with one paddle wheel immersed and the other beating the air. In this circumstance, she had a propensity to veer around, an action that had to be carefully counterbalanced by the rudder.

She was burning the last of her supply of coal when she approached the southern coast of Ireland. Sparks and a column of glowing vapor rose high over the flue. For naïfs at sea this light was an amazement. "Notwithstanding the wind and tide were averse to its approach," wrote one historian, "they saw with astonishment that it was rapidly coming toward them: and when it came so near that the noises of the machinery and paddles were heard, the crews in some instances shrunk beneath their decks from the terrific sight . . . while others again prostrated themselves, and besought Providence to protect them from the approach of the horrible monster which was marching on the tides, and lighting its path by the fires which it vomited."

The *Savannah's* paddles were biting into the water and she was in that state, described by a contemporary rhetorician, when the "stream of smoke from the orifice generally takes a horizontal direction in consequence of the movement of the vessel, forming a pendant of extraordinary length and of very singular appearance." Someone in the Cape Clear telegraph station took one surprised look and decided that he had seen a ship on fire. In minutes an urgent message was received by the admiral stationed in the Cove of Cork, and one of the King's swift revenue cutters, the *Kite*, was sent to the rescue of the apparently stricken vessel. Since the *Kite* came billowing on with all sails set while the *Savannah* rolled along under conspicuously bare poles, there was consternation aboard the cutter as she began to fall far behind the smoking ship. But when the *Kite* managed to fire several cautionary shots from her small cannon, the *Savannah* shut off her engines and permitted herself, in the name of the King, to be overtaken and boarded. The rescue mission was a matter of good-natured embarrassment that would eventually make amusing copy in the British papers. On the scene, the contretemps was most amiably resolved when Captain Rogers received the *Kite*'s officers as guests and took them on an inspection tour of the exhausted paddler.

"Shipped the wheels," reads the *Savannah*'s log for June 20, "and furled the sails and run into the River Murcer, and at 6 P.M. come to anchor off Liverpool with the small bower anchor." A low tide forced her to stay outside the bar, but scores of people came out in small boats to take a look. Charitable observers were "gratified and astonished" by the arrival of "a fine ship, without the assistance of a single sheet." Others felt that the *Savannah*'s Atlantic crossing was "the most dangerous thing that has occurred in the history of British shipping." Still others, according to her sailing master Stevens Rogers, suspected that the Americans had come over with "some design to release Napoleon from St. Helena."

Among the individuals who visited the *Savannah* in dock was Junius Smith, the expatriated American who, twenty years later, would make his own large contribution to steamship history. The idea that he might himself be involved in transatlantic shipping by steam had not at this time crossed his mind. Yet he carefully examined the *Savannah*'s machinery, took note of her fittings, and was told that, while she sailed most of the way across, her engines were used for six or seven days to test their efficiency. Many years later, when other ships, including his own, had made crossings entirely under steam power, Smith was outraged to find the *Savannah* being referred to as "the ocean pioneer." In his view, "the pretensions of the *Savannah* were obtruded upon the public notice." In the midst of the enormous public excitement that attended the first successful crossings under steam, he spoke out. "Now let any one of common sense ask himself the question if all this effervescence of the public mind could have happened, if there had been any previous idea of the practicability of navigating the ocean by steam power, much less if it had already been accomplished? Let him ask himself, if the pretence set up by the *Savannah* is not a manifest pretence, originating long after the death of the *Savannah,* and subsequent to the demonstration of a fact which gave birth to the assumption?"

The initial impact of a steamship from Georgia actually berthed in the Mersey was strong. But by the time the *Savannah's* visit stretched out to twenty-five days, curiosity on the part of Liverpudlians had waned, and there was no particular business interest to indicate that she might be sold, either as a steamer or as a sailer. She had nevertheless made her mark. Richard Rush, United States Ambassador to the Court of St. James, sent an official dispatch to the Department of State. The *Savannah,* he reported, had excited "equal admiration and astonishment" and was "a signal trophy of American enterprise and skill upon the ocean."

Recoaled, resupplied, she set off on July 23 for Stockholm, calling at Elsinor en route. Accompanied by an entourage in full regalia, the King of Sweden and Norway, Charles IV, came to look her over, had dinner aboard, and went for a cruise among the nearby islands. He was much taken with her, and it seemed for a time that the *Savannah* had found a purchaser. As it turned out, His Majesty was indeed interested in buying her. But he was still making payments on Norway, so to speak, and the great sums from his exchequer that had been paid out since he had become King of the Norse had put a serious dent in his newly balanced budget. Would Captain Rogers consider a trade— one hundred thousand dollars' worth of hemp and iron in lieu of cash? Captain Rogers, full of Yankee horse sense, would not; and sentiments he made known to Mr. Hughes, the American minister to Sweden, suggest he now regarded his voyage as a venture into public relations. "I know, Sir," he told Christopher Hughes, "that I am spending and losing money in this expedition; but I have satisfied the world that the thing is practicable. As I am in Europe, I wish to circulate the fame of my ship to all people especially to persons of distinction; if I make an exception it must be to Englishmen; for they sneer at us on all occasions, and in many instances were uncivil and insolent to me."

But he had not altogether given up the search for tangible specie and he thought he could get it from the imperial coffers of St. Petersburg, toward which the *Savannah* at once set sail. A new passenger boarding at Stockholm was Lord Lyndock of England. Since he happened to be on a tour of northern European capitals, the American minister in Sweden had offered him the convenience of a steamboat passage to Russia. He was glad to accept, for the token payment, it developed, of a gold snuff box.

Czar Alexander I was already something of a steamboat buff. When Robert Fulton had learned of this interest, he had proposed himself to imperial favor through the offices of the American minister to Russia, John Quincy Adams. "Being an inventor of Steam Boats," he declared, "having a claim on every Government for the use of my invention much superior to that of any other individual, and relying on the respect which the Government of Russia have for the arts," he had asked for exclusive rights in Russian waters. The Czar responded favorably and granted him a twenty-five-year contract to build and operate steam-driven vessels that would run between St. Petersburg and Cronstadt. The contract was exclusive, predicated on one condition: that Fulton provide the Emperor with a usable steamship by the beginning of 1818. When Robert Fulton died, in 1815, a big steamer that was to be christened *Emperor of Russia* lay unfinished in the shipyards. But this vessel never got to St. Petersburg. Instead, she was apparently given the name *Connecticut* and put into service and an illustrious career as a coastal steamer running between New York City and Stonington, and other ports in New England. By 1817 the Czar had forgotten about her in favor of a little paddler called *Elizabeth*, and she was now plying the Neva.

The *Savannah* steamed optimistically into Cronstadt. Marcus de Travys, the Russian Lord High Admiral, responded warmly to the American Minister's invitation to take a ride as far as St. Petersburg and back, and brought with him a company of naval and military officers. A good time was had by all but, once more, the little ship was welcomed, fêted, admired, and turned down. "This frigate is constructed of oak wood and surpasses in being solid and strong as it is in beauty," said a Russian newspaper—but Alexander I just could not be persuaded to buy her. However, he did very much want to have her remain in Russian waters. Again Captain Rogers was importuned by a reigning monarch to relax his demands and show some sense of compromise. Would the good Captain consider navigating the Black Sea, or even the Baltic Sea, under the protection of the Imperial Government? On trade routes in these waters that would be exclusively his? Once more Captain Rogers demurred. The Czar's notions were pleasant, and generous; but they were not cash on the barrelhead. His Imperial

Highness was disappointed yet, *noblesse oblige*, saw to it that Rogers did not leave his country empty-handed. When the *Savannah* sailed out into the Baltic, the Captain's effects included two new iron chairs, a gold watch, a guitar, a silver service and an ivory figurine—a miniature of himself.

After she had made stops at Copenhagen, and at Arendel in Norway, the *Savannah* entered upon a long drawn-out and stormy westward crossing. As if she refused to succumb to forces that would keep her from becoming a bona-fide ocean steamer, she managed to keep steam up, according to Stevens Rogers, even on some of the days when there was no one around to witness the fact. Back in Savannah by November 30, she had put American enterprise on the map, an American legend in the books, and her owners out of pocket to the tune of thirty thousand dollars. They kept her on hand for a while, but when the great Savannah fire of 1820 devoured what was left of their working capital they resolved once more to look for someone who might buy her. On President Monroe's old suggestion, she made a trip to the Delaware so that she might be evaluated as a possible addition to the Navy. Once again she failed to pass muster. Finally she was sold in New York, where she surrendered her engines for good and became, at long last, the sailing packet she started out to be. But her days as a coaster were few. She made eight round-trip voyages between New York and Georgia during 1821. On her ninth trip she lost her way on the turbulent night of November 5, 1821, and ran onto a sandbar, far off her course, near the community of Fire Place, Long Island. Pounding waves quickly broke her up; then, piece by piece, she was slowly buried in the long margin of sand that extends to Montauk.

❧ SECTION III ❧

T HE SAVANNAH's trip to Europe did not prove much—
perhaps only that the whims of monarchs are inscrutable
and that faith in the power of sails is never misplaced. In
the next few years her venture onto the North Atlantic was repeated by
ships flying the flags of several different countries. Listed only in record
offices and the fine print of columns devoted to arrivals and departures,
the movements of these ships constituted a far-flung enterprise that
would not come into focus for half a century. Nonetheless, wheeling
and sloshing, each on its own self-interested mission, ships driven by
steam power had begun to close drastically the distances between the
capitals of the Old World and the water-side settlements of the New.

One of these was the *Conde de Palmella,* an illusory vessel that
haunts research into early steamship trials on the ocean. Fifty feet long
and of seventy tons burden, built in Liverpool for a Portuguese trading firm, she sailed from the Mersey with one Captain Silva in command early in October, 1820, and made a fast four- or five-day passage
to Lisbon. Historical rumor has it that she refueled there, then paddled
on to "the Brazils." Since no one in Rio de Janeiro, or any other

South American port, seems ever to have witnessed or recorded her arrival, this part of her career remains mythical. However, a steamship of her name was plying the river Tagus in 1826—making it seem more than likely that the *Conde de Palmella*'s true role in life was that of a practical little riverboat, not that of an early sovereign of the southern seas.

In 1821, the *Rising Star*, a full-rigged ship notable for the oddity of two high black funnels abreast, came out of the Maudeslay shipping yard at Rotherhithe, and in October cast off from Gravesend for Chile. She spent the whole winter in getting there and did not reach Valparaiso until April. Her sponsor was Thomas Cochrane—later the tenth Earl of Dundonald—who, after a maverick's career in the British Navy, had accepted the offer of Chilean patriots to command their navy, such as it was, in their attempt to free themselves from Spanish domination. Apparently, Cochrane at first meant to steam out to Chile on the *Rising Star*. But when he heard that his services were urgently needed in the Pacific, he left the building of the ship to his brother's supervision and hurried to Valparaiso by wind and sail.

When she was fitted out, the *Rising Star* was dispatched in the belief "that the great disparity in numbers between the Chilean Navy and the Spanish Navy in the Pacific would be neutralized by the advantage obtained in utilizing a steam vessel for purposes of war." She was probably also dispatched in the hope of bringing a profit. Thomas Cochrane was happy to lend his nautical and military skills, first to rebel factions in Chile, then to others in Peru and Brazil; yet his services in the cause of liberation were not given free. By the time the *Rising Star* had got round the Horn, hostilities had ceased, the Spanish men-of-war she was supposed to stalk or entice into battle had all been driven away, and there was no money left in the Chilean national treasury to pay for her. Nevertheless, as the first steamship to sail on the Pacific Ocean, the *Rising Star* became a cynosure, visited by Governor Zenteno, parties of officials and by Mrs. Maria Graham, the widow of a British Naval captain, whose homiletic entry in her diary nicely catches the feeling of the time. "It was no small delight that I set my foot on the deck of the first steam vessel that ever navigated the Pacific," wrote Mrs. Graham, "and I thought with exultation of the triumphs of man over the obstacles nature seems to have placed between him and the accomplishment of his imagination."

The *Rising Star* could reputedly attain the speed of 12 knots. Yet she took all of six months to reach her destination. This fact suggests that, like those other ships which marine historian H. Philip Spratt has called "spasmodic pioneers," she depended far more on wind than she did on her 45-horsepower engines.

The real Flying Dutchman among early Atlantic ocean ships "impelled by fire or steam" is the *Curaçao*. A little wonder in her own time, she was too busy traipsing back and forth between the Lowlands and the West Indies ever to have caught the amazed attention even of those individuals whose reservoirs of misinformation start legends.

She did not begin her career as a Dutchman, however, but as an English vessel designated to fly an Irish flag—the Fitzgeraldine standard of the Knight of Kerry. In 1824, with only the experience of the *Savannah*, the *Rising Star* and a few coastal steamers to give them courage, a group of speculators came together under the leadership of the Rt. Hon. Maurice Fitzgerald who wanted to see that his own sea-girt ledge of Erin would be the point of departure for anything in the way of transatlantic service that might develop. He and his business friends called themselves The American and Colonial Steam Navigation Company and issued a prospectus outlining a plan whereby a small steamer would regularly set out from London, pick up passengers along the coasts of England and Ireland, and, in Valentia, transfer them to the decks of one big steamer that would carry them to Halifax and New York, another that would carry them by the Leeward Islands to Jamaica. The prospectus, thrilling as prose, was a flop when it came to raising money. The company nevertheless went ahead and ordered a 440-ton ship from the yards of the Messrs. J. H. and J. Duke in Dover. Christened *Calpe*—the ancient name for the Rock of Gibraltar—she was launched in September, 1825. But when it became obvious to the new company that they could not afford to run one steamship to the Americas, much less two, they shelved their plans and put the *Calpe* up for sale. She had been in the water just one year when she found a willing customer in the Dutch Government. They bought her, fully equipped, for about thirty-five thousand dollars, took her to the Netherlands, and made her the first steamship in the Dutch Navy.

Rechristened *Curaçao*, fitted out to carry mails to the Dutch Antilles, and mounted with two guns, she sailed from Hellevoetsluis, near Rotterdam, on April 26, 1827, got to the muddy waters of Paramaribo, Surinam, in twenty-eight days, twelve of them under steam, and reached the island colony of Curaçao five days later. She repeated this long voyage twice during the next two years, then was put on active duty as a man-of-war until 1848, when she was decommissioned, dismantled, and scrapped.

The only people who seemed to pay any attention to the transatlantic success of the *Curaçao* were the men who had brought her into being. Ten years after they had had to abandon their plans and sell her, a number of them, urged on by the indefatigable Knight of Kerry, tried once more to start a transoceanic service from the small island of Valentia. By this time other plans for direct England-to-America service—plans that entirely omitted the west coast of Ireland—were being forwarded. These, in the belief of Fitzgerald and his colleagues, were doomed to failure. They held a conviction that only a short Atlantic crossing—Valentia to Newfoundland or Nova Scotia, perhaps by way of the Azores—would work; and this was based on their certainty that no ship could be built large enough to carry the coals necessary for such a long passage.

In this they found a famous champion—Dr. Dionysius Lardner. The good doctor, attempting to give sanction to their claims, made one brief and handily quotable statement. Its effect was to ensure that nearly all the achievements of an honorable career would be poohpoohed and put aside. A wave of derision that began as soon as Dr. Lardner stood up to speak his mind was still rolling across the pages of maritime histories and chronicles of folly one hundred years after he sat down.

Lardner knew that transatlantic steamship service was feasible; but he believed, along with many other men of acumen and renown, that this could only be achieved by ships that would depart from the westernmost shore of Ireland and put in for recoaling at the Azores or in Newfoundland. Consequently, when plans for nonstop crossings were announced, he said what he believed: "As to the project . . . which is announced in the newspapers, of making the voyage directly from New York to Liverpool, it is, I have no hesitation in saying, perfectly chimerical, and they might as well talk of making a voyage from New York or Liverpool to the Moon."

"Upon what principle," asked one of his partisans, "is Dr. Lardner to be deprived of the use of the universally-employed language of metaphor?" But it was all too late; opening his mouth, the doctor had put his foot in it. When he continued to insist that he had no doubt "of the practicability of establishing a steam intercourse with the United States," he echoed only the particular ambitions of the British and American Intercourse Company. In 1835, this outfit had picked up where the *Calpe* left off and was trying to placate the Knight of Kerry by instituting, of all things, a tram-car line to run from Waterford to Valentia carrying crowds of passengers to an ever-ready fleet of ships for America. Not one ship of this Irish fleet, as it turned out, would ever hoist an anchor or turn a paddle.

This company or that, coastal steamers, men-o'-war or sometime sailers—the attempt to put a steamship on a transatlantic run was still but a very small part of history. Swift sea travel was largely a matter of rumors and wishes. Her voyage was *fait accompli*, yet the *Savannah*'s claims to historical priority as an ocean steamer are tenuous, tinted sentimentally by her connection with Georgia and made somewhat shrill by the chauvinist mindlessness of those who must put everything American first. The claims of a workaday Canadian vessel named the *Royal William* have more strength and more substance. This little ship from colonial Quebec set out on a commercial Atlantic voyage fourteen years after the proud and rejected *Savannah* had shipped her paddles, cracked on her dimity, and sailed back from her flirtation with the Czar on the banks of the Neva. Like her American predecessor, the *Royal William* also went looking for someone to bid high—not for her charms, which were conspicuously minimal, but for her well-tested engines and the ample space she provided for cargo. When she did go across the Atlantic, she went nearly all the way by steam; and this is the most important fact about her curiously brief and exotic career. Until the *Royal William* had proved the point, no one had been quite sure that, all ratios taken into account, "it does not require a coal mine to carry a steamer across the Atlantic, or an iron mine to make the machinery."

The *Royal William* was the pilot project of a new shipping firm— the Quebec and Halifax Steam Navigation Company—that proposed to offer dependable intercoastal service for passengers, cargo and mails from Quebec City to the Gulf ports of the St. Lawrence and the

Maritimes. (Included in the roster of its 235 stockholders were the names of the ambitious offspring of Abraham Cunard—Henry, Joseph and Samuel. Operating out of Halifax and into Cape Breton and New Brunswick, these men had already got themselves involved in cutting timber, mining coal and building ships.) The frame of the *Royal William* was put together in Cape Cove, Quebec, under the cliffs of Cape Diamond, in the shipyard of George Black and John Saxton Campbell, following the designs of a young man by the name of James Goudie. Born in Quebec in 1809, Goudie had been sent to Greenock, Scotland, at the age of fifteen, to learn the shipwright's trade. Back in Quebec and faced with his first big steamship job, Goudie found it only natural to copy plans he had seen used in the building of the *United Kingdom*, a steamer laid down in 1826 at the Scottish port for the London-Leith service. The *Royal William*'s 200-horsepower side-lever engines were made in Montreal by the firm of Bennet and Henderson. One of the partners, John Bennet, had like Goudie served an apprenticeship in Scotland, where he worked with Messrs. James Watt and Company, who had earlier supplied engines for Robert Fulton's famous *Clermont*. The new ship's crankshaft, forged by Robert Napier at Camlachie, was loaded onto a sailing ship and brought over to Montreal to be installed at St. Mary's foundry. Thus, the *Royal William* was almost wholly the product of the skill of shipwrights newly arrived in the unconfederated territories that were soon to become Canada.

Steamboats had been a familiar sight on the St. Lawrence River since 1809, the year when the little seventy-five-foot *Accommodation*, modeled after Fulton's *Clermont*, had emulated the American vessel's regular New York-to-Albany run by ferrying passengers between Quebec and Montreal. But a ship of 1,370 tons was by no means just another riverboat. All of Quebec turned out, on April 27, 1831, to see that she was hailed with honor. High on a launching dais, his Excellency the Governor General lent an official smile to the occasion as his wife, the Lady Aylmer, smashed a bottle over the bows and christened the ship after the reigning British monarch, William IV. To the strains of the Thirty-Second Regimental Band and the cheers and whistles of the townspeople, the new vessel carried her flags and pennons lightly down the ways until she floated in the St. Lawrence. Then, almost at once, she was taken in tow by the steamboat *British America* and urged upriver to Montreal to be fitted with her machinery.

By the end of August she was all set for her first trip—to Miramichi, in New Brunswick, then across to Prince Edward Island and down to Halifax. She made this maiden passage in six and a half days, without incident apparently, except for having aroused the curiosity of a British frigate on patrol in the Gulf of St. Lawrence. This warship fired a shot across the *Royal William*'s bows and forced her to heave to until the officers of the King's Navy could see for themselves "that there was nothing diabolical in her construction." In Halifax the *Royal William* stayed at her dock long enough to allow the town's most prominent shipping man, Samuel Cunard, to come aboard and look her over. During more than one visit he supposedly asked questions about her speed, sea-keeping qualities and fuel consumption. He noted the cozy parlor atmosphere of her saloon accommodation and put his head into the dining saloon, which, far in advance of its time, was actually set in a roundhouse on the open deck.

By the time ice in the St. Lawrence had put an end to water traffic for the year, the *Royal William* had completed three coastal trips. She then proceeded to a berth in Sorel, Quebec, to wait out the winter. In the spring of 1832 an epidemic of Asian cholera was imported full-blown into the city of Quebec, from which it spread all the way to the American midsouth. It probably arrived simultaneously on several ships (the disease was already rampant in Ireland and Scotland), but the brunt of the blame was borne by the sailing packet *Carricks* soon after she had disembarked her Irish emigrants. Three thousand people, mostly inhabitants of the Lower Town, were infected. As business life and social life slowed to the point of civic paralysis, the *Royal William* nonetheless resumed the schedule she was built to carry out, and sailed for Halifax on June 16. With eleven passengers in her staterooms, and fifty-two in the steerage, she reached Miramichi three days later. But by that time she was flying the yellow flag that signified cholera aboard. Her engineer was already dead and buried at sea; six of her crew were showing advanced symptoms. But an even greater horror was the news from Quebec. Once the letters in the mailbags designated for Miramichi were opened, panic swept the community. Local authorities quarantined the ship, marooned her passengers and stricken crewmen on Sheldrake Island and took armed precaution to see that they would stay there. Day and night, men in small boats circled the island to watch for any sign of escape.

Captain Nicolas of the *Royal William* appealed to the town magistrates for a chance to buy enough coal to enable him to sail on, but this request was flatly turned down. Timberman and leading citizen Joseph Cunard was Miramichi agent for the company that owned the *Royal William*, but not even he could persuade the civic authorities to let her go. The all-but-deserted ship had to languish offshore for a full month before she was given permission to hoist anchor. Pictou was next on her itinerary, but there she was met by armed men in a boat who stopped her from even entering the harbor. She sailed haplessly on to Halifax and was again promptly clamped into quarantine. By making a fiasco of her first trip of the year, the cholera epidemic had also brought the *Royal William* to an abrupt impasse in her career. She managed to get back to her home port in late August—fifty-five days after she had sailed out hoping for a breezy round trip. She brought back a paltry twelve passengers in her cabin and, in the steerage, twenty-seven demobilized militiamen from Bermuda who were aiming to settle in Lower Canada. Then she was tied up at Brunet's Wharf for the rest of the season. Deep in debt, with a spanking new and totally unemployed steamship on its hands, the Quebec and Halifax Steam Navigation Company made an attempt to retrieve at least some part of the nearly fifty thousand dollars they had laid out for her. She was sold by the sheriff, at the Sorel Parish Church door, for fifteen thousand dollars, to a group of buyers—all of them original stockholders—who had banded together to make a good thing out of the company's bankruptcy. But, man and boy, the Cunard clan were not among them; they had dropped out of the bidding before it ever got started.

In the late spring the *Royal William* was ready to try again. When John McDougall, a Scot from Oban, was given her command, a set of actions was put in motion that would, within four years, carry a mild-mannered sea captain from his house by the ramparts of the Plains of Abraham to the seaside battlefields of the Peninsular War. At first, for a month or so, the *Royal William* picked up a few dollars by giving up her pretensions as a liner for the ignominious role of tow boat for her inferiors—the sailing packets that came and went to the overseas landing depot on Grosse Isle. Then in June she was dispatched, via the Gaspé and Halifax, all the way to Boston, becoming the first British steamship ever to enter that port. When she fired a salute to the American flag as she was passing Fort Independence in Boston harbor, the fort's band answered with "God Save the King." Cordially welcomed, she again failed to turn a penny, in spite of the fact that she had proved herself swift, sea-worthy and, somewhat surprisingly, an object of admiration. Discouraged, her owners clung to the hope that if only they could find the right market, she would bring a price commensurate with her promise. That market, they felt, would most likely be in England. Without any hint of patriotic sentiment or any sign that they were doing something of historical importance, they decided to send her over under her own steam, simply as a means of enhancing her commercial potential.

Fourteen years before, the *Savannah's* modest advertisement for custom had been rebuffed with total silence; the *Royal William* did better by attracting all of seven passengers: a Reverend Mr. Seeney and his daughter, one Doctor Law, the Messrs. Causyer and Clark in the cabin and two persons in the steerage whose names, in the way of the times, were not worth mentioning. Each of the cabin passengers paid about twenty dollars for his passage, wines not included. The *Royal William* also got cargo: a collection of stuffed birds in a box, "natural curiosities" that a Dr. McCulloch was sending to London to be sold; six spars made of Nova Scotia pine; household furniture and a harp, made in England, that some disenchanted settler was apparently sending *back* to England. On August 4 she left Quebec, Captain McDougall in command. At Pictou she docked to take aboard a small mountain of Cape Breton coal and one passenger who had come over by schooner from Prince Edward Island. On August 17 she headed into the open ocean, "direct for London," as the advertisement in the Pictou paper promised. Laden with soft coal to almost half her total weight, she made the Grand Banks at a smart clip and was well on her way when, off the coast of Newfoundland, she was hit by a storm that crumpled the head of her foremast, put one of her two engines out of commission and poured so much water over her decks and into her hold that her engineer was convinced she would founder. As the gimpy little ship wallowed and shuddered, he was ready to take to the boats or, at least, to convince Captain Mc-Dougall that he should head for the Newfoundland shore. It was at this point, the Captain said later, that "things looked rather awk-ward." But luckily for the *Royal William*, she was rigged like a three-masted topsail schooner with long heavy spars. This gave her an auxiliary sea-keeping faculty that was probably crucial in her struggle to stay afloat. As she pounded eastward on her one remaining engine, it took all of ten days after the storm to pump her free of water and to patch her up. The second engine was repaired mid-Atlantic and, after a three-week passage, she made the Isle of Wight. There she put in at Cowes—as if to keep her slow time a secret, and to spruce up for any keen-eyed customer who might be on hand to witness her entrance into London. Her interior was damp but otherwise in good shape; newly painted stem to stern, she went up to Gravesend, reported her captain, "in fine style."

The whole voyage had taken twenty-five days. Since the sailing packets were now regularly doing better, this was nothing to boast of. But as an all-out test of the durability and persistence of marine steam engines, the trip was of signal importance. Except for rather long periods—twenty-four to twenty-six hours—every four days, when she had to stop in order to clean accumulations of salt from her boilers, the *Royal William* had indeed steamed all the way. This feat convinced British shipping interests of three things: the feasibility of transocean steamships; the possibility, under steam, of reducing the usual nine weeks out-and-home passages of the mail packets to five weeks; the availability and excellence of coal "in our colony of Nova Scotia."

Barely more than a week after the *Royal William*'s jaunty trip up the Thames, Messrs. George Wildes & Company, the agents to whom she had been consigned, disposed of her for a handsome ten thousand pounds sterling, to Joseph Somes, a shipowner from Ratcliffe. Not more than a year had passed since she had suffered the humiliation of being auctioned, like some broken-down country wagon, at the church door, and her price had doubled. She stayed in the Port of London for a few weeks; then, with Captain McDougall retained in command, she went on charter carrying British mercenaries on their way to join the forces of Dom Pedro, who was trying to secure the throne for the child-Queen Donna Maria. Charles Napier, the English Admiral who was also selling his services to the Queen's faction as Don Carlos da Ponza, commander of the Portuguese Constitutional Fleet, was offered the chance to acquire the *Royal William* but refused. He already had six English steamboats in Portuguese waters, using them as tow boats and supply ships for his men-of-war under sail, and finding them a nuisance. The trouble lay not so much in the steamboats themselves but in the truculence of the English engineers and crewmen who kept them going. Indifferent to internecine Portuguese struggles for power, these men tended to accept from the Admiral only those assignments they considered safe. Rejected once more, the *Royal William* picked up wounded or disbanded members of the British Legion and steamed back to London and a period of unemployment at the Deptford Victualling Office.

Midsummer, 1834, the *Royal William* received new orders: proceed to Portugal to institute steamship service between Oporto and Lisbon. She made one trip between these ports, then was dispatched to Cadiz to transport specie for the Portuguese treasury. On this short voyage her speed caught the covetous eyes of Spanish officials. When she got back to Lisbon the Spanish Ambassador, Don Evanster Castor da Perez, made representations to her owner that ultimately released her from charter to Portugal and transferred her ownership outright to Spain. The *Royal William* was then rechristened *Ysabel Segunda*, after the embattled princess who had become Queen of Spain in 1833. Armed with six cannon and a few other showy but ineffective military appurtenances, she became Spain's first modern warship. Again, Captain McDougall was part of a package deal; he was given the rank and pay of a commander in the Spanish Navy, a guaranteed bonus of nearly two thousand dollars a year, plus a contract to supply the whole squadron with provisions from Lisbon. Since he was probably the only man who could run the ship and, what's more, had no political axe to grind in England, Portugal, Spain or anywhere else, the Spaniards were clearly determined to keep Captain McDougall at the helm of their little behemoth. But neither change of name nor elevation to a military status were enough to divert the *Royal William* from her whimsical and checkered progress.

To get full fitting as a ship of war, she returned to Gravesend, where she was delivered up to the British Government and taken to its military dockyard at Sheerness. Then, bristling with armor and little guns, she sailed in full panoply for Saint Andero and San Sebastian. General Alava, the Spanish Ambassador to England, was aboard, along with General DeLacy Evans of the British Legion and his staff officers. At San Sebastian, the *Ysabel Segunda*, née *Royal William*, achieved a miniscule figure in the tapestry of history by becoming the first steamer of war ever to fire from her cannon a shot that was more than a ritual salute. This happened on May 5, 1836. Some of General Evans' troops, among them members of the Eighth Scottish Highlanders, had gone ashore to try to drive a band of Carlists out of the fieldworks in which they had entrenched themselves. Things were at a standstill when a well-placed volley from the decks of the *Ysabel Segunda* sent the surprised Carlists running and allowed the Highlanders to occupy their positions.

A year later she was dispatched to Portsmouth on what was becoming a Spain-to-Britain military run, then sent on to London. Minus Captain McDougall at last, she was to be turned over to the Spanish Ambassador with the idea that he would have her fitted out by British shipwrights for further military service. The Ambassador did his job, but when, pillar to post, the beleaguered ship got to Spain her hull was in such bad condition that she had to be sent to a shipyard in Bordeaux for repairs. When French shipwrights looked her over, they found her timbers so deeply decayed that they told the Spaniards she was beyond salvage. But her engines were still in good shape, they pointed out: Why not take them out of the old vessel and put them into a new one? Thus the pride of Quebec, not even ten years old, was turned into a hulk in the harbor of Bordeaux to rise and sink on tides from the Atlantic while a new man-of-war was being built to receive her engines, even her name.

Broken apart, the traducian entity that was once the *Royal William* was soon two ships, both unlucky. The one was left to rot; the other, going strong on engines from Montreal for still another twenty years, was finally undone by a sirocco that swept the coast of Algeria and sent her to the bottom. The little steamship that had once paddled merrily down the St. Lawrence had come to an ending as sorry as it was grotesque: while her cast-off hull, like the carapace of a hermit crab, lay on the mud flats of Bordeaux, the same engines that had made her the first steamship to make a bona-fide crossing of the Western Ocean were sinking slowly into the ooze of the Barbary Coast. Out of sight and out of mind for decades, the *Royal William* was eventually reborn in the bombastic imaginations of patriotic Canadians. By the end of the century, the tough little ship was no longer a hand-me-down piece of nautical hardware but "this young aurora of the seas, prepared to drive darkness, distances, and the winds before her, and constrain the elements themselves to be submissive."

❦ SECTION IV ❧

Junius Smith: Father of Ocean Steam Navigation / Yale Man and London Trader / The Royal Victoria

INTO THE DEPTHS of waters they had walked or into the abysmal indifference of time and the record office, one by one, the brave little smoke boxes made their crossings and disappeared. The *Savannah* had introduced an idea; the *Curaçao* gave substance to the notion of a liner; the *Royal William* accomplished the first North Atlantic passage primarily under the power of steam. They had proved beyond doubt that vessels making use of a conjunction of sail and steam could make reasonably safe and fast passages. Yet, long after they had done so, there was still no regular steam carrier on the busiest of the world's ocean routes. Bigger and more handsome every year, the sailing packets confidently kept the glamorous business of sea transport all to themselves. But as shipping fortunes were aggrandized, and captains with muttonchop whiskers became rich enough to retire to country estates among collections of silver plates, ceremonial pitchers, gravy boats and sugar bowls and other memorabilia scrawled with gratitude in rhyme and imprinted with kisses, minds of quite another persuasion were active.

Regular transatlantic steamship service was delayed, almost uncannily, for twenty long years after the notion had been proved entirely feasible. But when it came, it came all at once. The event that signaled it, decades in the making, was all over within a few hours. But those few hours sent the city of New York into raptures of excitement, united scientific research with human adventurousness, and introduced a touch of showmanship into the business of travel by sea that would never quite be erased.

When, almost simultaneously, two noisy and festooned steamships came trailing their cinders into Manhattan waters, the swath they cut had sliced the Atlantic Ocean in half. Founding an industry, they opened an era. Like an overfed idiot, that industry would soon grow out of its clothes and, within a hundred years, immobilize itself beyond the hope of house or home. But in its brave beginnings it united the pursuit of profits and the pursuit of mechanical, even aesthetic, ideals with a bravura that was irresistible.

Behind the pretty picture of two foreign steamships saluting one another off the seaward wedge of Manhattan Island lies a story of personal courage and crippling bad luck, imaginative capitalism in association with mechanical genius, Yankee canniness and British doggedness. Though it comes to its conclusion in one port, the story has its beginnings in two.

Junius Smith had one unwavering ambition: to be acknowledged as the one and only father of steam navigation on the Atlantic Ocean. When things were going well, he believed he had clear title to that distinction and even tried to commission Washington Irving to chronicle his success. "I will furnish all the necessary facts and documents and many interesting anecdotes," he told an associate in New York, "and in his hands I think it would be a work of interest to the general reader. If he will undertake the work, he shall have the profits and I will guarantee him against any losses." But the master refused to lend his florid quill to this plan and Smith had to look elsewhere. In a conviction of the "right and justice" of his claims, he waited for Queen Victoria to award him knighthood. But Her Majesty held back, and he had to take comfort in a Doctor of Law degree conferred on him by Yale College. Coming from "the seat of early associations," he told the college's president Jeremiah Day, "the home of my youth and the nurse of every kindly feeling, it comes with accumulated force and like good news from a far country cheers the heart and animates the pil-

grim on his onward journey." Having thus conveyed his felicities, he
came to the point. "Let me have the New Haven parchment," he
wrote from London. "It may be of some use to me here and fortify
my position."

Naïve in his hunger for glory, Junius Smith was nonetheless bucking
only for what he deserved. Defeated in the end, he would occupy his
considerable place in maritime history almost invisibly. Yet no one
can follow his story without flinching at the way in which a man of
the most engaging probity, easy humor and worldly wit, punished by
bad fortune throughout his career, continued to be pursued by furies
even beyond the grave.

Born at Plymouth, Connecticut, in 1780, a graduate of Yale in
the class of 1802, Smith for a time studied law with John C. Calhoun
in Litchfield, then moved to England where he set himself up as an
exporter of things like cast iron, lace, hemp and chalk, and as an
importer of cotton, turpentine and timber. In 1832, when he brought
his family back to America for a visit, they traveled on the sailing packet
St. Leonard and spent fifty-four days at sea. The length of the voyage
made Smith impatient, bored and finally desperate. It was, he said, a
"humbling" experience. As a London trader, he knew well the hazards
of weather that made consignments overdue, allowed apples and other
perishables to rot in the holds, and brought on angry cancellations of
orders for goods that were still wallowing somewhere mid-Atlantic. He
had heard accounts of packets stalled in calms for a week or more with
land in sight. He had seen weather put a freeze on commerce that was
dependent on the few ships that sailed in the winter months.

Now he had learned for himself why people refused to embark on a
packet voyage unless they had to. Paganini, for instance, when he was
offered an American concert tour that would have earned him a fortune,
had turned it down because, he said, he simply could not afford to spend
so many valuable months of his life at sea. Convinced that a steamer
would have made the same trip he made in one third the time, Smith
tried to enlist New York money in a scheme to start transatlantic service. "Dispatch is the life and delay the death of all business connected
with shipping," he said; but no one in New York would do more than
listen.

"New Yorkers seem at times *stupid* about steam navigation," he told
his nephew, who was also his business associate. "How can they shut

their eyes to the fact that steam ships do (and have done for years) navigate the tempestuous coast of Europe through the winter, at all seasons in all weather, whilst sailing ships lie in port." Returning to England on the *Westminster,* he spent another thirty-two impatient days under sail. "Thirty-two days from New York to Plymouth," he wrote to his nephew, "and forty to London is no trifle. Any ordinary steamer would have run it, the weather we had, in fifteen days with ease. I shall not relinquish this project until I find it absolutely impracticable."

In the heyday of marine tycoons like Preserved Fish, Pardon Gifford, Francis Skiddy and John Minturn, New York in the smugness of its great good fortune continued to rebuff Smith's overtures. But London was comparatively open to suggestion. "Doubtless you thought the enterprise too novel in itself," he reminded his nephew, "or too great in its object to be carried into practice. It is not so entertained in London. It is received indeed as a new guest but one of comely aspect and promising hopes." But when he applied for the privilege of an interview with the Duke of Wellington, all he got for his presumption was cold water. Presenting his compliments through a secretary, the Duke announced that he had "no leisure to receive the visits of gentlemen who have schemes in contemplation of the alteration of the public establishments." This cool response might have been anticipated. Wellington had already announced his antipathy to railways "because they would encourage the lower classes to move about."

Smith was of course not consciously aiming to undermine British traditions, but he did have a scheme that might allow him to monopolize the North Atlantic. Four steamers, he felt, would do the trick. This number would be fully equal to the twelve American sailing vessels regularly running between England and America. And if he could arrange to have two of the contemplated ships American-built and two British-built, he might "combine the interests of the two countries in their support."

Uncurbed by the coldness of the Iron Duke, Smith proceeded to canvass the city for more open-minded audience. "All this keeps me in a sweat in the month of July," he wrote his New York office. "But I see no reason to despair: on the contrary, every day affords fresh encouragement to go on, and I do not feel any doubt of raising the money to the very notch. But the patience and labour of forming a company in London is beyond all that you can imagine. It is the worst place in the whole world to bring out a new thing—the best when it is done. One hundred thousand pounds is but a drop to the great monied interests of London. The difficulty is to overcome the affinity which that drop has for its old birth, and to induce it to flow in a new channel. Do that, and it comes in a flood." Meanwhile he persisted. "Job's patience is much celebrated," he said, "but I don't think that he ever undertook to establish a steam company."

Smith became convinced that he must have big names from the world of finance if he was to attract lesser ones. Consequently, he was much heartened when the famous government contractor, Isaac Solly, a chairman of the Great Birmingham & London Railway Company, agreed to the use of his. With Solly behind him, Smith found that his prediction about money coming "in a flood" was correct. When MacGregor Laird of the Birkenhead shipping family also joined him, the company quickly began to come into shape. When it had announced itself as the British and American Steam Navigation Company and was preparing to open its books to the public in London, Liverpool and Dublin, Smith was thinking in terms of one million pounds—ten thousand shares to be offered at one hundred pounds each. At this point, having made his friendly gesture, Isaac Solly withdrew from any association as a director; but the prestige of the board remained high when two new directors were taken on: Colonel Aspinwall, the United States Consul in London; and James Beale, President of the Cork School of Art and Science.

In 1836 a contract was made with MacGregor Laird's firm to lay down the first ship, to be called the *Royal Victoria*. At a proposed 1,890 tons, she would be the largest steam-propelled vessel afloat. "The *Victoria* is now in frame and the finest frame that I ever saw," Smith reported to New York. "The best timber and the best workmanship. The nobility are beginning to cast their eyes upon her. I met the Marquis of Blandford at the ship yesterday. He was much delighted and called her the St. Paul's of naval architecture. The builders are proud of her and certainly are doing themselves great credit and the company great justice. I do hope by and by to see eight such ships traveling to New York."

The summer of 1837 on the North Atlantic was particularly boisterous. One sailing packet after another came in long overdue, causing serious trouble, sometimes bankruptcy, to men whose business depended on goods and monies from abroad. Junius Smith wasted little sympathy on the disappointed and irate traders who had ridiculed his early efforts to relieve them of just the sort of anxieties they were facing. "Multitudes cry out for a steamer," he wrote, "to get accounts from Canada and the States. I send them to the ship yard to look at her. I feel a little wicked on the subject, because these dogs only barked at us at first and were not aware that they would be the first to cast their tails between their legs."

He also took a swipe at Dionysius Lardner, who had been persisting in speaking his claim that plans for nonstop Atlantic crossings were "perfectly chimerical." In Smith's view, Lardner was "a perfect Quack and embarked in the Old Valentia Steam Company, now defunct for twelve years. But it won't do. We must have better evidence than Dr. Lardner can give us before any effectual obstruction can be given to steam navigation, Valentia and the Knight of Kerry notwithstanding." Yet, for all his fervor, Smith was modest in his claims, if not in his ambitions. "I do not mean to advocate the abandonment of sails," he wrote to Benjamin Silliman, "whilst I endeavor to show that it is not a philosophical method of propelling a ship. It will be sufficient if I show that the application of steam power is both safer and more philosophical than the power of wind in navigation."

As the Royal Victoria rose on the stocks, so began to rise another ship that would beat her both to the post and to the wire—the Great Western. Since the promoters of this vessel were to a man British, the challenge to be first across was viewed as another confrontation of England and the United States as maritime powers. In America, Yankee know-how and hard bargaining were still matters of the first account. Consequently, in some quarters at least, Junius Smith—that Yankee in London—was regarded as yet another of the homespun breed that had unshackled themselves from the British in 1776, bested them on the high seas in 1812, and would race them to China and back any time they wanted to put up a bet.

"Shall it be said," asked Ithiel Town, "that the far-famed and well-earned glory of Yankee enterprise is to be eclipsed—that the wreath which should encircle the brow of the noble Fulton is to be worn by our trans-Atlantic brethren in their higher and more perfect attainments in steam navigation?"

The answer was yes.

❈ SECTION V ❧

Isambard Kingdom Brunel / The Great Western / The
Sirius / The Race to New York / "The Broad Atlantic
Bridged at Last . . . Annihilation of Space and Time" / Daniel
Webster and Other Free-Loaders / The Fury of
James Gordon Bennett / "Farewell Nationality!"

I SAMBARD KINGDOM BRUNEL, the great civil engineer of the century, was present when the directors of the Great Western Railway held a meeting at a Blackfriars hotel in October, 1835. Of this body Brunel was merely an associate and sometime employee; yet one remark of his on this occasion would lead to a farreaching plan and to resonant events. Within a few years, his remark would also lead to the acute financial distress of those of the assembled company who were daring enough, or gullible enough, to take him at his word.

The Great Western Railway was looking into proposals for an extension of the already established line that would provide a connection from Paddington all the way to Bristol. In the course of talk, one of the more timorous directors shook his head: Was not the company overreaching itself? Need they really go all the way to Bristol? To confound reticence with bravado, Brunel spoke up. Why not make it even longer? Why not have a steamship meet a train at Bristol and carry its passengers all the way to New York? Why not give the good name of the Great Western to a steamship?

Nonsense like this was good for a laugh around the conference table, but only a mild one. Discussion turned upon other subjects. When the meeting was adjourned, Thomas Richard Guppy, a director known for his risible disposition, called Brunel aside and asked him to say something more of what he had in mind with his talk of an ocean steamship. What Brunel had in mind was a chance to prove still another of his theories, and a way to get the money that might support the effort. He believed he had found a way to build a bigger ship than any extant, and he believed that the bigger the ship the more profitable it could be. Against current opinion—which held that the doubling of the size of the hull of a vessel meant that twice the amount of coal would be necessary to power it—Brunel had come upon a simple formula: while the usable space of a hull increases as the cube of its dimensions, the resistance (or required driving power) increases only as the square of the same dimensions. Even as he was listening, Guppy apparently heard the blast of steam whistles setting off an Atlantic run. Within a few days he had convinced three other members of the Great Western's board to listen again to Brunel, and had begun to look with confidence toward further moral and financial support.

With Captain Christopher Claxton, R.N., an old and close friend of Brunel's, Guppy made a sort of reconnaissance tour around the country, calling at ports where steamboats were already a going thing and a good investment. What he found was encouraging; everyone wanted bigger ships and money to back them was readily available. When, to start things off, he personally put up fifteen thousand pounds, shipping men in Bristol were quick to follow his lead. In that city, as of June, 1836, the new firm—the Great Western Steam-Ship Company—came into being with a working capital of two hundred and fifty thousand pounds. Captain Claxton was appointed managing director. A contract for the first ship was given to a local builder, William Patterson, "known as a man open to conviction and not prejudiced in favor of either quaint or old-fashioned notions in ship building," with the understanding that he and his partner John Mercer would be under the close advisement of a Building Committee for the company composed of Brunel, Claxton and Guppy. The ship was to be designed to Brunel's specifications, and he would give his consulting services free of charge.

Already building in London, the *Royal Victoria* seemed quite certain to be the ship to get away first. The shipyards of Curling and Young were showing that their "great and deserving reputation" for punctual deliveries was justified. Then bad news arrived from Scotland, and auspicious signs were dimmed. The Messrs. Claude, Girdwood & Co., who had undertaken ,to construct the machinery for the ship, had accomplished two thirds of their job when financial troubles brought first a work stoppage, then bankruptcy. Junius Smith and his friends turned at once to the famous Robert Napier, and a new contract to provide engines was drawn up. Scheduled to be ready for the sea in the autumn of 1837, the *Royal Victoria*, it was now apparent, would not be ready until late in 1838.

The *Great Western* was meanwhile floated out of Patterson & Mercer's dock at Wapping, Bristol, on the morning of July 19, 1837. Before a crowd of fifty thousand people, Captain Claxton smashed a bottle of madeira on the figurehead, Mrs. Miles, the mother of Bristol's representative in Parliament, spoke the ship's name, and "the multitudes in every direction rent the air with their acclamations." A month later, accompanied by the tug *Lion* and a coastal packet, she left Cumberland Basin under sail and headed for London, where decorators were waiting to finish her saloon, engineers to install her machinery. The many visitors who came down from the City had never seen anything like her vast cabin; some of them felt that it was less a public room than it was a gallery of art. Seventy-five feet long by twenty-one feet wide, the saloon simply overwhelmed the curious. On its walls were fifty big panels picturing "rural scenery, agriculture, music, the arts and sciences, interior views and landscapes, and parties grouped, or engaged in elegant sports and amusements." Smaller panels "contained beautifully pencilled paintings of Cupid, Psyche, and other aerial figures." One local correspondent said it was an apartment "to vie with those of the clubhouses of London in luxury and magnificence." According to another, the overall effect gave the room "the appearance of a cabinet of old Dresden china." Brunel's own particular contribution to the saloon— pointed arches and quatrefoils in the spandrils—furthered the Gothic revival that was already well under way in England. Before long, students of such matters would note that the whole decorative scheme for the Great Western Railway tended to repeat this aspect of the ship's interior.

Spectators looking up at the *Great Western*'s bow saw a seminude figure of Neptune holding a gilded trident and, on each side of him, dolphins painted to look as though they had been dipped in bronze.

Not the least of the *Great Western's* marvels of engineering was a newly invented system of bells, allowing for communication between every cabin and the stewards' rooms. The *Civil Engineer and Architect's Journal* took special note of the innovation: "When the attendance of the steward is required, the passenger pulls the bell-rope in his berth, which rings the bell in the small box (in the stewards' room) and at the same time by means of a small lever forces up through a slit in the lid a small tin label with the number of the room painted requiring the services of the steward, and there remains, until the steward has ascertained the number of the room and pushed it down again. Thus, instead of an interminable number of bells there are only two. This arrangement, which is alike ingenious as it is useful, is deserving the notice of architects."

When a man from the London *Athenaeum* went down to investigate, he found himself at the scene of an endless social event. "With a hundred workmen on board," he wrote, "engaged in finishing her ornamental work, and her berths merely, they have had a complete levee of strangers, it seems, for some weeks past. One waterman, who had good reason to remember well, rated the number the day before at a thousand." In spite of his general grumpiness about new things, the Duke of Wellington came down to take the measure of the *Great Western* and was even gracious enough to scratch his autograph in the cabin's guest album. One reporter returning to the City said that he met "the Lord Mayor, with his state carriage and his four footmen rolling in gold, dashing down to Blackwall to get a last glimpse; all in pursuit, in a word, of the great animals of the day—the steamers now starting for the other side of the Atlantic."

While the *Great Western* was being primped like a queen and excitement about her was beginning to spread like a mild contagion, the *Royal Victoria* remained bogged down simply for want of driving power. Smith and his associates at first looked on with a patience that became chagrin, then desperation. Somehow they had to devise means for keeping the infant British and American Steam Navigation Company in the running of the great Atlantic race. Since it was obvious that the *Royal Victoria* would not be ready to go for many months, they conceived a drastically new alternative: to charter one or the other of the tough, dependable little steamships engaged in the coastal trade, fit her out for temporary long-distance travel and send her to New York under the banner of the new company. On the recommendation of MacGregor Laird and James Beale, who was familiar with the ship because of her frequent visits to his hometown of Cork, the vessel they chose was the *Sirius*—a wooden ship of 700 tons, 320 horsepower, with two masts and one funnel, "comely in her proportions." Built at Leith, she was bare and workmanlike in her general aspect, with rectangular paddle boxes instead of the conventional rounded ones. Her miniature superstructure was painted a sort of grim institutional green and black, and her hull was black. This austerity was modified, almost sentimentalized, by her figurehead—a winsome-looking mongrel dog that seemed to be proffering a star to anyone obliging enough to consider it. The *Sirius* belonged to the St. George Steam Packet Company and was regularly employed on a run that included London, Plymouth and Cork. When it was time to choose a captain for her transatlantic venture, James Beale suggested that his friend Dick Roberts, from Ardmore, Passage West, just outside of Cork, be named to take command.

By late March the *Sirius* was newly fitted out and on her mark; the *Great Western* was likewise polished, oiled and well advertised. "She stows with ease sufficient coals for 25 days' steaming at full consumption," said the Company. "It is unnecessary, therefore, to incur the delay of calling at Cork." She offered "128 sleeping places for one class of passengers, divided between upper Saloon State Rooms, under Saloon State Rooms, State Rooms in the Fore Cabin . . . and State Rooms in the poop or cuddy; besides which there are 20 good bed places for servants." She was scheduled to sail on April 7; the fare to New York would cost, on an average, thirty-five guineas.

Ready, each in her own way, the two ships were about to be introduced to one another for the first time. As the schooner bow of the *Sirius* carved the tidal waters of the Thames on March 28, and her bright-white little dog with his star put his nose downriver, she found herself coming abreast of the *Great Western*. The latter was simply out for a cruise, a little pleasure trip for the edification of a party of dignitaries. Inevitably, a race developed. By the time Gravesend was off her starboard, the *Sirius* had caught up with her rival and outdistanced her by more than a mile. But the laurels of priority were still to be awarded, the big test still to come.

In the gray first light of the morning of March 31, 1838, Isambard Kingdom Brunel, normally a brisk and slightly imperious man, was very likely a subdued and anxious one. He had followed the *Great West-ern* from the drafting boards to this moment; everything depended on her first voyage. At stake was not only the success of one already-celebrated ship, but also the reputation of a company that a suggestion of his had brought into being. Now, in his slightly dented stovepipe hat, as he walked the deck chomping the black stump of a cigar, he was about to witness proof. With him were his good friends Christopher Claxton and Tom Guppy and his famous old father, Isambard, Senior, along with a score of other men concerned in one way or another to see that the first steamer consciously planned to be a regular Atlantic runner came up to expectations.

When signals were exchanged between her captain, Lieutenant James Hosken, R.N., and George Pearne, Chief Engineer, the *Great Western* edged away from Brunswick Wharf into Blackwall Reach. It was 8:15 A.M., with hardly enough light in the sky to register the smudge left by her tall funnel as her big paddle wheels began to roil the filmy Thames. Devilishly smart and handsome in her lean black proportions, her quest at last begun, she sped downriver to Tilbury, on toward Gravesend, and was just feeling her way into the deep-water channel of the estuary when a tongue of flame reached wickedly out from the base of her funnel and in a moment covered her in smoke and flame. The underside of the deck was immediately enveloped; the fore stokehole and the engine rooms were dense with smoke. What had happened, as later investigation would reveal, was that the felt lagging around the boilers had been extended so far up that the red lead fastening the lagging in place became overheated, generating oil gas that spontane-ously ignited.

Choking and half blinded by smoke, Chief Engineer Pearne took a deep breath and scrambled below in an attempt to save the boilers by opening all the feed cocks. With the idea of beaching her before she could burn through, Captain Hosken headed the ship toward the re-claimed marshlands of Canvey Island. In the confusion of the moment, Isambard Brunel saw Christopher Claxton disappear below in smoke that now came pouring from every hatchway. To go to his assistance, he rushed to the fore hatch, put his foot on the top rung of a long ladder that reached to the keelson, and lost consciousness. Claxton, holding the nozzle of a fire hose that shot water onto the blazing beams over-head, suddenly found himself knocked down by a weighty bundle of something falling through the smoke. Stunned for a second, he recovered his wits quickly enough to realize that he had been hit by a human body and that this body was now lying unconscious in three or four inches of water on the boiler-room plating. He pulled it clear of the water, yelled for a rope to be lowered from above, and managed to get the unconscious man tied up and hauled onto the deck. When the fire was put out and the ship had come to a halt on the Chapman Sands, Claxton learned that he had probably saved the life of Isambard Brunel. When the latter had put his weight on the burned rung of the stokehole ladder he had plummeted eighteen feet. Unable to move, Brunel was bedded into a sail on deck, then lowered in a boat and rowed to Leigh, then to Southend. Since doctors were unavailable at either of these places, he was eventually treated for his injuries at Hole Haven.

The *Great Western* rested in the soft mud of Chapman Sands lightly. When the next high tide floated her off, she resumed her passage to Bristol. But the mishap was to prove costly. It allowed the *Sirius* to assume pride of place by a further twelve hours and it caused fifty nervous passengers to cancel plans they had made to cross on the maiden voyage. Her arrival at Bristol, where she anchored at Kingroad in the early evening of April 2, took even many of her own people by surprise. They had heard on good authority that she had burned in the Thames estuary.

At ten on the morning of April 4, 1838, the newly appointed captain of the *Sirius*, Richard Roberts, ordered the firing of a gun. As the salvo boomed out, his forty passengers (five ladies and six gentlemen in the first cabin; five ladies and three gentlemen in the second; one lady and twenty gentlemen in the steerage) knew they were about to cast off and stand on a course for the New World. Overloaded with 450 tons of coal, 20 tons of water and 58 casks of resin, the *Sirius* jauntily steamed down the River Lee and out into the island-sheltered harbor of Cork. "American colors at the fore, and the flag of old England at the stern," she rode the water nimbly, while smoke poured from her one funnel that somehow had the look of a cork-tipped cigarette. Thousands of people, including the residents of Passage West, Captain Roberts' home village, waved from both shores. As she approached Monkstown, the battery at Rock Lodge fired a parting salute. Among those who acknowledged greetings from the breezy open deck were the actor Davenport and his actress daughter, and one Mr. Ransome, who, with his wife and four children, was "proceeding," according to a local report, "to quell the Lower Canada Rebellion."

When the *Sirius* had sheered off from the attendant *Ocean* (a small steamer that had brought many of her voyagers down from Liverpool), and was off and away, all attentions were shifted toward her bigger and vastly more powerful rival. "The *Great Western*," said a London paper, "is roused at length. One may see her excited almost like a living thing. She heaves her huge whale-like sides with impatience. Her paddles instinctively dash into the water, as a war-horse, when he hears a trumpet, paws the ground. And see, how the fierce breath of a giant defiance pours out of her eager nostrils! Look to it, *Sirius!*"

Four days later, with all of her vaunted spaciousness housing a paltry six gentlemen passengers and Miss Eliza Cross, proprietress of Stay, Straw and Millinery Warerooms in Bristol, the *Great Western* went pounding out from Kingroad at about eleven A.M., "dragging slowly along while securing her very heavy anchor," and met the flood tide with "the wind blowing strong from West North-West" and a heavy sea. Then, hoisting at last "the lion-flag," she began "her march on the mountain-wave, with the motto, victory or death."

An important advantage enjoyed by both the *Sirius* and the *Great Western* over all other steamships that had previously labored across the Atlantic was "Mr. Hall's ingenious condensing apparatus." This was a device (invented by several men, but registered in the Patent Office by Samuel Hall) by which fresh distilled water could be fed to the boilers, making it unnecessary for steamers so equipped to break their voyages every three or four days in order to clean out salt. But there were still other kinks that had to be ironed out, other problems that might cause a ship to come to a halt midocean. Eight days from Cork, the *Sirius* had to hove to in order to refasten floats that had come loose and to repack her stuffing boxes. Twelve days out on a wild sea, however, she was "behaving nobly and riding like a duck," and on April 17, according to Captain Roberts, there was "a dangerous sea, and a bounteous fall of snow to cool our energies." From then on it was smooth sailing, a passage of such awesome sights that even the Captain himself was moved to epiphany. "It really appeared to me as if Providence smiled propitiously on our voyage," he wrote in his journal, "as we passed through, or, I may say, under, as it appeared to us, three of the most splendid arches (I may say triumphal) I have ever witnessed, extending from north to south about six miles, the centre hanging immediately over our trucks, the sun going down clear and resplendent. The dark, thick clouds hanging at our rear like an impenetrable mass, tinged along the margin by other clouds of a snowy whiteness, formed a most beautiful sight, such as the mind of man cannot truly imagine unless he has previously seen it."

Following closely behind, gaining on the pacesetter at the rate of two knots every hour, the *Great Western* was also having shakedown difficulties. Only a day out from Bristol, her bow took a deep plunge and Neptune's golden trident, broken off, sank into the ocean it had so briefly governed. "Sea sickness stalks in stifling horror among us," said a passenger, "and the dreadful cry of 'steward'—'steward'—the last ejaculation of despair, comes from a dozen nooks, hurried in a piercing treble, or growled forth, with muttered maledictions on the dilatory bucket bearer, in the deep tones of thorough bass." Then the stokers began to complain that they couldn't get enough sleep. Neither could the passengers. "The repose of last night," said one of them, "might be compared to a tossing in a blanket, and a dance of pot-hooks and frying pans was nothing to the din of the glorious clatter among the moveables that accompanied it." The larboard paddle wheel was discovered to be missing two essential bolts; a waterpipe broke and in a bad wind the fore topmast was swept away. Nine days out, the demands of speed began to overwhelm the efforts of weary stokers and trimmers. It became difficult to maintain steam "by reason the coal cannot be got from ends of ship and brought to the furnaces fast enough for consumption."

By promising them each an extra half dollar, Chief Engineer Pearne managed to put his crew to work at double time hauling coal from the extreme ends of the ship—all except for a stoker by the name of Crooks, who was obviously fed up with the whole business. He got drunk, quit work, and turned in. Next morning, when Pearne tried to get him back on the job, Crooks stuck to his bunk and his bottle. The situation was brought to the attention of Captain Hosken, who ordered that Crooks be "secured on the poop." This gesture proved to be unwise. Crooks got free, attacked the Captain and tried to heave him overboard from the ladder to the poop deck. When he was subdued and tied up again, his friends in the stokehole went on a sympathy strike, saying they would not lift a shovel until he was released. Crooks was freed of his fetters, but, early afternoon, his hangover caught up with him and he complained of illness. Chief Engineer Pearne "gave him medecine" and the *Great Western* plowed southwestward down the final arc of the Great Circle route.

The April 22 entry in the log book of the *Sirius* reads as follows: "To 10 P.M. 267 knots, light breeze and fine weather; observed the high lands of Neversink; at 8 P.M. stowed the engines; at 9 P.M. fired signals for pilot; then hove to for pilot, and scored off the Battery at 10 P.M." A long way off the Battery, indeed. Finding no pilot to guide her in, "all hands anxiously looking," the *Sirius* wallowed about for a bit and with a slight shudder nosed into a Sandy Hook mud bank.

Though pilots were nowhere in sight, newshawks were ready and waiting. As soon as the *Sirius* had stopped engines, her mission accomplished, she was boarded by a reporter on the news schooner *Eclipse*, chartered by the New York *Courier and Enquirer*. Within hours, headlines were being readied for early morning distribution: "Arrival of a Steamer from Europe," they read. "Seven Days Later from London, Six Days Later from Liverpool."

When the tide rose, the *Sirius* was freed from her grounding without damage or injury. April 23, 1838—it was St. George's Day; the two hundred seventy-fourth anniversary of Shakespeare's birth and the two hundred twenty-second anniversary of his death. Newsboys in the muddy streets of Manhattan were shouting the news of her arrival while the *Sirius* was still paddling up through the Narrows. "Arrival of the Steamer *Sirius* in Seventeen Days from Cork," they yelled. "The Broad Atlantic Bridged at Last . . . Annihilation of Space and Time."

"The news spread like wild fire through the city," said a local citizen, "and the river became literally dotted with boats conveying the curious to and from the stranger. There seemed to be an universal voice of congratulation, and every visage was illuminated with delight." Within the hour, "gracefully shaped and painted black all over, the water around her covered with boats," the *Sirius* rode at anchor off the Battery a short distance from Castle Garden. She had won the race; but it was a tortoise-fashion victory, and her term as holder of the transatlantic speed record would last barely twelve hours.

The *Great Western*, with "bunkers to spare," steaming serenely up the harbor as cheering spectators on shore got their second wind, was already marking the occasion with ceremonies of her own. One big table in her saloon had been christened Victoria; another one, The President. Around the buffets laid out on each of them, coveys of passengers were lifting toasts to just about everything when a gunfire salute from "Fort Ellises Island," of twenty-six guns—one for every state in the Union—made it clear that their arrival had been officially recognized. "The fire was electric," said one of them. "Our colours were lowered in acknowledgment of the compliment, and the burst which accompanied it from our decks was more loud and joyous than if at that moment we had unitedly overcome a common enemy. Proceeding still, the city became more distinct—trees, streets, the people—the announcement of the arrival of the ship by telegraph had brought thousands to every point of view upon the water-side; boats, too, in shoals, were out to welcome her, and every object seemed a super-added impulse to our feelings."

In *The Morning Herald,* James Gordon Bennett, "the cross-eyed Scot," a publisher whose normal tone was erinaceous, happily told his readers that "the approach of the *Great Western* to the harbour, and in front of the Battery, was most magnificent. The sky was clear—the crowds immense. The Battery was filled with the human multitude, one half of whom were females, their faces covered with smiles, and their delicate persons with the gayest attire. Below, on the broad blue water, appeared this huge thing of life, with four masts and emitting volumes of smoke. She looked black and blackguard, rakish, cool, reckless, fierce, and forbidding in sombre colours to the extreme." "As a whale among small fish, was the *Great Western* among the watercraft of our bay yesterday," said the man from *The Sun.* "The ships and battery furnished grand galleries for the spectators of the monuments in the naval amphitheatre. We thought of the artificial seas poured into the Roman theatres for the gratification of the emperors; and we thought that Rome in all her glory never witnessed a scene like this."

Noblesse oblige (she had crossed in 14½ days as against her rival's 19), the *Great Western,* "this immense moving mass," turned a pretty circle around the anchored *Sirius.* Receiving cheers, she returned them, then proceeded up the East River to Judd's Wharf at the foot of Pike Street, where a volatile swarm of men and boys, intent on boarding her, had to be held off with a show of muscle and firearms.

"With that strenuous abandon attainable only in the Empire City," New Yorkers were relentless in celebrating the achievement of the two steamers. They brought, said *The Enquirer,* "the most irrefragable testimony of the practicability of steam navigation between the Old and New Worlds . . . visions of future advantage to science, to commerce, to moral philosophy, began to float before the mind's eye." Since the War of 1812 the only comparable public commotion had been the visit of General Lafayette, the "Nation's Guest." Even while the two ships were still midocean, the Common Council had met to arrange for a proper welcome. These plans entailed a ceremonial collation on the *Sirius*, a banquet on the *Great Western*, and finally a big all-day party on Blackwell's Island for the commanders of both ships.

For the visit to the *Sirius* everyone gathered at Castle Garden stairs around noon. There the party stepped into "beautiful, sharp, long, low black row boats belonging to the United States Navy." Then, said one of the officials, we "led the way under the Battery Bridge and stretched out towards the Havre packet *Burgundy*, lying in the stream—went round the bow of the *Sirius*, and leaping into the larboard fore-chains, were soon welcomed on her quarter deck by her handsome, gallant and generous Commander Captain Roberts." In spite of a northeast storm that whipped them with sleet and snow, a company big enough to fill twenty boats embarked from the Battery and were rowed out to the ship. The flags and pennants of the *Sirius* snapped in the gale as a Navy Yard band on a barge played "God Save the Queen," and a band on the *Sirius'* afterdeck responded with "Hail, Columbia" and "Yankee Doodle."

Even in the wretchedly inclement weather the deck of the *Sirius* was crowded with sightseers. The official party, however, wasted no time in ducking below for a midday's repast. There was not enough room in the saloon and not enough air, but "the cheer was abundant on the heavily-laden table, and the wines soon made the compact crowd so happy that they forgot the pressure to which they were subjected. All tongues were soon in motion in commemoration of the great event." When it came time to respond to the main toast of the afternoon, Captain Roberts was apparently feeling no pain. "I am a happy man," he said. "This is an honour I could hardly dream of getting. Thanks to your great city, thanks to you all, gentlemen. If I could have a thousand years I would give them all up for the honour of this day. It is the happiest hour of my life: I am the proudest man in the world." The mayor closed the ceremonies with an eloquent address that "electrified the whole assembly, but of little of which," said a tactful reporter, "we have room to report." Another newspaperman, shivering and hungry on the open deck, could do no more than eavesdrop as the session in the saloon dragged on. "Judging by the length of time spent at it by their Honors of the city," he wrote, "ample justice was done by the corporate capacities of the city of New York."

Daniel Webster had a cold. Yet, three days later, he got into a boat with other dignitaries of similar corpulence to attend the feast on the *Great Western*. This company—"verily transported to the glorious saloons of France while yet under the luxurious rule of Louis XIV as they entered the main cabin"—was an eminent one. The British Consul was there, President Duer of Columbia College, Governor Mason of Michigan, along with most of the local lights who had already toasted the *Sirius*. After they had all looked at the "stupendous machinery," and the saloon which, according to one visitor, seemed "like a bower of bliss, a perfect garden of Armida" with sofas "wadded in a most luxuriant style of elegance never hitherto attempted, and only dreamed of in the descriptions of the Arabian Nights, and the tales of faëry," Alderman Hoxie led off the speeches. "Victoria Regina!" he shouted, and the company came to its feet. "The dominion of youth and beauty extends throughout the world!" Captain Hosken, speaking as an officer of the British Navy, lifted his glass: "The Navy of the United States! May we never be brought into other than friendly collision." Good feeling continued to flow as Daniel Webster rose to deliver one of his shortest speeches. "It is our fortune to live at a new epoch," he said. "We behold two continents approaching each other. The skill of your countrymen, sir, and my countrymen, is annihilating space." When Alderman Talmadge called upon John Ridge, Esquire, "of the Cherokee nation," the gathering was momentarily sobered. If the Indian was to be driven from the land he now inhabits, said Mr. Ridge, he "would retreat to the highest peaks of the Rocky Mountains, there to breathe a long, lingering farewell to the land of his fathers, and to die in defence of his life and liberty." The conviviality of the occasion was restored when, unexpectedly, Ridge concluded his speech with a toast, quite irrelevant to his theme, in which everyone was relieved to join: "The Queen of England! All ladies reign in the hearts of brave men."

Two days later the free-loading authorities were ready once more to hoist glasses of champagne and tuck into barons of beef. They met in the governor's room of the City Hall, then boarded a steamboat for Blackwell's Island. On the way they passed the Long Island poor farms.

The child inmates "were seen ranged along the bank, and as the steamboat neared the shore, they sent up from their shrill pipes a most joyous round of cheers, which," said a correspondent, was echoed "with hearty good will by all on board." Before sitting down to still another groaning table, the company also visited a new building "for the reception of proper lunatics." The mayor presided not only here but at the banquet which followed. Lieutenant Roberts was on his right, Lieutenant Hosken on his left. The "shrill pipes" of the cheering orphans were no longer heard as "with great zest and hilarity" the city fathers feasted until the ringing of a steamboat bell told them it was time to go home.

For all the cheers and gourmandizing, the arrival of the two steamships did far more than provide outings for *bon-vivant* councilmen. To a people who had every reason to believe that their future was here, the event was an affirmation. Confessing himself to be skeptical of the whole development, former Mayor Philip Hone nevertheless wrote: "Our countrymen, studious of change and pleased with novelty, will rush forward to visit the shores of Europe instead of resorting to Virginia or Saratoga Springs; and steamers will continue to be the fashion until some more dashing adventurer of the go-ahead tribe shall demonstrate the practicability of balloon navigation, and gratify their impatience on a voyage *over*, and not *upon*, the blue waters in two days instead of as many weeks, thereby escaping the rocks and shoals and headlands which continue to fright the minds of timid passengers and cautious navigators."

Brother Jonathan, feeling his oats, was quite prepared to take his place in the great world. All the flamboyant rhetoric was believable. "The advantages will be incalculable," said James Gordon Bennett, "no more petty rivalries, or national antipathies; no odious misconstructions and paltry jealousies, but a mutual love and respect growing out of an accurate knowledge of one another's good qualities, and a general emulation in the onward march of mind, genius, enterprise, and energy, towards the perfectability of man, and the amelioration of our physical, social, moral, and commercial condition. . . . They are founded in fact, and have nothing Utopian about them, and are deducible from positive data, as any demonstration of the Novum Organum, or any solution in the Mecanique Celeste. In the popular style of encouragement, and in one very appropriate to the subject, we most emphatically say, Go ahead!" So, that very week, did Captain Perkins of the steamboat *Moselle*. As he raced his high-funneled ship down the

Ohio River for the benefit of a big audience gathered on the banks near Cincinnati, "her boilers burst with a most awful and astounding noise, equal to the most violent clap of thunder. Heads, limbs, bodies and blood, were seen flying through the air in every direction, attended by the most horrible shrieks and groans from the wounded and the dying." One hundred and five passengers were killed. The Captain himself was "cast entirely into the street," where "his mangled carcase was gathered up."

By the first week in May, "the moral approximation of the two hemispheres" had been fully celebrated, the revels were finally ended and the two ships were set to make their return voyages to England. Publicity attending them had been unprecedented, yet words of wonder and admiration were still not persuasive enough to fill the berths of either. The *Sirius* drew 49 customers. The *Great Western*, expecting 250, got only 68 for her cabin accommodations and 3 for the steerage.

Among the voyagers who chose the *Sirius* was James Gordon Bennett, and he was in a fury. The cause of his anger was a suspicion of collusion between his archrival, publisher James Watson Webb, and the *Great Western*. This arose from the fact that, by having sent out a swift schooner, Webb's paper had scooped Bennett's when the *Sirius* arrived off Sandy Hook. When the *Great Western* came in, Webb was determined to get there first again. He sent a lackey out with the pilot boat with instructions to beg, borrow, or steal all the European papers the *Great Western* brought over. With uncommon resourcefulness— or common stupidity—the young man came back to the *Courier and Enquirer* offices triumphant. He had snagged the overseas newspapers, and he had also unwittingly purloined the ship's mailbags. Representatives of both Great Britain and the United States were quick to register complaints, but by that time the hot news from abroad was on the presses, the sacrosanct mailbags were in the post office where they belonged. The teapot tempest that ensued blew over—for everyone, that is, except James Gordon Bennett. In his own paper he castigated Webb for "the impertinent interference of this contemptible whippersnapper" and took umbrage at the *Great Western* herself.

Refusing to let the issue die, he began to circulate snide remarks about the ship and her company. Tit for tat, those who had become fans of the *Great Western* began spreading damaging tales about the *Sirius*. There had been a near mutiny on the crossing, they said. Captain

Roberts had had to send his black gang to their stations at gun point. Desperate to keep up steam, they said, Captain Roberts had been so heartless as to order one of the crew to snatch a doll from the arms of a child and stuff it into the maw of the furnace.

In the advertisement inserted in the New York papers, agents Wadsworth & Smith (the latter, Junius Smith's nephew Henry and constant correspondent) had emphasized the fact that the *Sirius*, for all her sudden eminence, was just a stopgap, a modest forerunner of greater things to come. She had been chartered, according to the notice, "to meet the pressing demands of the public, in anticipation of the steamship *British Queen*, now building." (This was the new name of Smith's *Royal Victoria*.) Of the 49 souls who elected to make the return voyage to England aboard her, 28 were accommodated in the cabin and the rest in the steerage. Among the latter, by the devices of someone already wise in the ways of public relations, were half of the New York Band of Music. When the publicity man had learned of their hankering to go to England, he offered them passage over in the *Sirius* for which they would pay him back by providing entertainment for two voyages: one on the *Sirius*, one on the maiden voyage of the *British Queen*.

It was still customary for sailing packets, as well as steam-powered vessels, to leave New York from an anchorage in midstream rather than wharfside. This called for the use of tugboats or tenders. As the *Sirius* prepared to sail on the first day of May, two of her passengers, finding themselves on the same tender, had become acquainted even before they boarded the steamer. Chevalier Henry Wyckoff, Chargé d'Affaires to the Court of St. Cloud, later recalled the incident.

"We moved off amid the hurrahs of excited people who came on every kind of craft to wish us God speed," said Wyckoff. "Perceiving a tall, slim man near me, I entered into conversation. His physiognomy was striking: lofty forehead, prominent nose, firm mouth, and the general expression, though somewhat stern, not forbidding. After chatting for some time I remarked: 'I hear the famous Bennett is aboard.'

" 'Yes, I believe he is,' said the tall man, with a smile.

" 'Do you feel at all nervous about it?'

" 'Not in the least.'

" 'Well, for my part,' I continued, 'I am not altogether comfortable on the point.'

" 'Why?' asked my companion.

" 'Because he is so given to saying sarcastic things of people.'

" 'That depends a good deal,' he answered, 'whether they are worth it.'

" 'Do you know him by sight?' I inquired.

" 'Very well.'

" 'Then do point him out if you see him on deck.'

" 'He is standing before you. My name is Bennett. . . . *Ecce homo!*' "

The indomitable Eliza Cross of Bristol was among the *Great Western's* passengers on the return sailing, and so was James Watson Webb, who, like Bennett, was going to London to see the coronation of the new sovereign, "to establish agents in Europe so that" he could "outstrip all other papers on this continent," and perhaps to witness the launching of the *British Queen*. With a week of sea water between the two editors, a combustible circumstance had been defused. But Webb could not resist a parting shot. In the column appearing in his newspaper next day, he indicated that the "out-pouring of public feeling" toward the *Great Western* was based on the conviction that the *Sirius* was, after all, an interloper "chartered for the purpose of snatching honours from those to whom they justly belonged."

Even after two solid weeks of steamer hullabaloo, New Yorkers had neither stopped talking about the wonder nor become blasé about her actual presence. Sailing day was still another red-letter occasion. One reporter told of "acres of solid flesh" around Pier 1, North River. Even as far uptown as the Astor House people stood on rooftops to watch. A reporter for *The American* elaborated: "Yesterday was a jubilee," he said. "About one o'clock, Broadway was thronged with carriages and pedestrians, in a steady and unreturning stream towards the Battery; and, when two o'clock, the hour of departure, had arrived, there seemed not a foot of ground on or around the Battery," which had become, said another New Yorker, "a mass of living witnesses to the event."

At two o'clock, the band struck up "Behold How Brightly Breaks the Morning," and "the noble ship, dressed out in colours, put off from the pier," carrying besides her passengers 5,500 letters, 1,760 newspapers and a cargo of cotton," and swept up the North River; the *Providence*, the *New York*, the *Vanderbilt*, the *Highland*, the *American Eagle*, the *Sun*, the *Arrow*, the *Brooklyn*, the *Hoboken*—"all decorated with colours, and many having on board bands of music, put out from different wharves, and circling around, formed for those on shore a *coup d'oeil*, while, in turn, the living pyramids at Castle Garden and the sea of human faces presented by a glance at the receding land, gave back a not-less-striking picture to those afloat."

The man from the *Courier and Enquirer* emphasized the harmony of nations, perhaps because this was something about which most Americans were still chary. "The meteor flag of England and the stars and stripes of the United States were displayed in friendly contiguity," he said. "It was as if the Old World and the New had shaken hands across the broad Atlantic, and a nation's voice had gone up to hail the glorious compact."

But the voice of one of America's most distinguished journalists, N. P. Willis, was not included in the national chorus. "There is one (to me) melancholy note in the Paean with which the *Great Western* was welcomed," he wrote. *"In literature we are no longer a distinct nation.* The triumph of Atlantic steam navigation has driven the smaller drop into the larger, and London has become the centre. Farewell nationality! The English language now marks the limits of a new literary empire, and America is a suburb. Our themes, our resources, the disappearing savage, and the retiring wilderness, the free thought, and the action as free, the spirit of daring innovation, and the irreverent question of usage, the picturesque mixing of many nations in an equal home, the feeling of expanse, of unsubserviency, of distance from time-hallowed authority and prejudice—all the elements which were working gradually but gloriously together to make us a nation by ourselves, have, in this approximation of shores, either perished for our using, or slipped within the clutch of England. In a year or two every feature and detail of our country will be as well known to English society as those of Margate and Brighton. Our similarity to themselves in most things will not add to their respect for us. We shall have the second place accorded to the indigenous society of well-known places of resort or travel, and to be an American will be in England like being a Maltese or an East Indian—every way inferior, in short, to a metropolitan in London." But a voice so gloomily vatic was destined to be a solitary and distant one.

Meanwhile, there was profit in the event, and by no means did it all go to the departing ship. Charging fifty cents to a dollar per head, employing everything that could chug, paddle or float, all of the Yankee boatmen made money and some of them struck bonanzas by filling their ships with as many as eight hundred excursionists. The coastal steamer *Providence* accompanied the *Great Western* down the harbor and drew alongside in the Narrows to take off visitors, among whom were former Governor William Learned Marcy and Governor William Henry Seward. Amid the noise of a final round of tootings and shouts of *bon voyage,* the *Great Western*'s paddles began to turn and she aimed her bowsprit toward the open sea. "When last seen," said a reporter, "she was gliding majestically over the waves, while a dark column of vapour marked her way toward the horizon." The *Sirius* by this time had paddled one third of the way to Europe.

❦ SECTION VI ❧

Haliburton and Howe: Two Men in a Boat / "*Is It the* Sirius?
Can It Be the Great Western?"

O N THE sixteen of May, 1838, twenty days out from
Halifax, the *Tyrian*, a ten-gun brig running mails to Falmouth—a ship precisely of the type that had given rise
to the term "coffin brig"—sat in an almost windless sea that was nonetheless disturbed enough to cause her to rise up on one wave and slide
down another as if she were riding in the wake of something enormous
and invisible that had just passed by.

Among her distinguished passengers—"As rich a cargo of intellect
as ever left our shores," according to a Halifax newspaper—were
Samuel P. Fairbanks, Master of the Rolls of Nova Scotia, who had
in his luggage maps and plans that he hoped would aid him in getting British money for the proposed Shubenacadie Canal to be cut
across the middle of the Province; an army man, Captain Robert
Carmichael-Smyth, who had been promoting British interests in the
building of railroads in North America; a physician named Walker
from St. John, New Brunswick; and two old and close friends, Judge
Joseph Howe and Judge Thomas C. Haliburton. The latter's official
titles were: First Justice of the Court of Common Pleas, and President

73

of the Courts of Session in the Middle Division of the Province of Nova Scotia. But he was internationally renowned (a few years hence he would be dubbed "the Nova Scotia Mark Twain") as Sam Slick, the humorist. Judge Howe was taking his first European vacation. Judge Haliburton was making his third eastward crossing and he was mostly on business: one part connected with the estate of a brother-in-law, the other concerned with terms to be arranged with the London publisher Richard Bentley for a sequel to his hugely successful book, *The Clockmaker; Or, The Sayings and Doings of Samuel Slick, of Slickville*. Celebrated public servants of the Bluenose province, they were about to take part in an unusual midocean rendezvous. Beginning as something like comic relief in the sober saga of the steamship, the event would eventually be recalled as a real, if somewhat intangible, contribution to Nova Scotia's part in the advance of ocean service.

It was dinnertime in the doldrums. Above the long table in the saloon, a rack of glassware, suspended from the ceiling by ropes, swung lazily back and forth as the *Tyrian* comfortably creaked and rolled. The gentleman diners, after nearly three weeks in the confines of a small ship designed strictly for carrying mails and hardy passengers without frills, were subdued. The voyage had been pleasant, according to Judge Howe, because "there was no fat dowager groaning in the next berth, or tumbling from side to side with the momentum of a water cask—no cross child howling like the east wind, to rack our nerves by day, or break our rest at night. Agreeable and intelligent society—a good table—books, newspapers, and a cigar on the Quarter Deck, helped to kill day after day, and yet with so much before and so much behind us, they died pretty hard after all."

Still, there had been diversions since the sandy shores of Sable Island had afforded them their last sight of land. They had caught halibut on the Porpoise Bank, cod on the Banks of Newfoundland; they had been bounced about by a three-day gale from the north; they had spoken a French brig from St. Pierre at anchor on the great Bank with "a numerous crew industriously engaged in the Fishery." They had honored the Saturday-night custom of "drinking Sweethearts and Wives," and Judge Howe had written a treacly poem about it:

SATURDAY NIGHT AT SEA

Sweethearts and Wives!—the Goblet pass—
A Bumper let it be;

Bright eyes are sparkling through each glass—
'Tis Saturday night at sea.

The Matron sits by her fireside,
   Her children at her knee:
They're breathing prayers that we may glide
   In safety o'er the sea.

The maiden droops in her shady Bower,
   What cause of grief has she?
The heart that heeds not bird or flower
   Is with us on the sea.

But brighter hours are yet in store,
   From ev'ry danger free—
We'll share the smiles of those on shore,
   We toasted on the sea.

When they had taken their places at dinner, they were, according to Joseph Howe, "repairing the waste which ennui and vexation, rather than any healthy exertion of mind or body, had occasioned." But they were hardly into the first of their meat courses "when the master rushed into the cabin to inform us that a steamer was in sight astern, and appeared to be running directly in our wake. Every knife was dropped— the half carved limbs of poultry were left hanging on the parent trunk —the half emptied glass hastily set down, and a general rush was made to the quarter deck. There she was sure enough—but a speck on the horizon—but with the line of black smoke above, leaving no doubt as to her character. On she came in gallant style with the speed of a hunter, while we were moving with the rapidity of an ox-cart loaded with marsh mud. Is it the *Sirius?* Can it be the *Great Western?* Shall we go in her? Will you send the Mail?—were the questions hastily put, but which for the moment none could answer."

When the steamer came within hailing distance, Captain Jennings of the *Tyrian* lifted his trumpet: "Will you take charge of the mail?"

"Yes," Captain Roberts shouted back, "but be quick. . . ." Apparently he also offered to accommodate any passenger who might like to make the switch. As Captain Carmichael-Smyth recalled, the gentlemen of the *Tyrian* made a "prompt decision not to quit our sailing craft, commanded as she was by so kind and excellent an officer." The

Sirius hove to, "an exciting and beautiful object," said Howe, "though painted black, her extreme length, red paddle wheels, and the state-room windows, opening like port-holes at the side, gave her a rakish look that was not unpleasing; and her height above the water (her quarter deck being above our davits), and ready obedience to her helm, dissipated at once any idea that might have been entertained of insecurity or danger."

As the mailbags were being lifted out of the hold of the *Tyrian* and lowered onto a small boat, the Honorable Messrs. Howe and Haliburton decided to go along for the ride. "Though there was some swell," said Howe, "we could not resist the temptation to pay even a momentary visit to this interesting stranger—got a seat on the mail bags, and while these were handed up the side, had five minutes to chat with the passengers on the quarter deck of the *Sirius*, and to take a glass of Champaigne with her Commander in the cabin. She had been 14 days making a much longer passage than we had made in 20—she would reach England in 2½ or 3 days certain, we might be a week, or a fortnight, or with a spell of easterly weather, three weeks more; with the novelty of the scene around us, and the positive advantages she possessed in point of speed, it required a strong effort to tear ourselves away from our new friend and be rowed on board our old one. Never did we feel so forcibly the contrast between the steamer and the sailing vessel, even for the deep sea passage. The difference is hardly greater between poetry and mathematics. We rowed back to the *Tyrian*, gratified perhaps that we had been the first Passengers that had boarded on the high seas the first Steamer that had made the voyage from Britain to America and back, but not at all pleased with the prospect of being left behind to the tender mercies of wind and canvas, when a few tons of coal would have done the business much better."

Back on board the packet, the two magistrates told their shipmates how the cabin of the *Sirius* was fitted up in a manner to suit the taste "of the most luxurious voluptuary," how the table, set for forty persons in the saloon, was reflected in every detail by immense mirrors which covered the walls, and how the *"coup d'oeil"* was altogether delightful.

Relieved of her mails, the *Tyrian* continued to wallow while her sails remained fecklessly slack. Meanwhile, charging and snorting, her big red wheels climbing the swells, her taffrail redolent with sides of beef and hanging strings of fresh vegetables, the *Sirius* disappeared into the east. Actually, this bravura performance was very much in the way of showing off. Still several days from her Falmouth landfall, the *Sirius* had almost run out of coal. For economy's sake, she was soon steaming toward England at a snail's pace, much to the displeasure of James Gordon Bennett, who complained of "grime, smut and smoke," and the "interminable racket." Yet before the voyage was over, Bennett was willing to put his name to a testimonial letter praising Captain Roberts and affirming that in the "present infant state of Atlantic navigation," he was quite sold on the ship's "security and speed, far outstripping any mode of conveyance hitherto known." As she groped through English Channel fog, the *Sirius* found at a sudden clearing that she was headed straight for one of the rocky Scilly Islands. But she veered off at the last second, proceeded dead slow through the resuming fog, rounded the Lizard, and reached port the next morning.

*Steamship Fever / The Second Royal William / The Sirius
on the Rocks / Enter Samuel Cunard*

THE EARLY summer of 1838 was a time of steamship fever for enthusiasts of progress, and for simple patriots as well. When the *Great Western* returned to her hometown, the Bristol *Mirror* reported, "The joy and pleasure announced by all classes upon her arrival have been unequalled in the city for many years, and they almost stand upon a level with the tidings from the Nile, Trafalgar Bay, and the plains of Waterloo." The port of Bristol, said another, "waking from her Rip Van Wynkle slumbers" had roused "English enterprise to a new maritime effort." But the tang of these joys and pleasures soon lost its piquancy. Citizens of Bristol, who wanted to visit the wonder ship were charged five shillings a head. When they learned that in New York ten thousand visitors had been not only welcomed aboard free of charge but even "regaled," they were furious. The correspondence columns of newspapers began to bristle with their complaints.

Across the Irish Sea, Captain Roberts was enjoying a wholly personal triumph. "Since the arrival of the *Sirius*," he wrote to a friend, "all is

alive about Atlantic steamers. I have been received in the most handsome manner; in Cork they are to present me with a service of silver,
value 200 pounds; in the town of Passage where I was born, a large
silver salver, and the Corporation of Cork present me with the freedom
of the city, in a silver box. The British and American Steam Navigation
Company are going to present me with a piece of plate, and I am to
be presented to her Majesty next court."

In the midst of the general euphoria, a man who signed himself
simply as "B" published a letter in the *Shipping and Mercantile Gazette*
which threw a little cold water on excessive puffs of steam. "John Bull
and Brother Jonathan appear in ecstasies at the recent voyages of the
Sirius and *Great Western* steamers," he wrote, "but on the results
. . . the anticipated velocity . . . the pecuniary benefit . . . I avow I have
always been and still am very skeptical." On present evidence, steamers
were much too slow, he felt, too costly to build, too expensive to
travel in. "I say, so long as we continue . . . blinded by coal-dust . . .
and roasted in the engine room, or soused round with the paddles, old
Boreas has nothing to do but puff his jolly good breezes, let jack set
plenty of canvass, brace up sharp or square his yards, as his good ship
pleases, mind well his helm, keep a bright look-out forward, three to
one the liners will do at all times as much as the smokers, if they don't
run them out of the line altogether." But new operations afloat and
big new plans ashore had taken irreversible impetus from the famous
crossings of the *Sirius* and the *Great Western*. Doubts like Mr. "B's"
were swamped. Junius Smith watched closely the progress of his already
beloved *Royal Victoria*—now about to be rechristened *British Queen*
in honor of the accession of Victoria—and to be launched on the sovereign's birthday. Confidently looking ahead, he had ordered an even
greater ship, to be named the *President,* and thus to fill out the balance
of his Anglo-American complement. The round trip of the *Sirius,* undoubtedly a *succès d'estime,* had nevertheless resulted in a loss to the
chartering company of nearly thirty-five hundred pounds. Smith did
not find this fact dismaying. It had proved a point, he felt, a point he
had argued long and hard with his fellow directors: a small ship on
the Atlantic run would not do: a successful ship would have to be a
big one—2,000 tons or more. When a newly formed Liverpool outfit
chartered the 617-ton *Royal William* (a second steamer of that name
built for the mail service between Liverpool and Kingstown) and sent
her "without touching any port in the Irish Channel" on a crossing with

a handful of passengers to New York in July, he took a wry view of their Johnny-come-lately efforts.

"Every man must *purchase* his experience," he said, "the Liverpool agents with their *Royal William* and twenty passengers not excepted." The Liverpool agents to whom he referred were the directors of the City of Dublin Steam Packet Company. The only experience they had "purchased" was in the coastal trade. Yet it was considerably deeper and more varied than Smith's experience; and they showed no hesitation in trying to put their city into the picture so far dominated by Bristol and Cork. Liverpool was, after all, *the* American threshold of Europe, as the sailing packets had been proving for ten years. As one American expressed it, the city was "bone of the bone of the United States. She has grown up with them, upon them, and like them—being still more now than she ever has been, the most American city in the Old World."

Herman Melville, assessing Liverpool with clear eyes, could only take what he saw with rueful resignation. More than any other seaport in the world, he said, the city "abounds in all the variety of land-sharks, land-rats, and other vermin, which makes the helpless mariner their prey. In the shape of landlords, barkers, clothiers, crimps, and boarding-house loungers, the land-sharks devour him, limb by limb; while the land-rats and mice constantly nibble at his purse.

"Other perils he runs also, far worse; from the denizens of notorious Carinthian haunts in the vicinity of the docks, which in depravity are not to be matched by anything this side of the pit that is bottomless.

"And yet, sailors love this Liverpool, and upon long voyages to distant parts of the globe will be continually dilating upon its charms and attractions, extolling it above all other seaports in the world."

The ship chartered by the ambitious Liverpudlians was not yet two years old, with cabin accommodations for eighty persons and a "peculiar construction (being divided into five sections, each water-tight)," which, as it soon developed, were most urgently needed. On her maiden voyage, she dispensed with cargo and took only passengers, one of whom was the son of President Martin van Buren, plus "heavy bags of intelligence." Even so, she was so laden down with coal in her bunkers, her holds and even in her deck well (she was prepared to steam nonstop for 4,500 miles) that when she sailed down the Mersey to cheers and the sound of cannon, according to a witness, "her paddles were buried six feet deep, her sponsons were submerged, and it was possible by leaning over the bulwarks to wash one's hands in the water that surged at the vessel's side."

The *Royal William* reached port in nineteen days, to become the first ship on the Liverpool–New York route that would in a short time be the most perpetually crowded on the ocean. Wildly encouraged by her modest success, Liverpudlians saw in their new ship "the first dawning of a new era in commerce, the first opening of a new mine of wealth, the first prospect of a new field of enterprise." The least they could do was to provide her with a running mate. Christened the *Liverpool* and sent out to New York in December, her consort, "a floating Leviathan," was the first two-funneled ship on the Atlantic.

But Junius Smith's remarks were prophetic. In early October the *Royal William*, with some sixty passengers aboard, had to burn spars, planks, and "a variety of spare articles" to make Sandy Hook, arriving in Manhattan not only out of fuel but dangerously short of water. "This is not," said an editor, "according to the usual English mode of doing business." Then the *Liverpool*, six days out, had to put into Cork because of a storm that threatened to overwhelm her. When it was learned that, when she should have been in New York Harbor, she was actually off Roche's Point at the mouth of Queenstown Harbor, the *Liverpool* gained a reputation for unreliability that dogged her brief career.

The *Great Western*, meantime, was happily plying back and forth, averaging about eighty passengers per crossing. The *Sirius*, with fifty-seven customers, made a second and final transatlantic trip under her old captain from the coasting days, Stephen Sayer Mowle. She then resumed her original career as a coaster. On the sixteenth of June, 1847, en route from Glasgow to Cork, she lost her way in fog and ran onto the rocky shore of Ballycotton Bay. Two of her crew and twelve passengers were drowned; and as her cargo began to be washed ashore, two hundred marines from nearby Cove were sent to protect it from pilferers. But some of the local villagers had already got to the caches of Guinness' porter that came floating in. When two of them died from drinking the stuff, the casualty list went up to sixteen.

More than fifty years later, deep-sea divers attracted by her legend, as well as by the value of her metal, went down into Ballycotton Bay to see what might be left of the *Sirius*. They found a number of relics—

pumps, part of the engine and its framework—and made a prize of her figurehead, which was sent to the Museum of Fisheries and Shipping, in Hull. This paved the way for a bigger salvage attempt in 1910. Henry Ensor, a Queenstown salvage contractor, writing to a shipping man in that year, describes the remains: "I send you herewith copy of photograph showing the shaft recovered from the Sirius. It is interesting to note that the Cast Iron hubs of Padle-wheels are in excellent condition while the wrot iron arms have almost entirely wasted away. The shaft in bearing where oil had been upon it was in fair condition. We also recovered one of her cylinders which we had to break up to get on board. The outside of the cylinder was covered with rust and marine growths like those on the shaft, but inside was quite bright and slippy with tallow in spite of 65 years under water. The piston-rod outside the cylinder was wasted away badly but inside the gland it was quite bright."

Behind scenes daily witnessed on the Avon, the Mersey and the Hudson, grander notions about steamships than had ever before been entertained were now being nurtured. When Haliburton and Howe, warmed by Captain Roberts' champagne, had been rowed back to the *Tyrian* and had stood on the slanting deck to watch the *Sirius* depart in bluster and muted histrionics, they were jealous of what they had observed. Their friend the promoter Carmichael-Smyth articulated just what they were thinking: Why should British mails and British passengers be steaming past their own front door? Why should not the deep-water harbor of Halifax be their proper terminus? They were not aware of it, but at the same moment Samuel Cunard was asking more or less the same questions.

On Sunday, May 20, 1838, they were coasting along the shores of Cornwall, where the spring verdure was so intense to Joseph Howe's eyes, he said, "that, to speak phrenologically upon the subject, our organ of color has become morbidly excited." Next day they anchored off Falmouth. Even before the Customs House Officer had clambered on board, outrunners from the town's two rival hotels "leaped upon the deck, made a hasty bow to each of the passengers, thrust cards into their hands, and poured out profuse recommendations—'Come to Pierce's House, Sir, principal hotel, center of town, near the Customs House, all the coaches start from there, Sir'—'Come to Selly's, Sir, fine house, good baths, beautiful view, fashionable place, near the

Terrace, boat alongside, Sir.' The honorable gentlemen chose Selly's, lowered themselves into a gig and scudded landward under a fresh breeze. The trip from ship to land cost a sovereign, "a rascally imposition, sanctioned by the usage of the place."

But soon they were again in good temper, delighted to feel that the floors did not roll under their feet as they became "comfortably esconced in Selly's best parlour." Howe's report to his Nova Scotian readers was rhapsodic: "The breakfast urn is hissing on the table— and oh! welcome exchange, once more female fingers are pouring out the coffee, and performing, with modest but assiduous promptitude, those little courtesies, through which Stewards and Cabin Boys have been bungling for nearly a month, but which women only have the delicacy to conceive, or the will gracefully to dispense. 'Tis good fun to see a party just landed eat their first breakfast—such mountains of muffins and hot rolls disappear, such slices of steaks and plates of eggs, to say nothing of tea and coffee, enriched by Devonshire clotted cream, welcome enough after the preserved milk of the voyage." After breakfast they went to the Customs House to claim their baggage ("they do overhaul things in capital style," Howe remarked, "scarcely allowing an inkstand to escape, for fear there might be some smuggled thought in it") and came back to Selly's to take their first warm baths since Halifax. "Well shampooed and decently dressed," they then "trotted around the town."

Here, to their surprise, they came upon a rumor they might have started themselves. The Government, it was said, contemplated the forwarding of mails to the Colonies by steamer, direct to Halifax or, more likely, via New York, with a branch line to the Maritimes. Since rumor insistently repeated what they had been privately thinking, they felt there was some cause for alarm. In a dispatch to his newspaper, Howe enjoined Nova Scotians to be alert to developments. If New York should be chosen as the terminal over Halifax, he indicated that it would be the sad lot of the Colonies to "see, instead of this natural nurture, the tide of importance and prosperity suicidally directed to strangers and rivals."

They meandered about the countryside for a week and eventually got to Bristol. Judge Haliburton paid a call on Captain Claxton, secretary of the Great Western Steam-Ship Company, and later attended a meeting of the owners. These men assured him that they had no objection to putting ships on a direct line to Halifax. But everything depended on the Government's willingness to commission them to carry the mails. Meanwhile, on the twenty-fourth of May, the *British Queen* had taken "leave of her moorings and majestically ploughed her way" into the Thames after the "Honourable Mrs. Dowson Damer, who occupied a conspicuous position upon a platform erected for the purpose, was seen to hurl at her the baptismal offering."

Judge Fairbanks, the erstwhile shipmate of the two Nova Scotians, was meanwhile talking to the proprietors of the newly launched ship about the very same matter. Encouraged by "most friendly and courteous treatment," Howe and Haliburton went up to London. There they were visited at their hotel by two men from the Maritime Provinces who were *also* seeking to bring steamers into one of the Canadian ports. They were William Crane, a member of the New Brunswick legislature, and Henry Bliss. As agent for the government of New Brunswick, and in behalf of trade committees in Quebec and Montreal, Bliss had already addressed a petition to the Earl of Litchfield, then Postmaster General. A modest petition, it asked merely for an inquiry into the possibility of a regular steam service that might supplement a proposed new sailing packet schedule.

With the prestige of Judge Howe to enhance its appeal, a new letter, signed by him and William Crane, went off to the Colonial Secretary, Lord Glenelg. A revision of packet service, they said, was not only extremely desirable but also "a measure of absolute necessity." Use of the ten-gun brigs had resulted in horrendous destruction of life and property, they pointed out, and slowness of dispatches had often allowed malicious rumors to gain foothold with, at times, unhappy political consequences. In fact, said the petitioners, "if Great Britain is to maintain her footing upon the North American Continent she must, at any hazard, establish such a line of rapid communication by steam as will ensure the speedy transmission of public despatches, commercial correspondence, and general information through channels exclusively British, and inferior to none in security and expedition." The signers confessed they acted on only their own authority in advancing this cause. Yet they trusted that his Lordship would "pardon the liberty and afford to a measure which cannot fail to strengthen and increase the prosperity of the Empire, the powerful aid of [his] countenance and support." Through his secretary the Colonial Secretary answered them politely. He told them that Her Majesty's Government was already quite aware of the matter they had so urgently broached, and otherwise patted them on the head for being such good boys and forward-looking subjects of the Queen.

In spite of his avuncular dismissal, Lord Glenelg was not behindhand in the matter Crane and Howe had advanced. After looking into prospects for a few months, the Post Office and the Admiralty decided the time was ripe. Subsidy support for the carrying of mails was nothing new, since the Government had been supplying this for decades. But the participation of the Admiralty was an innovation. In time of war, the Lords Commissioners felt, speedy mail steamers could be converted into auxiliary cruisers. With this in mind, they took the lead. In early November they advertised for offers: companies that might undertake to provide steamships of not less than 300 horsepower—each to carry Her Majesty's mails and dispatches from England to Halifax, and also between England, Halifax and New York, beginning April 1, 1839—were invited to reply.

The Government's wants were simple, and almost impossible to meet: What ships for this service could be built or made ready in the space of four months? Nonetheless, the Great Western Steam-Ship Company sent in its bid, and so did the owners of the *Sirius*. Meanwhile, a copy of the Admiralty's advertisement had reached Samuel Cunard. Something of a sly boots where business advantage offered itself, Cunard talked things over with no one but his son Edward, noted that the deadline was irretrievably past, and ignored the fact. He got his friend Sir Colin Campbell, Governor General of Nova Scotia, to write an extravagant personal commendation by way of introduction to Lord Glenelg. With that in his pocket, he set off on the Falmouth packet in January, 1839, for London. He was fifty-two years old; he was already addressed as "the Honourable"; and he probably knew as much about mails and ships and sea-going operations as any other man alive.

PART TWO

ASCENDANCY

1839-1889

✸ SECTION I ✸

The Loyalist Cunards of Halifax / The Halcyon Days of Joseph
Cunard / Colonel Samuel / Fanny Kemble Tells a Lie
The Lords of the Treasury Listen / Robert Napier: "The Tutelary
Deity" / "Three Good and Sufficient Steamships" / The British
and North American Royal Mail Steam Packet Company
Cunard Red / Bostonians Incensed / Return of the Heroes
Captain Ericsson's Plan / Clambake on MacNab's Island

C UNARD—the name that would most securely put its sterling imprint across the North Atlantic—did not come into the
chronicles of capitalism and sea-faring until its vowels and
consonants had survived the transmogrifications of one hundred and
fifty years. In its first appearance in North America it is Kunders; later
on it is Cunrad, or Conrad. Only after Thones Kunders with his wife
and their three sons had come to the end of wanderings that took
them from Crefeld on the Lower Rhine to William Penn's Quaker
community in the American wilds did the name assume its final six
characters. Then, bequeathed to their grandchild Abraham C., it
went on to Nova Scotia.

At the close of the Revolutionary War, Halifax was the one big
British seaport on the American side of the Atlantic; Nova Scotia the
most convenient haven for colonial families still loyal to the Crown
who wished to live in its dominions. In the course of a northward
migration of Loyalists in 1783, a convoy of twenty ships sailed from
New York—among them a vessel carrying Abraham C. Cunard and
a family named Murphy from Charleston, South Carolina. By the

time their ship had sailed into Halifax, twenty-seven-year-old Abraham had fallen in love with twenty-five-year-old Margaret, daughter of Thomas Murphy. While Cunard stayed in the port to look for work, the Murphys led their slaves and servants overland to the settlement of Rawdon, forty miles away. There, not long after their disembarkation, Abraham and Margaret were married.

The couple spent their first years together in an unpainted wooden shack on land that makes up the sloping back lot of what is now 257 Brunswick Street, Halifax. Here, where you could see the harbor and smell the ocean, their first son, Samuel, was born on November 21, 1787, followed in the space of ten years by Joseph and Henry, later by Thomas and William. A master carpenter by calling, Abraham Cunard worked as a joiner in the Halifax Naval Dockyard. Ship carpentering led to shipbuilding and shipbuilding to the purveying of fuel—for ships, to begin with, then for various business and domestic uses. (In Halifax, nearly two hundred years later, a familiar motto still appears on windows and the sides of delivery trucks: "Cunard Settles the Burning Question.")

Samuel and his brother Joseph went to the Halifax Grammar School, but they recited their catechism and most of their lessons to their mother at home. Samuel's clerical talent and head for figures got him a job in the civilian office of the army engineers attached to the militia garrisoned in the city while he was still an adolescent. Later he went to Boston and worked there for three years in the office of a ship broker. He had not yet come of age when he returned to Halifax and talked his father into founding—on a capital outlay of two hundred pounds—the firm of Abraham Cunard & Son.

The spoils of undeclared war brought good fortune to father and son almost at once. When an American square-rigger named *White Oak*, captured by a British privateer, was put up for auction by the Admiralty, the Cunards bought her and soon advertised that she would be loading for London, to sail under convoy, "with good accommodation for passengers." The *White Oak*'s first round voyage produced a fine profit; young Cunard had learned for himself what others had begun to suspect —that at either end of the arc made by the Great Circle route there was a pot of gold.

He was twenty-five when the War of 1812 actually broke out and already an operator of ships of sufficient value to make him a man of account in the highest councils. In spite of continuing Anglo-American hostilities, the Lieutenant Governor of Nova Scotia granted him a permit to trade with any port in the American colonies. The British Admiralty gave him a contract to provide, at his own risk, "conveyance by sailing vessels of His Majesty's mails between Halifax and Newfoundland, Boston and Bermuda." When he was twenty-seven years old he married Miss Susan Duffus, daughter of a Haligonian "Taylor and Habit Maker." His bride, though undoubtedly irreproachable, was, in the scarcity of reports about her, one of the town's less socially lustrous belles.

The firm of Abraham Cunard & Son soon had some forty vessels under its rubric, and Samuel himself was rich and patriotic enough to be listed as one of the most generous subscribers to a fund for soldiers wounded in the Battle of Waterloo. Cunard's Wharf, an important *entrepôt* for raw materials from the West Indies, had become a waterfront landmark; Lyle & Chappell's shipyards on the other side of the harbor in Dartmouth worked overtime in maintaining Cunard ships.

When the aging Abraham and Margaret Cunard retired to Rawdon to join the Murphy clan, the firm became his own—S. Cunard and Company. To expand its scope, he decided to go into whaling. But after three expeditions he had sent to the South Seas showed only scanty profit, he looked to other natural resources, and acquired timber rights to a vast section of wilderness in New Brunswick south of the Miramichi River. To get things started there he sent his brothers Joseph and Henry to the village of Chatham, where they opened a lumber office. As J. Cunard and Company, they were expected to supervise logging operations in the King's Wood from the cuttings to the sawmills, then to the many loading docks built out into the Miramichi.

Joseph Cunard apparently took to life in the boondocks as Imperial Caesar took to Gaul. A dashing figure in the raw settlements of Gloucester County, he lived, according to local report, "in a grandeur that has never been seen on our river." Within a few years (Henry Cunard having given up the business and gone into farming), J. Cunard and Company were involved not only with lumberyards, brick making and fisheries, but in building ships, mostly barques, in Richibucto, Kouchibouguiac, Bathurst and in Chatham, where they owned one of the first sawmills operated by steam power.

A lady bard from that neck of the woods has recalled Joseph's impact on the community in lines immortality has refused to relinquish:

FROM HALIFAX CAME JOE CUNARD:
HIS FATHER WORKED IN THE NAVY YARD.

But his brother Sam made the neighbors stare—
They said he would die a millionaire.

For Sam made money, and Sam took risks,
And he made a fortune in sailing ships.

He became a captain of industry
And he sent his brothers to Miramichi.

They landed here one day in June,
And that's when Chatham began to boom.

Henry the farmer settled down
At Woodburn Hill, a mile from town.

But Joseph lived like a lumber lord
In a style they said he couldn't afford.

He furnished the house in luxury
That the Hendersons built for Doctor Key

With a harpsichord and chandeliers
Calfbound books and mahogany chairs.

Peacocks paced on the terraced lawn,
The gardeners worked from early dawn.

There was a road to the porticoed door
For Joe Cunard and his coach and four.

A few years later the peacocks would be sent screaming into the wilderness, the harpsichord silenced, the porticoes strangled by creepers. There would come the momentous day that would end all the halcyon "days of Cunard." When creditors with a court order abruptly closed down all the enterprises of Joseph Cunard, the result according to a local historian, was "a crash that ruined the Miramichi and nearly wrecked the Cunard Line. The old-timers used to describe the Day of the Failure, how the mob roared about the streets of Chatham shouting 'Kill the villain!' and how Joseph faced them all, standing on the steps of his office with a pair of pistols thrust into the legs of his high-topped boots, defying a mob of thousands with, 'Now show me the man who will shoot Cunard!' "

Meanwhile, back in Halifax, the East India Company had made Samuel its agent for the Maritimes. By his single-handed efforts the first direct shipment of tea from China to Nova Scotia—six thousand chests of it—came into Halifax harbor in the hold of the *Countess of Harcourt*. S. Cunard and Company became the big teahouse for all of British North America. Branching out into coal mining, they became agents for Cape Breton coal fields, ready to provide the age of steam on the ocean with fuel long before that particular service was needed.

As late as 1829, in fact, even the very idea of steamship transportation was superfluous to Samuel's prosperity and, apparently, to his curiosity. In October of that year, when the Messrs. Ross and Primrose of Pictou wrote to him in the hope of getting him to lend his weight to plans for steamboats they were trying to initiate, Cunard's answer left no room for further importunity. "We have received your letter of the twenty-second instant," he replied. "We are entirely unacquainted with the cost of a steamboat, and would not like to embark in a business of which we are quite ignorant. Must, therefore, decline taking part in the one you propose getting up."

Within a few months—a whole year before the *Royal William* would first put into Halifax—Samuel Cunard's interest in steamship potentialities had obviously been piqued. What changed his mind so abruptly is not apparent, but the change itself was drastic, to the point where he had begun to say that "steamers properly built and manned might start and arrive at their destination with the punctuality of railroad trains on land. . . . The day will surely come when an ocean steamer will be signalled from Citadel Hill every day in the year."

"A bright, tight little man with keen eyes, firm lips and happy manners," Samuel Cunard possessed, and sometimes seemed actually to enjoy, power and wealth and the fawning esteem of those who coveted these advantages. With the ranking of colonel, he was one of the socially elitist "Scarlet Runners" of the Second Halifax Regiment of Militia. His high social standing was further confirmed by his membership in the Sun Fire Company, one of the "most exclusive" groups of citizens willing to come running, properly costumed, at the sound of a fire alarm. As a "consistent and outspoken supporter of the ancient Tory regime," he was appointed commissioner of lighthouses and, for a time, served as chief administrator in charge of soup kitchens and other relief measures for indigent immigrants. As the Honorable Samuel Cunard, he sat as a member of the Nova Scotia Legislative Council—the famous and all-powerful "Council of Twelve," whose banking and commercial interests dominated both the city and the province. A merchant friend who had opportunity to observe Cunard's rise from ambitious obscurity to unruffled eminence regarded him as an outstanding "diplomatist," and otherwise characterized him as "a very able man, and, I am happy to say, a good man. In early life he was somewhat imperious. He believed in himself—he made both men and things bend to his will."

He was also one of that race of countinghouse bookkeepers to whom education was solely an instrument. Among the very few of his personal letters that have survived is one written to the headmaster of a private school in Pictou about his two youngest brothers. He is willing to have the boys learn Latin if the headmaster insists, he says, but wants the man to remember "that they are intended for business, and that a plain English education answers the purpose." Another passage in the same letter suggests that his humane concerns were not backward. "I shall feel much obliged if you will have the kindness to supply the little wants of the boys from time to time; they will require as the winter approaches worsted socks, and strong shoes which can be had at Pictou better than here . . . any other thing that you may conceive they stand in need of and that will add to their comfort please to order for them."

When old Abraham Cunard died, Samuel's inheritance swelled his own resources to something in the neighborhood of two hundred thousand pounds—a fortune, in those days, beyond ordinary comprehension. He was the father of nine children and, at the age of forty-one, a widower who on Sundays escorted to the front pew of St. George's Church on Brunswick Street a graduated procession of seven daughters and two sons.

Early in January, 1838, three Cunards—Samuel, Joseph and Samuel's twelve-year-old son William—took ship from Halifax. The brothers had business to look into in England; and Samuel, at fifty, was just old enough and rich enough to begin to relax into the graces and large society that London might offer a reasonably well-endowed widower from the colonies. During his months in London the impending voyages of the *Sirius* and the *Great Western* were the talk of the maritime world; and just as his visit was about over and he was waiting to hear that his homeward packet was ready to go, news of their crossings to New York brought the speculations of a long season to an exciting climax. Then, on the eve of Samuel's departure, Joseph Howe came bouncing into London to tell him all about the *Tyrian's* midocean encounter with the *Sirius*. When they dined in Piccadilly that evening, Howe rehearsed his recent talks with steamship people in Bristol. In the circumstance, Cunard could not have been entirely pleased with Howe's proprietary stance or the news of his untoward gadding about in the interests of steamships—*any* steamships. But their evening was at least overtly congenial, and Samuel and his son sailed from Gravesend the next day.

For the remainder of that year Cunard's energies went in one direction. He could by himself have been quite able to swing the cost of a steamship or two—or even a small fleet of them. Yet he was too innately cautious to act without an official commitment, too canny to assume the whole financial risk alone. Looking for partners, he broached his ideas to merchant friends in Halifax but found not one of them responsive. In Boston it was the same thing. Frustrated but resolute, he set off for England in Her Majesty's packet *Reindeer* in mid-January, 1839.

While Samuel Cunard was enduring a rough winter's passage eastward, the *Nova Scotian*, a Halifax newspaper, came out with a story about a request for a "Tender for Performing by Steam Vessels the Mail Service between England and Halifax and New York." This was the request that had recently been put in circulation by the British Admiralty. Oddly unaware that the one man who could—and in the long run would—satisfy the requirements of the tender was at that moment en route to his momentous appointment, the newspaper's unnamed correspondent (he was, no doubt, the ubiquitous Joseph Howe) assumed a dim view of steamships for Halifax. "It is absurd to suppose that any set of men would embark the large amount of Capital required for the undertaking," he wrote; the subsidy needed would be too high, the time in which to build ships too short. Yet he felt that someone charged with the interests of Nova Scotia ought to go to London, that "some representations upon the subject should be sent from this quarter without delay."

In a coincidence almost too good to be true, Samuel Cunard, having checked into his old Piccadilly hotel, was at the very moment beginning to make his presence known and his intentions clear. Yet on his own word, he was ignorant of developments in regard to the tender that had led others to court the Admiralty's favor. Seven years later, when the transatlantic mail contracts were under review, his interrogation by a parliamentary committee proceeded as follows:

" 'Were you aware of an advertisement having been issued for conveyance of the mails?'

" 'No. I was not.'

" 'Before you left Halifax, had you no idea of any intention on the part of the Government to issue an advertisement?'

" 'No, not at all. There had been some conversation about the *Great Western*. It had been discussed in Parliament frequently. I saw those things in the papers, but I knew nothing of any arrangement, or proposed arrangement.' "

Accounts of Samuel Cunard's mission to London suggest, almost invariably, that his success there was promoted by his acquaintance with the celebrated hostess Mrs. George Norton, née Caroline Sheridan. The basis of these accounts is the story of a dinner party recounted in the memoirs of the actress Fanny Kemble: "She [Mrs. Norton] came often to parties at our house, and I remember her asking us to dine at her uncle's, when among the people we met were Lord Lansdowne and Lord Normanby, both then in the Ministry, whose good-will and influence she was exerting herself to *captivate* in behalf of a certain shy, silent, rather rustic gentleman from the far-away province of New Brunswick, Mr. Samuel Cunard, afterwards Sir Samuel Cunard of the great mail-packet line of steamers between England and America. He had come to London an obscure and humble individual, endeavouring to procure from the Government the sole privilege of carrying the transatlantic mails for his line of steamers. Fortunately for him he had some acquaintance with Mrs. Norton, and the powerful beauty, who was kind-hearted and good-natured to all but her natural enemies (i.e., the members of her own London society), exerted all her interest with her admirers in high place in favour of Cunard, and had made this very dinner for the express purpose of bringing her provincial *protégé* into pleasant personal relations with Lord Lansdowne and Lord Normanby, who were likely to be of great service to him in the special object which had brought him to England. Years after, when the Halifax projector had become Sir Samuel Cunard, a man of fame in the worlds of commerce and business of New York and London, a baronet of large fortune, and a sort of proprietor of the Atlantic Ocean between England and the United States, he reminded me of this charming dinner in which Mrs. Norton had so successfully found the means of forwarding his interests, and spoke with enthusiasm of her kindheartedness as well as her beauty and talents; he, of course, passed under the Caudine Forks, beneath which all men encountering her had to bow and throw down their arms."

The trouble with this account is that it reports an event that could not possibly have taken place until 1841, the year when Miss Kemble, on her own admission, began a two-year visit to England. And by 1841, far from being a rustic petitioner for the favors of royalty, Samuel Cunard was already the chief stockholder in a company whose four hard-working liners were the talk of the ocean. His indisputably helpful acquaintances in London were not habitués of fashionable salons but two men, both highly placed, to whom Cunard's good name and character were well known. They were James Melvill and William Edward Parry.

As secretary of the East India Company, Melvill was able to keep an eye on maritime business as if he were stationed in a conning tower. He saw at once what Cunard most specifically needed and directed his attention to Robert Napier—the most famous marine engineer on the banks of the Clyde, and soon to be acknowledged as "the tutelary deity of the art and science of shipbuilding." Napier had supplied machinery for the steamship *Berenice,* put into service by the East India Company between Bombay and Suez in 1837; and his relations with the Admiralty were most amiable. The Lords Commissioners deferred to his judgment, trusting, as he himself said, "to my honour in everything."

Cunard's other London acquaintance was, in the nature of the game, his ace in the hole.

In the years following the War of 1812, there was a young man, William Edward Parry, garrisoned at the Halifax naval base, who used to visit the Cunard household. When naval orders took him elsewhere, Parry's purely social acquaintance with Samuel Cunard had lapsed. His talents had eventually taken him upward until, in 1839, he was the Admiralty's Comptroller of Steam Machinery and Packet Service. When Samuel got to London the prospect of renewing his old friendship on quite a new footing was too promising to ignore. And as it happened, he was preparing his steamship proposals just when Parry was courting proposals of precisely the same nature. Acting for the Admiralty, Parry had written to George Burns, a Glasgow shipbuilder, asking him if he would possibly be interested in bidding for the rights to a Government-sponsored Atlantic packet service under steam. No, said Burns, he would not. Rebuffed, Parry was able to turn quite conveniently to Cunard. The Admiralty was not much impressed with offers made by the Great Western people and by the St. George Steam Packet people, he told him; was there a chance that a bid signed by S. Cunard might be in the making? Cunard at once put down and dispatched to the Lords of the Admiralty explicit proposals. "I hereby offer to furnish steamboats of not less than 300 horsepower," he wrote, "to convey the mails from a point in England to Halifax and back, twice each month . . ." to provide feeder services, to have the ships ready by the first of May, 1840, and to do it all for the sum of fifty-five thousand pounds subsidy per annum.

Their Lordships were taken with this straightforward offer and sent the text of it on to the Treasury with a memorandum: "The sum is not unreasonable for the proposed service, if the Lords of the Treasury are prepared to entertain a proposition of this kind." Their Lordships were indeed prepared and, as soon as Cunard was confident of that, he made his first bid for Napier's cooperation in a letter that at once outlined his needs and established his penuriousness. "I shall require one or two steamboats of 300 horse-power and about 800 tons," he informed his agent in Glasgow. "I shall want these vessels to be of the very best description, plain and comfortable, not the least unnecessary expense for show. I prefer plain woodwork in the cabin, and it will save a large amount in the cost."

Napier had long ago earned his great reputation, and he was now in a mood to risk it. Like Cunard, he had been speculating about steam on the Atlantic for years. As far back as 1833, a London merchant by the name of Patrick Wallace had sought his advice in regard to ocean-going steamships. "I have not the smallest doubt upon my own mind but that in a very short time it will be one of the best and most lucrative businesses in the country," Napier told him. But Wallace's dream of ocean liners was a bubble; six years had passed; events in the time between had only confirmed what Napier had predicted. Then, as if an inevitable event had found its place to happen, quite out of the blue came Samuel Cunard.

In his letter to the agent, Cunard said he would come to Glasgow at once if Napier and his partner Wood were inclined to receive him. Napier wrote back within the day, spelling out for Cunard the whole roster of his own accomplishments. "If your friend is really in want of vessels," he told the agent, "I shall be happy to go to London to meet him, and I have no doubt but that we would in a very short time understand one another."

He was right. Cunard went up to Lancefield, Napier's home near Glasgow, in early March and, as Napier recalled, "waited upon me at my house with specifications." Before the meeting was over they had come to a simple agreement: Mr. Napier would within the year supply Mr. Cunard with two vessels, for thirty thousand pounds each. These would satisfy the advertised requirements of the Admiralty and the "plain and comfortable" vision of Cunard. "I am of opinion Mr. Cunard got a good contract," Napier wrote to a friend, "and that he will make a good thing of it. From the frank off-hand manner in which he contracted with me, I have given him the vessels cheap, and I am certain they will be very good and very strong ships."

Napier did not hold this opinion for long. When he reviewed plans worked out at Lancefield, he began to suspect that in the general good feeling of the interview he had perhaps agreed to something less than what he really wanted to supply. Without consulting Cunard, he made new calculations and came up with a list of improvements. These would add as much as two thousand pounds to the cost of each vessel, but he had come to feel they were essential. Without them the ships would be run-of-the-mill; for the self-conscious master of marine engineering nothing run-of-the-mill would serve. Determined to have his way, he said he would even make an outright gift of all the extra work and materials involved.

Cunard was simply bewildered. He had to admit that Napier's proposals were extraordinarily generous, but the annoying thing was his upsetting of an apple cart that had been carefully, even delicately, loaded. He was dealing, he knew, with a man who would give him "twenty shillings to the pound," but probably not aware that he was up against a creative personality that would insist on its own prerogatives.

The truth was that Cunard's goals could be measured by return on investment, Napier's only by his own sense of the fitness, rightness and harmonious resolutions of the job in hand. In sketches of the articulations of marine machinery, Napier had produced work that struck some people as "enchanting as a Japanese print." This extra margin of concern, involving only the aesthetics of the thing, was something Cunard could not understand and it would in time give him a lot of trouble. He put aside his reluctance, nonetheless, and went back to Scotland.

There, on March 18, 1839, he and Napier arrived at a formal agreement and had it put in writing. "Three good and sufficient steamships," the contract stipulated, "each not less than two hundred feet long keel, and fore-rakes not less than thirty-two feet broad between the paddles, properly finished in every respect, having boats, masts, rigging, sails, anchors, cables, with cabins finished in a neat and comfortable manner for sixty to seventy passengers, or a greater number in case the said Robert Napier shall find that the space will conveniently and commodiously admit thereof." The first vessel was to be ready for delivery in the Clyde on the twelfth of March, the second on the twelfth of April, the third on the eighteenth of May. Should Napier be remiss in meeting these deadlines, he stood the chance of having to forfeit five thousand pounds in each instance.

Back in London with the contract and new specifications, Cunard wrote to Napier: "The Admiralty and Treasury are highly pleased . . ." and in the same letter reported another less cheering reaction. He may of course have been moved to report this for its own sake, but it is hard to avoid suspecting him of a bit of one-upmanship. "You have no idea," he told Napier, "of the prejudice of some of our English builders. I have had several offers from Liverpool and this place; and when I replied that I have contracted to Scotland they invariably say, 'You will neither have substantial work nor completed in time.'" Napier took this unnecessary piece of intelligence soberly and with grace. "I was quite prepared," he wrote back, "for your being beset with all the schemers in the country and in this state of the business. I am sorry that some of the English tradesmen should indulge in speaking ill of their competitors in Scotland. I shall not follow their example, having hitherto made it my practice to let deeds, not words, prove who is right or wrong. At present I shall not say more than court comparison of my work with any other in the kingdom, only let it be done by honest and competent men."

Pride—and a perhaps obsessive determination not to be found want-ing—once more led Napier to make new demands. He was in the process of supplying engines for the *British Queen*, then being readied for her maiden voyage, and he had become acquainted with Junius Smith's other new ship, the *President*. Alongside these cynosures, the ships Cunard had in mind could only have struck him as mean and runty. He was revising plans once more, he told Cunard. The ships would just have to be bigger and grander if they were not to be the poor cousins of the Atlantic. Incredulous, Cunard threw up his hands. Napier was squandering money on royal galleons before there was money in view to pay even for the "plain and comfortable" ferryboats he had specified. Further increase in the costs was out of the question. The Admiralty was satisfied, the Treasury was satisfied—why wasn't Robert Napier? Cunard went to James Melvill and said, in effect, that he had had enough. Why did not Napier get on with the job instead of endlessly proposing changes that meant only more money and longer delay? No matter what the cost, Melvill told him, he would be wise to go along with the Scotsman's requests; and urged him to go to Glas-gow and talk the matter out. Hat in hand, Cunard went north again.

Napier was sympathetic, and quick to see what was muddying every-thing: money, and the lack of it. As engineer and a builder of marine machinery, he was also one of the directors of the City of Glasgow Steam-Packet Company. Among his colleagues were two men Napier particularly respected: George Burns; and David MacIver, who managed the Glasgow Steam-Packet's offices. Napier more or less promised Burns the position of agent for Cunard if he would help in raising the neces-sary capital. For management of the steamships themselves, Napier had kept MacIver in mind. To further matters, he arranged a meeting between Cunard and Burns at the latter's office.

For all Cunard knew, he was entering into fresh territory with a new scheme. But for Burns, this was actually the second time in the same year that he was faced with an opportunity to come in on the ground floor of a transatlantic undertaking. As William Parry had opened a door for Cunard, so had he opened one for Burns. But when Burns saw what the demands of such a project were, he was over-whelmed, and said he would stick to coastal trading. Now, in the pres-ence of enterprise itself, he was as interested as if he had never before heard of such an astonishing thing.

The old Burns would likely have settled for some comfortably peripheral interest in any new mail-carrying scheme. The new Burns, oddly enough, was swept up in the enthusiasm—or converted by the manifest rectitude—of a man from the colonies no one had ever cited for magnetism, let alone charisma. He asked Cunard to take dinner with him—a dinner during which they could explore all phases of the project with David MacIver. When this was arranged, MacIver listened but showed no sign that he approved. The proposed subsidy was tempting, he granted, but what about the strings attached? Should the new ships not keep to their schedules, he reminded Cunard and his host, the Government would collect a fine of five hundred pounds for every twelve hours by which a sailing might be delayed either in getting off or in arriving. This meant that only one day's delay in each fortnightly sailing during the course of a year would eat up every shilling of the subsidy. This was putting matters in the very worst light, MacIver knew; yet he would have none of it. Before the dinner was over, he took Burns aside and told him to make it known to Cunard that he was wasting his time and theirs.

Burns could not bring himself to act upon MacIver's bad manners. Let's let everything ride over until the morning, he suggested, and the party broke up. When they regathered early for breakfast at Napier's big Lancefield House, Cunard was primed to make the most of his last chance. He began by emphasizing what everyone might have known: with Napier's engines, risk of breakdowns and delays would be minor. Hoping MacIver would acquiesce if not approve, Burns still felt Cunard's sense of urgency. He would like to bring some of his Glaswegian friends in on the deal, he told Cunard. It would perhaps take as long as a month to canvass them all, he thought: would Cunard wait that long? Cunard said that he would. Within just one week the subscription lists were closed; the biggest single investor on them was S. Cunard, with an outlay of fifty-five thousand pounds.

An executive division of labor was promptly set up. By early May the new British and North American Royal Mail Steam Packet Company announced its corporate entity and registered its cumbersome name. The amended contract called for four vessels instead of three and each of them were to satisfy Napier's specifications to the very letter. Cabin accommodations were to exhibit even a slightly illicit touch of the luxurious. Otherwise, to stamp his personality on the enterprise (and to keep it there indelibly for more than a hundred years) Napier made sure that the funnels of the company's ships were of a color he had already made his own unofficial trademark. This was a highly distinctive orange-red—a mixture of bright ocher and buttermilk—with a broad black band at the top and black lines on the flanges, which had for years identified Isle of Man steamers for which Napier had been responsible.

Somewhat ironically, the most assuring factor in the Admiralty's decision to favor Cunard and his new friends with a seven-year contract was the success of the *Great Western*. Her owners knew this, and they were determined not to let Cunard and his associates assume precedence without the delays a Parliamentary investigation would make inevitable. Unable to claim collusion or chicanery, they put the burden of their case where it was most telling—on their moral right to precedence. They were first on the Atlantic, they said, a place not achieved without great expense and risk. Why should the public be taxed for a service from which one company alone would derive all the profit? Why should not governmental subsidy be prorated among all ships that would guarantee the conveyance of mails? These entirely reasonable questions were answered by the investigation committee with a blanket endorsement of everything Cunard was up to.

When news of the contract—calling for a direct run to Halifax, with a feeder service to Boston—reached home in April, Haligonians took heart. They passed a civic resolution thanking Cunard; then they subscribed eight thousand pounds for a new hotel to receive boatload upon boatload of transatlantic voyagers. Bostonians, on the other hand, were incensed. The Hub of the Universe was utterly indisposed to regard itself as a branch line of anything. A number of merchants met in the Tremont Bank and whipped off a series of resolutions, one of which, craven to the point of pusillanimity, offered to Cunard an advantage he himself would not have dared to assume. "Resolved. That it is the sense of this meeting, that a suitable Pier and Dock should be provided for a term of years, for the reception of the Liverpool steam packets to this port, where they may receive and discharge their lading, free from expense to the owners of the steamers, and that such other facilities be afforded as the importance of the subject may require." The big point of it all was "that the larger class of steam packets should run entirely through from Liverpool to Boston," with a concession to Halifax, "for the reception of fuel, and to receive and discharge passengers and freight."

These resolutions reached Cunard in London, just as he was preparing to sail for New York. He took them to the Admiralty and found their Lordships to be acutely sympathetic to the Bostonians' wounded feelings and pleas for justice. They were moved not only to guarantee service to Boston but to increase the subsidy so that the new line could carry the Cunard flag directly to Massachusetts.

Joseph Cunard had joined his brother in the late winter of 1839, but just what he was doing in England is not clear. Samuel would not very likely covet his business advice; perhaps he simply needed a brother's moral support. In any case, Joseph was importantly on the scene where Samuel brought off his big deal. This country-style clannishness of the Cunards made some people think that the new steamship venture was a family affair. As a result, credit that should have gone exclusively to Samuel was, in the early stages at least, often assigned to his younger brother.

When Joseph reached Halifax in late April, he told everyone about the marvelous new contract in the offing and sent the town into a whirl of avaricious excitement. When the good word galloped ahead of Joseph and spread through the woods of New Brunswick, plans for a gala of gratitude were swiftly put into effect. The settlers of Richibucto and Kouchibouguiac and all the villages along the Miramichi, to whom the sign *J. Cunard & Co.* was as potent as a coat-of-arms, began arranging ceremonial gatherings and boisterous acts of homage. When Joseph finally descended, he was cheered like a returning hero by crowds gathered under the eaves of his showplace residence, given the place of honor at a public banquet, and toasted by his serfs and vassals for every beatitude in the history of grace. Then, with the pomp of medieval guildsmen, they marched for his review in the following order:

HEAD MARSHALL
Gentlemen composing the Amateur Band
Two of the Deputation, with the Address,
HAMMERMEN,
in the following order,
Vulcan
Two Cyclops, with emblems of Office

Two　　do　　do.
Supported on each side by a Cyclop in uni-
form, with battle axe.
Banner,
On which was painted the Hammermen's Coat
of Arms, supported by a Crown,
Supported on each side by Cyclops, with
battle axes,
Two Cyclops, with emblems of Office
Two　　do　　do.
Banner,
Inscription—God Save the Queen,
Supported on each side by Cyclops bearing
crown and anvil.
Then followed a body of Mechanics, carrying
Crowns and Emblems of Trade,
Piece of Ordnance,
Supported by Cyclops, bearing battle axes,
SHIPWRIGHTS,
in the following order, handsomely dressed
with blue silk scarfs,
Model of Ship, on Launch ways,
Company's Signal, Union Jack,
Master shipwrights, arm in arm, attended by
Two Lads of the trade,
First and second Foremen, arm in arm,
Six Shipwrights, as Builder's Guard,
Handsomely furnished with broad-axes and adzes,
Thirty Shipwrights, with axes, two and
two, handsomely furnished,
Flag
CAULKERS,
Two and two, handsomely furnished,
Flag
BLACKSMITHS,
Two and two
JOINERS,
Two and two,
Flag,
RIGGERS,
With Model of a Full-Rigged Ship
SAWYERS,

Two and two.
Then followed in succession, the Engineers,
Carpenters and others, belonging to the
Steam Mill Company,
Banner
On which was painted a representation of the
Steam Mill, Saw, Plane, &c.
CARPENTERS AND BUILDERS,
Two and two.
Then followed Members of various trades
promiscuously mingled,
two and two.

With everything finally set in motion, Samuel Cunard had taken his good time about going home. He lingered in London for a couple of months, then booked passage with the intention of arriving in Saratoga Springs while the season was at its height. When he sailed from Liverpool, one of his shipmates was his old Bluenose colleague Judge Haliburton. The voyage was inordinately rough for a summer crossing, so rough in fact that the *Great Western* took longer to get to New York than at any other time since she had dogged the *Sirius* into port more than a year earlier.

Except for weather, the trip was without event—at least without event of which her passengers were aware. Actually, the *Great Western* had shared a sea lane with a mosquito-sized rival whose virtues—a hull of iron and a screw propeller—would before long make her own celebrated features quite obsolete. This embryonic rival was the *Robert F. Stockton*, an almost ridiculously tiny steamer of a kind that never before had dared an Atlantic crossing. Schooner-rigged, she was all of 35 tons burden—71 feet long and 10 feet wide—and the showpiece model ship for the screw propeller invented by a Swede, Captain John Ericsson.

Even after he had sent a propeller-driven boat smartly down the Thames for the edification of scouts from the Admiralty, Ericsson found no support for his invention in England, except from two resident Americans: Francis B. Ogden, the United States Consul at Liverpool; and Robert F. Stockton, a commodore in the American Navy. These men urged Ericsson to take the little experimental model to America— and so it was that the ship came to make her crossing just when Cunard did. She lost a man overboard when a mountainous sea engulfed her deck, and she had to fight the same foul weather that caused the *Great Western* to hove to—yet her Captain John R. Crane navigated her from Gravesend to New York in forty-five days.

The only newspaper to give the *Stockton* much attention in New York was James Gordon Bennett's. Obviously still mindful of the buffeting he had endured on the *Sirius* a year before, Bennett even called for the Corporation to present the freedom of the city to Captain "Mad-Jack" Crane. "The fact is," he wrote, "as the years slip by, there will not be a steamer ploughing the Atlantic on the old jarring-and-racking principle. Every steam packet will be constructed on Captain Ericsson's plan, and they will move through the waters, the passengers scarcely knowing how. But this is not all. The vessels are more compact; they have much more space for cargo and passengers, and there is such a material saving in fuel. They sail faster, and there is not that disagreeable jar and noise that we suffer in steamers on the old principle."

Philip Hone agreed. The arrival of the *Robert F. Stockton* was, he believed, one of the greatest of maritime exploits, adding that he felt the midget ship was lucky not to have "come across a whale, one of the descendants of 'Mocha Dick,' the white whale of the Pacific."

Halifax had to wait for its favorite son to quit the turreted pleasure domes of Saratoga, but its citizens knew he was coming and prepared for the day. All Nova Scotians were invited to contribute to a fund for a "liberal present" of silver plate; and as soon as he got back a group of local patriarchs waited upon Cunard at his residence, hailed him "with feelings of unfeigned delight," and forced him to stand at attention while, one by one, they spoke their paeans of Haligonian pride. "You have, Sir," said one of them, "on all occasions, been anxious liberally to encourage and forward every measure having a tendency to call forth the resources and promote the prosperity of this your native land." Cunard's response was couched equally in the fulsome formality that custom expected. "Having embarked so largely in this enterprise," he said, "I need not assure you that every exertion will be used on my part to carry into effect the intentions of the Government, and to afford every facility to the public convenience; but did I require anything to stimulate me to renewed exertion, it would have been the approbation of my fellow townsmen: the warm manner in which they have hailed this undertaking assures me of its success."

Even in an era of scrupulously studied felicity, the interview was painful and all too much for everyone. Instead of going ahead with the big public dinner they had planned, the committee took note of Cunard's "disinclination to anything like display," and invited him to a clambake.

It was chill and rainy in Halifax on the morning of August 28, 1839. The local newspaper later reported that "appearances strongly favoured the idea that it would be necessary to postpone the feast"; but it suddenly cleared up about one o'clock, and everyone headed for MacNab's Island near the mouth of Halifax Harbor. The Eighth Regiment's band and a few optimists had already gone over to the island by steamer. By two o'clock, confident "that no more cold water would be thrown on the event," whole boatloads of gentlemen were being ferried down the harbor. On a hill in front of the house of MacNab himself a pavilion formed of flags had been erected, underneath which tables were spread, covered with substantial and delicate fare. The *pièces de résistance* were two frosted cakes in the form of pyramids surmounted by miniature flags on which were imprinted inscriptions "suitable to the event." One hundred and fifty citizens sat down to buckets of oysters and clams at four o'clock and did not get up until nearly eight. Thirteen toasts— each a "full and flowing bumper"—were drunk. For the prodigiousness of his personal triumph, the main one was directed to Samuel Cunard.

⚜ SECTION II ⚜

The British Queen / *Junius Smith Comes Across*

TRANSATLANTIC victory would come neither by swiftness, resourcefulness, brilliance nor even by tenacity. Like
a reward from heaven, it would come by providence and
good husbandry. Early in 1839, while Samuel Cunard was merely
carrying on negotiations, the *Great Western* was already carrying out
passengers. Two other steamships, the *Royal William* and the *Liverpool*,
were taking bookings and laying in supplies. Over all of these well-
endowed front runners, Cunard's good engines and good sense would
win conclusively.

And now the *British Queen* was getting ready to claim, if not, alas,
to assume, preeminence. Junius Smith could not resist joining her
maiden voyage. "She is a nice girl," he wrote to his nephew, "and I
can't do better, and I know she will take me in." When his nephew
said that it seemed to him that the *Queen* was taking an awfully long
time to come into shape, Smith replied snappishly. "Englishmen," he
said, "had rather spend a few months in *completing* their work than be
blown up in default. They leave that part for the Americans, who seem
to have profited very little by the death of others." Within three years,

these were words he would have to eat. In this instance, however, it was not an Englishman, but a Scotsman, whose finicky sense of craft was making the ship late. Snubbed and ignored when the contracts for the *British Queen*'s engines were given out, Robert Napier had finally been asked to take over. Now he was taking his time installing machinery at a price that seemed almost vengefully higher than that which he had originally named.

Napier's irritating tardiness was but one of Smith's troubles. While his "floating colossus," as a London paper called the 2,016-ton ship, was being fitted out, he found himself in an altercation with his fellow directors. The issue was absurd. They had proposed that, as in the case of many of the sailing packets, the victualing of the *British Queen*'s passengers be made at the discretion and to the taste of her captain. Although, Smith said generously, Richard Roberts was surely not a man to stint on what might be placed on the *British Queen*'s tables, he had, on principle, to object to such a demeaning role for an ocean liner's captain. He went "upon the ground of the impolicy," he said, "of placing the captain in a position that his remuneration should depend upon the degree of starvation to which his passengers were subject." But Smith was overruled. Captain Roberts would lay his own table and pare his own cheese.

No beauty, in one report, "a big lump of a boat" in another, with her "hideous old stern, old-fashioned square ports, one of her anchors abreast of her fore-mast," the *British Queen*, with a blue smoke stack and a full-length figurehead of her namesake carrying a scepter in her right hand, an orb in her left, was at last ready to set off. Captain Roberts—already dubbed "the Columbus of steam" for his voyage in the *Sirius*—was at the helm when she sailed from London on July 10, 1839, and from Spithead the next day. The happiest man among her passengers was Junius Smith. After six long years of struggle and connivance, he was going to New York, as ruddy and forward as a figurehead, in the biggest and swiftest ship, "the greatest of all lions by far," that the Empire City had the chance to welcome. To make sure that the thing would be done with style and point, he sent ahead instructions for a banquet that was to be laid out in the saloon of the ship a day or two after she arrived. In the matter of toasts, he suggested that "after the President of the United States, Queen, etc., are given, my name as father of the Atlantic steam navigation should follow in right and justice. Let a subscription be opened upon the spur of the occasion to purchase a full-length (and no great length either) portrait of your very humble servant to be painted in London and placed in your Chamber of Commerce."

Once more, a new ship off the Battery allowed New Yorkers to exhibit their strenuous abandon. Storied, sung, fêted, the *British Queen* remained at her berth at the foot of Clinton Street for four days, visited by thousands of sightseers and nautical connoisseurs, among whom were Philip Hone and his daughter. "Her cabin is superbly fitted up," Hone wrote in his diary, "and the staterooms adjoining it are convenient and pleasant as possible; but the sleeping apartments below are dark and confined, and I doubt whether the whole amount of sleeping accommodations is equal to that of the *Great Western*. The scene on deck was a perfect show; discharging in one place and receiving and stowing cargo in another; boxes and barrels of stores; cartloads of fresh meat; great lumps of ice; mountains of coal sinking into the crater of the lower hold; live cows and poultry wondering what part of the pandemonia is intended for them; sentinels employed in the unthankful office of keeping back disappointed visitors; and officers more agreeably engaged in doing the genteel thing by our more favored selves."

On August 1, "the guns of the fort proclaimed our departure," wrote Junius Smith, "and the voices of one hundred thousand spectators threw their acclamations upon the gentle breeze." Music in his ears, he said goodbye to well-wishers who, "in their fairy steamers," accompanied the *Queen* downriver, into the Bay, for all of twenty-two miles before she stood out to sea. Seldom has a steamboat been so clearly a man's ward, protégé and heart's delight. "Ship quiet and steady as time," he noted in his journal on August 3; and on the sixth: "*Queen* dancing merrily over the seas." Next day she was still "leaping over the billows with infinite grace; when she pitched, she pitched 'kindly,' not the slightest strain."

Halfway over she was "going ahead with all imaginable dignity," then "dancing over the waves light-footed as a fox." Careering "over the mighty waters in all the plenitude of majesty," she was nearing landfall on August 13. "The *Queen*," Smith asserted, "approaches her dominions, quick of step, always solicitous to let her subjects know that she is still mistress of the seas."

Lyricism merely glossed the matter; pedestrian demands for good food and physical ease exposed it. Two voyages later the passengers of the *British Queen* were so disgusted with their accommodations (Captain Roberts offered a bribe of free daily champagne to anyone who would occupy the hated fore cabin) and with the food provided that all sixty-seven of them signed a letter protesting poor "bread, butter, water," and stating that the line as now conducted was not worthy of patronage. This attack on the hands that fed them might have been damaging, but disgruntled passengers did little to slow the marked progress of the new *Queen.* Running well in all weathers, the crack ship of her time, she was a scrappy veteran before even the first of Cunard's ships had made her way across. In June, 1840, Captain Roberts boasted to a friend in New York that he was in command of the fastest sea-going vessel in the world. "We have beat the *Great Western* every voyage this year," he said, "and last year I have made the passage from Plymouth to New York shorter than ever performed, only 13 days 11 hours from Pilot to Pilot. Let *Great Western* do that if she can."

❦ SECTION III ❦

Nova Scotians: Samuel Cunard and Donald McKay / The Sweet Singer of Hartford / The Sovereign of the Seas vs. the Canada

THE BEST of packet ships, according to the experts, were those built in New England by a man from Nova Scotia —Donald McKay. As time would tell, the most successful of steamship operators was another Nova Scotian—Samuel Cunard. Their careers were parallel, yet the acumen of Cunard the entrepreneur would quite overshadow the genius of McKay the artisan. A poor businessman, McKay was a worker in a tradition of craftsmanship and taste—with its contempt for mere utility—that had been an element of enlightened societies since the Renaissance. Cunard was an operator in a comparatively new tradition of acquisitiveness, a soberly statistical man whose triumphs, like those achieved in the gouged-out landscapes and sooty slums of the Industrial Revolution, were largely mercenary.

In spite of the prevailing steamship fever, sailing packets and clipper ships would for another thirty years crowd the seas on which rode but a few smudged and clanking steamers with auxiliary sails. Americans in particular were unwilling to accept the superiority of steamships over their masterful sailing vessels. "When a packet ship running before a strong westerly gale in mid-ocean overhauled a wallowing side-wheeler steamer," said one sailing captain, "the joyous shouts and derisive yells of the steerage passengers on board the packet, as she ranged alongside and swept past the 'tea-kettle,' were good for the ears of sailormen to hear. In those days no sailors liked steamships, not even those who went to sea in them. If a packet captain sighted a steamer ahead going in the same way, he usually steered for her and passed to windward as close as possible, in order that the dramatic effect of the exploit might not be lost upon the passengers of either vessel."

Clippers had been refined to such a point that they stood for the sailing ship in its final elegant decadence. Clippers were "the orchids, the Borzois, of sea-faring." Yet well-appointed packets-on-schedule left those with a mind to travel little to be desired in the way of transatlantic service; and they delighted in instances when packets would best the graceless steamers just as, a few decades later, their grandchildren liked to shout "Get a horse!" to motorists whose chugging Daimlers and Willys-Overlands had left them stranded. To them the idea of a ship was still a sailing ship—not an assemblage of engines that had somehow been made buoyant. "In light head winds and moderate weather," said a New Yorker, "a steamer would go wheezing and bubbling along side of the proudest ship in the British or American navy, and passing, laugh her to scorn; but let the ocean be lashed, and let the waves run high as the topmast, and how is this long stiff vessel, overburthened with the weight of machinery, with a burning volcano in her bowels, to ride on the crested billows and sink again into their dark, deep caverns? It may answer—and if it does, heigh for the Downs, the Mersey, or the Seine in ten days."

But, more than ever, time was money—and money would answer. Romantics and patriots might eulogize the beauty and clean-cut slant of Yankee sails ("One wanted her to stay there, frozen in motion," said a man in love with a clipper, "to be an undying delight for the eye and a correction of heresies."), but men who had business to attend to overseas, or consignments for profit to dispatch, put their faith in the dependability of steam. And gradually even those voyagers who boarded steamers in fear and awe were forced to recognize their virtues. Among these was an analyst of social schemata who saw technology as rendering old pretensions absurd. "Steam is the great democratic power of our age," he said, "annihilating the conventional distinctions, differences, and social distance between man and man, as well as the natural distances between place and place. Observe that high and mighty Exclusive, sitting all by himself on the bench of the quarter-deck, wrapped up in his own self-importance and his blue traveling-cloak lined with white. . . . What a great personage this I-by-myself traveler would have been in the day of postchaises-and-four and sailing packets! Now, in the steam-boat, not a soul, not even the ship-dog, takes the least notice of his touch-me-not dignity. The dinner bell rings, and down must this great personage scramble with the rest of us; must eat, and drink, and carve—and ask, and help, or be helped, and talk, listen, and live with the other passengers, or go without dinner, or starve."

When the sweet singer of Hartford, Lydia Huntley Sigourney, came home from abroad in 1841, she was lucky to have chosen to cross on a steamer, and wanted everyone to know about it. When the *Great Western* ran into a drift of icebergs, "the engine accommodated itself every moment," she wrote, "like a living and intelligent thing, to the commands of the captain. 'Half a stroke!' and its tumultuous action was controlled; 'a quarter of a stroke!' and its breath seemed suspended; 'stand still!' and our huge bulk lay motionless upon the waters, till two or three of the icy squadron drifted by us; 'let her go!' and with the velocity of lightning we darted by another detachment of our deadly foes. It was then that we were made sensible of the advantages of steam, to whose agency, at our embarkation, many of us had committed ourselves with extreme reluctance. Yet a vessel more under the dominion of the winds, and beleaguered as we were amid walls of ice, in a rough sea, must inevitably have been destroyed."

But as sails were being folded, and famous old sailing stagers retired to the status of hulks and barges, the bright particular star of the ship-building profession did not himself give up the contest without a saucy demonstration of what, given the challenge, a scudding sail could still accomplish. One day James Baines of Liverpool, "the first man in England to appreciate McKay's genius," came with his associates in the Australia Black Ball Line to the McKay yards in Boston. They wanted to place an order for vessels to service immigrant ports down under. McKay was happy to oblige them; a contract was drawn up. Then, to show off his handicraft and, at the same time, make a gracious gesture, McKay invited Baines and his party to return to England on his new clipper *Sovereign of the Seas*. But the men from Liverpool turned him down because, they said, they were too busy to afford the leisure of a crossing under sail. Instead, they would have to hurry back on the next Cunarder which, in this case, was the *Canada*. Piqued by their refusal, McKay bade them a cool *bon voyage*. On the day his clients left Boston under steam, he sailed out of New York on the *Sovereign of the Seas*. For five days the sailing packet led the way, attaining in one 24-hour period the sensational figure of 340 nautical miles. But the steamer gradually overtook her and won out by forty-eight hours—even though the *Sovereign of the Seas* had covered the distance between the Grand Banks to Cape Clear at an average of 12.75 knots.

While she sailed proudly over the Mersey Bar, the *Sovereign* had to acknowledge that her best efforts were wanting. Yet she had proved that she and her scudding sisters could still give any steamer a run for its money. Two extra days at sea were, to some travelers, a crucial disadvantage. But there were still many others to whom the silken hiss of the passing sea under the shadow of white sails was an enchantment not to be traded for a sky perpetually smudged by the iron-works of engines that turned paddle wheels.

✥ SECTION IV ✥

The Unicorn *to Boston / Henry Wadsworth Longfellow in Faneuil Hall / The* Britannia *Sets the Rules / News for Halifax: God Saves Queen Victoria / The "Cunard Festival" The Four Sisters Come to Stay*

J UST BACK HOME from his enthralling voyage on the *British Queen,* Junius Smith read in the London *Times* of the awarding of a contract to Cunard and his new associates. With a note saying that the story was worth notice, he sent the newspaper to his nephew in New York, along with an advertisement for still another steamship enterprise—the Royal Mail Steam Packet Company. The name "Cunard" seemed, at the time, of little consequence to Smith. The interpretation he put upon the story in the newspaper was, characteristically, his own: "So we go," he said. "A gentleman called at my counting house yesterday and speaking of this [Cunard's] company remarked, 'It is all owing to you.'" The gentleman caller was not entirely alone in this opinion. An editorial in a contemporary issue of *Railway Magazine* also told Smith just what he wanted to hear: "It will appear," said the writer, "that that enterprising gentleman, Mr. Junius Smith, has the honor of having had the sagacity, as long since as 1833, to discover not only the practicability, but the profitableness of the undertaking. His first proposals, it seems, were, as all

117

other great enterprises usually are, laconically declined by the parties to whom they were addressed. This, however, does not lessen Mr. Smith's claim to a mind capable of conceiving a project in advance of the times, and as beneficial to the world as it was bold in conception."

Junius Smith was out for *la gloire*, knighthood and a pedestal in the pantheon; Samuel Cunard was simply out for business. Even while the first of his ships was in the building stage, he decided to look around for a vessel that might serve as a feeder for the Halifax service—a sturdy boat that might take over the Gulf of St. Lawrence routes of the old *Royal William*. Directorates had begun to interlock; he did not have to look far. Among the ships running between Glasgow and Liverpool for the firm of G. and J. Burns was the *Unicorn*. Not quite four years old, she was small—a mere 700 tons—but smart and efficient with a bowsprit jutting out from a figurehead in the form of the fabulous beast for which she was named. She would do for the coastal waterways, Cunard thought; but first she would go as a sort of herald—she would pioneer the route to Halifax, then introduce the Cunard flag to Boston.

The question of command was settled when he chose Captain Walter Douglas. Ever since 1825, Douglas had sailed the St. Lawrence on riverboats between Quebec and Montreal, and even acted as sailing master on His Majesty's Surveying Ship *Gulnare*, engaged in charting the River's channels.

On the fifteenth of May, 1840, the *Unicorn* "hauled out of the Clarence Dock into the stream," and on the sixteenth left Liverpool with twenty-four passengers, among them Samuel Cunard's son Edward. For sixteen long tempestuous days she pitched and rolled toward Halifax. As Captain Douglas wrote to a friend a few days after her arrival there, "I dare say you have heard before this time of our arrival, after a passage of 16 days, although a very boisterous one, nothing but gales of wind from west to northwest. The *Unicorn* is a most splendid seaboat; it blew one night a perfect hurricane, so that we could not carry our close-reefed foresail. We eased the engine to about half-speed, keeping the sea about a point or two points on the bow; she then went ahead about two knots as easy and dry as possible." She stayed in Halifax long enough to take welcome cheers and salutations, receive on board three thousand visitors, unload her provincial mails, disembark half of her passengers and give those bound for Boston a chance to drink and dally in the purple parlors of Water Street and Barrack Street.

Boston's Long Wharf, reaching back into the city then much deeper than it does today, was new enough and big enough to be considered a "wonder of the Western world." On the third of June, the great stone pier was the very best point of vantage for thousands of people who came down to the harbor to greet the first steamer from Europe ever to pass Boston Light. The *Unicorn* was first spotted from Mr. Parker's observatory on Central Wharf at twelve minutes to five; within no time, American and British flags were hoisted over the City Hall, civic buildings and on flagstaffs erected especially for the event.

Welcomed by martial airs from the band of the American ship-of-the-line *Columbus* and salutes fired from the cannon of the revenue cutter *Hamilton*, the *Unicorn* passed Castle Island and dropped anchor close enough to Long Wharf to allow the crowd to watch Captain Sturgis of the *Hamilton* personally give his greetings to Captain Douglas of the steamship. To the cheers of other crowds on every dock and pier, she steamed along the North End wharves and the Navy Yard, then by Copp's Hill and crossed over to the new Cunard wharf in East Boston. The windows of her cabin were shattered by the boom of one of the guns that bade her welcome, but at last she was able to disembark her passengers and deliver her papers. "Sixteen days later from Europe!" the newsboys yelled, and Bostonians paid their good money for the sobrieties of the *Times* and the levities of *Punch*.

"When the first signal was hoisted, announcing the anxiously expected vessel, I, sir, was at my post, among the earliest of the citizens who thronged to the water's side." The speaker was Thomas Colley Grattan, a writer of novels who was at the time British Consul in Boston. "There was no wind abroad, no sunshine in the sky, as the smoky standard of the steam ship floated in the distance. Soon she appeared manifest, moving through the mist in dignified celerity, independent of elemental aid. . . . It would be a waste of words . . . to attempt a further description of the scene—the roar of the artillery, the ringing of the city bells, the strains of music from the ships of war, and above all the pealing shouts of the great mass of men out-voicing all the rest. . . . As I saw the cable fastening the vessel to the Boston wharf, it required a small effort of poetical imagining to consider it less as a material substance, which might next be coiled around the pier at Liverpool, than as an emblem of the tie of interests and affections, which stretches across the ocean from shore to shore. . . ."

Mayor Jonathan Chapman presided at ceremonies, three days later, in Faneuil Hall, where "toasts, song, puns and punch filled up a very pleasant hour." Four hundred and fifty guests marched to the tables in procession from a point of assembly at the old City Hall. Toasting Captain Douglas and Edward Cunard, the mayor reminded his audience of the happy conjunction that was about to be achieved: steamships on the Boston docks would soon be able to unload their goods directly onto the trains of the nearly completed Boston & Albany Railroad and send them speeding westward. "Commercial enterprise!" he said, and lifted his glass. "It waked up the Dark Ages! It launched mankind on the sea of improvement; it launched their bark and spread their sails until a sail is no longer needed to join the two Continents together."

Edward Cunard said he was sorry his father was not on hand to respond to the city's welcome. Then Mr. Grattan rose to compliment his Yankee friends. "The inhabitants of New England have been compared to the granite and ice which are their chief articles of export," he said. "But I have not found this so—unless it is intended to compare them to granite in point of firmness in good resolves, and ice in the purity of their moral characters." In the murmur of self-approval that followed, Henry Wadsworth Longfellow gave a toast, "not distinctly heard in all parts of the hall," that was perhaps meant to temper the heavy commercial zeal of the occasion. "Steamships!" he proposed. "The pillar of fire by night and the cloud by day," and then concluded with laureate banality, "which guide the wanderer over the sea." The real poetic bite of the evening was given by Captain Sturgis; his toast was spare. "The Cunard steamers!" he offered. "May they cut their way through friends and foes."

The *Britannia*, flagship and prototype of the first Cunard fleet, sailed from the Mersey on the Fourth of July, 1840, thus inaugurating a steamship line that would outlast all of its competitors. For almost 125 years, the Cunard Line would have no enduring rival on the North Atlantic. From the very beginning, rules, orders, meticulous regulations were its hallmarks. On the *Britannia*, for instance, staterooms were to be swept every morning, beginning at five o'clock.

The wine and spirits bar would be opened to passengers at the astonishingly liberal hour of 6 A.M. Slops were to be emptied while passengers were at breakfast (stewards would have to queue up, *pots de chambres* in hand, on the leeward side of the ship to discharge the accumulations of the night), and breakfast was to be attended by boys "in becoming apparel." Bed linens were to be changed every eight days. Passengers were requested to keep their scuttles shut and to quash the candles in their staterooms at midnight. "A cheerful acquiescence" in these matters was expected. Captain Woodruff of the *Britannia* had himself to suffer the further advices of his employers. "It will be obvious to you," they said, "that it is of the first importance to the Partners of the *Britannia* that she attains a Character for Speed and Safety. We trust in your vigilance of this: good steering, good look-outs, taking advantage of every slant of wind, and precautions against fire are principal elements." They also admonished him against waste: "Burn up all the ashes—throw nothing overboard," they said, and assured him that there would be sieves aboard to help in the process. They established the hierarchy of the officers' mess: "Mate, Second, Third, First Engineer, Chaplain, Surgeon, and any respectable Second-Class Passenger."

Only five months off the stocks and into the water, the *Britannia* was so small that she could be fitted, like a boat in a bottle, into the lounges of some of the Cunard ships that would come after her. Yet she was so remarkably big for her time that it was "necessary to swing her out into mid-stream and place passengers aboard from a tender owing to her immense size." She had space in her cabins for 124 passengers, but not enough drawing power, even on her maiden voyage, to fill more than half of them. More spacious and glamorous ships were already crisscrossing the ocean; ships far more handsome were being built. As the memoirs of a generation of travelers would indicate, the *Britannia* lacked that faculty of affectionate engagement that every now and then transforms a working ship from a records-office statistic to a legend. But, in the language of the times, she had "something to the back of her"—a subsidy big enough to float her in champagne and the guidance of a team of blue-eyed Scots whose minds worked like budgets.

Samuel Cunard was aboard when she started on her maiden voyage, and with him was his daughter Ann and her girlfriend Laura Haliburton, daughter of the judge. The ocean was turbulent nearly all the way over, but, to one of the passengers at least, this was of small account. "I had a good steak, with a bottle of hock, for my breakfast," he told a friend. "There were too many good things for any man of taste to even think of sickness." The *Britannia* encountered icebergs in the near distance on July 14; and on her last day's run she logged 273 nautical miles—a greater distance, in the space of twenty-four hours, than any steamer had yet traversed. She arrived at Cunard's wharf in Halifax at 2 A.M. on Friday the 17th. When she was ready to cast off for Boston at nine that morning, some of her passengers had already departed by coach and steamer for New Brunswick, while others had boarded the *Unicorn* for a three-day feeder run to Quebec. Hometown crowds swarmed over all the adjacent wharves "to get a look at this elegant creation of British skill and Nova Scotia enterprise." As they waved and shouted, Samuel Cunard, "hale and hearty, and in excellent spirits" lifted a plump little hand and with the reserve of royalty waved back.

The *Britannia* had brought illustrious passengers to Halifax, among them the Lord Bishop of Nova Scotia, two American consuls, the Earl of Caledon and one Mr. Featherstonhaugh, Commissioner of the Maine Boundary Question. She had also brought "intelligence of much interest." This was news of the attempted assassination of Queen Victoria, and perhaps of Prince Albert, though no one could quite guess why. The Queen, with the Prince Consort at her side, had set off in a low open carriage for an evening's drive up Constitution Hill, when Edward Oxford, a mentally retarded undersized adolescent, had sent two pot shots in their direction. There were small explosions, a mêlée, and shouts of "Kill him! Kill him!" but the Queen, rumpled but unscathed, got back to the palace and Oxford got sent to gaol for most of his life. "The affair," observed the Halifax *Times* with detachment, "notwithstanding the excitement which it caused at the time, magnified to an unnatural degree by the press, appears from all that has transpired, to have been the act of a half-mad individual, and harmless in its intent, inasmuch as it cannot be satisfactorily discovered that the pistols were loaded with ball."

Boston was meanwhile getting ready to extend the welcome of the port and to stage a grand festival. But the awkward thing was the

Britannia's timing. Since she docked on a Saturday evening at ten o'clock, most Bostonians—not including the Reverend Ezra S. Gannett —were unaware of her arrival until they went to church next morning. At the Federal Street Meeting-House, the Reverend's sermon for the day tried masterfully to reconcile the ways of Cunard shareholders and Cunard clients with the ways of God. "We are a mercantile community," he reminded the feathered bonnets and silken top hats, "this is a commercial place. . . . Money, commerce, industry, are among the means which the Divine Providence has embraced in its plan of education for man." The coming of the *Britannia* was a triumph, he felt, but also, he feared, a threat and a challenge. She and her sister ships would bring wealth to Boston, but they would also bring Europe to Boston, and those European influences that were, inevitably, nefarious.

By midday, everyone in town knew that the ship was at her berth in East Boston, but they had to wait until Tuesday for the opening rituals of the "Cunard Festival." Then, in ranks of eight, citizens by the thousands marched behind a phalanx of civic officials and bewhiskered merchants. The mayors of every city in New England walked in the van of foreign consuls and local politicians. An immense pavilion, grand enough to attract the attention "of all classes," was erected on the western front of the elegant Maverick House, East Boston's new hotel. Porches were converted into galleries where two thousand people sat to a banquet, including ladies who, for the first time, "graced, by their presence, a public dinner in Boston." An arch rising over a flag-filled piazza bore an inscription: "Liverpool-Halifax-Boston" with the name "Cunard" at its base, along with the names of his first four ships—*Britannia, Caledonia, Acadia, Columbia.* Dinner and speeches went on for a full five hours.

Colonel Josiah Quincy, Jr., President of the Day—and also President of Harvard College—began things on a note that was never relinquished. He told Samuel Cunard that he "had a head to contrive, a tongue to advocate, and a hand to execute" the great achievement the company had gathered to celebrate. Daniel Webster made his obligatory speech; George Bancroft topped it "by an immeasurable distance." Among the racier toasts was one volunteered from the crowd: "The Honorable Samuel Cunard—the only man who has dared to *beat* the British Queen." (Laughter.)

Mr. Grattan, the British consul, again came to the fore, to emphasize Anglo-American harmonies, and to observe that "like Paganini, who played on one string," he was always stuck with one subject. As usual, Cunard himself had nothing to say—except that he could not find the language to express his gratitude.

A song, composed especially for the occasion, was sung by George H. Andrews. Its last verses were these:

> East Boston, one day, I have heard people say,
>   Was nought but a desolate *Island*;
> But working by steam, they fill'd up the stream,
>   And turned the wet dock into *dry land*;
> Then with a steam chain, it grappled the main,
>   What noddle but follows my ditty,
> We're no longer alone—"but have bone of our bone,
>   Yea, and flesh of our flesh" from the city.
>
> Oh dear, think of a scheme, *odd though* it may seem—
> 'Tis sure to succeed if you work it by steam.
>
> How timid and slow, but a few years ago,
>   The world hobbled on in its motion,
> Old Europe seem'd far as the fix'd Northern star,
>   On the boundless expanse of the ocean;
> But though it were hard—at the word of Cunard
>   *Britannia* herself is a rover,
> Old England awhile, that fast anchor'd isle,
>   By steam is now here—half seas over.
>
> Oh dear, think of a scheme, *odd though* it may seem—
> 'Tis sure to succeed if you work it by steam.

Statesman and orator joined with merchant and banker: not since the *Mayflower*, 220 years earlier, had there been a landing of such importance to the Commonwealth of Massachusetts. Boston still felt that the umbilical cord rudely cut in the days of the Tea Party and the Massacre could not be repaired; yet the line to Liverpool was, in its way, a life line.

Legend would come to suggest that Samuel Cunard was the Vasco da Gama of the Age of Steam. Yet to his contemporaries, Cunard was preeminently a merchant trader and a capitalist of extraordinary acumen. When the crowds in Boston poured out, they came not to celebrate the feat of Captain Woodruff, the man at the tiller, but that of Cunard, the man at the till. His steamships promised them a profit, a chance to beat out New York by providing a quick transfer of goods from landing pier to train, then to Albany and the limitless West. Philip Hone, who could not conceal something of a patronizing smirk at the hoopla in Boston, was nonetheless aware of the commercial advantages these doings heralded. "The good people of Boston," he wrote, "are so delighted at the prospect of rivalling New York that they are in perfect ecstasies at the arrival of the steamship *Britannia*, and have made a glorification of my little friend Cunard. The roar of the cannon might have been heard, had the wind been easterly, by the unwilling ears of the chopfallen New Yorkers."

With his "quiet manners and not overflowing speech," Cunard accepted homage in the terms it was offered. He also accepted the gift of a silver cup, thirty inches high, "the largest cup in existence," embossed with an outline of the *Britannia*. But he had to refuse invitations to dine in Boston houses which, had he accepted them all, would have taken him out every evening for the next five years.

The cutter *Hamilton*, at anchor in sight of the Maverick House festivities, lamps alight and swinging from masts and rigging, sent up rockets when darkness fell, thus signaling the start of fireworks from the top of every hill around. As the cow in her cow house bedded down for the night, as water quietly lapped at her stilled paddles while dazzling showers broke over her foremast, the little *Britannia* lay snug at her new berth. As far as Boston was concerned, she was the only ship on the ocean.

In effect, Boston was right. During the next year, the *Britannia* and her three sister ships made forty successive crossings of the Atlantic. Foreign trade in Boston went up one hundred percent. Decades before the laying of the Atlantic cable, the rope that bound the *Britannia* to East Boston (as Colley Grattan had observed of the *Unicorn*) was the same that bound her to Liverpool. There were, statistics showed, 150 sailing ships for every single steamship, yet one fifth of all freight came and went under steam. The service to Boston was a journeyman's run compared with the operations of larger and more handsome ships to New York; and, stem to stern, the *Britannia* and her sisters could not disguise the stodgy solidity and penny-turning austerity of her owners.

Nor, in spite of the marvelous regularity established by forty crossings in a row, could ocean steamers dispel the chariness of travelers. "A successful trip is expected by all," said a passenger about to board the *Britannia*, "but I cannot help wondering what we would do if the Monster exploded in mid-ocean." Yet the Cunard ships were there to stay. They would eventually have the North Atlantic pretty much to themselves—but not before they had, almost smugly, survived disasters to other ships and the bankruptcy of men more imaginative and, to their cost, more precipitous than Samuel Cunard.

☙ SECTION V ❧

The Britannia *Icebound / Merchants to the Rescue*

NEW YORK never quite forgave Cunard for choosing Boston as his first American terminus. Chauvinists among newspapermen there lost no opportunity to register the lingering resentment. When the Cunard Line's *Columbia* foundered off Cape Sable, Nova Scotia, there was no loss of life, but journalists in New York implicitly blamed the loss of the ship on Boston. Most navigators did not feel that Boston Light was any harder to find than Sandy Hook, but the New York *Herald* had its own notions of peril on the sea. These were the extra "four hundred and fifty miles of rock, ledge, shoal, fog and narrow intricate channels" that ships into Boston from Europe supposedly had to deal with. Other charges of the sort amounted to a continuous whispering campaign aimed at discrediting the Port of Boston.

Sensitive on the point, Bostonians were put on their mettle in 1844 by a cold spell that brought an embargo of thick-ribbed ice to Boston Harbor and locked the *Britannia* tight in her berth. For most of the population this extraordinary Arctic interlude was fun. As the whole distance between the wharves and Fort Warren became frozen over, "men, women, and children enjoyed the novel experience of walking all over the harbor, skaters went to the outer-most edge of the ice. Horses and sleighs entered on the ice-field from South Boston. Booths were established for the supply of creature comforts, bonfires lighted to warm the hands and feet of pedestrians. The earliest ice-craft with extended sail was seen skimming over the smooth surface, and the days and nights on the harbor partook of a carnival." But to merchants and shipping men the big freeze was not a lark. How delighted New York would be to hear that the famous Cunarder was detained by the sub-arctic climate of Massachusetts! Sharing the general alarm, Boston businessmen decided to call a meeting at the Exchange. With Mayor Martin Brimmer in the chair, they debated what might best be done. By whatever method might serve, they agreed that they had to get the *Britannia* out of Boston as close to her schedule as possible, and without a penny's cost to Cunard.

The best idea was to make a miracle—to part the walls of ice so that, like Moses, Captain Woodruff could lead his passengers into the land their tickets promised. This would cost money, but the reputation of the city as a dependable seaport was at stake. The men designated to pass the hat were those of only sterling credentials: Benjamin Rich, Caleb Curtis, Ozias Goodwin, Thomas C. Smith, Samuel Quincy, Thomas Gray, Charles Brown, Thomas B. Curtis, Ammi C. Lombard. When they had amassed enough instant capital to proceed, they made a succinct little contract meant to brook no delay, and put it in writing: "Mr. John Hill in connexion with Messrs. Gage Hittinger & Co. agree to cut a passage for the Steamship *Britannia* to proceed to sea tomorrow night and to cut the passage from the Eastern Ferry as far as India Wharf, the whole passage to be 200 feet wide at least; the whole to be accomplished within three days from the First day of February at sunrise, and they agree to receive in full for their services the Sum of Fifteen Hundred dollars . . . to be paid when the work is accomplished and to receive no pay if they do not accomplish it as stipulated."

The channel was made by ice ploughs cutting straight furrows from between which hundred-foot-square cakes of ice were hoisted up on ropes by men in squads of fifty and hauled away by teams of horses. With new iron blades affixed to her bow, the *Britannia* made a daring 7-knot run for it on February 3. She "moved majestically through the canal to the open ocean," said a reporter, "amid firing of cannon and the cheering of thousands, the multitudes not only lining all the wharves but flocking upon the solid ice in countless numbers." Bostonian pluck and ingenuity had saved the day: sprung free, the *Britannia* was off on a voyage that got her to Liverpool only two days behind schedule.

"Probably never again," said a Bostonian, "will we witness the spectacle of an ocean steamer moving down the harbor accompanied by thousands of people running or skating by her side." He was almost right. A few years later, with an obeisance to Cunard that was beginning to run thin, the same thing had to be done all over again. When the *America* got caught in the big freeze of 1857, the city government, the Board of Trade and the merchants "all pulled together in their noble efforts to raise the siege" and set her frosty paddles churning toward Liverpool.

❦ SECTION VI ❧

The President: Sine Qua Non / *Captain* Roberts: *"To Sea in a
Washing Tub" / Lost Without Trace, Almost*

PROMOTING any hint and rumor that might bring him
knightship, Junius Smith scanned the cloudy Atlantic skies for
signs and portents. The *British Queen* was buoyantly at sea;
the new *President* was rising in the shipyards; he had come into his
majority. His joy in the *British Queen* was hardly to be contained; yet
as his new prodigy began to show herself his loyalty began to waver.

The *President*, a little bigger than her predecessor, was notably more
handsome and more trig: a bust of George Washington sent out a hyperthyroid glare from the base of her bowsprit; on her stern the American
eagle and the British lion supported their respective coats-of-arms in
splashes of gold and filigree. On each of the white boxes covering her
paddle wheels was a big, crisp five-pointed star.

After she was launched at Limehouse in December, 1839, the *President* ran up sails and proceeded to Liverpool to receive her engines and
paddles. But her first venture in open water proved ominous. Barely into
the Channel "she became unmanageable as she was ill-ballasted and
nearly rolled the masts out of herself." By good fortune, the *Royal
William* (the Liverpool steamer, not the one from Quebec) was able

to pick her up and tow her into Plymouth, where she was put back into proper balance. She eventually made Liverpool, where meticulous artisans were determined to give her the best-furnished and best-dressed interior of any ship in England. The long fitting-out period delayed her entrance into service until August, 1840.

A consequence of her tardiness was the chance to come into the Atlantic picture just when things were looking up. Speculators noted that the Cunarders ran with almost pedestrian regularity into Boston; that the *Great Western* was a fixed new feature on the North Atlantic; that the *British Queen* carried cargoes that spelled hefty profits; and that her passenger lists were long and distinguished. Sceptics might note that both the *Royal William* and the *Liverpool* had quit the great race, but these ships were always regarded as makeshifts and substitutes anyway.

When she arrived in New York in August, 1840, the *President* in the eyes of some observers was the *sine qua non* of safety at sea. But in the eyes of some nautical experts who had studied the development of steamships, she was not safe simply because she was too long. Seven feet longer than the *British Queen,* a full thirty feet longer than the *Great Western,* she exceeded those dimensions which, to the thinking of some marine architects, would guarantee sea-worthiness. What these men were chary of was "hogging." This is the term given to the dangerous strain on a vessel when the midship part of her hull is lifted high on a wave that leaves her fore and aft ends comparatively without support. Small ships would easily rise and fall with a wave of any size; a ship as long as the *President,* lifted in the middle, might droop at both ends and so break her back. The *Great Western* herself had almost suffered just such a fate, after which the red streak painted on her hull about five feet above the waterline so clearly charted the effects of stress that her owners thought it wise to erase the evidence with a solid coat of paint.

The *President's* maiden voyage was not impressive, because she took more than sixteen days in coming over and Cunard's newly launched *Acadia* bested this time by a full three days. Nonetheless, she was quietly settling into a schedule and a career when, once more, her fitness was brought into question.

She was five days out of New York in November, 1840, when her Captain Keane surprised his passengers by calling a meeting to tell them he could not take them to Liverpool except in extreme jeopardy. Bad weather had slowed the ship; there was not nearly enough coal in the bunkers to ensure a safe landfall. Consequently, he informed them, he was taking the ship back to New York. Unaware of this development, Junius Smith wrote to his nephew on November 17: "We have no *President* yet and how she can manage to keep out supposing she had no engines and was under bare poles is a mystery to me, seeing we have had a gale of wind almost constantly from the westward for the last week." Back in the Hudson River when they should have been gliding over the Mersey bar, the *President*'s disgruntled passengers were not behindhand in publishing their experience with a shipping line careless enough to send a vessel on a winter's passage without adequate fuel. Later in the month, with a handful of passengers, she made it to Liverpool and was laid up there until the following February.

As a matter of courtesy and deserved priority, Captain Richard Roberts had been asked to assume the *President*'s command. But he did not like the idea. To a man of his outspoken self-regard, the offer was something less than a boon. While he was at times minded to give up sea-going for a berth ashore, his fame as a pioneer on the ocean had made him hungry for even greater eminence. He seemed not to be aware of the fact, but the one thing he was hoping for—to be at the helm of the first iron ship to cross the Atlantic—had just been removed from his grasp by the voyage of the *Robert F. Stockton*. As for the *President*, he felt that, all things considered, he was himself the more remarkable maritime phenomenon. "It is too bad," he told a friend, "to be forced into a vessel to give her character."

But finally he allowed himself to be persuaded to give over the command of the *British Queen* in order to take the *President* to New York and back. On the day before he left Liverpool, James Murphy, an old friend of his, came to lunch on the *President*. In the course of it he told Roberts that he felt the ship showed serious evidences of strain— of having been "hogged"—and questioned the wisdom of taking her to sea. "My dear James," said Roberts, "I would go to sea in a washing tub."

The *President* arrived in New York on March 4, 1841. When she steamed out of the Lower Bay one week later, her passenger list included the names of a son of the Duke of Richmond, Lord Fitzroy Lennox, and the Irish comedian Tyrone Power, who was a favorite of the music halls of both London and Manhattan. The full complement of the ship came to 136. The *Orpheus*, an American packet en route to Liverpool, sailed out alongside her. Within hours both ships were caught in a gale so savage that the tightly furled sails of the *Orpheus* were ripped open and torn to shreds. In the toils of a storm that blew without respite for two days, Captain Cole of the *Orpheus* caught sight of the *President* "rising on top of a tremendous sea, pitching and laboring very heavily." Somewhere between Nantucket Shoals and George's Bank, mountains of water washed the two ships from each others' sight. Riding out the tempest, the sailing ship eventually sloughed her way into Liverpool. The *President* simply disappeared.

Since ships frequently went unreported and overdue for days and even weeks, fears for the steamer were not given voice until about a month after her departure. In the period of waiting, the new President of the United States, William Henry Harrison, died in the White House, and the superstitious crossed themselves. The *President* had sailed into absolute, baffling oblivion. On May 3, Junius Smith told his nephew, "I suppose the *President* is lost. I have slight hopes of ever hearing of her again." His London office was daily besieged by people hoping for some word: the Duke of Richmond, sorrowing for his son, sent members of his staff, and there were repeated visits from representatives of Queen Victoria.

Looking for an answer, one versifier, with the approval of the London *Times*, apostrophized the sea itself:

> Speak! for thou hast a voice, perpetual sea!
> Lift up thy surges with some signal word,
> Show where the pilgrims of the water be,
> For whom a nation's thrilling heart is stirr'd.
>
> Down to thy waves they went in joyous pride.
> They trod with steadfast feet thy billowy way;
> The eyes of wondering men beheld them glide
> Swift in the arrowy distance—where are they?

Where were they, indeed. With nothing to feed on, rumor fed on everything; as weeks became months, newspapers kept the event of the disappearance alive with a morbidity that catered to popular appetite while it prolonged the anguish of those personally bereaved. Nathaniel Currier, who would later be half of Currier & Ives, did not let so rich an opportunity pass; within weeks of the ship's disappearance he provided his connoisseurs of disaster with a print of the *President* showing her practically on beam ends "as last seen from the packet ship *Orpheus*, Captain Cole, in the terrific gale of March the 12th, 1841."

False-hope mongering was good business. It was, one should not forget, a period in history when a book entitled *Interesting Narratives of Popular Shipwrecks and Other Calamities* could become the equivalent of a modern best seller. Inventive and mischievous minds came up with all sorts of speculation and fantasy designed to hold the public in suspense. "That ever-present pest," said one sceptic, "the finder of the floating bottle with its message of despair, reported that the bottle, picked up at sea, contained this: 'The *President* is sinking. God help us all. Tyrone Power.'" When this arid little dispatch from the deep (written, naturally, by the most famous man on board) proved anticlimactic, other notions were advanced. A mutiny theory became an obsession. When that began to wear out, speculation turned upon piracy and the thrilling possibility that the ladies and gentlemen of the *President* were captives of one-eyed brutes somewhere in the Caribbees.

Pharisiacal editorials meaning to condemn the more ghoulish flights of speculation served, covertly, to color it with all the melodrama the fragile stuff could bear. "Every surmise on this awful subject," said one of them, "is not only painful but equally fruitless and vain. One appalling fact impresses itself upon the bewildered mind with a weight that ensures shuddering conviction: the steamship *President* was—and is no more. She has gone, and left no track upon the pathless sea. The last faint ray of hope has long departed, and the darkness of uncertainty has settled over her fate. In the beautiful language of Washington Irving, we exclaim, 'What sighs have been wafted after that ship! What prayers offered up at the deserted fireside of home! How often has the sister, the wife, the mother, pored over daily news to catch some casual intelligence of this dark rover of the deep! How has expectation darkened into anxiety—anxiety into dread—and dread into despair! Alas! not one memento shall ever return for love to cherish. All that shall ever be known is, that she sailed from her port, and was never heard of more.'"

Along with her captain, Lieutenant Roberts, "the Columbus of Steam," and the scroll, encased in a silver casket, that gave him the freedom of the City of Cork, the *President* had taken all of her 136 souls to the bottom of the Atlantic. Clues as to the fate of the liner were few and insubstantial, but eventually they began to seem conclusive.

Midocean, on the twenty-third of April, a Portuguese brig came in sight of a paddle-wheeler moving along under sail, her big funnel smokeless. The brig, only a few miles away from the silently drifting steamer, assumed the big ship was simply resting on her engines, and sailed on. Some time later, an entry in the log of the brig *Poultney*, en route from New York to Smyrna, noted an encounter with "a large piece of wreckage, sixty feet long and 30 to 40 feet wide, that looked like the broadside of a steamboat, the main-channel having four dead-eyes, with turned mouldings and long iron straps. Her bulk was black with a broad white streak and large, painted ports. There was a bight of hawser over a piece of wood apparently a part of the guards."

Without much hope, Junius Smith began to do his own detective work. Following up one rumor, he went aboard the sailing ship *Lord Saumarez* at her dock in London on May 11. He learned from the ship's log book that a steamship had been sighted on the tenth of April between three and four P.M., lying close to the wind and heading, as the *President* would have been, NNW. She had three masts, it was noted, and a huge funnel. The first mate of the *Lord Saumarez* thought that the sighted ship might have been the *Earl of Hardwicke* en route from Calcutta and now berthed at the East India Dock basin. Smith persisted, and boarded the newly arrived steamer, only to learn that, on April 10, she could not have been anywhere near the *Lord Saumarez*. Besides, the *Earl of Hardwicke* had a small funnel and was not a regular steamer "but a kind of hermaphrodite, intended to steam in calm." Finally, he came to believe that the ship the *Lord Saumarez* saw was indeed the *President*. Since no other steamship had arrived just before or just after the *Earl of Hardwicke* and the *Saumarez*, what other vessel could the steamship on the horizon have been? The *President*, he felt, must have been trying to reach the Cape Verde Islands. "I do not want to affirm that such is a fact," he said, "but, under all circumstance, I apprehend we may fairly indulge a strong hope that the ship seen was the *President*." Not long after this, Captain Jensen of the schooner *Moniko* told of finding the stern boat of the *President* and of hauling out of the sea several casks with the steamer's name on them. Similar casks, he reported, had been washing ashore from time to time at St. Nicholas, one of the Cape Verde Islands.

At best, the *President* was flotsam and jetsam, and so were the ambitions of Junius Smith. The reputation of his company was irreparably damaged, his chances of knightship sadly crimped. As a frisson of fear ran through the maritime world in the aftermath of the disaster, the traveling public turned back to the sailing packets in frightened droves. Not even Smith's illustrious *British Queen* could save the day. Westward bound, she had in fact been hobbled by the same wild slant of weather that had swallowed the *President*. With all of the floats on her portside wheel torn off and half of those on the starboard wheel transferred to replace them, she wallowed almost helpless for a week and finally ended a twenty-day voyage not in New York but in Halifax. When she got back to England she was still trig and handsome; but she was, after all, the sister ship of the *President* and, in the eyes of the public, tainted by the family resemblance. Forced to give up, she was soon sold to the Belgian government.

When—at an inquiry in New York—statements were made to the effect that the *President* had left port markedly out of trim, partisans of Junius Smith were outraged. "The entertaining for one moment the idea that Captain Roberts would have taken his vessel to sea, had she been out of trim," said one of them, "is the greatest insult that could be offered to his memory." How could any one in New York have heard the lost captain boast that he "would go to sea in a washing tub"?

Even the *Great Western* had to sail under a long shadow of doubt and suspicion. Within a year after the *President*'s disappearance, her passenger lists were so thin that her owners were ready to put her up for sale for sheer lack of patronage. The four Cunard sisters were all working the Boston run, but they remained afloat and solvent solely by virtue of their big subsidy. They got people back and forth from Liverpool to Boston all right, and they were quietly building the reputation for safe, sure transit that would make the Cunard Line invincible. But they lacked that rakish bent and bearing that had made the business of ocean steamships one of the romances of the century.

In spite of financial jeopardy, the *Great Western* ultimately managed to avoid the auction block. She was soon making enough money to encourage her owners to plan for a new ship, to be named the *City of New York*. A cargo of African timber for the hull of this new sister ship was ordered and her keel was about to be laid when Isambard Brunel put forth objections. Why merely repeat the *Great Western*? he asked. Why not build a vastly greater ship with unprecedented features? Once again his colleagues listened and were persuaded. They urged him to begin to work on any new design on which his inventive mind and heart might be set.

❧ SECTION VII ❧

The Letter Bag of the Great Western */ Captain Halfront's
Complaint / "A Glorious Fleet of Snowy Canvas"*

PUNCTUALITY, plush, dash and fortitude had made the
Great Western the steamship *par excellence* on the Atlantic
Ocean, the peerless first lady of a new age. "The movements
of this fine vessel," said a New Yorker, "have gotten to be as regular
as the rising and setting of the sun, or the flux and reflux of the tides."

But in the continuing reports of voyagers, punctuality came to be a
comparatively small and negligible comfort. After he had crossed on
the same voyage that had brought Samuel Cunard in triumph from
Liverpool to Saratoga Springs, Thomas Haliburton entertained himself
and his readers with a series of mock epistles written by fictitious passengers, and published them in a thin volume entitled *The Letter Bag
of the Great Western.*

His "Captain Halfront" is quite definitely Haliburton's own persona,
with a slightly Hogarthian twist: "You will naturally inquire how I
like the *Great Western,* the speed and splendour of which has been the
theme of every newspaper for the last year. . . . My first disappointment . . . was not enjoying, as I had hoped from the payment of

forty-two sovereigns, the exclusive occupation of my stateroom. This
is indispensable, I will not say to comfort, but to common decency. I
have the honour and pleasure of having a most delectable chum, who
. . . chews tobacco, spits furiously, talks through his nose, and snores
like a Newfoundland dog. Many of his habits are too offensive even
to mention, and you may therefore easily imagine what the endurance
of them for twenty-two days must have been. . . . Bad as the air of
my room is, I cannot venture at night to open my cabin door for the
purpose of ventilation, for the black servants sleep on the floor of the
saloon, and the effluvia is worse than that of a slaver. Driven from my
dormitory at daylight . . . I find myself involved . . . in a mob of some
hundred and twenty passengers hurrying to breakfast, where cold tea,
hard biscuits, greasy toast, stale eggs, and mountains of cold meat, the
intervening valleys of which are decorated with beef steaks floating
in grease, await me. . . . Waiters who never wait, and servants who
order everything, and though deaf are never dumb, fly from one end
of the saloon to the other. . . . Vociferous claims for attendance that
is never given, and the still louder response of 'Coming, sir,' from him
that never comes, the clatter of many dishes, the confusion of many
tongues, the explosion of soda bottles, the rattle of knives and forks,
the uproarious laugh, the ferocious oath, the deep-toned voice of the
steward, and the shrill discordant note of the Mulatto women, create
a confusion that no head can stand and no pen describe. . . . I return
to the vacant saloon, where lo, two Africans, each bearing immense
piles of plates, commence dealing them out like experienced whist
players. . . . These are followed by two others, who pitch, by a sleight
of hand, the knives and forks into their respective places, like quoits.
. . . I once more reluctantly mount the deck . . . where I fall heavily,
tripped by some kind protruding feet, and am dreadfully cut in my
face and hands by angular nutshells, which are scattered about with
the same liberality as the rind of the orange."

"Captain Halfront" reveals finally that, while his subject is annoyances—a whole litany of them—his theme is nostalgia and the particular memory of the long congenial voyage when the *Tyrian* was overtaken by the *Sirius*. "There is no conversation," says the "Captain."
"The progress of the ship, Niagara, machinery, and the price of cotton
and tobacco, are the only topics. If I should still survive, which I do
not expect and cannot wish, I return not by steamer. I shall go to
Halifax and take passage in a Falmouth packet, where there is more of

society and less of a mob; where there is more cleanliness and less splendour; where eating is not the whole business of life, but time is given you to eat; where the company is so agreeable you seldom wish to be alone, but where you can be alone if you wish—in short, where you can be among gentlemen."

Passengers and their idiosyncrasies were but small part of the *Great Western*'s troubles: she developed a disconcerting roll because she had been allowed to become top-heavy. This was due to the fact that, over the years, a scullery, a larder and a blacksmith shop were built on her sponsons, and a huge lifeboat, 28 feet long by 10 feet broad, had been stowed bottom-up on her deck. To correct this tendency to roll she was fitted with bilge keels.

Yet even in the blasts of the Atlantic she continued to inspire confidence, as a passenger on one of her worst voyages confirms. "I took my passage, and in the end of October we put to sea," he wrote. "The next day a heavy westerly storm set in, the rudder was unshipped, a wheel was broken; the bowsprit was shivered, and part of the bulwarks carried away. The storm lasted nine days, and as we saw no sun, no one could tell our whereabouts. Yet I had never felt more assured. In seaman's phrase, the vessel swam like a duck. One day, in the cabin, a lady said to me, "Good God, you sit there as quietly as if this were all play.' 'I am really quiet, madam,' I replied, 'because I feel safe.' 'God bless your confidence, sir,' were her words, as she lay down. The next morning the storm lulled, the necessary repairs were made, and the lady said to me, 'Well, sir, it seems you were quite right, after all.' Nine days after, we reached New York . . . the longest recorded passage of a steamer; but then 18 days seemed little to me, compared with my 58 days' voyage in 1816."

People did not like long, invariably grim voyages under sail; but neither did they like the clatter, soot and anxiety that went with steamships. A sea voyage was simply a thing to be endured with a minimal show of civility and complacency. "As soon as the labors of the faithful engine ceased," said one disheartened traveler, "the passengers began to tumble out of their berths, and in a few minutes were bustling up and down the cabin aisles as if they feared the haven would recede, or the ship take a notion to turn upon her tracks and go to sea again. All order and courtesy were forgotten. Those who had been most familiar during the sojourn upon the waters, passed each other almost without recognition. The formalities of friendship, now that nothing more was to be made of them, went by the board in the revival of special selfishness. It was a sad picture of a larger stage of life."

Eighteen years after the *Sirius* and the *Great Western* had come to the wire neck and neck, there was still no regular steamship service between England and New York except that supplied by the *Great Western* herself. Dr. Dionysius Lardner could not resist a bit of crowing over this development. On an American lecture tour he struck back at his critics with a histrionic cry to his listeners in the second balcony. Where are all the steamships that had started their Liverpool to New York careers? he wanted to know. "Again and again, I ask, where are they? Echo answers, Where?"

Just when steamships should have begun to monopolize the ocean, passenger lists on the sailing packets were growing longer and longer as the vessels themselves became more capacious and more comfortably appointed. America had met the onslaught of the age of steam, according to F. Lawrence Babcock, "by putting to sea a glorious fleet of snowy canvas," an activity that constituted "one of the few truly quixotic gestures in the commercial history of our nation."

"In 1847 the ascendancy of steam still lay in an undreamed future," wrote Carl Cutler. "Men were still saying that it might do on short hauls but could never replace sail on the long runs, just as they were saying fifty years later that sail would always be needed on the Great Circle routes to the Orient and on the hard Cape Horn passage. In spite of the ominous preparations of the steamerites for the construction of a dozen liners of unprecedented power, the canvas-backers were supremely confident of their ability to meet any conceivable competition. It was the inconceivable that put them out of business."

One by one, eight steamers had pushed open doors to a future which, most social observers felt, would belong to science and the skill of engineers. Yet, instead of expanding, the fleet of ocean steamships had diminished. Only five of them were still in operation; the stodgy Cunarders coursing into Boston, and the *Great Western*. As she awaited the debut of her consort, the *Great Western* alone continued to carry customers by the power of steam to and from the Port of New York.

SECTION VIII

The Great Britain / "Stupendous Progeny of the Genius of Mr. Brunel" / Mrs. Miles Off the Mark / The Rainbow and the Boast of Archimedes / The Shoals of Nantucket / Beached in Dundrum Bay / Brunel Heartbroken / Oblivion in the Antipodes / The Very Lazarus of Ships Comes Home

THE GREAT BRITAIN changed all that. She took her time in coming and her descent was a painful comedy of errors. But when she finally dipped her expensive bows into sea water, she was not only the biggest ship ever, with the greatest number of decks and masts, she also represented a sea-going revolution after which nothing would ever be the same. Designed to be constructed of wood, she arrived iron clad. Engined for paddle wheels, she came propeller driven. With a clipper bow, a sheer with lines drawn so economically that they approached the hydrodynamic, a flat double bottom, a watertight bulkhead and, instead of bulwarks, iron rails with nettings, she was a showpiece of features not to be duplicated for more than a decade.

A maritime prodigy, a glimpse of things to come, the *Great Britain* commanded professional respect and evoked endless public curiosity. Otherwise, almost from the moment of her inception, she was, like her original name—the *Mammoth*—a bunglesome nuisance responsible for more trouble than she would ever be worth. Buxom, wayward and intractable, she began her career in Bristol under gilt-edged auspices, crossed the Atlantic a few times and then, beached like a whale and rolled over on her side, lay helpless for a whole winter being battered by waves on the coast of Ireland. Pulled free and repaired, this "awkward, ill-fated monstrosity" became a carrier of emigrants to Australia for a period of over twenty years. Then, relieved of her superb engines, she resumed her career as a full-rigged sailing ship. Attempting to round Cape Horn in 1886 with a cargo of coal from Penarth for San Francisco, she caught on fire, sprang a leak, and had to put into Port Stanley in the Falkland Islands. There, after attempts had been made to repair her fire damage and opened seams, she was declared, in the language of the insurance business, "a constructive loss." She was sold to the Falkland Islands Company and used for storing coal and wood. In this circumstance she faded into the mists of an oblivion that held her for nearly fifty years. Then, just as the sad old bones of the ship seemed about to dissolve, she was lifted up bodily, cradled on a barge, and laboriously towed eight thousand miles back to the place where she was born.

The keel of this "stupendous progeny of the genius of Mr. Brunel" was laid in July, 1839. All of four years later, polished and brightly pennoned, she was still squarely in the dock where she had been put together. Announcements were out, and at last she was ready to be eased into the water. Down from London on the Royal Train, actually conducted by Isambard K. Brunel himself, came Prince Albert, "dressed as a private gentlemen." With him came the Marquis of Exeter, Lord Wharncliffe, the Earl of Lincoln and "a large concourse of noblemen and gentlemen, and families of the first distinction from nearly every quarter of the kingdom." After they had lent their presences to the launching, they assembled for a banquet at which, according to one fawning eye, "the demolitions of the various delicacies proceeded quietly, and it was gratifying to observe that the West Country air appeared to have in no wise disagreed with the Royal appetite."

The christening itself was once more to be performed by Mrs. Miles, who had already named the *Great Western* and should have been in top form; but the ship, yanked by a tugboat, "slewed away" when Mrs. Miles tried to hit her with a bottle, much to the disgust of a schoolboy who was watching. "Mrs. Miles tried to perform the ceremony," he said, "and being clumsy or nervous instead of throwing the bottle let it drop out of her hands into the water." With a second bottle the Prince Consort hit the target, but the force of the thrust sent splintered glass and foaming champagne showering upon a gang of workmen desperately trying to urge the ship out of her imprisoning walls. The *Great Britain* had a name and a blessing; but when the little tug *Avon* started to pull her from one basin of her dock to another she balked, and the tug's hawsers snapped like string. On a second try the *Avon* managed to tow her into the fitting-out basin; and there she stayed, and stayed. Five years after the laying of her keel, while her older sister the *Great Western* went on wrestling the waves of the Atlantic year by year, the *Great Britain* still sat like a sluggard.

There were two strangers in the life of the *Great Britain;* each of them contributed crucially to her character and thus to her career. The first was the *Rainbow*—a ship of iron that so impressed the directors of the Great Western Steam-Ship Company that they canceled plans for a wooden hull and told their builder Patterson to incorporate into their new ship all the advantageous features they had observed. The second stranger was the *Archimedes*. She was a little three-masted topsail schooner of 240 tons launched at Poplar in October, 1838, and fitted with a screw propeller designed by Francis Pettit Smith. A gentleman farmer of Hendon, Smith had first tested his notions of screw propulsion by sending a model of a ship across the length of his duck pond. When this worked, he ordered a six-ton boat in which he installed a wooden screw propeller. On a trial run in the Paddington Canal, the screw took two complete turns of the shaft until it hit something floating, lost one of its turns and, to the surprise of Smith and other spectators, at once scooted forward. The happy accident helped the inventor to perfect his propeller and encouraged him to found the Screw Propeller Company to develop the invention and to build a full-scale ship, the *Archimedes*. A frankly experimental proposition, the *Archimedes* was out to prove herself to the sceptical and did so by traveling to Holland at the invitation of the Dutch Government, and then by making a tour of British ports "to provide oracular proof to all interested." When she got to Bristol in May, 1840, the frames for the paddle boxes of the *Great Britain* were already installed.

In spite of this advanced stage of affairs, Guppy of the board of directors confessed himself to be wholly seduced by the performance of the *Archimedes*. He had studied her workings as she went through a series of trials in the mouth of the Avon and then he had gone with her as a passenger all the way to Liverpool. Screw propulsion, he could see, was not only feasible but inevitable. When he said as much to Brunel and won his agreement, together they asked the other members of the company to hold everything. Within weeks, new plans had reversed all the essential engineering of the ship.

The biggest immediate problem, it developed, was how to tone down a screw ship's noise. To look at, the *Archimedes* was saucy, rakish and sleek; but the noise of her churning screw, particularly at high speeds, was intolerable. To be condemned to hearing it for the length of a transatlantic voyage would be to court madness. Determined to reduce the decibel level, Brunel dedicated himself exclusively to the problem. Experimenting first with leather, then with heavy chains, he eventually brought the noise down to a comparative purr. Next, the cumbersome paddle wheels and their bandbox casings (Claxton said they gave the ship a "dromedary hump") were taken down, and the transformation of the *Great Britain* was complete.

For some inscrutable reason, the hull of the ship was built wider than the entrance to the lock she would have to negotiate in order to reach the Avon. When the time came to float her out into Cumberland Basin, the bridge of the lock was removed, along with a portion of its masonry. The "long and ludicrous durance" of the *Great Britain* seemed, at last, to be over. Before daybreak on a bleak December morning, when the ground was shining with a severe frost and swept by an easterly wind that cut to the bone, tens of thousands of people gathered on both sides of the lock to see the ship eased out of her cage. Great barrels of burning tar, lined up for six hundred feet, illuminated the scene and, according to a sketch made on the spot, gave the mufflered spectators under the arklike walls of the hull a kind of biblical gravity.

At a moment carefully calculated to take advantage of the tide, a steam tug named *Samson* began to pull the ship through the lock into high water. As Christopher Claxton, aboard the tug, directed the operation, he became aware that the tide was not going to rise to the height he had figured upon. The *Great Britain* was not going to make it. As if caught in a vise, she had begun to settle between the lock openings. Should she be sitting there as the tide fell away from her flat bottom, the damage she would incur would very likely be serious. He gave orders to have her hauled back.

All day, under the "scientific and practised eye" of Isambard Brunel, large gangs of masons worked to clear the lock. On a second attempt that evening, she was finally pulled through. The day's delay caused Brunel to cancel a trip to Wales. A letter he wrote that night explained why: "We have had an unexpected difficulty with the *Great Britain*," he wrote. "She stuck in the lock; we *did* get her back. I have been hard at work all day altering the masonry of the lock. Tonight . . . we have succeeded in getting her through; but, being dark, we have been obliged to ground her outside, and I confess I cannot leave her till I see her float again. . . . I have, as you will admit, much at stake here and I am too anxious about it to leave her."

On the next rising of the tide, the elaborate figurehead of the *Great Britain*—royal arms flanked by a beehive, two cog wheels, a dove, a square, and the caduceus of Mercury in bronze on white—also rose. Taken in tow by the tug *Samson*, the stubborn vessel was eased past Round Point and out to Kingroad, seven miles away, in just over an hour. There, while her engines were started up in a first modest test, her tables were laid with a cold collation. As the *Great Britain* rolled along in her natural element, her first passengers lifted glasses to her freedom, her future and each other. But the men of Bristol did little but sigh with relief. She was, they suspected, the whitest of elephants. Until, more than a hundred years later, she returned to the harbor of her birthplace as a celebrated relic—the very Lazarus of ships— few of her townsmen ever regretted her absence.

She steamed up to London late in January, 1845. Her sojourn there as she was fitting out took on the character of a perpetual levee: at an average of fifteen hundred visitors per day, everyone from Queen Victoria and Prince Albert to bootblacks and chimney sweeps came to stare at the widely publicized "mammoth." When the papers reported that a thousand and more yards of Brussels carpeting were laid on the floors of her saloons and staterooms, Managing Director Claxton was moved to point out that the company had not lost its senses. "A large sum of money has not been uselessly squandered in procuring gaudy decoration," he said. "Its fittings are alike chaste and elegant." Down the center of the dining saloon were twelve columns of white and gold ornamented with capitals "in the Arabesque style." Looking glasses were so placed as to reflect the room lengthwise. Walls were lemon-tinted drab, relieved with blue, white and gold. A special interior feature of the ship was a whole section of staterooms, reserved for the exclusive use of female passengers, that adjoined a combined boudoir and sitting room. "The advantages of this arrangement," said Claxton, "must be obvious, as ladies who may be indisposed, or in negligee, will be enabled to reach their sleeping berths without there being the slightest necessity for their appearing in public."

With sixty passengers—a mere one sixth of the number she was prepared to carry—the *Great Britain* got away under the command of the famous Captain Hosken at the end of July and took fifteen days to reach New York. She was greeted with inspirational prose, but neither her appearance nor her speed made much of an impression on the citizens of Manhattan. Contrasted with the lithe tall look of the typical American ship, her six low sails seemed clumsy and supernumerary. Her funnel, barely visible without an eye-straining search among her seventeen hundred yards of canvas, gave little indication of power. Her severely flush deck made her look truncated, as if she had been dismasted and somehow put together again. Still, she was visible proof that iron could float, and it was obvious that her new kind of propulsion was workable. As one New York observer put it: "The boast of Archimedes, that his screw might overturn the globe, if he had a place to stand it, does not seem so hyperbolical, after all; and iron is likely to form a better *floating* capital than gold and silver, or even bank-notes. What would our grandsires have thought of crossing the ocean on plates of iron, and shoving vessels ahead by screws!"

The *Great Britain* seemed to be ready to settle into a New York shuttle service with her running mate, but she was not. On her second trip, much to the surprise of her navigators, soundings showed that she was over the shoals of Nantucket when she should have been approaching Sandy Hook. "A strong set to the northward" was in fact so strong that her captain decided to take shelter at Holmes' Hole in Vineyard Sound where he found a pilot to guide him to New York. When she was put into dry dock there, her propeller was found to be missing two arms and a blade. To even the balance, shipwrights removed another blade, allowing her to drag back to Liverpool by sail and steam in twenty days. Examination there showed that the steam supply lines from her boilers were defective. Repairs to correct these and installation of a new screw kept her laid up all winter. Once more, the *Great Western* was carrying all the New York traffic by herself.

In the following spring the *Great Britain* began a series of crossings which, except for a breakdown in a guard for an air pump, were uneventful and therefore promising. On September 22, 1845, she left the Mersey with 180 passengers—the largest number so far to embark on an Atlantic voyage by steamer. Among these was a troupe of young Viennese dancers bound for a tour of American cities. Only a few hours from Liverpool, when she was supposed to be skirting the shores of the Isle of Man, the *Great Britain* ran onto a shoal of sand and stuck fast. Since there appeared to be no immediate danger to passengers and no damage to the hull, Captain Hosken decided to wait upon assistance from nearby Liverpool on the next day. When daylight broke, however, the commander learned, to his embarrassment, that he had not run onto the Isle of Man but onto the shores of Dundrum Bay close to Tyrella watchhouse in the northeast of Ireland.

It would be a long while before the mystery of this total loss of bearings would be solved. Brunel suspected that the compass had been thrown out of kilter by the magnetic attraction of the unprecedented amount of iron that had been built into the ship. But the trouble turned out to have more than one source. Captain Hosken had been issued an erroneous chart of the waters of the Irish Sea. "I was betrayed," he said, "through the omission of a notice of St. John's light in the chart of this year, and the want of knowledge on my part of such a light having been established."

When the tide ebbed, all passengers were taken off, safe but shaken. "We have, indeed, been in fearful peril," wrote a lady to a friend. "All was confusion; men and women rushed from their berths, some threw themselves into the arms of strangers; one could with difficulty stand. Mr. ——'s first words to me were, 'I think there will be no loss of life, but the ship is gone.'

"What fearful words on such a dark night! Oh! I cannot tell you of the anguish of that night! The sea broke over the ship, the waves struck her like thunder claps, the gravel grated below. There was the throwing overboard of coal, the cries of children, the groans of women, the blue lights, the signal guns, even the tears of men, and amidst all, the Voice of Prayer, and this for long dark hours. Oh! What a fearful night!

"The day dawned and we lay between two long ledges of rock while another stretched across our front, five hundred yards to right and left; the ship had been dashed to pieces. I cannot think of that night without tears. I feel and gratefully acknowledge that the Hand of a Merciful Providence was stretched out to protect and save us. The conduct of Captain Hoskins through the night was admirable.

"At dawn we were lowered over the ship's side and carried on shore in carts of seaweed manure, and Mrs. —— and I lay upon the floor of an Irish cabin where we found plenty of bread, some bacon, and divided an egg among three."

Most of the passengers returned to Liverpool in hope of finding another ship; the dancers from Vienna found places aboard the sailing packet *Yorkshire* and cheered her onward as she made her fastest crossing.

When news of the mishap reached Bristol, Captain Claxton at once started off for Ireland. He found the *Great Britain* wedged solidly into sand that covered a shoal of detached rocks, her bottom already gashed open in several places. Claxton's first notion was to wait for the next spring tide a few days hence and hire steam tugs to try to pull the ship free. But meanwhile a strong southern gale blew in; flood tides breaking over the ship threatened to reduce her to splinters. To maneuver her into a position of comparative safety, Captain Hosken ordered sails to be set and then urged her, not out to sea, but up the beach. She lay there for weeks while her owners tried to learn what means of salvage would be most feasible. Her builder, Patterson, went north to look her over, taking with him James Bremner, a civil engineer expert in the floating of stranded ships. Together they worked out a system of breakwaters designed to keep the ship safe at least through the winter. Hastily built, these were washed away in a November gale that "in a moment laid this labour of man's hands prostrate, smashing the beams like so many reeds."

The directors were on the point of giving up in favor of collecting insurance when Isambard Brunel went to Dundrum Bay to see for himself. What he saw broke his heart. Two days after he got there, he reported back to Claxton. "I have returned from Dundrum with very mixed feelings of satisfaction and pain, almost amounting to anger, with whom I don't know. I was delighted to find our fine ship, in spite of all the discouraging accounts received, even from you, almost as sound as the day she was launched, and ten times stronger and sounder in character. I was grieved to see this fine ship lying unprotected, deserted and abandoned by all those who ought to know her value, and ought to have protected her, instead of being humbugged by schemers and underwriters. Don't let me be understood as wishing to read a lecture to our directors; but the result, whoever is to blame, is, at least in my opinion, that the finest ship in the world, in excellent condition, such that 4000 or 5000 would repair all damage done, has been left, and is lying, like a useless saucepan kicking about on the most exposed shores that you can imagine, with no more effort or skill applied to protect the property than the said saucepan would have received on the beach at Brighton."

While the directors were looking to the salvage of their fortunes, Brunel looked only toward a way to salvage his ship. Unwilling to permit her to break up on "an awfully exposed shore, as if her own parents and guardians meant her to die there," he devised a new system of breakwaters and sent a detailed account of his plans to the home office. The directors listened, approved, and sent Captain Claxton back to Ireland to supervise the new attempt. This time the breakwaters held. The ship was given makeshift haven for the winter and, late in the following August, was floated off and with great effort hauled, in an almost sinking condition, into Liverpool. Rescued, resuscitated, the *Great Britain* looked quite like her old self as she lay in the North Docks. But her career as the glamorous paragon—"the stupendous steamship" of "unparalleled vastness"—was over.

She had proved that an iron hull would stay intact even under the most savage poundings of the winter ocean. She had remained comparatively whole in conditions that would have seen any other ship in shambles. But this was of little consolation to the directors of the owning company. They had succeeded in salvaging their famous ship, but the cost and the delay had so stripped them of operating funds that they were forced into liquidation. In hopes of a different sort of salvage, they sold the big ship lying in the Bramley-Moore Dock "like a huge mass of iron suffering from premature rust" to the Liverpool and London Steam Navigation Company. (At the same time they also sold the doughty *Great Western*—with forty-five round trips on the Atlantic to her credit—to the West India Royal Mail Packet Company. Except for a brief interlude when she had to go trooping off to the Crimea, she sailed for this firm with veteran aplomb and profit for another ten years.)

The *Great Britain*'s new owners reduced the number of her masts from six to four, and sent her off to New York. Assisted by six thousand square yards of canvas, she got to Sandy Hook by sail and steam in 13 days, 6 hours, 40 minutes. But after one voyage out and back she was assigned to new pastures. "Gold fever" was sweeping over England like an epidemic, and, to meet the demand of the thousands of men who wanted to get to Australia in a hurry, the *Great Britain* was put onto the long run to the Antipodes. She continued on this route around the Cape of Good Hope for many years, and then, long after a working term that would have found any ordinary ship worn out or washed up, she surrendered her engines and was converted into a sailing vessel. Worked to the bone, she was still traipsing about the seven seas decades after steam had put most of the old sailers out of business.

On her last trip, when her seams opened up off Punta Arenas and she had to head for the Falklands, she sailed into a trap that had already snared scores of other vessels that had limped into the infamous "port of little comfort." Charges demanded by island shipwrights to repair the *Great Britain*'s hull were so high as to amount to blackmail. Unwilling to put a great sum of money into fixing up an obviously moribund carrier, her owners decided to abandon her, in other words, to sell her to the Falkland Islands Company, which was in need of just such a big iron hull to serve as a storehouse for wool.

All but forgotten, the *Great Britain* sat on the bleak tides of the Antipodes for decades. Then, in 1933, local interests proposed to tow her up one of the creeks of the island and deliberately sink her in order that she might be used as the foundation of a bridge for a sheep crossing. When this was found to be unworkable, the Falkland Islands Company offered her to the British Royal Navy as a target for gunnery practice in the hope that she might at last be taken off their hands, towed out to sea and sunk. But out of respect for the sad old relic the Navy refused. In 1936 the company, still not quite done with her, offered to give her outright to the British Government as a living memorial, if only the Government would pay the charges of salvage. But a public subscription to raise the necessary costs fell far short of its goal in depression-ridden England and the offer was turned down. The *Great Britain* was towed to Sparrow Cove, Port William, early in 1937. Some of her decking was ripped out and found to be still solid enough to be used for building a bridge and a jetty, the former over the Fitzroy River, the latter at Port Stanley.

The rustiest emblem of the Industrial Revolution, she sat in utter desuetude on the beach at Port Sparrow. She would end, it seemed, as she had begun—"in long and ludicrous durance" while only penguins and mollyauks promenaded decks that once echoed the footsteps of Victoria Regina and her bewhiskered consort. But the day of her delivery was at hand, and soon the day of her total resurrection would be predictable.

When a self-styled "ship nut" by the name of William G. Swigert learned that the *Great Britain* was not—as even some marine historians had assumed—a sunken carcass but a hulk afloat, he was determined to save her, transport her, and have her in his own back yard. He not only had the means for so grand a salvage operation, but also just the place to put her once she was pulled out of the shallows of Sparrow Cove. Swigert, who is president of the Pacific Bridge and Engineering Company in San Francisco, worked with the San Francisco Maritime Museum to put in motion a plan to bring the *Great Britain* to his home city as part of a permanent waterfront exhibition. More or less at the same time, a British naval architect, Ewan Corlett, wrote a letter to *The Times* of London setting in motion quite the same sort of plan, differing only in that it was to be carried out by Englishmen.

By 1968, the British public had become aware that, unless something was done at once, the *Great Britain* would meet her ultimate fate in one of two ways and that each was of a morbidity too awful to contemplate: death by dissolution in the Falkland Islands or "salvation" at the hands of an American entrepreneur. With a rally of sentiment and purposiveness that heartened everyone—including the man from San Francisco himself, who relinquished all his claims—Britons formed committees, initiated plans, sent Ewan Corlett on an exploratory mission to the Falklands, and with the support—to the tune of fifty thousand pounds supplied by their *own* millionaire entrepreneur, Jack Hayward—saved the *Great Britain* for Great Britain.

Coddled and cradled, borne upon a submersible pontoon, she was towed eight thousand miles from her oozy anchorage to the tidal waters of Avonmouth. After a trip that lasted from April to June, 1970, the *Great Britain* was eased back into the very launching dock where poor flustered Mrs. Miles had dropped into the water the bottle she should have smashed on the bow. And there the avatar of iron vessels sits for all to see, as precious to the lover of ships as, to the true believer, timber from the Holy Land.

A vast antediluvian relict, all moss and eyes, close up she looks like something unearthed. Barnacles in serrated, almost evenly spaced rows, decorate the lower sides of her bulging hull. Grass in tufts grows side-wise out of the wooden cladding that was affixed to her in 1882. Minus masts that were cut off and left in the Falklands, her deck is merely scattered sections of rotted flooring and tangles of rusty iron; the few lifeboat stanchions still remaining are wrenched and twisted as though they had been bent by a blast. The cavernous inside depths of the ship are ribbed by iron, belly-of-the-whale archings of such breadth and power as to make a contemporary suddenly aware of just what the Industrial Revolution was all about. As she rests in her cobblestone dry-dock, her huge rudder hangs in the air. The bulk of her, looked at fore to aft, seems curiously tumefied and her bow with its gaping anchor sockets seems to fix a basilisk stare on the water just out of reach. Her figurehead, the most humanly lively part of her, is entirely gone. But what is left of the golden unicorn on the portside bow and what is left of the golden lion on the starboard are marked even now by the jaunty lift of tails.

❦ SECTION IX ❦

The Preposterous Voyage: Charles Dickens Supine

CHARLES DICKENS—since General Lafayette the most illustrious European to visit the United States—took passage on the *Britannia* early in January, 1842. Like everyone else, he was acutely aware that the wreckage of the vanished *President* was still floating somewhere in the ocean, but good and sufficient reasons committed him to America. His purposes were to give dramatic readings of his works, to lecture variously and to do "something" about the lack of an international copyright law by which he had been deprived of every cent of royalties earned by his books in the United States. He was also going to realize an old ambition: to set foot "upon the soil I have trodden in my day-dreams many times and whose sons (and daughters) I yearn to know and be among." Not least, he proposed to keep a record of his travels that would be published.

A resounding social and commercial success during the months he was making it, Dickens' visit was a great scandal when he reviewed it. Yet the most enduring of his observations, curiously enough, were those specifically concerned with the voyage over. His sometimes hilarious yet largely lugubrious report was so widely read and taken so deeply to heart for generations that, almost single-handedly, he fixed on ocean travel an unhappy image that nothing could modify. More than one hundred and twenty years afterwards, when the American poet Anne Sexton came to recount her own first Atlantic voyage, Dickens' experience still served as a touchstone:

> We sail out of season into an oyster-gray wind,
> over a terrible hardness.
> Where Dickens crossed with *mal de mer*
> in twenty weeks or twenty days
> I cross toward him in five . . .
>
> I have read each page of my mother's voyage.
> I have reached each page of her mother's voyage.
> I have learned their words as they learned Dickens'.
> I have swallowed these words like bullets.

When Dickens got to the Liverpool landing stage (he was traveling with his wife Kate and her maid, whose name was Anne) and was about to board the tender that would take him out to the *Britannia* anchored in the Mersey, he found that "every gallant ship was riding slowly up and down, and every little boat was splashing noisily in the water; and knots of people stood upon the wharf, gazing with a kind of 'dread delight' on the far-famed fast American steamer; and one party of men were 'taking in the milk,' or, in other words, getting the cow on board; and another were filling the icehouses to the very throat with fresh provisions; with butchers'-meat and garden-stuff, pale suckling-pigs, calves' heads in scores, beef, veal, and pork, and poultry out of all proportions; and others were coiling ropes and busy with oakum yarns; and others were lowering heavy packages into the hold; and the purser's head was barely visible as it loomed in a state of exquisite perplexity from the midst of a vast pile of passengers' luggage; and there seemed to be nothing going on anywhere, or uppermost in the mind of anybody, but preparations for this mighty voyage."

Weighed down with enough cargo to steady a liner ten times her size, the little tender puffed into midstream. "We are made fast alongside the packet, whose huge red funnel is smoking bravely," Dickens goes on, "giving rich promise of serious intentions. Packing-cases, portmanteaus, carpet-bags, and boxes, are already passed from hand to hand,

and hauled on board with breathless rapidity. The officers, smartly dressed, are at the gangway handing the passengers up the side, and hurrying the men. In five minutes' time, the little steamer is utterly deserted, and the packet is beset and over-run by its late freight, who instantly pervade the whole ship, and are to be met with by the dozen in every nook and corner: swarming down below with their own baggage, and stumbling over other peoples'; disposing themselves comfortably in wrong cabins, and creating a most horrible confusion by having to turn out again; madly bent upon opening locked doors, and on forcing a passage into all kinds of out-of-the-way places where there is no thoroughfare; sending wild stewards, with elfin hair, to and fro upon the breezy decks on unintelligible errands, impossible of execution; and in short, creating most extraordinary and bewildering tumult.

"In the midst of all this, a lazy gentleman, who seems to have no luggage of any kind—not so much as a friend, even—lounges up and down the hurricane deck, cooly puffing a cigar; and, as this unconcerned demeanour . . . exalts him in the opinion of those who have leisure to observe his proceedings, every time he looks up at the masts, or down at the decks, or over the side, they look there too, as wondering whether he sees anything wrong anywhere, and hoping that, in case he should, he will have the goodness to mention it."

What Dickens was least prepared for was the sight of his stateroom: an "utterly impracticable, thoroughly hopeless, and profoundly preposterous box." His bunk itself was a kind of shelf with a thin mattress covered, "like a surgical plaster," by a flat quilt. "Nothing smaller for sleeping in was ever made," he said, "except coffins." The chance that his wife's luggage might be fitted into this cramped cabin was as remote as the possibility that "a giraffe could be persuaded . . . into a flower pot."

In the office of the Cunard agency in London he had seen an artist's rendering of the saloon. He remembered this as "a chamber of almost interminable perspective, furnished . . . in a style of more than Eastern splendour, and filled . . . with groups of ladies and gentlemen in the very highest state of enjoyment and vivacity." The actual saloon was "a long narrow apartment, not unlike a gigantic hearse with windows."

Afraid to go to bed, he walked the deck the first night out, observing "the melancholy sighing of the wind through block, and rope, and chain; the gleaming forth of light from every crevice, nook, and tiny piece of glass . . . as though the ship were filled with fire in hiding, ready to

burst through any outlet, with its resistless power of death and ruin."
His feet got cold and his hands got cold, and by midnight he was ready
to turn in. Below, he found his wife in seasick silence on a sofa, her
maid "a mere bundle on the floor, execrating her destiny, and pounding
her curl-papers among the stray boxes. Everything sloped the wrong
way . . . I had left the door open, a moment before, in the bosom of
a gentle declivity, and, when I tried to shut it, it was on the summit
of a lofty eminence. Now every plank and timber creaked, as if the ship
were made of wicker-work; and now crackled, like an enormous fire of
the driest possible twigs. There was nothing for it but bed; so I went
to bed."

Seasick himself, he remained hallucinated and largely comatose for
about ten days, unable to read the pocket Shakespeare he had been
given as a *bon-voyage* present, unable even to keep his thoughts consecutive. When the weather finally abated somewhat, he managed to
get up and out. "Ocean and sky were all of one dull, heavy, uniform,
lead colour," he wrote. "There was no extent of prospect even over
the dreary waste . . . for the sea ran high, and the horizon encompassed
us like a large black hoop. . . . In the gale of last night the lifeboat had
been crushed by one blow of the sea like a walnut-shell; and there it
hung dangling in the air; a mere faggot of crazy boards. The planking
of the paddle-boxes had been torn sheer away. The wheels were exposed
and bare; and they swirled and dashed their spray about the decks at
random. Chimney, white with crusted salt; top-masts struck; storm-sails
set; rigging all knotted, tangled, wet, and drooping; a gloomier picture
it would be hard to look upon."

Dickens remained upright for the rest of the trip and, though seldom
comfortable, tried to make himself useful. To a friend who had presented him with a traveler's medicine chest, he wrote: "If you could
only have seen me . . . endeavoring (with that impossible pair of scales,
and those weights, invisible to the naked eye) to make up pills in the
heavy weather, on the rolling Atlantic! If you could only have seen me,
when Kate and Anne were deadly fearful of shipwreck, bent on raising
their spirits with calomel, and ringing the changes on all the bottles in
that mahogany box, to restore their peace of mind!"

For general publication, his observations were quite in the same key.
"The weather continuing obstinately and almost unprecedentedly bad,"
he wrote, "we usually struggled into [the] cabin, more or less faint and
miserable, about an hour before noon. and lay down on the sofas to

recover; during which interval, the captain would look in to communicate the state of the wind, the moral certainty of its changing to-morrow (the weather is always going to improve to-morrow, at sea), the vessel's rate of sailing, and so forth. . . . But a description of one day will serve for all the rest. Here it is.

"The captain being gone, we compose ourselves to read, if the place be light enough, and if not, we doze and talk alternately. At one, a bell rings, and the stewardess comes down with a steaming dish of baked potatoes, and another of roasted apples; and plates of pig's faces, cold ham, salt beef; or perhaps a smoking mess of hot collops. We fall to upon these dainties; eat as much as we can (we have great appetites now); and are as long as possible about it. If the fire will burn (it *will* sometimes) we are pretty cheerful. If it won't, we all remark to each other that it's very cold, rub our hands, cover ourselves with coats and cloaks, and lie down again to doze, talk, and read . . . until dinner time. At five, another bell rings, and the stewardess re-appears with another dish of potatoes—boiled this time—and store of hot meat of various kinds: not forgetting the roast pig, to be taken medicinally. We sit down at table again (rather more cheerfully than before); prolong the meal with a rather mouldy dessert of apples, grapes, and oranges; and drink our wine and brandy-and-water. The bottles and glasses are still upon the table . . . when the doctor comes down, by special nightly invitation, to join our evening rubber: immediately on whose arrival we make a party at whist, and as it is a rough night and the cards will not lie on the cloth, we put the tricks in our pockets as we take them. At whist we remain with exemplary gravity (deducting a short time for tea and toast) until eleven o'clock, or thereabouts; when the captain comes down again, in a sou'wester hat tied under his chin, and a pilot-coat: making the ground wet where he stands. By this time the card-playing is over, and the bottles and glasses are again upon the table; and after an hour's pleasant conversation about the ship, the passengers, and things in general, the captain (who never goes to bed, and is never out of humour) turns up his coat collar for the deck again: shakes hands all round; and goes laughing out into the weather as merrily as to a birthday party.

"As to daily news, there is no dearth of that commodity. This passenger is reported to have lost fourteen pounds at Vingt-et-un in the saloon yesterday; and that passenger drinks his bottle of champagne every day, and how he does it (being only a clerk), nobody knows. The head engineer has distinctly said that there never was such times—meaning weather—and four good hands are ill, and have given in, dead beat. Several berths are full of water, and all the cabins are leaky. The ship's cook, secretly swigging damaged whiskey, has been found drunk; and has been played upon by the fire-engine until quite sober. All the stewards have fallen down-stairs at various dinner times, and go about with plasters in various places. The baker is ill, and so is the pastry-cook. A new man, horribly indisposed, has been required to fill the place of the latter officers; and has been propped and jammed up with empty casks in a little house upon deck, and commanded to roll out pie-crust, which he protests (being highly bilious) it is death to him to look at. News! A dozen murders on shore would lack the interest of these slight incidents at sea."

When the *Britannia* finally reached Nova Scotia she ran aground in a shoal of mud. But her captain was able to work her free and to ease her into Eastern Passage, the "wrong" entrance to Halifax Harbor, where he dropped anchor to await daylight. After a seven-hour stopover in Halifax, where some of the sea-crazed passengers, "having indulged too freely in oysters and champagne," according to Dickens, "were found lying insensible on their backs in unfrequented streets," they sailed on to Boston. The passage from Liverpool had taken, in all, eighteen days.

❦ SECTION X ❧

An American Pioneer: The Washington / *A Memo for*
Henry Clay / Junius Smith: Lobbyist / The British
Rub It In / Joy in Southampton

JUST as the *Great Britain* was being prised like a starfish off the
rocks of Dundrum Bay, a brand-new American ship was making
a bid to match the performance of the *Great Western* as a
regular New York to Europe carrier and—for the benefit of zealots in
Congress—to "drive the Cunarders off the ocean." This pioneer was
the *Washington*. Described in her home port as the "most complete
and beautiful ship ever constructed," she was actually a graceless tub
of a boat that seemed to have been hammered together by journeymen
carpenters rather than joined together by shipwrights. Charged with a
mission she could in no way fulfill, the *Washington* had a career at sea
that was over and done with almost before anyone knew it had begun.
But even in her brief time as an emissary on the high seas—sponsored
by Congress—her many mistakes and her dismal performance set a
sorry American standard on the ocean that would never be quite forgotten for nearly half a century.

To some Americans, British success with steamships was a national
embarrassment. To others, like Christopher Hughes, who was now the

159

United States' Chargé d'Affaires at the Hague, the behavior of class-conscious Englishmen on the Atlantic was an abomination no true Yankee should have to put up with. In the course of a westward crossing aboard the *Great Western,* Hughes made his feelings known to Henry Clay, who had held the office of Secretary of State and who was now a Senator. "The honest-hearted and independent Yankee makes no difference in his attention and deportment to his passengers," wrote Hughes. "He is equally courteous, careful, and anxious about *all* his passengers. The Bull deals out his cold civilities with a view to what he considers the relative *rank* of individuals! To some, he is careless, rude, and even insolent. All this is the fruit of *institutions.* The Yankee never thinks of rank—all of proper conduct are equal in his eyes! He feels himself to be the equal of all—superior to none. This is his birthright—he neither claims nor yields superiority. In a word, we surpass immeasurably our English cousins in courtesy and justice, and I believe that every American aboard this ship (even to the coloured servants), and we form three-fourths of the passengers, think as I do; nothing but necessity induces Americans to use these English steamers. And we generally feel humiliated at the fact, that this *monopoly* has been allowed to fall into English hands. The fact has lowered us in the opinions of foreign nations, as a nautical and enterprising people. *We ought to build steamers.*"

Congressmen also worried about national honor, resented having to entrust their overseas mail to foreign hands and foreign hulls, and deplored as well the Navy's lack of any kind of steam auxiliary power. To put an end to such mortification, Congress passed in 1845 a bill designed to expand naval power, establish a transatlantic service, and set up a line of American ships for Yankee travelers. The substance of this bill was a provision for a mail subsidy and a ten-year contract to be awarded to a company willing and able to undertake to run four steamships of about 2,000 tons each between New York and some English Channel port. The vessels, by contract, would have to be so designed as to be quickly convertible to armed ships of the line. They would also have to prove themselves crack transports, outshining in every respect the plain-Jane Cunarders and, of course, beating their time.

The most ardent promoter of this bill was none other than Junius Smith, returning to the lists as an obstreperous one-man lobby, who acted as if he could not finally be denied. After his London-based company had been reduced to shambles, Smith had come back to America in 1843 to live with his nephew Henry in Astoria, Long Island. He still quite rightfully saw himself as the unrecognized and unrewarded pioneer of the North Atlantic—the Sophoclean protagonist who had overcome every obstacle men had put in his path, only to bow finally to the whims of gods who swept the *President* off the face of the ocean. "It was no slight affair for an individual without fortune, without influence, and without cooperation," he told a friend, "to devise, shape, and follow out measures which were to change the commercial intercourse between Europe and America, and establish a new system of navigation, against the interests of commercial and nautical men, the uniform practice of past ages, and the prejudices of men."

At his nephew's country home Smith somewhat occupied himself with experimental gardening, but he continued to brood on the growing disparity between British and American enterprise on the sea lanes. When he could no longer bear his puttering with celery and breadcorn, he started to buttonhole importers and shipping men in New York, then went to Washington where he elbowed his way into the offices of everyone from the greenest member of the House of Representatives to the Secretary of the Navy. Smith was concerned with rehabilitation on two scores: the nation's recovery of maritime importance, if not supremacy; and his own reentry into the transatlantic picture.

When in 1845 the Congressional bill was passed and tenders invited, six potential steamship operators responded. Of these, E. K. Collins' bid was put aside because it came late, and the one by Smith himself, proposing a service between New York and Liverpool, was underbid. The contract went to Edward Mills, a promoter completely unknown in shipping circles. New Yorker Mills was a businessman of many interests; passenger and mail ships were but one. He had asked for a subsidy of 300,000 dollars per annum for a line serving New York and Le Havre. By the time the Government had bestowed its full favor, *arriviste* Mills was promised 400,000 dollars per annum for a period of five years if he would guarantee a biweekly service to Bremen by way of a British Channel port. Bitter but resigned, Junius Smith gave up steamships for good and went back to cultivating his own garden in Astoria.

Edward Mills' lack of experience in the business of shipping soon began to register—on him and his associates, as well as upon the watchdogs of the United States Treasury. He could not raise enough money to build even two ships, much less the four that would be needed to ensure a biweekly schedule. As the whole venture began to show signs of sagging, Mills was lucky to be bailed out of a worsening situation when a newly formed group of capitalists took over his Government contract. This was the Ocean Steam Navigation Company of New York, headed by C. H. Sand and Mortimer Livingston. Impatient with such developments, the Government cut the original amount of the subsidy in half.

Her background was cloudy, her beginnings inauspicious, yet, signs and portents aside, the first American transatlantic steam packet was about to run up the Stars and Stripes. To the general public, that was all that mattered. When the *Washington* was launched in the New York shipyards of Westervelt and Mackey on January 30, 1847, the hopes she carried were confirmed by a citywide volley of guns, bells and cheers. A wooden paddle-wheeler, 260 feet long, she was barque-rigged with lots of canvas and had sides painted in traditional man-of-war fashion—a wide white strip, below her maindeck bulwarks, on which gun ports were painted in black. She carried no guns and the ports were fake, yet her long hull, square stem and great bulk gave her a comforting look, as if she had power to spare.

Four months later, carrying 127 passengers—among them Major Hobbie, Special Trans-Marine Agent for the Post Office Department, who was going over to arrange an Anglo-American postal treaty—she was put to the proof. Since she was scheduled to sail from New York just as Cunard's *Britannia* was setting out from Boston, the first ocean race between an American steamship and a British one was joined. The New York *Herald* voiced a common expectation: "We shall have to say that, if the *Britannia* beats the *Washington* over, she will have to run by the deep mines, and put in more coal. We shall have, in two years' time, a system of Atlantic, Gulf, and Pacific steamers in operation that will tell a brilliant story of the enterprise of Brother Jonathan. We are about to go ahead, and steam is the agent of the age."

Steam may have been the agent, but Brother Jonathan still needed the assistance of trained men. When it turned out to be impossible to locate practiced marine engineers to work her engines, the *Washington* had to sail off with but one first-class engineer and a corps of helpers whose experience was limited to New York riverboats. Almost as soon as the ship got into the swells of the Atlantic, all of the makeshift crew, including the firemen, were laid low by seasickness and stayed that way for three days. Meanwhile, with only half of the *Washington*'s power in her boilers, the little seven-year-old *Britannia* was outrunning the American ship with ease. Two days before the *Washington* was even sighted from the Isle of Wight, the *Britannia* was resting, like an actress between shows, at her familiar dock in Liverpool.

To Americans, that news was bad enough. Then the British rubbed it in. "In point of size," wrote the London *Times* correspondent in Spithead, "she looked like an elongated three-decker, with only one streak around her, but about as ugly a specimen of steam-ship building as ever went through this anchorage. She did not appear to make much use of her 2,000 horse-power either, but seemed rather to roll along than steam through the water." Worse was to come. If the English press might be accused of rudeness, the English Government might be charged with open hostility. While the *Washington* was still at sea, the British Lords of the Treasury and Her Majesty's Post Office joined forces to issue an order: all American letters and newspapers for France and the Continent put off by the *Washington* at Southampton would not be treated as "closed mail," but subject to prevailing rates of postage via London. Since the American government had for many years allowed British mail for Canada to be landed at New York without any levy of overland charges, this was curiously narrow behavior on the part of the British Post Office. The upshot was retaliation: "closed mail" for Canada was no longer a British privilege. Instead of signing a treaty, the major who had sailed on the *Washington* to arrange for a beneficent exchange returned to his own country to build barriers.

British rebuffs and sneers came almost exclusively from London. Southampton received the *Washington* with joy and shouts of encouragement. Port and shipping interests there cared not a whit whether she was a paragon of marine architecture or a rub-a-dub tub. The big point was that she had steamed up Southampton Water and not the Mersey, thus preparing the way for other ships that might also be persuaded to bypass Liverpool. Across the Channel, the city of Bremen, equally delighted, greeted her with bunting, bells and a state procession. The burgomeister with his entourage paid a formal call aboard; at a banquet in the town hall toasts were offered in endless variation upon the theme of hands across the sea.

Back in Southampton, the *Washington* was fêted at a dinner given on board by the directors of the local docks to honor her officers, with the American ambassador and the American consul prominently in attendance. Word of the ship's disappointing debut had by this time spread to New York and gone on to Washington. No longer carrying the hopes of anyone but the boosters of Southampton, she had begun a brief and depressing career. She left Southampton on July 10. But before she had dropped her pilot just beyond the Needles, it was discovered that the fire bars on her furnaces were beginning to melt because the coal she burned was too powerful. She turned back to port, exchanged her "anthracite for the common sort," and did not sail away until four days later.

For all her lack of auspice, the *Washington* had the distinction of being the first American steamship to fly, by grace of Congress, the dollar sign; and the first to go beyond the Cunard ships, which carried only saloon passengers, in enlarging the scope of the bourgeoisie by providing, between the infernal rats' alleys of steerage and the pearly portals of first, a respectable second class. She must also be credited— if, in retrospect, credit is the word—with having opened the door to the princely imprudence of Edward Knight Collins, and with having confirmed a suspicion that Americans, try as they might, just could not run steamships.

☙ SECTION XI ❧

THE BIG, broad and only American chance on the North Atlantic came and went in the space of just one decade. Riding luck and a Government subsidy, the Collins Line came into the picture with a fine show of rosewood paneling, enscrolled mirrors and great elbowing shafts of machinery that pounded to Liverpool in ten days.

To give a sassy Yankee answer to the schedule-keeping sobriety of Cunard and his pinch-penny Scottish colleagues, Collins provided chambers of marble and gilt, tonsorial parlors, speed and *haute cuisine.* From the moment they set out, the Collins steamers carried a sense of bravado and devil-may-care that thrilled even those Americans who were still felling trees in Indian territory. "In nothing was American pride more interested and gratified," said a British historian, "than in this signal triumph of national industry and enterprise."

During a few brilliant years before the company foundered in a sudden, sad confluence of tragedy, ineptitude and debt, American supremacy on the most traveled of sea lanes was absolute. In the histrionic verbosity of the day, the United States was said to have "wrested the

Tyrian trident from Britain's grasp," torn "the proud title of Mistress of the Seas from her breast." But then, alack and alas, having done this, "she flung her heritage away like a witless wastrel—with the abandon of a drunkard."

All known accounts of the career of Edward Knight Collins say that he sought support from Congress for steamships to Europe during the last years of the 1840s. However, remarks in a letter written by David MacIver to Samuel Cunard in April, 1841, show that Collins was laying down plans a good number of years earlier. "I have yours of Saturday," wrote MacIver from Liverpool to Cunard in London, "enclosing the Prospectus of an Iron Steam Coy. to New York—Quackery—not worth noticing—would only do harm to publish it—would excite more attention than it deserves. 'Delano and Rathburn' spoke the other night as if Collins had no chance of getting up his Steamers—All he is asking from the American Government is, liberty to tax the settlers he carries."

A few years even earlier—just after the *Sirius* and *Great Western* had come smoking into New York—Collins had told a friend he was convinced there was "no longer chance for enterprise with sail," that steam "must win the day." Collins' deeds followed long after his express thoughts on the subject. Yet when he was ready to propose himself as the American standard bearer in the great ocean race, no man could list better credentials or claim more expertise in the business of sea transport.

His father was Captain Israel Gross Collins, his uncle, Captain John Collins, both masters of sailing vessels. Captain Israel had met and married Mary Ann Knight on one of his frequent voyages to England. Then the couple crossed to America to settle on Cape Cod, in Truro, where Edward Knight Collins was born on August 5, 1802. His mother died a few months later and he became a ward of his uncle John Collins. Never much of a nautical man as far as actual sea-going was concerned, Edward was from the first caught up in commercial aspects of sea-faring. When he was barely more than a youngster he left the shores of Cape Cod for the docks of Manhattan and became an apprentice in a South Street commission house. This gave him a chance to see for himself the magnitude of maritime operations in the port of New York. For a time he made voyages to coastal cities—Wilmington, Savannah, St. Augustine, Pensacola—on ships laden with cotton, sugar and hard lumber. Later he served as supercargo—a position roughly akin to that of purser—on ships to Cuba and Florida chartered by a New York merchant, John F. Delaplaine. When his father gave up the command of sailing ships in order to establish an agency trading between New York and Vera Cruz, Edward was already an experienced hand with ships' manifests and schedules. A new firm—Israel G. Collins & Son—opened an office in the shadow of the tall masts and bowsprits at Burling Slip and South Street. The senior Collins died a few years later. Then the biggest firm operating sailing packets between New York and Mexico, as well as the first on-schedule packet service to New Orleans, was known simply as E. K. Collins & Co.

A close observer of ship performance, Collins had over the years developed certain notions of his own about ship design. Flat-bottomed vessels, he noted, were at times faster than those with V bottoms and could often negotiate shallow waters where ordinary ships could not. Consequently, he ordered a broad flat bottom for his ship *Mississippi*— at 750 tons, with space for 2,600 bales of cotton, the largest carrier in the American merchant marine—and, later, for his packet ship *Shakespeare*, which he sent across to Liverpool in 1836. In command of the *Shakespeare* was his uncle John, a man who could obviously turn a penny as deftly as he could hoist a sail. As soon as he arrived in the Mersey, Captain Collins set his crew to work. They touched up the broad-bottomed *Shakespeare* with paint and polish, holystoned her decks, festooned her with long pennants and banners. Then she was opened to public inspection for a week. Ship-wise Liverpudlians agreed: this was the finest packet ship going. Travelers applying for passage were three times in number what the *Shakespeare* could handle. On her voyage back to New York she carried the largest cargo any ship had ever brought into that port.

Collins' ambitions were newly charged. On the profits of his freight-carrying packets he built a whole new fleet of vessels, each named after some theatrical figure of the century—*Garrick, Siddons, Sheridan* and, after the Roman actor, *Roscius*. Before long, everyone had taken to referring to this operation as the "Dramatic Line." The deluxe transports of their day, Collins' vessels were considerably more comfortable than the first steamships with their clatter and splash and, on the eastward run at least, almost as swift. Roomy and airy, free of smoke and smuts, they were ingeniously appointed in ways meant to exploit theatricality. Brightly painted effigies of their namesakes served as figure-heads. Interior decorations took their cues from the Forest of Arden or the shrubberies of Dunsinane. Under such inducements, fashionable travelers were soon in the habit of coming over on one of the Cunarders, then returning in the ease and quietude provided by the swelling sails of the Dramatic Line. In this way they would, like Dickens, avoid "a second experience in a British smoke-box."

Owner of the most prestigious line of sailing packets—including the *Roscius*, the first of them to exceed 1,000 tons—Collins was already a rich man when the sooty signatures of the *Sirius* and the *Great Western* put new handwriting on the wall. Restless, ambitious, he was still smarting under the rebuffs to his first attempts to get into the steamship business by way of Government support when luck brought him a second chance. Ruefully, he had accepted the Government's decision favoring Edward Mills and had put the matter out of his mind. But while he was in Washington on business of a quite unrelated nature a few months afterward, he learned from his friend Hobbie of the Postmaster General's office that Mills' contract to carry the mails was not necessarily an exclusive one. When Hobbie then introduced Collins to Postmaster General Johnson, that surprising piece of information was confirmed. Collins now had an opportunity to make proposals of his own.

Congress in general wanted a dependable mail service to Europe in bona-fide, Yankee-crafted, all-American ships. Congressmen in particular —James Asheton Bayard of Delaware was one—wanted nothing short of American maritime supremacy. The Senator said he was tired of listening to reports of British triumphs on the ocean. "I suggest cost must not be considered," he told his colleagues. "I suggest, too, that Congress grant a carefully selected American shipping expert a completely free hand *to proceed with the absolute conquest of this man Cunard.*" The sea-minded public wanted steamships to match the excitements of the sailing packets; ships that would shatter records; captains whose blue-eyed rectitude and muttonchop dignity would continue to provide models of American manliness; big statistics and awesome dimensions. The Navy wanted steamships that could be converted into military transports capable of outrunning anything afloat. Edward Knight Collins was prepared to satisfy each of them and to come up with a few embellishments no one could foresee.

In a proposal made to Postmaster General Johnson, Collins offered to carry mails between New York and Liverpool on a schedule of twenty round trips per year—once a month during the winter, twice a month in other seasons. For the guarantee of a subsidy in the amount of 385,000 dollars per year, payable in quarterly installments, he would build five new steam vessels superior to all others on the ocean. Johnson forwarded his letter to the Senate, recommending Collins as "a gentleman of the highest reputation for his judgment and skill, as well as ability to perform the service he proposes." Collins' ideas were bounced around the halls of Congress for more than a year and a half. When, at last, a score of Senators had had their chance to speak out, and the Navy and the Post Office had been brought into something approaching harmony, a contract incorporating nearly everything Collins had proposed was given approval and passage on the first of November, 1847. This contract was signed for the Navy by Secretary John Young Mason; for The New York and Liverpool United States Mail Steamship Company by Collins and two associates, the Brown brothers, James and Stewart. These men were bankers who had joined with Elisha Riggs and W. S. Wetmore to provide Collins with financial backing for the firm that, in spite of its long name, would always be known simply as the Collins Line.

Collins was a man with a demonstrated taste and flair for showmanship. His Dramatic Line of ships already represented the class of the packets; he was determined that his steamships would be the aristocrats of the Great Circle. Constructed entirely in New York—the birthplace, ever since the *Savannah*, of most American transatlantic candidates— these vessels would incorporate refinements of marine engineering made since Robert Fulton went puffing up the Hudson and they would exhibit all of the baroque fantasy and plushy pretentiousness of the Mississippi and Ohio riverboats. Since they would also have to meet requirements laid down by the Navy for their potential use as transports or cruisers, Commodore Matthew Calbraith Perry was detailed to oversee the military aspects of construction.

"Meddlesome Matty," as the Commodore dubbed himself, was charged to exercise over the ships "a parental official influence." The hulls of two of Collins' steamers were already completed when Perry came into the picture. He found this dismaying. In his reports to the Secretary of the Navy he hinted that, had he been party to the original contracts and had been able to oversee construction from the time the keels were laid, the Collins steamers would be more practical and not so "extravagantly showy."

As a young officer (he was now in his late fifties) Perry had been involved in the earliest application of steam power to ships of war and had himself commanded the *Fulton*, the first steam vessel in the American Navy. In the planning stages of the new Collins ships, when the comparative merits of paddle wheels and the newly introduced screw propellers were discussed, Perry held out for paddles. Like most of his nautical colleagues at home and abroad—and in agreement with the public that liked to see with their own eyes what made a ship run— Perry felt that paddle wheels were more trustworthy. This conviction was enforced when, at the very beginning of his voyage to the Orient that would "open up" Japan, the screw steamer *Princeton* broke down and had to be left behind while Perry and his staff splashed halfway around the world in the dependable paddle-wheeler *Mississippi*.

In all, there were to be five Collins steamships. Two of them, the *Atlantic* and the *Pacific*—2,856 tons burden, 282 feet long, and bigger than anything except the *Great Britain*—were launched on the same day, February 1, 1849. The *Atlantic* was the first to get away to sea, and it was the bold address and power of this vessel that brought the Collins Line a singularity and a charismatic appeal not even disaster could erase.

At a glance, the striking thing about the *Atlantic* was her shape. She was abruptly rounded at the stern, and instead of a bowsprit she had a straight cutwater. These features gave her a tublike, or battering-ram, appearance. There was something self-contained and pugnacious about her, as if she would just as soon fight the sea as sail it. No one could call her graceful. Yet when her enormous paddle wheels gouged the water and hot black smoke issued from her tall black funnel with its red top, she was, to New Yorkers, at least, the very picture of the Behemoth. Riding relatively high out of the water, she was drier and more comfortable than ships with a scantier margin of freeboard. Built of live oak, planed with pitch pine, her forbidding arklike hull nevertheless enclosed sea-going niceties previously unknown.

Steam-heated, she carried 40 tons of ice in a huge ice room, and she had not only bathrooms, but a barber shop which, for its time, ranked as nothing short of a marvel. "It is fitted up with all necessary appa-

1. The *Great Western* opens an era

2. Sir Samuel Cunard, Bart

3. P. T. Barnum brings
Jenny Lind to New York
aboard the Collins
liner *Atlantic*

4. Edward Knight Collins:
America's magnificent failure

5. 1970: the exhumed bones of Brunel's *Great Britain*
passing under Brunel's suspension bridge at Bristol

6. The apotheosis of Isambard Kingdom Brunel

GREAT EASTERN

GREAT WESTERN

GREAT BRITAIN

SALTASH

HUNGERFORD

BRUNEL

7. Brunel at the end of his life, the chains of
the *Great Eastern*'s checking drum as background

8. "Not since the Ark. . . .": the *Great Eastern* under construction

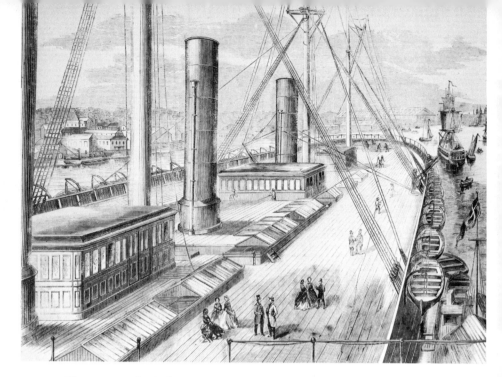

9. The promenade deck: "People bowed and spoke to each other in passing," said Jules Verne, "as formally as if they were walking in Hyde Park."

10. A stateroom: all the comforts of home, including "oilcloth and Turkey rugs" on the floor

11. An extremely rare photograph, source unknown, proving the *Great Eastern* was as plush as her reputation

12. The grand saloon in the great storm of 1861

13. The grand saloon on calm seas

14. The elite stroll in the shadows
of sails and funnels

15. Elegance comes to the steerage: tables, chairs and stewards
on Inman's *City of Brussels*

ISMAY, IMRIE & CO.
10 WATER ST. LIVERPOOL.
34 LEADENHALL ST. LONDON.

16. Cloud-flown canvas and painted stacks:
a White Star liner of the transitional period,
when steamships were most beautiful

17. At the taffrail: the lady and the officer

18. Leaving Liverpool, the tender pulling away

19. A musical soirée: "It is difficult to imagine, from the homelike appearance of the scene, that the great ship is tearing along at full speed..."

ratus," reported an overseas correspondent, "with glass cases containing perfumery, etc.; and in the center is the 'barber's chair.' This is a comfortable, well-stuffed seat, with an inclined back. In front is a stuffed trestle, on which to rest the feet and legs; and behind is a little stuffed apparatus like a crutch on which to rest the head. These are movable, so as to suit people of all sizes; and in this comfortable horizontal position the passenger lies, and his beard is taken off in a twinkling, let the American waves roll as they may."

Woodwork fittings in the *Atlantic* were various and costly: white holly, satinwood and rosewood paneled the walls of two large saloons divided by a steward's pantry. One of these was the dining room—67 feet long and 20 feet wide—and the other, of the same dimensions, was a drawing room, "the most beautiful and gorgeous apartment of the kind that was ever seen," heavily carpeted, furnished with plumply upholstered chairs and sofas, tables with tops of Brocatelli marble, walls lavishly brightened with mirrors and by "windows ornamented with designs emblematical of American freedom." There were so many mirrors, in fact, that a man of normal vanity was apt to find them obstreperous. "I was one day reading," said Yale professor Benjamin Silliman, "looked up, and saw six repetitions of myself, and the original made seven. Surely the most inordinate self-love would be satisfied with so many reduplications."

There were also amenities of a more practical nature. "I remember very little of that morning," said an *Atlantic* lady passenger on her second day out, "except it be the incident of my finding out, as if by instinct, the use of a queer little utensil of painted tin, a sort of elongated spittoon, which stood by my washstand."

Coats of arms of the States were affixed to panels between staterooms; upholding a carved and gilded ceiling were pillars inlaid with mirrors and bronzed seashells. Among a patriotic plethora of five-pointed stars and spread eagles in the grand saloon, an oil painting depicted the figure of Liberty trampling a feudal prince. After making a dockside tour of her, a proud but anonymous citizen sent a letter to the New York *Herald* saying that he felt the whole thing, "the landscape panelings, the tresseled gildings, the sash-work of stained glass, filled with device of rainbow tints, proudly elevates the character of our mechanics and artists." An English writer turned a patronizing eye on the "handsome spittoons—the upper part fashioned like a shell and painted a sea green or sky blue." These curious artifacts, he went on, gave "ample facility for indulging in that practice of which Americans are so fond." Another could not resist pointing out the hazards of Collins Line dining arrangements. "The seats are covered with leather or American cloth, the surface of which is slippery, and occasionally a passenger who has neglected for the moment to balance himself properly, will slide suddenly from his seat and under the table."

One of the *Atlantic*'s most practical and enduring innovations was a smoking room. This was a claustrophobic den of narcosis situated in a sort of outhouse on deck. It was bare, cramped and rancid; but as a masculine retreat it was the precursor of a feature of ships that would be zealously perpetuated into the middle of the twentieth century. The *Atlantic*'s staterooms, according to one gentleman traveler, were little improvement on the one Dickens had complained of. "There is a fatal mistake in the construction of these," he said. "They are designed for *two*. In the family relation this may be tolerated perhaps. But for single men—single men to be made double, Siamese for the voyage— is utterly abominable. In the first place, the state-room is almost too small for the healthy respiration of one full grown person. In it are two berths, or sleeping shelves, with a narrow board in front to keep the sleeper, or the sick, from rolling out. The mattress of course harmonizes in width with the shelf. He who has neither lung fever, nor pleurisy, may sleep 'this side up' and get along pretty well; but he who is reduced to the back, must look out for his hips and ribs. I have known one or two men who could only get along by genuflection, which answers well on Sundays ashore, but for every night of the week, might possibly be troublesome. Dressing is a mystery, when two men, strangers, are up in such quarters, and try to dress at the same time. It is embarrassing, even after a treaty that only one should get up at a time. Some could only get along in putting on a coat by opening a door, and so thrusting an arm into the corridor; and by a jump from the bed shelf get into their pantaloons."

The only way in which to obviate this uncomfortable proximity, according to the same traveler, "is *to take a whole state-room to one's self*. No matter what the cost. Sacrifice a month or more of foreign travel, wear old clothes, eat but one meal a day, rather than have a fellow-citizen so near you as to breathe half your air, and make you breathe all his."

Only a few months from the day that would precisely mark the point of midcentury—April 27, 1850—the *Atlantic* sailed out on her maiden voyage carrying one hundred passengers. There seemed little reason not to believe that the second half of the century would see American ships propelled by steam joining in the same ascendancy that had carried American sailing packets and American clippers to maritime preeminence. But little snags and setbacks that should have spelled warnings went unregarded.

Sailing only half full when she should have been crowded with fashionable ladies and gentlemen to her deck rails, the *Atlantic* was hardly outside of Sandy Hook when she went crunching through a wide, low-lying field of ice. Some of her paddle blades were damaged; the sea was too rough to allow for repairs; and she had to "prosecute her voyage" at a cautiously reduced speed. Six days out, one of her condensers gave way and she hove to for forty hours. Instead of breaking all records as she was expected and primed to do, she took a dawdling thirteen days to get into the Mersey. To Americans awaiting news of a triumphant dash across the ocean, the report of this slow crossing was anguish. To British reporters it was a nice, cruel chance to enlarge upon the shortcomings of the new boat from New York with its "dumpy funnel and bulky lines," and to take pot shots at Yankee pretensions. People were speculating about the meaning of her figurehead, wrote a Liverpool journalist. Some thought it represented Neptune; some felt it must be Wordsworth's old Triton blowing his wreathéd horn. No, said others, it could only be Edward Knight Collins, blowing his own trumpet.

But the *Atlantic* was to have the last laugh. When her paddles were repaired and she was otherwise tightened down and tuned up, she tore back to New York in the record time of 10 days, 16 hours. She had delivered what she promised; the American public was delighted, American optimism newly enhanced. "It is the common notion," said George Wilkes, "that monster vessels are not safe, but while this is the common notion, Science, which is never deceived by prejudice, has been quietly increasing the size of ships, until the vessels of the Collins Line exceed the bulk of the *President* and *Great Britain*. Science will increase them larger still, though obliged to rib them with refined steel and line their enormous sides with double engines. Then ocean travel will be squared and ordered like lines upon the land; these new monsters of the deep will lie steadily upon the great bed of the ocean, beneath the motion of the waves, or that surface agitation, the greatest height of which has been ascertained to be only 25 feet, with an average of 18. This will veto sea-sickness; large saloons will take the place of ocean cells and coffins; luxury, safety and utility will be united, and those who enjoy the combined advantages will look back with surprise to the time when a world of one hundred millions of inhabitants were content to make their travel, and conduct their exchanges, in little acorns of 1000 tons, many of which once spread sheets of cotton goods to catch the chance breeze of the ocean as their only means of motion."

Thus began a long series of record-breaking crossings of the ocean that were watched, clocked, analyzed, and argued over with the statistical passion that later generations would give only to closely contested events at Shea Stadium, Le Mans or Wimbledon. The *Atlantic* was quickly followed into service by the *Pacific*, the *Arctic* and the *Baltic*. Together this foursome cornered the market on transatlantic luxury, and passed the speed record among themselves like runners in a relay race.

Unruffled, the Cunard Line added the *Asia*, a fine ship with a hull of British oak and engines by Napier that could drive her at a cruising speed of 12½ knots. Collins travelers were given to hyperbole and flights of chauvinist excitement; yet voyagers on the new Cunard ship also found cause for rapture. In a letter written as the *Asia* was getting ready to sail from Liverpool and sent off by tender, the English writer Martin Tupper described the departure for his wife. When "you mount the side and stand on the top deck . . . what a noble craft it is! Though so high-seeming above the water—there are 22 feet more of her beneath it; and though the splendid Saloon be 60 feet long, it is less than a quarter of her whole length. However, everybody knows what these miracles of man's art are, and with what quietness and ease that leisurely monster the engine does its work. . . . Well: it's eleven—and the multitudinous mail-bags . . . have been flung aboard; and the pair of pop-guns fired— and the American flag is 'broken down' at the foremast head—and the crew in musical time are pulling at all manner of hawsers, and painters, and sheets and so forth—and off we go: never to stop, please Heaven, till we've spanned the broad Atlantic. Amen."

But that keen taste for novelty, that propensity toward the epicene that Collins passengers had developed was no part of the Cunard ethos, and its famous conservatism had begun to look like backwardness. Within two years after the sailing of the *Atlantic*, Collins ships were carrying fifty percent more of first-class passengers than Cunard. Ocean travelers had come flocking to ships with a reputation for fashion, dash and a broad hint of recklessness nearly everyone seemed quite willing to countenance.

Developments in the age of steam commanded first attention, yet sailing ships still carried most of the people, rich and poor alike, who were minded to cross the ocean. One of these ships, small and anonymous in maritime history, became a morbid footnote in cultural history.

One midsummer day in 1850, the rich, slightly eccentric follower of Swedenborg, Henry James, took his seven-year-old boy, Henry Junior, on an excursion boat ride around New York Harbor. As father and son were studying the movements of water traffic running between the tip of Manhattan and Fort Hamilton, they were joined along the deck rail by a family friend, Washington Irving. In the ensuing talk, young Henry James overheard a sad piece of intelligence that meant very little to him, but very much to the community of American letters. The wild storm which had passed over the city yesterday, Washington Irving told the elder James, had driven the barque *Elizabeth* smash up against Fire Island, and Margaret Fuller was among those who had been drowned.

"I have a vague expectation of some crisis," Margaret Fuller had written to her mother from Italy. "My life proceeds as regularly as the fates of a Greek tragedy, and I can but accept the pages as they turn." Even more explicit as self-fulfilling prophecy was a last note sent to her Italian friend Constanza Arconati. "I had intended if I went by way of France to take the packet-ship *Argo* from Havre," she wrote. "I read of the wreck of the *Argo* returning from America to France. There were also notices of the wreck of the *Royal Adelaide*, a fine English steamer, and of the *John Skiddy*, one of the fine American packets. Thus it seems safety is not to be found in the wisest calculation. I shall embark more composedly in my merchant ship; praying, indeed fervently, that it may not be my lot to lose my babe at sea, either by unsolaced sickness, or amid the howling waves. Or that, if I should, it may be brief anguish, and Ossoli, he and I go together."

Soon after writing this, she had embarked with her new husband, Giovanni Angelo Ossoli, and her infant son Angelino, at Leghorn on a vessel affording them the most inexpensive passage they could find. The voyage, presumed to take the better part of two months, was made under the black shadows of a whole pack of Eumenides. When the

Elizabeth was still in the Mediterranean her captain came down with confluent smallpox. By the time they got to Gibraltar he was dead. Held in quarantine for a week there, the barque was finally allowed to proceed through the Pillars of Hercules with the first mate in command, and with the captain's widow more or less going along for the ride. They were hardly into the Atlantic when the baby Angelino, of whom the dead captain had made a pet to fondle and dandle, came down with smallpox, and the whole company went into a panic of apprehension. But as she nursed the infant back to health, the doom-conscious Marchesa d'Ossoli was not without kind help and passionately attentive company: traveling with her and her husband in a sort of *ménage à trois flottant* was Horace Sumner, a young and heartsick admirer from New England who had gone to Europe "to see cathedrals and Margaret," whom he had first known in the days at Brook Farm.

By July 18, the *Elizabeth* had come almost to her New World landfall; prospects for landing in New York on the following morning were considered to be good. According to the calculations of the first mate, the barque was somewhere between Cape May and Barnegat. Actually, she was much farther north—headed straight for the notoriously treacherous low-lying sands of the spit named Fire Island. When a crackling storm swept over New York City and up the coast in a series of drenching gales, the little ship was tossed and twisted out of control. Then the tons of Carrara marble and the bust of John C. Calhoun by Hiram Powers that she was carrying in her hold got loose and plunged through the bottom, sending her careening inshore while waves in great floods began to break over her deck. Imbedded in the soft sands, she was in sight of groups of men and women on shore—but these turned out to be human harpies from settlements on the Island waiting for wreckage to drift in, or for the waters to subside enough to allow them to board the ship and help themselves to anything of value that could be extracted from its cabins or the pockets of its cadavers. A few of the crew and passengers, including the widow of the captain buried at Gibraltar, did manage to swim or wade ashore. But, twelve hours after the barque had struck, Margaret Fuller, her husband and child, were still aboard along with others who innocently believed that the sight of shore was a promise of rescue—especially since so many landsmen were witness to their plight. But when rescue failed to come, and it was evident that the ship was breaking up, a steward offered to take the infant Angelino and try to carry him ashore in his arms. He would, he told Madame Ossoli, save him, or die in the attempt. Within twenty minutes his body and that of the child were washed up on the beach. Still clinging to disintegrating bits of rigging, the Ossolis were finally overcome and swept away. Neither of their bodies or that of the young swain Sumner were ever found.

"On Friday, July 19," wrote Ralph Waldo Emerson in his journal, "Margaret dies on rocks of Fire Island Beach within sight of and within sixty rods of shore. To the last her country proves inhospitable to her; brave, eloquent, subtle, accomplished, devoted, constant soul!"

Henry David Thoreau came to the scene of the wreck in the hope of salvaging any of Margaret's possessions and papers that might not have floated away. He found a few trifles that he thought were hers, but whatever manuscripts Madame Ossoli may have been bringing home, including her magnum opus *The History of the Roman Republic*, had been ruined or dispersed by the looters as they ransacked the passengers' quarters.

Many years later, recalling the Hudson River boat ride with his father, Henry James took a surprisingly detached view of the event. "The unfortunate lady," he wrote, "was essentially of the Boston connection; [she] must have been a friend of my parents." But most of the dynamic Margaret's literary colleagues were disconsolate. "I have lost in her my audience," said Emerson. "There should be a gathering of her friends and some Beethoven should play the dirge."

Jenny Lind, the miniature lady known as the Swedish Nightingale, came to America in September, 1850, aboard the *Atlantic*, "a most fitting fiddle-case, a suitable cage for such a bird." Phineas T. Barnum, the showman and author of fabulous hoaxes who was responsible for importing the songstress, was determined to be the first American to offer her a word of welcome. To make sure, he enl'sted the help of his friend D. A. Sidney Doane who, most conveniently, held the title of Health Officer of the Port of New York. Doane put Barnum up for the night in his house on Staten Island, then provided him with official clearance and a boat to take him out to the *Atlantic* as she lay at anchorage in Quarantine. But when Barnum climbed aboard and was escorted to Miss Lind's stateroom, there, big as life, was Edward Knight Collins. To make matters worse, the petite soprano was almost hidden by a huge bunch of roses just presented to her by the shipowner. But the effects of this contretemps were dissolved in the éclat of the occasion, and the party maintained civilities; the *Atlantic*, carrying the biggest number of passengers yet to travel on a single crossing, proceeded serenely to her Canal Street dock. Then Barnum's foresight turned things distinctly in his own favor. Jenny Lind's arrival was, in fact, a production in itself. "Thousands of persons covered the shipping and piers," wrote Barnum, "and other thousands had congregated on the wharf. The wildest enthusiasm prevailed as the steamer approached the dock. A bower of green trees, decorated with beautiful flags, was discovered on the wharf, together with two triumphal arches, one of which was inscribed 'Welcome, Jenny Lind!' The second was surmounted by the American eagle, and bore the inscription 'Welcome to America!' These decorations were not produced by magic, and I do not know that I can reasonably find fault with those who suspected I had a hand in their erection. My private carriage was waiting and Jenny Lind was escorted to it by Captain West [of the *Atlantic*]. The rest of the musical party entered the carriage, and, mounting the box at the driver's side, I directed him to the Irving House. I took that seat as a legitimate advertisement, and my presence on the outside of the carriage aided those who filled the windows and sidewalks along the whole route, in coming to the conclusion that Jenny Lind had arrived."

Barnum's embarrassing brush with Collins may have given him an idea of the power wielded by men who owned steamships. Within a year of the episode at Quarantine, he himself had become part owner of the 1,500-ton wooden paddle steamer *North America*. He and his partners planned to carry passengers and freight on a fast run to Ireland. The first sailing, advertised to take place on June 17, 1851, was postponed for a week. Then, when her passengers were all aboard, they were told that the sailing was canceled altogether and that they must disembark and take their luggage with them. With so bad a start, this project came to nothing. Cornelius Vanderbilt bought one half-interest in the steamer, allowing Barnum and two associates to retain the other half, and sent her around the Cape to San Francisco. Even such sterling auspices could not detain Barnum for long, however, and he quit the fleeting venture into shipping by selling his share in the *North America* to Daniel Drew. The Atlantic was thus denied the Barnum Line to Galway Bay with a shore excursion to Blarney. But, as history soon would show, not even Barnum in his prime could have outdone the showplace frivolities of ships that were already in the making.

On April 19, 1852, the *Pacific* breezed across from Liverpool to Sandy

Hook in 9 days, 20 hours, 15 minutes, to become the first ship, sail or steam, paddle or screw, ever to cross the Atlantic Ocean in less than ten days. Said *Punch*:

> A steamer of the Collins Line,
> A Yankee Doodle notion,
> Has also quickest cut the brine
> Across the Atlantic Ocean.
> And British agents, no way slow,
> Her merits to discover,
> Have been and bought her—just to tow
> The Cunard packets over.

Speed was the thing. "Speed!" shouted Senator Bayard. "Speed against which these British can never hope to compete. Speed of such magnitude as the Government of Britain and its chosen instrument, this man Cunard, ever visualized or could ever hope to achieve against America!" Representative Olds from Ohio seconded the Senator. "We have the fastest horses, the prettiest women, and the best shooting-guns in the world," said Mr. Olds, "and we must also have the fastest steamers. The Collins Line must beat the British steamers. Our people expect this of Mr. Collins and he has not disappointed them."

The only people Collins was disappointing were those with something more tangible than an emotional investment in his operations—the stockholders and the governors of the United States Treasury. His ships might swipe passengers from Cunard, break records and gain headlines, but his account books were written mostly in red. For anyone with an eye to see, it was clear before all the world that Collins was well ahead of "this man Cunard." But appearances were profoundly deceiving. The cost of running the new liners was prohibitive, and Collins' rigorous extravagance was not open to curbs or compromise. The pace at which the ships were driven—"vibration in a choppy sea," said one expert, "almost shook the Collins ships apart"—resulted in frantic patchings and overhaulings after every voyage. Speed demanded extra coal and larger crews. The sumptuous table set by the ships of the Collins Line made the Cunard Line menus look like boarding school fare, but the outlay for such largess was crippling. "No vegetable, fruit, game," noted one traveler, "or other rarity that can be kept for fifteen days in large masses of ice, is neglected."

Here, for instance, is an example of an ordinary day's bill of fare for dinner:

SOUPS—*Green turtle   Potage au choux*
BOILED—*Hams   Tongues   Cold corned beef   Turkeys, oyster sauce
    Fowl, parsley sauce   Leg of mutton, caper sauce*
FISH—*Cod, stuffed and baked   Boiled bass, Hollander sauce*
ROAST—*Beef   Veal   Mutton   Lamb   Geese, champagne sauce   Ducks
    Pigs   Turkey   Fowls*
ENTRÉES—*Macaroni au gratin   Filet of pigeon au Cronstaugh
    Croquette de poisson à la Richelieu   Salmi de canard sauvage
    Poulets, pique, sauce tomato   Côtelette de veau à la St. Gara
    Fricandeau de tortue au petit pois   d'Oyeis en cassis
    Epigram d'agneau, sauce truppe*
VEGETABLES—*Green corn   Green peas*
SALADS—*Potato and plain*
PASTRY—*Baked vermicelli pudding   Apple fritters, hard sauce
    Almond cup custards   Red currant tartlets   Apple tarts
    Open puffs   Cranberry tarts   Coventry puffs, &c.*
DESSERT—*Fruit   Nuts   Olives   Cakes, &c., &c.
    Coffee   Lemonade (frozen)*

One index to comparative costs assumed by Collins and Cunard was provided by the salaries they paid their captains: the Collins skippers got 6,000 dollars per year, the Cunard men 2,500. Little wonder that on the first twenty-eight voyages of the Collins Line the average loss per trip was almost 17,000 dollars.

By the end of his first year of operations, Collins could see his financial picture with clarity: his subsidy was going to be totally inadequate. To set about getting better terms from the Government, he threw one of the most novel parties in American history. Just when excitement about the Collins Line's record breakers was at its height, he sent the handsome new *Baltic* to the Potomac—in February, 1852. His gesture had the look of fun and exhibitionistic patriotism, but it was really bare-faced lobbying. Mooring his ship off Alexandria, he bid all official Washington to come and see what he had wrought. Down from the capital in boat-loads came President Millard Fillmore and a party of Cabinet members, Senators and Congressmen—anyone whose favor might be bought—or bent in the right direction—by food, wine and the Collins touch. There were holdouts, of course—teetotalers and incorruptibles—and a few, like Jefferson Davis, who took the reasonable line that if English ships could carry American mails at half the price charged by American ships they ought to be allowed thus to serve American interests.

But to men like Representative Polk, brother of the ex-President, this attitude was venial. "May I stand upon the floor of the American Congress," he said, "and find men who are willing to measure our greatness by the circumference of the dollar—a dollar sir!—measure American greatness by a round dollar—and thus pander to British interests, to bow the pliant knee, and say to the power that assailed us at Lexington, that flashed the first gun from Bunker's Hill—that fought us upon sea and land in 1812—that has been jealous of our prosperity and greatness ever since—'Good mother, won't you carry our mails for us?' Why, sir, I scorn, I despair this anti-American policy and sentiment!"

This sort of oratorical music was still ringing in Collins' ears when, within a few months, he learned that his subsidy had been almost doubled: instead of a mere 19,250 dollars per voyage, he would get 33,000, or 858,000 dollars per annum. The marvelous aggrandizement represented a boon hardly to be expected. Yet the Government's magnanimity was even more extensive: Collins was relieved of his contractual obligation to build a fifth ship. Some citizens were dubious about the whole thing, but everyone found it easy to agree with Senator Borland of Arkansas, who said, "Mr. Collins' tongue seems to have been gifted with the spell of the 'open sesame' to the heart of Congress."

Others came to feel that the subsidy helped to provoke the ruin of the Collins Line. "The managing owners," said one of the doubters, "seem to have acted upon the presumption that they had the national treasury to fall back upon, that prudence and economy were unnecessary." Yet the decision to give a boost to the Collins enterprise was a popular one. What was better or more visible evidence of the self-conscious nation's new place in the world than peerless steamships flying the Stars and Stripes?

More than ever the Atlantic was the arena where champions were proved. After the discovery of gold in California, packets and clippers had gone away in scores to round the Horn, or to deliver passengers like cattle at Chagres for the jungle trek across the Isthmus of Panama. "The United States has never yet done anything," said a man in *Harper's*, "which has contributed so much to their honor in Europe, as the construction of this Collins line of steamers. We have made a step in advance of the whole world. Nothing before floated equal to these ships."

Such statements sounded like expressions of open or nascent chauvinism, but they were nothing of the sort. One Captain McKinnon of the British Royal Navy, writing in the same periodical, compared his "sailor's experience" on a trip to New York on a Cunard ship with a return to England in a Collins liner. He found the officers of Cunard cold and unobliging, sadly lacking in "the universal and cordial civility and attention in Yankee vessels." He had read some of the snide and patronizing reports of American steamships that had appeared ever since the colorless *Washington* had lumbered into Southampton. He had heard praises heaped on the Cunard Line and its already "old" traditions and, though he considered himself a patriotic Briton, he had had enough. "The vast and heavy bowsprit of the Cunard Line is an absolute excrescence," he wrote, "a bow-plunging, speed-stopping, money-spending, and absurd acquiescence in old-fashioned prejudices about appearance, and what the old school attempt to swamp all arguments by condemning as *not ship-shape!* Pshaw! What confounded stuff! This is the sort of feeling that prevents improvements, and allows Brother Jonathan to build the finest sea-going steamers in the world, which the Collins liners undoubtedly are."

The robust *Atlantic* was grinding through heavy seas midway between Cape Clear and New York early in January, 1851, when she broke her mainshaft and became mechanically inoperable. To divert her toward the shorter run to Halifax, her captain ordered all sail spread. But when weather continued to buffet his ship, he decided to steer for Bermuda. This change of course brought only further damage and more frustration. When wild seas had snapped off his bowsprit and his jib boom, smashed his paddle boxes and dented his paddle wheels, he turned about in an attempt to ride prevailing winds back to Queenstown.

For nearly a month, anxiety about the fate or whereabouts of the overdue liner sent chills of rumor through the City of New York. It is inflated, foolish and antique in its phrasing, yet the following account from the New York *Herald* of the ultimate arrival of news about the missing ship suggests the degree of fascination Americans found in Collins and his vessels: "By the arrival of the steamship *Africa* at this port . . . we received the most welcome and gratifying intelligence that it has ever been our pleasure to place before our readers, namely, the safety of the steamship *Atlantic*. We congratulate our readers and the community at large on the receipt of this welcome intelligence. The *Atlantic*, it seems, experienced a similar accident to that which the steamship

Niagara, of the Cunard Line, met with about a year ago, and which disabled her on her trip to New York. Now, having made this joyful announcement, let us describe, if we can, the sensation with which the arrival of the *Africa*, and the expectation of her bringing intelligence of the *Atlantic*, created in New York and vicinity. No sooner were her guns heard in the city, than hundreds, and we may say thousands, of our citizens rushed to the Battery and to all the docks on the North River from the depot of the Collins' Line of steamships to Castle Garden, to ascertain whether the *Atlantic* had been heard from. They were tantalized by the reports of the *Africa's* guns, as they fired, one after another, for upwards of an hour, and many an eye was strained in looking for the blue and red lights, the signs of the vessels of the Collins Line. At length a steamship was seen approaching the city from Quarantine; but the signals which she bore were not those of the *Atlantic* or any vessel of the Collins Line. 'But if this is not the *Atlantic* it must be the *Africa*, and she will, no doubt, bring some intelligence of the *Atlantic*,' argued the more intelligent of the anxious multitude. It was the *Africa*; and as she came up the bay, firing gun after gun, it was believed by the thousands on the lookout that the vessel would not expend so much powder to announce her own arrival only. 'It must be that the *Africa* brings good news of the *Atlantic*, or she would not fire so many guns,' said the multitude. 'What can it mean? What is the object of this uncommon firing?' was the inquiry on every side, and the response was, 'The *Atlantic* is safe; the *Atlantic* has been heard from.' Soon the *Africa* approached her dock; but she did not move half fast enough to satisfy the impetuosity of the thousands who felt as if every moment was an hour until her arrival. At length the *Africa* reached her wharf in Jersey City and when she got within hailing distance one of the officers ascended the paddle-box and with his trumpet announced, 'The *Atlantic* is safe; she has put into Cork with a broken shaft.' A shout of rejoicing at once went up, which made the welkin ring, which was continued for several minutes. During all this time the crowd grew larger, while many of those who heard the glad news ran home to tell it to their families and friends.

"But what shall we say of the excitement which the account of the safety of the *Atlantic* created in New York, and especially in the lower part of the city? No sooner were the guns of the *Africa* heard than every one living on the north side of the city hurried to the docks in the neighborhood of the North River, and eagerly sought for any information concerning this favourite vessel. The publication office of this paper was crowded to such an extent that it was with great difficulty the gentlemen connected with the establishment could find a way of ingress or egress. From our establishment the excitement was carried to all parts of the city. 'The *Atlantic* is safe' was announced from the stages of the different theatres. The performances were temporarily suspended in those places of amusement by the cheering which ensued; and out of doors the welcome intelligence was passed from person to person, that 'the *Atlantic* is safe,' until every one in the city was acquainted with the gratifying intelligence. We confine ourselves within the limits of truth and fact, when we say that every man, woman, and child in our great metropolis went to bed last night with a 'thank God' on their lips that the *Atlantic* was safe."

The big, tough-looking *Atlantic* with her imp of a figurehead trumpeting over the waves remains the archetypal liner of her decade. First, fast and indestructible, she stands for the brash and lighthearted moment of American success on the ocean. Her sister ship, the *Arctic*, stands for just the opposite.

With her broadside push and power the *Atlantic* may have opened an era, but it was the doomed and far more beautiful *Arctic*—the ship whose "melancholy fate, accompanied with such a fearful sacrifice of life as filled the Republic with grief and consternation"—that conclusively closed it.

When the *Arctic* was launched early in 1850, thirty thousand people came to see what one reporter (who forgot the *Great Britain*) called "the most stupendous vessel ever constructed in the United States, or the world, since the patriarchal days of Noah." The carriages of the fashionable crowded all nearby streets and yards as "every point of eminence presented masses of heads, forming a *coup d'oeil* of surprising interest." The *Arctic* was far more handsome than the *Atlantic*, more graceful, and more meticulously tricked out in the stuff of the period that spelled opulence, including a Spirits Room. Of her grand saloon a passenger wrote: "Magnificent mirrors, stained glass, silver plate, costly carpets, marble centre tables and pier tables, luxurious sofas and arm-chairs, and a profusion of rich gilding give an air of almost Oriental magnificence to a room one hundred feet in length and twenty-five feet in breadth." In aspect and proportion she was, in effect, legendary. "Even the ancients," said one benumbed observer, "endeavoring to form a craft worthy of Neptune, god of the Ocean, never contrived a car so magnificent as this." Within months of her maiden voyage, almost everyone agreed that the *Arctic* was the finest and fastest ship Collins had yet put to sea.

When this "pride of the nation, the clipper of the seas, with everything auspicious about her," sailed from Liverpool on September 20, 1854, the occasion had the air of a Collins family party. Among the 233 passengers were Edward Knight Collins' wife Mary Ann, his youngest son Henry Coit, his only daughter, also named Mary Ann, and seven members of the family of James Brown, one of the banker brothers whose support had made the Collins Line possible in the first place. Other passengers traveling as guests of the line were Collins' brother-in-law Samuel M. Woodruff, whose wife was with him, and a little boy who was making the voyage for his health—the crippled eight-year-old son of the ship's commander, Captain James C. Luce. The grandest passenger was the Duc de Gramont, who was en route to Washington to present his papers as *attaché libre* to the French legation, accompanied by his valet. A number of well-to-do New York businessmen were on board, and so was Henry Hope Reed, Professor of Rhetoric and English Literature at the University of Pennsylvania. The professor had just made a tour of literary England, in the course of which he renewed an acquaintance he had made with William Makepeace Thackeray in America two years before. Bidding the professor *bon voyage*, Thackeray had said that he wished he himself were going over on the *Arctic*, and promised he would soon come once more to lecture to American audiences. Another passenger was a new American citizen, English-born Frederick Catherwood, an artist and an archeologist whose drawings, inspired by Piranesi, had grandly depicted the ruins of the Ancient World from Rome to Karnak and Baalbec. Later, Catherwood had been perhaps the first of his profession to make the discovery that Mayan culture was indigenous to the New World.

"What a freight was that!" said a preacher just a few weeks later. "There was manhood in its strength and daring, and woman in her trust and beauty, and youth with its sunny gladness and buoyant expectancy; there was the professional man with his clustering honors, the government messenger entrusted with important document, the scholar whose name was adorned with literary distinction, the artist with his renown, the merchant with his commissions and treasures, and the man of elegant leisure and refined tastes." Distinction, alas, would confer neither immunity nor exemption.

Seven days out on a voyage that had been businesslike and without event, the *Arctic* began to slip in and out of patches of heavy fog off the Grand Banks. But such enveloping pockets were familiar to anyone who had sailed those waters, and only to be expected. Captain Luce, one of the group of old packet skippers whom Collins had enlisted to drive his steamers, sent the *Arctic* full speed ahead in the risky and fearless manner that had become a Collins tradition. Fog was a nuisance— but not much more than that. In fact, the, first Commodore of the Cunard Line, the famous Captain Judkins, felt that the way to overcome fog was not by reducing the paddles to half speed but by tearing through the gloom at full speed. In that way, he said, you are "sooner out of it." Another thick-skinned voyager reported a not uncommon experience. "The fog hung heavy over the Banks," he wrote, "keeping the look-out in the forecastle busy jamming his wind in the fog-horn, warning the fishermen of our approach. From all accounts the warning often came too late, for the steamers were often on them before they could avail themselves of it. There was often only a scream heard, then, a slight crash, the rattling of timbers along the side of the destroying vessel, and all was over with the fishermen, but the steamer kept right on her course." His ship, "somewhere near the Banks, actually cut right through the centre of a barque in a fog, but happily without injury to herself save the loss of her bowsprit and figurehead."

As the *Arctic* cut full speed through a blinding wad of fog, even the sound of a toy horn was not heard by those on board the little 250-ton iron-hulled French steamship *Vesta*, en route to France with all sails set, one day out from the island of St. Pierre. Its childish warning would perhaps not have mattered anyway. As he peered through the murk about noon on the twenty-seventh of September, the lookout in the bow of the *Arctic* suddenly gave a shout. "I rushed to the deck," said Captain Luce, "and just got out when I felt a crash forward and at the same moment saw a stranger steamer under the starboard bow. In another moment she struck against the guards of the *Arctic* and passed astern of us. The bows of the strange ship appeared to be cut off literally for about ten feet. Seeing that in all probability she must sink in a few minutes, after taking a hasty glance at our own ship and believing that we were comparatively uninjured, my first impulse was to try to save the lives of those on board the stranger."

"As a swordfish might wound a whale," the propeller-driven *Vesta* had plunged her long sharp stem lethally into the *Arctic*'s hull. Some men among the *Vesta*'s 147 passengers—fishermen and salters—also believing their ship to be sinking, rushed to lifeboats that might take them to the safety of the *Arctic*. In the confusion, one boat was lowered, swamped, and thirteen people were drowned. Captain Luce by this time had lowered one of his own boats and sent it to the *Vesta*'s side. This gesture was humane, but, in making it, he had lost time that would soon appear unredeemable. The damage to his own ship, which he at first regarded as negligible, suddenly became shockingly clear. When the *Vesta*, lost in the fog from any view of the *Arctic*, was found by her engineers to be badly maimed but easily afloat, her captain headed for the harbor of St. John's, Newfoundland. With three holes punched in her hull below the waterline, and her officers finally aware of her mortal jeopardy, the *Arctic* was set speeding for Cape Race, sixty miles away. In a feckless attempt to cover the gouges in the hull, sails were draped over the prow. But water continued to pour in over her furnaces at the rate of a thousand gallons per second. The ship was slowed, then altogether silenced. The race for land was over almost before it had begun.

As the *Arctic*'s paddles relaxed to a lazy churning, Captain Luce assigned women and children to the five remaining lifeboats and ordered his men to hammer together the biggest raft that time would allow for. Young Stuart Holland, from Washington, an apprentice engineer, was detailed to fire the ship's signal gun once every minute. The sea remained calm, the fog had dissolved into mere wisps. The ship was intact, land was near, and the presence of other vessels in the area seemed likely. Then the great dripping paddles stopped altogether. The eerie stillness, the list and drag of the ship, were too much for some members of the crew. In a sudden "extinction of all authority on board," they commandeered all but one of the lifeboats, then cut themselves free of the *Arctic* and the jurisdiction of Captain Luce.

If these men had ever heard the decision reached in the case of the United States versus Alexander Holmes in 1842 in the Circuit Court, Philadelphia, they were now choosing to ignore it. This decision had it that "in case of extreme danger, the sailors are bound by law, if need be, to sacrifice their lives to save the lives of the passengers; that the sailors had no right to sacrifice the lives of passengers to save their own; and that while two sailors might struggle with each other for the same plank which can save but one, if the passenger is on the plank even the law of necessity will not justify the sailor in taking it away from him." If it were only a matter of sailors, the Court held, "all should have an equal chance for life, and where the sacrifice of life is necessary the doomed one should be fairly selected by lot." How this lottery was going to be set up and agreed upon by two or more sailors on a drifting plank was not spelled out. On the *Arctic*, in any case, only one lifeboat, under the command of the chief engineer, was left for the use of passengers. Otherwise, it was *sauve qui peut.*

About four hours after the collision, the bow of the *Arctic* rose high in the air. Then, sinking backward in a grotesque chord of wailing sounds caused by air through her funnel, she sank in a hiss of steam and a bubbling up of wreckage. On the raft, floated free, were seventy-two men and four women. Captain Luce stood by his post to the end. As his ship plunged down he held his crippled youngster in his arms. Together they were dragged under by suction, then sent spiraling to the surface. As he floated among splinters and spars, he was pulled under a second time, separated from his son, then reunited with him in the swirling waters. There, said the Captain, who, miraculously, was to survive, "a most awful and heartrending scene presented itself to my view; women and children struggling amidst pieces of wreckage of every kind, calling on each other and God to assist them. Such another appalling scene may God preserve me from ever witnessing—I was in the act of trying to save my child again when a portion of the paddle-box came crashing up edgewise and just grazed my head and fell with its whole weight on the head of my darling child. In another moment I beheld him a lifeless corpse on the surface of the waves."

Young Holland, heroic as the boy who stood on the burning deck "whence all but he had fled," had fired his last signal and died at his post. "Unmoved by the base desertion of others," said a published eulogy, "he continued firing the signal gun, that boomed like a death-knell over the waters, and when the wreck sank to its gloomy grave, he too became numbered with the dead. Was death ever more heroic?"

The century had a penchant for those who stuck to their guns, yet Holland's action soon became symbolic of far more than that. According to one historian, the whole American Merchant Marine was "scuttled and deserted on the 27th of September, 1854, when the *Arctic* sank with her commander at his post and the Washington lad, the young hero, at his gun, sending homeward the sad signal of distress and farewell, as if a premonition of the doom of American honor on the Atlantic."

The makeshift raft and its desolate waterlogged company had meanwhile floated into the clammy haze. By early evening the sea turned choppy, sending icy dousings over the edges and slopping up through the slatted flooring. Through the long night, at intervals of fifteen minutes or so, one survivor after another lost his grip, or released it, and, alive or dead, was washed away. By daybreak only a handful of men lay miserably clinging to the boards around which and under floated whitening bodies. When the ship *Huron*, out of St. Andrews, New Brunswick, bound for Quebec, spotted the raft, its human cargo consisted of just one man alive. His name was Peter McCabe and he was a member of the *Arctic's* crew.

Within three days, the *Vesta* had made her way into the harbor of St. John's. Not far away, two of the *Arctic's* lifeboats had reached the fishing village of Broad Cove on the Newfoundland shore.

Ten-day crossings were commonplace by this time. So were incidents of breakdowns or uncommonly bad weather that delayed ships for many days beyond their expected arrival times. Still, the *Arctic* was something special. When she did not come up the Narrows on September 30, and there was no sign of her on October 1, a little *frisson* of anxiety touched those who were waiting for her. Slightly puzzled, but not alarmed, E. K. Collins was moved to speculate publicly upon what might have delayed her. The *Arctic* had actually been at the bottom of the ocean for ten days when, on Saturday, October 8, the New York *Tribune* carried a reassuring statement: "Mr. Collins attributes the detention of the *Arctic* to the breaking down of her machinery. He is of the opinion that, instead of putting back, she is coming on under sail, and may be expected to arrive at this port today or Sunday." This seemed a reasonable speculation. Everyone in the city remembered how, three years earlier, the long-overdue *Atlantic* had turned up in Ireland. But Sunday came and went, and so did Monday and Tuesday. On the evening of October 10, the barque *Lebanon*, carrying eighteen *Arctic* survivors, arrived off Sandy Hook. These men, transferred to the pilot boat *Christian Berg*, were brought up the harbor in the dark morning hours of October 11 like so many ancient mariners with tales to tell.

"I was waked this morning by the voices of newsboys," wrote a young lawyer, George Templeton Strong, in his diary, "something about 'the *Arctic* and four hundred lives,' and sent out at once for the extra. What a chill that proclamation must have sent into scores of households! How many people sprang up at the sound of that half-inarticulate nasal cry, and hurried off to get the paper and refused to entertain the idea that they had heard the announcement right, and paid their sixpences and unfolded their purchases in desperate haste and saw the terrible truth in print! Allen, I. G. Pearson, James Brown, Woodruff—to those households and many more it was the voice of death."

In a sad session quickly dismissed, the Board of Aldermen passed a resolution instructing City Hall to lower its flags to half mast for three days. By midmorning "the metropolis assumed the appearance of one great funeral." Business at the Merchants' Exchange was canceled for the day; the Corn Exchange rooms were shrouded in crepe. The city was draped in mourning from Bowling Green to Fourteenth Street. "The business streets," said James Gordon Bennett, "usually so gay and bustling, were filled with little groups of men whose solemn countenances showed that they were fully impressed with the belief that no common disaster had befallen the city. In the home circle, the matter was talked over in whispers, and everywhere was expressed the deepest regret. . . .

"The feeling extended beyond those who had any relatives, friends, or acquaintances, for the Collins steamships are the pride and glory of New York, and our citizens regard their triumphs or their defeats—their safety or their dangers—as those of the city itself. This will account for the great depression which could be seen everywhere in the city. It is beyond description. It appeared that a great pall had been lowered upon us, and that everything was overshadowed in its gloom."

Edward Knight Collins was on his way home from Washington when the story of the *Arctic* preceded him to New York. When his train reached its Hudson River depot, he took the Jersey ferry across to Manhattan. It was four A.M. when, disembarking, he was given the calamitous news. He went at once into seclusion at his house in Larchmont, where, some days later, he received a letter, posted at Quebec, from Captain Luce. "It becomes my painful duty," wrote the Captain, "to inform you of the total loss of the *Arctic*, under my command, with many lives, and I fear among them must be included your own wife, daughter and son, of whom I took a last leave at the moment when the ship was going down."

With four days to prepare their sermons, clergymen were ready on the Sunday with jeremiads and elegiacs from, so to speak, the horse's mouth—Jeremiah, 49:23: "for they have heard evil tidings; they are faint-hearted; there is sorrow on the sea."

"The past week will be an epoch in the history of public sorrow," said one minister. "The loved and honored, the strong and beautiful, have found a grave together, the waves their winding sheet, the winds shrieking, the billows resounding their requiem."

In his evening sermon at Plymouth Church, Brooklyn, the Reverend Henry Ward Beecher deftly mingled sociology with hints of predestination. "Death was the plot that steered the craft," he told his flock, "and no one knew it. He neither revealed his presence nor whispered his errand. And in the morning the waiters served the titled and the rich. In the evening the lusty strength of the engineer was a greater title than money or coronets."

Unlike the newspapers, already speaking with arrant hypocrisy about the "wicked recklessness of speed," Reverend Beecher acceded to the hand of God: "Oh, what a burial was there!" he shouted over the pews. "It was an ocean grave. The mists alone shrouded them. No spade prepared the grave, no sexton filled up the hollow earth. Down, down they sank, and the quick returning waves smoothed out every ripple and left the sea as if it had not been and the place which knew them knows them no more for ever."

To others, the event served as an index: technology, civilization, the conduct of daily affairs—all were getting out of hand. "What becomes of the whole theory of progress," asked a journalist, "when men approaching or leaving, or resting in this metropolitan City of the United States have little more security than among the nomadic tribes of the desert? Is this an exaggeration? Look at our steamers— look at our railways—look at our streets. We have now no promise in traveling a hundred miles, that a misturned switch or a concussion will not smash trains palpitating with humanity into shrieking despair and mortal anguish. Our great street, Broadway, at this instant is so greasily filthy that variously from one hundred to five hundred horses fall down in the muck each day. May we not accept the old average of uncertainties and vibrate between the crib and the coffin with a less menacing swing of life's pendulum?"

Johnny-on-the-spot, Nathaniel Currier lost no time in capitalizing upon the mournful music of these elegies. As he had in the case of the *President*, he produced a handsome print of the foundering *Arctic*, surrounded by drowning figures while one top-hatted figure floated away on a raft—and saw that it was available to the public while the cries of grief were still reverberating.

Winter came on and for months the city mourned its many dead. Yet passenger lists of the remaining Collins liners were still long and distinguished, including large and affluent families setting out en masse on the grand tour of Continental spas and monuments that had almost become obligatory. In the following June, for instance, *paterfamilias* Henry James, Sr., "marched aboard the S.S. *Atlantic* of the Collins Line with his wife and five offspring and a French maid." Before the year was out, more than seven thousand voyagers had dallied in the plum-colored plush saloons of the *Atlantic*, the *Pacific*, the *Baltic*, and had lingered over their gourmet tables. A good part of this booming traffic was the consequence of the withdrawal of all of Cunard's ships so that they could be sent trooping to the Black Sea with boatloads of men and horses for the Crimean War. But most of the bookings were due to the still-untarnished glamor of the Collins operation and its two-fold promise: food and service on the scale of Delmonico's, speed in all weathers that no other ships could match.

The Crimean War had to come to an end before the Cunard Line could regroup its forces and reenter the Atlantic lists. When hostilities did finally cease, Cunard was more than ready to challenge Collins every inch of the way from Tuskar Light to Sandy Hook. The ship groomed to do this was the *Persia*—one of the most beautiful steamships of all time. Although she was advanced enough to have an iron hull, she was still driven by paddle wheels powered by Robert Napier's masterwork engines; and she kept voluminous sails in reserve. Her iron bow stretched out like an eagle's beak 390 feet from her stern; her two black and Cunard-red funnels stood sturdily fore and aft of great humped and embossed paddle boxes. Primed to race

Collins' *Pacific* across the wintry ocean and so regain the speed record for Britain, the *Persia* made her bid and was almost totally wrecked in the effort. Trumpeted as the finest and largest vessel afloat, she came hangdog and overdue into New York only to learn that, by tragic default, she was the victor after all.

On January 23, 1856, the *Pacific*—the ship that was the first ever to cross the ocean in nine days—sailed from Liverpool with an oddly balanced complement: 141 crew members and 45 passengers—statistics that reflected the hesitancy of travelers to venture, even in the "equable temperature" of steam-heated accommodations, onto the midwinter sea. Moored at the Huskisson Dock in Liverpool when the *Pacific* sailed away was the new Cunard liner *Persia*. While the competitive notion was not official, the *Persia* was prepared to give the *Pacific* the advantage of days at sea before she would attempt to catch up with her. Meantime, she hung back, to lay in supplies and to entertain her admirers.

The *Pacific* was hardly out of sight when the *Persia* welcomed aboard visitors who were expected to scan her "noble proportions," linger in her "*salle des dames*, magnificently fitted up in true Oriental taste," and sit down to "a *déjeuner* laid out in the main saloon, consisting of every delicacy the season afforded." In the course of many toasts, one of the party of civic authorities and shipping magnates rose to drink the health of the *Persia*'s captain, C. H. E. Judkins. It was his hope, he said, that in spite of the fact that the *Pacific* was already at sea, the good Captain would make sure that the new Cunard ship would overtake and pass her. Captain Judkins responded with personal modesty and a Cunard officer's innate reserve. He had a new career before him, he said: he was now entrusted with the command of an iron ship. But, as in the past, he would simply do his duty and "ever have regard to safety before speed." The disclaimer was a formality; everyone was convinced that when the *Persia* dropped her hawsers and cast off, the chips in the great ocean stakes would be down.

As she followed in the wake of her American rival, her captain was ignorant of one fact—a fact that would prove literally inescapable. Ice in the proportions of sea-borne glaciers had moved far down into the North Atlantic and now, like a drifting continent, covered all of that part of it cut by sea lanes. Five days out—hot in pursuit of the

Pacific as well as the reputation of E. K. Collins—the *Persia*, her paddles churning at 11 knots, pounded head-on into a field of ice. Her graceful fiddle bow was blunted, sixteen feet of her starboard rivets were snapped off like buttons, the rims of her paddles turned and twisted into tangles of disjointed metal. Nothing like this had ever before happened to a Cunard ship. But, unlike all of her predecessors, the *Persia* had a hull made of iron and was thus able to withstand a concussion that would have sent any of her ancestors to the bottom. Buckled under, her head heavy in the water but still buoyant, she kept her course, forgot all about a race for supremacy, and set her big wheels working toward New York. There, expecting to be greeted by her chosen rival, she found no sign, no word.

The *Pacific* had disappeared, and without a trace—except, possibly, for some ornamental doors "with white or glass handles." These were observed in a field of floating ice by the *Edinburgh*, New York to Glasgow, steaming along a few days later in the same sea lane the Collins steamer had likely traversed. Most maritime experts came to feel that she had crashed into an iceberg or, like the *Persia*, into a shelf of ice, against which her straight bow and wooden hull were no defense. This belief was strengthened by reports from ships that had made hazardous crossings at the very same time.

"At seven o'clock in the morning," wrote a passenger on one of them, "we saw a spectacle which none on board will ever forget; it was, in fact, the finger of Providence, and some more deserving than I and others must have been on board. The whole veil of fog rose like a curtain, and we looked upon an ocean scene beautiful, fearful, and grand. The atmosphere as far as the eye could reach was clear; the sun shone brightly on a continuous chain of icebergs about a hundred feet high, intermingled with fields of ice. Chain after chain burst upon the sight, and the sight was awfully impressive. In less time than it has taken to write this the curtain descended, and all became obscurity again. The captain took the hint and turned his ship towards England for the remainder of the day, and towards the south at night, not resuming his course to America until the following morning."

While the *Pacific* left no tangible record or conclusive trace, her fate may be even more tellingly inferred from an account left by a passenger on the *Persia* as the Cunard ship sailed the very same waters that closed over the *Pacific*. "The *Persia* rode the buffetings of a strong sea without incident for almost three days," according to this passenger.

"But on Tuesday the wind and the sea both got very strong, and everything indicated that a storm would soon prove [her] powers. . . . Accordingly sails were set, but the wind increased . . . and saved us the trouble of taking in our main try-sail by snapping the gaff in two. It blew a fearful hurricane for sixteen hours. One sea struck her so heavily as to carry away one of her large sponson boats."

This storm was only the beginning of a relentlessly perilous passage. "We encountered another storm on Friday," reported the log-keeping passenger, "which carried away our head boards and very nearly walked off with another of our boats. . . . This hurricane blew from the southeast, and lasted about fourteen hours. Saturday evening was moderately calm, and we all went to bed that night in comfort, thinking we would have one night's quiet rest after so much tossing and tumbling; but this night proved the most dangerous of all to us, for about 2 o'clock, A.M., the inhabitants of the *Persia* were roused from sleep by a violent concussion, which we afterwards ascertained was caused by striking a small iceberg. Fortunately the officer of the watch had stopped the engines before she struck, but her impetus was so great that she cut through this floating mass of ice, and ran far into a field of ice before she stopped. It was then necessary to steam out of this unpleasant position, and in doing so the ice got entangled in our paddle-wheels, tearing off five of our floats, and even breaking up the immense iron bars upon which the floats are fastened. As soon as we got clear of the ice we had to set about repairing our legs . . . [the paddle wheels] which kept us like a log upon the water the most part of Sunday. While we were doing this the ice was slowly sailing past us, and as far as the eye could reach ice was seen upon the waters north, south, east and west; we appeared surrounded and hemmed in. . . ."

Facing up to the fact that its famous fleet had been cut in half by two reverberant disasters within two years, the Collins Line revised its advertisements. "The ships of this Line have improved watertight bulkheads," read the new notices, "and to avoid danger from ice, will not cross the Banks north of 42 degrees until after the first of August."

It persevered bravely, but the Collins Line was in deep trouble. Even before the disappearance of the *Pacific*, the line's staggering financial losses had supplied fresh ammunition to forces in Congress that had long nursed resentment at what they felt was the Government's untoward generosity to a select group of New York businessmen. As a "catspaw against the lion," E. K. Collins had done well. Whenever one Congressman or another showed consternation at the cost of Government support for his "palaces of the ocean," still another Congressman pointed to his unequivocal conquest of "this man Cunard." But, in the face of the company's relentless losses, first of money, then of ships, men who resented Collins' *persona grata* relationship with powerful influences in Washington opened fire.

Among them was the Democrat from Arkansas, Senator Borland. "The influence of this line has already full sway in the *executive* counsels of this Government," he said. "It has already the monopoly of the newspaper press of this metropolis; and, remorseless still, like some huge and hungry boa constrictor, is fast winding its torturous and fearful holds about the body and limbs of this Congress, until our strong ribs give way and our very heart seems ready to be squeezed out, in the ghastly form of appropriations, which, if this pressure be not removed, will pour the life-blood of the National Treasury into the capacious and rapacious maws of bankers and speculators."

Beset and beleaguered, Collins and his faithful backers nevertheless went ahead with the construction of the greatest ship of all, the *Adriatic*. Of 3,760 tons burden, designed by George Steers, the man responsible for the triumphant racing yacht *America*, she was a full seventy feet longer than her three famous sisters, queen of the United States merchant fleet, and the last word in those interior refinements and excesses associated with the name of Collins. She also sported something brand new to navigation—a calcium light, a sort of embryonic searchlight, affixed to her masthead, that was designed to extend the helmsman's vision at night for miles. But the April air in which she was launched was frigid, and continued to get colder. Under continual attack from Congress, faith in the Collins subsidy was being whittled away. By February, 1857, the subsidy was cut back from its handsome largess to its mean first figure of 385,000 dollars. Inadequate in 1853, this was hopelessly insufficient in 1857. Readying its masterpiece in one part of the city, the Collins Line was just about ready to close up shop in another.

Delays in the fitting of machinery caused the *Adriatic* to be late in coming to the rescue of Collins and Company. When she was finally declared in shape to put to sea, public interest had waned. Instead of assuming her place as the contemporary Leviathan, the *Adriatic* made her debut as a white elephant. When she got off to Liverpool in November, only one out of ten of all of her expensively fitted berths was occupied. She came back with a trifling few travelers in December, whereupon she was laid up and put into the deep freeze of a Manhattan winter.

Early in 1858, in spite of widespread sentiment that Collins ships had "elevated the American name and character" and "wrested from Great Britain the palm of the maritime dominion," the Government subsidy was withdrawn altogether. The *Adriatic*, advertised to sail for England mid-February, did not sail; and when the *Baltic* came in from Liverpool on the evening of February 18 and was secured to her berth, the Collins adventure on the ocean was at last a matter only of history. *Harper's* gave voice to a general feeling of impatience: "The Collins steamer which was advertised to leave this port on Saturday last did not do so. If the United States, with their peculiar advantages, can not maintain a line of ocean steamers without taxing the entire people of the Union to keep them afloat, then we had best stick to sailing ships, and leave the steam navigation of the ocean to John Bull."

A couple of months later, in a pathetic April Fool's Day ceremony at the foot of Canal Street, from which E. K. Collins absented himself, the little mothball fleet was auctioned off as a package to the highest bidder. He was Dudley B. Fuller, and he was the only one interested in bidding at all. For a mere fifty thousand dollars, the three great ships were delivered into the hands of a man whose only concern was to see that they would be employed, dismantled or painted blue—just as long as they returned a profit.

Before long the *Atlantic* and the *Baltic* were chartered for service as military transports by the United States Army. After the Civil War, the *Atlantic* was broken up at Cold Spring Harbor, New York. The *Baltic* lasted longer. With her engines removed, she became a sailing vessel carrying wheat from San Francisco to Europe. She was not sent to the breakers until 1880. For a little while, the *Adriatic* ran for the Havre Line. Then she was sold to the Lever Line, to carry British mails between Galway and New York. She set a record in this service, making the run from Ireland to Newfoundland in 5 days and 19 hours. At once, old regrets were aired. "This magnificent steamer," said one patriot, "alienated from the country that had refused to protect her and receiving the subsidy and flying the flag of our persistent and victorious rival, was an eloquent object lesson of the causes that had wrought ruin of the

American Merchant Marine." According to another, when the Stars and Stripes came down from the *Adriatic*'s peak, and the red ensign was run up, it was "a vivid sign of our national defeat and humiliation." The *Adriatic* could break records, but she could not pay her way. After a short life under British colors, she became a store ship off the coast of Africa. Beached there in 1885, she was left to rot.

As for Collins, his concern with the sea and shipping ended with the auction. He tried to make something of the discovery of coal and iron on some farm property he owned in Ohio, but little came of this, or of a succession of speculative ventures that preoccupied him for another twenty years. When he died in 1878, the name of Collins, like the Collins flag itself, was but a wrinkled and faded standard from the past.

❦ SECTION XII ❦

Commodore Vanderbilt: "Laboring for Daily Bread" / The North Star / Laughter in Southampton / Gazed at by the Sultan / Competition with Collins

N O IMAGE was more resonant to Americans of the 1850s than the figure of Edward Knight Collins in the glassy-eyed guise of Father Neptune, trumpeting his sovereignty from the prow of the S.S. *Atlantic*. But during the very same years of his comet-like rise and plummeting fall, men of less executive dash but more real financial acumen were risking fortunes on steamships—and one of these was Cornelius Vanderbilt. Collins' rivalry with Samuel Cunard abroad has tended to obscure his running battle with this equally power-ful rival at home. But the truth is that in Vanderbilt he encountered a man who would dog his every step through the most vital part of his career. Vanderbilt was jealous of Collins' triumphs, "officially" outraged—and perhaps genuinely appalled—by his extravagance, and eager to preempt his role as New York's king-pin shipping magnate. From the ordeal of the contest that ensued, Vanderbilt emerged with his temper frayed, his ocean ships scattered and unemployed, but with his riches intact and sacrosanct.

For years, just about all of the crisscrossing water traffic of New York and New Jersey and most of the traffic on Long Island Sound was under the control of Commodore Cornelius Vanderbilt. But when gold was discovered in California the subsequent demand for transportation by fortune hunters led him out of domestic waters onto the broad ocean. At first he concentrated solely on carrying packed boatloads of prospectors to the coast of Nicaragua, from which they might make their way across the isthmus to the Pacific and take ship northward. But as his fortunes swelled, Vanderbilt began to feel the tug of an ambition. After years of devotion to business he wanted to do something on the sea more daring than trucking goods between Staten Island and Fisher's Island, more satisfying to his tycoon's taste than running the sea-going equivalent of boarding houses for bachelors with banjos on their knees and California on their mind. He was a man who could do anything he pleased: his annual income already came to something in the neighborhood of three million dollars. Fifty-nine years old, he had worked all of his life, and he was in a mood to take his first vacation. True to his character—a mixture of the naïve and magniloquent— and the demands of his ego, this holiday would be no meditative retreat into some sylvan glade, but the grandest of grand tours. He would "do" the capitals of Europe, he decided, and do them literally under his own steam. He would take his eleven children with him, and, though he had started out in life as a bumpkin from the hills of Staten Island, his tour would come as close to the notion of a royal progress as money, ostentation and the protocols of capitalism would allow.

In these plans lay the seeds of two large developments: the Commodore's rise to a tit-for-tat rivalry with E. K. Collins on the Atlantic; the still unforeseen business of pleasure cruising that would, in the longest run, overwhelm every other kind of passenger travel.

Other people had yachts, some even had steam yachts. Vanderbilt would have nothing less than his own ocean liner. The result was the 2,500-ton *North Star*, built by Simonson under the Commodore's close supervision, at the cost of five hundred thousand dollars. When she was launched in the spring of 1853, she took the water like Cleopatra's barge. The rosewood furniture of the main saloon—two sofas, four couches, six armchairs—was Louis Quinze, updated by Victorian upholsteries of figured velvet plushes with green grounds filled with stylized bouquets of flowers. Leading off from the saloon were a cozy family's quarters of ten staterooms, enameled in white, each with a plate-glass door, berths fitted with silk lambrequins and hung with heavy lace curtains. Green and gold, crimson and gold, orange and gold—each stateroom had its own color scheme and, like the main saloon, was kept at a comfortable temperature by one of Van Horn's steam heaters hidden under an elaborate bronze trelliswork. A homey touch on the carved staircase leading from the saloon was a picture of Vanderbilt's Staten Island residence. The dining room carried further the indigenous American fancy of steamboat baroque: panels of Naples granite, the style of Breschia jasper, the surface of yellow Pyrenees marble. On the ceiling, scrollwork of purple, light green and gold surrounded medallions from which the faces of Webster, Clay, Calhoun, Washington and Franklin stared down upon a long table set with a glittering armory of silver, cups and dishes of ruby-colored china embellished with gold. The effect of it all was just what Vanderbilt had counted upon. "What," asked a local paper, "will the wealthy noblemen of England—the proprietors of sailing yachts of fifty and a hundred tons—say to a citizen of the United States appearing in their waters with a steamship yacht of twenty-five hundred tons burthen; a vessel large enough to carry the armament of a British seventy-four?"

A good part of the *North Star*'s crew was made up of young men from prominent families who simply wanted to be part of the Vanderbilt entourage. The steward of the Racquet Club was enticed aboard to serve as Purser and the ship had her own resident clergyman, a sacerdotal toady by the name of John Overton Choules ("The Commodore does the swearing," said the Reverend, "I do the praying")—and her own physician. The *North Star* was ready to go by mid-May. As sailing time drew near, patriarch Vanderbilt became a little misty-eyed. "I have a little pride," he said, "to sail over the waters of England and France, up the Baltic and through the Mediterranean and elsewhere, under this flag without a reflection of any kind that it is a voyage for gain— with such a vessel as will give credit to the enterprise of our country."

When it came time for the Commodore and his guests to board her on the morning of May 19, the only sea trial to which the *North Star* had been subject was a modest *giro* down the bay to Sandy Hook. This trip, judged as thoroughly satisfactory, was going to be partly repeated for the five hundred friends of the sailing party who came to bid *bon voyage*. The plan was to dine and wine them for a couple of hours, then send them all back from Sandy Hook in a harbor boat. Everything was set to go when the *North Star*'s firemen decided that the moment was propitious for calling a strike that might win them higher wages. The Commodore heard their complaints with contempt. Within the hour he dismissed every last man of them and hired a dockside collection of green hands, some of them "fresh from the rural occupations of life." One of them was so green in fact that, when he was told to strike two bells, he came back in a while to say that he could find only one.

At 10:30 A.M. the wheels of the grandest private yacht in modern history began slowly to turn. Three minutes later the *North Star* was caught on the tidal reef that lay just off the pier. Stalled, stuck, in the very first flight of his dream, the Commodore lost neither his self-possession nor his flair for the big gesture. He dispatched two telegrams: one to the Secretary of State, one to the Navy Department, requesting emergency space in the Navy's New York dry dock. Washington was of course happy to oblige. The *North Star* was allowed in for inspection and detained overnight. Damage was slight—the vessel had merely "lost her shoe." Next morning, eased through the gates of the dry dock to the cheers of a few faithful friends, she went boldly down the river firing salutes left and right as if to inform everyone in earshot that she was all right and on her way.

The voyage across was smooth, life aboard pious and even merry. Grace was said before every meal, prayer meetings held every evening. Otherwise the hours of the day were passed in leisure; the hours of the night in song. Soloists among the company modestly proposed themselves; choristers banded into volunteer groups; minstrels with riverboat repertoires emerged from the lower depths.

The *North Star* took on her English pilot on the first of June. Not far from the Needles he steered her nicely onto a bank of soft mud. But the next flood tide lifted her off and she went on to anchor that night in Southampton Water.

Some English journalists were awed; others saw the Commodore as an avatar, a living representative of the legends of Eldorado. "Mr. Vanderbilt is immensely rich," said one. "Such a costly and magnificent mode of travelling as that adopted by the owner of the *North Star* is perhaps without example. Brother Jonathan has certainly gone ahead of himself, and has, at least, surpassed everything of the kind hitherto done by millionaire Englishmen." The London *Daily News* reported: "An American merchant has just arrived in Europe on a pleasure trip. He has come by train from Southampton, and left his private yacht behind him in dock at that port. This yacht is a monster steamer. Her saloon is described as larger and more magnificent than that of any ocean steamer afloat, and is said to surpass in splendour the Queen's yacht. Listening to the details of this new floating palace, it seems natural to think upon the riches of her owner, and to associate him with the Cosmo de Medicis, the Andrea Fuggers, the Jacques Coeurs, the Richard Whittingtons of the past, but this is wrong. It took Florence nearly fifteen centuries to produce one Cosmo, and she never brought forth another. America was not known four centuries ago, yet she turns out her Vanderbilts, small and large, every year. The great feature to be noted in America is that all its citizens have full permission to run the race in which Mr. Vanderbilt has gained such immense prizes."

Encomiums aside, the only public event of any consequence involving the *North Star* travelers in England was a banquet given at the Victoria Rooms in Southampton by the Lord Mayor and leading citizens. All the eminent British and Americans who were invited sent regrets; some of these were stated curtly, some elaborately. Taken all together, the weight of their negations suggested that Vanderbilt and his party had set in motion a mass exodus. But these defections failed to curb the enthusiasm of the indefatigable boosters of the port of Southampton. Still aware of the defeat of the many promises the already defunct *Washington* had set up, they tended to view the Commodore as another forerunner, his *North Star* as the Judas goat that would lead the great ships of the North Atlantic into Southampton water instead of the well-traveled sea roads of the Mersey.

In the course of a long afternoon of toasts and responses, the Commodore contributed little more than his presence, but that in itself was edifying. He was extolled, as might be expected, as "a gentleman who owed his present high position entirely to his own industry and perseverance," and as an example of the new dispensation of enlightenment into which mankind had walked. "It is significant," said one of the suppliants for American trade, "of the advanced state of the world at this time, to behold a gentleman freighting a vessel with those who are nearest and dearest to him on earth, and confidently setting out to traverse the greater half of the globe, and pay his respects to the chief civilized nations." Finally he was cited, in the extravagance of the moment, "for the extent of his knowledge of mankind." Coaxed from his lumpish silence, Vanderbilt rose to the occasion. He was glad to see them, he said. It gave him sincere pleasure to make their acquaint-

ance, because they were all one people, he and they, newly bound by
the power of steam. He could not make a speech, he said. "It is not
in my trade. (Laughter.)" To show how grateful he was, he invited
all of the assembled company to board his ship next day for an excursion
around the Isle of Wight and on to Spithead.

Immediately after a day-long picnic on her open deck, the *North Star*,
"carrying with her the good wishes of all the lieges of Southampton,"
steamed off for ports in the Baltic. In Cronstadt, at last, a real royal
personage, in the form of the Grand Duke Constantine, came aboard for
a collation with an entourage of courtiers who clambered over the yacht
like schoolboys. Then the party sailed on to France.

In the course of the three weeks that the Vanderbilt party devoted to
Paris, a group of capitalists with close connections among old aristocratic families were bold enough to importune the Commodore. They
wanted him to join them in establishing a transatlantic steamship line
that would serve all the Americas—North, Central and South. "To
those overtures," reported a friend, "Mr. Vanderbilt gave no encouragement." When the *North Star* had sailed on into the Mediterranean and
reached Constantinople, the Frenchmen tried once more to interest
him in their plans. But the Commodore would not be diverted, even
by so vast a scheme for the ocean from "personal enjoyment and the
happiness of his circle."

Just folks from the hills of Staten Island, he and Mrs. Vanderbilt
went on depositing their calling cards in the astonished hands of major
domos who guarded the doors of palace and embassy all along the shores
of the Mediterranean. By the time the *North Star* was ready to make her
exit through the Straits of Gibraltar, the grandest of all private yachts
had "been admired by the Russian Court, gazed at by the Sultan . . .
astonished John Bull and frightened the Pope."

A good time, it seems, had been had by all. As she steamed past
Sandy Hook on the twenty-third of September and wound her way upstream toward Manhattan, gunfire from her afterdeck told the Commodore's mother that her wandering boy was home. The legends of
Horatio Alger had not yet spread their blight upon young American
manhood. But the prototype of their hero had already arrived in the
person of Cornelius Vanderbilt—one lad "laboring for daily bread,"
who had come to "the moment when, as a merchant prince, he was
returning from a voyage in his own steam yacht to almost every great

port of Europe, having received the respect and admiration of the Old World as the successful architect of his own fortunes."

When the Crimean War broke out in 1854, E. K. Collins lost for a time his old competitor Cunard, whose ways he understood, and gained a new rival in Vanderbilt, whose ambitions and methods he found inscrutable. Cunard had met his obligation to the British Admiralty by supplying, on demand, eleven good and sufficient steamers. This meant that he had to withdraw all of his ships from the Boston run and drastically reduce the service to New York. The contingency gave Vanderbilt his chance, not only to fill the gap created by Cunard's withdrawal, but also to show Congress and the public that the right man could run a steamship line at a profit without resorting to inflated subsidies or pursuing the philosophy of "rosewood and mirrors."

His first step was to contract for a new ship, to be christened *Ariel*. Then he set about plans to buy back or charter his *North Star*, which he had sold to a company running to Panama. His mind was made up on two accounts: he would put himself into competition with Collins by taking up the slack left by Cunard; he would finally demonstrate to Cunard and Company that an American could operate a transatlantic service as cheaply and efficiently as any combination of cheese-paring Scots.

When Collins got wind of Vanderbilt's intentions—especially his proposal to ask the Government for a subsidy of a mere 16,000 dollars per round-trip voyage—he knew that his own operation (supported at the rate of 33,000 dollars per round trip) would soon be open to question. Consequently he bearded Vanderbilt in the latter's office. He sought one assurance: a statement from the Commodore saying that he would raise the amount of his subsidy request to a figure matching Collins' own. No one, said Collins, could run ships across the ocean for less. Vanderbilt disagreed, and was otherwise deaf to entreaty. He said he would not dream of asking for a subsidy bigger than the one the British were giving Cunard. He was "patriotic in the matter. If an Englishman can do it for 16,000 dollars, I can . . . I won't admit that a Britisher can beat us in anything." Since Vanderbilt had set his course, Collins could only retreat with no assurances whatever.

But before Vanderbilt actually made his appeal to Congress, the *Arctic* disaster gave him a chance to be magnanimous—to convince Collins that he was not an ogre and to prove that, assured of a reasonable profit, he was not without fellow feeling. When news of the sinking reached New York, Vanderbilt sent word to Collins that the *North Star* was at his disposal. No other American ship had speed enough to carry out the Collins schedule, or was sufficiently grand in its appointments to maintain the Collins style. Collins refused, with thanks. The *North Star* might have the required speed but, when you came down to it, she was a grandiose version of a private yacht, with severely limited passenger accommodations.

Fifteen thousand dollars per voyage was the figure Vanderbilt finally asked for. As long as the Cunard ships would be occupied in the Crimea, he told Congress, his own ships would alternate with Collins on a semi-monthly basis, thus providing weekly service from New York to Europe. The modesty of his request caught the legislators off guard. An even greater surprise were expressions of support for Collins, attesting to the fact that he had won wide sympathy in an ocean enterprise that was still very young. The exemplary role of the Cunard liners as troop transports newly convinced some Congressmen of the wisdom of Government support for passenger ships that could, like Collins', be enlisted in time of war. Others knew that Collins, for all his combined flair and reclusiveness, had since the loss of the *Arctic* become a figure of pathos. The spectacle of the hard-driving Vanderbilt moving in at this unhappy juncture was, to some members, repugnant. The Commodore's petition was turned down.

Subsidy or not, Vanderbilt was determined to compete with Collins on the high seas. His new ship *Ariel* and the *North Star*, refurbished, were announced as ready for service. Since the Cunard ships had by this time come back from the wars and were running regularly into New York from Liverpool, Vanderbilt declined to enter into rivalry with Cunard. He decided instead to take on the challenge of a hapless little outfit called the New York and Havre Steam Navigation Company. This firm had started with two ships, the *Franklin* and the *Humboldt* and a Government subsidy of 150,000 dollars per annum, to carry mails to France via Southampton. But the *Humboldt* had cracked up near Halifax, the *Franklin* on Long Island, and now two new ships, the *Arago* and the *Fulton* were being brought in to replace them. From April until October, 1855, Vanderbilt ships left New York at intervals of three weeks for France, with a stop at Cowes. But after six months of it, Vanderbilt was sorry about the whole thing. He had carried more passengers to and from Le Havre than his rivals, but the effort had opened his eyes to the proportions of the largess in which the Collins Liners stayed afloat. "It is utterly impossible," he said, "for a private individual to start in competition with a line drawing nearly one million dollars per annum from the National Treasury . . ." and concluded with a hefty swipe at Collins: "The extravagance which a compensation so munificent naturally engenders is utterly inconsistent with the exercise of that economy and prudence essential to the successful management of any private enterprise."

In strategic retreat, Vanderbilt was moved by a single new idea: to build a ship far bigger than anything associated with Collins, so big that it might undercut everyone's rates and still turn a profit. With this in mind, he proceeded to construct the *Vanderbilt*, a ship of nearly 5,000 tons, 355 feet long, costing almost a million dollars. By the time this "largest vessel which has ever floated on the Atlantic Ocean" was ready to sail, Collins had faded out of the picture. By cutting ocean rates, the Commodore made it impossible for the ships of his only rival, the Bremen Line, to compete with him. For a while, with departures every forty days, the new ship was the whole complement of the Vanderbilt Line. Thus, for a brief span of years—until the Civil War canceled all overseas plans—Commodore Vanderbilt achieved his ambition of dominating the American Merchant Marine on the Atlantic.

❧ SECTION XIII ❧

Inman's Iron Screws / *The* Princeton *Shows Off* / *The*
Massachusetts Ill-Conceived / *Henry Morford Astride a Screw*

WHILE E. K. COLLINS was outracing Cunard and trying to keep Commodore Vanderbilt at arm's length, a
canny young Englishman from nowhere was quietly
overtaking them all. His name was William Inman and he had come
into the transatlantic forefront with a whole folio of innovations: his
ships were made of iron and they were screw-propelled; instead of catering to the ocean-going elite, he concentrated upon the needs of emigrants; instead of waiting for refugees from the great Irish famine to
come to his docks in Liverpool, he went to their docks in Queenstown.
His luck in keeping his steamers from plummeting to the bottom of
the ocean was no better than Collins', but his talent for management
was equal to that of the Cunard Line's Scotsmen. By 1857 he was carrying one third of all individuals traveling across the ocean.

Inman, born in 1825, was a native of Leicester. His family moved
to Liverpool when he was thirteen and there he attended the Liverpool
Collegiate Institute and was soon drawn quite naturally into the main
business of the port. He began as an apprentice in one provision house,
specializing in groceries, and soon moved to another, Richardson Broth-

ers and Company, specializing in linen and foodstuffs. Not long afterward he became manager of their shipping department, provisioning packets that ran from Liverpool to Philadelphia, and then the Richardsons took him on as a partner. In this capacity he began to think of transport itself instead of supplies, and became particularly taken with the performance of a new Clyde-side product, the *City of Glasgow*, as she made her first very successful voyages from Scotland to New York. This 1,600-ton ship, "of screw motive power," so intrigued him that he persuaded his partners to buy her and begin, in 1850, their own service from Liverpool to Philadelphia.

Four years later, by a twist of moral circumstance, Inman was able to buy out his partners and so establish the Inman Line with a complement of vessels that included the original *City of Glasgow*, to which were added the *City of Philadelphia* and the *City of Manchester*. His opportunity had come with the Crimean War. When the Admiralty commandeered some of the ships he owned in partnership with the Richardsons, the brothers, who were Quakers, could not in conscience support the idea that their ships, even as mere troop transports, would be armed. While the Quaker "Meeting for Sufferings" was preparing, on the very eve of the war, to send a delegation to Moscow to plead with the Czar for peace, the Richardsons found themselves helplessly in the position of preparing for war. After a short wrestle with the ethics of the situation, they decided they would retire, sell out to the twenty-nine-year-old Inman and leave him to carry on, in peace and in war, quite by himself.

At first this advantage only left him to face adversity alone: in March, 1854, with 480 people aboard, the *City of Glasgow* disappeared midocean. Then in September, less than two weeks before the *Arctic* went down, the *City of Philadelphia*, on her maiden voyage, came to grief at Chance Cove, Newfoundland. All of her passengers and crew were rescued, but the ship was a total loss.

Overcoming these setbacks, the Inman company grew because it offered services no other steamship line had introduced. Inman was the first to send impoverished emigrants across the ocean at a cheap rate by steamship, the first to send his vessels to Queenstown, thereby sparing Irish emigrants the expense and misery of an Irish Sea crossing to Liverpool. He was also the first to conduct a steamship line as a family affair.

Mrs. Inman put herself into the thick of decisions about decor and sailing schedules, and it was "owing to the weight of that excellent lady's views" that Inman steamers offered home comforts. On one occasion, crossing with her husband from Liverpool to Queenstown, she passed herself off as an emigrant in order to inspect steerage accommodations from the point of view of one who would have to endure them. Some-how—but most likely through the promotional desk of the Inman Line —the story of her overnight passage incognito came to be widely published. The figures of Mother Inman and Father Inman benevolently watching over their ragged charges became an endearing, and notably profitable, part of the Inman legend.

For thirty dollars, Inman would carry an emigrant three thousand miles, feed him three meals a day—arrowroot with sugar and milk, oatmeal porridge and molasses for breakfast; one half fresh beef, one half mess beef for dinner; tea and gruel for supper—and invite him to his "matutinal ablutions" with a clean towel, fresh soap and a "plentiful supply of water and mirrors." Prospective passengers scanning the flimsy little publicity brochures he distributed through the hungry parishes were beguiled. "Three thousand miles at a halfpenny a mile," they read, "and this nourishment thrown in for nothing! Emigration made easy! Luxurious would be a better term." And who could resist the brochure's final promise? At the end of the voyage, "our emigrants march to the railway depot, enter the cars, and—Go West! In a few brief months the almighty dollar rolls across the pond, and the dear ones left behind follow in the footsteps of the pioneers."

In an age of side-wheelers, Inman's iron screws had also demonstrated an efficiency that indicated paddles were about to become obsolete. Compared with the Cunard ships' consumption of more than 75 tons of coal per day, the *City of Glasgow* had used up only 20. Compared with Cunard's cargo capacity of 500 tons, the Inman ship had room for 1,200.

Americans had of course experimented with screw propulsion by this time. But in instances both military and commercial, results were not clear enough to turn either Collins or Vanderbilt away from their grand new side-wheel projects. On the military side was the case of the *Princeton*—an iron frigatelike Navy ship fitted with a screw designed by the illustrious Swede John Ericsson. When the *Princeton* came to New York in 1843 to have armament installed, she took it upon herself to entertain the waterfront populace and, in the process, to humiliate the *Great Western*.

When she arrived in the Lower Bay around noontime on October 19, she made her way toward Manhattan "serene as a duck on a horse pond," and dropped anchor in the North River. Without a yard of canvas on her masts, she looked naked and innocent. But she was neither. Sly boots, she waited until the *Great Western*, setting out on her regularly scheduled run to Liverpool, had left her East River pier and, steam up, had begun to pound away from the Battery toward the sea. Then the *Princeton*, with a lion's-tail slosh of her propeller, started in pursuit. She came on, "no paddle-wheels or smoke-pipe visible, propelled by a noiseless and unseen agency, without a rag of canvas on her lithe and beautiful spars." She overtook the *Great Western* in full view of crowds on the banks, circled her once, then again, and glided back to her anchorage in the North River. She had cruised with the speed of a shark against the *Great Western*'s dogpaddle; she had made her grandstand play. "The Great Aquatic Race," headlined *The Herald*. "Great Britain Against America, and America Against the World!"

But the *Princeton* was still to have her comeuppance, still to miss her own biggest chance to prove her mettle. Her reputation was great enough to survive the explosion of three of her "Peace Maker" guns which, in 1844, killed six people aboard her, including two Cabinet members, and almost blew President Tyler into the Potomac. But it could not survive an ill-timed breakdown. All set to escort Commodore Perry to Japan, she came a cropper when her screw propulsion machinery gave out and she had to stand by, helpless, as preparations for the great venture to the Orient were being made all about her. Unable to be made ready in time, she had to undergo the disgrace of being superseded by a paddle-wheeler on one of the most important voyages of a seafaring century.

The first attempt to establish a ship with a screw propeller as a commercial ocean carrier was made by a group of Bostonians led by Captain Robert Bennett Forbes. Their idea was the *Massachusetts*—a fully rigged sailing ship fitted with an auxiliary propeller, a little funnel abaft the mainmast, and cabins accommodating thirty people in the poop forward of the mainmast. The *Massachusetts* was designed to sail when the wind was right and to steam when sails were of small or no use. Her owners were not so ambitious as to compete with Cunard, but merely with the vast fleet of sailing ships that still carried by far the greater part of transatlantic cargo and passengers.

Their all-purpose ship came down the ways in the early morning of July 23, 1845, observed by a reporter from the Boston *Post*, whose pen was probably plumed. "The beautiful packet ship *Massachusetts*," he wrote, "was launched from the yard of Mr. Samuel Hall, East Boston, between one and two o'clock on Tuesday morning. Few were present, except the workmen, to witness the beautiful sight. The moon herself, 'pale regent of the night,' was oft obscured by passing clouds, and shed at best, a dull and broken light. But the sheet lightning seemed with one continuous blaze to light the vaulted firmament. When all was ready and the 'tide brim full,' the last connecting plank was cut in twain, and, smooth and swiftly down the inclined ways, the noble ship descended to the main, and plunging through it, cut the swelling foam, and floated lightly on her destined home."

Each piece of furniture on the *Massachusetts* was ingeniously equipped with an air-tight compartment so that, at a point of emergency, it might be used as a lifebuoy. She carried lensed lights on each bow, her ventilators were as advanced as those on the Cunard liners and, to assist or to relieve her engines, she carried skysails on three masts covering an area of nearly four thousand yards.

For all her gimmicks, the *Massachusetts* was ill-conceived. Her maiden trip from New York to Liverpool—the first American crossing under steam since that of the *Savannah*—took all of seventeen and a half days, six of them under sail alone. The homeward-bound trip—during which the Welsh coal she had taken on in England refused to burn in her furnaces—took twenty-eight days. Her poor first-time-out performance was only confirmed by a second round-trip voyage when rough weather made the use of steam impossible. She was then sent to the East Indies. Within a year she was chartered by the United States Government to serve in the Mexican War and later as a store ship at Acapulco. When she continued to be bunglesome, neither one thing nor the other, her engines were finally removed. Renamed *Alaska*, she was stripped of all of her pretensions and returned to the role of the simple packet ship that, in the moonlit waters of East Boston, she was.

"I think you had better not have anything to do with screws," Junius Smith had cautioned his nephew, "least you be screwed harder than you would like." Though such advice had long been rejected, even shipping companies progressive enough to employ the new device failed to do anything about making the sounds and vibrations of the screw propeller tolerable. The medieval tradition that royalty and other categories of the socially eminent travel high in the after part of a ship still obtained. In a paddle-wheeler, this meant that first-class passengers would likely inhabit quarters far from the source of locomotion. It also meant that they would have to put up with absurd inconveniences while dining, especially during bad weather. Then, according to one Cunard passenger, the stewards who waited on you wore oilskins and sea boots. "The galley was situated in the forward part of the vessel, and the dining-room aft. Food was conveyed in silver dishes along an open deck, and exposed to the full fury of seas coming aboard, so that, in the absence of hot presses, when your roast beef was placed before you it was well-nigh cold, and firmly embedded in a lake frozen over with fat."

But in a screw-driven ship, this old custom meant that ordinarily privileged persons would have to spend most of their passage time in a little honeycomb hump of cabins only a few feet above the spinning blades. When a ship pitched in heavy weather, propellers tended to race wildly in the air. On calm seas, a voyage by propeller-driven ship was in the nature of a perpetual massage. Aware of these disturbing tendencies, cautious Samuel Cunard did not acknowledge the inevitability of screw propulsion until 1853. Then the company, which believed that it was only good policy that "others should experimentalize, and when the novel principle has been proved by indubitable tests, then, and not til then, to introduce it into their next vessel," ordered its first iron ships to be so fitted. (At the same time—as if to recognize Inman's extraordinary success on the Philadelphia run—Cunard specified that accommodations for emigrants be part of the new design.)

When actor Henry Morford, against the advice of his fellow thespian Billy Florence, decided to take a chance with one of the new propeller-driven ships to Liverpool, he wrote a farewell poem beginning:

> Though Billy Florence o'er the sea
>   Ran off last week, per mail Cunarder
> A different fate remained for me—
>   A narrower and harder.

> Gotham's Wise Men obtained a bowl
>> When they went gayly seaward rowing;
> I, dense of body as of soul,
>> Astride a *screw* am going.

Once at sea, Morford began his journal: "Within a few hours of leaving the wharf, the saloon passengers are 'messed.' Then one by one and two by two to the deck, to books, and cigars, and reading, and promenade—to the lee of the hot funnel if the morning is cool, to very quiet chairs, for ladies doubtful of stomach . . . the dirty steerage passengers trooping out from their kennels to wash up their dirty tins and foul crockery at the pumps. To listening to the whistle of the boatswain—listening to that ever-recurring whistle, and wondering 'what is he going to do, *now?*' "

By the time he was halfway over, Morford's doubts about the wisdom of choosing a screw-propelled ship over a paddle-wheeler had vanished. "When I wrote that farewell poem," he said, "to my fancy the screw steamer was a mere apology as compared to the paddle—the *dernier* resort of poor people who could afford nothing better. Billy Florence, booked for the *Scotia*, had said to me in one of the boxes of the Winter Garden: 'Pshaw!—come over with me, on a paddle-wheeler! I wouldn't cross in a screw if I had to stay home the balance of my life!' And I believed him and wrote accordingly of the "narrower and harder fate" of "going on a screw." So much for theory—now for what experience has taught me. That the screw steamship, full of power and full-rigged, is the perfection of sailing ship with propelling power added —no clumsy paddle-boxes to catch the sea and cause constant heeling to starboard and larboard, with beating blows that shake ship and passenger as if in the last throes of dissolution . . . rolling a little more, sometimes, than the paddle-wheeler, but always easier, and always pitching far less laboriously (the pitch being *the* misery at sea), and the additional immense advantage secured, against disablement, that *if* the machinery of the screw chances to give away, the screw being unhooked and left to play at free will, a full-rigged and properly-modelled sailing-ship remains, capable of making average sailing speed and weather . . . and I have no more doubt, to-day, that within five years the last paddle-wheel transatlantic steamer will be broken up or sold for mere coast service, than I have of the inevitable broadening and acceleration of human intelligence."

Yet, while ocean trade was booming for those who catered to such new appetites, the greater number of passengers by far traveled only because they had to. Among them were cynics who would not be fooled by grand saloons that aped the fretwork and scallops of bordello baroque, the well-padded hush of gaming establishments, and who would not be taken in by staterooms hung with silks like bowers of illicit bliss. The sea was still the enemy of the human psyche and soma. Over the raptures of travel brochures and travel agents came cries from the heart. "Going across the Atlantic is humbug," said one of the disenchanted, "there isn't a particle of sense in it; it is worse than folly—it is madness. . . . Goodness! to be laid up on a narrow shelf, with a tin pan fastened to the rim of it, for unmentionable purposes; with a tight bandage around your stomach, another around your head, the shelf twisting and grinding and rocking from side to side, and head to foot alternately—goodness! I say, where is the poetry, or comfort, or fun, or anything else but misery in crossing the sea."

Of all new features, the one most continually heralded was the screw. For all the abuse heaped upon it and all the doubts it magnified, the screw was efficient and cheap; and it had come to stay. Since it could be placed in no other part of a ship's anatomy than its tail, the only thing to do about the nuisance of it all was to remove passengers from its shuddering proximity. Sociology and technology had come to a juncture—to maintain the ladies and gentlemen of the elite in the quarters to which they were accustomed would be to subject them to torture. The technology of the thing was unalterable, but at least the sociology of it could bend. It would take another decade and more for them to make the adjustment, but the elite were bound to find their own special place on shipboard, and they did.

The Great Eastern: "Canst Thou Draw Out Leviathan with an
Hook?" / Brunel's "Great Babe" / Explosion Aboard and the
Death of Brunel / Jules Verne on Deck / The Great Storm
of 1861 / A Harvard Man to the Rescue / Show Business
The Ghosts of the Great Eastern

ONCE a romance, now a commodity, steamships had lost
much of the magnetism that had kept people enthralled—
even people who would never think of traveling on them.
Something was needed to recharge old currents of interest, to recover the
fascination that had attended the *Britannia* from the Mersey to Halifax
Lights, the *Washington* from the Narrows to Bremerhaven, the *Arctic*
from the drawing boards of Corlaer's Hook to the cold deeps off Cape
Race.

In 1859 this need was fulfilled beyond anyone's dreams by the *Great
Eastern*—"a Triton among minnows," *une ville flottant*, "a great swollen
hunk of a premature Leviathan," a ship stillborn, a ship out of epoch.
Five times bigger than the next biggest ship afloat (no other vessel
would exceed her in tonnage displacement for nearly fifty years), she
was huge, busy and slightly grotesque—not only because of her awesome dimensions, but also because, like a giant born with the brain of
a cretin, she lacked the power, if not the will, to govern herself. She had
a propeller as big as a windmill, ponderous paddle engines that worked
"with the steadiness and patience of a London drayhorse," paddle boxes

capacious enough to contain Ferris wheels, and six masts, tall as trees, spread with sheetings sufficient to bed a regiment. Yet she was weak and clumsy, given to rolling and to bumping into things, and developed an appetite for soft coal so big that she was never worth her keep.

Oddities and deficiencies apart, she was a wonder, a leap into the future, a product of technological imagination operating conspicuously beyond the control of her profit-seeking sponsors. Nearly seven hundred feet long, she looked like a fortified town. She had five smoking chimneys, and a sixty-foot-high wall of black iron punched through by portholes in tiers. Three million rivets went into her hull, each one of which had to be affixed by the coordinated efforts of a whole team of shipwrights. "In riveting," a shipyard guide explained, "the men are arranged in gangs, or sets, each containing two riveters, one holder up, and three boys; two boys are stationed at the fire, or portable forge, and one is with the holder up; this boy's duty is to receive the red hot rivet with his pincers from the boy at the forge, and insert it in the hole destined for its reception, the point protruding about an inch. The holder up immediately places his heavy hammer against the head of the rivet, holding it firmly there, while the two riveters assail it with alternate blows, so as to completely fill it; and directly this is done, one of them takes up a kind of chisel, round which a pliant hazel rod, serving as a handle, is twisted; and holding it against the protruding end of the rivet, the other by two or three blows chips it off fair and smooth with the face of the plate, the whole operation scarce occupying a minute."

From the first, the *Great Eastern* promised big money and, from the first, lost money with a prodigality that confounded every man who ever had anything to do with her. As a result, she went through the hands of one group of owners after another like a hot potato. The public found her astonishing; nautical men feared her; some considered her an abomination. In an era when seamanship was still a matter of ingenuity, courage and even honor, she threatened to turn sailors into blacksmiths. To those who felt that, in her presence, "the intellect expands, and takes such exulting flights that we can rationally regard that huge vessel as the latest wonder of the world," she was "destined to bridge oceans, and bring the nations of the earth closer together." Her promoters hoped that she would be a magnet that would exert its pull on both sides of the ocean. They envisioned her shuttling hordes of Europeans to Portland, Maine, from which port they would be trundled into overland coaches for Niagara Falls and Mammoth Cave. They saw

Americans being sent in teeming boatloads to "improve their acquaintance with Europe, and learn that art is not yet dead there, civilization at a standstill, nor talent and invention entirely resident on the Hudson, or the Mississippi."

The *Great Eastern* did eventually bridge an ocean and she did bring the nations of the earth immeasurably closer together—but not in the way anyone had foreseen. Long after her owners had run out of hope that passengers from either side of the Atlantic might still occupy the endless long rows of her cabins, she became the ship to lay the first Atlantic cable. In this long, torturous, but ultimately successful undertaking, she at last achieved a working role commensurate with her size and abilities. But when the second of two cables had been payed out, and a sensitive finger in Brest, Normandy, could tap out its message to a receiving station in Duxbury, Massachusetts, she at once returned to the ranks of the unemployed. Big and everlastingly promising, she could not be overlooked for long, and soon she had new owners—the Great Eastern Company Ltd. This outfit was composed of Frenchmen who, with the enthusiastic but discreet support of Louis Philippe, planned to urge great numbers of passengers, Americans in particular, to use her as a ferry to the Paris Exhibition. But Americans would not be so urged. The hopes and efforts of the Frenchmen constituted but one more short-lived episode of failure in the sad story of the great iron ship. After thirty-one years of vicissitudes and ephemeral success, long past a prime she never really had, the *Great Eastern* was ready to call it a day. Yet the men who owned her then had as hard a time in getting her out of the water as the men who built her had in getting her into the water.

A lineal descendant of the Crystal Palace's Great Exhibition of 1851, "the fairy tale and success story" that "proclaimed . . . the visibility of human progress," this "epic of iron," this "sublime embodiment of the might and majesty of England," was many things to many different men. To some she was an ark more fabulous than Noah's. Hearkening to the authority of Sir Isaac Newton—who said that a cubit was twenty and sixty-two hundredths inches—or to the pontifical word of Bishop Wilkins—who said that a cubit was twenty-one and sixty-eight hundredths inches—they were assured that both science and theology denominated the *Great Eastern* the bigger vessel, in everything except breadth. To John Scott Russell, who was responsible for

her lines and dimensions and whose own company built her at Millwall, she was both a notorious triumph of nautical architecture and a
crushing burden. To Isambard Kingdom Brunel, that historically pre-
cocious mind whose every creation was "outsize, brilliant and radical,"
she was his "great babe," the penultimate gesture of a career abound-
ing in prodigal flights of fancy wrought in iron. Speaking of the *Great
Eastern*, "the fact is," said Brunel, "that I never embarked on any one
thing to which I have so entirely devoted myself, and to which I have
given so much time, thought, and labour, on the success of which I have
staked so much reputation, and to which I have so largely committed
myself and those who were disposed to place faith in me."

He was still a comparatively young man when he conceived the
great ship and watched her grow. Yet time was running out for Brunel,
and a premonitory sense of urgency may have led him to conserve all
his efforts. For swift travel he designed for himself a britska with a
boxlike body, protected by a hood and a screen, in which he could
stretch out and go to sleep. On many occasions, while its owner lay
quite dead to the world inside, this carriage would be lifted onto a
truck of a train at Paddington Station and dispatched to a designated
point along the Great Western Railway. There the britska would be
met by four post-horses and a new stage of the journey would begin.
This "flying hearse," as people along the railway came to call it, was
for weeks on end Brunel's only bedroom, and from its draped confines
he would descend to oversee the *Great Eastern* as she was being put
together.

One day, as the mighty vessel was rising to her final height, he would
stand before the Promethean tangle of the sixty-pound links of the
launching drum cables in his black top hat and rumpled pants to be
photographed. Before his ship was out of her cradle he would die of a
stroke. Spared the ignominy of her illustrious failure, he did not have
to stand by helplessly as his maritime wonder was forced into roles she
was never meant to play, dispatched to waters she was never meant to
ply.

In Brunel's conception the logic of the ship was a matter of form
following function: the mammoth proportions of the *Great Eastern* were
dictated by the service she was expected to perform. This service was
specific: to undertake nonstop voyages around the Cape of Good Hope
to India and Australia. Other steamships had to depend upon coaling

stops in remote places. The *Great Eastern* was designed to carry her own vast supply of fuel. Her dimensions were in fact bound by the limitations upon navigation that would be encountered in getting to Calcutta, fifty miles up the river Hooghly—the one coaling station at which she would call en route to or from Australia. Since coal-carrying capacity was the main thing, early plans for passengers called only for "500 cabins . . . of the highest class, with ample space for troops and lower class passengers." When the businessmen who owned her ignored the purpose for which she was built and chose, first, to exhibit her as a showboat, a kind of Cardiff Giant afloat, and then to enter her in the ocean marathon against sleek, swift and confident Atlantic runners, she was already doomed to the life of a misfit.

Other ships were built; the *Great Eastern* seemed to grow, as if she were the reincarnation of "some pre-Adamitic colossus." "The voyager up and down the Thames," wrote a London observer, "had noticed with astonishment the slow growth of a huge structure on the southern extremity of the Isle of Dogs. At first a few enormous poles alone cut the sky-line and arrested his attention; then, vast plates of iron, that seemed big enough to form shields for the gods, reared themselves edgeways at great distances apart; and as months elapsed, a wall of metal slowly rose between him and the horizon. . . . Neither Grosvenor nor Belgrave Square would take the *Great Eastern* in. Berkeley Square would barely admit her, in its long dimension, and when rigged not at all; for her mizzen-boom would project up Davis Street, and her bowsprit would hang a long way over the Marquis of Lansdowne's garden."

Ten thousand people came to see "the heaviest object that man had yet attempted to move" launched broadside into the Thames. Unknown to Brunel, more than three thousand tickets allowing admission to the yard had been sold. By turning a delicate feat of engineering into a public entertainment, the *Great Eastern*'s owners had put Brunel in an abhorrent position that left him embittered. Instead of waiting until the ship was ready to be floated off, the directors wanted a launching ceremony to be held long before operations were actually begun, so that Miss Hope, the chairman's daughter, could break a bottle of champagne on the ship's prows without danger of being launched herself.

Leviathan was the company's name for the vessel; the public had already settled permanently on *Great Eastern*. In the impasse, entirely new names were put down on a list and, on the very morning of the launching, submitted to Brunel. Exasperated, he waved the man who brought the list aside. "As far as I am concerned," he said, "you can call her *Tom Thumb*." In a letter written to Samuel Baker, one of the directors, he later made his feelings clear. "In the midst of all this anxiety, I learnt to my horror that all the world was invited to 'The Launch' and that I was committed to it *coûte que coûte*. It was not right; it was cruel; and nothing but a sense of necessity of calming all feelings that could disturb my mind enabled me to bear it."

In spite of the powerful efforts of enormous tackles and two hydraulic rams, the *Great Eastern* stuck halfway down the stocks, tipped like a tub on a beach, and would not be budged. Instead of being "as remarkable an event as any in the calendar of human invention," the launching was a flop. During the next two months a long series of launching attempts was made, more than a half-million dollars spent, yet the truculent *Great Eastern* continued to squat on her hunkers. Bored with this reluctant Leviathan, Londoners had given up rushing down to Millwall in response to still another invitation to see her into the water.

Some sceptics began to doubt that she would ever be water-borne; some predicted that she might very well just sit where she was, rusting away, "a monument to human folly and presumption." To others her ponderous dilemma was a fine source of amusement. The *Morning Advertiser* quoted the Book of Job: "Canst thou draw out Leviathan with an hook?" "The Hero of Millwall, Mr. Brunel," said *Punch*, "is undaunted by the scoffs launched at his launch. He may be observed in the evenings, gazing hopefully on the Leviathan, ejaculating like another Galileo, *Epur se muove*." Finally, by the boon of an abnormally high tide, "as if to give the lie to the carping and quibbling of amateur engineers, the great ship rose substantially from her cradles, buoyant on the bosom of the rising tide." But there was no one around, neither to gasp nor to applaud.

The company that had originally commissioned the *Great Eastern* went broke in getting her ready. A second company rescued her and announced that she was being fitted out for the transatlantic trade on the main route, except that Portland, Maine (the closest American city to Europe), instead of New York would be her western terminus. She would never get to Portland, in spite of preparations made there to berth her at the specially constructed Victoria Pier. Cancellation of this plan sent the citizens of Portland into righteous fury and even caused some of them to bring suit for loss against the Great Ship Company. But confusion generated by the *Great Eastern* was already *de rigeur*. From the very outset of her life on the water, the monster ship showed that she was prone to trouble on the scale that suited her.

Except for the sad circumstance on the occasion of her first trial run that Brunel, the man whose "head . . . had devised the mighty structure, was lying on his pillow, sore and aching, and was not there to enjoy the triumph," the big ship seemed to have emerged in all the brightness of her promise. As watchers on the shore looked "for the slightest indication of life in the mighty mass of matter upon which their eyes were riveted, it was as if they were looking for an illustration of the miracle to be performed by the man with a mustard-seed of faith, that he should say unto the mountain, 'Be removed into the sea,' and that it should be so." But on another trial run in September she was playing hostess to a number of dignitaries and citizens interested in marine development when the fore part of her simply blew up. By chance, most of the excursion party was at the time in the dining saloon for an early evening meal. But a number of others, hoping for a sunset view of the town of Hastings, had gathered in the bow. As the *Great Eastern* was passing Dungeness Light, the group on deck were suddenly aware of a rising hiss of steam. Turning their heads to investigate, they saw the huge forward funnel rise on a cloud of steam and, like a dud rocket from a launching pad, lift into the air, and tumble over. "The forward part of the deck," said a man from the *Times* who was on board, "appeared to spring like a mine, blowing the funnel up into the air. There was a confused roar amid which came the awful crash of timber and iron mingled together in frightful uproar, and then all was hidden in a rush of steam. Blinded and almost stunned by the overwhelming concussion, those on the bridge stood motionless in the white vapour till they were reminded of the necessity of seeking shelter by the shower of wreck—glass, gilt work, saloon ornaments and pieces of wood which began to fall like rain in all directions." When news of the explosion reached Brunel, he was too weak to analyze its source or to suggest how its recurrence might be forestalled. "From that time he gradually sank until Thursday night, the 15th inst., when he expired, in his fifty-fourth year."

Major repairs to her superstructure and minor readjustments in the logistics of the *Great Eastern's* first voyage caused many delays. Nearly all of the passengers booked for the maiden voyage canceled their reservations and demanded their money back. Scheduled to start for New York on June 16, 1860, she had to wait over for an extra day because all the firemen in the forecastle reported for duty in a condition described as "hilarious." With accommodation ample enough to take care of four thousand passengers—a far greater number than any nonmilitary ship before or since—she finally sailed with only thirty-eight—and of these eight were deadheads. The circumstance allowed the exclusive company of ladies and gentlemen to travel in a grandeur of proportions approaching the Babylonian. The most cramped stateroom on the *Great Eastern* was double the size of the roomiest stateroom on any other ship. Every one of her cabins was equipped with a wash basin, a dressing table, a rocking chair and a settee ingeniously designed to conceal a bathtub with hot and cold running water. The bathtub alone represented regality attuned to enlightenment—an advance in the march of sanitation that had, so far, reached only a handful of houses in the whole of England.

Deceitful advertising had led Charles Dickens to expect Oriental pavilions of awesome perspective on Cunard's modest spit-and-polish *Britannia*; on the *Great Eastern* all the claims of the advertising men at last delivered just what they had promised. Broad skylights, huge golden pillars, ornate staircases with steps of silver-oxidized ironwork and mahogany balusters—all the accouterments were elegant, all dimensions sacerdotal. Flanked by gigantic mirrors and surrounded by velvet couches, even the huge funnels were by "decorative deception" turned into "positive ornaments." The walls of her great dining room were grained in imitation of bird's-eye and curled maple; the arched crossribs of its ceiling striped boldly with blue and red. Even the hitherto scruffy and vaguely illicit smoking room had come into a new dispensation; the *Great Eastern's* retreat for gentlemen had fourteen windows, a ceiling of white and gold with a wainscotting of lemon yellow. If the reports of particularly sensitive travelers are credible, she was also a soundbox of aeolian resonance. Her first captain was a musician—a sensitive soul who quit the ship with a nervous breakdown at the end of her maiden voyage to New York—and would not sail without his flute and his own private grand piano; and there were so many chords wafted from the keyboards of other instruments scattered about that some passengers begged to be changed to cabins far away from the reverberant saloons—deep in the bows or any other place out of earshot.

Running flush from stem to stern, more than a furlong in length down each side of the hatchways, her upper deck allowed for promenades as wide as boulevards. Never before could sea-going travelers walk upon such broad open areas. Jules Verne, who made a voyage to New York, recorded a fair-weather scene. "Vegetation is sometimes behindhand," he said, "but fashion never. Soon the Boulevards, filled with groups of promenaders, looked like the Champs Elysées on a fine Sunday afternoon in May." The sound of a trumpet echoing a call to the tables down the companionways interrupted the progress of the fashionables for a while, but "lunch over, the decks were again filled; people bowed and spoke to each other in passing as formally as if they were walking in Hyde Park; children played and ran about, throwing their balls and bowling hoops as they might have done on the gravel walks of the Tuileries; the greater part of the men walked up and down smoking; the ladies, seated on folding-chairs, worked, read, or talked together, whilst the governesses and nurses looked after the children. A few corpulent Americans swung themselves backwards and forwards in their rocking-chairs; the ship's officers were continually passing to and fro, some going to their watch on the bridge, others answering the absurd questions put to them by some of the passengers; whilst the tones of an organ and two or three grand pianos making a distracting discord, reached us through the lulls in the wind."

In the matter of speed, the *Great Eastern* was something less than an ocean greyhound. She was supposed to do fifteen knots, "without diminution and without cessation, under any weather." But sailing vessels, at least on the eastward run, consistently logged as many miles per day as she did. To those passengers who believed that, because she was longer than the trough of even the largest recorded storm wave, she would ride unperturbed through tempests and thus make seasickness a thing of the past, she was, literally, a nauseating disappointment. She rolled like a drowsy walrus and, to everyone's surprise, pitched with the abandon of a coasting schooner. As one queasy customer reported: "I became aware that the ship had added to her usual roll a peculiar lifting of her forefoot, producing a gastric complication by no means enviable."

Since there were so many tasseled hangings to swing, so many Louis Quatorze furnishings to slide about and such vast enclosures to be tipped on end like the chambers of a Coney Island fun house, the *Great Eastern* in a storm gave new scale to life on the bounding main. "On one bad night," said M. Verne, "my balance was strangely variable. . . . Portmanteaus and bags came in and out of my cabin; an unusual hubbub reigned in the adjoining saloon, in which two or three hundred packages were making expeditions from one end to the other, knocking the tables and chairs with loud crashes. I left my cabin, and helping myself with my hands and feet through the billows of luggage, I crossed the saloon, scrambling up the stairs on my knees, like a Roman peasant devoutly climbing the steps of the Scala Santa of Pontius Pilate; and at last, reaching the deck, I hung on firmly to the nearest kevel."

Experiences of this nature on another voyage led one passenger to ask: "Is the *Great Eastern* destined to revolutionise ocean voyaging as her sanguine projectors have anticipated? Or, is she fated to be ultimately moored in some river as a floating hospital and exhibited to our passing grandchildren as one of the most monstrous crazes of the nineteenth century?" "How will the winds and waves affect this leviathan mass," asked another, "when they chance to be in their surly and uncongenial moods? A connected mass of 27,000 tons is not as easily heaved as a cork or a cockle-shell; but the storm-winds and the storm-waves of the open ocean have a tremendous power. What will they do then, with this stupendous morsel, when they have it fairly within their clutches?"

The answer came in September, 1861. On a crossing from Liverpool to New York, the *Great Eastern* encountered a storm that stripped her to the gunwales and battered her reputation beyond the hope of salvage. A correspondent of the *Constitution: Or, Cork Advertiser*, who identifies himself only as "A Passenger," tells the story.

"We sailed from the Mersey amid the cheers of thousands of spectators, not one of whom could have imagined how small was the chance of their ever seeing her again. We proceeded very satisfactorily until Tuesday night and Wednesday, our speed averaging from 12 to 14 knots. We last sighted land soon after noon on Wednesday, and later the wind changed from south-east to north-west, blowing fresh. Thursday—A fresh gale with a rough sea. Noon—A heavy gale; wind, from north to west; sea tremendous. We roll heavily, and ship many seas. I begin to understand the true meaning of a gale in the Atlantic. The captain looks anxious, but the passengers have faith in 'the big ship.' The rolling is fearful, and quite upsets all persons' notions of the steadiness of the *Great Eastern*. One of our cows has her leg broken; in a short time they are both 'rolled' to death. [According to another passenger—Sir William Forwood, a Liverpool shipowner—the cowhouse was one of the first parts of the superstructure to be destroyed, releasing not only the two cows but a swan that had made its nest beside them. One of the cows got caught in the skylight of the forward saloon where it hung, head down, until it dropped to its death. The swan skittered about, doubling itself in the great panels of mirrors until it was pierced by a sliver of shattered glass.]

"2 o'clock—Things look worse. The captain tries to put our head to the wind. The port paddle gives away with a crash. The jib is set, but it is blown to ribands in moments. The rolling increases; the deck presents an angle of 45 degrees and none but experienced seamen can walk about. Attention is drawn to the boats; they are suspended on either side, mostly on fixed davits. The heavy rolling brings the boats in violent contact with the waves. The tackling of the long boat becomes deranged; a man and a boy enter it to remedy the evil, but the wind strikes the boat, and gives the occupants forcible ejection—happily upon deck—and in a moment it is floating far away from us. Four other boats share a similar fate in rapid succession. I watch the men at the wheel, an army of them. They are contending with an element whose power they cannot fully estimate. They will stand to their post and we have hope. 5:45—Our position is becoming critical. A tremendous sea has struck our stern, broken her rudder head and done serious damage to her stern-post. Still we are not quite at the mercy of the waves; we have our screw, and we have our starboard paddle.

"I now leave the deck, where I have been studying the great lesson of the deep, and feel anxious to know how matters are progressing below. As I descend the staircase I hear a crashing which even deadens the roaring of the wind and waves. I pass the store-room; its shelves are empty, and the crockery fighting a fierce battle on the floor below. I pass in to the grand saloon, but a change has come over the scene. Everyone who has visited this ship must have been struck with the gorgeous magnificence of her saloons, her easy lounges, her brilliant chandeliers, her numerous and extensive mirrors, the regard to comfort and elegance in every shape. But the lounges are now over-turned, the tables are thrown down and broken, the chairs are frantically chasing those who but a few moments before had been their fair occupants. The stove from the centre of the room is adrift; it has wreaked its vengeance upon a large mirror, but has mischief in it yet. Books leave their shelves without the slightest solicitation. But the ladies and children!—where can they seek protection? Some have, indeed, sought their cabins but the majority are huddled in corners on the floor, and terror is strongly marked in their faces. The stewards are capturing the various articles of furniture, and binding them down as they would so many wild and savage beasts. I venture in to assist, and am rewarded for my indiscretion by being hurled violently against the mirror, which had been 'starred' by the stove. It falls into a thousand pieces, and inflicts injury upon many. I have cut my head, my little finger dislocated, and a tooth knocked out.

"The ship, I now learn confidentially, is considered unmanageable. The snapping of the rudder-head is a double misfortune. It allows the rudder to swing round upon the screw, and entirely prevents it from being worked. The ship has begun to drift into the trough of the sea. Another effort is made with the remaining paddle to turn its head. The effort is too much—this paddle now gives way; we are at the entire mercy of the waves. May the great Ruler of the waves have mercy upon us this night! The trysail just set is blowing in ribands.

"Friday, 6 A.M.—The gale is still furious. We are drifting before the wind. The pumps are all going. I do not like the sound, but am assured that they have complete mastery over the water. The water has got in through the ports and by way of the deck. The captain is a brave fellow, and keeps his spirits up wonderfully. He is ever keeping the men steadily at the wheel, although the rudder has been gone for many hours. He knows the alarm a knowledge of this would create. I overhear a conversation between the captain and some officers. Something must be done to try and turn the ship's head, and then, if the wind abates, sail will be set, and we may reach a port in safety. How is it to be done? A large spar, marked as weighing four tons, is to be heavily loaded with iron, then fastened to an immense hawser, and thrown overboard. Luncheon is set in the dining saloon; some cannot eat, but still many seats are occupied. The rolling—or, now, more properly speaking, 'rocking,' for the movement is violently from side to side—comes on again with renewed force. The passengers catch hold to support themselves. The tables are not fastened, for whoever supposed the big ship would become so rampant? The tables give way, and the scene of the grand saloon is enacted again. The stewards rush in to the rescue, but in two minutes every piece of crockery on the tables is smashed, knives and forks fly about, and the scene closed by a general accumulation of tables, chairs, crockery, passengers, and stewards in the middle of the saloon.

"I return to the deck. The spar is being thrown over, and it certainly steadies our movements. But we are still in the trough of the sea. It is the second day of our misfortunes, and we do not see the end of them. A meeting of the passengers is held. They face the difficulties manfully. We are out of the track of vessels. It may be some days before we meet with aid. We must be careful of our resources. A committee is appointed to confer with the captain, and a working committee to watch and protect the interest of the passengers. The captain and the officers must save the ship—we must aid in preserving discipline. I am appointed chairman of the working committee and go through the ship by virtue of my office. The noise produced by the continued rocking of the vessel is dreadful. Bottles, broken crockery, knives, forks, and plated articles, constantly dashed from side to side of an iron ship, produce the very agony of discord; and the chorus is brought up by a tallow cask and a chain cable which have got loose in a large compartment, and spread consternation and terror.

"Saturday, 5:30 A.M.—A friend comes to tell my cabin companion that the water is making fast on the pumps; all hopes of safety are now over; it is only a question of time when the boats shall be lowered. I dress quickly, and take a farewell view of my cabin. On getting to deck I find the alarm false. He had only learnt what I already knew as to the steerage, and the water was not gaining upon the pumps; but the hatches were open, and the noise of the water rushing from side to side, with the rocking of the ship, is really alarming. The gale has in a great measure subsided, but there is still a strong swell. We are drifting steadily along, whither we hardly know. Yesterday we were going nearly due north, to-day we are going south-west. Our chief hope lies in sighting some vessel; but we are miles from the line of ships.

"A new subject of interests arises. There is scarcely a cabin to which water has not found its way. The baggage stores are opened. The water has got in, and in sufficient force to float even many of the larger articles. The rocking of the ship has set the whole mass in motion. It has the free range of a compartment some 60 feet square, and 24 hours of such friction has reduced portmanteaus, hat-boxes, dressing-cases, and all the personal chattels incidental to 400 passengers into a mass of pulp such as could not be rivalled by one of the most powerful shoddy mills in the West Riding of Yorkshire. I go down, for I have a personal interest in the mass of ruin. Identity is out of the question. Here are the spangles of the dress of an actress; there the sleeves of an officer's coat. On this side the rim of a hat, on that the leg of a dress boot. Later, I see men feeling cautiously with bare feet for jewels and money, in which this desolation is said to be rich. How they will identify their own, and resist the temptation of taking that which is not theirs, is beyond my philosophy.

"The sea is getting quiet, and a new hope springs up."

This hope came in the form of a thirty-eight-year-old civil engineer, Hamilton E. Towle, a Harvard graduate who lived in Exeter, Massachusetts. Towle had learned that, three feet above the point where the rudder entered the hull, a ten-inch pin of wrought iron on which the rudder turned, had broken off. For the want of this tiny pin the ship known around the world as the greatest of mechanical marvels was at the moment helpless. He worked out a plan for getting the flapping rudder under control, but Captain Walker, "a slightly built, nervously organized, and rather undersized Scotchman," was no man to accept advice from a passenger. Towle's suggestions were turned aside. But as the storm waxed and it became prudent to send up rockets as signals of distress, Captain Walker gave in. He put the engineering department of the ship at Towle's disposal and allowed him to carry out a plan that involved swinging a man on a rope over the stern, which rose and fell about five stories every couple of minutes, plunging him down to, and sometimes under, the surface. After a number of painful and tricky efforts the rudder was brought under control, and the ship could again be driven by her propeller. A short while after Towle had completed his triumphant job of repair, everything took a turn for the better.

"A sail! A sail!" continued "A Passenger." "I look. It is close upon us. A small brig. She speaks us. She is the *Magnet* of Halifax. Now there are signs of rejoicing on board. Husbands embrace their wives; fathers and mothers their children; she agrees to lie by us for the night, and we retire with renewed hopes.

"Sunday—we have drifted about 100 miles in two days, at first in the wrong direction but are now getting right again. I ask the doctor how many casualties have come under his charge. He says 27, but adds there are others. He has dealt only with the worst. We have had no loaf bread for two days. This is chiefly occasioned by a severe accident to the baker, who was thrown across the bake-house and has a compound fracture of the leg. Barrels of biscuits are lashed in various places and we help ourselves. The steering arrangements are going on well, and hope is expressed on all sides—it is written upon the faces. 5:30—There is a joy which does not find its expression in words or cheers. The ship moves by means of her screw, and her head is being brought round; her direction is home. Neither the temporary expedient steering us nor the general conditions justify the captain remaining in the Atlantic. We are 280 miles from Cape Clear. We may hope the screw will take us 8 knots per hour, and we shall see land in 36. The moon shines brightly; the sea has assumed almost a dead calm; the decks are gay, and we are all comparatively happy. Monday—Progressing steadily in a dead calm. At 10 A.M. we sight the *Persia*. She left her port four days after us, and will carry obscure tidings of our misfortune to New York, for we cannot stop our engines without imperilling our temporary steering arrangements. She sees we are distressed, and comes round us. She clearly does not understand why we do not stay our course; and she proceeds on her way for she carries the mails."

About this meeting with Cunard's *Persia*, another *Great Eastern* passenger reported: "A board was held up stating we had lost our rudder, and that she might go to our lee side. She did as requested, but we were running before her nine knots an hour (only by the screw), and I do not wonder that the captain of the *Persia* thought us rather foolish. He stopped and made off, probably not seeing a board on which was written, 'We cannot stop the machine,' and which was held up too late."

When the *Great Eastern* got to Queenstown after her week of going nowhere, the composure of her passengers had quite returned. In a general meeting called while the ship was still offshore, they passed resolutions freely distributing praise and blame. For Captain Walker— who had taken over command only ten days before the ship sailed from Liverpool—they had only praise. They were also grateful to Mr. Towle and voted to present him with "some suitable testimonial to our appreciation." (Whatever this was, it was not enough. When

Towle later sued the Great Ship Company—claiming salvage money in the amount of 100,000.00 dollars—an out-of-court settlement brought him 10,000.00 dollars for his efforts.) Then they expressed their "unanimous and heartfelt thanks" to the captain of the brig *Magnet*. But for the managers of the *Great Eastern* in offices ashore they had nothing but contumely. These men, they said, had allowed their ship to put to sea "unprepared to face the storms which every one must expect to meet in the crossing of the Atlantic." Everything, they declared, was wrong or inadequate; only the great strength of the ship herself had saved them.

Battered, broken, her tail between her legs, the *Great Eastern* had nonetheless proved her mettle and confirmed the opinion of marine experts who wished her well. Ugly and outsized, she still boasted a hull that had been masterfully joined. Her structural excellence was borrowed: her builders, copying new techniques in bridge building introduced by Brunel, had seen to it that these were adapted to the stresses of the ocean. Then, supplying her with an inner bottom and inner sides that "constituted in all respects a second ship inserted within the outer one," they greatly enhanced her safety in the chance of collision with icebergs, or grounding on rocks, and at the same time provided space for a water ballast of 2,500 tons.

The virtue of this double-strength hull was soon confirmed. Approaching New York off Montauk at the outer tip of Long Island, the *Great Eastern* was pierced by an uncharted needle of shoal rock that tore holes in her bottom and opened her up for a hundred feet. The mishap caused her to be stranded for months, more or less on the spot where she had been gouged; but it otherwise involved loss of nothing but a little time and money.

For a few short unprofitable years, sailing in and out of the unlikely terminus of Flushing, Long Island, the *Great Eastern* was a bona-fide transatlantic liner carrying thin lists of hundreds, in space prepared for thousands, of passengers. Then, commissioned as a trooper, she made one voyage to Quebec, followed by the tedious years when, like a fabulous spider on the water, she laboriously spun out the length of the Atlantic cable. Otherwise she was exploited for her value as entertainment in a period of history when the biggest of anything had the power to draw almost everyone.

Had Brunel lived to see his prodigy so reduced, he would have been saddened, no doubt, and perhaps humiliated. He might have even remembered the words spoken by his friend W. L. Lindsay one day in 1858 when the two men were surveying the hull of the *Great Eastern* still on the stocks. "You're premature," Lindsay had said. "The world hasn't grown up to her. Turn her into a show, Brunel, something to attract the masses. Send her to Brighton, dig a hole in the beach and bed her stern in it . . . she will make a substantial pier and her decks a splendid promenade."

Phineas T. Barnum was never able to get his hands on the *Great Eastern,* but she attracted to her decks the same great population of impressionable citizens that had made the showman's New York museum one of the permanent attractions of the city. Some Americans had been so glad to see the ship, in fact, that at the end of her first crossing a crowd broke its way into the docking area, grabbed hold of her hawsers and pulled in the "great babe" as enthusiastically as if she were Paul Bunyan's instead of Brunel's. Tied up between Hudson and Fourteenth Streets, she was a "part of the country, detached from English soil which after having crossed the sea, unites itself to the American continent." Within twenty-four hours a whole carnival of sideshows and pitchmen sprang up within a stone's throw of her moorings. At a dollar a head, and no restriction on the length of time during which they might explore her heights and depths, nearly twenty-five thousand people came every day to gawk, picnic and scribble postcards to their friends back in Skaneateles and Sneden's Landing.

Walt Whitman was impressed with the ship, even though she was much longer than he supposed. In his poem "Year of Meteors," he reduces the length of the *Great Eastern* by more than eighty feet. Otherwise he grants her a laureate's acknowledgment:

> Nor forget I to sing of the wonder, the ship as she swam up my bay,
> Well-shaped and stately the *Great Eastern* swam up my bay, she was
>   600 feet long,
> Her moving swiftly surrounded by myriads of small craft. . . .

Some Americans noted that she lacked a figurehead or a bowsprit; all of them admired her vast proportions and graceful lines; but a few could not refrain from saying tut-tut to her bad housekeeping. "There was much surprise expressed at the neglected condition of the decks," said a reporter, "which appeared as if they neither had been cleaned, scraped, holystoned, or varnished since she was launched. The smoke-pipes look as if they had encountered the storms of a voyage from India instead of England."

On an excursion to Cape May, the *Great Eastern* earned a quick bundle of greenbacks and evoked a torrent of ill-will. After paying ten dollars for the passage down the New Jersey shore and back, excursionists were outraged to find that they had nothing to eat, no place to sleep except on mattresses hawked by small-time profiteers—that they had, in fact, bought a pig in a poke. By the end of the summer, even New Yorkers who did not themselves feel they had been somehow swindled by the *Great Eastern* were sick of her. When she finally pulled anchor and sailed off, "the throng that assembled on the wharves and shores was by no means great, and as she moved off not a cheer greeted her."

Back in England and pleading poverty in spite of all the American dollars she had garnered, she was finally given the chance to make a token gesture toward fulfilling the role she was made for—a long voyage around the Cape of Good Hope to India. Then, almost as soon as she had quit the bazaars of the Orient she was put into the thrall of the new mass-market bazaars of the Occident. A dry goods merchant had her sides painted with huge letters that made the bulk of her look like one gigantic billboard.

Decks aloud with flacks and spielers and calliopes, the mighty *Great Eastern* ended her days in the odd role of a maritime monarch pretending to be a show-biz pasha. To people who could remember the days of Brunel, her appearance offshore was a sad embarrassment. A young student of naval architecture attending a summer conference in Liverpool in 1866 reported that the first thing he saw when he set out on a water excursion was "the unfortunate *Great Eastern*. She was moored in the River Mersey, and had been transformed as a speculation by a syndicate into a floating palace, concert hall and gymnasium, and as we passed the band was playing and the trapeze was at full work, the acrobats, both male and female, flying from trapeze to trapeze: a deplorable exhibition which would have broken the heart of Mr. Brunel."

In 1888, anything that could be removed from the old ship was sold piece by piece at public auctions. To give a touch of elegance to this disposal of things there was even issued a catalogue soberly detailing items of plumbing, joining and carpentering. But the effect of this piece of literature was to reduce one of the legends of a century to a hardware salesman's collection of component parts. Not the least notable thing about the event was the name of its presiding auctioneer. In an ironic little turn of the course of maritime history, the man above the auction block, gavel in hand, was none other than Samuel Cunard's scapegrace brother Joe. After the collapse of his miniature sawmill empire in New Brunswick, Joseph Cunard had moved or, as his compatriots implied, fled to Liverpool. There, on his way toward becoming "esteemed for his good business qualities and uprightness of character," he went into partnership with a man named Wilson and organized a firm advertising itself as "Ship Valuers and Brokers for the Sale of Ships and Steamers." The demise of the *Great Eastern*, for this company at least, had produced a bonanza.

Denuded and dismantled, thirty-one years old, the great ship was towed away to the breakers in 1889. In the matter of size, she was still without peer on the seven seas. But in the matter of power she had long been superseded by ships whose dimensions by comparison were puny.

The ghosts of the *Great Eastern!* Since their story is not burdened with the onus of truth, probably nothing will ever lay them. But the fact is that the most enduring and famous thing about the ship is the legend of two workmen supposedly entombed alive in the black caverns of her hull. While the ship was still under construction, the story goes, a riveter and his assistant fell from a scaffolding and their cries for help went unheard in the clangor of the shipyard. Through all of her years at sea, the legend assumes, the desiccated bones of these two men, sailing everywhere with the *Great Eastern*, kept her accursed. The story is thrilling in a morbid sort of way, but it is false.

"The breaking up of the *Great Eastern* was remarkable for two things," said the English writer L. T. C. Holt, "for the stubbornness with which her splendid hull resisted the efforts of her despoilers and for the birth of a fantastic legend, that the skeletons of a riveter and his boy were discovered sealed within her double hull. That throughout her chequered career the ship had been accompanied by two such grisly stowaways was just the kind of macabre nonsense which a credulous public would swallow whole without pausing to think. Moreover, to the superstitiously inclined it explained her every misfortune. In the first place, as any shipbuilder will confirm, the possibility of a riveter and his mate becoming trapped in this way is so remote as to be almost inconceivable and in the second it is on record that twice, once at the time of floating off and again in July 1859 during the fitting out, Brunel gave orders for the space between the two hulls to be scrupulously cleaned out. When we recall the tonnage of water ballast that was pumped in and out of her the reason for these orders will be obvious. Finally, the firm of Henry Bath & Sons which broke up the ship is still in being and has no record of any such discovery, nor do the records of the appropriate coroner's court yield any trace of the inquest which must have followed such a find."

❦ SECTION XV ❦

IN THE THIRD quarter of the century the nature of ocean transport, past and future, showed a pattern and a temper. The courses it *had* taken were—with the exception of those pursued by Samuel Cunard—risky, profitless and short-lived. The courses it *would* take in the next thirty years or so were equally perilous, profitless and in most instances brief. Almost totally unhampered by competition from the United States, Europeans would launch ships technologically sophisticated, aesthetically overblown and socially stratified. Each of them in turn would strain to break records that had, in turn, just *been* broken. "The passenger market"—as potential customers soon came to be regarded—was an amorphous entity; yet a little beyond midcentury it contained a newly discernible element: Americans to whom travel was edification, an ingredient of social *finesse,* an essential correction to provincial points of view.

But the passenger market was still largely made up of people who traveled out of necessity. Among businessmen there were some who had actually become transatlantic commuters. "Commercial men are naturally in favor of comfortable and fast Atlantic steamers," said one of them, "and declaim against slow ships as vehemently as they would against a railway parliamentary train. They may be found in their usual corner of a London City restaurant on the first day of the month, and at the same table on the last day will be able to tell you what they had for dinner in Delmonico's, New York, or in the chief restaurants of the Western towns, as well as on board the vessel out and home in the interim."

Still wary of putting to sea on vessels with boilers, timid travelers continued to book cabins as far from the infernal heart of these monsters as possible. Of the advance of science or the promise of ease in transit—at least as it was represented by steamers—such travelers refused to be persuaded. "In planning a trip abroad," said one, "the voyage across should not be numbered among its pleasures." To which a clergyman added, "If God would forgive us, we should not commit the sin of going to sea a second time." "When I hear people who profess to enjoy the steamer passage to Liverpool," said an American lady, "I always think how unhappy they must have been at home." "Sleep in the stateroom is the offspring of asphyxiation," said another, "the parent of cramp and the writhing of a doomed body in a coffin." "There I was," moaned a bluestocking, "in helpless agony, clinging to the sides of the berth, and underneath me the Evil Screw."

Yet there had begun to appear people convinced that a round trip to Europe might be as good for one's physical condition as for the enlargement of one's spiritual purview. A sea cure, it came to be felt, was also just the thing for damaged emotions. Young women who had fallen inconveniently in love with ne'er-do-wells, or who had been left waiting in their veils on the church steps by cads and scoundrels, were bundled off to Liverpool in the notion that the one sure antidote to lovesickness was seasickness. There were even individuals—Nathaniel Hawthorne was one of them—who saw in steamship travel the invigoration and uplift that had long been supposed to follow only in the wake of snowy sails. Among Hawthorne's shipmates on a voyage from England to Boston were James Ticknor Fields and Harriet Beecher Stowe. His "love of the sea amounted to passionate worship," said Fields, "and while I (the worst sailor probably in this planet) was longing, in spite of the good company on board, to reach land as soon as possible, Hawthorne was constantly saying in his quiet, earnest way,

'I should like to sail on and on for ever and never touch land again.' "

Hawthorne's compatriot Henry James did not share his rapture. To James an Atlantic voyage "even with the ocean in fairly good humor" was "an emphatic zero in the sum of one's better experience." Soot, oil, stench, the murky vomitings of furnaces and every other kind of fallout engendered by the spawn of the Industrial Revolution were germane to the operation of ships and largely taken for granted.

But to any humane and sensitive soul, the means by which steamships were made to work were discomfitting. Richard Henry Dana, Jr., had survived two years before the mast. Yet when, in the course of a voyage on the *Persia*, his seaman's curiosity led him to investigate the abysmal no-man's-land into which passengers seldom descended, he was scarcely prepared for what he saw. "In these deep and unknown regions," he reported, "down by the keelson of the ship, led to by stories of winding stairs, in the glare of the opening and closing furnace doors, live and toil a body of grim, blackened and oily men, stokers and machinists, coal-carriers, fire-feeders and machine tenders, who know as little of the upper ship as the upper ship knows of them. When down among them on the brick and iron floors between the walls of brick and iron, amid the sights and sounds of their work and care, I lost all sense of being at sea, or even on ship-board, and, for aught that I could hear or see, might have been in the subterranean recesses of a steam factory in Staffordshire. . . ."

While many travelers became resigned to the reality of liners as "purgatorial tubs, overflowing with the mixed reek of engines, cooking, and oil-lamps," to some high hearts ships were still subjects for epiphany. "Shipshape and Bristol fashion, point-device in paint and polish," said one sea lover, "the massive hull glides over the quiet waters of the basin; you catch the sheen of shining brasses, of glistening air-ports, of glazed white, and lacquered black."

For the ordinary man, going to sea was still the source of a pedestrian worry kept lively by reports of collisions, fires, groundings and by two phrases that were chillingly familiar: "never heard of" and "disappeared without trace." In either of these, according to the Jeremianic prose of the period, might lie "the only tale of how a noble vessel and her living freight were suddenly engulfed in eternity." John S. C. Abbott, a clergyman of a sentimental cast and a wholly endearing nature, wrote of his departure from New York bound to Liverpool: "No one can leave his home, to traverse weary leagues of land and sea, without emo-

tion. Images of the loved, who may never be seen again, will rush into
the mind. And even if the most resolute retire for a moment to their
state-rooms, throw themselves upon the sofa, bury their faces in the
pillow, and, with moistened eye, plead with God for a blessing upon
those who are left behind, it is not to be condemned as a weakness. I
soon returned to the deck."

As late as 1863, said an Englishman, "a trip to the States was held
to be quite a serious enterprise. You made your will before you sailed.
Your friends gave you farewell dinners and accompanied you to the
Euston Terminus to see you off by the limited mail for Queenstown,
via Holyhead." In New York, the Equitable Life Assurance Association
stressed the point. "Comfortable Reflections at Sea and Confidence
to the Loved Ones at Home," read their advertising copy, "Can Be
Best Assured by the Husband and Father Going Abroad, Providing for
Their Welfare in the Best System of Life Insurance Extant."

Yet by this time assurances, emphasizing safety and detailing ingenious
safety devices, had almost disappeared from advertisements. Instead,
prospective travelers were invited to savor refinements of life at sea
that had begun to approach the epicene. Unvarnished truth and plain
fact would never insinuate themselves into the shiny pages of travel
brochures, yet the emergence of luxury as a demand rather than as a
marginal provision began to force the steamship companies to deliver
something appreciably close to what their sleek prose promised. To
affluent passengers, the idea of a ship as a great house one could rent—
even as a segment of high society one could enter for a fee—began to
take precedence over the idea of a ship as a mere conveyance.

To emigrants the new ships offered only a cellar on the ocean as
crowded and foul-smelling as the slums they came from or had passed
through on their way to the landing stage. Since international travelers
tended to be either very well off or next to destitution, shipowners
took the distinction into close account. This meant silken largess for
the hundreds, bare-board austerity for the thousands. The division between was immutable. "The passengers of the First and Second Class,"
read a shipboard notice, "are requested not to throw money or eatables
to the steerage passengers, thereby creating disturbance and annoyance."
In the same cautionary spirit, one company went so far as to make
its private instructions public: "Commanders are requested to discourage communication between saloon and steerage passengers, for

should it become known to the Health or Quarantine Officers that such communication had existed on a voyage in the course of which any contagious or infectious disease had occurred, saloon passengers would probably be made subject to quarantine."

On some ships, a spirit of Christian community was allowed to prevail over the rigid social isolation. "At night," wrote a girl traveler from Boston, "we descended into the depths of the steamer to worship with the steerage passengers. It was like one of Rembrandt's pictures— the darkness, the wild, strangely-attired people, the weird light from the lanterns piercing the gloom, and bringing out group after group with fearful distinctness."

Steerage was separated from first class by an unquestioned and invisible chasm. The separation of second class from first was not as decisive, yet in the regard of the more smug and fatuous, even persons traveling second were regarded as a race apart. "They nurse their babies," said one observer as he studied them from the altitudes of his upper deck, "gossip and sing with music and games, and have generally that very good time which people in their walks of life know so well how to enjoy."

Once Inman had shown the way, traffic in emigrants provided the bulk of the income and profits of most shipping lines. Yet emigrants hardly figured in the publicity releases the companies handed out to the press. Competition among ships seemed to turn almost wholly on what any one of them could offer saloon passengers in the way of speed, comfort and social—or societal—security. Since the affluent paid even more deference to class distinctions than the impoverished—and since poverty, more often than not, was viewed as a moral rather than an economic condition—the steamship companies openly courted the rich while they quietly maintained solvency by serving the poor. Passengers with a taste for green-gold livery, glistening mahogany and upholsteries of pneumatic plumpness on land wanted nothing less at sea. Consequently the Great Circle route of the Atlantic was not only a race track but a sort of Peacock Alley. The race was important, but lean ocean greyhounds were soon overtaken by rotund Leviathans. Floating hyperboles, absurdly caparisoned in brocades of silver, weighted and hung with the swag of the Western world like Hannibal's elephants—these new ships would at first alter the picture, then change it completely.

The great change, technologically speaking, was based on two developments: iron hulls and screw propellers. Until vessels of this type had proved themselves capable of superseding everything, most immigrants still came by sailing ship. Cabin passengers, given the choice, consistently preferred paddle-wheelers. But when the companies discovered how much cheaper it was to cross the ocean under screw power, that preference did not matter—except to veteran old skippers who insisted that paddles gripped the water better than screws, that wind in the sails was cleaner and more economical than burning coal, and that a clipper bow could cut the seas more cleanly than a straight stem.

The turbine engine, still many years hence, would usher in the operatic phase of transatlantic travel and all its cheerful decadence. Meanwhile, there was a period when steamships were not only tolerably comfortable but astonishingly handsome. Not since the days of Donald McKay had ocean-going vessels been so indisputably objects of beauty. These were the liners constructed when sails still complemented engines—at least as tokens or auxiliaries—so that clipper bows and yacht-like lines, raked funnels and tall masts in a row, united the compact power of steam with the nearly obsolescent charm of cloud-flown canvas.

The most notable ship of this period was the very first of a new breed—the *Oceanic*. Built by the young firm of Harland & Wolff in Belfast, she was the forerunner and archetype of six sister ships that sailed under the red swallowtail burgee imprinted with the five-pointed star of the White Star Line.

Like the long-defunct Collins Line, this company had its beginnings in the great days of sail, when its American-built wooden ships took emigrants and cargo to Australia.

The White Star was already a well-known operation when, acquiring the clipper ship *Red Jacket*, its directors found their company's image enhanced by a touch of primitive Americana. The *Red Jacket*, built in Rockland, Maine, was named for the Senecan Sagoyewatha, an Indian chief rewarded for his aid, as a scout for British forces in the War of Independence, by the gift of a red tunic. When the White Star Line took the *Red Jacket* on charter to Australia and later bought her outright, the figure of Sagoyewatha in his red coat, open at the chest to show a white, five-pointed star, quite naturally struck the public with the force of a trademark. But by 1867 the Messrs. Pilkington & Wilson were ready to sell out name and image. Thomas H. Ismay bought the flag and the goodwill of the firm for one thousand pounds and began to send new iron ships across the old routes to the Antipodes. Successful in this, he turned his eyes on the North Atlantic and, in 1869, organized the Oceanic Steam Navigation Company, or, in the mind of the public, the White Star Line.

Launched without ceremony in the late summer of 1870, the *Oceanic* spent six months being fitted out with appurtenances that would make her the eponymous instance of the modern ocean liner. When she sailed into the Mersey on February 26, 1871, even the most case-hardened observers of maritime prodigies saw something to make them blink. The *Oceanic* was ten times longer than she was wide. Her open deck was an iron promenade enclosed with railings instead of bulwarks, thus allowing sea wash to run off freely instead of gurgling through scuppers. She had a straight-stemmed cutwater, a single low funnel, and four cylindrical iron masts laden with sail. Of stately rig, long and low in the water, she came to Liverpool "more like an imperial yacht than a passenger steamer."

The *Oceanic*'s outer appearance was but the first of a score of surprises. Her biggest—and, as it turned out, definitive—innovation was the placement of her grand saloon. This "great square parlor" which was not "the usual plush coffin in our steamers," was placed high and squarely amidships. Thus was ended the custom, in force since the Middle Ages and continuing through the eras of the galleon and the caravel, of confining privileged travelers to quarters in the high rump of the stern. Extending the full width of the ship, the *Oceanic*'s grand saloon was lighted by circular bull's-eyes, fourteen inches in diameter, that looked onto the sea. At each end of the room stood coal-burning fireplaces with marble mantels. The great thing for passengers at meal times was the introduction of separate armchairs. At last a man could dine without having to get up from his long settee "of indefined capacity," napkin in hand, for late-comers; without having continually to push over and make room for others; and with confidence that, in a moment of dreadful urgency, he could make a quick exit. After dinner, when it was time for the segregation of the sexes that gentility still demanded, ladies could retire to a boudoir encased in brocades and hung with mirrors. Gentlemen could go to a smoking room on the main deck that was "quite a narcotic paradise," open "to sea and sky, or closed to both." For the first time since the *Great Eastern*, smokers did not have to go, so to speak, behind the barn.

Staterooms on the *Oceanic* were bigger and brighter than those on any other ship. They had electric bells which, at the "touch of the finger to the ivory disc," commanded the instant attention of stewards. Instead of jugs, rattling in holders affixed to the walls, there were taps for water, fresh and salt; instead of candles there were adjustable oil lamps; instead of a suffocating burden of blankets to cover him at night a passenger could count on the balm of steam heat. Steam, in fact, had become the genius of the ship. "Like the elephant that picks up a needle and tears down a tree," said the Sapphic echoes of White Star's brochure, "there is no task too small, no work too great for the giant, Steam. He warms the child's berth; he weighs the anchor; he turns the barber's brush; he loads and discharges the ship; and rests not night nor day."

For those who could afford to pay for her choice midships cabins, the *Oceanic* was blessedly quiet. In these apartments, the noises of the screw were muted, the creaking of the steering apparatus muffled. In fact, some people of sharply refined tastes had already come to prefer the hermitage of a well-appointed stateroom to the uncertain pleasures of mixing with strangers in showily decorated saloons. It was a regular practice of one of Henry James' rich but minor heroines "to spend the voyage in her cabin, which smelt good (such was the refinement of her art), and she had a secret peculiar to herself for keeping her port open without shipping seas. She hated what she called the mess of the ship and the idea, if she should go above, of meeting stewards with plates of superogatory food." Nevertheless, it seemed that the notion of a transatlantic voyage as a pleasure and not as a dread necessity might finally take hold. "Never was more beauty or greater strength and stability wrought in iron since the metal was introduced into shipbuilding," said T. H. Ismay. Yet, besides himself, only 64 passengers showed up to occupy the *Oceanic*'s 1,200 berths when she sailed on her maiden voyage.

Their trip was a trial—in more ways than one. As soon as the *Oceanic* gained headway in the Irish Sea, her main bearings and crankpins were found to be overheating dangerously. She put into Holyhead with the idea of making adjustments to correct this trouble; but more than adjustment was needed. She had to give up all notions of an Atlantic dash in order to sidle sheepishly back into Liverpool under the eyes of the thousands who had just bidden her Godspeed. But on March 16, 1871, mended, oiled and on her mark, she started off again, only to spend fifteen long days before getting to Sandy Hook. Speed, her owners insisted, was but a secondary consideration; in the new era, comfort was the thing.

Whatever concern Thomas Ismay may have felt about his new ship's drawing power was at once allayed by the response of New Yorkers. When she was docked at the foot of Pavonia Avenue in Jersey City, fifty thousand people piled onto ferryboats and crossed the Hudson in order to walk her decks. Not since the first visit of the *Great Eastern* had any liner created such a stir or generated so much of a carnival atmosphere. "It was acknowledged," said a report sent back to England, "that this new type of ship had, in the striking phraseology of America, 'come to stay.' " She even had bathtubs.

Within a year of her maiden voyage the *Oceanic* was joined by identical sister ships—*Atlantic, Baltic, Republic,* and, one year still later, by two slightly larger vessels, *Adriatic* and *Celtic.* To cap all of White Star's thrilling innovations, the last two ships were lighted by gas. But there was so much foul-smelling leakage caused by the normal working of a ship at sea that gas lights had to be replaced by conventional oil lamps. This was but a minor setback in a swift series of developments that had brought the White Star Company into control of a fleet of express liners superior to anything else on the Atlantic.

Not since the days of Edward Knight Collins had Cunard ships been so thoroughly superseded. Making the most of speed and comfort, the White Star Line was preeminent, not only over Cunard, but over a lively group of competitors that also included the National, Guion and Inman Lines. In fact, innovations on White Star ships were so widely publicized that voyagers on the Cunard Line who had read about them began to feel themselves underprivileged. One of these was John W. Burgess, the American historian, who took passage on Cunard's *Tarifa* from Boston just a few months after the *Oceanic* had welcomed sightseers up her gangplanks in Jersey City.

"All the accommodations for the passengers," said Burgess, "staterooms, dining saloons, toilettes and deck were in the extreme stern of the vessel so that we were exposed to the greatest motion of the vessel at all times and at every turn. There were no bells to call the steward. If a steward was wanted, the passenger must go out into the gangway and shout for him. There were only two toilettes in the ship, and there was no bath at all. The dining saloon was just above the staterooms, also in the stern of the vessel. There were no swivel chairs, no chairs at all at the tables, only long benches, and at every meal there was a free fight for the end seats so that in case of nausea one might quickly rush out on deck. There were no napkins at the table and when our passengers made a sort of protest to the Company in regard to what we considered hardships, referring in it to the absence of table napkins, old Mr. MacIver replied that going to sea was a hardship, that the Cunard Company did *not* undertake to make anything else out of it, and that if people wanted to wipe their mouths at a ship's table they could use their pocket handkerchiefs."

MacIver's response put the Cunard philosophy in a nutshell. The spectacular Collins Line had come and gone; the *Great Eastern*'s commercial career was a shambles. Cunard ships alone had maintained an unblemished record for safety, as well as a Scottish determination on the part of their owners to avoid frivolities that were threatening to turn hard-working transports into pleasure pavilions.

While travelers faithful to Cunard—and frightened of anyone else— continued in their pedestrian ways, White Star customers were becoming the jolliest people on the ocean. "How splendid are these passage boats!" said Mr. Hepworth Dixon. "The *Republic* is a floating palace, with the style and comfort of a Swiss hotel. I am ready to despair of finding any vessel more completely to my mind. We measure more than 400 feet in length, and have a saloon amidships, gay with gold and soft with cushions, in which the young ladies can flirt, and their elders dawdle over books and prints."

The *Republic*'s Captain Digby Murray was less given to enthusiasm. Only a short time before Mr. Dixon's rapturous voyage, the Captain had reported to the home office of the White Star Line troubles with his ship and trials with his crew. His attitude toward the grimy, ignorant, ill-fed and underpaid seamen over whom he ruled is no doubt an index to attitudes generally held in the eighth decade of the Century of Progress.

"Gentlemen," he wrote. "In my letter to you from Queenstown, I told you of the detention from leakage in upper between-decks, forward of the saloon. I am sorry to say it still continues, and we have many other difficulties to contend with; the saloon and state-rooms have been flooded through the new ventilations; the windows of the wheelhouse have been dashed in by the sea, and compass unshipped and broken, thermometers broken, etc.; the stanchions of the bridge and bridge compass carried away; gangway abreast of saloon unshipped and carried aft; chocks of two boats washed away; a great deal of water washing down companion-way into women's quarters aft. The new ventilators, as before mentioned, are a perfect failure, drowning the passengers out, nor can we make them tight.

"No canvas was set during the gale. It was ordered at one time, but the utter worthlessness of the crew, skulking and stowing away, crying like children, made it difficult to do anything. Our carpenters are precious little account in bad weather, and a very slow lot at any time; our crew often a lot of curs. To have got a sail up, or cut away for use, I should have had to ask assistance from the passengers. I had our fireman (so-called) rope's-ended for stowing away in the coal bunkers for the fourth time; it had become really a serious question. We could only get four men of the starboard watch the other night; I therefore consulted with the officers and chief engineer, and we have decided that the safety of the ship requires decisive measures, and that after this we will strip and flog every man stowing away while on watch."

Such gloomy reports from the bridge were not echoed by passengers below—at least by the time Captain Digby had been transferred to the better-beloved *Atlantic*. "The splendid accommodations," wrote the Reverend A. A. Willits, "the charming weather, the distinguished and talented character of the company on board, and the novel, instructive, and delightful entertainments in the saloon every evening . . . have together made this a most remarkable and memorable voyage; so much so that many gentlemen on board, who have crossed the ocean repeatedly, declare they have never seen anything comparable with it before, and that it really initiates a new era in ocean navigation."

The clergyman's summer voyage was darkened, but only very briefly, by a tragic mishap. On July 4 he wrote in his diary: "Sad accident occurred today. The Quartermaster, whilst firing a salute in honor of the day, was so severely wounded in his arms that it became necessary for Dr. Sims to amputate both limbs, one at the wrist and the other at the forearm. The greatest sympathy was felt for the poor fellow." This regrettable event did not curb the celebrations planned in honor of the long Fourth. On the next evening Reverend Willitts was delighted to see "a party of young ladies and gentlemen dancing the Lancers to the music of a piano!" On the following night he delivered a lecture to an overflow crowd in the saloon. His topic was "Sunshine, or the Secret of Happiness." This talk went so well that Dr. Sims was also persuaded to contribute to the inspirational fare. His lecture subject was "The Ambulance Service in the Late Franco-Prussian War." The attention span of the passengers on the *Atlantic* was notable, if not inordinate. On the last night out, among a series of poems written en route and delivered en masse was George Francis Train's valedictory, which concluded:

Whereas,
No steamers ever make such perfect time,
As the floating palaces of the "White Star" Line;

Whereas,
They give to each a daily chart,
To mark the passage from the hour of start;
And Church and Theatre, Concert, Legislative Hall,
Song, Recitation, Speech—a programme for us all—
Each night they organise in the grand saloon!
(Where width of ship gives forty feet of room)
And the "tableau vivant" with its sixty lights,
Illuminates the debate on "Womens' Rights";

And Whereas,
Obliging officers, and smart, attentive crew,
Strain every nerve to please, like men both brave and true;

Resolved,
That we, the voyagers, some hundred and thirty souls,
Fair bumpers fill, and wave aloft our flowing bowls:
"To Captain Murray! May he always shine,
As Admiral of the famous 'White Star' Line!"

Not quite one out of five ocean passengers had the money to pay for these new indulgences; four out of five traveled in the bare wooden stalls of the steerage. Mostly emigrants, bedraggled "bog-trotters" combed out of the stricken parishes of Ireland, these travelers were subject to examination before being allowed to board ship. Any one of them found to be "lunatic, idiot, deaf, dumb, blind, maimed, infirm or above the age of sixty years," or "any woman without a husband with a child or children," was liable to be turned away at the last minute, his possessions bundled around him and no place to go.

There was also a mild concern for bodily cleanliness, but this was continually frustrated. Emigrants had never been introduced to the sanitary solutions of the middle class, the gurglings of the water closet, or the marvels of other bathroom apparatuses. The joys of ablution were something to which they would not subscribe. Somehow they had been instilled with "hygienic obscurantism," in the phrase of one historian, and were wary of the rites of purification, reluctant to part with that sense of identity residing in their own smells.

Those who could pass muster and were allowed aboard entered a whole new dispensation in emigrant services. Almost everything had been upgraded; for instance, there was the innovation of the combined dining-room-cum-lounge and bedroom. This was made possible by a "clever contrivance"—sleeping berths made of canvas that could be folded away, so that a table with attached seats might be lowered from the ceiling and stowed away again after meals.

In the ambience of unaired bedclothes, stale food and handy chamber pots, steerage passengers could now count upon table fare regulated by the British Government. For breakfast they could have coffee with fresh bread and butter; and for dinner they were entitled to soup, beef, pork or fish, with bread and potatoes and, on Sundays, pudding. "After each meal," said a gentleman who was reduced to traveling in the steerage, "a long line of men, women and children could be seen going up the stairs, each with their dinner dishes in their hands—like a line of convicts at State prisons leaving their cells—and waiting for an opportunity to dry them after washing."

For every one hundred souls in the steerage there were two toilets. Anyone who wanted a place to sit on the open deck had to look for coils of rope or boxes—part of the cargo—that had been lashed down. Really indigent passengers slept in a bare canvas bunk, six feet long, eighteen inches wide; those with a little money could buy straw mattresses which would be thrown overboard as the ship sailed into New York Harbor.

In the early years of emigrant traffic there was no segregation of the sexes. This confinement of twenty people or more in one compartment often led to episodes that the vast Victorian vocabulary of moral turpitude was taxed to describe. Eventually the White Star Line was moved to provide separate quarters for men, women and married couples. But even these improved circumstances could widen the eyes of the genteel observer. A lady from Queenstown who paid a visit to the

Germanic reported to a London newspaper that the ship was "a whited sepulchre, haunted by the memories of sin, full of ravening wickedness and all uncleanness."

The hopes of emigrants for a new life, often fortified by absolute rejection of their old lives, gave them, besides endurance, a sort of grim, indomitable merriment. Thomas Moore, one of the century's lyricists of kitsch, could write of the emigrant ship's "trembling pennant," which

> Still look'd back
> On that dear Isle 'twas leaving.
>
> Thus loath we part from all we love,
> From all the links that bind us.
> So turn our hearts, where'er we rove,
> To those we've left behind us.

To one Atlantic captain, at least, this was nonsense. He had noted time and again that once they were out of sight of Queenstown and its "tall veledictory cathedral" with a "steeple silhouetted above the little town and its bay like a last blessing," emigrants did not look back. "They all seemed glad to leave their native land," he said. "We hardly got outside the harbour before fiddles and concertinas would be produced, and they would be dancing away on the foredeck. If there happened to be any sea on after passing the Fastnet they would disappear, and no amount of persuasion would get them out of the bunks when the sea calmed down till 'stink-pots,' otherwise pans of sulphur, were lighted in their quarters. Then they would discover that they had more life in them than they thought they had, and would come rushing on deck gasping for breath."

The hare and tortoise race between slowpoke Cunard and its flashy rivals seemed once again to be coming down to the wire with victory for Cunard. Just as, one by one, the glamor girls of the Collins Line had foundered while the dowdy dowagers of Cunard sailed serenely on, so for a time did it seem that the bedighted new White Star ships might not be able to keep the pace they had set for themselves.

When the two-year-old *Atlantic* sailed from Liverpool via Queenstown for New York on March 20, 1873, she left the Irish port with an unusually large passenger and crew complement of 942, enough coal in her bunkers to keep her steaming for just over fifteen days, and, according to one passenger, "with a crew disorderly and infamous," among whom were officers "carousing the whole voyage." From the start, heavy weather seriously slowed the *Atlantic*'s progress. Eleven days out from Ireland, she was still 400 miles from Sandy Hook. Chief Engineer Foxley told her Captain James Agnew Williams that the coal supply was down to 127 tons. Captain Williams, afraid that further bad weather en route to New York might leave his ship with a perilously narrow margin of fuel, decided to head for Halifax, only 170 miles away. At 1 P.M. on March 31, the *Atlantic*'s course was changed from southwest to northeast and she proceeded in clear weather toward the coast of Nova Scotia. Under full steam, doing about 12 knots, at 3 A.M., April 1, she smashed head-on into rocks at Meagher's Head, at the extreme point of Point Prospect, less than 20 miles from Halifax Harbor.

Twenty-eight hours later, a telegram arrived at the White Star offices in Liverpool:

> BRADY THIRD OFFICER ARRIVED HALIFAX ATLANTIC ILLEGITIMATE CAPE PROSPECT ABOUT CHESHIRE CHAIN BOULOGNE PEOPLE IN-CLUDING CAPTAIN SAVED INTENDED IMPRECATION HAVE DES-PATCHED PENNELL NAVAL

When this message was decoded, the owners of the *Atlantic* learned that their ship was a total wreck and that of the 942 men, women and children aboard, some 700 (the figure was later revised to 481) had perished. Eventually they would learn that before the ship's boilers had exploded and she had sunk by her beam ends, two hundred people had made it to shore on lines attached to rocks. When they had to deal with insurance claims, they would learn that local scavenging parties had cruised the area in rowboats, seizing bodies as they floated by or lifting them up with gaffs so that they could search the sodden clothing for valuables before dropping them back. And finally they had to learn that the contents of trunks and suitcases were offered for sale to the curious in a grim little *marché aux puces* laid out like a church fair on the granite ledges of Nova Scotia.

It was the century's worst transatlantic disaster. A court of inquiry established at Halifax elicited the banal facts: leaving orders to be awakened at 3 A.M., Captain Williams had retired to the chart room a little after midnight; at twenty minutes to three, his "tiger" came to the adjoining wheelhouse with a pot of cocoa and was about to rap on the Captain's door when Fourth Officer John Brown said, "No—let him sleep." The Captain did sleep, forgotten by everyone, until he was jolted awake by the crunch of the collision.

The newspapers loved it all—the grisly eyewitness reports of a night of sublime horror, the court of inquiry which confirmed, on very thin evidence, the general suspicion that the *Atlantic* had indeed started across the ocean with insufficient coal. The New York *Herald* printed an interview with a young Irishman, Patrick Leahy, who, as he hung in the rigging "saw the first and awful sight. It was just gleaming day; a large mass of something drifted past the ship on the top of the waves, and then was lost to view in the trough of the sea. As it passed by, a moan—it must have been a shriek, but the tempest dulled the sound— seemed to surge up from the mass, which extended over fifty yards of water; it was the women. The sea swept them out of the steerage, and with their children, to the number of 200 or 300, they drifted thus to eternity."

Chief Officer John Firth was meanwhile hanging in another part of the rigging. As the battered ship waited for rescue by fishing craft and tug boats from Halifax, he tried, he said, to comfort a woman passenger. But the cold was too severe and she succumbed. When he last had sight of her, he reported, "Her half-nude body was still fast in the rigging, her eyes protruding, her mouth foaming, a terribly ghastly spectacle rendered more ghastly by contrast with the numerous jewels which sparkled on her hands."

Within a matter of weeks the disaster had entered show business. Episodes from the night of the wreck "were painted on canvas and rolled on a big wooden cylinder. This was turned by a crank and the pictures moved across the front of theatre stages." This picture show toured the Maritime Provinces with sensational success, especially for that part of the story in which the canvas unrolled "a beautiful and almost nude girl being cast upon a rocky shore at the feet of a hardy fisherman." According to a report from New Brunswick, "Women became hysterical gazing at it, and some fainted." Sigmund Freud was seventeen years old at this time; exercises in hysteria were still ascribed to delicacy of sensibility.

Such outbursts and breakdowns had been encouraged by an artful mixture of poesy and clinical morbidity. A couple of days after the *Atlantic* had grounded, the Halifax *Chronicle* had dispatched two reporters to the scene. The account turned in by one of them significantly expanded the archives of Victorian journalism.

"A boat was speedily engaged to convey the anxious news seekers, first to the Hill of Death," said the *Chronicle*'s man, "secondly to the spot where the broken and dismembered *Atlantic* lay. As the skiff shot round the points and passed among the numerous islets and rock masses that stud the coast here, glimpses were obtained of the wrecking fleet, comprising schooners and boats beyond number. Row boats, manned by hardy fishermen, sped full quick to a cove where were already made fast more than one embarcation whose equipment of grappling irons, drags and ropes told plainly the mission on which its crew was bent. The curiosity of the *Chronicle* messengers was now roused to its highest pitch, and every rock face, every grass slope, every earth terrace, was scanned in hopes of discovering the first traces of the dread harvest of the sea. This curiosity was not to be so easily satisfied, and by a strange chance the first glimpse of the dead bodies was to be dramatic in the highest degree. A slow climb of a steep declevity marked by huge projecting granite masses, a glance at the distant breakers seen from the top of the rock, then on turning a vast block of stone, the visitor gasped for breath as, at his very feet, still and stark and cold, with glassy eyes opened out to widest extent and gazing up into the 'lone and sunny idleness of heaven,' lay in rows what, not many hours before, had been human beings, sharing with him light, air, passions and all things earthly.

"A feeling deeper than reverential awe, a sensation as might be experienced by one standing on the threshold of death, chilled to the very marrow the bones of the looker-on, and it was with slow steps, subdued mien, and half-averted glance that the gleaner of news approached this solemn assembly. Then what a sight met the eye! There, on the brow of that rocky island, partly on the stones, partly on the grassy earth, wet with last night's rain and cut up by brown patches of peaty moss, exposed to the wind and to the heat and cold of heaven, lay the aged and the young, the strong and the feeble, equalized at last by the blow that fell so sudden on them. Ay, man, woman, and child had been alike swallowed up by the greedy deep that strove hard to keep its human prey, and fought for it with angry breakers and sullen roar of surf. Side by side lay they, these corpses whose expression varied not greatly, for of them some bore the imprint of that peace so much spoken of and so little believed in, and which shone here wonderously evident; others set resolutely as if the last thought of the living ever conjured had been 'duty!'; and others again revealing nothing of the final emotions that must have crossed the few, fast passing minutes that lapsed ere eternity opened up before the dead. In all positions too . . . but one and all carefully and reverently covered where mutilations disfigured the form.

"For, alas! the work of rescue needs a bold and unscrupulous hand, and the floating body must be gaffed as it washes by, and no matter where the sharp hook strikes, whether on face, or neck, or body, it cuts and tears frightfully. Some corpses had been so terribly lacerated that sail cloth had been used to cover up the features and limbs which love itself could no longer recognize. Hands, arms, feet and legs that were bared, showed around, and all were bleached white; all were shrunken horribly; faces were discolored and blotched red, green—yes, all manner of hideous colors, and again were fair and rosy as in life. . . ."

When the Halifax court published its findings, dismayed White Star executives tried urgently to prove that their ship did *not* sail short of coal. Eventually they succeeded in having the case referred to the Chief Surveyor, and the London Surveyor to the Board of Trade. These gentlemen issued a shocking statement which the desperate company accepted with pleasure: "The loss [of the *Atlantic*] was not through being driven on a lee shore, helpless, her fuel spent and the engines without fire. She was run at full speed, engines and boilers all in perfect order, upon well known rocks, in fine weather."

Captain Williams himself was dealt with mildly. The presiding judge at Halifax could not forbear stating his belief that the Captain's conduct "in the management of the ship during the twelve or fourteen hours preceding the disaster was so gravely at variance with what ought to have been the conduct of a man placed in his responsible position, as to call for severe censure." Yet it was the merciful judgment of the court that the Captain had shown great personal courage and heroism in the fearful hours after the wreck. To placate angry public opinion, Captain Williams was relieved of his mariner's certificate—but only as a token punishment. Within two years he was back on the bridge of a White Star liner.

⚛ SECTION XVI ⚛

S.S. City of Boston: "The Wonderful Narrative of Julia Dean" / "I've Got Pluck and I've Got Money, and I'm Going to Have You, Honey"

WHITE STAR was not the only line that was losing ships to the gods of chance and customers to Cunard. The Inman Line was having troubles, too. Its *City of New York* went aground on Daunt's Rock near Queenstown and became a total wreck; its *Glasgow* caught fire at sea and had to be abandoned. Yet the line continued to grow at a pace; travelers were obviously just as taken by a bargain in a transatlantic ticket as they were in safety. Then, in 1870, the company sustained still another jolt.

In January of that year its *City of Boston* left her namesake port on schedule with a small midwinter's complement of 177, including passengers and crew. She put into Halifax, en route to Liverpool, and on the twenty-eighth of the month sailed out to oblivion.

Overdue, unreported, the *City of Boston* left not a spar or a rumor to cling to. The baffling months went by without a clue. Finally, in June, William Inman said to his stockholders what little there was to say. "I can no longer conceal from myself the overwhelming possibility that the total loss of this company's steamship, with all on board, has taken place."

The demise of the *City of Boston*, involving neither a great ship nor a large number of passengers, was soon on its way to becoming a mere footnote in the history of losses at sea. Then, in 1880, rising out of a decade of silence, came the one voice to tell what had happened to the *City of Boston* and what had happened to the sole survivor herself. She was Julia Dean, and she put her story into a little pamphlet of very fine print entitled "The Wonderful Narrative of Miss Julia Dean, the Only Survivor of the Steamship *City of Boston*, Lost at Sea in 1870." Miss Dean, now Mrs. Charles Vollar, claimed by an affidavit reproduced with her pamphlet, that she had been floated onto a volcanic island after the sinking of the *City of Boston*; that she had lived alone there for more than eight years, and was only returned to civilization when, having noticed that her island was about to disappear, she had put to sea in a small boat and was picked up by a schooner, en route from Liverpool to New York, by the name of *Sally Briggs*.

As her story goes, Miss Dean as a girl lives in rural Pennsylvania, where society, modeled on the lines of an English county, is somehow made up only of squires, tenants and wastrel sons with spirited horses. An indifferent girl, but not a cruel one, Miss Dean rebuffs the sighing overtures of Charles Vollar, a fine young man whose honest affection fails to thrill her—even after he has literally snatched her from the unwelcome embrace of a villainous squire named Bradley Adams. Years later, long after unrequited love has caused Vollar to leave the neighborhood, Julia Dean must still cope with the relentless importunities of "Brad" Adams and, upon his rather timely death, with the equally obnoxious advances of his brother and heir, Thomas Adams. "I'm bound to have you one of these days," Thomas tells her. " 'I've got pluck and I've got money, and I'm going to have you, honey'—that's poetry, but it's true as gospel, see if it ain't." Without waiting for this prediction to fulfill itself, Julia leaves Pennsylvania in her father's company to visit relatives in England. The ship they choose is the *City of Boston*, and they are only two days out of Halifax when a tempest arises, lightning stabs the ship and sets her ablaze. Amid scenes of instant horror the liner founders—leaving Julia Dean alone on a raft. She drifts for many hours. Then, half drowned and comatose, she is deposited on a volcanic shore. There, Christian fortitude plus good basic training in household management serve her well. She makes a home for herself in a cave, picks berries, traps animals and skins them, learns to live in a perpetual state of *déshabille*. For eight years, lonely at times but always glad to be alive, she makes the most of this hermitage. Then, one summer day, a storm of great velocity breaks over the island, floods her cavern home, and washes out Miss Dean, along with her domestic effects. When the storm subsides, she opens her eyes in the presence of a man.

"I awoke to find a handsome man bending over me, dashing water in my face from the keg (which fortunately I always kept just outside my now sunken cave), and rubbing my hands vigorously.

"My first feeling was one of peace, rest and thankfulness for my miraculous delivery, the next was one of intense astonishment at again beholding a human being, and on that island.

"Strange, but nevertheless true, no sense or feeling of shame came to me at my half-naked appearance. I had long since come to look upon my thin costume as the proper and only thing.

"My large eyes, opened so wide in amazement, attracted the man's attention, and, seeing that I had recovered, he asked. 'Who are you? What are you? How came you there—here?'

"Tears sprang unbidden to my eyes, as I heard for the first time in eight long years words thus spoken, and spoken by an American. I sprang up to my feet, and all unwomanly as it may seem, dear reader, I kissed his hands, his face, and threw my arms around his neck, sobbing like a child.

" 'Poor woman,' he said, 'she does not understand English. I wonder how came she here? She must have been alone on this island a long while, judging from her looks, action, and costume.'

"Controlling myself, I knelt at his feet, and cried: 'Thank God! I see and converse with a human being once more. Thanks, oh, thanks my more than preserver! I see in this, O kind Providence, the beginning of the end, when my rescue shall be all complete.'

"It was his turn to be astonished now, and seeing how great his astonishment was I hastened to relieve him, saying: 'You see before you a poor girl who was tossed upon this island over eight years ago, and who has lived here alone ever since, never beholding the face of man during all that time.'

" 'Great Heaven! This is indeed a strange story,' he exclaimed. 'Why you are a *real* Crusoe, a female Crusoe at that. My poor child, you must have suffered greatly. Your rapture at beholding me, and wild caresses, were extremely natural under the circumstance. But how came you on this island? Surely no ship was wrecked here. It must be many miles out of the course of all vessels.'

" 'I might ask you the same question, sir,' I replied, 'and with as much reason.'

" 'True, true,' he said, 'mine is a strange story.'

" 'Mine may be equally as strange,' said I.

" 'Your vessel was lost at sea? Burned, perhaps, and you floated hither on a raft. I see by your looks that I have partly guessed it. Tell me your story, and I'll tell mine. Was it a sailing vessel?'

" 'No. It was the steamship *City of Boston* and I have every reason to believe that you see before you the only survivor of that ill-fated craft.'

" 'Lost at sea in 1870?' he said musingly. 'Yes, I remember the year well, for I had several dear friends on board that steamer, and they have never been heard from since.'

" 'What were their names?' I asked, 'Had you none nearer and dearer than friends?'

" 'There was one on board that vessel,' he exclaimed vehemently, 'that I would have laid down my life for, though she spurned my—'

" 'Spurned your love,' I interrupted, 'and—great God! I see it all now, you are *Charles Vollar!*'

" 'Merciful heavens,' he shouted, 'and you are—no, no, it cannot be—'

" 'Yes, I am Julia Dean!' "

When this recognition scene has run its course, and Charles Vollar tells the story of *his* shipwreck, they face their situation together. Orphans of the storm, they start to make out of flotsam and jetsam a house and a home. But propinquity soon makes them uneasy and restless. Spending their days together and their nights apart is more than they can bear. Putting aside scruples, they agree to declare themselves wed. " 'Then,' " said Charles, " 'we are married in the sight of heaven, and only lacking the ceremony devised by man to make us man and wife. Let us stand hand in hand, asking God to make us one in all things. Let us swear, with no witness present save the moon just risen, and the weird music of yonder waves for our marriage bells, that we will Love, Honor and Obey each other even until death shall part us.' "

Mutterings from the volcano confirm what they have begun to sense: the island is getting too hot for comfort. In fear that the earth is going to disappear from under them, they build a boat and sail away just as the island gives a great sigh, gulps, and goes under. Then the *Sally*

Briggs, with Captain A. Downey Brease in command, comes scudding along. They are sighted, assisted aboard, and carried to New York.

After their miraculous rescue the happy couple settle in Philadelphia. When Mrs. Vollar finally gets around to telling her story, she has it illustrated—mainly with drawings of herself in scanty costume dismembering animals—and publishes it at her own expense. Downey Brease cooperates by signing the affidavit reproduced on the pamphlet's cover, and by stating, "The lady's name, Miss Dean, appears on the passenger list of the steamer *City of Boston*, lost at sea in 1870." Few of her readers took the trouble to learn whether or not this was true. Sadly enough—on the evidence preserved in the Archives of Nova Scotia in Halifax—it was not. And Downey Brease had by this time no doubt retired to the breezy downs.

❦ SECTION XVII ❦

Inman Advances / The City of Berlin / Robert Louis Stevenson: Amateur Immigrant / Sarah Bernhardt and the Lady in Black

UNDER THE BURDEN of universal approval and their own exemplary behavior Cunard ships had begun to fade as objects of popular attention. Six in a row, the White Star sisters became the crack liners of the Great Circle route. At this point the prosperous Inman Line decided to step out of its strictly utilitarian character and enter the glamor stakes. The phrase "Inman's iron screws," and its connotations of the troop ship weighed down with a cargo of faceless emigrants, was suddenly a thing of the past.

Inman's loss of the *City of Boston* was baffling and dismaying, but the loss was comparatively minor in light of the fact that the line had already carried more than a half-million passengers safely across the ocean. Suspicions that the ship was overloaded and in bad repair cast only a small shadow over the company's good name. Two and a half years later, the *City of Washington* cracked up on the coast of Nova Scotia near Cape Sable. This time there was no loss of life, but the shadow of doubt was amplified. Still, by the end of 1873, with a fleet of thirty-one ships, an aggregate tonnage of nearly 80,000, the Inman people had the means to challenge the gate crashers of the North

Atlantic and to put down all doubts about the validity of their own hard-earned reputation.

The Inman ship designed to recapture the Blue Riband from White Star's *Adriatic* and to match her trappings, tassel for tassel, was the *City of Berlin*. Within a year of her launching late in 1874, the new flagship could claim priority on all counts. Her engines hurried her from Queenstown to New York in 7 days, 18 hours, 2 minutes, for a new westbound record. Her tonnage, with the exception of the now *hors de combat Great Eastern*, was unmatched. Her first-class appointments and overall spaciousness made the White Star ships seem cramped. "You can have a promenade of nearly five hundred feet straight ahead," reported a happy passenger. "The lower deck looks like a little town, and it is a great deal pleasanter than most little towns. There is a row of handsome-looking houses, with a street open to the sea on either side. These houses, bright and neat, with their descriptions engraved on each in English, French, and German, are the officers' rooms, ladies' room, smoking-room, etc., all opening upon the deck on both sides. The ladies' public room is spacious, and filled with sofas and seats, so that the occupants can sit and chat with their male friends outside, or draw a curtain and shut themselves from all observation. The washing conveniences are such that you turn the taps in your stateroom to wash with more confidence than if you had a London reservoir to draw from, there being between three and four miles of lead piping in the ship. The bathtubs are all of white marble. You arrange the business of getting a bath with the steward. At the entrance of each bath is a slate, on which is inscribed the passenger's name and the time at which the bath is devoted to him. Should he fail to appear, the others go on in rotation. The saloon is furnished in Spanish mahogany and purple velvet. There are four rows of tables. The captain presides at one, the purser at another, the surgeon at a third, and some favored passenger at the fourth. Sleeping accommodations are so arranged that families or parties of eight, sixteen, and twenty-four can be berthed in private rooms."

Such leaps forward in amenity on the ocean were widely heralded, yet the people who could afford them were few—and Robert Louis Stevenson was not among this privileged number. When Stevenson was contemplating a voyage to New York in 1879 he had several considerations in mind. He wanted to go cheaply; and he wanted a chance, as an "amateur immigrant," to see for himself just what went on in the steerage of a transatlantic liner. He also wanted a writing table on which he might be able to put the finishing touches to a new work entitled "The Story of a Lie." There was neither space nor table for a working writer in the steerage, so he had to pay a few pounds more for a second-cabin booking on the *Devonia*, of the Anchor Line, sailing from Greenock early in August. This accommodation was, he said, "a modified oasis in the very heart of the steerage. Through the thin partition you can hear the steerage passengers being sick, the rattle of tin dishes as they sit at meals, the varied accents in which they converse, the crying of their children terrified by this new experience. . . ."

The only differences between true steerage and second cabin, as far as Stevenson could detect, were a reserved dining table, crockery plates and the fact that "in the steerage there are males and females; in the second cabin, ladies and gentlemen." He set off on his voyage to collect material for a travel book, but almost before it was begun he had lost his objectivity as a reporter and become a much concerned participant. "At breakfast," he said, "we had a choice between tea and coffee . . . a choice not easy to make, the two were so surprisingly alike. I found that I could sleep after the coffee and lay awake after the tea, which is proof conclusive of some alchemical disparity . . . and twice a week, on pudding days, instead of duff, we had a saddle-bag filled with currants under the name of plum-pudding. At tea we were served with some broken meat from the saloon. . . ."

To the voluminous literature of optimism in which Americans read continuously of the high-hearted people who breasted toward the promise of a new world, Stevenson contributed nothing. "We were a company of the rejected," he said, "the drunken, the incompetent, the weak, the prodigal, all who had been unable to prevail against circumstances in the one land, were now fleeing pitifully to another; and though one or two might still succeed, all had already failed."

When he found himself unable to sleep in his cabin because of its foul dead air, Stevenson made a bed for himself on the second-cabin floor and returned to it nightly for the length of the crossing. Like his between-decks companions, he sought out company and possible acquaintance among those in the steerage just below. On one of these descents he "found a little company of our acquaintances seated together at the triangular foremost table. A more forlorn party, in more dismal circumstances, it would be hard to imagine. The motion here in the ship's nose was very violent; the uproar of the sea often overpoweringly loud. The yellow flicker of the lantern spun round and round and tossed the shadows in masses. The air was hot, but it struck a chill from its foetor. From all round in the dark bunks, the scarcely human noises of the sick joined into a kind of farmyard chorus."

But finally the weather cleared, the sea became easy, and the pent-up emigrants took to the open deck. Fiddles and concertinas came out, and suddenly singing and dancing was the order of the afternoon. Then fell the shadow of cold-hearted privilege. Although it was a generally accepted principle that it was "a gross breach of the etiquette of sea life, and a shocking exhibition of bad manners and low inquisitiveness, for passengers to visit unasked the quarters of an inferior class," Stevenson had to witness just such a contretemps. "Through this merry and good-hearted scene," he reported, "there came three cabin passengers, a gentleman and two young ladies, picking their way with little gracious titters of indulgence, and a Lady-Bountiful air about nothing, which galled me to the quick. I have little of the radical in social questions, and have always nourished an idea that one person was as good as another. But I began to be troubled by the episode. It was astonishing what insults these people managed to convey by their presence. They seemed to throw their clothes in our faces. Their eyes searched us for tatters and incongruities. A laugh was ready at their lips; but they were too well-mannered to indulge it in our hearing. Wait a bit, till they were all back in the saloon, and then hear how wittily they would depict the manners of the steerage. We were in truth very innocently, cheerfully, and sensibly engaged, and there was no shadow of excuse for the swaying elegant superiority with which these damsels passed among us, or the stiff and waggish glances of their squire. Not a word was said . . . but we were all conscious of an icy influence and a dead break in the course of our enjoyment."

By the time the voyage was over, said Stevenson, "the steerage conquered me; I conformed more and more to the type of the place, not only in manner but at heart, growing hostile to the officers and cabin passengers who looked down upon me. It seemed no disgrace to be confounded with my company; for I may as well declare at once I found their manners as gentle and becoming as those of any other class. . . ."

The grandest of the new ships did not attract everyone—sometimes because of national loyalty, sometimes out of a feeling that a voyage was a voyage and not to be eased with *coquillage* and swags of silk; sometimes, as in the case of Sarah Bernhardt, one was famous enough and canny enough to make a good deal with a steamship company willing to carry a celebrity in style and on the cuff. For her first voyage to the United States, in October, 1880, the Divine Sarah chose a battered old French stager named *L'Amerique*, whose history was so lamentable in the way of groundings and floodings and other bungled mishaps that almost no one could be prevailed to travel on her. But when, through her impresario, Madame Sarah was offered "excellent terms" for herself and a legion of attendants, she packed up her own bed sheets and linens and sailed from Le Havre, weeping copiously among the five pillows of a large brass bed covered with a sable throw, in a stateroom embowered with roses and imperially embossed throughout with the letters "SB."

Despair at parting from her son Maurice and from her native land was soon deepened by the effects of the rough Atlantic. For three days she was sick and weepy, miserable enough to deny access to the hothouse cabin even to her leading man Angelo, who normally could be counted upon to comfort her distress. But on the fourth day she was fit enough to dress and venture a promenade on the open deck. As she was striding along in the bracing salt air, she several times passed a heavy-set little woman swathed in black and wreathed in melancholy. The ocean seemed comparatively calm, yet out of nowhere came a rolling billow that sent the old steamer into a violent lurch. Sarah, grabbing hold of a bench as she was thrown off-balance, saw that the lady in black was being pitched forward at the very top of an open companionway. She clutched the hem of the stranger's skirt, broke her headlong fall, and held on until a sailor and the actress' maid Felicie rushed to help them. When the two women, lifted upright, had pulled themselves together, the following conversation, according to Sarah, ensued.

"You might have been killed, Madame, down that horrible staircase."

"Yes . . . but it was not God's will. Are you not Madame Hessler?"

"No, Madame, my name is Sarah Bernhardt."

"I am the widow of President Lincoln."

With this revelation, Sarah stepped back, brought the back of her hand to the flat of her brow, and allowed "a thrill of anguish" to run through her. She felt she had done the lugubrious lady the only service she ought not to have done—pulled her from the brink of death. The episode was shattering enough to send her back to her brass bed for two whole days. But on the twenty-third of the month, her thirty-sixth birthday, she was feeling fine. Admirers in Paris had put gifts into the hands of Felicie, and as these were being presented to her there came a delegation of three sailors, representing the entire crew, bearing "a superb bouquet." At first glance, the illusion was complete. But the flowers were actually vegetables. "Magnificent roses were cut out of carrots," wrote Sarah, "camellias out of turnips, small radishes had furnished sprays of rose-buds stuck on to long leeks dyed green, and all these relieved by carrot leaves artistically arranged to imitate the grassy plants used for elegant bouquets."

Four days later *L'Amerique*—on what must have been the coldest Indian summer day in the history of New York or the imagination of Sarah Bernhardt—came up through the Narrows toward Manhattan. "The Hudson was frozen hard," said Sarah, "and the heavy vessel could only advance with the aid of pick-axes cutting away the blocks of ice."

℁ SECTION XVIII ℁

Captains Courageous / "His Telescope Was Ever at Her Service" / Captain Murray and Oscar Wilde / The Arizona Story / Lily Langtry's Rat

AS SHIPS got to be big enough to carry whole segments of stateside society across the ocean, the captain's social role was as active as he cared to make it. As in the case of the old packet masters, some of them loathed having to mix seamanship with *savoir faire*. (Of one dour commander it was said that he "cares nothing for the *suaviter in modo*, but demands credit for his *fortiter in re*.") Tamed by the hum of engines and by company injunctions to be civil if they could not be congenial, captains were no longer the whip-cracking autocrats of square-rigger days.

Yet, to landsmen, these silent men on windy decks were still figures of wonder and surmise—even to a landsman as sophisticated as James Russell Lowell. "He used to walk the deck," said Lowell of a captain he knew, "with his hands in his pockets, in seeming abstraction, yet nothing escaped his eye. He is as impervious to cold as a polar bear. On the Atlantic, if the wind blew a gale from the northeast, and it was cold as an English summer, he was sure to run out in a calico shirt and trousers, his fuzzy brown chest half bare, and slippers without stockings. He always combs his hair, and works himself into a black frock-coat (on Sundays he adds a waistcoat) before he comes to meals, sacrificing himself nobly and painfully to the social proprieties."

Other captains found it no sacrifice at all. Among these was an Inman Line commander whose propensities came under the scrutiny of a magazine writer. " 'For there always is a Belle!'—[the Captain] colloquized, over a neat bottle of Chablis—'One fair spirit whom I can promenade up and down deck, exhibit the machinery to, converse with at night about the planets and cosmogony, and use for the purposes of staving off other women, and making the old maids furious. Yes, the Belle of the Voyage is something more than a painter's dream or a title out of a Book of Beauty; she is one of the Captain's Rights, and a piece of his furniture.'

"His preference," said the journalist, "for the exquisite Miss Pettitoes had been flagrant. He had walked with her, bragged to her, and lent her his fleeciest wraps on cool days. His telescope was ever at her service, and was usually to be seen glued to one of her dark eyes. They had played off 'practicals' upon each other: she had put him through a course of absurd attitudes, under pretense of teaching him the 'Boston Dip'; he had induced her to extend their promenade to the forecastle-deck—where as quick as thought, the old salt had chalked around her pretty feet a magic circle, a zone from which she only escaped after her little Vienna *portemonnaie* had opened to its widest extension.

" 'There is always a Belle,' continued the Captain. 'Sometimes it is a Juno; sometimes it is a Psyche. I hardly know which I prefer, the experienced or the verdant. Last trip there was Mrs. Allweather, who had been to India, and whose trunks were stained with the sweat of filthy Arabs on the Nile. With her I could talk of anything and everything, and she turned a brandy-tumbler upside down like a horse-guard! Another advantage she had, her promenading was perfect—she never missed the step in turning about. But I hardly know whether, for steady diet, I don't prefer the dear little greenhorns! Their astonishment at everything is so delicious! They are so proud at discovering a sail which the maintopman has been watching for the last half hour! They are so sure of seeing land, half-way over, if some steamer's smoke happens to lift over the horizon! They so constantly feel rocks bumping against the keel in mid-channel! The dear little hearts; how comfortably they cling to one's arm! It is only fair that a profession so thoroughly salted as ours should be allowed an occasional touch of something fresh.' "

A captain likely to be inflamed by a pretty ankle could hardly be expected to respond to the likes of Oscar Wilde. When Captain George Siddons Murray brought the *Arizona* into New York early in January, 1882, an exceptionally large number of reporters came clambering aboard. Wilde received them in full fig: a bottle-green fur-lined overcoat with a broad fur collar, lemon yellow kid gloves. From under a round sealskin hat his hair fell almost to his shoulders.

City editors had instructed their men to come back with epigrams and anecdotes. When Wilde failed to supply them with either, they sought out Captain Murray and asked him if Oscar Wilde lived up to the words of the Gilbert and Sullivan lyric supposedly about him:

> A most intense young man,
> A soulful-eyed young man,
> An ultra poetical, super-aesthetical
> Out-of-the-way young man?

Whatever he was, the Captain was reported to have said, he didn't care for him. "I wish I had that man lashed to the bowsprit on the windward side."

It has never been established just who was on hand to immortalize the terse exchange, but the *mot* of the morning was Oscar's. As the customs officer was examining his luggage, he asked Mr. Wilde the routine question "Have you anything to declare?"

"Nothing," replied Oscar, "but my genius"—and swept across town to breakfast at Delmonico's and on to his suite in the Grand Hotel.

When Wilde chose to come over on the *Arizona*, he showed either a flip of daring or a tendency to play it safe. The nature of the *Arizona's* recent history would support the one as firmly as the other.

Two years before Oscar Wilde had walked up her gangplank in Liverpool, the *Arizona*, already the holder of the Atlantic speed record, became doubly famous by smashing full speed, head-on, into an enormous iceberg off the Grand Banks. "You can't imagine the appalling suddenness of the thing," wrote a young passenger. "At one moment nothing was further from our thoughts than an accident. Then came that awful crash and those on their feet in the smoking room were either flung to the deck or thrown into a struggling heap on a settee at the forward end of the room. The throb of the engine stopped almost instantly and there was a moment of deathly stillness. Then a hubbub of voices arose and we heard the hysterical screaming of a woman from the saloon. A moment later there was a rush for the deck, not a rush for the boats, you understand, but a wild scramble to get on deck to see what had happened. Dad and I were among the first to reach the door. A glance forward told the story. The *Arizona*'s bow, or what was left of it, was literally buried in a huge iceberg which towered sixty or seventy feet above us. Tons of shattered ice from the face of the berg lay on the turtle deck and made it impossible to see much of the bow. Captain Jones had been below when the ship struck and as he reached the bridge above he called out, 'My God, where were your eyes?' "

Her celebrated greyhound's nose crumpled and gaping, gashed open all the way back to the wall of her collision bulkhead, the *Arizona* crawled slowly into the harbor of St. John's, Newfoundland. William H. Guion, managing director of the Guion Line, was on board. With a nice touch of showmanship he ordered a false wooden bow to be installed over the ship's bashed-in nose. When this was securely in place, the *Arizona* tore back to Liverpool in a roaring 6 days, 17 hours, 30 minutes. In the whole episode not a soul had been lost. The *Arizona* had survived a midocean encounter with ice which, many people felt, was the real but uncorroborated cause of the disappearance of nearly every North Atlantic ship posted as "missing without trace."

When the *Arizona*'s story was told, the incident was viewed in two distinct ways: From one perspective, the ship had demonstrated her enormous strength in an ultimate test of sea-worthiness and had strengthened the conviction of seamen who believed that when a collision was inevitable, a big, fast ship could "cut the obstructing vessel in two with comparatively little injury to themselves." From another point of view, her captain—whose license was suspended—was exposed as a mariner foolhardy enough to maintain full speed in the known tracks of drifting icebergs. Travelers, wayward and unpredictable, tended to favor the first view. Any ship powerful enough to go pounding into an iceberg and still stay afloat was good enough for them, and they continued to make the *Arizona* one of the most highly patronized ships in Atlantic service. Once more, prompted by William H. Guion, adversity had found its uses.

After almost a full year of lecturing in "aesthetic dress" (as demanded by the terms of the contract he had made with impresario Richard

D'Oyly Carte) and allowing himself to be exhibited "like a calf with two heads" through thirty-six States, Oscar Wilde was back in New York to welcome his beloved Lily Langtry ("Lily of love, pure and inviolate,/Tower of ivory, red rose of fire") as she also arrived on the *Arizona*. At dawn one morning, his long hair crowned by a cowboy's hat, Oscar went out to Quarantine on the press boat to greet her with an armful of lilies. "There are rats on the *Arizona*," the Jersey Lily informed him, "long-coated and tame." One of them used to listen to her read aloud; when he got thirsty he would rattle the chain in the wash basin. As for the voyage, that was tame, too. "I wanted to see the ocean run mountains high," she said. "It ran only hills high."

Oscar Wilde himself chose to return to England in the comparative old-shoe comfort of the Cunard liner *Bothnia*. Late in December, still wearing his wide-brimmed Western hat, he sailed from New York almost unnoticed. As one columnist ironically lamented, "Oscar Wilde has abandoned us without a line of farewell, slipped away without giving us a last goodly glance, left without a wave of his chiselled hand or a friendly nod of his classic head." His American sojourn had begun with a fanfare, broad caricatures and heavy-witted jokes in all the papers and a wide smile of national amusement. But in the space of twelve months, the importance of Oscar Wilde for Americans had been seriously diminished. For Wilde, in turn, the good-hearted, open-handed American of European fancy had been reduced to a paltry figure indeed. "For him," said Oscar, "Art has no marvel, Beauty no meaning, the Past no message." When reporters met his ship at Liverpool, his opinions were rueful, and a bit saucy. "What about the trip?" asked one of the newspapermen.

"I was disappointed . . . the Atlantic is greatly misunderstood."

"What about Anglo-American relations?"

"The English and Americans have everything in common," said Oscar, "except, of course, their language."

❧ SECTION XIX ❧

The Death of Sir Samuel / Cunard Redivivus / The Servia
The End of the Oregon

B Y THE middle years of the 1860s a score of companies were fighting one another for warm bodies to fill their berths and bunks. From a little auxiliary enterprise enabling people to get back and forth from the Old World to the New, transatlantic shipping had become a business where dog ate dog. On one of the days when jostlings for advantage and pride of place were at their most intense, old George Burns of Glasgow and the Cunard Line opened a letter. It came from Edward Cunard: "My father just now desired me to send his sincerest wishes to you for your welfare and all your family, and this is the last message, I fear, you will ever receive from him. He has passed through a week of intense suffering, has never once uttered a complaint since he has been ill, and has been constant in his thanks to God for His support through a long life, and the blessings He has bestowed upon him. He took the communion today with all who are with him. Mr. Gordon, the clergyman, said he never saw any one more happy in his mind, or better prepared to die. He expresses his firm belief in the mediation of our Saviour, and feels that he can only be saved through Him. He may yet linger a short time, but he thinks himself

270

that his hours are numbered, and we shall soon have to close his aged eyes, and fold his aged hands, when their owner will be no longer old."

Cunard had quarreled with Burns over the issue of the screw propeller versus the paddle wheel. The sea-keeping power of the *Great Eastern* had convinced Burns that screws for the company's new ships were imperative. Cunard was not impressed. Paddles had served him well; they still *looked* safer to his passengers; and he was determined that his ships would continue to be driven by them. The difference resulted in an angry impasse. Discord had finally replaced the extraordinary harmony that had long governed the Cunard inner sanctum. On his death bed, Samuel's conscience had moved him to a healing gesture.

But by the time the olive branch had come into Burns' grasp, Samuel Cunard, true to his own last prediction, had already passed away. The youngster whose momentous career had begun on the muddy streets and slatted sidewalks of Halifax had died a baronet. On the recommendation of Lord Palmerston, he had been knighted by Queen Victoria for the services rendered by his ships in the Crimean campaign. Now his son Edward would inherit his baronetcy and his estate, including what was left of a fortune strained in the payment of debts incurred years before by his improvident Uncle Joseph in New Brunswick. Sir Samuel's worth was variously estimated. One report had it as being in the region of three hundred and fifty thousand pounds; a letter that passed between two of his friends contained the remark, "I miss our old friend Sir Samuel Cunard, I think he has left 600,000 pounds. So much for steam in twenty years." Edward survived his father by a scant four years, when the baronetcy passed to his son Sir Bache Cunard.

Within another ten years, put on the shelf by the success of its brash and more imaginative competitors, the Cunard Company was driven to take drastic steps. Once upon a time, deficiencies ranging from stateroom space to table napkins could be made to seem minor by the invocation of magic words—"the Cunard never lost a life." But that time was past. Notions of caution, care, good service and plain food had governed old Samuel Cunard, but these were now inadequate to the demands of an expanding flow of ocean travel. Taking a new lease on its business life, the line relaxed the policy that had kept financial control exclusively in the hands of Cunards, Burnses and MacIvers and went public under the Companies (Limited Liability) Act. Early on in the company's career, the three pioneer families had bought out all of the original Scottish shareholders. Now, retaining 1,200,000 pounds of shares for themselves, they agreed to put 800,000 pounds' worth on the market. These were snapped up at once.

Because of its unblemished record of safety, the all-weather punctuality of its vessels and its hand-and-glove relations with Her Majesty's Government, the Cunard Company had acquired a gilt-edged luster. Who did not agree with the encomium of Mark Twain? "The Cunard people would not take Noah himself as first mate," said Twain, "till they had worked him up through all the lower grades and tried him ten years or such matter. They make every officer serve an apprenticeship under their eyes in their own ships before they advance him or trust him. It takes them about ten or fifteen years to manufacture a captain; but when they have got him manufactured to suit at last, they have full confidence in him. The only order they give a captain is this, brief and to the point: 'Your ship is loaded, take her; speed is nothing; follow your own road, deliver her safe, bring her back safe—safety is all that is required.'"

Such sentiments were all fine and reassuring, but financial progress was calculated on grounds less commendable. A first step in the new Cunard dispensation was to get rid of the company's long-winded name. The British and North American Royal Mail Steam Packet Company became the Cunard Steam-Ship Company. The famous old granddaddy of all steamship lines was now ready to come to grips with every upstart on the Great Circle. New money in hand, the company acted with unprecedented bravura. Samuel Cunard had "thought in services when other people thought in ships," in punctuality when other people thought in speed records. "Never in advance of the times, but never far behind them; never experimenting, but always ready to adopt any improvement thoroughly tested by others; avoiding equally extravagance and parsimony; carefully studying the nature of the service in which it is engaged, guarding against every contingency," the Cunard Company had become a standard bearer of Victorian prudence, congratulated equally for its ethical caution and its cash profit.

Now that Samuel Cunard was no longer around to cut a corner and save a penny, the company was free to take services for granted and to spend money competitively. The result was the *Servia*, the biggest vessel since the *Great Eastern*, the first big steel-hulled ship on the Atlantic, and the first to be lighted by incandescent electric lamps. Fast, though not a record breaker, she was designed to carry a greater number of first-class passengers than any other ship running, and to transport them in a manner to which White Star and Inman had forced Cunard to conform. "An enormous but shapely mass of steel," the *Servia* had five decks, a saloon with the grandest staircase on the Atlantic and "columns fluted and girded in a chaste style." Some of her staterooms were even fitted with Broadwood's patent lavatories. She carried 480 first-class passengers, 750 in third class. Her big engines preempted space that other ships kept for cargo; but her vast accommodation for saloon passengers allowed her to turn a profit even when she sailed all but empty of freightage. In establishing this ratio, she was the first in a flotilla of ever larger ships crossing the Atlantic on an express service, i.e., one catering primarily to passengers and leaving the haulage of cargo to second-class liners or freighters.

The *Servia* soon became an archetype of the "comfortable" ship— the liner that wore an air of retirement from the race that used up the energies of other ships and kept them in a state of fractious competition. When Henry James, no devotee of sea travel, described the pleasures of a voyage from Boston to Liverpool, he had a ship just like the *Servia* in mind. Leisure and security was the new emphasis—virtues that James promoted with an eloquence Cunard's publicists could not have matched if they tried. She was slow, said James, "but she was spacious and comfortable, and there was a kind of motherly decency in her long, nursing rock and her rustling, old-fashioned gait. It was as if she wished not to present herself in port with the splashed eagerness of a young creature. . . . I had never liked the sea so much before, indeed I have never liked it at all; but now I had a revelation of how, in a midsummer mood, it could please. It was darkly and magnificently blue and imperturbably quiet—save for the great regular swell of its heart-beats, the pulse of its life, and there grew to be something so agreeable in the sense of floating there in infinite isolation and leisure that it was a positive satisfaction that [the ship] was not a racer."

When the *Servia* got a consort, the *Aurania*, Cunard had come handsomely back into the forefront. There were still many travelers, it became apparent, who would respond to modest virtue and stable reputation rather than to glitter and implicit promises of adventure. With profits rising, the Cunard management became a bit daring—to the point where they would reach out to buy, at a bargain price, just the sort of ship upon which they would normally look askance.

The *Oregon* had been ordered from Elders' Fairfield Yard by the Guion Line to serve as a running mate for their two greyhounds, the *Arizona* and the *Alaska*. But soon after the Guion people took delivery of the ship and put her on the Liverpool–New York route they found that they could not keep up the payments on her. The shipbuilders foreclosed, and sold her to Cunard—thus adding to Cunard's collection a slightly second-hand jewel that nevertheless outshone all of its own.

"Elegant and majestic," with "the sharpness of a racing yacht," the *Oregon* held the speed record for only the eastward crossing, yet she was generally regarded as the fastest ship on the Western Ocean. Her grand saloon glowed in the light of day filtered through a dome of many-colored glass twenty feet high. The saloon's floors were parquetry, its panels of polished satinwood, its pilasters of walnut with capitals of gilt, its ceilings white and gold. Like Collins' *Atlantic*—more than thirty years earlier—the *Oregon* had a "barber's shop, with two luxurious American shaving chairs and hairbrushing machinery overhead."

A correspondent of the Liverpool *Mercury* who had gone along on her maiden voyage as far as Queenstown felt that she was the only ship that he would admit to the company of his own two paragons— the *Great Eastern* and Collins' *Adriatic*. The ladies' cabin, he wrote, "is a perfect gem. The pale sea-green cushions and seats are just the tone suitable for complexions of every hue, and we think their fair occupants will never be disturbed by more water than the neighbouring bathrooms afford."

The *Mercury*'s correspondent was wrong. In the early morning of March 14, 1885, as she was nearing Fire Island Light with 896 passengers and crew abroad, the *Oregon* was pierced by the bow of a schooner that came silently out of nowhere and disappeared at once back into nowhere. The ghostly encounter—the schooner's name and nature would never be learned—was nevertheless fatal. The sailing ship had opened an enormous hole in the *Oregon*'s side between her two boiler rooms. When her captain ordered the watertight doors to be closed, there was no response: coal dust accumulated on the sills had made the doors inoperable. The *Oregon* began slowly to fill—so slowly, in fact, that there was time to remove every soul on board, first to a passing pilot boat and later to the North German Lloyd ship *Fulda*. Eight hours after the anonymous schooner had slid out of the morning murk, the great *Oregon* went down in a mere 120 feet of water ten miles off the shore of Long Island.

The Cunard Company had once again been spared having to rack up its first loss of a passenger. There was still more good fortune in the fact that, in the mind of the public, the vulnerable *Oregon* was associated with the iceberg-smashing *Arizona* and the racing *Alaska*, and not with the high-decked dowagers that fluttered the red pennants of Cunard.

❈ SECTION XX ❈

S.S. Umbria *and S.S.* Etruria: *The End of the Single Screw / The Saving of the* Spree

UNDAUNTED by this excursion into other peoples' notions of ease on the Atlantic, Cunard went back to the familiar way and image of Cunard and ordered two big comfortable ships propelled by single screws. These were launched in successive years: the *Umbria* in 1884, the *Etruria* in 1885. At once the company was congratulated for its courage. Revenues on the North Atlantic were falling; the shipping business had already entered a period of desuetude. Some of the most famous carriers were threatened with dissolution. The decline would soon put the Guion Line into bankruptcy, send the National Line into oblivion and humiliate the Inman Line by forcing it to lose its identity under the American flag and the canopy of the American dollar.

Patriarchal John Burns, keynoting ceremonies that launched the *Etruria,* spoke words that, fifty years later, would be reinvoked to hearten the men of Cunard when, in the abysmal depths of another depression, they would launch the *Queen Mary.* "I have been told that it is an anomaly in shipping to talk of bad times," said Burns, "and yet to build such immense ships . . . but I believe that . . . the Company which reduces the time in crossing the Atlantic . . . will ensure success in the long run. There is no courage in entering upon great enterprises in prosperous times, but I have faith in the future, a confidence that the Cunard Company will hold its own upon the Atlantic."

In the *Umbria* and *Etruria* Cunard had also acquired the two particular ships that, quite contrary to anyone's intentions, would make it evident that the era of the single screw was over. Auxiliary sails as adjuncts to the equipment of an 8,000-ton liner already had a pitifully inadequate look, and soon they were removed. But, said one officer, "mechanical confidence went too far when the auxiliary sails were discarded." He was soon to be proved correct. First, the *Umbria* would fracture her shaft midocean and wallow about helplessly for days; then the *Etruria* would find herself in precisely the same predicament.

"The *Etruria* was just about in mid-Atlantic," her captain recalled, "when we felt a peculiar shock. I was on the bridge with the First Officer. We thought, at first, we had struck some large piece of submerged wreckage. After the apparent bump, there fell an uncanny stillness on the ship. The engines had been stopped; and when this occurs at sea without previous warning, it causes anxiety. The binnacle showed she was more than 20 degrees off her course, but from the rudder telltale it could be seen that the helm was hard over the correct way. There was still a speed of 15 knots on the ship although the engines were stopped; and, wondering why she was not steering, I called down the speaking tube to the Quarter Master and asked him how long the helm had been hard-a-starboard.

" 'Oh,' he replied, 'not many seconds after that there big bump she got a couple of minutes ago.' I went aft and looked over the stern, and, as we expected, the rudder was gone. The shock we had felt was not only the rudder dropping off, but also the propeller. As the latter broke away, it smashed up against the rudder-post and tore it off from close to the keel to about one foot above the waterline. The combined weight of the missing parts was well over sixty tons; and this, dropping off at the very after-end of the ship, caused a sudden plunge of the bow, making us think we had hit something. The *Etruria* and *Umbria* were the last of the single-propeller ships; and we could have provided no better advertisement of the value of twin-screw ships to the world in general and to our own passengers in particular."

Twenty-eight days after the accident, after having made port at Fayal, in the Azores, first by being towed by a small steamer out of

New Orleans for Liverpool—the *William Cliff*—then by a passing oil tanker, and finally by having put over a jury rudder, the *Etruria* was towed into the Mersey by three ocean-going tugs. Alarm over the fate of the most famous ship in the world was at once relieved. But the public, as well as the shipping fraternity, knew that the accident was absurd and humiliating. This was simply not the way for a Cunard thoroughbred to behave—or, for that matter, no way for one of Cunard's *gemütlich* German emulators to behave.

The lesson of the *Etruria* had hardly time to be taken in when North German Lloyd's new *Spree* also broke her screw. "We drifted about at the mercy of the wind and waves from six in the morning of Saturday until early Monday morning," a lady passenger wrote to a friend. "We would sit all day looking eagerly for some speck on the vast waters, and when night settled . . . and rockets were resorted to, we would strain our eyes into the darkness, hoping in vain to see an answering gleam. . . . Then added to all of this, we had the second class and steerage passengers with us, and many of them were desperate-looking fellows, as they stood near the life-boats with their life-preservers on and such dreadful expressions on their faces—which made escape that way impossible, even if the high sea had allowed it.

"We were rapidly drifting out of the track of all steamers and if the least storm broke over us, our watertight compartments would never hold the five hundred tons of water in our poor boat. It was not until Monday morning, after forty-eight hours of this dreadful drifting, that a light was sighted. This second night our good Captain had had an enormous fire of pitch pine built in a tank on the prow of our ship. This fire, which was kept up all night, was seen twenty miles away by the captain of a little Montreal cattle steamer, the *Lake Huron*. He thought it was a ship on fire and came to save one or two sailors, and saved 800 souls!"

The *Lake Huron* also did her bit to save the fortunes of the Beaver Line, for whom she worked: the grateful cheers of rescued passengers were still echoing, the badges of heroism still being distributed, when her owners collected a cool one hundred thousand dollars in salvage money, on demand.

Such well-publicized misfortunes eventually caught up with the reputations of the *Umbria* and *Etruria* and turned the two ships into Jonahs. (The *Spree* escaped this when her single screw was replaced by twin screws.) But before this happened they enjoyed a span of years in which they not only were great commercial successes, but in which they also became the absolute doyennes of social life on the ocean. Commercial success came from their speed (between them they held Atlantic records for nearly five years) and their size; social success came from the gentility of their appointments and the fact that they were snobbish enough to eliminate any but cabin passengers. Steerage was done away with in the *Umbria* altogether; on the *Etruria,* a section of cabin quarters was convertible to third-class trade in the slack season only.

In both of these Cunard showpieces, innovation continued to be the thing. Instead of "ice rooms," they carried the first refrigerating machinery ever installed in Atlantic liners. Oil lamps were dispensed with in favor of electric light "produced by four of Siemens's machines." There were even pipe organs in the music rooms. A number of staterooms were laid out *en suite* for the use of affluent families and celebrities traveling with entourages; and all of them featured a hot-water heater, an electric light and a life-saving cork jacket. There were thirteen marble baths on each ship, all of them fitted with steam and shower apparatus; and lavatory accommodation was "dispersed throughout." At their disposition lady passengers could loll away their time in a sort of midocean harem—a boudoir that formed a vestibule leading to a whole series of scented baths and mirrored lavatories set aside just for them.

✵ SECTION XXI ✵

*The Beautiful City of Rome / Society at Sea
Alta Moda and Haute Cuisine*

T HE MOST beautiful ship of the period—the most beautiful ship, in the view of many people, in the whole era of steamships on the ocean—was the *City of Rome.* Prototype of the three-funneled liner with auxiliary sails, she emerged in splendor, the biggest and most exquisitely appointed of all ships, and was almost at once retired from the race she was groomed to win. Her maiden voyages to New York in October, 1881, out and back, were so slow that she was returned to her builders' shipyards to sit out the winter. With engines overhauled and retuned, she resumed her career the following spring. After six disappointing round voyages she was again sent back to her builders as a bad example. A legal tangle involving them and her owners kept her enisled and out of commission for a long time; then she was sold at a cut rate to the prosperous new Anchor Line. Taking her for what she was and not for a speed demon, her new owners sailed her with pride and profit for many years.

The trouble with the *City of Rome* was greed and exigency—demands visited upon her even before the extraordinary plans of her designers could be fulfilled. Blueprinted to be constructed of steel, she was built of iron because her owners, threatened by a steel shortage, could not countenance a delay in the date they had set for taking delivery. Their impatience doomed the ship as a candidate for the Blue Riband; and they did not want her as anything less. When most of her internal features and her long sleek lines were incorporated into the designs of their new *City of New York* and *City of Paris*, they seemed glad to forget her.

Worked to a point of breakdown, rejected, then sold to strangers in a spirit of good riddance, the *City of Rome*, overcoming all such vicissitudes, remains the serene highness among the greyhounds and pleasure barges of the latter half of the century. A figurehead of the Emperor Hadrian, three times larger than life, leaned out over the waves she breasted. On her stern, embossed in gold, glittered the arms and crest of the Eternal City. Her trio of black, white-banded funnels set close together made a pattern and established an image of power in reserve that would obtain until the demise of the *Queen Mary*, eighty-six years later. Five hundred and sixty feet long, with a schooner bow thrust forward in a slant of heraldic grace, an acre of "glistening sail and flowing sheet" rising above fittings outlined in polished brass, she united the aerial qualities of the flying clippers with the humming dynamism of engines encased in iron.

Her hull was jet black, her superstructure the color of Devonshire cream. Her music room was paneled in ebony and gold. Her grand saloon, dressed in a scheme of neutral hues and pastel tapestries, was brightly lighted by an oval skylight twenty feet long and ten feet wide. The ladies' boudoir had walls of brocaded silk, a ceiling of Japanese leather paper, chairs and couches upholstered in blue velvet, window hangings of Roman cloth with banded stripes of plush. Even the smoking room exhibited a delicacy not heretofore evident in the dark panelings and mohair coverings of the typical gentleman's retreat. Its walls were covered with Japanese watercolors of birds and flowers, its seats upholstered in pigskin, and it had a parquet floor.

Expanded, reconstituted, and known as Inman & International, the company that had turned its back on the doomed beauty of the *City of Rome* now put all of its faith in the *City of New York* and the *City of Paris*. Handsome and swift, these ships carried the first great age of opulence at sea one step further than anything before.

Each of them offered fourteen private suites that contained a bedroom with a brass bed, a sitting room furnished like a "den" in a private house, as well as their own lavatory and bath. Their midship dining saloons were lighted by a roof of glass 53 feet long, 25 feet wide; and their walls were aswim with naiads, dolphins, tritons, mermaids and friezes of decorative shellfish. Swivel chairs permanently affixed to the floor beside long tables were still the convention; but these new ships also had dining alcoves with small tables where families or parties of friends might choose to dine together. Smoking rooms paneled in black walnut, furnished with scarlet leather couches and chairs, added a touch of the grandee to the old sense of masculine sanctuary. The libraries, lined with oak wainscotting, contained nine thousand volumes on shelves over which were carved the names of literary figures. Upon these, stained-glass windows inscribed with poems referring to the sea threw a purplish light. The kitchens were "isolated in a steel shell," from which cooking odors were carried off into ventilation shafts and directed up into the funnels. Passengers who did not care to climb stairs could take advantage of "constantly ascending and descending electric chambers."

"Luxury," said an American whose instincts were uncommonly humane, "has been carried just as far as the present human invention and imagination can take it. Suites for families are arranged with private sitting-rooms and private tables, so that, barring the roll so uneasy to the unhappy landsman, one could scarce know the change from the most luxurious apartment of the Brevoort. Let us hope that genius will yet invent a mechanical stoker and that we may not of necessity subject our fellow-beings to the 140 degrees too frequently found in our modern fire-rooms."

Provided with settings so felicitous, the rich had begun to make the ocean liner crossing a normal part of the yearly round. "The lovely season," said a journalist, "called in America by that tender name, the Fall, is closing; the children of Fashion, who have made of Europe one vast watering-place, are loading the homeward steamers—they will exchange the chance meetings at Spa and Homburg for flirtations as light and as meaningless in Washington or New York. The season is closing; the vessel is loaded, the gallant captain escorts the belle of the company up and down the monstrous decks, and the commercial travelers play shovel-board on the sunny planks, over the ears of sea-sick dowagers, wretched in their staterooms."

There was a time, wrote Van Wyck Brooks, "when a voyage to Europe was like a voyage in Charon's ferry-boat." But by the end of the century that feeling had passed as the social coziness of first-class sea travel took precedence. How dense this coziness actually was is suggested by an entry from a diary kept by Marian Lawrence Peabody, whose family, then and now, contributed a prominent set of sculptured busts to the pantheon of Boston Brahminism. The ship Miss Lawrence took was the *Umbria*, still sailing high in spite of the irascibility of a single screw.

"July 27, 1896," wrote Miss Lawrence. "We got aboard . . . at eight, after spending the night at the Fifth Avenue Hotel. There was a huge crowd on board, rather awful-seeming people, but we were glad to see that many of them left before we sailed at nine, leaving us with about 475 saloon passengers. About three hours out of New York we suddenly rolled and shook and stopped! We had run aground and there we stayed until ten that night. All the steamers that sailed after us passed by with cheers or offers of help and we were surrounded by tugs and reporters all day. With the help of a dozen little tugs we were finally set free at high tide. We had run onto a wrecked coal barge which had two buoys to mark it, so it was very *stupide* of the pilot.

"At ten o'clock we heard that a diver was going down to see if the bottom of the ship was in shape to continue our voyage. He was beneath us on a tug, all dressed up for his task, but we heard him say it was too rough to go down. So we started across the ocean! This made Mamma very nervous as she thought there must be a hole in the ship's bottom. The first morning was warm and I got out of the stateroom as soon as I could to get some air. On deck one of the awful Cook's tourists men came up and asked me 'if I hadn't thrown up yet,' and related his experiences before I could get away from him. Leaving him abruptly I walked around the deck and saw at least six horrible exhibitions which sent me scurrying below, where, though I didn't eat much breakfast, I felt restored in spirit.

"We heard that 100 Yale men were to be on board, but it turned out there were only forty-five, going over with their crew to race at Henley. Knowing Redmond Cross, who is on the Yale crew, we quickly met others of the Yale boys including Cheney, a friend of George Gray's, and Thorne, captain of the football team. Another good friend was B. Learned Hand. He and his friend Davy Vail had just graduated from Harvard Law School and became our steady escorts. The family we saw most of was Judge and Mrs. Howland and their daughter Fanny. In the evening our particular group gathered in the saloon—the Howlands, Brink Thorne, Cheney, Mr. Amory Gardner, Cecil Baring and George Booth—and had roast beef sandwiches and drinks, about 11 o'clock at night."

❧ SECTION XXII ❧

Campania and Lucania: *"The Limits of Human Possibility"*
Thomas Cook and "The Tribes of Unlettered British" / Americans
on the Arno / Pure Unadulterated Fun / Immorality in Steerage

SOMEWHERE in the fourth quarter of the century Cunard had lost clear title to preeminence on the North Atlantic. Stable and solvent, it continued to keep to schedule and to ride on even keel; yet many years would pass before the line would again be the standard by which service on the ocean was measured.

However, as their competitors got plushier and more sumptuous, Cunard's mentors began to entertain notions previously unheard of— especially notions about what to offer the growing numbers of genteel customers from the western United States who came to New York and Boston to embark for Liverpool. They decided to ignore the indigenous British pragmatism that had governed their shipping operations and to cater to those alien forms of hedonism that seemed to follow in the wake of the dollar. It was as if they had at last become aware of a pointed difference between the character of the British traveler and of the American traveler which inn-keepers on the Continent had long taken for granted.

When the typical British subject went abroad, he naturally assumed that nothing would quite measure up to what he had left behind;

nothing would be remotely as pleasurable or comfortable as it was at home. His breakfast tray would carry neither eggs, grilled sausage nor an intelligible morning paper; peckish at four o'clock, he would be left at the mercy of people just awakening from siesta, dubious *bistros* advertising "Tea Within." He expected on the whole to rough it and forebear, to tolerate all those things of which he could not approve, from Spanish brandy to German feather beds. Traveling Americans, on the other hand, seemed to bring their maddening optimism and provincial appetites to Europe with them; expecting everything to be *better* than it was at home, they were delighted to find their wishes granted; all those slightly sinful comforts and suave services they were embarrassed even to dream about in Milwaukee were quite naturally theirs to enjoy in Granada and Salzburg.

When the liner as a sea-borne hotel was expanded to the proportions of the floating palace, Cunard executives began to indicate a willingness to shift their emphasis from plain service to the particular enticements of high life and *haute cuisine*. But generations of insistent conservatism were not to be easily overcome. The hominess and homeliness of British interior decoration and the parochialism of British graphic art were sorry preparation for a contest in which the frivolous chic of the new thing was a far greater selling point than well-oiled engines and safe passage.

But toward the end of the century, as one line after another—Inman, National, Guion—disappeared or was swallowed up in a merger, the Cunard directors saw their chance to take a big step forward in re-establishing their firm as the premier carrier on the Atlantic. They determined to build two ships that would surpass every steamer, past, present, or on the drawing boards. The machinery for these "floating cities" would be unique in magnitude and power and, according to a publicity release, their fumes would be channeled into funnels "as high as the Eddystone lighthouse." The two new Cunard flag bearers were the *Campania* and *Lucania*, and they came to the fore with heavy-set British aplomb and a burst of patriotic puffery.

Built on the Clyde, their length was greater than the width of the Clyde itself. They had to be launched diagonally—a circumstance that signaled the thrilling fact that the old cradle of Cunarders had been outgrown. "Judging by these last products of the skill of my country-men," said a maritime chronicler, "the feasibility of propelling vessels by steam has developed to the limits of human possibility." Each sporting two funnels so enormous and tall as to make them seem dangerously top-heavy, these ships gave "a tremendous, if somewhat masculine, impression of nobility," and had speed enough to pass the Blue Riband between themselves at will. Their interior chambers, cold and grand, were dictated by the taste for sculptured wood, stained glass and enveloping upholsteries commonly associated with barons and earls. Its appeal to American customers was direct—especially to those for whom the baronial carried not only the aura of Runnymede but of Fifth Avenue mansions and Newport cottages.

By the end of the century the interior decorator had pretty well usurped the role of the company director in deciding what the enclosed spaces of ocean liners should look like. Yet, without much concern for the structural curves of a vessel, decorators simply installed in her given confines what was currently fashionable on land. Thus, cosseted and corseted, the pale flowers of Victorian society could travel at sea in all the security, comfort and familiar decor of their own drawing rooms. The ladies' saloon in the *Campania,* for instance, was "their own reservation, into the precincts of which man is only admitted on a special permit. It is a charming retreat, the carpets are of a very pretty pattern; the lounges are wide, the cushions impart an exquisite sensation of buoyancy, geraniums are blooming, and the mignonette is exhaling its sweetness. It is a club-house and boudoir combined; if my lady has a nervous headache, or wishes to escape the importunities of an ardent but obtrusive admirer, or if she wants to read in quiet, or to gossip, or to fritter her time away in *dolce far niente,* she steals in here, and here is sanctuary."

The sea with its mysteries and moods was thus beginning to be obscured behind accouterments devised to remind the passenger of home comforts. The seasick, the homesick or the merely ill-at-ease were provided the sedation of the familiar. A passenger who wished to sail for a week or more, hermetically sealed, could finally do so. If he were willing to pay as much as six hundred dollars a day he might, according to a brochure, have "the privilege . . . of seeing nothing at all that has to do with a ship, not even the sea."

The smoking room of the *Campania,* with its coach roof and piazzala arrangement of chairs along the sides, had the air of a cathedral choir, slightly cheered by the brassy glow of an open fire grate, a hearth shiny with Persian tiles, an Oriental rug in front of it. "The whole tone of the room," said an erudite passenger, "is suggestive of *otium cum dignitate.*"

A Collard grand piano and an American organ stood on the Persian carpet of the drawing room, the forward end of which was an inglenook meant, somehow, to suggest cozy, homelike ambience. Electric lamps in the shapes of rosettes of beaten copper lighted the reading room. What it all added up to, said Cunard publicity, was "a silent sermon in good taste."

The *Campania*'s dining saloon was sensational. It could seat 430 persons in revolving armchairs, with the Cunard lion rampant on the back of each; these were placed in rows beside tables so long that they diminished in perspective like railroad ties. The whole room was illuminated by a vast crystal dome that covered a light well extending downward through three decks. "Its general style is Italian," said an observer, "somewhat sobered down by an air of British substantiability." This conservative reminder was seconded by another, issued under the imprimatur of Cunard itself. "It is not usual to dress in the evening for dinner," said a company guide, "dresses of serge will be found very serviceable."

Staterooms were "lofty and well ventilated"; a particular feature was the replacement of the old wooden berths by "Hopkins' 'triptic' beds, which are so constructed that the upper bed folds up against the bulkhead." For those to whom money was no object, there were "suites of rooms fitted in satinwood and mahogany, with everything to match; parlour and bedroom, the former fitted up with tables and chairs after the style of a lady's boudoir; the latter fitted with a brass bedstead, hangings, wardrobe."

Samuel Cunard and the grand old men of Lancefield would have bridled at these excesses. But their respective heirs had seen to it that a British tradition was flexible enough to bend with times that demanded "the greatest possible luxury" along with "perfect sanitary arrangements."

At the same time that shipping companies were strenuously wooing an elite, real or pretended, a new breed of ocean traveler caring little about social status on the high seas or anywhere else began to appear in numbers. These were young Americans of "good" background but modest means who simply wanted to see the Louvre and the Prado, sign their names in the guest book in Keats' study above the Spanish Steps and shout "Prosit!" in the beer halls of Heidelberg. *Wanderjahre* was a notion still pretty much confined to young men of well-to-do families along the Eastern seaboard. But the idea that a few summer months abroad might be profitable and edifying had become widespread.

"American women go on trips not only alone," observed a European, "but in large, almost frightening bands. During the last few years large assemblages of unmarried women, grotesquely denominated Kentucky belles, or Jersey beauties, or Kansas peaches, have traversed Europe." A good part of this development was due to the success of Thomas Cook, the man who had introduced mass travel into the Western world. In the space of four decades, the modest domestic day-trips that Cook had first organized in the English midlands had grown into grand tours. Now so many tourists were advancing in cordons and phalanxes over the landscapes of Andalusia and Tuscany that, to some people, what had once seemed a boon had become a blight. The novelist Charles Lever, who was also Her Majesty's consul at La Spezia, had observed, from his Italian post, Cook's "devil's-dust tourists, the tribes of unlettered British," as they came in waves. Registering his distaste for the readers of *Blackwood's Magazine,* he said: "Anything so uncouth I never saw before, the men, mostly elderly, dreary, sad-looking; the women, somewhat younger, travel-tossed and crumpled." Such people, he said, were spreading over Europe "injuring our credit and damaging our character."

Thomas Cook's reply to his critic was mild and incontrovertibly sensible. "Let me ask why Mr. Lever's susceptibilities should be outraged, and his refinement trampled on, because thirty or forty Englishmen and Englishwomen find it convenient to travel in the same train, to coalesce for mutual benefit, and to sojourn for a . . . time in the same cities?"

But like his literary colleague Lever, the poet James Kenneth Stephen also had his reservations about those tourists who seemed to proliferate under the aegis of Thomas Cook. In Stephen's case, it was Americans who offended the proprieties—at least those particular Americans he had rubbed elbows with on a riverboat. In a poem entitled "On a Rhine Steamer," he most likely speaks for others who thought as he did:

> Republic of the West,
>   Enlightened, free, sublime,
> Unquestionably best
>   Production of our time.

The telephone is thine,
   And thine the Pullman Car,
The caucus, the divine
   Intense electric star.

To thee we likewise owe
   The venerable names
Of Edgar Allan Poe,
   And Mr. Henry James.

In short it's due to thee,
   Thou kind of Western star,
That we have come to be
   Precisely what we are.

But every now and then,
   It cannot be denied,
You breed a kind of men
   Who are not dignified,

Or courteous or refined,
   Benevolent or wise,
Or gifted with a mind
   Beyond the common size,

Or notable for tact,
   Agreeable to me,
Or anything, in fact,
   That people ought to be.

Led by contingents of blue-stockinged ladies and Unitarian clergymen mustered on the village greens of New England, the devotees of high culture had begun to descend upon the Continent with an avidity that would not spend itself for a hundred years. In spite of populist celebrations of native talent and fresh young voices from the west of the Mississippi, America had, aesthetically speaking, begun to "inherit" Europe in a development that the twentieth century would make explicit. But in the nineteenth century this slow process of appropriation only made many Americans impatient and they simply went ahead and grabbed of Europe what they could. "They read *Hyperion* on the Rhine," said Van Wyck Brooks, "they read Longfellow's sonnet about the Ponte Vecchio, with the twisting dragon of the Arno underneath it. They strolled through the Via de' Bardi, where Romola lived, and they visited the grave of Theodore Parker, who resembled Savonarola in certain respects. They rowed into the Blue Grotto, climbed Vesuvius, drove to Amalfi; they were punctual at St. Peter's on Palm Sunday. They spent a day at Fontainebleau, a day at Rambouillet, an hour in front of Rubens's *Descent from the Cross*; and they lingered at Gibbon's house in Lausanne and the Iron Virgin of Nuremberg and the organs of Freiburg and Haarlem. They sniffed the fog of Johnson's London and visited Chester and Coventry, where they faithfully murmured Tennyson on the bridge, rejoicing in the random corners and feasts of crookedness that satisfied their passion for the picturesque. The English lawns, the castle towers, the woods, the village churches brought tears of recognition to their eyes, as of the previous state that Plato spoke of; and, eager as they might be to improve conditions at home, there were no such tories—in Europe— as traveling Yankees. They longed for the picturesque at any price, regardless of dampness, injustices or any abuses."

Then, when a sufficiently large number of genteel young persons had reported that they survived the rigors of the steerage and had "seen" Europe for less than the cost of a single first-class passage on one of the luxury liners, an endless army of students on their own began to move.

"Pure unadulterated fun," promised a Boston travel agent; anyone, willing to go steerage, who had a bicycle and could hustle up a hundred dollars could spend a summer in Europe. The agents' advice was detailed. "Go first and buy a bottle or two of coffee essence, some lump sugar and a couple cans of condensed milk. Get a couple of bottles of pickles. Bring your own towels and a cake of soap. Bring a pillow, then get a camp stool for a cheap steamer's chair. It will not cost much and you can leave it at Southampton till you return. Sitting accommodation is always bad and hard to be got going steerage.

"When you get your ticket stamped in the office at the head of the wharf and are at last on deck, scuttle down into the steerage hold, and throw your satchel into the vacant top bunk, as near the middle of the vessel as possible, and stay by it until the bunks are all taken up. You will find a clean colored blanket in your bunk and a straw mattress. There will probably be twenty bunks in your compartment, and you will find that the stewards have put all English-speaking people together. They will all be single men when you are; married couples and children in the other side, and further from you, where you will not be allowed to go, the single women.

"You will find in your bunk a large block tin cup, a deep soup plate, with 'Cunard Line' stamped on its white surface, a knife, fork and large spoon, all of which you are expected to keep clean yourself. This will be your bill of fare: Beef soup or pea soup, with a scrap or two of meat in your plate, a tin of coffee, and plenty of very good bread and butter, breakfast, at eight o'clock; at eleven, your tin full of nice beef soup, plenty of beef, very good, but nearly always fresh, and potatoes; at supper, five o'clock, bread, butter and tea. On Friday you will have soup in the morning, but no meat, and fish at dinner; you will have pudding at Sunday's dinner, and a little marmalade once or twice in the evening. You will find every thing scrupulously neat on board, and try to help that thing by keeping your bunk and your dishes neat. Keep a watch, too, of fellows who will try to steal your clean dishes and leave their dirty ones in place of yours; that is about the only kind of stealing you need fear.

"There is, of course, a deal of quiet flirtation going on, some of the prettiest girls finding it not difficult to pick up admirers even among the first- and second-class passengers, who occasionally come to the steerage deck. In this amusement the lines of nationality are not drawn. The crew, on the whole, are jolly good fellows, willing to oblige and be obliged, being always ready to take a quarter out of you if they can.

"At nine o'clock all women go below, very reluctantly. Then, if you are a wise man, is the time to take your exercise. The air is deliciously cool, there is no crowd, and a calm moonlight or starlight night at sea, if you are alone with a companion who has sense enough to keep silent, is beautiful. If you are an imaginative man, the vastness of this great earth then first dawns upon you, when you see yourself rushing day after day with such speed over it, and yet know how little of its mighty circle you have turned."

Such beguiling versions of romanticism in steerage came in for severe questioning when the American Immigration Commission put its agents, disguised as impoverished travelers, on a number of different trans-atlantic ships. One of these agents was a woman who, having been "miserably insulted and compelled to withstand privations which were repulsive to her nature," made a report that shriveled all the claims of the travel agents. "The disorder and surroundings offended every sense," she said. "Everything was dirty, sticky and disagreeable to the touch. No sick pans are furnished and the vomitings of the seasick are often permitted to remain a long time before being removed." Worse was the "general air of immorality," including incorrigible behavior on the part of peeping toms. "During the hour preceding the breakfast bell," she said, "while the women were rising and dressing, several men usually went through and returned for no ostensible reason." The real meat of the lady's indictment was saved for the end. "Several of the crew told me that many of them marry girls from the steerage. When I insinuated that they could scarcely become well enough acquainted to marry during the passage, the answer was that the acquaintance had already gone so far that marriage was imperative."

❧ SECTION XXIII ❧

The American Line / Ocean Liners to War
"Is That You, St. Paul?"

S TARS AND STRIPES at the mastheads of superb clipper
ships had put an American stamp on the seven seas from Salem,
Massachusetts, to Hong Kong. But on the Great Circle route,
especially after the demise of the Collins Line, the American flag
turned up infrequently and without signifying anything more than
that Americans were still crossing the Atlantic with a kind of workaday persistence. Since the Great Circle was not only a sea route but a
showcase into which nations put their greatest ships, the decline of
the American mercantile fleet was inescapably evident. For a period
in the 1860s, in fact, there was not a single American steamship
crossing the Atlantic in the merchant service. But at last, in 1892,
the United States came upon an opportunity to meet and best the
competition, and to restore a measure of glamor to the American
way at sea.

The rescue of American fortunes and the restoration of American
prestige was undertaken by a Philadelphia concern called the International Navigation Company. Back in 1873, this company was ingenious enough to have started a service between Philadelphia and

Antwerp under an arrangement by which their ships flew the Belgian flag, were manned by Belgian crews, and subsidized by the Belgian Government. The only thing American about the arrangement was its financing: except for a few shares sold to Belgian subjects in order to make them eligible to serve as resident directors of the company, all the stock was kept in the hands of Philadelphians.

Making good money in this modest hands-across-the-sea collusion, the International Navigation Company was in a position to take advantage of a much bigger deal. After the death of founder William Inman, the line that bore his name was put up for sale, and the Philadelphia company bought it. This meant that an American shipping firm was now owner of one of the three big British steamship lines—the others being White Star and Cunard—that were granted yearly mail subsidies from the British Exchequer. In an access of gratitude for this advantage and with, as it developed, overreaching Yankee ambition, the Americans changed their name to Inman and International, and almost at once made plans to build two ships bigger and more lavishly accoutered than anything in either the White Star or the Cunard fleet.

To Her Majesty's ministers, this show of go-ahead aggressiveness was apparently just another instance of American bad form. When the two new ships—*City of Paris* and *City of New York*—were in the process of being built, the British Government abruptly pulled the rug from under the feet of the Philadelphians. With thin-lipped curtness they announced that the services of the Inman Line as a mail carrier would be at once dispensed with.

The men from Philadelphia were taken aback, then bewildered. What were they to do with two dazzling new steamships, the first ever to be propelled by twin screws, faster and more powerful than any other ships, more grandly appointed and more costly? Since they could not compete with White Star and Cunard without the British Post Office and Admiralty subsidy, and since Congress had long before decreed that the American flag could fly only above ships built in American shipyards, the directors of the company decided they had nowhere to go but, hat in hand, heart in mouth, to the Halls of Congress. There they frankly outlined their predicament, pled their case and quickly persuaded the legislators to bail them out. A bill was soon passed allowing the new *City of New York* and *City of Paris* to come under American registry—with only one modest proviso. For the privilege of American registry, the company was to build, in an American shipyard under the supervision of the Department of the Navy, two big passenger ships that could be converted overnight to wartime uses.

Delighted to comply, the company contracted with the Cramp Ship and Engine Building Company of Philadelphia to build for them two 12,000-ton ships that would be as American as the Old Homestead. These vessels were the *St. Louis* and the *St. Paul*; along with the company's two other liners—with their names now shortened to plain *New York* and *Paris*—they made up a transatlantic fleet capable of putting the steamship lines of England, Germany, France and any other foreign carrier on its mettle.

America at last had its own floating palaces—not the clamorous little monsters of the days of Collins, but serene, long, broad-decked beauties that moved with the brazen ease to which their preeminence gave them title. "Their beauty," said a nautical man of the *New York* and *Paris*, "could be appreciated even by confirmed wind-ship men, for they had the hulls of giant clippers, long and slim and full of grace. Their three slim funnels raked smartly aft, along with their three tall masts, and though they carried no sail, they carried the tapered, questing bowsprits of sailing ships."

In their grand saloons, each capable of sitting 420 people at one meal, delicacies came flaming to the table under a roof of glass domed like the Crystal Palace. Overhead, in its niche in a loft, an organ pumped out tranquilizing melodies. Mermaids "in the form of intermediate brackets," competed with paneled representations of other marine exotica along walls fifty-three feet long and almost as wide as the ship. But here, in a room most fit for revels, piety was still a force to contend with.

One issue of the newspaper printed aboard the *New York* and distributed free to her passengers recounts a typical evening. Every seat in the grand saloon was taken, said the paper, when the Reverend Dr. Hoge began his sermon, and everyone was rewarded. The evening's "discourse was strewn with gems of thought," but since the reporter had room for only one "from this speaker's Tray of Diamonds," he offered the following: " 'A little child's grave, though it is very small, is large enough to cast a deep, broad shadow across a fond parent's life.' "

Other passengers sought comfort in the hourglass-shaped library where the stained-glass windows were inscribed with quotations from poems about the sea; and where eight hundred volumes stamped with gold lettering awaited the pleasure of the literate. The *New York's* smoking room, big enough to accommodate 130 fuming devotees of the weed at one seance, was paneled in American walnut and furnished with couches and chairs of leather dyed scarlet.

Suites de luxe that could be entered—as if they were small private houses—from the open deck delighted even those passengers who could not afford to live in them. "Looking astern from the forecastle," wrote a traveler on the *New York,* "the broad surface on each side of the deck-house stretches back for over five hundred feet. At intervals there are passage ways opened through the deck-house to give convenient access between the two sides of the ship; and these also contain the entrance doors to the suites of apartments that are so attractive to the traveler. Each suite has its drawing-room, boudoir and bed-chamber, a little flat in miniature, with lavatory and bath, and windows that look out upon the sea."

With the slightly dazed look of a newly naturalized citizen, the *New York* first flew the Stars and Stripes on Washington's birthday, 1893. Thousands of patriots came to the sea wall at the Battery to watch President Harrison "fling 'Old Glory' to the breeze while Naval Reserves presented arms and cannons thundered forth the national salute from the decks of the cruiser *Chicago* and from the batteries of *Castle William.*"

When the *New York* and *Paris* came to New York, the Blue Riband came with them since, quite early on in their careers, they had swiped it for good from Cunard's fastest runners. But, for the booming American Line—as the Philadelphia-based company was now called —this was not enough. They were out to get the speed record for a ship that was American-*built* as well as merely of American registry.

William Cramp, whose company was contracted to build the two new all-American ships, saw them as agents of redress. "Their advent upon the world's highway of the North Atlantic is awaited by the American public with anticipation," he said, "and by the English public with apprehension. Since 1861, the period of a generation, the English have enjoyed a monopoly of the ocean traffic of the world, scarcely disturbed by the comparatively feeble efforts of their Continental neighbors, and they have built most of the ships employed by the latter at that. This long reign of undisputed supremacy has bred in the English mind a sense of proprietary right to the sea and of lien upon the carrying trade of the United States, which at last has become so arrogant that they resent any effort at emancipation on our part as an invasion of prerogative.

"Remembering unkindly the competition of our merchant marine in the old days, the English shipbuilders and shipowners of our time watch the development of a new commercial fleet under our flag with bitter hostility. To all these manifestations of ungenerous rivalry the American answer is simply 'Wait and see!' The ships will be on the line next summer."

In planning for the *St. Paul* and the *St. Louis*, the builders had to abide by the orders of Congress to heed certain decisions made by Navy personnel assigned to the shipyard to see that the liners would make good auxiliary cruisers. But everyone was in agreement about speed—with the result that the *St. Louis* and *St. Paul*, launched in December, 1894, and April, 1895, respectively, lost little time in capturing the passage records between Sandy Hook and England. In doing so they outsped not only their own running mates but the fastest that Cunard and White Star had to offer.

"One of the ways to keep in front," said a captain of the *St. Louis* who had a good old Yankee sense of foxiness and ethical vacuity, "was to tear into a fog. The *St. Louis* would steam at full speed through the murk, her bridge officers bending over the canvas dodger, all at high tension, the captain standing by the telegraph trying for a few extra miles in the race that would land our people in time to make the London train before the rival liners could get their passengers to the metropolis from Liverpool. After one such night, as the day came, we saw the rigging and part of a topmast lying across the windlass on the forecastle head. Some small craft, never again reported, had left her card. This was quickly hove overboard by Boatswain Crockett, working under instruction of the chief officer; the incident never found mention in the log."

As for beauty—the *St. Louis* and *St. Paul* were about as remarkable as a cellar door. Two inordinately tall funnels rose out of a big bastion of a hulk that might have been hammered together by blacksmiths obsessed by cubic space. The sister ships were in fact so ugly and so strikingly lacking in anything like sea-borne suavity, that American commentators were driven to justifications from the past. "Both," said one of the die-hards, "are thoroughly American in design as well as in construction. The trained eye of the seaman could recognize them as Yankee vessels a dozen miles away. In their external aspect they are like our splendid coastwise steamers magnified. They have the straight bow, curving slightly away at the waterline, the long, fine Yankee sheer, the graceful stern, the wholesome freeboard, and the bridge and pilot house forward, where the steersman can hold the ship well in hand—all the salient characteristics of the modern seagoing steam merchantman of the United States. They have even the two clean taper schooner masts, which American naval architects adopted years ago as the best rig for steamers, while foreign craft were still dragging about the cumbersome square yards and canvas, now everywhere abandoned."

Perhaps it was because the Navy wanted to be sure that the ships could be converted into floating barracks overnight; or perhaps because the taste of American decorators was in a phase as dismal, if not as assertive, as their British counterparts. Whatever the reason, the interiors of the new American flagships were serviceable, stark and largely forbidding. "Gold leaf and effects usually associated with 'floating palaces' have been disregarded," said the company, which then arrived at a sort of apologia for saloons and cabins that must have struck even the most parochial of its directors as *reductium ad absurdum*. "The large sums which are spent on the interior decorations of the modern steamship are not always spent wisely," they said. "There is a great and ever-increasing luxury of equipment, but the taste displayed is commonly that of the abstract upholsterer, and whatever effect is produced is attained simply by the lavish use of expensive material. It was to avoid this pitfall that the company determined to put the general scheme of decoration, after the marine architect had drawn the deck plan, into the hands of a land architect." This landsman was frivolous enough to install a gallery housing a pipe organ at one end of the grand saloon, but otherwise his contributions to the art of marine decoration simply repeated the barren adequacy of meetinghouse and courtroom. High life, of a sort, still took place in American sporting houses among the wonderful trappings of cathouse rococo—but the *St. Louis* and *St. Paul* would have none of this. Their austerity made even the respectable Cunarders look like cockney gin palaces.

Yet, to many of their passengers, and even to their captains, these paramilitary ships were pleasure pavilions to rival the floating houses of Kashmir. "In those days," said a former captain of the *St. Paul*, "she knew the caressing swish of silken petticoats and the gay laughter of the elite. Her passenger lists were like the social registers of two continents. . . .

"Her famous saloon, with its deep-toned organ, was to hear the voices of celebrated men and women, to know the splendor of those fine dinners of the past sparkling with wit and wine and the flashing of jewels. Beauty chose her because she herself was beautiful and young. Those were the days when languorous-looking pea-green ladies with large hips and ripe breasts, dressed only in semi-discreet poses, filled the walls in *bas-relief*; it was the height of decorative art. To the last these voluptuous sirens clung to the insides of the ancient liner."

For most of a decade, the quadrivium of American Line ships brought new zest to the endless contest on the sea lanes of the North Atlantic and satisfaction to Americans who for generations had deplored the senescence of their country's maritime enterprise. The American renaissance-at-sea, however, was severely checked when the Germans came steaming into the picture with a big show of decorative afflatus and invincible power. Then the Spanish-American War ended it altogether. True to their promise and purpose, the *St. Louis* and *St. Paul* were commandeered almost at once and turned into warships capable of engaging even orthodox military cruisers in battle. Both had brief and furiously busy careers as ships of war; and the *St. Paul* did a good turn for Theodore Roosevelt and his rough-riding gentlemen by cutting the Spain-to-Cuba cable, off Santiago. Following the entry of the *St. Louis* and the *St. Paul* into hostilities, the *New York* and the *Paris*, rechristened the *Harvard* and the *Yale*, respectively, were stripped, armed, and dispatched to the Caribbean. Thus, said a naval authority, "It fell to the American Navy to be the first to put into practice the modern principle of using the fastest mail and merchant steamers as auxiliary cruisers for naval warfare."

The Spanish-American War was such a brief, frantic and old-fashioned skirmish in the Antilles that within a year these ships were back, skimming the cream off the Atlantic milk run and carrying the slim hopes of the American merchant marine across the shoals of the twentieth century. Just before the momentous turning, the *St. Paul* herself was instrumental in advancing one of the greatest developments of the new age.

This occurred at the end of her fifty-second eastward voyage, when her most illustrious passenger was Guglielmo Marconi. The inventor had it in mind to prove the efficacy of ship-to-shore wireless by sending messages, via a receiving station at the Needles, to all parts of Europe. As the ship was about to leave her New York dock early in November, Marconi sent a cable to London saying that he would attempt to speak to the Needles just as soon as the *St. Paul* was in English waters. To be on hand for the historical moment, Major Flood Page, one of the directors of Marconi's Wireless Telegraph Company, went down to the receiving station the night before the expected transmission. In the morning, he reported, "the Needles resembled pillars of salt as one after the other they were lighted up by the brilliant sunrise. There was a thick haze over the sea, and it would have been possible for the liner to pass the Needles without our catching sight of her. Breakfast over, the sun was delicious as we paced the lawn, but at sea the haze increased to fog; no ordinary signals could have been read from any ship passing the place. . . .

"The idea of failure never entered our minds. So far as we were concerned, we were ready, and we felt complete confidence that the ship would be all right with Mr. Marconi himself on board. Yet . . . we felt in a state of nervous tension . . . it was not anxiety, it was certainly not doubt, not lack of confidence, but it was waiting.

"We sent out our signals over and over again, when, in the most natural and ordinary way, our bell rang. It was 4:45 P.M.

"Is that you, *St. Paul?*"

"Yes."

"Where are you?"

"Sixty-six nautical miles away."

By the time the *St. Paul* got to Southampton, a copy of *The Transatlantic Times*, the first ocean newspaper to be serviced by wireless, was ready for any of those of her passengers willing to pay one dollar for the souvenir. "There are 375 passengers on board," said the paper, "counting the distinguished and the extinguished."

This minor triumph could not compensate for the fact that by deferring to the American Navy, the American merchant marine had surrendered all of its candidates for honors on the North Atlantic and allowed itself to be overtaken by a succession of new ships from Europe. So reduced, it would have a long and discouraging wait for the moment when one of its own ships would take the Blue Riband in her teeth and bring it back to American shores. It would, in fact, have to wait until a summer morning in 1952. Then, upon half a century of decline and desuetude, Margaret Truman, the President's daughter, would blow the whistle.

PART THREE

APOGEE
1890-1919

⚘ SECTION I ⚘

Wilhelm II Piped Aboard / *The* Teutonic: *"We Must Have Some of These"* / Turbinia: *"A Thing Bewitched"* / *Charles Algernon Parsons* / *Imperial Germany to the Fore* / *Mark Twain: "The Modern Idea Is Right"* / *The Sad Case of the* Kaiser Friedrich *The Fearsome* Kaiser Wilhelm der Grosse

ONE AUGUST AFTERNOON in 1889, the German Emperor Wilhelm II was piped aboard the new White Star liner *Teutonic* and into the embrace of his uncle the Prince of Wales. The occasion was a naval review at Spithead to which Thomas Ismay, the White Star chairman, had invited three hundred and seventy guests, "the greater part of whom," said *The Times*, "enjoyed his hospitality, while he endured their society." The Emperor had sailed across the Channel on a ship of the German Navy that had then joined the British fleet in a ceremony, overtly cordial, that was really a matter of making muscles and flaunting military hardware.

The thing about the *Teutonic* that both the Prince of Wales and Ismay most wanted their visitor to see was her armor. For the first time, a merchant ship had been transformed, almost overnight, into an armed cruiser supposedly able to withstand attack, as well as to pursue and destroy a potential enemy. But somehow the Emperor was not much impressed by a few guns placed here and there, or by armor platings and the military bleakness to which the great ship was reduced. What took his attention was that aspect of the liner that most appealed to her passengers. After all, what German ship had a barber shop with an entrance resembling a cathedral vestry, with electric motors to drive hairbrushes, electric fans to dry ladies' hair after shampooing? What German ship could offer such a litany of rapture as those details recently enumerated in the press?

"The smoking-room is the cosiest and most handsome shrine of tobacco ever seen ashore or afloat," said a London reporter. "It is difficult to conceive such a room outside of our Pall Mall clubhouses. The woodwork is that rich dark mahogany seen in old mansions. The handsome, lazy-looking couches are upholstered with leather of a colour to match the above. The walls are covered with a richly-gilt embossed leather of the same tone. The panels are bright oil-paintings representing the picturesque ships of the Middle Ages. The ceiling reproduces a very handsome old English plaster pattern in aquatint and variously shaped designs. In the day-time the room is lighted through square windows opening out on the deck, screened at will by stained-glass blinds, and at night by electric lamps in the ceiling, placed behind stained glass. Here, then, one can smoke and dream in a voluptuous corner, spanning the ages which have intervened between the times of the argosies depicted on the walls until steamships were invented, or further still, from Jason's ship to this one of the White Star Line."

Long and uncluttered, the *Teutonic* was one of the first ships to abandon masts supporting sails in favor of short masts that served merely as flag poles. Consequently her silhouette was meticulously modern, and her power and interior refinements quite beyond anything the Emperor had ever seen. His Imperial Highness spent an hour and a half roaming through the ship's interior. Then, with the casual covetousness of a man who spots a new brand of cigar or golf ball, he was overheard to say, "We must have some of these."

Whether or not this remark sparked it all, the big maritime news of the final decade of the century was the emergence of Imperial Germany as the most eminent power on sea lanes that had for generations been regarded as an exclusive British preserve. But before this could happen, a British engineer in the great heritage of Napier and Brunel had to make it possible.

"It was a sight positively staggering while it lasted," wrote a London journalist, "there was almost an uncanny element about it." What he saw were three men of certified Victorian aplomb—Thomas Ismay, his son Bruce and their friend Sir George Baden-Powell—"holding on to the rails, bending almost double to withstand the wind" created by a ship with "flames belching from her funnel, with a good third of her keel fairly forced out of the water leaving a high curling wake behind."

The little vessel they rode, long and lean as a pencil, tearing "through the seas like a thing bewitched" was named *Turbinia*. When they could step back onto the *Teutonic*, and the *Turbinia* was again tied up alongside like a calf nuzzling its mother, these gentlemen could claim to have traveled on water at a greater speed than any men before them. They had also offered themselves as part of a demonstration of a new kind of marine propulsion—one that would in a very few years revolutionize ocean travel.

It was a day in June, 1897; the occasion was the Grand Naval Review in the course of the celebration of Victoria's Diamond Jubilee when all things commemorated the Queen's sixty-year reign—even the ships' menus on which Balmoral puddings, Victoria creams and Windsor biscuits were conspicuous; and the place was a stretch of open water off Spithead. The Prince of Wales, the future Edward VII, was there, and so was the confidante of his nephew the Kaiser, Prince Henry of Prussia. A scandal, an outrage, the event was a striking success for those who planned it, simply because the main point of the escapade was to let everyone in on the secret power of the new steam turbine engine developed by Charles Algernon Parsons.

Years before, Parsons had constructed a steam turbine to generate electricity on land. Then, in 1894, he organized the Marine Steam Turbine Company and turned his thoughts toward developing the same principle for use at sea. Working with scale models, testing tanks and many shapes of propellers, Parsons worked for years to perfect the turbine blade that would unlock the power to drive a ship. By 1896 he had sketched out a design that satisfied him. This design would remain serviceable for forty years—until the time when the aging inventor, denominated *Sir* Charles, was called in as a consultant on the *Queen Mary*, for which, almost on the spot, he devised an even more sophisticated model of his invention.

Parsons knew that he had got hold of something with implications that would be enormous. He was also aware that the shipbuilding fraternity was cautious and conservative, sometimes to the point of immobility. "If you believe in a principle, never damage it with a poor impression," he said. Consequently he was ready to go "the whole hog" to "startle people." With canny showmanship he picked just the occasion that would serve, and quite illicitly managed to sneak his little 40-ton prodigy into the mighty armada of dreadnoughts and armed merchant ships assembled for review in the Solent. To those observing the show, nothing at first seemed amiss. At a signal known only to its crew, the *Turbinia* moved out of the area reserved for spectators, "entered the long sea lane between serried rows of naval vessels," and "in a mad dash of Nelsonic impertinence" began to skim over the water like a traveling fountain. "Her speed," said the man from *The Times*, "was simply astonishing, but its manifestation was accompanied by a mighty rushing sound and by a stream of flame from her funnel at least as long as the funnel itself."

Torpedo boats enlisted to patrol the general area were at once sent after her to bring her back into line. But C. J. Leyland, the *Turbinia*'s captain, was not going to allow himself to be overtaken. Whizzing past the ships on review he met one of the vedettes dashing through an opening to head him off. "It was a close shave," he admitted later. "I just had space to avoid her. Her crew dashed into the bows and her lieutenant unbuckled his sword, expecting to have to swim. He evidently spoke to me and I said something to him, but as we were passing at a speed of nearly forty-five knots, it may have been just as well that our impromptu remarks did not carry."

When she had completed her star turn, the saucy little cynosure shut down her power and allowed herself to be tied up alongside the *Teutonic* long enough for the Ismays and Sir George Baden-Powell to board her for another joyride. As one observer remarked, she had already become "the most important topic of conversation in technical circles between the two Poles," generating curiosity on the same scale that she had generated power. Driven by nine propellers arranged in sets of three on three shafts, the little bladelike ship—100 feet long and only 9 feet wide—had achieved 2,000 horsepower while shooting over the water at nearly 40 miles per hour.

Navy brass, not particularly amused by Parsons' "proper box of tricks," was out for his blood. But before the admirals could apply sanctions, Prince Henry of Prussia sent his congratulations and asked if the *Turbinia*'s run might not be repeated. Such approval from an honored guest stayed the hand of the Admiralty long enough to allow Navy men to see for themselves just what Parsons had wrought. Once their lordships had recovered equilibrium they became covetous. Within a short time the British Navy was enlarged by two destroyers—H.M.S. *Viper* and H.M.S. *Cobra*—powered by Parsons' turbines. In the early part of their careers these small and powerful ships were the fastest things on water anywhere.

Shipping magnates, almost as conservative as the Lords of the Admiralty, were also reluctant to allow that hi-jinks in the Solent might have signaled a change in the established order of things. But ranks were broken when a Scottish operator of coastal steamers gave an order to the Dumbarton firm of Denny Brothers to build a ship for passenger service on the Clyde. This was the *King Edward,* and beginning in July, 1901, she ran happily, efficiently and safely between Fairlie and Campbeltown. Other firms still needed convincing. One company built two ships, alike as peas, except that one was driven by the conventional reciprocating engines, and one by turbines. These twin vessels were tested and compared in the Irish Sea on runs between Heysham and Belfast.

The Cunard Steam-Ship Company meanwhile decided to make comparisons on a big scale. They put reciprocating engines into their new *Caronia,* while the *Carmania,* her sister ship, was given turbines. But even before the *Carmania* had proved that she was easily superior, the enterprising Allan Line (the same company had introduced the first steel ship, the *Buenos Ayrean,* in 1881, just before the arrival of Cunard's steel *Servia*) again stepped to the forefront. This line's two new ships, the *Virginian* and the *Victorian,* each equipped with three screws driven by turbines, were commissioned in 1905.

Once the turbine had proved its efficiency, the penultimate phase of transatlantic travel was begun. Sea lanes that were once romantic avenues to freedom, golden tracks of commerce or invitations to realms of culture, adventure, history, now became pedestrian highways for hundreds of thousands of people who insisted on being pampered, beguiled, entertained day and night, and delivered on the dot. The broad Atlantic had long ago been narrowed; now it was regulated. Instead of challenging the whims of the sea gods with his fingers crossed, the traveler merely tested the limits of his self-indulgence. Now, among a plethora of offerings, the finicky voyager could pick and choose the convenient time, the right ship, the most tasteful accommodations and the companions most likely to prove congenial. "Even the least eventful sea-voyages," said novelist Edith Wharton, "lend themselves to favorable propinquities," and thousands of lighthearted travelers agreed with her.

The Great Circle had become a waterway crowded with ferryboats. To some people, this had all happened too swiftly; the vaunted progress of science threatened to abolish the fear of God. "After all," said one gloomy observer, "the Atlantic and the other oceans were made by the Great Designer as barriers between separate continents, and although we speak of them casually as rather of the nature of a herring-pond, and build our ships to act as ferries, yet are we not flying in the face of Nature, and asking for trouble?" Above the blasts of the steam whistles of all the mighty liners, the voice of Cassandra sounded rather like grandmotherly maundering. No one—least of all those people who rode in caravans of trunks, hatboxes, portmanteaus and fruit baskets to the Liverpool landing stage and the docks at the foot of East Fourteenth Street—paid any attention to it.

Imperceptibly at first, then with a splash that brought everyone to attention, great new German ships—built for the first time in German shipyards—were beginning to set the pace, and the style as well. In the matter of style, the German emphasis had for years been in the direction of the *gemütlich*, the home-away-from-home familiarity of an unpretentious hotel in, say, Bavaria. In the dining rooms of the Hamburg-Amerika ships, said the *European Tourist Gazette*, "The tables sparkle with silver ware and crystal spread over white damask cloths. The large brass lamps, polished until they shine again, are lit by electric light, and the rays glint among the pink and green glasses and slender goblets, ranged in racks overhead, which sway to and fro with the motion of the ship. All the objects are multiplied indefinitely by the mirrors at each end, which open interminable vistas of moving color." In almost the same breath, the prospective traveler was assured that "neither cattle, nor pigs nor sheep are carried on these steamers."

Speed was still the irresistible genius and prime factor in the minds of shipowners. But among growing signs that speed *per se* might soon lose its drawing power, German builders were moved to give the designer a free hand. The most eminent of decorators brought in to apply his talents to aesthetics on the sea lanes was Johannes Poppe of Bremen, an architect to whom marine design was a fresh field. After he had carried through designs for the city library and the Cotton Exchange in his native city, Poppe was invited by the directors of the Norddeutscher Lloyd to do the interiors for their new ship *Lahn*. Challenged to make something out of the limitations of ship space that would be both beautiful and edifying, Poppe went to work. "Necessity and compulsion prevailed everywhere," said one of his admiring contemporaries, "and artistic forms were the very last thing considered. They were nothing but the glittering robe, as it were, which was made to cover enforced exigencies."

In 1877, when the *Lahn*, with all of her massive and ponderous forms, her gilded railings, allegorical statuary and trumpeting cherubs, came into service her arrival marked "the momentous turning point in the history of interior decoration of ships." Under the auspices of the German Empire, the age of magnificence afloat had been launched. German ships became temples of high baroque, grand galleries of an aspiration so Valkeyrian that only megalomaniacs might dally there in comfort or good conscience. Eventually, the restraining lambency of *art nouveau* would overtake the apostles of gigantism. But for twenty years and more the operatic excesses of German marine decor would be admired, ridiculed, and emulated. Lasting right up until the outbreak of World War I, this period of art-at-sea would meticulously reflect a world that, for all its pretensions, was moribund and doomed. Its temper was hyperbolic and its mode was elephantine. Part Richard Wagner, part Victor Herbert, its harmonies were sufficiently viable to juxtapose the classic with the kitsch in a symphony of uncertain taste that was nevertheless appropriate to its audience.

German shipowners had for decades done well on the North Atlantic. The services they offered were sound, unspectacular, largely concerned with transporting endless streams of America-bound emigrants from *Mittel-Europa* and its more easterly neighbors. As early as 1847, with the appearance in New York of the sailing ship *Deutschland*, the company that became the Hamburg Amerikanische Packetfahrt Actien Gesellschaft had inaugurated a passenger service that continued unbroken through the century. In 1856, the same company had introduced the first German transatlantic steamship. This was followed within two years by a steamer from Bremen belonging to the Norddeutscher Lloyd Company. The two German firms competed with one another for emigrants in all the corners of Europe and carried on rate wars that were at times so intense that emigrants were transported almost free of charge. At the height of one of these contests, Norddeutscher Lloyd went so far as "to lend every steerage passenger an enameled dinner service, a spoon and a fork, and to present him or her with a blanket which might be taken away at the end of the voyage." The rivalry of the cities of Hamburg and Bremen reached all the way back to medieval times. For the last eighty years of the nineteenth century this rivalry all but played itself into a mutual death grip as, ship for ship, German marine ingenuity built its bridge across the Atlantic.

Riding the waves in a Teutonic merriment of lager beer, Schweitzer-käse and pretzeln while bands—composed mainly of versatile stewards from the second class—puffed in three-quarter time through leisurely dinners and digestive siestas on deck, the famous German lines had grown rich. "It is pleasant to be summoned to one's meals," said a passenger on Norddeutscher Lloyd's *Havel*, "not by a barbarous gong, but by a civilized and inspiring bugle. Only musicians are employed as second-class stewards, and an excellent band plays on deck every morning, so that even sea-sick passengers are reheartened. Who of us will ever forget the sweet, deep pleasure of being awakened on Sunday morning by the playing of 'Nearer, my God, to Thee'?"

Mark Twain, well on his way toward becoming a transatlantic commuter, was equally delighted with the *Havel*. He recorded his pleasure in a little essay entitled "The Modern Steamer and the Obsolete Steamer." "I should not have supposed that the modern ship could be a surprise to me," wrote Twain, "but it is. It seems to be as much a surprise to me as it could have been if I never read anything about it. I walk about this great vessel, the *Havel*, as she ploughs her way through the Atlantic, and every detail that comes under my eye brings up the miniature counterpart of it as it existed in the little ships I crossed the ocean in fourteen, seventeen, eighteen, and twenty years ago. For instance, she has several bathrooms, and they are as convenient and as nicely equipped as the bathrooms in a fine private house in America. . . .

"In the steamer *Batavia*, twenty years ago, one candle, set in the bulkhead between two staterooms, was there to light both rooms, but did not light either of them. It was extinguished at eleven at night, and so were all the saloon lamps except one or two, which were left burning to help the passenger see how to break his neck trying to get around in the dark.

"The old ships offered the passenger no chance to smoke except in the place that was called the 'fiddle.' It was a repulsive den made of rough boards . . . and its office was to protect the main hatch. It was grimy and dirty; there were no seats; the only light was a lamp of the rancid-oil-and-rag kind; the place was very cold, and never dry, for the seas broke in through the cracks every little while and drenched the cavern thoroughly.

"One curious thing which is at once noticeable in the great modern ship is the absence of hubbub, clatter, rush of feet, roaring of orders. . . . A Sabbath stillness and solemnity reign . . . I observe stateroom doors three inches thick, of solid oak and polished. I note companion-way vestibules with walls, doors and ceilings paneled in polished hardwoods . . . all dainty and delicate joiner-work, and yet every join compact and tight; with beautiful pictures containing as many as sixty tiles—and the joinings of these tiles perfect. These are daring experiments. I find the walls of the dining-saloon upholstered with mellow pictures wrought in tapestry and the ceiling aglow with pictures done in oil. In other places of assembly I find great panels filled with embossed Spanish leather, the figures rich with gilding and bronze. Everywhere I find sumptuous masses of color—color, color—color all about, color of every shade and tint and variety; and, as a result, the ship is bright and cheery to the eye, and this cheeriness invades one's spirit and contents it.

"The old-time ships were dull, plain, graceless, gloomy, and horribly depressing. They compelled the blues; one could not escape the blues in them. The modern idea is right, to surround the passenger with conveniences, luxuries, and abundance of inspiriting color."

In a letter to a physician friend about the same voyage, which took place in June, 1892, Twain's pleasure makes him speculative. "This is the delightfulest ship I was ever in," he says. "One can write in her as comfortably as he can at home. . . . If I were going to write a book I think I would try to get my family's leave to take a room in the *Havel* and ferry back and forth till the book was finished. I will give that idea to some bachelor author."

Lovers of ease and Wagnerian artifacts were drawn to the ships of the two German lines, yet neither of these lines commanded anything of that volatile thrill of interest that had made steamships on the Atlantic an issue of zealous nationalism. Germany was swiftly coming into her majority as an economic and imperialist power, and her need for a mercantile fleet was becoming crucial. Shipbuilding was already among the first of the empire's expansionist priorities. Instead of commissioning ships to be built on the Tyne or the Clyde, as they had been used to doing, shipowners of Bremen and Hamburg took to importing British engineers and craftsmen and to setting them to work at high pay in German shipyards. When their own shipwrights had learned what they needed to know, the services of the Englishmen and Scotsmen were dispensed with and, save for a few experts who acted as foremen, sent home.

By the early years of the 1890s, German firms had become notably prosperous. In one decade, Hamburg-Amerika alone had carried half a million passengers to New York—half again as much as either Cunard or White Star. The German companies basked in Imperial favor, were staffed by brilliant, ambitious executives and, as time would tell, competitive to the point of madness. The motto on the Hamburg-Amerika house flag was indicative: *Mein Feld Ist Die Welt* ("My field is the world").

The "noble example" of Germany in its surge to the forefront of maritime power had rallied the waning hopes of sea-minded Americans, and led directly to Congressional support for the rehabilitation of the American Line. "Germany has a scant foothold on the deep sea," said one patriot, "and none of the splendid nautical traditions of America. What the empire has done, the republic can do more readily. No race like ours with a grasp upon two oceans and the mingled blood of Viking and pioneer can long be cheated of its birthright."

Kaiser Wilhelm himself was caught up in the nobility of it all. After a short cruise on one of the great ships he wrote a letter to his mother. "Any man who, standing on the deck of a ship with the starlit firmament of the Almighty as his canopy and the boundless seas as the only object of his vision," said His Imperial Highness, "takes occasion to question his conscience, to weigh his responsibilities, and to contrast them with his inclination to do good and keep in the path of righteousness, will not hesitate to pronounce a sea voyage a salutary thing for himself and those depending upon him."

To put an end to the dominance of rivals like the *Campania* and the *Lucania* and to halt the leapfrog way in which Cunard alternated with White Star in claiming the fastest speed, the longest menus and the most ornate grand saloons, the North German Lloyd Company adopted Prussian measures. They went to the Vulcan shipbuilding company in Stettin with a simple, stark proposal: build us the fastest ship in the world and we'll buy it; give us anything less, and you can keep it.

Though they would have only one round-trip voyage to New York in which to prove they had delivered the goods, the Vulcan people accepted the risk and came up with a winner. Presented with the same proposition, the Schichau yard in Danzig came up with the sorriest ship of modern times. In the hope of getting a share of the business that normally fell to Vulcan, the Schichau people said they would build a liner with a guaranteed speed of 22 knots, and proceeded to turn out the long, lithe, trifunneled *Kaiser Friedrich*. But when the new ship from Danzig took 7 days, 11 hours getting to Fire Island lightship and came home in a dismal 9 days, 2 hours, 30 minutes, her second round trip was canceled and she spent three months back in the shipyard being generally tightened up. But nothing worked. She just could not cross the ocean in much less than seven days. Fed up with these poor performances, the North German Lloyd announced that they were giving the ship back to her builders. But, said the proud firm of F. Schichau, you can't give her back since you've never officially accepted her; we ourselves will withdraw her from service and dispose of her in our own way. Thus began a legal dispute that went on for years and was eventually settled out of court. Robbing Peter to pay Paul, the Schichau people chartered the *Kaiser Friedrich* to the Hamburg-Amerika Line. Under the latter's flag her transocean time was worse than ever —in ten voyages she could never do better than seven days.

With her 24,000-horsepower engines under wraps, the cornices and scrolls of her gilded saloons packed with dust, the *Kaiser Friedrich* lay gently rocking at her moorings in the harbor of Hamburg for twelve long, empty years. The biggest white elephant in captivity since the *Great Eastern*, the *Kaiser Friedrich* was also the most expensive to keep. As maintenance charges and storage costs rose year by year, the humiliated vessel rusted and flaked in full view of the Port of Hamburg. Finally, in 1912, she was taken out of bondage. A new company operating between France and South America—the Sud Atlantique Line— bought her, gave her the name *Burdigala*, affixed red roosters to either side of her three buff funnels, and sent her off to Brazil and the River Plate. But that run was also more than the old ship could handle and within a year she was laid up, this time in the harbor of Bordeaux. She was still there when World War I broke out. In March, 1915, the French Government requisitioned her for service as a troop ship, then had her rigged out as an auxiliary cruiser. Lumbering along with little 5.5-inch guns staring incongruously out of peep holes on her huge decks, she was spotted by a German submarine in the Mediterranean, torpedoed, and sunk in November, 1916.

The take-it-or-leave-it, all-or-nothing deal proposed by North German Lloyd was much more happily realized in the career of another ship. When the Vulcan yards took the challenge, the immediate result was the tall, fast, always fearsome-looking *Kaiser Wilhelm der Grosse*. This was the ship that would open a new era, a period in steamship history when the landscapes of Valhalla enscrolled on the walls and ceilings of grand saloons would all but collapse under their own weight, as well as a period when Teutonic efficiency united with matchless engine power would give Germany all the honors of the northern seas. And when the wits of the first decade of the century began to say that something or other was "hideously," or "divinely," "late North German Lloyd," they meant, according to an American contemporary, "two of everything but the kitchen range, and then gilded."

Sporting four stiffly erect tall funnels, a white superstructure and a black hull with a greater carrying capacity than even the *Great Eastern*, 649 feet in length, driven by twin screws and spacious enough to take care of 2,300 passengers, the *Kaiser Wilhelm der Grosse* was nothing short of a sea-going boast. The ceilings of her public rooms were higher than those of any other ship, their walls were loaded with paintings, carvings and bas-reliefs that glowed in the sacerdotal radiance of stained glass. In every respect, old standards of comfort and luxury had given way to outsized magnificence. Instead of quietly charming the well-to-do passenger by reminding him of his home, his club, or a familiar country inn, the new designers overawed and overwhelmed him. For his week or so at sea he lived in noble apartments of cathedral proportions; in steady weather he might forget the sea and imagine himself to be the castellan of some turreted eyrie on the Upper Rhine.

On her first crucial trip, in 1897, the *Kaiser Wilhelm der Grosse* raced across the Atlantic at a rate of more than 21 knots to snatch the Blue Riband. To ship-conscious England, that romp across the preserves of Cunard and Thomas H. Ismay was an affront. "In that jubilee year," said Humfrey Jordan, "England was not feeling modest. She despised foreigners without troubling to conceal the fact; she recognized herself, with complete assurance, as a great nation, the head of a mighty empire, the ruler of the seas. But, with the jubilee mood still warming her citizens to a fine self-satisfaction in being Britons, England lost, and lost most decisively, the speed record of the Atlantic ferry to a German ship. The *Kaiser Wilhelm der Grosse* was a nasty blow to British shipping; her triumphant appearance on the Atlantic came at a moment peculiarly unacceptable to the English public."

Within a year, even though her top-heaviness and lubberly propensities had earned her the nickname "Rolling Billy," the *Kaiser* was so successful as to preempt twenty-four percent of all transatlantic passenger revenue. Within three years she had become the first European liner to be equipped with wireless, not only as a device of safety but as a convenience for travelers. Never before in its history had the Cunard Line so clearly dipped its flag to a superior money maker. Never had the White Star Line been so flabbergasted: the emergence, overnight, of one ship had made all of its own carriers obsolete. It was cold comfort to recognize that English know-how in German hands had produced the *Kaiser*. The White Star directors were in fact so stunned that they were reduced to petulance. Let the Germans drive themselves to pieces with their belching behemoths, they said; from now on the White Star will concentrate on comfort, grace, spaciousness. As if speed were suddenly anathema, they even began to speak with pride of the virtues of "the nine-day boat."

✄ SECTION II ✄

Germany Über Alles / *"The Man from San Francisco"* / *Henry James: "A Shapeless Bundle of Shawls"* / *The Lavish Hand of Johannes Poppe* / *Blueprints Marked:* Mauretania, Lusitania

A S THE CENTURY turned, new German ships asserted and reasserted their claims to the Atlantic speed record and paraded their finery on the sea lanes as though they were floating in review down Unter den Linden.

"The rise of German prosperity," said a captious Englishman, "and, therefore, the appearance of what economists demonstrate to be the immediate sequel—an instant desire to spend money in all sorts of self-indulgence—has been followed by a readiness on the part of steamship companies to put forth the greatest material comfort that is practicable on board ship." One notable German gesture toward self-indulgence on a new scale was the introduction of *à la carte* restaurants. The traveler could now buy his ticket marked "With Meals" or "Without Meals." If he chose the latter he would dine in a Ritz-Carlton Restaurant, where "it may be taken for granted that a brigade of chefs trained by Escoffier and a brigade of waiters trained by Ritz make the cuisine and service as renowned as that of the famous restaurants ashore."

Allowing for dining at no fixed time and no *prix fixe*, this new arrangement pleased a sufficient number of first-class passengers to allow for its continuance for many years. Among these was an editor of the *New York Times*. "There will be . . . general rejoicing over the abolition of the bugle call at half-past seven," he wrote. "That piercing strain has its attractions for those with whose habits or inclinations its summons happens to coincide, but for others it is a most terrible affliction." Some travelers found the lack of schedule in dining hours oppressive. "The new plan of eating at all hours spoils the voyage for good sailors and delights the poor sailor," said a veteran American lady traveler. "People were eating white asparagus with their meat and all kinds of vegetables together on one side of us, and on the other side, they were eating ice-cream and nuts!" Escoffier and Ritz might attempt to bring their Continental touch to Teutonic dining rooms, but a caustic English observer would not be taken in by such refinements. "German decorative art," he said, "is in a particularly happy position to supply all that is necessary to make a steel tank resemble a palace."

In a similar vein of undeclared huffiness, an American arbiter of social behavior warned her lady readers not to forget that German propriety aboard ship might be something to be regarded with tolerance, but certainly not to be taken as a standard. "On the German steamers it is considered no breach of etiquette," she advised, "for a woman to go after dinner with a man friend, or with her chaperon, or husband, or brother to the smoking-room and enjoy her coffee, but on the English, French and American liners, this custom is not in vogue and must not be enforced by even the most innocently gay and venturesome young lady."

What more graphic mark of imperial afflatus could the Germans exhibit than that gracing the forward wall of their crack new liner's dining saloon? "One of the main ornaments," wrote a journalist, "is the large picture of His Majesty the Emperor William II, painted by Ludwig Noster. The painting is surrounded by a richly carved gilt frame, and on both sides of it are elaborately ornamented broad pilasters connecting the floor with the ceiling. In the middle fields of the frame are allegoric figures of Loyalty and Sagacity, and in each of the upper fields is a large cartouche of carved work, the central fields of which again contain emblems of loyalty and sagacity. Four ornamental eagles act as shield bearers. The arched fields of the light well are ornamented with handsome paintings of Hohenzollern Castle and the castles of Augustenburg, flanked by allegoric cherubs representing the Trades, Commerce, Shipping."

Among an idiotic plethora of steamship statistics, what more zany notion could the Germans offer than that one of their new ships had a carrying capacity "in excess of the number of men engaged in the Seminole War of 1856–1858?" When the Russian writer Ivan Bunin needed the metaphorical possibilities of a great liner in his story "The Man from San Francisco," he created a fictional ship, the *Atlantis*, and furnished her with trappings and passengers in the new Germanic image. "A siren on the forecastle howled ceaseless in hellish sullenness," wrote Bunin, "and whined in frenzied malice, but not many of the diners heard the siren—it was drowned by the strains of a splendid string orchestra, playing exquisitely and without pause in the two-tiered hall, decorated with marble, its floors covered with velvet rugs; festively flooded with the lights of crystal lusters and gilded *girandoles*, filled to capacity with diamond-bedecked ladies in *décolleté* and men in smoking jackets, graceful waiters and deferential maîtres d'hôtel—among whom one, who took orders for wines exclusively, even walked about with a chain around his neck, like a lord mayor."

The term of the *Kaiser Wilhelm der Grosse* was ended by the spectacular performance of a new ship from Hamburg—the long, low, four-funneled *Deutschland*. As shipbuilders began to turn out top-lofty superstructures, she was one of the last ships to have the sleek look of a greyhound. But this was no help at all in preventing her from becoming superseded, almost at once, by the Bremen Company's *Kaiser Wilhelm II*.

Like every new ship, the second *Kaiser Wilhelm* had her term of precedence and fashionability. In August, 1904, one of her passengers, returning to his native land after twenty-one years abroad, was Henry James, who had been enticed into making this particular voyage by the mother and sister of a friend of his. These ladies had apparently made most of the necessary arrangements for his voyage. A midsummer letter addressed to them spells out anticipations of pleasure that were not to be realized. "Now that I have beautifully heard from you on the great *K.W. II* question," wrote James, "I feel delightfully launched and settled, and the spell of the protected and 'done for' state is but too promptly and prematurely working. I seem already in possession of that lovely elongated sea-chair (I know I shall have the best on the ship) with my heels tucked up, my shawls becomingly arranged, my smelling bottle serenely clasped and an occasional graceful female form bending over me to ask how I feel *now?* I am feeling 'now,' as I say, very much as I expect to feel '*then*,' so perfectly, thanks to your admirably kind offices, has the condition of peace descended on me. When you ask me, airily, if you may take for granted that you 'arrange' for my place at table and the deck-chair aforesaid, I respond with a roaring '*Rather*, please!' I expect to cross the sea in the simple form of a shapeless bundle of shawls, without human feature, semblance or identity, transported hither and thither, according to wind and weather, by discreet stewards (in *your* pay) but not revealing to the casual observer the shape or the sentiments of man."

The passage was smooth, but James, according to his friends, could "hardly be said to have enjoyed the voyage." Sick a good part of the time, the man who had made his first trip to Europe on the already historic *Great Western*, had to be fed toast and tea on occasion, and otherwise left, minus his shawls, alone. He was, as he later told the ladies, their "forlorn friend on the *Kaiser*," and the shock of reentry into America through the waterfront sheds of Hoboken only prolonged his phase of melancholy. Once, not long before, James had made harborside New York the subject of an epiphany when he wrote that "memory and the actual impression keep investing New York with the tone, predominantly, of summer dawns and winter frosts, of sea-foam, of bleached sails and stretched awnings, of blanched hulls, of scoured decks, of new ropes, of polished brasses, of streamers clear in the blue air; and it is by this harmony, doubtless, that the projection of the individual character of the place, of the candour of its avidity, and the freshness of its audacity, is most conveyed." But the years had taken their toll—of him and of his city. Now, emerging "from the comparatively assured order of the great berth of the ship," he found that "there, only too confoundingly familiar and too serenely exempt from change, the waterside squalor of the great city put forth again its most inimitable notes, showed so true the barbarisms it had not outlived that one could only fall to wondering what obscure inward virtue had preserved it."

Playing fast and loose with all the ships at sea, the Germans were planning still swifter, more sumptuous liners. The light well of the

Kaiser Wilhelm might rise through three stories; the light well in the new *Kronprinzessin Cecilie* would rise through four. The lavish hand of Johannes Poppe would guarantee the grandeur of the *Cecilie's* public rooms, and the artists of the *nouveau* would introduce a delicacy and a sense of marine *aesthétique* previously unknown.

Where was the British counterpart of Rudolf A. Schroeder? What British firm could say that its designer "is a man of poetic temperament, and while his interiors are free from affectation or fidgitiness, they are dominated by a rhythm of line and harmony of color which give them a charming effect?" How could the British, with their obsession with cosiness, match bedrooms with "pale stripes of gold-tinted blue—the combination seemed to have been borrowed from peacock feathers— otherwise decorated all in white, whilst the walls and the furniture of the adjoining parlor were covered with a silvery leather?" How could the British match the big fish tanks on the awning deck where passengers could catch their own carp, pike, tench and trout and have them cooked to order? When the time came, the first thing besides speed the British did try to emulate was the number of funnels carried on all the new German liners. The four great paired stacks on the *Wilhelm der Grosse* and her successors had come, in the mind of the public, to stand for ultimate marine power and safety. There were many instances where agents dealing with emigrants could not talk their potential clients into sailing on any ship with less than four funnels. Most ships did not need that many, but, to meet public expectations, British shipowners ordered them anyway.

White Star soon gave up trying to catch the Germans, but Cunard was merely biding its time. The *Carmania*, with new turbine engines, had proved to be a faster and more economical proposition than her conventional sister *Caronia*—and on that fact Cunard based its next move.

The high curve of steamship history—that time when variation begins to replace innovation—makes its arc across those months of 1905 and 1906 when designers were leaning over blueprints marked, respectively, *Mauretania* and *Lusitania*. Nowadays, when a man dreams of the sea and a ship, the figure he sees is likely to have their features. When a child draws a ship, it is apt to look like them. Archetypes of marine excellence, these ships brought the shipbuilders of Scotland and England back to their old eminence and the Cunard Company back to its old role of leadership. But not before the company had managed to ensure that position by threatening to abandon it.

At the moment of its majority, Cunard showed itself ready—if only the price were right—to abdicate. To tell this story of commotion in the palace and consternation in the countinghouse it is necessary to go back a few years. Then it is possible to rehearse the steps by which American capitalism tried, at one fell swoop, to buy a dominating place on the ocean to which it had neither right nor title.

❧ SECTION III ❧

Junius Pierpont Morgan and the International Mercantile Marine
Albert Ballin: Hamburg-Amerika's Wünderkind / The Kaiser's
Hunting Lodge / Cunard for Sale / Cunard Ransomed / "The
Ocean Was Too Big for the Old Man" / Caronia and Carmania

RICH MEN with covetous eyes and voracious ambitions, the "robber barons" of the New World were beginning to have designs on the Old. In the same decades when these men were amassing the equivalent of imperial fortunes from railroading, oil, meat packing, steel, America's share of overseas freightage dropped from 86 to a mere 12 percent. Sea traffic was a great source of profit to the British, the Germans, the French and the Scandinavians. Why should it not—like meat packing—be "Americanized" into one vast and peerless trust? It was only a matter of time before one of the new tycoons was going to take a long look at the bright, scurrying ships of the North Atlantic sea lanes and feel a sudden itch to put them all in his pocket. In the very first year of the new century, when this figure showed himself and published his intentions, he turned out to be the most powerful of them all—Junius Pierpont Morgan.

In league with American railroad owners, Morgan dreamed up an economic weapon he hoped would open the way to an American monopoly of freight from Europe. This was the "through bill of lading" whereby goods from England or Germany would be carried by ship and train directly to, say, Cincinnati for little more than the cost of transporting goods from New York to Cincinnati. Since no British or Continental company would have access to this sea-land route, the American interests would virtually control the carriage rates on all imports. In regard to passenger ships, the aim was to establish something close to an American monopoly. To do away with competitive advertising and to regularize schedules, Morgan hoped to have a first-class steamer leaving New York almost every day in the week. Instead of having to book far in advance, or to accommodate his travel plans to those of any one of a dozen steamship lines, a traveler would be able to set off on a voyage to Southampton as easily as he might go to Grand Central Station and take a train for Chicago.

As a first move, Morgan bought up the only two American companies of any importance in North Atlantic trade—the International Navigation Company and the American Transport Company. Gulping down these lines as though they were mere appetizers, he looked hungrily overseas. In 1901 he added the Red Star Line, the Leyland Line, the Dominion Line and, in 1902, to the chagrin and embarrassment of many British subjects, the great White Star Line. With this much accomplished, and with feelers going out in all directions—including one that reached seductively into the very board room of the Cunard Steam-Ship Company—Morgan and his colleagues told the public just what they were up to. The announcement itself was bland, yet it sent a shudder through British shipping interests that was "almost like a declaration of war." They had formed the International Mercantile Marine Company, they said, and under its rubric had arrived at a working alliance with the Hamburg-Amerika Line and the North German Lloyd. The news of the German deal had the effect of a *coup de grâce*.

Morgan's chance to outstrip the British on the Atlantic was provided mainly by just one man. He was Albert Ballin, one of the most imaginative and humane figures in the whole cold, Roman-eyed pantheon of shipping executives. Ballin had come up the hard way and in the course of his ascent had brought Germany to first place on the waterways of the world. Starting with a job in a small Hamburg agency that, for a fee, packed off emigrants to New York and Baltimore, Ballin soon became an operator of ships himself. Still in his early twenties when he joined the Carr Line, he parlayed that company's six rusty little ships into a combine with two other emigrant services—Sloman's

American Line and the Union Line—and gave Hamburg-Amerika so much competition that they decided to get rid of him. To do this they simply incorporated him and his hard-working fleet into their own operations. Their drastic step proved to be a brilliant one. In no time at all, Ballin rose from manager of Hamburg-Amerika's passenger department to become director of the whole company. Since it had by then become the biggest shipping firm on earth, Ballin's position, at the age of thirty-one, made him the *wünderkind*.

In the unusual swiftness of his rise to the top, Ballin had helped to give his company the edge over its Bremen rival by taking quick advantage of a Norddeutscher Lloyd miscalculation. The men of Bremen had persisted in building single-screw ships when everything pointed to the success of twin-screw liners. Just when North German Lloyd was producing the *Havel* and the *Spree*, Hamburg-Amerika under Ballin's insistence came out with the twin-screw *Normannia*, *Fürst Bismarck*, *Auguste Victoria* and *Columbia*. The consequence was a sudden leap in business for the Hamburg Company that left the North German Lloyd far behind.

His executive authority was firm and his canniness was widely acknowledged, yet Ballin could not help being awed by Junius Pierpont Morgan. The American was, according to Ballin, "a man of whom it is said that he combines the possession of an enormous fortune with an intelligence that is simply astounding." He did not hesitate to enter into the proposed combine under an arrangement by which the American tycoon would control fifty-one percent of Hamburg-Amerika's shares while still allowing the company to maintain nominal autonomy. Germany's rivalry with England on the seas had by this time become so keen that, even to gain one point, the Kaiser himself was quite ready to countenance the takeover of a Teutonic shipping empire by an American plutocrat.

When the deal was still being negotiated, Ballin received a telegram This dispatch, he said, commanded "my presence on the following day for dinner at the Hubertsstock hunting lodge of the Kaiser, where I was invited to stay until the afternoon of the second day following my journey to Eberswalde. At that town a special carriage conveyed us to Hubertsstock, where we arrived after a two-hours' drive, and where I was privileged to spend two unforgettable days in most intimate intercourse with the Kaiser. The Chancellor had previously informed me that the Kaiser did not like the terms of the agreement, because Metternich had told him that the Americans would have the right to acquire 20 million marks' worth of our shares.

"During an after-dinner walk with the Kaiser, on which we were accompanied by the Chancellor and the Kaiser's A.D.C., Captain v. Grumme, I explained the whole proposal in detail. I pointed out to the Kaiser that whereas the British lines engaged in the North Atlantic business were simply absorbed by the trust, the proposed agreement would leave the independence of the German lines intact. This made the Kaiser inquire what was to become of the North German Lloyd, and I had to promise that I would see to it that the Lloyd would not be exposed to any immediate danger arising out of our agreement, and that it would be given an opportunity of becoming a partner as well. The Kaiser then wanted to see the actual text of the agreement as drafted in London. When I produced it from my pocket we entered the room adjacent to the entrance of the lodge, which happened to be the small bedroom of Captain v. Grumme; and there a meeting, which lasted several hours, was held, the Kaiser reading out loud every article of the agreement, and discussing every single item.

"The Kaiser himself was sitting on Captain v. Grumme's bed; the Chancellor and myself occupied the only two chairs available in the room, the Captain comfortably seating himself on a table. The outcome of the proceedings was that the Kaiser declared himself completely satisfied with the proposals commissioning me to look after the interests of the North German Lloyd."

Albert Ballin did what he was told, saw to it that his rivals from Bremen were brought in on the deal, and was rewarded with the Order of the Red Eagle, "second class with crown." His reward from Morgan was considerably greater—an annual salary rumored to be in the neighborhood of one million dollars.

When the combined might of the German mercantile marine was in his pocket, Morgan came steaming across the Atlantic in his own little ocean liner, the *Corsair*, and was received by Kaiser Wilhelm like the visiting potentate he was. The German press was jubilant. "The blow to England," said Berlin's *National Zeitung*, "is all the greater since the German companies have been able to keep out of the trust and maintain their independence."

More than ever the pressure was on Cunard. New German ships, from Hamburg and Bremen alike, had outclassed the *Lucania* and *Cam-*

pania, and there were still newer and bigger German liners on the ways. The *Umbria* and *Etruria* had maintained their dignity but not their youth, and the fact that they were single-screw ships made them even more passé. In fact, the *Etruria*'s misadventure of the fractured screw and her subsequent towing to Liverpool via the Azores, occurred just when Morgan and his German friends had begun to show their collective hand. The widely reported accident tended to involve public opinion and led to "questions in Parliament." But the Government was reluctant to answer any question until the Morgan-Cunard matter was settled.

True to the memory of its shilling-minded founders, the Cunard Company assessed the situation, saw where its advantage lay, and realized at once that its best strategy would be a pose of simple helplessness under the enormity of the Yankee threat. After a series of maneuvers, a wringing of hands and a great sigh of anguish, the company in effect blackmailed the Government into keeping it British, free and solvent.

The man Morgan had mainly to deal with was young Lord Inverclyde, grandson of Samuel Cunard's partner George Burns, and chairman of the Cunard Line. When representatives of the Morgan Combine asked Cunard to join them, or allow them to buy control, Lord Inverclyde went them one further. Why not, he said, buy us outright? When the Morgan people wanted to know the going price, Inverclyde told them: make us an offer. When they came through with an offer of 18 pounds per share for 55 percent of all Cunard stock, Inverclyde informed them that this was not enough.

From the beginning of these overtures, Inverclyde had scrupulously detailed for the British Government what was going on. Just as scrupulously, he had indicated to the Government that it alone had the power to rescue Cunard from the blandishments of the American colossus. But when the Government took the attitude that to join or not to join was Cunard's own affair, Inverclyde no longer felt obliged to make the Admiralty party to his company's dealings. Lord Selborne, First Lord of the Admiralty, became worried about what Cunard might be up to. Somewhat ruefully, he told Inverclyde that "when such vast issues are at stake a patriotic company is bound to keep its Government informed as you have hitherto done." Inverclyde replied that his stockholders were tired of the Government's delaying tactics. At this point, Sir Christopher Furness entered the picture.

Sir Christopher's idea was to form a British shipping combine—an anticombine strong enough to withstand the Morgan juggernaut. Lord Selborne was charmed by this unexpected development, and indicated as much to Lord Inverclyde. But since the latter was still nursing the hope that the Government would step forward with cash enough to reinvigorate Cunard and send it back into the lists against the new trust, he regarded the idea of a makeshift British combine as abhorrent. When Inverclyde showed his distaste, Lord Selborne became impatient. There are, he said, only three courses open to Cunard: (1) join the American combine; (2) fight the combine, with Government assistance unspecified; (3) join a British anticombine. The Government, Selborne let it be known, was strenuously opposed to the first possibility, unenthusiastic about the second, and quite preferred the last.

When he had absorbed these sentiments, Inverclyde apparently felt that the moment had come to bear down hard. He let it out that his company was being faced with "absorption or annihilation," and made it clear to the Admiralty that Cunard was either going to stay afloat on Government money or deliver itself without a qualm into the captivity of Morgan's money. "Frankly," he said, "I think the time has come when you should say what you intend to do with regard to the Cunard Company and not continue on the present indefinite course. If you do not intend to make any arrangement with us but prefer to work with somebody else I would much rather that you would say so and let us know where we are. In any case a time is coming when I must let my shareholders know what has been going on, so that they may judge for themselves whether their interests have been properly looked after, and moreover the Directors of the Company cannot longer put off certain arrangements which they have had in view, but which latterly have been held in abeyance, to give you time to make up your mind whether you would do anything or not."

Faced with a barely veiled ultimatum of "certain arrangements," which Cunard "had in view," the Government tried once more to persuade its willful directors to consider entering into the anticombine proposed by Sir Christopher Furness. The penultimate attempt proved fruitless. The only thing left to do, it seemed, was to give in to the demands that Cunard had covertly persisted in keeping alive from the first word of the Morgan threat—a threat now magnified and made sensational by the press of London.

"Licenses to remain on earth" were sold in the streets for a penny a piece, complete with the signature: J. Pierpont Morgan. Who was to rule the waves—Morgan or Britannia? Was there no end to the man's avarice? Once he had "Morganized" the Atlantic Ocean, would he not take over British collieries and British factories? Would not this Yankee *magnifico* strip the walls of the stately homes of England of their Tintorettos and Rembrandts? Dismantle the ancient libraries and send them, volume by volume, back to his own library in New York? The warning voiced by historian James Anthony Froude, not many years before, suddenly rang with urgency. "Take away her merchant fleets," said Froude, "take away the navy that guards them; her empire will come to an end; her colonies will fall off like leaves from a withered tree; and Britain will become once more an insignificant island in the North Sea."

Its hands and wrists fettered, its beautiful white body tied to the tracks while the glinty-eyed locomotive from Wall Street came bearing down the line, Cunard cowered and blinked in the mock terror of those who know they are going to be snatched to safety. Some observers of the scene felt that the British Government was being humiliated—that it was being forced into an act of capitulation to the demands of a private company. But others felt that to bolster up Cunard would be to make a gesture of legitimate national self-interest. After all, said one of them, "a Cunard liner, like an Armstrong gun, is a familiar object to the greater part of the civilized world." Joseph Chamberlain, the Colonial Secretary, was one of those who looked upon the Morgan combine as a menace. To preserve its independence, he said, British shipping should have direct construction subsidies from the national treasury. Parliament was inclined to give him generous support. In their ignorance of the fact that Cunard had stood aloof to Morgan's advances only because his price was not right, the sentimental British public also stood up for the beloved old institution. With so much power and favor enlisted in its cause, Cunard could not lose.

The upshot was a Government loan of 2,600,000 pounds, at the low interest rate of 2¾ percent, to be paid in 20 annual installments—plus an annual subsidy of 150,000 pounds. The only strings attached were two: that Cunard remain a British concern; that, as always in the past, the Government have the right, in the event of a national emergency, to use of the company's ships at preferred rates.

A strong new strain of xenophobia marked the Government's condition that the company remain true-blue British. Foreigners were not to be

20. A North River *bon voyage*

21. The girls in the grand saloon

22. Dinner: first course, first casualty

23. Deck scenes: (ABOVE) sailing day, circa 1890;
(BELOW) the pleasures of the voyage

24. *Deutschland über Alles*: the triumph of Johannes Poppe

25. British dining room: "a silent sermon in good taste"

26. Tall funnels, emblems of power, symbols of status

27. *Art nouveau* at sea: the trend toward the grandiose curbed
in two interiors of the North German Lloyd's S.S. *George Washington*

28. Captain Edward J. Smith (RIGHT) with his officers on the *Olympic*.
Seven months after this photograph was taken, Captain Smith,
in command of the *Titanic*, was swept from the bridge and drowned.

29. The "black gang": they died, too

30. The *Lusitania* carries on: a first-class deck scene photographed
two months after the sinking of the *Titanic*

31. Emigrants in *their* deck space

32. The *Imperator*'s eagle, its claws clutching a globe on which
is inscribed, "Mein Feld Ist Die Welt"

33. The *Imperator*, before she lost her eagle,
before she became Cunard's *Berengaria*

34. The smoking room, when it was still a masculine sanctuary

35. The *Mauretania*: a dining room detail

36. The *Aquitania*: looking aft

allowed to serve as directors, even as principal officers, including men who might qualify as "masters and officers and engineers in charge of watch on board any of the company's ocean steamships." Shares in the company even were not to be held "by or in trust for, or be in any way under the control of any foreigner or foreign corporation or any corporation under foreign control." Fear of Morgan and jealousy of German accomplishment at sea had provided nationalist elements in Britain with a new charter.

Ransomed and rehabilitated, Cunard was able to set about plans for new ships—beginning with the *Caronia* and *Carmania*—and, in a very short time, was in a position to challenge successfully the power of everything that the American-German consortium could put into the water. Rewarded for its intransigeance, the British company went on to become the big thorn in Morgan's side. Heartened by resistance across the Channel, France's Compagnie Générale Transatlantique no longer felt it had to listen to American promises, threats or jingles of silver.

In a surprisingly short time the Morgan combine was in trouble. The New York Stock Exchange refused to list the watered stock on its Board; potential shareholders became shy of a company so obviously overcapitalized. "The ocean," said the *Wall Street Journal*, "was too big for the old man." "Everyone," said *The Marine Engineer*, in 1905, "now knows what a miserable fiasco the great Morgan plan has turned out to be." Nevertheless, the corporate entity of the Morgan maritime organization was kept intact for nearly two decades. Then, finding it wise to sell the White Star Line back to British interests, it lost its main source of income and faded out of transatlantic competition.

Given the powerful thrust of ten million dollars, the fortunes of the Cunard Line shot up. At first the company could barely hold its own as German shipyards began to turn over to Hamburg-Amerika and North German Lloyd liners of an elegance and dash that nothing on the oceans could touch. But then things changed as Cunard became sponsor of a royal succession of liners that would for all time remain the archetypes of the Era of the Big Ship.

The first of these were the *Caronia* and the *Carmania*—smoking, big-funneled vessels with black hulls and cluttered high white superstructures. Somehow, these ships gained for themselves the fatuous sobriquet of "the pretty sisters." Their real distinction lay not in their prettiness, which anyone who has seen even a postcard version of the *City of Rome* or the *Deutschland* would find debatable, but in their character. While German ships churned the sea lanes in pursuit of speed records, these ships sailed, *hors de combat,* a bit slower but with un-assailable dignity. In contrast to the heavy Teutonic splendors of the German saloons and smoking rooms, they offered Britishness—the equivalents, at sea, of the tea cosy, the hot-water bottle and the Afghan throw. Early on, they gained a reputation for solid comfort, high quality and absolute dependability. Through a period when ships were supposed to be awesome, each of them developed an affectionate fol-lowing of contented customers who remained faithful for decades.

Even before she was completed the *Caronia* began to spawn hyperbole. "When I was at school," wrote an English wit, "we used to sing about the gentlemen who stayed at home at ease while the mariners of England swept the stormy seas. Now it's the other way. You've got to pity the poor devils that have to stay on land. It's the most perilous place in the world. Yesterday, I almost had a free shave from a slate that fell from a roof. A sailor crossed from the opposite side, 'Do you mind piloting me to the Cunard docks?' he says. 'I'm nearly dead with fright at the dangers of the shore,' he says. 'Come to sea and you'll live to a ripe age.' And when I read about the *Caronia* I'm tempted to pack my bag. . . . [She's] that big you'd think they wanted a brewery of champagne to christen her. If you need a ten mile walk you can do it on the decks, and never meet the same man twice. If you go for a really long walk on her, when you return the young man at the next seat has forgotten your face. I'm not sure whether there are electric cars aboard. I think there must be.

"In the *Caronia* you can hire a room, apartments, a flat, a house, a mansion, or a street of mansions, meals included in the rent. You can live in *Caronia* society or you can keep to your own house. You can dine in public or in the privacy of your own mansion. You could meet your brother in Liverpool. 'I've just come over on the Cunarder,' he says. 'So have I,' you say. 'I missed seeing you,' he says. 'You couldn't have lived in the same street as me.'"

Wonders were manifest, but behind the scenes there were still re-minders that steamship travel was often awkward, primitive and down-right dangerous. Young James Bisset (later Sir James Bisset, Commodore of the Cunard Line) was Fourth Officer on the new ship. Many years later he recalled his first crossing. "When I joined the *Caronia*," he wrote, "she was coaling. She required 5,000 tons of coal for the voyage from Liverpool to New York and return. While the ship was being coaled, all the passenger compartments were kept closed. The furniture in the saloons, smoking-rooms, and lounges were protected with linen covers. Despite these precautions, some coal dust penetrated to all parts of the ship. The stewards and cleaners had the task of removing this grime before the passengers came aboard. How they hated coaling! But it was a necessary ordeal in those days before oil fuel had come into general use."

On the bridge, twentieth-century technology had brought other problems in the form of "newfangled loudspeaking telephones, with brass fittings." These, Bisset recalled, "were connected from forward and aft to the bridge, and also from the engine room, as an addition to the old-fashioned speaking tubes. But the telephones were far from perfect. Words came through them distorted to such an extent that they were often unintelligible, and sounded like a foreign lingo. At such times, especially when the ship was being docked or undocked, the average captain would grab a megaphone and sing out his orders."

The most serious oversight in the *Caronia's* general equipment was one that only the greatest of all maritime disasters would serve to rectify. This was, incredibly, the lack of a sufficient number of lifeboats. "The liner carried forty boats," wrote Bisset, "each capable of accommodating forty persons. That is, if the order were given to abandon ship and to take to the boats, there would be accommodation for only half of the 3,336 souls aboard the liner. This deficiency was in no sense unusual or contrary to prevailing practice. The ship and her lifeboats were inspected and approved by the Board of Trade and conformed in every way with the laws, rules and regulations, and all other requirements of that period. The rules and regulations were a legacy of bygone years, when ships were much smaller and carried far fewer souls than the transatlantic Ocean Greyhounds. The lifeboat accommodation in Cunarders was similar to that in all other large liners, that is, capable of carrying one-half of the total ship's company. It had not occurred to anyone in authority, either ashore or afloat, that this was a portentous lapse in logic, capable in the event of a disaster, such as fire at sea, collision with an iceberg or a derelict, or the foundering of the vessel from any cause, of dooming one-half of the ship's company to a watery grave."

❧ SECTION IV ❧

The Germans Set the Pace / The Scottish Lusitania *and the English* Mauretania */ Museums at Sea / Grand Hotels with Engines / The Captain as Social Arbiter / Theodore Dreiser Dazzled / Franklin Delano Roosevelt on the* Mauretania *One-Upmanship on the Atlantic / "Where Will It All End?"*

CUNARD *redivivus* and Morgan-on-the-make had entered into a mighty struggle for primacy. In this contest the *Caronia* and the *Carmania* were but pawns in a delaying action. For the real push, which involved Morgan incidentally and Germany primarily, Cunard was laying plans to give the British Government what it had paid for—two ships that would outweigh, outrun, and overtake anything else on the oceans.

Thus, in the decade leading toward the outbreak of World War I, the era of the steamship moved on to its apogee. As the German mercantile marine was racing toward extinction, the British toward decimation, the waters of the North Atlantic were roiled by ships in the spit and image of their respective national characters. Moribund empires were producing moribund vessels. The contest for speed, splendor and profit on water reflected a struggle on land that even the threat of suicide would not relax. "May the time not come," asked the eminent old marine historian E. Keble Chatterton, "when rest and simplicity will again replace excessive strenuousness and restore to the Atlantic something of its plain expansiveness, and take back the

334

character which it has now developed as being merely a race-track for ocean greyhounds?"

The time would come; it was not now. The Germans had a message for the British and when the British got it, *mea culpa* became a sort of national pastime. When the *Kaiser Wilhelm II*, designed and built by Germans in a German shipyard, passed through Southampton en route to New York, journalists caught their breath.

"It is little less than remarkable," said one of them, "that a nation which in the eighties was more or less dependent on this country for the construction of her mail ships should have so rapidly developed her shipbuilding talents that she now produces a vessel which is the largest in the world and which in point of speed promises to equal any steamship yet afloat . . . and there are features about the *Kaiser Wilhelm II* which represent an approach to luxury in voyaging which has as yet been unattained. And here, perhaps, we touch a secret of German success in steamship enterprise which has not even yet been acknowledged.

"We allude to the abandonment of the old-time theory that the passenger should accommodate his requirements to the ideas of the ship, and the setting up of the newer standard which ensures that a traveler afloat shall have his wishes and even his prejudices recognized as fully as if he were ashore. In a word, the Germans have got rid of a good deal of that rigidity in the matter of life on shipboard which too often seems a sort of inevitable by-product of British ownership. The explanation is, perhaps, that we have played the game on certain lines for so many years, and with such marked success, that anything which does not quite conform to tradition is perforce regarded with a certain amount of resentment.

"The Germans, on the other hand, are comparatively young as shipbuilders and as shipowners on a large and enterprising scale. They started out hampered by no traditions, and with eager and receptive minds, and to-day we see them not only beating us soundly on the Atlantic, but doing it practically unaided. Our shipowners have been declaring that excessively high speeds do not pay, and yet here we have two German lines contending for supremacy—not over us, for we are 'out of it,' but over each other—in this very respect, and doing it practically without state assistance. It is some consolation to the British public to know that the German flag is not going to have all its own way on the Atlantic a year or two hence. The two new Cunarders, with their speed of 24½ or 25 knots, will be able to show a clean pair of heels to the vessels of any other flag, and to this extent there will be widespread gratification, especially as Lord Inverclyde has formally contradicted the report that it was impossible to get the vessels built according to the company's ideas. But what naturally occurs to the mind is to inquire whether, supposing there had been no Atlantic Combine, and no necessity for the British Government to step in, our shipowners would still have been content to stand by and see the Germans turning out greyhound after greyhound?"

The Scottish *Lusitania* slid down the ways of the Clyde, the English *Mauretania* down those of the Tyne. At last the two cynosures —bearers of hope, national honor and the hedged bets of Cunard— had arrived. Old chroniclers like Keble Chatterton who had seen everything that steamships could do and who knew everything that steamships had ever done, were reduced to God-fearing awe. "And so we come," he said, "to those two leviathans which form, without exception, the most extraordinary, the most massive, the fastest, and the most luxurious ships that ever crossed an ocean. Caligula's galleys, which were wondrously furnished with trees, marbles and other luxuries which ought never to desecrate the sweet, dignified character of the ship, were less sea-craft than floating villas exuding decadence at every feature. There are some characteristics of the *Mauretania* and *Lusitania*, with their lifts, their marbles, curtains, ceilings, trees, and other expressions of twentieth century luxury, which, while appreciated by the landsman and his wife, are nauseating to the man who loves the sea and its ships for their own sakes, and not for the chance of enjoying self-indulgence in some new form. But whichever way you regard them, from whatever standpoint you choose, there is nothing comparable to them, there are no standards whatsoever by which to judge them.

"Cover them with tier upon tier of decks, scatter over them a forest of ventilators, roofs and chimneys, till they look like the tops of a small town; fill them inside with handsome furniture, line their walls with costly decorations; throw in a few electric cranes, a coal mine, several restaurants, the population of a large-sized village and a good many other things besides; give them each a length equal to that of the Houses of Parliament, a height greater than the buildings in

Northumberland Avenue, disguise them in any way you please, and for all that these are *ships,* which have to obey the laws of Nature, of the Great Sea, just as the first sailing ship and the first Atlantic steamship had to show their submission. I submit that to look upon these two ships as mere speed-manufacturers engaged in the record industry, as palatial abodes, or even as dividend-earners is an insult to the brains that conceived them, to the honourable name of 'ship' which they bear." So, to an old salt came the twilight of the gods, of seamanship, of the genius of marine engineering. The sybarites had taken over: "Barring a bridle path for the equestrian, a smooth road for the automobilist, and a forest for lovers to walk in, everything else seems to have been provided."

Still, to quite another man who loved the sea and was learned in its history, the sight of the *Lusitania* sliding down the Clyde toward the open ocean was an intimation of millennium. Recalling a childhood experience, Glaswegian George Blake wrote: "Was it the size of her, that great cliff of upperworks bearing down upon him? Was it her majesty, the manifest fitness of her to rule the waves? I think what brought the lump to the boy's throat was just her beauty, by which I mean her fitness in every way; for this was a vessel at once large and gracious, elegant and manifestly efficient. That men could fashion such a thing by their hands out of metal and wood was a happy realization. Ships he had seen by the hundred thousand, but this was a ship in a million; and there came to him then as he saw her, glorious in the evening sunlight, the joy of the knowledge that this was what his own kindred could do, this was what the men of his own race, labouring on the banks of his own familiar River, were granted by Providence the privilege to create. In that moment he knew that he had witnessed a triumph of achievement such as no God of battles or panoplied monarch had ever brought about."

The ship as a sea-borne museum was an idea initiated by the Germans; the decor of the new British dispensation furthered it. Eclecticism was the philosophy—an unrelated variety of styles and periods with, now and then, "pleasant glimpses of modern art to give relief." Thus was begun, said one cynic, "an irresistible movement towards a second Renaissance; in other words, the craze for period decoration on the cocktail principle." To another it was the beginning of the "Piccadilly period of steamship decoration," culminating "in that quintessence of aesthetic shams which guides to ocean travel term *de luxe*."

This consciousness of a large seam of vulgarity running through ocean travel was not confined to an awareness merely of ships as overdone hostelries. To fastidious sensibilities, the most offensive thing was the deportment of traveling companions and the inevitability of being thrown in with people whom, on shore, they would avoid or ignore. "Our table neighbors were of a queer sort," said a New York hostess with the hauteur of Margaret Dumont, "a harmless quiet man in company with two impossible 'ladies,' and a woman who must have been Altman's 'sales lady.' Miss Anna Held was our 'star'; she did not give us her great 'undressing act,' but she *did* give us two songs at the concert that were beyond the 'limit.' The upper, enclosed glass deck we did not like; it shut out all the fresh air and shut in all the tobacco smoke and other odors, but the majority of the passengers adored it! They could wear their silly, thin *neckless* (I say, reckless) waists, their silly openwork stockings and low shoes with very high heels and the hideous 'hobble' skirt and 'hobble' hat."

The main staircase of the *Mauretania* was paneled in French walnut with carved pilasters and capitals. The scheme for the writing room and library came out of the era of Louis Seize: panels of gray sycamore highlighted with gold and ivory and even the bookcases were copied from originals in the Trianon. The main lounge and ballroom were also French, of an eighteenth-century cast, while the main dining room went back to François I. In the smoking room the 'influence' was fifteenth-century Italy. The model for the Verandah Cafe was the Old English Orangery at Hampton Court. For all that, the ship was somehow supposed to remind its customers of "a stately British country home."

The ocean liner as a floating castle on the Rhine had been introduced by Johannes Poppe. The ship as a grand hotel with engines was the slightly different contribution of British designers. Shipowners of London and Liverpool had by and large furnished their liners in the same spirit, and with the same taste, that might have been appropriate to their country homes and their town houses. For one thing, it gave their wives and daughters something to do (a notion that persisted, incredibly, until as late as 1966 when Lady Brocklebank, swatches of flowered chintz and dyed leatherette in hand, descended upon the mock-up deck plans of the *Queen Elizabeth 2*; but the word got out, and public uproar forced Lady Brocklebank to desist in her kind efforts as the newspapers recorded a general sigh of relief. "Those who have feared everything would come up roses, horse brasses, chintz and Tally ho prints," said a lady columnist, "are, no doubt, sitting easier in their Barcelona chairs.") and it provided insurance against the shameless floridity of taste on that general foreign outback known as "the Continent."

But by the time the Germans had recognized the role of the interior designer in outfitting a ship and had enlisted first-rate artisans, if not first-rate artists, the English had come to see that even the bravest efforts of directors' wives would simply not do. "Ship decoration has lately come to the front with a rush," said a London decorator. "When it was seen what could be done to royal and other steam yachts in the way of refined and graceful furnishings, the directors of the big steamship companies began to realise that decoration was a profitable investment for attracting the best class of passengers. For the requirements of comfort, not to say luxury, are becoming more persistently voiced every day."

To meet the competition, British shipping companies turned their decorating problems over to the London architectural team of Mewès and Bischoff, which later became Mewès and Davis. This was the firm responsible for the monumental pile of the Royal Automobile Club, in Pall Mall, as well as for the Louis Seize interiors behind the sooty arches of the London Ritz. Another factor in the new dispensation was the work of an architect by the name of J. J. Stevenson, who had come under the influence of his friend William Morris. Together with the designers H. A. Peto and James Miller, these men scrawled an eclectic but nevertheless discernibly British signature across the upper decks of some of the grandest of all Atlantic liners. Thus was born the terms "White Star Roman" and "Berengaria Baroque"—good-humored epithets that still aimed to derogate a style of decoration that represented a ruthless pillage of "the dressing-up box of history."

"Hotelism," wrote C. R. Benstead, "is a modern disease that arrived with the steam-engine, a sort of artistic hydrophobia in that those responsible for the internal decoration of a modern liner are mortally afraid to leave any indication that the scenes of their efforts belong to an ocean-going vessel. Thus afflicted, they run amok with a rainbow and a few acres of gold leaf, trailing behind them a devastation that would have made Solomon in all his glory appear mean and dingy."

In 1912, a leading marine historian said flatly: "The main consideration is to convey the idea that one is not at sea, but on terra firma."

To travel on a ship was in no way to admit to a love for the sea, or certainly not to affirm a taste for the kind of ship-matey intimacy that the long voyages of the nineteenth century tended to enforce. Distinguished citizens did choose to leave their moorings and travel abroad; but geography was one thing, social stratification quite another. Introductions on shipboard were sought and made with the most scrupulous guard against overstepping, on the one hand, reclusiveness on the other. According to one authority on etiquette, the way to propose oneself to the pleasure of acquaintance with Mrs. Brown was, once you were sure of your ground, simple. Finding yourself in her company on promenade deck, you would turn to her and, without stopping for breath, say, "Mrs. Brown, I saw your name in the passenger list and I am going to ask you to let me introduce myself to you on the strength of my long acquaintance with and great affection for your sister, Mrs. William Barr, of Cleveland."

Women like Mrs. Brown would, perforce, submit to the waywardness and archaic inconvenience imposed by foreigners if they were to get about the Continent. But this did not mean that they were prepared to swing out of a familiar social orbit. To cater to the self-regard of his clientele, a ship's captain had become a social arbiter. His position aboard ship gave him absolute discretion; his skill in dealing with the inflated egos of the affluent demanded a degree of diplomacy for which he had perpetually to remain in training.

Once his ship's safety was assured, the captain was expected to act as host to the company's guests and to do all in his power to induce them to travel again in the same ship or in another of the line. According to one captain, it was his role "to adjust disputes, pacify angry women, comfort frightened ones, and judge correctly just when to send one whose conduct is questionable to her room for the rest of the passage. He must know when to forbid the bartender to serve more liquor to a passenger who is drinking too much and just when to post the notice in the smoking room that gamblers are on board. Passengers must not be antagonized unless they antagonize others more valuable to the company than themselves, for the company exists to carry the public over the ferry, not to better their morals. A master, under English maritime law, is a magistrate at sea. He may, if he wishes, perform marriages on board, and such ceremonies are as binding as though performed on shore. He may require a woman of suspicious appearance to sequester herself, and if she refuses order force to be used in removing her. He may put the President and Board of Directors in irons if they interfere with the navigation of the ship, and though it is probable that he will soon be out of a berth if he pursues such courses, he will suffer no legal punishment."

With his purser, the captain had to pore over *Who's Who*, the *Almanach de Gotha* and the tip-off lists from the home office before he could select "that frieze of simulated order" that would make up the captain's table, or prepare the roster of others who naturally expected that, some time during the voyage, the captain would request the pleasure of their company. In spite of this meticulous preparation, the captain's table on the crossing tended, by and large, to reflect his own personal tastes, perhaps his own ambitions. Instead of choosing aristocrats of birth and title, or members of the community of arts, letters and the professions, most captains courted the conspicuously rich—men whose identities belonged to corporations, free-floating women whose distinction was estimated in the number of trunks that had accompanied them to the dock. One commander put the matter succinctly: "Although the Company never exert any pressure as to who is to sit where, there is naturally a tendency to consider its commercial interests where influential passengers are concerned."

The many-shelved library of memoirs by retired captains of the great liners confirms the suspicion that nearly all of them were yokels in braid—men with horizons limited to what their binoculars might explore and to what, otherwise, the company-man's vision could discreetly encompass. Contrary to all they had, perforce, to witness in the way of jostling for privilege, arrant shows of what money can buy, drunken bad manners, the gaping yawns of businessmen trussed up in their soup-and-fish, women groaning at the weight of diamond earrings and the pinch of jeweled slippers, their social observations were often indistinguishable from the blurbs of travel folders. Thus, to one retired commodore at least, night life at sea was a working girl's daydream: "Hundreds of multi-coloured fairy lamps shed their soft radiance on the forms of beautiful women gloriously gowned and handsome men in immaculate evening dress who dance the hours away to the music provided by jolly orchestras."

Brilliant seamen undoubtedly, they had to train themselves to act with a social grace for which they had not the background, the disposition or the aptitude. Their pragmatic view of the ways of the world sometimes afforded them insights into the social stratum they entered voyage to voyage. "Rich men," said one skipper, "spend their lives ashore at work and once it is put aside they become as bewildered as dogs who have temporarily mislaid their masters." But more often than not the autocrats of the Great Circle were as giddy as schoolboys in the presence of multimillionaires, prize fighters and ladies whose divorces had provided them with as many names as their bracelets had charms.

The *Lusitania* was the first of the great sister ships to be launched, and thus the first to demonstrate that the still-new turbine engine could make a racer of a marine mastodon. With full steam up, the *Lusitania*'s 3,000,000 individual turbine blades generated a force of 70,000 horsepower. On her trial runs, in spite of the fact that her bottom was "heavily coated with the chemically-saturated mud of the river Clyde," she reached a speed of 25 knots. She was also the first great ship to employ electricity to operate her steering apparatus, to close and open her 175 watertight compartments, to detect fire, and to control her lifeboat davits.

To see that she was prepared to sail from Liverpool, 22 trains, hauling 300 tons of coal each, had to chug into port and empty their loads into her bunkers. Her waterworks could have served to supply the needs of a city as big as London: just to cool the spent steam from her engines, 65,000 gallons of sea water per minute were driven through her stills. From stem to stern, her form ran in one continuous curve. Her fine bow, her long forecastle that extended far back into the superstructure, her graceful stern and the heavy rake of her four huge funnels made her the apotheosis of speed, might and sea-going efficiency.

Her beam was so great that her average-sized cabins were half again as spacious as those on any other steamship. On her arrival in New York she "created a furor," according to a reporter, "for which one must go back several decades to the day on which that other great ship, the *Great Eastern*, entered this port." On her second voyage she became the first ship ever to earn the right to be called "a four-day boat."

Yet circumstance of an almost astrological whimsicality would some-how contrive to make the *Lusitania* only another ship. She would come to a spectacular end, and so find a place in the annals of war and infamy; but meanwhile she would have to defer in almost every way to the magnetism of her English sister. It was the *Mauretania* that was des-tined to emerge as a prodigy and to live as a legend. And in spite of an encyclopedia of words that might explain the phenomenon, no one will ever quite know why. Statistics, dimensions, sea-worthiness, effi-ciency, speed—nothing measurable can account for the difference, since the two ships had almost everything measurable in common.

The distinction was a matter of feeling. Theodore Dreiser was just one among hundreds of thousands of people to whom the *Mauretania* offered a vision of a way of life. "There were several things about this great ship that were unique," wrote Dreiser. "It was a beautiful thing all told—its long cherry-wood, panelled halls . . . its heavy porcelain baths, its dainty staterooms fitted with lamps, bureaus, writing-desks, wash-stands, closets and the like. I liked the idea of dressing for dinner and seeing everything quite stately and formal. The little be-buttoned call-boys in their tight-fitting blue suits amused me. And the bugler who bugled for dinner! That was a most musical sound he made, trill-ing the various quarters gaily, as much as to say, 'This is a very joyous event, ladies and gentlemen; we are all happy; come, come; it is a delightful feast.'"

From the very first, the *Mauretania* won a homey sort of affection that by its nature qualified and humanized the awesomeness the greatest ship afloat could not help emanating. She was not so much "beautiful," in the view of the times, as she was "handsome." With the simplicity, if not the scale, of a yacht, she cut the water with a force that brought grace into mind, with power as a mere afterthought.

"When she was born in 1907," said Franklin Delano Roosevelt, "the *Mauretania* was the largest thing ever put together by man . . . she always fascinated me with her graceful, yachtlike lines, her four enormous black-topped red funnels, and her appearance of power and good breeding. . . ." Although, with bewildering honesty, he con-fessed himself as having no taste for traveling either on her or on her sister ship. "Why? Heaven knows!" he said. "Yet, not for one minute did I ever fail to realize that if there ever was a ship which possessed the thing called 'soul,' the *Mauretania* did. . . . Every ship has a soul. But the *Mauretania* had one you could talk to. At times she could be wayward and contrary as a thoroughbred. To no other ship belonged that trick of hers—that thrust and dip and drive into the seas and through them, which would wreck the rails of the Monkey Island with solid sea, or playfully spatter salt water on the Captain's boiled shirt as he took a turn on the bridge before going down to dinner. At other times, she would do everything her Master wanted her to, with a right good will. As Captain Rostron once said to me, she had the manners and deportment of a great lady and behaved herself as such."

Burning 1,000 tons of coal per day, her furnaces attended by a 'Black Squad' of 324 firemen and trimmers, the *Mauretania* took the Blue Riband from Germany in 1907. She proceeded to nail that figurative ensign to her foremast; and she kept it there against all comers for the incredibly long space of twenty-two years. In a period when speed was the crucial thing in ocean rivalry, she sailed serenely in the vanguard of every ingenious new shape or device that the builders of ships could exploit. Thus, in the words of her own biographer, Humfrey Jordan, the *Mauretania* became "the most popular of all the carriers of human freight in service on the Atlantic. She was, as men say of a horse, all quality. Beauty is a different thing; there are some people, though they are rare, who deny that she was beautiful; there are none who can deny symmetry, proportion, the fineness of line which distinguish quality from commonness. To continue the horse simile, she might be hot at times, but she was always a beautiful ride. She did not wallow in a sea way, although she might be wet in one; in good weather and in bad she had a grace of action which made most other ships look like labouring tugs. That was her primary distinction; even the sea-timid and sea-careless recognized it at once. To that she added speed, comfort, reliability and her own atmosphere."

For long periods the *Mauretania* arrived at one side of the ocean or the other within a range of time that, unbelievably, never exceeded ten minutes. Just when the German flotilla seemed to have brought Hanoverian afflatus permanently into the sea-going prospect, the *Mauretania* reminded everyone that there was still such a thing as understated ornamentation and quiet taste, decor of a modesty that would not offend, just as it would not particularly beguile, people of discrimination. Yet she could still satisfy the expectations of the snobbish.

"This," said the caption under a view of her Verandah Cafe, "might be a particularly charming corner in your favorite country club or an enclosed verandah in your Oyster Bay house." Above all, the lure was an insistent kind of British cheerfulness, as opposed to the disciplinarian orderliness of ships of a Junker temperament.

The gradual ascendancy of shipbuilders over shipowners was one of the crucial developments in shipping as a business during the latter part of the nineteenth century. In the early days of transocean enterprise, owners or operators went to shipbuilders with a set of requirements and paid them to turn out profitable carriers. But as technological advances in shipbuilding were introduced at an always-accelerating pace, owners were apt not to know quite what they wanted or what they should have. Builders had to tell them what was available. Consequently, builders moved into the vanguard and worked with an imagination and bravura that caused a breach between the director in the shipyard and the director in the board room that has been maintained until this day.

In the early part of the twentieth century, more than ever the big game on the Atlantic was one-upmanship. Just as the *Teutonic* and the *Majestic* were continually racing Inman's *City of New York* and *City of Paris* from the Needles to Sandy Hook, along came the *Kaiser Wilhelm der Grosse* to swipe the baton from both of them. Challenged anew, White Star put the second *Oceanic* into the water in 1899, only to be met with the German response of the *Kaiser Wilhelm II*, followed swiftly by the *Deutschland* and the *Kronprinzessin Cecilie*. Sidling into the picture with the *Carmania* and *Caronia*, Cunard made a modest yet notably dignified showing. The company was really biding its time, waiting for the moment when the huge turbines and triple screws of the *Lusitania* and *Mauretania* would leave everything in their wake. In the nature of the contest, however, it was inevitable that, even before these ships became champions, they also became targets on which the ambitious eyes of other companies were fixed. Ships even more fabulous *could* be built, and with about fifty thousand passengers afloat in every single week of the year there were always other companies ready to build them.

"As a result," said one marine historian, "no other shipping route in the world has ever spawned such extravagances or such follies. Where else have ships had Byzantine chapels and Pompeiian swimming pools, dining rooms styled like the palace of Versailles, lounges decorated in mock Inigo Jones, and Turkish baths like Eastern harems?" Yet as the liners got swifter, more gargantuan and more heavily burdened with the kitsch of European history, insistent questions were more frequently asked. Where are we headed? Where will it all end?

With a premonitory chill, one answer to both of these questions had been made by an editorial writer as early as 1890. "Some of these days one of these record breakers will break a record he does not wish to break," he wrote, "and then, too late, a howl will go up over the whole civilized world of the criminal folly of driving steamers at full speed through dense fogs and waters filled with icebergs."

❄ SECTION V ❄

W IRELESS, introduced into ships at the turn of the century, was widely in use on the ocean for more than ten years before people were aware of the ways in which it might change their lives and, on occasion, save their lives. Then occurred two unrelated events—of sensational concern on both sides of the Atlantic—that brought home to Americans and Europeans the fact that Marconi's invention had made the world not only smaller and safer, but also vastly more interesting. The first of these was the mass rescue in a midwinter sea of a crack liner's passengers and crew. The second involved the apprehension and arrest, by means of dots and dashes transmitted across ocean wastes, of one quiet little anonymity of a man who had poisoned and dismembered his wife.

On January 23, 1909, the 15,000-ton White Star liner *Republic* was not quite one day out of New York on her way to the Mediterranean with 440 passengers. She was lumbering wetly through thick fog southwest of Nantucket Island when, about 6 A.M., the small ship *Florida*

347

of the Lloyd Italiano Line—loaded with 900 emigrants bound for New York—pierced her side with the thrust of a flung harpoon. "At 5:47 A.M.," recalled one of the *Republic*'s officers, "we heard a whistle about three to four points on our port bow. We had 'heard steam before sound,' and the helm was immediately put hard-a-port, and the engines run 'stop' and then 'full speed astern.' The engines had been going full astern for two minutes when I saw a vessel. I saw her masthead light on our port beam, and could see by the direction of her lights that she was coming round at a great speed on her starboard helm. Our engines were rung to 'full speed ahead.' She struck us a right-angle blow in the engine-room at 5:51 A.M. At the time we were making a little headway through the water. From the impact I thought that she was going right through us, and as I saw her penetrate further and further into us, I thought that we might float for about three minutes, but apparently the *Florida* was a very weak-built ship, and her bows simply crumpled up."

Three of the *Republic*'s passengers were instantly killed in the bunks where they slept. Her engine room was awash within minutes. The radio shack on her upper deck lost a wall and half of its roof. Almost at once she developed an ominous list. The *Florida*, minus an anchor she had deposited in one of the *Republic*'s staterooms, and with her bow squashed like a shut accordion to the length of thirty feet, nevertheless remained buoyant by virtue of a collision bulkhead that did not give. As the two wounded ships drifted out of sight of one another and through the fog, the power of the *Republic* failed and her lights went out. Her radioman, Jack Binns, quickly rigged up a set of emergency batteries. These gave him a transmitting range of about sixty miles. He tapped out CQD: All Stations—Distress.

Meanwhile, Captain Sealby of the *Republic* assembled his passengers on deck and gave them coffee. Ships to rescue them all would be on the way, he told them through a megaphone, there was no immediate cause for alarm. As it turned out, the Captain was right. The nearest station to hear Binns' call was in Siasconset, at the eastern end of Nantucket. Jerked awake by the message on his head phones, A. H. Ginman, the local radioman, learned from Binns only the basic facts: the *Republic* had been struck by an unknown ship that might also need help. As soon as he knew his own ship's position, said Binns, he would call back. Ginman cleared the surrounding air. In a few minutes he was ready to rebroadcast Binns' message: *Republic* Rammed by Unknown Steamship, 26 Miles Southwest of Nantucket. Badly in Need of Assistance.

This message was soon acknowledged by the French ship *La Touraine* and the White Star *Baltic*, both of which changed course.

Guided by fog signals, the *Florida* had nosed her way back to the scene of the collision. Captain Angelo Ruspini offered to take aboard all of the passengers of the ship he had rammed. Captain Sealby did not hesitate to accept. In the space of two hours, a procession of little boats ferried all of his passengers to the *Florida* without a hitch.

Along with Captain Sealby and the crew, Binns remained on the *Republic*. He kept sending signals to the *La Touraine* and to the *Baltic*, and otherwise tried to reach any ship within the range of his emergency transmitter. Exposed to the freezing wet and without food, Binns stayed at the Marconi instrument for fourteen hours. When he finally decided to take a break, he got down a companionway, swam to the kitchen and salvaged a few crackers and some almonds from the ship's stores.

As she came on full steam, the *La Touraine*'s wireless operator asked Binns how things were going. "I'm on the job," tapped Binns, "ship sinking, but will stick to the end." Overhearing this, the wireless man on the *Baltic* horned in with a word of cheer: "Don't worry, old man, we are bursting our boilers to get to you." The *Baltic* did get within range, but thick fog entirely obscured her presence. Mere miles apart but lost in the murk, the three ships floated about for twelve hours, fecklessly sending up rockets and detonating bombs. Finally the *Baltic* was down to her last bomb, but this proved to be the saving one. The sound of its detonation was heard on the *Republic*, followed by a lugubrious but recognizable moan. Binns tapped out: "You are right on course; we can hear your fog horn." Within minutes, all her portholes lighted, her deck rails lined with excited passengers, the mighty *Baltic* came into view like a traveling carnival.

Once they were in range of one another's voices, the captains of the White Star ships conferred by megaphone. Since the *Republic* was likely doomed, and the *Florida* uncomfortably, if not dangerously, overloaded, they agreed that the best thing to do was to take everybody onto the *Baltic* and return to New York. The fog had lifted completely, but now an icy rain was drilling into the sea. In this hazard and misery, 1,650 people were transported to the safety and warmth of the *Baltic*—but only after a potential mutiny by Italian emigrants on the *Florida* had been put down by the *force majeur* of those who might, in the circumstance, have exercised *noblesse oblige*. The cause of the trouble was simple class privilege and the prerogatives that presumably went with it. As the boats that would bear the *Florida*'s combined burden of passengers to the *Baltic* were being loaded, the *Republic*'s first-class male passengers were given precedence over the *Florida*'s women emigrants. One of the unwritten laws of the sea, quite like established custom ashore, was that persons of means were exempt from the stricter applications of democracy. When this law clashed with the also unwritten rule of women and children first, something had to give. As they watched Privilege stepping, as it were, over Innocent Help-lessness, the emigrants quite naturally reacted to what they saw and set up a clamor. "Discipline, however, was maintained and the privilege of class upheld," by officers who, controlling the rescue boats, were sole arbiters of who should get into them, and when. As for democ-racy, that could wait until the emigrants had passed the Statue of Liberty.

Day was breaking when the last of the passengers was lifted onto the *Baltic*. Those with curiosity enough to look around them could see a flotilla of sea craft perhaps never again to be duplicated. In later years, it would be a maritime rule that only the nearest vessel to a dis-tressed ship should take the role of rescuer. But Binns' call had brought every ship within a three-hundred-mile range to the assistance of the *Republic*. The surrounding waters were full of revenue cutters, freighters, liners of several nations, even the famous old whaleback freighter, *City of Everett*. The magnetism residing in wireless had been demonstrated conclusively; the loneliness of a ship at sea was now only an impression and not a fact.

As the *Baltic* went steaming toward Sandy Hook, and the *Florida* with a big canvas patch on her prow resumed her slow passage, new efforts were made to save the *Republic*. Along with Binns and a few other members of his crew, Captain Sealby had actually abandoned ship. All night he kept watch nearby in a small boat, and when at dawn he saw that his ship was still afloat, determined to board her again in the last hope of starting a salvage operation. The Revenue Cutter *Gresham* from Wood's Hole, Massachusetts, and the old Navy de-stroyer *Seneca*, took the *Republic* in tow, while the Anchor Line's *Furnessia* was made fast to her stern to act as a rudder. The idea was to beach the *Republic* on the nearest shelf of shallow water. But, in the event, this effort was all too little and too late. The weird little sea-going procession of the halt and the lame moved slowly; the wounded *Republic* continued to sink, inch by inch, foot by foot. When her demise seemed merely a matter of minutes, Captain Sealby ordered Jack Binns to abandon ship. Exhausted after nearly thirty-six hours at his post, Binns was first hoisted aboard the *Gresham*, then transferred to the *Seneca*. Finally dried out and bedded down, he went into a semicomatose sleep that lasted around the clock. Almost thirty-six hours after she had been struck, the *Republic* took her final dive. At the time she was the largest ship ever to have sunk in the Atlantic Ocean. Captain Sealby and one of his officers went down with her, but they were thrown free and eventually fished out by the Coast Guard.

It was Excelsior! all over again—Jack Binns was the new boy on the burning deck whence, except for Captain Sealby and his officers, all but he had fled. Every detail of his ordeal was relayed by newspapers to millions of readers. The picture of the half-frozen young man tapping out his message while his ship sank deeper and deeper beneath his feet was a new image in the mythology of fortitude. As for Binns himself, the message he tapped out on his little key had found its mark and then had returned to overwhelm him. As he stepped ashore in New York he was hoisted on the shoulders of stewards and paraded around the streets adjacent to the White Star pier while trumpets blew, crowds shouted and girls threw flowers. When he went to a show at the Hippodrome, a spotlight picked him out and the audience, to a man, rose to tender him an ovation. When he arrived at Liverpool on the *Baltic*, crowds were waiting for him at the landing stage. In his hometown, Peterborough, he drove with the mayor to the Guildhall where, as his fiancée sat beaming at his side, he took the encomiums of his townspeople. The first in a long line of overnight sensations for which the early part of the century would be noted, Jack Binns was the instant hero—dashed, within a few months, into oblivion with almost the same speed and force with which he had been pulled from it.

The second thrilling incident involving ocean liners and wireless came a year later, when a man who lived at 39 Hilltop Crescent, Camden Town, in London, was arrested for uxoricide and taken into custody off the barren plains of Father Point, Quebec, more than three thousand miles way. In the annals of criminology, as well as maritime history, the significant thing was the unprecedented use of Marconi's invention to catch a culprit across the breadth of an ocean. The reading public was fascinated by the scientific ingenuity of it all, but its deeper fascination was held by the audacious details of still another *crime passionelle*.

Harvey Hawley Crippen, a little man with a disproportionately large and straggly moustache, was born in Coldwater, Michigan. In the course of a business career on the shady margins of medicine, he had drifted to London. Without a medical degree, he was nevertheless addressed as "Doctor" and worked for a firm dealing in patent medicines and dental equipment. By the time he was forty-eight years old, he was doing reasonably well, financially speaking, but at home he lived like a mouse in a cage. His wife, a large blowzy woman with a marked resemblance to the Red Queen, was, to some of her friends, "a bird of paradise." To less affectionate observers she was a species of gorgon— a large, ugly, ambitious, overaged girl, conspicuously lacking in talent, who lived in a hopeless dream of imminent stardom. To herself she was a celebrity—a singer and an entertainer whom the great music halls had still to discover.

She had been rudely booed and whistled from every stage she had allowed her presence to grace, but this seems not to have affected her self-esteem or to have checked her persistence. Born Kunigunde Mackamotski, she called herself Belle Elmore. When accumulating evidence began to suggest that her career in the music halls might be limited, she solved matters quite simply: the world itself would be her stage. Thus she moved about unfashionable London in furs and jewels provided by her Milquetoast of a husband, mixed with theatrical people and carried on flirtations of a fairly sweaty intensity. The "avenue to her affections," said an acquaintance, "was not very narrow or difficult of access." Tantrums at midnight, threats to leave Doctor Crippen and to flee into the open arms of any one of several big spenders she could, and did, name, had begun to undermine the fragile domestic harmony in which the couple had once managed to live.

To compound irritations for the Doctor, Belle had given up all pretense even to keeping his house. A neighbor who came to visit reported: "I followed her into the kitchen one morning when she was busy. It was a warm, humid day, and the grimy windows were all tightly closed. On the dresser was a heterogeneous mass, consisting of dirty crockery, edibles, collars of the doctor's, false curls of her own, hairpins, brushes, letters, a gold jewelled purse. The kitchen and gas stove were brown with rust and cooking stains. The table was littered with packages, saucepans, dirty knives, plates, flat-irons, a washing basin, and a coffee pot. Thrown carelessly across a chair was a lovely white chiffon gown embroidered with silk flowers and mounted over white glacé. The little lady cat, who was a prisoner, was scratching idly at a window in a vain attempt to attract the attention of a passing Don Juan. . . ."

Doctor and Mrs. Crippen no longer slept together, and they no longer cared about connubial arrangements, except for the sake of appearances. This led them, now and then, into the deception of spending evenings of false congeniality as husband and wife with friends, mostly of Belle's, either at home or in the gin palaces of outer London.

Early in 1910, they had a particularly violent quarrel: Belle apparently told Harvey that she was going to leave him and that she was going to clean out everything on deposit in their joint bank account. This fair warning allowed matters to come into focus. Unknown to his wife, the Doctor was in love, perhaps for the first time in his life, and his passion was reciprocated. The demure young woman who worked in his office as secretary and bookkeeper was already his mistress. Her name, for all of its fictitious overtones, was real and her own: Ethel Le Neve. Belle did not leave when she said she would, and her presence in the house gradually became an intolerable burden to Harvey Crippen. As she went on with a life of her own—dressing up to the nines, leaving and arriving at all hours, singing to herself one moment, sulking the next—the placid little pseudo-doctor worked out a scheme.

In mid-January, hypnotized by love, or driven by detestation, or both, he went to the chemist's shop of Lewis & Burrows in New Oxford Street and came away with a small packet. In it were five grams of hyoscin hydrobromide, a vegetable mydriatic alkaloid produced from the plant called henbane—a narcotic poison so strong that one quarter to one half a grain of it was considered a lethal dose. On the last day of the month, after he and his wife had spent a long, somewhat fractious, evening at home with some friends by the name of Martinetti, the Doctor had come to zero hour. He induced Belle to drink something to which his hyoscin—all five grains of it—had been added, and watched her die. Then he cut off her head, her arms and legs, and carefully saw to it that, by virtue of his surgeon's training, she was expertly drawn and quartered. He wrapped part of the cadaver in the jacket part of a pair of striped pyjamas, took it downstairs into a coal cellar, buried it under a brick flooring, and sprinkled the area with lime. The rest of the corpse he stashed away for safekeeping in a place where it would remain inconspicuous until he could decide how to dispose of it.

A few weeks later he let it be known that Belle Elmore had left his bed and board to travel in America. A chill she caught on the passage over, he said, had led to her coming down with pneumonia in California and, according to a cablegram he had just received, the illness had been fatal. Meanwhile, Ethel Le Neve had given up her job in the Doctor's office and come to live with him on Hilltop Crescent. She was sorry, she said, for the Doctor's sake, about the disappearance of his wife; but her sorrow did not prevent her from wearing the furs, silks and diamonds of the wayward woman who, as she thought, had spitefully deserted a man who, in her own view, was the soul of kindness. In March, at Easter time, traveling as husband and wife, the Doctor and his inamorata took a brief holiday trip across the Channel to Dieppe. En route, the Doctor dropped overboard a bunglesome package full of bones, hair and teeth. Refreshed by their excursion, the lovers returned to the anonymity of Hilltop Crescent and there continued to play house.

Life in this cozily illicit menage proceeded on even tenor through the course of the spring. Then, in June, an old friend of Belle's, who had just returned from a vaudeville tour in the United States, came to see Doctor Crippen. The woman's stage name was Lil Hawthorne, but she was really Mrs. Nash. She and her husband had seen a notice of Belle's death in a theatrical journal, and were so upset that they just had to know more about it. Doctor Crippen was short with them, gave no details, and was incautious enough to let them catch a glimpse of Ethel Le Neve handsomely decked out in items of finery that had either belonged to Belle, or looked as though they had.

The Nashes turned out to be a prime pair of Nosey Parkers. The Doctor's account did not sound "right" to them, and the sight of the girl typist in Belle's clothing was an affront that cut them to the quick. In fact, the story and the circumstance were so fishy, they felt, that they were moved to pay a visit to Scotland Yard. There the man they were ushered in to see was Chief Inspector Walter Dew. He heard them out and decided, a little wearily, that he had still another missing-person case to check out. He promised the Nashes he would talk to some of Belle's friends at the Music Hall Artists' Guild, then have a chat with Doctor Crippen himself.

Belle's music hall friends had nothing of interest to contribute: they had, of course, received the cards of mourning Doctor Crippen had sent out; it was all very sad; California was far away. Dutifully, the Inspector proceeded to Hilltop Crescent. When he got to the semi-detached villa with its leafy front garden, he was met at the door by a maid with a French accent who asked him to wait while she summoned Miss Le Neve. Ethel, "neatly and quietly dressed," according to Inspector Dew, was nevertheless wearing a diamond brooch of unignorable brilliance.

No, she said, Doctor Crippen was not home—he was at his place of business in Oxford Street—and identified herself as his housekeeper. When the Inspector told her that he wanted rather urgently to see the Doctor and that he would like her to take him to his office, she quite readily complied. When they got to the entrance of the building, Miss Le Neve slipped away, ran up the stairs before the Inspector was able to stop her, but soon came down with Harvey himself. "This is Doctor Crippen," she said. Their formal introduction having been made, cat and mouse began to play their ancient roles.

The Inspector informed Doctor Crippen that Belle Elmore's friends were "not satisfied" with the story of her demise and indicated that he wasn't either. Without hesitation, the Doctor admitted that the information he had given out was false: the bereavement cards were fraudulent, a device to explain his embarrassment. As far as he knew, Belle Elmore had simply cleared out as, for years, she had threatened to do, and was still alive.

This was not much to go on, but the Inspector's curiosity was now totally engaged. First, he took down a written statement from the Doctor in an interview that lasted for five hours. Then he and a deputy assistant, along with Miss Le Neve and the Doctor, all climbed into a cab and went back to Hilltop Crescent. As the Doctor hovered by, passive but cooperative, the police officers searched the house for any evidence of the remains of Belle Elmore and finally came to the coal cellar. As Doctor Crippen kept an eye on them from the top of the stairs, they poked about, tried the brick flooring, and tapped the walls. They concluded their on-the-spot investigation with thanks to their host, who then put forward a notion of his own: why not insert an advertisement in American newspapers that might serve to flush the missing Belle from her hiding place? This, Inspector Dew allowed, was a fine idea. Together they composed a notice: "Mackamotzki. Will Belle

Elmore communicate with H.H.C.—or authorities at once. Serious trouble through your absence. Twenty-five dollars reward to anyone communicating her whereabouts—"

The Inspector was now convinced that Doctor Crippen was a liar. But his intuition had produced no evidence and he had to stop where he was. Troubled and sober-faced, he called it a day, and took his leave.

As soon as the police officers were out of sight, Harvey Crippen squashed the little advertisement in his hand. The lies he had spread about his wife's death, he told Miss Le Neve, were catching up with him. They would continue to cause him bad trouble; they would be a constant source of distress to her. Until the mischievous Belle would reveal her whereabouts, he said, things would continue to go badly; they would have no peace together. The only action to take was to go away, leave the country until things blew over, or until that day when Belle would come back to retrieve her feathers and amethysts. He then sat down and wrote a note to his business partner: "I now find that in order to escape trouble I shall be obliged to absent myself for a time. I believe that with the business as it is going now you will run on all right so far as money matters go. I shall write you later on more fully. With kind wishes for your success, Yours very sincerely, H. H. Crippen."

Early next morning, a Saturday, putting newly devised plans into effect, he and Ethel went to the office to place the note on the colleague's desk. About nine o'clock, a "dental mechanic" by the name of William Long came in. Surprised, the young man asked Crippen if anything was wrong. "Only a little scandal," replied the Doctor, then asked Long whether he would mind running an errand for him. What he wanted, he said, was a complete oufit of clothes for a boy. Would Long be good enough to find a shop in Oxford Street where he could get a brown tweed suit, a brown felt hat, two shirts, two collars, a tie and a pair of shoes? Long went out, came back with every item he was asked to buy, then excused himself and went about his morning's tasks. Ethel, who had been keeping out of sight in a back room, at once put on her new clothes. The Doctor cut her hair, then shaved off his own moustache. The clothes did not fit well, but Ethel made the best of her disguise and was soon on her way with the Doctor out the back door. Within the hour they were at Victoria Station en route to Dover and a boat to the Continent.

They got to Rotterdam on Sunday, July 10, then went on to Brussels where they registered as "John Hilo Robinson and son," at the Hotel des Ardennes. But their real destination was Antwerp, where Doctor Crippen thought it most likely that he could buy inexpensive passage tickets to Quebec. His hunch was correct; the Canadian Pacific liner *Montrose* was sailing on July 20. With a good week to spare, the bogus father and son took many long walks, visited the zoo, and otherwise spent their time as sightseers.

When Inspector Dew reported to his headquarters on Saturday morning, he was still deeply uneasy about his Friday afternoon's investigation of the Crippen house. Yet he hesitated to go back, at least so soon. To give some official substance to the still-nebulous case, he issued a conventional missing-person report on Belle Elmore and had it posted in all police stations in London. The gesture left him free to pursue his own thoughts—and to review the long statement the Doctor had signed —in the hope of turning up some lead or spotting a loophole that might determine his next step. After a restless weekend, he put his hesitations aside. He simply had to have another talk with the Doctor himself. Early Monday morning he went to Crippen's office.

There he was shown the leave-taking note, and William Long told him about his being sent out to buy clothes to outfit an adolescent boy. The suspects had flown the coop, yet there was still nothing sufficiently concrete in the matter to warrant laying a charge against them. Unregistered and unnoticed (it was still a time when passports were not essential to international travel), the Doctor and his girl-in-disguise could by this time be anywhere within a range of a thousand miles or so. The only thing to do was to find some item of evidence that would give sanction and point to a manhunt.

Inspector Dew went back to Hilltop Crescent with an assistant, Sergeant Mitchell, and started all over again. For two days they picked, pried and dug inside the house and in the adjoining garden. On Wednesday, as he was probing the coal cellar with a poker, Inspector Dew dislodged one brick, two bricks, a whole square of bricks. Then he took a garden spade and began to dig. In minutes the atmosphere in the cellar was so foul and nauseating that he had to climb the stairs for a breath of fresh air and a tot of brandy. When he went back to the cellar he picked up his spade and shoved it into something soft that turned out to be a mass of putrefied flesh.

A police guard was put around the house; coroners and physicians and other detectives were brought to the scene. A police bill headlined

"MURDER and Mutilation," bearing photographs of both the Doctor and Ethel was printed up and sent out worldwide. A warrant for the arrest of the pair was issued on July 16. On the twentieth, lugging one sad little suitcase up the gangplank of the S.S. *Montrose*, John Hilo Robinson, clean shaven, and his effeminate son sailed from Antwerp for the New World.

Like everybody else, Captain Henry George Kendall of the S.S. *Montrose* had been reading the English newspapers, following every new speculation as to the whereabouts of Doctor Crippen and his mistress. He had also read the police reports that carried photographs of the suspects and samples of their handwriting, as well as details about their habits. The Doctor was described thus: "Complexion fresh, hair light brown, inclined sandy, scanty, bald on top, rather long scanty moustache, somewhat straggly, eyes grey, bridge of nose rather flat, false teeth, medium build, throws his feet outwards when walking." The report also noted: "Somewhat slovenly appearance, wears his hat rather at back of head. Very plausible and quiet spoken, remarkably cool and collected demeanor." Ethel Le Neve's appearance was briefly described, but details of her wardrobe took up more space than anything else: "Dresses well, but quietly, and may wear a blue serge costume (coat reaching to hips) trimmed heavy braid, about ½ inch wide round edge, over shoulders and pockets, three large braid buttons down front, about size of a florin, three small ones on each pocket, two on each cuff, several rows of stitching round bottom of skirt; or a light grey shadow-stripe costume, same style as above, but trimmed grey moire silk instead of braid, and two rows of silk round bottom of skirt; or a white princess robe with gold sequins; or a mole coloured striped costume with a black moire silk collar; or a dark *vieux rose* cloth costume, trimmed black velvet collar; or a light heliotrope dress."

Two hours out of Antwerp, Captain Kendall was making a routine inspection patrol of his ship when, on the boat deck, he noticed a middle-aged man and a young man standing intimately close together by the rail. What caught his attention was the fact that the younger man was squeezing the older man's hand "immoderately." As he said later, "It seemed to me unnatural for two males, so I suspected them at once." The Captain was not alone in his suspicions about male travelers who showed more than ordinary affection for one another. As the manhunt went on, a London paper reported that attention was concentrated on the Allan liner *Sardinian* because on that ship, traveling together, were "a person in clerical attire and his 'son,' a good-looking youth of an effeminate type."

"On the scent," as he put it, Captain Kendall became his own blood-hound. When the Robinsons were having lunch, he went to a cloak-room and examined their hats. The older man's was stamped: *Jackson, Boulevard le Nord*; the young man's carried no shop name, but had tissue paper packed inside the rim to make it fit a head smaller than the one it was designed for. To make sure that his suspect wore false teeth, the Captain told funny stories in the hope of making the elder Robinson laugh. To see what would happen if he suddenly called out "Mr. Robinson!" he shouted to him on an open deck. At first he got no response. Then young Robinson nudged his father, who in turn apologized to the Captain, saying that the icy weather had made him hard of hearing. When Captain Kendall was certain of his quarry, he radioed the Liverpool City Police.

Inspector Dew's long term of frustration was over. As soon as the message to Liverpool had been transmitted to his office in London, he checked steamship sailings and found that the White Star *Laurentic* was leaving for Quebec the next day. A fast ship, the *Laurentic* was scheduled to reach Quebec nearly two full days ahead of the *Montrose*. He left London by rail early next morning and, barely disguised as a "Mr. Dewhurst," was ushered in secrecy aboard the *Laurentic*. All through the voyage, as newspapers printed charts and diagrams to show the proximity of the pursued and the pursuer, he tried to get through to Captain Kendall by wireless to say that he was on the way. But the transmitting power of the *Laurentic* was too weak to arouse a response from the *Montrose*. Not until he disembarked at Father Point was the Inspector able to make a connection via the local wireless operator who, by this time, was reporting that Captain Kendall was more certain than ever that the Robinsons were Crippen and Le Neve.

Along with two constables of the Canadian Provincial Police—all of them disguised as pilots with blue suits and white caps—Inspector Dew went out in a lifeboat rowed by four sailors to meet the *Montrose* at her usual anchoring place. He climbed a rope ladder, and was being greeted on the bridge by the Captain, when "his attention was caught and riveted by a smallish man who had emerged unconcernedly from behind a funnel on the deck below." But this man had no moustache and wore no glasses. Only when he was close enough to look into his "bulgy" eyes was Inspector Dew sure.

"Good morning, Doctor Crippen," he said. Startled to be so addressed by a river pilot, Mr. Robinson stared, then twitched.

"Good morning, Mr. Dew."

The fugitives were put into a Quebec prison, then escorted back to England on the White Star *Megantic*. After a long trial that was reported, day by day, around the world, Doctor Crippen was sentenced to be hanged in Pentonville Prison and Ethel Le Neve was acquitted. The squawk and crackle of the wireless had become part of the web of circumstance. From the moment when they had been identified by Captain Kendall, said the London *Times*, they "have been encased in waves of wireless telegraphy as securely as if they had been within the four walls of a prison."

✖ SECTION VI ✖

J. Bruce Ismay: Havanas and Napoleon / Counter Measures:
Olympic, Titanic, Britannic / *"Olympic Is a Marvel"*
H.M.S. Hawke *and the Twenty Millionaires*

ONE ORDINARY evening in 1907, a large Mercedes ton-
neau with an elegant Roi-de-Belge body pulled up in front
of 27 Chesham Street, Belgravia, London, S.W. In a few
moments, Mr. J. Bruce Ismay, head of the White Star Line, and Mrs.
Ismay were handed into the automobile by a chauffeur liveried in green
and gold who then drove them the short distance to Downshire House,
Belgrave Square. This was the residence of Lord Pirrie, head of the
shipbuilding firm of Harland & Wolff, and the occasion was an intimate
dinner party. As the evening progressed and, in the command of custom,
ladies absented themselves from gentlemen for an hour of post-prandial
ease, the social occasion became an impromptu business conference.
Over Havanas and snifters of Napoleon, the shipping tycoons sketched
and doodled a scratchpad of plans that would, in effect, usher in a new
age of ocean travel. These same doodles would also set in motion a
sequence of events that would overwhelm the man who drew them—
J. Bruce Ismay—and make it certain that he would spend his last years
on earth as a pariah and a living ghost.

Both men were acutely aware that evening of two incontrovertible facts: the *Lusitania* and the *Mauretania*. The *Lusitania* had already raced to New York in something close to four and one half days; the *Mauretania* was about to go into service with a power plant engined to drive her even faster. After many years of resting on their oars, the Cunard people had produced ships that were, in popular report and in the eyes of experts, "the marvel of this age, no matter from what point of view they are regarded." To Ismay and Lord Pirrie these words amounted to a challenge they could not allow to pass. The consequence was a grand conception: they would build three new ships, all of them half again as large as the superlative new Cunarders, just as swift, and as chock full of paintings, tapestries and other kinds of period art as a national museum. The tonnage of these ships would be fixed at something around 45,000 to 50,000 tons. As a trio they would institute a ferry service with a regularity and a passenger-carrying capacity no other liners could touch. They would be called: *Olympic, Titanic, Britannic* or, as rumor soon would have it, *Olympic, Titanic* and *Gigantic*.

Thus opened the penultimate stage of great passenger ships. Subsequent decades would produce examples of the supership, but only a handful would supersede the proposed White Star ships in tonnage. And these late comers would enter the scene in a strung-out sequence, regarded more as individual prodigies than as part of a fleet or of a company.

Laid down in Lord Pirrie's Belfast yards mere months after the evening in Belgrave Square, the *Olympic* came first, on October 20, 1910. At slightly over 45,000 tons, she was the biggest ship in the world, with triple screws, four funnels, a Louis Seize dining saloon 114 feet long that could seat, at one time, 532 persons, and the first "plunge bath," as her swimming pool was generally called, ever to be placed in an ocean liner. Eight months later, her fitting-out period was over and her selling points could be revealed. These were of a refinement to make a sybarite purr—her Turkish baths, for instance, with cooling rooms in the style of seventeenth-century Arabia. Here the portholes were kept out of sight by an intricately carved Cairo curtain through which, its designers hoped, the light would fitfully suggest "something of the grandeur of the mysterious East."

"Variety and purity of styles," wrote one of the experts who came to look her over, "are the characteristics of present-day ship decoration." Juxtaposed on the *Olympic* one could find, in aura and in detail, the influence of the several Louis', Seize, Quinze and Quatorze; Jacobean, Adam, Empire, Italian Renaissance, Georgian, Queen Anne, Modern Dutch and Old Dutch. Such a glut of period-piece riches on the *Olympic* led one commentator to anticipate that passenger ships would become what they in fact soon did become—not means of travel but points of destination in themselves. "On the *Olympic*," he wrote, "the artists ransacked the seventeenth century for their ideas, and have displayed the prevailing tendency in ship decoration by copying details from several Jacobean houses of the period, so as to secure purity of style. The reproduction of decorative details of famous residences and mansions of distinctive periods on board ship is becoming quite fashionable. Instead of the original suggesting an idea, as has been the vogue hitherto, it is being reproduced in facsimile, even to the smallest detail. If this development is carried to the extreme, we shall see the public saloons of the future liner presenting replicas of the famous British castles and historic seats—a dining-room from Penshurst Place, a drawing-room from Chatsworth, a baronial hall from Holyrood, and so on. The tourist will then be spared the round of visits through these islands —he will become familiarised with our historic architectural treasures while crossing the ocean by rambling through his temporary floating home."

In the uncommonly happy history of the White Star Line, no date was more auspicious than May 31, 1911. All in one day, the *Olympic* was handed over to her owners and the great hulk of the *Titanic* was christened and sent splashing into the waters of the Irish Sea. On hand for the launching was J. Pierpont Morgan, who had traveled all the way from London to witness the event. As a prospective passenger, he had already picked out just the right location for the suite that would be henceforth designated as his alone. As part owner, he was of course keen to see what the *Titanic* might promise in the way of rehabilitation for his sluggish International Mercantile Marine Company.

Attended by many more reams of publicity and far more public excitement than would greet her sister the *Titanic*, the big black *Olympic*, nearly 900 feet long and 11 decks high, sailed down Southampton Water on her maiden voyage two weeks later. The most jubilant and, at the same time, the most critical man on board was J. Bruce Ismay himself. Leaving his wife to her own devices, he spent most of his time studying the ship's appointments, conferring with Thomas Andrews, who had overseen her building in the Belfast yards, and in attempting to overhear the comments of passengers. By the time she had reached New York, Mr. Ismay's list of corrective memoranda was full: there should be a glass-enclosed screen on B Deck, he noted, so that passengers in the luxury suites on both the *Olympic* and the *Titanic* might have their own private promenade space. There should be holders for cigars and cigarettes in the W.C.s. The beds were too comfortable, he thought, too springy; the whole ship vibrated through them and kept people awake. Lath bottoms should be fitted, to stiffen matters. There should be a potato peeler in the crew's galley. Otherwise, as he cabled Lord Pirrie, "*Olympic* is a marvel, and has given unbounded satisfaction."

In New York, however, he became aware of the inadequacy of the piers where his new trio of ships would have to dock. They were too small and their facilities were not geared to handling so many people at one time. Someone made a suggestion that Montauk Point at the end of Long Island would cause much less inconvenience if a terminal pier were established there. The Long Island Railroad warmed to this idea; but after a flurry of discussion, nothing came of the daring new plan and the White Star ships continued to dock in Manhattan.

Grander and greater than anything going, the new sovereign of the Atlantic steamed on schedule back and forth between Southampton and New York all through the high summer. But then, as if to remind everyone concerned with her that she was made by the hand of man and that she was vulnerable, she was suddenly stopped in her tracks. On the morning of September 20, just as she had begun to head westward once again, out of the blue His Majesty's warship *Hawke* rammed into her backside and all but put her out of commission for good.

The accident, hashed over in courts of inquiry for years, seems ultimately baffling and inexcusable. It happened in clear weather in calm waters when each of the ships involved was under the control of a master mariner. First sighting one another when they were nearly four miles apart, the two ships somehow managed to get through the finest meshings of the network of navigational safety and into a violent contact that battered the *Hawke*'s imperially embossed nose and relieved the *Olympic*'s vast quarter of forty feet of plating. Immediately after the collision, as the cruiser was sent spinning free and away, the liner's watertight doors were closed, her collision mats rigged. But happily, as it turned out, these were merely precautionary measures.

Never in danger of sinking, yet thoroughly abashed, the *Olympic* put into Osborne Bay, dropped her anchor for a period of inspection, then went on to Cowes to disembark "twenty millionaires whose aggregate wealth is estimated at five hundred million dollars," along with a heavy list of passengers whose bank accounts were matters of less esteem. The subsequent interruption of service in the busy end of the season was of course costly to the White Star Line. But when the *Olympic* was sent back to Belfast for repairs, and was docked near the berth where her sister ship, the *Titanic,* was being fitted out, the sight of the two wonder ships together was like a promise of invincibility.

The age of the great liners was nearing its apex. The contest for supremacy continued to be both earnest and amusing as articles about horsepower and turbines were frosted with details of outrageous frivolity. The cooling rooms in the *Titanic's* Turkish bath, for instance, were just as fascinating as those in the *Olympic.* Who would not want to disport himself in the ambience of bronze Arab lamps in a setting determinedly Moorish, with tables of inlaid Damascus and drinking fountains of chromatic marble?

As still another sunny season on the Great Circle was approaching, the London *Standard* was in a mood to handicap express liners as though they were entrants in the Grand National. "To the battle of Transatlantic passenger service," said the *Standard,* "the *Titanic* adds a new and important factor, of value to the aristocracy and the plutocracy attracted from East to West and West to East. With the *Mauretania* and the *Lusitania* of the Cunard, the *Olympic* and *Titanic* of the White Star, the *Imperator* and *Kronprinzessin Cecilie* of the Hamburg-American, in the fight during the coming season, there will be a scent of battle all the way from New York to the shores of this country—a contest of sea giants in which the *Titanic* will doubtless take high honours."

𝔖 SECTION VII 𝔚

The Titanic: Ten Lethal Seconds / Ice . . . Fields of It / "Good Morning, Old Man." / "CQD CQD SOS SOS CQD SOS, Come at Once" / Carpathia: "Ship of Gloom and Succor."
"ALL SAVED FROM TITANIC AFTER COLLISION" / The Cheerful Embalmer / A Microcosm of Civilized Society / Theodore Dreiser: "A Great Rage in My Heart against the Fortuity of Life" / Joseph Conrad Outraged / Elbert Hubbard's Eulogy Henry Adams Shattered / "The Convergence of the Twain"

FOR TEN lethal seconds on the night of April 14, 1912, the starboard hull of the greatest ship on the high seas came into contact with the submerged shelf of a drifting island of ice. Smudged with a bit of paint from the shipyards of Belfast, the iceberg then slid back into the dark and floated away on the Labrador Current. Her engines stopped, her signals silent as she continued to travel on the momentum of 46,000 tons, the ship began to fill, to lurch into a list that would never be righted. Through a gash three hundred feet long, torrents of sea water were already pouring in. "All of a sudden the starboard side came in upon us," said one of the stokers. "It burst like a big gun going off; the water came pouring in and swilled our legs." The encounter was as brief as a glancing blow; the meeting of ice and steel a matter of dreadful efficiency. Three hours later the 882-foot-long *Titanic* stood almost vertical, a weird black and white column in the middle of the ocean. Then she dived down, head first, to a depth of two miles. Trapped in the dark companionways and wooden dormitories of the third-class quarters, hundreds of emigrants were first overwhelmed, then entombed. On the upright afterdecks, passengers clinging to stanchions and ventilators were washed from the ship like insects from the trunk of a tree. The water temperature was 28 degrees Fahrenheit.

Adrift in lifeboats, some seven hundred other people heard the tumbling crash of boilers and engines dragging the ship under, then a vast silence like a sudden intake of breath, then "one long continuous wailing chant" as their shipmates succumbed to the cold or drowned among pieces of wreckage. To one man in a lifeboat, the sound they made was like that of "locusts on a mid-summer's night." To another, theirs was "a cry that called to heaven for the very injustice of its own existence; a cry that clamored for its own destruction." An accident at sea was already on its way to becoming a metaphor: the arm of a wrathful God lifted against the vanity of earthly riches and the presumptions of science.

In simple fact, the loss of the *Titanic* was a maritime disaster without equal. But in the broad resonance of its notoriety, the sinking of the *Titanic* became an event in the psychological makeup of a generation. "The pleasure and comfort which all of us enjoyed upon this floating palace," said one passenger, "seemed an ominous feature to many of us, including myself, who felt it almost too good to last without some terrible retribution inflicted by the hand of an angry omnipotence." In the space of three appalling hours, vague guilts and elusive anxieties that had dogged one hundred years of material progress came into focus.

The unsinkable ship, the most superb technological achievement of her time, the dreamed-of sign and symbol that man's mechanical skill would carry him into a luminous new world of power, freedom and affluence had become, in the words of one contemporary dirge, "the most imposing mausoleum that ever housed the bones of men since the Pyramids rose from the desert sand." Nothing had gone wrong. Everything had gone wrong. The odds on a ship such as the *Titanic* hitting an iceberg and foundering under the blow were calculated at a million to one. With devastating and absolute precision the *Titanic* and her officers had in the space of four days surmounted these odds. Designed to survive anything that man or nature could bring to bear against her, the great ship could not survive even the first voyage of the twenty-five or thirty long years of sea-going for which she was built.

Courts of inquiry on both sides of the Atlantic would sift every detail, rehearse every movement, accuse, exonerate, and recommend. Yet all of their columns of facts would be swamped by an overwhelming sense of incredulity, all their tediously rational explanations would be surrendered with a primitive bow toward the irrational. To the man in the street, not one of the answers to the more than twenty-five thousand questions asked in court about the loss of the *Titanic* would do. The only explanation was Fate, a bolt from the sky that conclusively demolished two of his most important articles of faith: an awed belief in the sovereignty of science, a generous conviction that the rights and privileges of wealth were both real and deserved. When scores of the richest and most influential men on earth, men "to whom life itself seemed subservient and obedient," could freeze to death clinging to pieces of wreckage in the middle of the ocean, something in the order of things was amiss. The unfolding marvels of science and the Olympian preserves of privilege were suddenly made human, vulnerable and hardly worth his affection or his fealty.

The course of the event itself was brief, its sequence of incidents entirely explicable. Four days out of Southampton, via Cherbourg and Queenstown, the *Titanic* was running at about 22½ knots—her highest speed to date—cutting the water along the southwestward arc of the Great Circle on a remarkably calm sea. During the day, her Commander, Captain E. J. Smith, had received routine wireless messages, followed by urgent warnings, each telling him about ice—fields of it, towering pinnacles of it—directly in the path of his ship.

Three days earlier, in fact, and less than ten miles from the scene of the *Titanic*'s collision, the French liner *Niagara*, carrying 1,100 passengers from Le Havre to New York, had smashed into an iceberg with a force that opened up her hull to such an extent that she had to call for help. Cunard's *Carmania*, responding to the call, "entered the ice field at noon and by 1:30 P.M.," according to the New York *Herald*, "was so reduced in speed that her engines were barely turning. . . . Twenty-five icebergs, many of them of monster size, were counted by passengers of the Cunarder. One berg was reported as towering 500 feet in the air." But when the *Niagara* reported that her pumps were working and that the damage was under control, the *Carmania* was able to go on her way. In spite of such known jeopardy, the *Titanic*'s speed was not reduced by so much as a fraction of a knot.

At about 11:40 P.M., Lookout Frederick Fleet, posted high in the bow, caught sight of just one great chunk of the massive archipelago of icebergs which, by this time, everyone knew was there. At once he banged the clapper of the crow's-nest bell, and telephoned the bridge. Responding to the alarm, Robert Hitchens, the man at the helm, sent the *Titanic* veering "hard-a-starboard," causing her to scrape the iceberg she would otherwise have smashed into and to slice open the hull that would almost certainly have withstood even a head-on collision.

The well deck forward was littered with ice knocked or scooped from the iceberg. But from the point of view of most of the passengers, contact between the ship and the ice was so slight as to be negligible. "I wound my watch—it was 11:45 P.M.," one of them recalled, "—and was just about to step into bed, when I seemed to sway slightly. I realized that the ship had veered to port as though she had been gently pushed. If I had had a brimful glass of water in my hand not a drop would have been spilled, the shock was so slight." But, almost as if she had been gutted by a fishhook, the huge starboard hull of the ship was already opened lengthwise. In moments, watertight bulkheads were transformed from bastions of protection against the sea to deadly containers weighted with tons of salt water.

Insofar as the structure, capacity and operation of the ship were concerned, the most knowledgeable man on board was Thomas Andrews of Belfast. A nephew of Lord Pirrie, Andrews had overseen the building of both the *Olympic* and the *Titanic* in the yards of Harland and Wolff, had accompanied the newer ship on her sea trials and had kept up a worried surveillance of her performance and her amenities from the moment she sailed from Southampton. Andrews had filled a whole notebook with small points of concern: the hot press in the restaurant galley was inefficient; there were too many screws in the stateroom hat hooks; there was too much dark woodwork in some of the public rooms; the wicker furniture in the veranda garden should be stained green. As soon as the *Titanic* had come to a drifting stop, Andrews descended into the forepart of the hull to investigate the degree of damage that might have been incurred. What he saw left no doubt in his mind that the ship had taken a blow from which she would never recover. He told Captain Smith what he had seen and unequivocally emphasized what it meant. He then repeated his story to the one man on board who had most to lose because he had most at stake—J. Bruce Ismay, President of the White Star Line, whose flag the *Titanic* flew. At once Captain Smith gave orders to signal distress. Dumfounded, his wireless operator complied by sending out CQD, the general call of distress, six times, adding MGY, the *Titanic*'s own call sign, and the message "Have struck iceberg. We are badly damaged. lat. 41.46 N., long. 50.14 W."

Fifty-eight miles away, the comfortable old Cunard liner *Carpathia*, carrying a few American tourists and a lot of emigrants going home on visits, was steaming westward out of New York at the beginning of a voyage to the Mediterranean. Usually by this time of night, her radio officer, whose name was Harold Cottam, would have closed down his Marconi shack and gone to bed. But tonight, for no reason at all, he lingered in his dimly glowing cubicle, reluctant to shut off the world that had beeped and crackled through his headphones all day. He had gone so far as to unlace his shoes and to get rid of the weight of the earphones, thus missing the first message sent out by the *Titanic*. Ten minutes later, still not quite ready to close up shop, he again picked up the headset. The air waves were clear; he decided to have a chat with his colleague Phillips on the *Titanic*. He got through, heard "K," the go-ahead signal, and was in the process of tapping out a cheery "GMOM" (Good morning, old man) when the *Titanic*'s message blasted him out of his seat. "CQD CQD SOS SOS CQD SOS. Come at once. We have struck a berg. CQD OM position 41.46 N. 50.14 W. CQD SOS." Within minutes, responding to the first SOS ever sent out by a liner at sea, the *Carpathia*'s 14-knot engines were outdoing themselves at 16 knots as, at her own jeopardy, she zigzagged around icebergs coming out of the night like floating cathedrals.

Aboard the *Titanic*, stewards obeyed orders from Captain Smith: all passengers were to be commanded to don life jackets and to assemble on the open decks where they might be assisted into boats. So began the calm, all but somnambulistic series of little events marked by "an inborn dominion over circumstance" and "a conformity to a normal standard of conduct" that characterized the human drama of that night. "It is not the slightest exaggeration," wrote young English scientist Lawrence Beesley, "to say that no signs of alarm were exhibited by anyone: there was no indication of panic or hysteria; no cries of fear; and no one running to and fro to discover what was the matter, why we had been summoned on deck with life-belts, and what was to be done with us now that we were there." What was to be done was tragic and criminally inexcusable: 2,207 passengers and crew were somehow expected to fit into life boats with a total capacity of 1,178. Few of the passengers knew this, and most of them believed that getting into the boats was nothing more than a cautionary gesture. The ship would right herself, they felt; if not, she would at least remain buoyant until help arrived from the several ships already known to be on the way to her side. Women and children began to be loaded into the swung-out boats, along with a few men who were expected to handle the oars and man the rudders. The sea remained calm as a meadow, the passengers largely silent, stunned, and orderly. By the time all of the boats had been lowered, the ship was settling deep in the water by the head. Lights continued to burn quite as if everything were normal. The big windows of saloons illuminated the broad decks; long rows of lighted portholes showed at a slant. The ship's band, eight members in all, stationed themselves on the sloping promenade deck and played medleys of ragtime tunes. Later, wearing life jackets, they continued their serenade on the boat deck. Very few passengers were in a mood or a position to hear them when they decided to change their stations at about 12:30, yet they were still as intent upon their music-making as they would have been with a full house to play to. "Soon after the men had left the starboard side," said a survivor, "I saw a bandsman—a 'cellist—come round the vestibule corner from the staircase entrance and run down the now deserted starboard deck, his 'cello trailing behind him, the spike dragging along the floor." The band's final rendition was the Church of England hymn "Autumn." The plea it made was grotesquely pertinent: "God of Mercy and Compassion!" sang their brasses, "Look with pity on my pain. . . . Hold me up in mighty waters,/Keep my eyes on things above. . . ."

But the ship went down and, to a man, they went down with her. "The filling of the forward compartment brought her down by the head," said the *Scientific American*, "and gradually, to an almost vertical position. Here she hung awhile, stern high in the air, like a huge weighted buoy. As she swung to the perpendicular, her heavy engines and boilers, tearing loose from their foundations, crashed forward (downward); and the water pressure, increasing as she sank, burst in the so-far-intact after compartments. It was the muffled roar of this 'death rattle' of the dying ship that caused some survivors to tell of bursting boilers and a hull broken apart. The shell of the ship, except for the injuries received in the collision, went to the bottom intact. When the after compartments finally gave way, the stricken vessel, weighted at her forward end, sank, to bury herself, bows down, in the soft ooze of the Atlantic, two miles below."

Since very few people outside of the ship's officers knew J. Bruce Ismay when they saw him, the main owner of the *Titanic* was able to mix with the maiden-voyage passengers without suffering more than his usual shyness. Though he realized, directly after she struck, that his ship was going to sink, he worked for nearly two hours side by side with other male passengers and officers assisting women and children into the lifeboats. When the last boat on his stretch of deck was ready to be lowered away, there was still room in it for several more people. Urged, if not ordered, to do so by Chief Officer Wilde, according to witnesses, he and E. E. Carter of Philadelphia made a leap into the boat—or, as Jack Thayer later reported, "I saw Ismay . . . push his way into it. It was really every man for himself." In either version, Ismay had in one moment crossed from the land of the living to the limbo of the living dead.

The matters of his duty, his impropriety or his cowardice found their crux in two opposing statements made at the British inquiry into the *Titanic* disaster. One statement was made by A. C. Edwards, M.P., counsel for the Dock Workers' Union, in response to a question from Lord Mersey, who was presiding. "Your point," said His Lordship, "is that, having regard for his position as managing director, it was his duty to remain on the ship until she went to the bottom?"

"Frankly, that is so," said Mr. Edwards. "I do not flinch from it."

Lord Mersey felt otherwise. "The attack on Mr. Ismay resolved itself," he said, "into a suggestion that . . . some moral duty was imposed upon him to wait on board until the vessel foundered. I do not agree. Mr. Ismay, after rendering assistance to many passengers, found 'C' collapsible, the last boat on the starboard side, actually being lowered. No other people were there at the time. There was room for him and he jumped in. Had he not jumped in, he would merely have added one more life, namely his own, to the number of those lost."

Many months earlier, Ismay had made known his intention to resign as President of the International Mercantile Marine in June, 1913. When the American and British inquiries into the sinking were concluded, he did not have to look far to learn that his immediate associates in the White Star Line would be relieved to have him remove himself from a picture in which he had so prominently figured. Reluctantly, he retired from both companies and took up residence in a house he had bought in Costello, Galway. For the next twenty-five years he divided his time between this Irish retreat and London. His wife gave parties he did not attend and took motor trips on the Continent without him. He had always loved the ceremonial processions that were forever taking place in the still imperial and sumptuary capital of London. These he continued to attend—not in the grandstand seats where his wife and children sat with their friends, but as a well-brushed, entirely anonymous, spectator among the crowds at the curbstone.

The awesome dignity of the circumstance, a sense of a vast dumb show playing itself out in the middle of nowhere, seems to have been the most lasting impression of all of those survivors who were safe and sound enough to witness the event and sufficiently self-possessed to take it in. But long before the people who had lived the story could tell it as it was, newspapers told it in terms of the overheated imaginations of staff writers. The grave sequence of events by which the disaster unrolled, and the quiet courage of those caught up in it were some of the most incredible things about that night. What the reading public was given, and what it believed—even long after the truth was told— were versions more or less like the following account published in a New York newspaper: "Stunned by the terrific impact, the dazed passengers rushed from their staterooms into the main saloon amid the crash of splintering steel, rending of plates, and shattering of girders, while the boom of falling pinnacles of ice upon the broken deck of the great vessel added to the horror. . . . In a wild ungovernable mob they poured out of the saloons to witness one of the most appalling scenes possible to conceive. . . . For a hundred feet the bow was a shapeless mass of bent, broken, and splintered steel and iron."

Long lines of lighted discs, the *Titanic*'s portholes shifted gradually from horizontal to almost vertical. The little boats drifted or were rowed away into the chilling dark. Young Beesley later recalled intimately things that most of the bewildered survivors neither saw nor could comprehend. "The night was one of the most beautiful I have ever seen," he wrote. "The sky without a single cloud to mar the perfect brilliance of the stars, clustered so thickly together that in places there seemed almost more dazzling points of light set in the black sky than background of sky itself; and each star seemed, in the keen atmosphere, free from any haze, to have increased its brilliance tenfold and to twinkle and glitter with a staccato flash that made the sky seem nothing but a setting made for them in which to display their wonder. . . . The complete absence of haze produced a phenomenon I had never seen before: where the sky met the sea the line was as clear and definite as the edge of a knife, so that the water and the air never merged gradually into each other and blended to a softened rounded horizon, but each element was so exclusively separate that where a star came low down in the sky near the clear-cut edge of the waterline, it still lost none of its brilliance. As the earth revolved and the water edge came up and covered partially the star, as it were, it simply cut the star in two, the upper half continuing to sparkle as long as it was not entirely hidden, and throwing a long beam of light along the sea to us."

The *Carpathia,* only one of many ships in answering range, was the first to reach the scene, at four A.M. Seven hundred and three of the eight hundred and fifty passengers who had left the *Titanic* in lifeboats were hoisted aboard in bosun's chairs and canvas bags. By daylight, the bodies of nearly fourteen hundred other passengers and crewmen were drifting like "a flock of white gulls at rest on the sea" when the *Carpathia* finally moved out of the scattered flotilla of ships that had responded to the SOS and remained standing by. One of these was the Russian vessel *Birma,* whose young English radio officer sent private word of the disaster to his parents. "There is no untruths to this affair," he wrote. "I was the first to hear the Distress Call and we were 100 miles away, but at 6.0 A.M. we arrived at the position given us, but not a sign of any wreckage only dam great icebergs and it was awfully cold."

As ocean currents continued to disperse hundreds of floating corpses and the *Carpathia,* "a ship of gloom and succor," headed southwest under full steam, *The New York Evening Sun* hit the street with its Baseball Final. "ALL SAVED FROM *TITANIC* AFTER COLLISION," read a banner headline, "Liner Is Being Towed to Halifax/ After Smashing into an Iceberg." But across the page, top right, the news was lugubrious: "Giants Drop/ Game at Hub/ Boston Braves Win/ From McGrawites." In Boston itself, *The Evening Transcript's* report was just as comforting, just as precipitous. "TITANIC'S DANGER OVER," said the headline, "Hours of Anxiety at Last Relieved." The reassuring report was based on an interview with a vice-president of the White Star Line. "The Allan Line, Montreal, confirms the report that the *Virginian, Parisian* and *Carpathia* are in attendance, standing by the *Titanic,*" he said. "We are absolutely satisfied that even if she was in collision with an iceberg she is in no danger. With her numerous water-tight compartments she is absolutely unsinkable, and it makes no difference what she hit. The report should not cause any serious anxiety." Another page of the same edition of the *Transcript* carried a big three-column advertisement announcing that the *Titanic* would sail on her first eastbound passage, from New York, at noon on Saturday next, April 20. "Passengers Safe," was the word from Toronto's *Evening Telegram*, "Leaving *Titanic*—Two Liners Assisting in Rescue." Meanwhile the White Star Line had arranged with the New York, New Haven and Hartford Railroad to dispatch a special train of twenty-three sleepers, two dining cars and a number of day coaches to Halifax as a convenience to the great number of passengers who would be disembarked there. But by early Monday evening, rattling northward along the coast of Maine, the train was stopped in its tracks and turned back to Boston. Reporters who had badgered White Star executives all day long were finally satisfied when an official statement confirming what they knew was handed to them.

A reading public that had long fed on the numinous ways of the Four Hundred and the imperious whims and manners of the rich and superrich hurried to the groaning board of juicy items the press was quick to lay out. John Jacob Astor, "the world's greatest monument to unearned increment," had died with twenty-five hundred dollars in his pockets. His crushed corpse, "found dressed in a blue suit, standing almost erect in his lifebelt," was hauled into Halifax on a rusty cable boat. In the same boat with him, laid in rough coffins and heaped with Nova Scotia ice, were nearly two hundred other men whose names suggested gold watchchains, waistcoats piped with satin, the aroma of fifty-cent cigars. Speculating on the "untold wealth" among the richest of them, a New York paper made up a litany of dollar signs. Astor's reputed fortune came to 150,000,000 dollars; Benjamin Guggenheim's to 95,000,000; Widener's and Straus's to 50,000,000 each; Ismay's to 40,000-000. By the merest chance, they could not include that of Alfred Gwynne Vanderbilt. Intending to sail on the *Titanic*, he had changed his mind at the last minute, as his mother in New York learned when she got a cable saying he was "safe in London."

In the course of the grim expedition made by the Commercial Cable Company's ship *Mackay Bennett*, other bodies had been merely consigned to the sea. The diary of Cable Engineer Frederick A. Hamilton tells how it was done: "April 17th, 1912. Having taken in a supply of

ice and a large number of coffins, cast off. . . . The Reverend Canon
Hind of "All Saints" Cathedral, Halifax, is accompanying the expedition; we also have an expert Embalmer on board.

"April 20th. A large iceberg, faintly discernible to our north, we are
now very near the area where lie the ruins of so many human hopes
and prayers. The Embalmer becomes more and more cheerful as we
approach the scene. . . .

"April 21st. The ocean is strewn with a litter of woodwork, chairs
and bodies, and there are several growlers about. . . . The cutter lowered,
and work commenced and kept up continuously all day, picking up
bodies. Hauling the soaked remains in saturated clothing over the side
of the cutter is no light task. Fifty-one we have taken on board today,
two children, three women, and forty-six men, and still the sea seems
strewn. With the exception of ourselves, the bosun bird is the only
living creature here. 8 P.M. The tolling of the bell summoned all hands
to the forecastle where thirty bodies are ready to be committed to the
deep, each carefully weighted and carefully sewn up in canvas. It is a
weird scene, this gathering. The crescent moon is shedding a faint light
on us, as the ship lays wallowing in the great rollers. The funeral service
is conducted by the Reverend Canon Hind, for nearly an hour the words
"For as much as it hath pleased . . . we therefore commit his body to
the deep" are repeated and at each interval comes, splash! as the
weighted body plunges into the sea, there to sink to a depth of about
two miles. Splash, splash, splash."

Meanwhile their widows—dressed in hand-me-down garments of
mourning provided by passengers on the *Carpathia* and weary of a voyage from nowhere during which the ship's band endlessly played
"hymns and other quietly beautiful selections"—had filed down the
gangplank of Pier 54 at the foot of West Fourteenth Street in New
York. They were met by an audience of ten thousand curiosity seekers.
They were also greeted by their own limousines, private trains and
phalanxes of servants, secretaries and other kinds of amanuenses and
factotums ready to envelop their sorrows in whatever creature comforts
might serve. The fashionable Hotel Belmont was as good as its word:
since many of the first-class passengers had engaged rooms there before
sailing from Southampton, the manager saw to it that six large automobiles were waiting for the hostelry's clients as they disembarked, not
at the White Star Pier, as earlier arranged, but at the Cunard. How she
managed it, nobody knew, but Mrs. John Jacob Astor kept up the side

of the seriously rich when, "to the wonderment of all," she "walked off the *Carpathia* perfectly composed. She was dressed in a black broadtail coat with an enormous sable rever. Around her neck was a circle of diamonds" and she carried a muff. Nothing was made of the fact that the illustrious Madeleine Force Astor was a teen-aged girl, or that she was five months pregnant.

"What daring flight of imagination," asked a journalist, "would have ventured the prediction that within the span of six days a stately ship, humbled, shattered, and torn asunder, would lie two thousand fathoms deep at the bottom of the Atlantic, that the benign face that peered from the bridge would be set in the rigor of death and that the happy bevy of voyaging brides would be sorrowing widows?"

Every fourth or fifth family among first-class passengers on the *Titanic* was attended by a maid, a valet, a nurse or a governess. In a period when the average American family income was well below one thousand dollars, a number of passengers had paid well over four thousand dollars for the privilege of crossing the ocean on the maiden voyage of an already famous ship—"a ship built," said *The Nation*, "for the great men of the earth, for the financial giants of our time, men who could lightly pay for this single voyage the year's keep of ten British families." Somehow, for that social season, crossing on the maiden voyage of the *Titanic* was *the* thing to do: in their bouffant hairdos and corsets, high collars and high-buttoned shoes, ancestors of the jet set had come flocking from all over the Continent to embark at Cherbourg or Southampton. "No one consulted the Passenger List," said one outsider. "They met on deck as one big party."

This sort of exclusiveness had already been taken for granted. The notion of an upper crust, defined and self-aware, was not fancy but a reality that the nature of the *Titanic*'s complement only emphasized. "If," said a contemporary, "thinking of the *Titanic* . . . you could imagine her to be split in half from bow to stern so that you could look, as one looks at the section of a hive, upon all her manifold life thus suddenly laid bare, you would find in her a microcosm of civilized society. Up on the top are the rulers, surrounded by the rich and the luxurious, enjoying the best of everything; a little way below them their servants and parasites, ministering not so much to their necessities as to their luxuries; lower down still, at the base and foundation of all, the fierce and terrible labour of the stokeholds, where the black slaves are shovelling as though for dear life, endlessly pouring coal into furnaces that devoured it and yet ever demanded a new supply—horrible labour, joyless life; and yet the labour that gives life and movement to the whole ship. Up above are all the beautiful things, the pleasant things. Up above are the people who rest and enjoy; down below the people who sweat and suffer."

When the *Titanic* vanished, so did the sanctions that had somehow attended a way of life that few people could actually follow except vicariously and by overblown report. To the man of 1912, technology was a general promise of better things; social stratification, a consequence of wealth and the natural disposition of power. When these were brought to chaos in an instant, a frisson of fear and doubt ran through his world like a cold wind. "When," asked the Bishop of Winchester, "has such a mighty lesson against our confidence and trust in power, machinery, and money been shot through the nation? . . . The *Titanic*, name and thing, will stand for a monument and warning to human presumption."

To millions of Americans and Britons in particular, the wreckage of this greatest toy in the playground of the rich was morbidly fascinating. It became, almost at once, something to be reenacted for thrills on vaudeville stages; the subject of a painting by the German Expressionist Max Beckmann; the story of an anonymous ballad, "De Titanic," that echoed the sort of dialect that once passed for Negro speech. Black troops sailing for France in World War I liked to sing:

> De rich folks 'cided to take a trip
> On de fines' ship dat was ever built.
> De cap'n presuaded dese peeples to think
> Dis Titanic too safe to sink.

> De ship lef' de harbor at a rapid speed,
> 'Twuz carryin' everythin' dat de peepels need.
> She sailed six-hundred miles away,
> Met an icebug in her way.

> .   .   .

> Up come Bill from de bottom flo'
> Said de water wuz runnin' in de boiler do'.
> Go back, Bill, an' shut yo' mouth,
> Got forty-eight pumps to keep de water out!

> .   .   .

On de fifteenth day of May nineteen-twelve,
De ship wrecked by an icebug out in de ocean dwell,
De people wuz thinkin' o' Jesus o' Nazaree,
While de band played "Nearer My God to Thee!"

It was as though the only order in society and the great world that most people could recognize had found its moment of chaos. If John Jacob Astor's faith in the titanic might of the century was so sorrily misplaced, how could they justify their own? The hands of the great clock that stood at the head of the *Titanic*'s grand staircase were paralyzed; its two bronze figures—Honor and Glory—crowning Time, were engulfed. What now would signify? Nothing would ever be as it was. The long run of the good old days was suddenly broken, leaving only a series of horrifying close-ups in a huge dark theater.

Theodore Dreiser's first visit to Europe was in its last days, and he was fretting to be on his homeward way. When he inquired about sailings, he was told that the next available ship would be the *Titanic*. But a friend of his pointed out that the White Star liner would be expensive and, because of her newness, very likely uncomfortable. To save money, Dreiser sailed on the Red Star Line's *Kroonland* and went second class. Three days out from Dover, he was having conversation with some men friends in the smoking room. "A damp wind had arisen," he wrote, "bringing with it the dreaded fog. . . . The great fog-horn began mooing like some vast Brobdingnagian sea-cow wandering on endless watery pastures." A German passenger, "pale and trembling," approached the novelist and his companions, whispered that he had something to tell them, and shepherded them onto the open deck. "Gentlemen," he said, "the Captain's given orders to keep it a secret until we reach New York. But I got it straight from the wireless man: the *Titanic* went down last night with nearly all on board. . . ." Then, said Dreiser, "with one accord we went to the rail and looked out into the blackness ahead. The swish of the sea could be heard and the insistent moo of the fog-horn. . . . I went to my berth thinking of the pains and terrors of those doomed two thousand, a great rage in my heart against the fortuity of life. . . ."

One of the most difficult things for the man in the street to do was to account for the behavior of passengers unwilling to take simple steps to save themselves. Blasé, disbelieving, or simply unwilling to be roughly handled, many of them showed themselves to be reluctant to enter the lifeboats; many responded to the orders of officers and stewards with outright truculence. The myth of the unsinkable ship and the signs of wealth and elegance they could, even in jeopardy, still see and touch combined to atrophy even the sense of self-preservation. "All the people on board existed under a false security," said Joseph Conrad. "And the fact which seems undoubted, that some of them actually were reluctant to enter the boats, when told to do so, shows the strength of that falsehood. These people seemed to imagine it an optional matter." But what else could you expect, Conrad implied, of "a sort of marine Ritz, proclaimed unsinkable, and sent adrift with its casual population upon the sea, without enough boats, without enough seamen (but with a Parisian café, and four hundreds of poor devils of waiters). . . .

"The water-tight doors in the bulkheads of that wonder of naval architecture could be opened down below by any irresponsible person. Thus, the famous closing apparatus of the bridge, paraded as a device of greater safety, with those attachments of warning bells, colored lights, and all those pretty-pretties was in the case of this ship little better than a technical farce. . . ."

Editorials and sermons dwelt with zest on the wages of human arrogance. "There was issued a challenge to the god of chance," said one of them, "and the result is measured by a sacrifice that has had few parallels in history." "God is not responsible for this calamity," said the Reverend Doctor Joseph Silverman of Temple Emanuel in New York, "man is responsible. God is the law-giver. He created the laws of nature by which we are to live. He created man with free will to go forth and study and obey his law. This calamity is the punishment for disobedience of those laws. . . . That iceberg had a right to be where it was, but that ship had no right to be where it was. . . ."

In the shock of it all, even the heinous reputations of plutocrats were modified. Addressing the damp ghost of John Jacob Astor, Elbert Hubbard played upon the last shreds of decency in those who had read the grisly stories of drowning millionaires with immense satisfaction at the meting out of justice. "Words unkind, ill-considered, were sometimes flung at you, Colonel Astor," wrote Hubbard. "We admit your handicap of wealth—pity you for the accident of birth—but we congratulate you that as your mouth was stopped with the brine of the sea, so you stopped the mouths of carpers and critics with the dust of the tomb. If any think unkindly of you now, be he priest or plebeian, let it be with finger to his lips, and a look of shame into his own calloused heart." In the same breath the Sage of Aurora eulogized friends and acquaintances who had disappeared with the ship. "And so all you I knew, and all that thousand and a half a thousand more I did not know, passed out of this Earth-Life into the Unknown upon the restless, unforgetting tide. You were sacrificed to the greedy Goddess of Luxury and her consort the Demon of Speed. Was it worth while? Who shall say? The great lessons of life are learned only in blood and tears. Fate decreed that they should die for us. Happily, the world has passed forever from the time when it feels a sorrow for the dead. The dead are at rest, their work is ended, they have drunk of the waters of Lethe, and these are rocked in the cradle of the deep. We kiss our hands to them and cry, 'Hail and Farewell—until we meet again.'" As it turned out, Hubbard would not have to wait long for this meeting. Just five years hence, he would himself be unexpectedly hurried into the Unknown from the deck of a sinking ocean liner.

In Washington on April 16, Henry Adams wrote a spluttering letter to a friend. "The foundering of the *Titanic* . . . strikes at confidence in our mechanical success," he said. "By my blessed Virgin, it is awful! This *Titanic* blow shatters one's nerves. We can't grapple it. . . . I've shifted my passage to the *Olympic* on May 4 . . . but nerves are now so shaken that no ship seems safe, and if I am wrecked I might as well go under." Adams had expected to make the eastward maiden voyage of the *Titanic*, for which he had booked "another extravagant apartment." But ten days after he had first learned of the sinking, he suffered a stroke. His friends, along with his physician, felt that the disaster was perhaps the strongest contributing factor.

Overseas, Thomas Hardy was grieved and appalled by still another evidence that man and the world were toys in the hands of a whimsical deity. Hardy's good friend, journalist W. T. Stead, had gone down with the ship, and so had a number of other people he knew as acquaintances. When the sponsors of the charity known as The Titanic Relief Fund asked him to join the roster of eminent people to be represented in their "Dramatic and Operatic Matinee" at Covent Garden, Hardy was obliging. He gave them a poem, "The Convergence of the Twain: Lines in Memory of the Loss of the *Titanic*." In this he recapitulated the event in terms that had long defined the Hardyesque message and its preoccupation with divine inscrutability. The result, nevertheless, was the one piece of imaginative literature occasioned by the *Titanic* that seems likely to survive all journalistic accounts and all fictional recreations.

THE CONVERGENCE OF THE TWAIN

In a solitude of the sea
Deep from human vanity,
And the Pride of Life that planned her, stilly couches she.

Steel chambers, late the pyres
Of her salamandrine fires,
Cold currents thrid, and turn to rhythmic tidal lyres.

Over the mirrors meant
To glass the opulent
The sea-worm crawls—grotesque, slimed, dumb, indifferent.

Jewels in joy designed
To ravish the sensuous mind
Lie lightless, all their sparkles bleared and black and blind.

Dim moon-eyed fishes near
Gaze at the gilded gear
And query: "What does this vaingloriousness down here?" . . .

Well: while was fashioning
This creature of cleaving wing,
The Immanent Will that stirs and urges everything

Prepared a sinister mate
For her—so gaily great—
A Shape of Ice, for the time far and dissociate.

And as the smart ship grew,
In stature, grace, and hue,
In shadowy silent distance grew the Iceberg too.

Alien they seemed to be:
No mortal eye could see
The intimate welding of their later history.

Or sign that they were bent
On paths coincident
On being anon twin halves of one august event.

Till the Spinner of the Years
Said "Now!" And each one hears,
And consummation comes, and jars two hemispheres.

❧ SECTION VIII ❧

DISASTER may have brought the divine rights of privilege into question—but not the rights of owners and builders to launch ships of even more exaggerated pretensions. Top-heavy and ornate, dynamic, powerful and stratified, ocean liners continued to have the resonance of metaphors. They were, in fact, acceptable models of twentieth-century cities afloat: people wearing fedoras and sables lived on the sunniest elevations, people wearing cloth caps and shawls lived down by the boiler works; Rotarians met on Tuesday afternoons in the forward lounge; on Saturday nights parties in evening dress left the dance floor to go slumming in the beer halls of the lower decks. Distinction between classes, theoretically a moribund idea, was in practice rigorously upheld. The only places where rich and poor were likely to catch sight of one another were on the dock or in sick bay. Even as the *Titanic*, "name and thing," was going under, the walls of still another sea-going metropolis were rising on the stocks of Harland & Wolff's Belfast yards.

The new giantess was supposed to be a sister and running mate to the *Olympic* and *Titanic*—third in a trio that would allow the White

Star Line to maintain a weekly express service between Southampton and New York. In spite of persistent rumor, the name *"Gigantic"* was probably never really meant for her, yet the sort of megalomania that had overtaken the shipping fraternity gave credibility to the idea. In any case, by the time the *Titanic* had come to be regarded not merely as a ship of doom but as an affront to Heaven, the directors of the line would hardly have dared to emblazon such a name on any ship, much less one that actually *was* gigantic. When she was launched in February, 1914, the new ship assumed a quietly traditional name— *S.S. Britannic.* When she was ready to sail she offered, and widely advertised, new safety features: a double bottom (just like the one on the *Great Eastern,* nearly sixty years earlier), a system of watertight bulkheads designed to obviate weaknesses uncovered in the *Titanic,* and a visible plethora of lifeboats in cantilevered davits, like the cars of a Ferris wheel.

Restrictions imposed by World War I soon halted the installation of the luxurious interior that was to make the *Britannic* richer and handsomer than anything else at sea. By the end of 1915—painted white, marked with huge red crosses and a red strip that ran from stem to stern—she was commissioned as a hospital ship. For almost a year she sailed between Southampton and ports in the Mediterranean, collecting wounded soldiers and bringing them home in the care of a large medical staff of doctors and nurses. On November 18, 1916, en route from Salonika to Mudros, where hundreds of wounded men were waiting to be embarked, she hit a mine, slumped forward, and quickly sank 620 feet into the Aegean Sea. The clouds of war had all but obscured the career of the greatest ship extant. She disappeared, it seems, almost before anyone knew where she was or, indeed, who she was.

"Among the gifts to humanity," said the somewhat gloomy prophet Keble Chatterton, "there is not included that of taming the sea. She is tyrannical in her strength, untamable, dominant; and when you launch into her bosom heavy masses of iron and steel, and deceive yourself with high-sounding names—call them *Great Easterns, Majestics, Indomitables, Titanics,* and all the rest—the Sea only laughs at you, for she knows perfectly well that a blow or two from her mighty arm will end their days and settle their fate for all time."

These feelings were not widely shared by men who owned and directed the destinies of ships. But to the men who actually kept their engines running and their gear intact, such sentiments were a confirmation of old suspicions. Too far away to go to the rescue of her sinking sister ship, the *Olympic* had continued eastward to reach Southampton on schedule, and was about to set off once more for New York when, without warning, all of her firemen and trimmers simply put down their tools and walked off the ship. Undaunted, her engineering officers managed to get the ship downriver to Ryde, where they dropped anchor. While the *Olympic* waited there in hope that a new gang of men might be enlisted, the walkout was joined by all the sailors aboard. Parleys between management and labor were fruitless. The voyage was abandoned, the passengers put ashore. "I have no doubt," said an officer, "the recent tragedy has been too much for their nerves. Suddenly becoming panic-stricken, they concluded that the best thing for themselves and their frightened families, was to have a voyage off home."

The loss of the *Titanic* was awesome and dreadful, yet it resulted in only a slight gap in the front ranks of the armada of mammoth steamships. With the ascendancy of the White Star abruptly checked, its peers and rivals in Germany, France and England lost no time in pressing the advantage misfortune had opened to them. Hamburg-Amerika's new *Imperator*, to be followed by the *Vaterland* and the *Bismarck*, was almost ready, and the Compagnie Générale Transatlantique, after decades as a quiet competitor, was about to produce its *pièce de résistance* in the shape of the *France*. Meanwhile, Cunard had thrown away the book in fitting out a sea-going museum that would offer a retrospective exhibition of European culture.

This floating anthology would be christened *Aquitania*. Even before the rude intrusion of World War I that would send ships scattering and foundering, the appearance on the sea lanes of these giants (the *Bismarck* would not be completed until 1922) definitively closed still another era in the saga of Atlantic carriers. When they had left the drawing boards and had slid down the ways, the stridently operatic phase of shipbuilding was over. With the exception of the *Bismarck* (later to be named *Majestic*), no other ship capable of challenging these Amphitrites of the Victorian twilight would come over the horizon until 1926.

The 52,000-ton *Imperator* was the first in that succession of ships Albert Ballin believed would make his company preeminent over his German rivals in Bremen, as well as his competitors abroad, especially the White Star Line with its frustrated plans for a three-ship weekly express service. And certainly nothing but a troop transport had accommodations for so great a number of passengers and crew. As originally equipped, the *Imperator* could carry 908 passengers in first class, 592 in second, and 1,772 in steerage. Her crew numbered about 1,200. Fully booked, she would sail with nearly 5,500 souls on board— a figure ships of later decades would not even remotely approach. Her debut in the resonance of the *Titanic* disaster and its worldwide dirge hardly seemed propitious. Yet the appearance of an even greater ship than the *Titanic* guaranteed that she would be scrutinized with a degree of fascinated attention her owners could in no way have promoted. One notable feature of the *Imperator* was a pillar-free vista the whole end-to-end length of her enormous first-class lounge. This was made possible when architects divided the uptakes of her two functional smoke stacks (the third was a dummy) so that they ran up the sides of the superstructure rather than through the middle of the ship. Another feature was a swimming pool that gave the appearance of being set in a mosaic temple supported by Doric columns. Another was a large searchlight, set up on its own platform on the foremast, presumably meant to comfort passengers by giving them visible evidence of an eye out for icebergs. But to the eyes of later generations—eyes perhaps glazed by the elaborations of grandeur in the ships of the period— the oddest feature of the *Imperator* was the modesty of her plumbing appointments. "Particular attention," said a brochure that was otherwise heavy with hyperbole, "is called to the almost total elimination in the first cabin of the folding wash-stand. In its place is a commodious marble wash-stand with running hot and cold water . . . which serves as a dressing table."

Without question, the most striking thing about the *Imperator* was a crudely grotesque and scarifying figurehead. Ugly as sin, this device was a huge bland-eyed eagle with a dinky little crown on its snakelike head. Its cast-iron claws gripped a cast-iron globe that was bolted to a cast-iron sunburst of flashing golden spikes. Around the globe ran a gilded ribbon of iron embossed boldly with the familiar Hamburg-Amerika motto, "*Mein Feld Ist die Welt.*" Straining for length, the *Imperator*'s architects had also given her a deep overhang out of all proportion. These fore and aft features made her the longest thing afloat, but were scant help in modifying her bulkiness or her worrisome top-heaviness.

Enthroned in its flashy gear, the imperial eagle ruffled the Atlantic waves until the ship's third voyage. Then an angry sea reached up, ripped the whole business from the prow and drowned it. Soon came other heavy seas to indicate that something was radically wrong with the sea-keeping qualities of the matchlessly grand *Imperator*. When her helm was shifted in rough weather she listed so deeply and would "hang on the roll" so unendurably long that her sea-hardened crew were almost as terrified as her passengers. To overcome this, her owners decided upon a drastic series of dismantlings. First they ordered the removal of truckloads of ponderous ornamented furniture, then of the marble baths in the luxury suites. The mahogany and marble fixtures in the Continental Grill on promenade deck were taken away and the space transformed into a garden with lightweight cane furniture. Still unsatisfied, they ordered workmen to clip nine feet off the top of each of her three cavernous funnels.

Denuded inside and slightly disfigured outside, the *Imperator* had still to endure further ignominy: 2,000 tons of concrete were poured into her bottom. This extreme measure would allow her to keep a reasonably even keel through a long career; yet her basic sea-worthiness was not a feature to win the ship more than a small measure of confidence or affection. "She was a ship of gloomy paneled majesty," said one of her captains, "hard to handle, clumsy and Teutonic, a creation of industry without pretensions to beauty."

The French Line (the common name for Compagnie Générale Transatlantique Cie.) was never concerned with emigrant transportation on the scale of the British and German companies. Instead, it had for years maintained standards of comfort and touches of modest luxury appealing exclusively to the well-to-do. But by 1912 the line had caught the prevalent fever for a sort of eclectic exhibitionism. Thus, beginning with the *France*, French ships would develop on an ascending scale of charm, chic and tapestried ambience that would eventually give them priority among passengers to whom congeniality counted for more than grandiosity, *haute cuisine* for more than speed. French taste on the Atlantic was almost as appalling as that of other nations, but somehow its burden was mitigated by the worldliness and *joie de vivre* of the passengers who elected to put up with it. French ships as carriers of the Smart Set would come into their own with the debut of the *Ile de France*; then with the *Normandie* they would just about wrap up the business of the North Atlantic. These "Who's Whos" afloat were still far in the future; but at least in the *France* of 1912, "a castle on the Atlantic," the French had a ship capable of making a strong inroad upon the Anglo-German hegemony.

At about 24,000 tons, the *France* was considerably smaller than her rivals and, like them, she sported, almost *de rigeur*, four big black funnels. Sitting low in the water, with low funnels placed unusually far forward, she gave an impression of high style and efficient ease. But "she rolled like a sick headache," said one passenger; on her first voyage she broke two thousand dollars' worth of crockery. One of the *France's* big and widely advertised features was the upgrading of the conventional *cabine de luxe* to an out-and-out *de grand luxe*, or "regal flat." These "princely suites of rooms" were large enough to accommodate six persons, thus allowing a family or a party of friends to cross the ocean "in complete isolation" from the *nouveau riche* upstarts in first class and the *canaille* in other remote and obscure parts of the ship. Each suite had three canopied beds, and two others with brass bedsteads. Its occupants had their own Empire-style dining room, a drawing room copied from a salon in a Touraine château, a bathroom and, in the shy language of the period, "other domestic conveniences."

As for cuisine, the *France* carried on the *boulevardier* traditions of La Belle Epoque. At the beginning of every voyage, eighteen barrels of *pâté de foie gras* were trundled aboard to whet the appetites of diners in a salon on two levels with decorations, borrowed from the country seat of the Comte de Toulouse, that had been adapted by a pupil of Mansard. A life-sized portrait of Louis XIV by Hyacinthe Rigaud, after a painting in the Louvre, welcomed passengers into the main lounge. Other portraits—of Princesse de la Tour du Pin, Madame de Maintenon, Henriette d'Angleterre, la Duchesse de Bourgogne—smiled wanly down upon the *causeries* of the well-heeled. To pass the evening, first-class passengers might choose the Moorish salon where they could listen to the sounds of a fountain that played continuously under an Algerian fresco executed by a painter named Poisson.

An impressionable visitor to the *France* believed that he had at last found Utopia. "One is even spared the tedious climb and descent of the staircase," he said. "The citizen of the floating town presses a button, a grille rolls back to reveal an elevator, and he is whisked to the desired floor." He was charmed by the saddlebag easy chairs in the smoking room and the refreshing waters of the swimming bath. "Even the luxury of a Turkish bath," he said, "is not denied to its votaries." On the dressing table in each of the expensive cabins, he noted, there was "a natty device" which "with the turn of a button" would allow a lady "to heat the intricate implements for completing the coiffure."

But one unreconstructed British connoisseur of sea-gong amenities would not be taken in by such Gallic fripperies. French Line ships, he said, "are beautifully decorated, and fitted with every luxury; but they do not suit British taste, inasmuch as no notice is taken of the Sabbath day. The cuisine, wines, and attendance," he conceded, "are excellent."

The new *France* nevertheless brought the French mercantile marine importantly into transatlantic competition. "Our *paquebots* are fragments of French territory which move about," said a historian. "In a confined space we produce our country: its cuisine, its cordiality without familiarity, its grace of decoration, its harmonious ensembles of color in which there is nothing too loud or shocking."

Luxury travel *à la Française* in time of peace was one thing; a wartime crossing in the stripped-down grimness of one of France's veteran steamers quite another. When Edward Estlin Cummings, a young poet, critic and recent Harvard graduate volunteered to join the Norton-Harjes Ambulance Corps, he was ticketed on the French Line's *La Touraine*. This grand old ship—the first twin-screw vessel France had put into the Atlantic run—had once held the Blue Riband. She was the last of all liners of her size to carry auxiliary sails, the first to have offered fifteen courses on her *carte du jour*. It was said of her that, "if there was one ship the Germans tried to sink and kept missing, it was the *La Touraine*, which, full of American war workers, plodded to and fro across the Atlantic thumbing her dowagiac nose at submarines as she tortured the poor devils who had to cross on her. Suffer! Ten days on the *La Touraine* in war time was all of that. She was always overcrowded. There were plenty of cooties, yet she got her people through."

Cummings' letters to his parents in the course of the voyage from New York to Bordeaux suggest that the once reigning queen of the

French merchant service had quite lost her charms. "À bord de *Touraine* le 4me mai 1917," he wrote, "*Parentes carissimi!* I am pro-German henceforth. And why not? Yesterday I partially emerged into consciousness; last night I visited the *salle à manger* for the first time since Saturday: today I am sitting in the *salon de conversation* writing this—a feat unparalleled. Should you ask why, I must name names. O name fore'er accursed—thy sinister initials peek at me from every impossible corner: C.G.T. French Line, a murrain on thee! Should the blond captain of a U boat consent to waste a torpedo on thy torpid bowels, I'd grasp his Hunnish hand.

"Understand that it's a beautifully calm day, warm, sunny, etc.—yet this thunder mug of a boat jabbers and jogs and gapes from side to side so as to make writing an achievement equal to the Pyramids. I refrain from describing its conduct during the 'northeaster' which we have been having for the past 5 days. Nor will I—ah no!—give generalities, even, concerning *my* conduct. Suffice it to say that after the *honest sickness* of Sunday and Monday, plus the *genteel misery* of Tuesday and Wednesday, I am barely capable of making my respects to ye. . . . The cabins (or state-rooms, or something) are dependent for ventilation . . . on half a dozen—nay, two or three—'portholes.' These, naturally, were shut during the N.E.'er. Hence I dragged up and down, sleeping mostly on deck till the hoze-man tapped me on the leg at 5:30 A.M., or leaping from top to sides of my bunk with my stomach grinning at me from the mast-head. . . .

"The 'boat' is a funny thing, made of wood and stone, with a few bricks loose in the hold. Everytime the rudder is moved a 2000 sack of Fords is kicked down-stairs. When the 'boat' wants to whistle, 'she' shuts her eyes, stops her heart-beats, buttons her vest, and goes off with a heart-rending scream that reminds you of Cambridge policemen at busy traffic corners. 'She' has a way of dying in the grip of a fair-sized wave, which is heartily amusing."

As the *Touraine*, "that swanlike barque," approached the coast of France, precautions against submarine attack were increased. In a second letter, on May 6, Cummings writes: "All life-boats are cleared; the rail is taken up and off all around the stern; and there's an esquimo in the Crow's-nest. People are threatening every night to sleep on deck, but nobody does. Perhaps they will tonight. My graciousness toward empirical submarines continues.

"Having missed most of the ships, fish, drift-wood, et cetera, hitherto

—I yesterday saw a 3 masted square-rigger under full sail. It was the best thing I ever saw."

Slightly longer and a little bigger than her sister ship *Imperator*, the *Vaterland* was another overdecorated hostelry in the disguise of an ocean liner. "Everything on the *Vaterland*," said an admirer, "has been designed to look as much like a sumptuous hotel and as little like a ship as human imagination can do it. The windows are shaped and curtained like a private house." Steaming up the harbor at the end of her maiden voyage in 1914, she encountered an outbound tide and a heavy wind blowing down the Hudson. She was met off Hoboken by fourteen tug boats, but before she could be taken in hand, a harbor tug, having trouble in managing the barges she was towing, drifted between the *Vaterland* and Pier 2. Stopped still to wait for the interloper to pass, the *Vaterland*, with a draft of very nearly forty feet, began drifting herself—toward the Lackawanna Ferry Landing where the depth of water was only twenty-seven feet. Desperate, her attendant tugs signaled for others, and soon there were six tugs pulling at her hawsers, three on her starboard side, fifteen on her port side, and twenty-five others racing to the rescue. Her four great propellers were already churning up mud and sand when, at last, the drifting was halted and she allowed herself to be eased into a berth.

The *Vaterland* had reached New York just as war was declared. To guarantee her safety in a neutral haven, her owners decided to keep her there. Consequently she was laid up for three years. When the United States entered the war in 1917, the German crew that had kept her a "live" ship subjected her to a thoroughgoing act of sabotage. They removed essential parts of her engines, disconnected lines carrying fuel and water, destroyed or erased all signs with information that might identify a fixture or point a direction.

The American Government claimed the ship as a prize of war. But when a boarding party was dispatched to take control, they found the *Vaterland's* internal workings in a tangled mess. Live steam hissed out of flushed toilets, bilge water and fuel oil poured out of shower installations, ropes of wires petered out in useless knots and ravelings. Expert American crews had to work for months to restudy and reconnect wires, pipes and nozzles. But eventually the ship was returned to working order and grandly rechristened *Leviathan*. The largest liner ever to carry the American flag, she was given a new start in life as a troop transport. On a shakedown cruise in her new role, to Guantanamo, Cuba, even more damage was uncovered. The ventilating system worked backwards, almost suffocating men in their bunks, among whom was a signalman by the name of Humphrey Bogart. But when the great ship was finally made habitable and sea-worthy, she carried more than 110,000 soldiers to Liverpool and Brest.

The other prodigy that sailed in all her *folie de grandeur* up the Narrows in 1914 was Cunard's *Aquitania*. "If the limit of any art exists," said one fatuous enthusiast, "it is nearly as possible attained in the *Aquitania*." With a well-placed lift from the publicity department, she was "the ship beautiful," and almost everything about her was as arty and slyly phony as that inverted description. The gin-palace pretensions of the ships of the middle of the nineteenth century seemed modest and very far away. The new mode was eclectic anonymity on the largest possible scale. Nothing was consistent, stylistically or historically, and the passengers themselves soon reflected the rampant confusion. Dress and deportment no longer distinguished aristocrats and scions of First Families from Hoi Polloi. When there was enough money in hand, appearance could quite easily be made to deceive. Said one bewildered but bemused traveler: "The woman whom we picked for Mrs. H. van Resselaer Somebody (traveling with two maids, two valets, a Pomeranian, one husband, and no children) proves to be a Broadway show-girl; and the one we dubbed a duchess, the proprietor of a Fifth Avenue frock-foundry. Show-girls, milliners, and dressmakers are very often the 'smart' people of the ship, and it must be regretfully admitted that duchesses too often fail to mark themselves by that arrogance and overdress which free-born American citizens have a right to expect of them."

A tendency toward *mélange* had become a principle. Sober enumerations of the ship's interior features turned inevitably into self-parody. "As regards the decorations," said an account in a shipbuilder's journal, "a faint echo only of Tudor times and the days of Hans Holbein will be found in some of the decorative details of the *Aquitania*. From this we pass to the days of Sir 'Anthonie' van Dyck and Inigo Jones, but the periods of domestic architecture and decorations most completely illustrated in the ship are those which lie between the Restoration of Charles II and the middle of the reign of George III. From the stern classic style of Inigo Jones, Christopher Wren, and the French masters who flourished in the early part of the reign of Louis the Magnificent, we pass gradually to the lighter motives of the Adams and Dances. Full justice is done to the Dutch influences which made themselves strongly felt towards the end of the 17th century. If the first thing which meets the eye on the grand staircase is a fine original example of Giovanni Antonio Pannini, conjuring up a pleasant visit to those picturesque Roman ruins he loved to paint, we are soon face to face with the carving of Grinling Gibbons, the portraits of Lely and Kneller, and the ironwork of Jean Trijou, who published his 'New Book of Drawings of Iron Work' in 1693, and did so much to beautify the 'palace of the gods' at Hampton Court. It need only be added here that the engraver's art has been as effectively illustrated in the decoration of the *Aquitania* as that of the painter, the sculptor, and the tapestry makers of Mortlake."

"You may," said one observer, "sleep in a bed depicting one ruler's fancy, breakfast under another dynasty altogether, lunch under a different flag and furniture scheme, play cards or smoke, or indulge in music under three other monarchs, have your afternoon cup of tea in a verandah which is essentially modern and cosmopolitan, and return to one of the historical periods experienced earlier in the day for your dinner in the evening at which meal, whatever may be the imperial style or the degree of Colonial simplicity, you will appear in very modern evening dress."

Nonetheless, passengers did try to live up to what ships expected of them—especially those to whom the manner of travel was an index to social position. This was the time, wrote Lucius Beebe, "when twenty pieces of hold luggage were an absolute basic minimum for social survival and when even a gentleman required a wardrobe or innovation trunk in the corridor outside his stateroom to hold the four changes of clothes he was expected to make daily on an eight-or-nine day passage. They went with valets and maids, hatboxes and shoe trunks, jewel cases, and in some fastidious instances, their own personal bed linen. Invalids brought their own doctors and nurses, dog lovers traveled with mastiffs and St. Bernards. Occasional magnificoes or eccentrics brought their own barbers, and food faddists carried their special rations of sanitized lettuce leaves or graham nut bread. The transatlantic entourage of a well-placed man or woman might well number half a dozen persons, while there was no limit at all to the number of secretaries and couriers that could be kept usefully at hand. Traveling was a ritual, mannered, planned, orderly, and a matter of massive logistics. Not the least of its details was that of money."

The *bon voyage* party was not only a sentimental ritual but a social occasion. To the luxuries awaiting the voyager on shipboard, friends added a surfeit of comestibles designed not so much to nourish him as to regale him. "Such a send-off," wrote a veteran traveler, "the most splendid we ever had—cream, butter, fresh eggs, fruit, candy, boxes of cake, boxes of biscuits, growing plants for turning one of our port-holes into a pretty window box; a pot of fifty growing tulips, which adorned our table in the dining room for the whole voyage, nineteen books from one friend—all carefully selected—and twelve others, separate gifts; a dainty little basket holding six spools of sewing silk and six spools of cotton, each threaded with six needlefuls. One sumptuous gilt basket had twelve little bottles, each containing a different kind of jam for breakfast; hung up between were little bags of choice tea, all ready for use, and on the top of this basket were what looked like bunches of grapes—each grape being really a delicious drop of candy— it was a fairy basket!"

Gradually, those sophisticated trippers who had been everywhere— twice—came to be joined by a new breed of traveler who, in a sense, would never go anywhere simply because he found no lack of advantage in where he was. This was the self-confident American yokel, the endearing ignoramus who, hearkening to the blast of the alpenhorn, had left his hay-and-feed business in Three Rivers, Michigan, to see more rarefied parts of the world. He, said Irvin S. Cobb, was the one "who would swap any Old Master he ever saw for one peep at a set of sanitary bath fixtures." Yet he was just as knowledgeable about ocean travel as the tycoon whose matched items of luggage from Louis Vuitton were piled up in pyramids at the customs sheds of Le Havre and Hoboken. "Yes, sir," said Mr. Cobb's voyager, "my idee is that a fellow ought to go over on an English ship, if he likes the exclusability, and come back on a German ship, if he likes the sociableness. Take my case. The last trip I made I come over on the *Lucy Tanner* and went back agin on the *Grocer K. First* and enjoyed it both ways immense."

To other naïfs, the sacerdotal trappings of the new ships were so edifying as to cause even hard-drinking men to behave themselves. "On the modern liner," said one virtuous soul, "it is the custom for men to put on their evening clothes at dinner time while the women array themselves in their most attractive costumes. Under these conditions there is no necessity for resorting to drink."

The last of the four-funneled ships, the *Aquitania* was also the last word and ultimate extension of a kind of interior decoration reflecting a way of life on which World War I would draw a curtain. Since acquisition defined wealth, nothing but accumulations of objects could assure a rich man that he was indeed rich. Artifacts of any worth were always identified with power. Consequently, styles evoking nostalgia for capitals of finance and seats of privilege, and any kind of emblem that suggested royalty, were subject to appropriation. The lunettes in the *Aquitania*'s first-class drawing room, for instance, were "made in the same way as the lead lights which were originally made by the Brothers Adam to be placed over the front door of many London houses in the neighbourhood of Portman Square."

The *Aquitania* also had the advantage of a crew trained—in a sort of father-to-son heritage of stewardship that marked whole families in Liverpool and Southampton—to give service on a scale of British tact, grace and professionalism that positively dizzied American travelers. "On shipboard," said Theodore Dreiser, "I noticed for the first time in my life that there was an aloofness about the service rendered by the servant which was entirely different from that which we know in America. They did not look at one so brutally and critically as does the American menial; their eyes did not seem to say, 'I am your equal or better,' and their motions did not indicate that they were doing anything unwillingly. In America—and I am a good American—I have always had the feeling that the American hotel or house servant or store clerk . . . was doing me a great favor if he did anything at all for me. However . . . when I went aboard the English ship . . . I felt this burden of a serfdom to the American servant lifted. These people . . . did not seem anxious to fight with me. They were actually civil. They did not stare me out of countenance; they did not order me gruffly about. Yes, and it was so in the dining-saloon, in the bath, on deck, everywhere, with 'yes, sirs,' and 'thank you, sirs' and two fingers raised to cap visors occasionally for good measure. Were they acting? Was this a fiercely suppressed class I was looking upon here? I could scarcely believe it. But as to manner: Heaven save the mark! These people are civil. They are nice. They are willing. 'Yes, sir! Thank you, sir! This way, sir! No trouble about that, sir! Certainly, sir! Very well, sir!' I heard these things on all sides and they were like balm to a fevered brain."

If money were no object, your accommodations on the *Aquitania* could be any one of a number of suites that took their aesthetic cue from the painters after whom they were named: Holbein, Gainsborough, Romney, Raeburn, Reynolds, Rembrandt, Van Dyck or Velasquez. You could begin your day with a plunge in the Pompeiian swimming bath, followed, if you liked, by a Turkish bath. "They are as comfortable as can be," said a votary. "The bather can perspire as happily and healthfully in one as the other, the attendant of either will liberate him spotlessly clean; the cooling room, where coffee and cigars will be enjoyed, will enable him to regain an agreeable temperature and catch no cold afterwards, and he will return to the company of his fellows immaculate physically and charmingly placid."

You might have your elevenses in the Garden Lounge where the decorative idea was to make you think that you were in an old English garden; the walls of the deckhouse on one side of the lounge had been tricked out to resemble stone covered with trellises. A close observer might in fact realize that he was in the midst of a history lesson as room by room told him the story of the British nation "from the far-off days when that 'goodlie ship the *Great Harry*' was one of the world's wonders down to the end of Europe's struggles for supremacy with Napoleon."

In a setting designed to give you the illusion that you were in a chamber of the Palace of Versailles looking onto the Park of the Grand Trianon—"the palace itself being visible in the distance through a colonnade of flower-decked Doric columns"—you could also study walls hung with blue tabourette silk to which were affixed the mezzotint portraits of eighteenth-century court favorites. Then you might wish to taper off with a cigar in the Carolean smoking room. Even if you were but an unlettered butter-and-egg man from the Oklahoma panhandle, you could be uplifted—because, as the publicity man put it, "the power of the *Aquitania*'s Smoking Room can be felt by the least erudite." If, on the other hand, you were already aware of the darker turns of ecclesiastical history, you might be enthralled, since the smoking room "is said to recall Jesuits whispering their 'dark secret of the warming pan'—dimly heard by 'men whose ears had been torn away by the hangman's blunted shears.'" In any case, you would be constantly assured that you were at sea in a rolling "Temple of Taste in general and Anglo-Saxon art in particular."

In 1914, along with the world to which it belonged, all this was wrapped up in tarpaulin and put away. When the *Aquitania* resumed her career in the sad years after the war, her pretensions were matters of only muted comedy and decadence.

Decadence in decor was a comparatively minor shame; but in an age that tended to go gaga over arrant assertions of wealth and to extend an easy tolerance to even the most craven displays of social preferment, decadence of ethics and humane concern was not a very pretty thing. Two years after the *Titanic* had gone down in a trumpet blast of thrilling publicity, more than a thousand souls were drowned in an accident hardly noted in the annals of maritime disasters and remembered, if at all, only with a yawn by those who tracked the corpse of John Jacob Astor from the grand saloon to the morgue.

No one had ever designated the *Empress of Ireland* a floating palace. Her passenger list when she left Quebec on the afternoon of May 28, 1914, could offer nothing better than the names of a lot of middle-class Anglo-Saxons and a long roster of Salvation Army officers and executives from one end of Canada to the other.

After she had dropped her pilot at Father Point that night, her Captain Kendall—the man who had nabbed Harvey Crippen at the very same place four years earlier—set his 15,000-ton ship on a course for the open sea. But fog rolled in and disaster struck in the form of a little Norwegian freighter named *Storstad* carrying 10,000 tons of coal from Sydney, Nova Scotia, to Montreal. The collision—still another one of those incidents in which everyone sees everything and does everything except the one thing that might have forestalled contact—left the *Empress* with a door-sized hole in her hull. More quickly than any other ship on record, she filled in less than fifteen minutes, turned over on her beam ends, and sank before her passengers could get into lifeboats or even onto her upper decks.

A commission of inquiry was shortly set up, an encyclopedia of details was sifted, but out of a tome of claims and counterclaims, only the evidence of the indomitable Captain Kendall got to the heart of the matter. When the *Storstad* had done what she could to save those aboard the *Empress* and the latter's Captain had been pulled aboard, he went onto the Norwegian's bridge, where the following exchange took place.

"Are you the captain of this ship?"

"Yes," said the Norwegian.

"You have sunk my ship," said Captain Kendall. "You were going full speed, and in that dense fog."

"I was not going full speed," said the Norwegian. "*You* were going full speed."

The whole incident, said the Commission of Inquiry, was a "great shock to the confidence which people were beginning to feel in the floating capacity of these large passenger ships."

The first salvos of World War I signaled the shrouding of the grand saloons, and a day-by-day peril for passenger-carrying ships that would deepen as the years of hostilities dragged on. Many of these ships would be torpedoed in encounters marked only by little black Xs on the maps of the North Atlantic and the South Atlantic. Others would be sabotaged, burned, or sunk in the course of tricky military assignments. Some would be interned and left to rust in coastal backwaters. Some would be transformed into troop transports or airplane carriers. Some would become floating hospitals, their glass-enclosed promenade decks transformed into airy hospital wards. In the *Aquitania*, for instance, white iron bedsteads would be ranged in rows across the length of the Adam Drawing Room. Wounded soldiers lying in traction could study the chimneypiece carved of statuary marble and the copy of a painting by Giovanni Cipriani that hung above it.

In the case of the Germans, the greatest of their ships would be claimed as prizes of war, or handed over to the enemy as part of war reparations. From the point of view of steamship development and its social ramifications, the war provided a great lacuna that lasted for nearly six years, followed by another six years when the steamship business could make only faltering efforts to find its way back to prosperity. The most eventful days for the ships of the great international fleet of Atlantic carriers were the very first after the resounding incident at Sarajevo.

❧ SECTION IX ❧

The Kronprinzessin Cecilie *Turns About / Fiddler's Green,
Maine / Sojourn at Bar Harbor: "Has a German Skipper
Turned Jules Verne?" / Captain Polack and the Social
Whirl / Germans in Night School*

DER *Doppelschrauben Schnelldampfer Kronprinzessin Cecilie,*
loaded with about eleven million dollars' worth of gold
and silver bullion and more than one thousand passengers,
was halfway to Plymouth, en route to Bremerhaven. On the night of
July 31, 1914, the man on duty in the little shack on deck that housed
the wireless was subjected to an intense crackling on his earset. "Urgent
and Confidential . . . Urgent and Confidential," followed by a message
addressed to the ship's captain: "Erhard has suffered attack of catarrh
of the bladder. Siegfried." The Marconi man at once took this message
to the bridge. Captain Polack—"our precious Polack" to many Americans who had known him since the days, twenty years before, when he
was Second Officer on the *Spree*—recognized it as instructions in code
—a code he had months before been supplied with the means to de-
cipher.

The burden of the message was twofold: war was about to be declared
between the Central and Allied Powers; the Captain was to take every
precaution to prevent the capture of his ship by the British. He ordered
the course of the *Kronprinzessin Cecilie* to be reversed, then gravely

descended to the grand saloon that was ornamented with paintings representing "ideal" landscapes—motifs from the gardens of the Italian Renaissance palaces of Lante, Farnese, Palmieri, Gorgoni, Albani, Doria, Borghese and d'Este, and from the Vatican gardens. He silenced an orchestra playing for an after dinner dance, and summoned a few socially prominent individuals among the passengers to join him in that "acme of cosiness," the *Rauchzimmer*. There, as the Welte-Mignon player piano waited for someone to pump out *The Whistler and His Dog* or *The Skater's Waltz*, the chosen few lit cigars beneath busts of Silenus, Apollo and Minerva. "Gentlemen," said the Captain, "it is my duty to inform you that I have orders from the Imperial German Government to take this ship to a neutral port in the United States."

In no time at all the word had spread to the Vienna Café (where a single *à-la-carte* meal cost just about as much as a steerage passage ticket for the whole crossing), to the wind shelters on deck, "an ingenious invention of Director von Helmholt, of Bremen, which has been patented in all civilized states," to the Imperial Suites with their dining and drawing rooms, to the nether regions of the ship where hearty German-Americans played cards in the dim light of barren lounges or slept off big dinners in their iron bunks. In spite of general consternation and disbelief, any one with an eye to see could tell that the backtracking of the great liner was already *fait accompli*: the moon that had lately shone on the starboard was now coldly eyeing the port.

Captain Polack, assuring his passengers that their ship had ample fuel and food to bring them safely into port, asked them "to keep their heads." Most passengers accepted the circumstance, since there was nothing else to be done anyway. But for men of affairs dismay was unrelieved. Among the first-class passengers were American executives on financial missions, United States senators en route to an international conference, a large shooting party on the way to Scotland for the grouse. The most affluent of these got together and made up a purse. Then, ready to plunk their cash on the barrel head, they went to Captain Polack. If he would replace the German Imperial standard with the American flag, they said—and thus proceed in safety right under the bowsprits of the British Royal Navy—they would pay five million dollars for the ship and throw in a hefty bonus for the Captain himself. The Captain refused to be rescued by these Yankee plutocrats. He thanked them, had his ship's name blacked out, ordered black bands to be painted around the tops of her four yellowish funnels, and proceeded to carry out the instructions he had received from Berlin. His notion was to make his ship look, at least at a distance, like the four-funneled *Olympic.*

In this naïve disguise (almost everyone knew that funnels on German ships were placed in double pairs instead of equidistant, as on the British liners), the *Kronprinzessin* sped for the nearest American port. This, of all places, turned out to be Bar Harbor—and at the very *height* of the season. The breakneck pace of the ship through fog and black of night made some passengers uneasy, some panicky. They chose a delegation and sent it to the Captain begging him to slow down. But his only concession to their fears was a more liberal use of his foghorn. He knew what passengers did not: the French liner *La Savoie,* having discovered his position, had alerted the several French and British warships that were in a position to intercept the *Cecilie* and lay claim to her treasure trove. Three nights after the dramatic turnabout, her portholes covered over with canvas, not a gleam of light along her length, the big ship, guided by the American yachtsman C. Ledyard Blair standing at the Captain's side, moseyed into Frenchman's Bay and shut off her engines. A few hours later, early risers among the summer people looked out of their windows. There, riding at anchor among their own little flotilla of yachts and sailboats and Old Town canoes, they saw what most of them took to be the great *Olympic,* sister ship of the *Titanic.*

The *Kronprinzessin* had "dropped her starboard anchor in the inner harbor about midway between the steamboat wharves and the Porcupines," said a local reporter. "The telephone operators were soon aware of her presence, and those early upon the streets became excited as they learned of the presence here of the big German ship, and spread the news. By the middle of the forenoon the shore path was well covered with people and the boat ships did a big business taking people out and back." By the time the resort had learned that its own gilt and wicker environs had provided safe haven for what the newspapers termed "the German gold ship," it had also learned of the unexpected return of two of its very own: Mrs. A. Howard Hinkle and her daughter, of Cincinnati, who were summer residents in one of Bar Harbor's big villas, did not disembark in Plymouth, England, but in their own back yard.

Faced with the option of internment in New England or capture by the British destroyers that were already hungrily cruising just beyond the International Limit, Captain Polack chose to stay for the season. Bar Harbor suddenly became Fiddler's Green. (A good number of the resort's summer people knew the Captain—"a moustachioed giant, over six feet tall" of "urbane charm and social graces"—because they had crossed on ships under his command.) The United States Coast Guard cutter *Androscoggin* had meanwhile sidled up to the *Kronprinzessin* and relieved her of her king's ransom in gold and silver bars. Special trains carried the bullion back to the vaults of New York's Guaranty Trust Company and the National Trust Company, from which, barely a week before, it had been removed for shipment to Germany.

Americans were still far enough away from the war and partisan emotions to see the whole thing as a great sport. "Has a German skipper turned Jules Verne?" asked a columnist. "While the Pierre Lotis and the Joseph Conrads of literature compose dashing sea yarns with a pen, Captain Polack is penning his adventure with an ocean leviathan, to accessories of wireless, gun play, fog and foreign war. We figured that he was somewhere off the Pentland Firth . . . and he pushes his huge bow past the Porpoises into Frenchman's Bay. All the elements of the popular novel are in the exploit: international complications; hostile cruisers in pursuit; a huge treasure of gold bullion in the hold; the mystery of fog; the uncertain effects of wireless communication; a group of American financiers in the smoking-room able and willing to buy the five-million-dollar craft in order that they might go where they pleased. The thing has a lordly sound. It has stupendous humor. A transatlantic chase in fog for a 15-million-dollar international stake. Here is a sporting event for money kings. . . . The *Cecilie* is safe until further notice. She is there, behind the spruce-bristled, granite-backed Porpoises, and to have put her there, Captain Polack, is something of a prodigious stunt. . . . Who told her she might carry people from New York to Bar Harbor? What ruinous competition with the Eastern Steamship Company!"

So began the love fest of Bar Harbor and its German guests. Captain Polack and his officers became part of a summer's social whirl that saw them kissing the hands of hostesses at lawn parties, dancing at balls, going out on fishing and lobstering expeditions and sailing parties. A local man hired the Star movie theater to entertain the *Kronprinzessin*'s crew; the ship's band gave concerts on the Village Green. Of the first of these the *Bar Harbor Record* reported: "A large crowd assembled to hear the music and showed their appreciation by their applause, which in itself is most unusual for a crowd in Bar Harbor. For the last piece the band played *America*. This called for cheers and the blowing of horns by the large number of automobiles which had gathered to hear the music. The band then played *Watch on the Rhine*, which was so well received the crowd demanded an encore."

But soon upon these revels fell the shadow of the long arm of the law. Annoyed by the failure of the *Kronprinzessin* to deliver their gold bullion to Plymouth, the bankers concerned sued the North German Lloyd Steamship Company for damages in the amount of 1,040,467 dollars, plus interest. When this action was brought in the Bar Harbor Federal Court, doughty Deputy Marshal Eugene C. Harmon, according to the local paper, "left at noon to seize the ship." And he did.

Watched day and night by the cutter *Mohawk* and a torpedo boat, caught in the custodial web of the United States Marshal for Maine, the great ship lay swinging at anchor late into the fall. With the approach of winter and the possible threat of ice damage, not only Captain Polack but also his legal guardians were concerned to have the ship moved to a less hazardous anchorage. When a rumor that the *Kronprinzessin* might be taken to Portland was spread about, Bar Harbor was both angry and sad. The "ice charge" made its citizens furious; the possible loss of the ship made them prematurely nostalgic. "The streets of the town have been made interesting by the presence of the officers and the crew of the big liner," said *The Record*, "and Captain Polack has been the recipient of many social courtesies and has proven to be a most delightful gentleman as well as the notable and exceedingly efficient navigator he is known to be. Bar Harbor citizens have hoped that the big liner would stay here until the conclusion of the big European war, for business and social reasons."

But the rumors of removal were well founded. "The complication of moving the *Kronprinzessin Cecilie* is less military than legal," said the Boston *Transcript*. "The navigation problem is not insuperable. The course suggested by local pilots would be outside of the Cranberry Isles and Isle au Haute off Penobscot Bay, to Matinicus, passing either inside or outside of that rockpile; thence to Monhegan keeping preferably to eastward of it . . . and from Monhegan to Portland Head."

When Captain Polack heard of this devious coastal voyage so gratuitously planned for him, he was appalled. The *Kronprinzessin*, he said, "was not a canoe."

The problem was not resolved until the Captain himself went to Washington to confer with the Acting Secretary of the Navy, Franklin D. Roosevelt. There it was decided that the ship should be guided to Boston by destroyers. Dogged by British cruisers still patrolling off shore, the ship was towed to Boston for safe keeping, in mid-November. There she was interned afloat in President Roads, just off Shirley Point and Deer Island, between the German ships *Köln* and *Ockenfels*. "Now that the Bar Harbor season is over," said a pundit, "perhaps the *Cecilie* would enjoy Palm Beach." But Boston would have to do. "You know," said Captain Polack to a group of Hub reporters as he pointed to his heart, "down here I am glad that I am in Boston. It was getting to be cold and lonesome at Bar Harbor."

Members of the *Cecilie*'s crew were allowed to go off now and then on fishing expeditions, and before long some of them were attending Boston night schools, taking books out of the Boston Public Library, and being otherwise swept up into the cultural climate of the Hub of the Universe. But when the United States entered the war, their ship was overhauled and converted into a troop transport. With most of her Teutonic features obliterated, the long lean *Kronprinzessin Cecilie* became the good old S.S. *Mount Vernon*. Soon newspaper photographs would show her decks packed with doughboys grinning under the Stars and Stripes as they set off for the mud of France and the task of making the world safe for democracy.

❦ SECTION X ❧

S.S. Carmania: *The Pretty Sister Slugs It Out / Encounter off Trinidad Island / A Good Fight / Return to the Luxury Trade*

O NE FACTUALLY grim but unavoidably amusing episode of the war at sea was a vicious little eighty-minute blast of mutual attrition that saw two great passenger liners slugging it out to the death, while flying fish went scudding all about them in the shiny waters of the South Atlantic.

Like all of the Cunard ships, the eleven-year-old *Carmania* was still subject to the agreement made in 1903 when the British Government rescued the company from the apish paws of J. P. Morgan. This meant that, in the event of hostilities, the Government had the right to commandeer any part of the Cunard fleet for military purposes. The *Carmania* was docked in Manhattan when the several nations made their declarations of war. But not even a continent in flames could interrupt her heavily booked summer schedule, and she faithfully sailed back to Liverpool on the preappointed date. There she was greeted by men from the Government who had big plans for her. They watched over her as she discharged her dauntless American passengers to their summer holidays in Europe, then ordered gangs of workmen to board her and to set to work. They painted her hull black and her Cunard-red funnels a military gray; they riveted armored plate onto all of her most vulnerable parts, packed her decks with "protection" coal and bags of sand, removed the scrolled woodwork from her passenger quarters and installed emplacements to hold eight 4.7-inch-caliber guns with a firing range calculated at about 9,300 yards.

Transformed in the space of a week, the *Carmania* was no longer one of "the pretty sisters," but a big drab cruiser, decks cleared of wicker and tea trays, waiting for a kind of action that had nothing to do with the click of the discs used in shuffleboard. At first the Admiralty ordered her on an inspection trip—to look over merchant shipping in the Irish Channel, get used to her role as protector, and perhaps find occasion to become a pursuer. Then she was to proceed at full steam across the ocean to Halifax for patrol duty. But, one day out, she received countermanding orders: proceed directly to Bermuda. She arrived there on August 23 and took on coal while her officers and men went shopping in Hamilton for clothing that would keep them comfortable in the tropics. Five days later she headed southward to join a British squadron under Admiral Craddock that was searching the coastal waters and river mouths of Venezuela in an attempt to flush the German cruisers *Dresden* and *Karlsruhe* out of their supposed hiding places.

But almost as soon as she had joined this squadron she was detached from it in order to pursue a mission quite on her own. Correctly, as it would soon appear, the British Admiralty suspected that the German Navy had established a number of secret depots in the South Atlantic where colliers from Europe could rendezvous with the German sea raiders. One of the most obvious places for such meetings, they figured, was Trinidad (not to be confused with Trinidad in the West Indies), some seven hundred miles east of Brazil, a barren volcanic island four miles long and two miles wide with a nicely protected anchorage on its southwest side. When the *Carmania* arrived off Trinidad one bright morning and coasted around Nine-Pin Peak, her officers, lifting their binoculars, saw just what they were looking for: a ship as big as their own, quietly riding at anchor while two small ships, all derricks up, busily filled her bunkers with coal.

This was the *Cap Trafalgar*, the finest liner on Hamburg-Amerika's South American run. Far grander in the matter of palm gardens and suites *de luxe* than the *Carmania*, and considerably newer, she had been a cruiser for hardly two weeks. Docked in the River Plate when war was declared, she had made a successful run for it and rendezvoused with a German gunboat from South Africa that supplied her with officers and armament. Then, quite like the *Carmania*, she had immediately started looking for enemy ships to sink—in the natural expectation that any she might find would be far smaller and more vulnerable than herself.

Almost as soon as she was spotted, on the morning of September 14, the *Cap Trafalgar* put up steam, indicating to the *Carmania*'s officers that she was aware of being observed and that she was getting ready for whatever the encounter might lead to. The *Carmania*'s commander thought that the ship in view was North German Lloyd's *Berlin*. His mistake was explicable: while the *Cap Trafalgar* was known to have three funnels, one of these—a dummy ventilator—had been jettisoned when the ship cleared Montevideo. The *Cap Trafalgar*'s captain, on the other hand, knew exactly who the British ship was and that she was far bigger game than anything he had ever expected to meet in the remote waters of Trinidad Island. As the two erstwhile floating palaces looked each other over through telescopes and glasses, they could see that they were more or less the same size, wore the same hastily assumed disguises, and guessed that they were about evenly matched in the matter of speed and perhaps of armament. "It promised," said a British chronicler, "to be an equal fight, and in preparation for it dinner was ordered for all hands that could be excused duty, for the hour of 11:30, in accordance with the old naval principle—food before fighting."

In a brief ballet of chivalric thrusts and maneuvers that seem hardly credible in the century of total war, the two ships moved almost merrily toward the fray, guns up and banners flying. The *Carmania*'s ensigns flew from both the flagstaff aft and the masthead. The *Cap Trafalgar* ran up the white flag with the black cross of the German Navy. As if to throw down the gauntlet, the *Carmania* fired a shot across the *Cap Trafalgar*'s bows. The German ship replied in kind and the battle was joined. Within minutes, both were on fire, paint began to flake from blistered gun emplacements, and both began to list. As the two ships closed in, the Germans brought out machine guns and raked the *Carmania*'s open decks. The British plugged away at the *Cap Trafalgar*'s waterline as if it were a jugular vein. German shells demolished the *Carmania*'s bridge, rendered almost all of her controls inactive and penetrated her side seventy-nine times. As bucket brigades were attempting to dampen down the worst fires on the decks of the British ship, the *Cap Trafalgar* suddenly veered to port and started for shore. Her list had increased steeply, her boats were being swung out, yet she kept on going, perhaps with the idea of beaching herself. "More and more," said an eyewitness, "the big liner fell over until at last her funnels lay upon the water, and then, after a moment's apparent hesitation, with her bow submerged, she heaved herself upright and sank bodily. It had been a good fight and she had fought honourably to the end and gone down with her ensign flying, and when, as she vanished, the men of the *Carmania* raised a cheer, it was hardly less for their own victory as a tribute to the enemy."

These manly cheers were still ringing when a blazon of black smoke on the northern horizon stopped them cold: an enormous ship with four funnels and scowling like a bear was pounding down on the battered *Carmania*. This was the great *Kronprinz Wilhelm,* the terror of the Southern Seas. Alerted by signals of SOS from the *Cap Trafalgar* —the first of which advised of her engagement with the *Carmania,* the second reporting that her fires were out of control—the *Kronprinz* had answered the call to rush to longitude 35 degrees west, latitude 26 degrees south. But when the calls for help had suddenly ceased, the commander of the *Kronprinz* drew his own conclusions. (He had meanwhile come close enough to be sighted by the *Carmania.*) Wary of steaming into an area that might very likely be infested with British cruisers, he turned about and steamed away. Racked, limping and still afire, the *Carmania* was herself choosing the better part of valor by trying to get lost. During the night, her crew rigged up an emergency wireless with signals strong enough to reach the cruiser *Bristol.* The warship came alongside the *Carmania* next morning, and doused her stubborn fires with powerful hoses. Then the cruiser *Cromwell* also arrived on the scene. Using both ships as floating chandlers, the *Carmania* borrowed enough navigating gear and patches of sorts to enable her to make Pernambuco, Brazil, under the escort of the auxiliary liner *Macedonia.* There she was repaired sufficiently to allow her to venture an Atlantic crossing.

Rehabilitated in Gibraltar, she was returned to service within two months. When she had survived the dangerous years that saw nearly all of her sister ships heeling over with great wounds in their sides and sinking out of sight, the *Carmania* washed off her war paint, took back her potted palm trees, her snow-white napery and her apricot-colored plush, and sailed unflustered back and forth across the Atlantic. Among her cozy clientele, who would have guessed she was the same ship that, riddled like a sieve, had fought her way out of a Gilbert and Sullivan gunfight in an obscure corner of the horse latitudes?

❈ SECTION XI ❈

May 7, 1915: "Mein Gott, Es Ist die Lusitania!" / *The Warning in the Paper* / *Alfred Gwynne Vanderbilt and Shipmates* / *The Outline of a Torpedo* / Unterseeboot-20 / *Divergent Opinions The Claims against Cunard* / *The Eloquence of Consul Frost* / *An Embarrassment of Coffins*

THE OUTBREAK of war changed at once the natures, the careers and the destinies of nearly all of the great passenger liners. Some were reconverted, some interned, some sent flaming into the deep. But one of the proudest of them all, the *Lusitania*, kept to her purpose of serving passengers on the Great Circle route. Punctual and courageous, she had learned to be chary. Only a few hours after she sailed from New York on August 4, 1914, a malfunction in one of her turbines was discovered. Just as her engineers were trying to correct this, the lookout in the forecastle sighted an enemy warship, obviously aware of her sailing time and lying in wait. The *Lusitania's* captain, changing course at once, asked the British cruiser *Essex* "to come to us quick," then steered his ship northward until she was able to slip into a fog bank and drift about unseen. When the threat seemed to be over, she steamed north at the best speed she could get up, traveled in a state of blackout every night, and reached Liverpool after a slow passage of nearly eight days.

A few months later, as the *Lusitania* was approaching Ireland en route to her home port, her captain was warned by wireless that the

Irish Sea was infested with undersea raiders and told to hoist the flag of some neutral country. This *ruse de guerre* must have seemed childish to the captain, or to anybody else, but he had no choice but to follow instructions. Since his ship was carrying tons of United States mail and four hundred American citizens, he decided that the flag best suiting his purposes was the American. Thus, disguised as an American passenger liner when there was no remotely comparable ship in the registry, the greatest of British ships rushed full steam across the Irish Sea, refused to stop even to take on a pilot, and shot into the Mersey as if pursued by a bear. Only then were the Stars and Stripes lowered down and folded away.

Theoretically, the *Lusitania* could outrun any submarine bold enough to come near. Yet, to save coal and labor costs on wartime passages—seldom were more than half of the ship's available berths occupied—her owners had ordered a drastic reduction of power. Six of her boilers had been shut down, leaving her with a maximum speed of 21 knots. This meant that she was still the fastest passenger ship anywhere and, supposedly, speedy enough to outrun all attackers on the water or under it. This may have been so. But in the sad event, taken unawares and sitting, big as a house, in the eye of a periscope, she never got the chance.

Most of the embarking passengers who came crowding onto the Cunard Line pier on May 1, 1915, had seen the warning placed in the morning's papers. "NOTICE! Travellers intending to embark on the Atlantic voyage are reminded that a state of war exists between Germany and her allies and Great Britain and her allies; that the zone of war includes the waters adjacent to the British Isles; that, in accordance with formal notice given by the Imperial German Government, vessels flying the flag of Great Britain, or of any of her allies, are liable to destruction in those waters and that travellers sailing in the war zone on ships of Great Britain or her allies do so at their own risk. Imperial German Embassy. Washington, D.C., April 22, 1915." This statement had actually been in the hands of the German Ambassador, Count Johann von Bernstorff, for more than a week. But he was somehow annoyed by the way it was phrased. Instead of releasing it to the press at once, he simply put the cablegram in a desk drawer "and hoped that Berlin would forget about it." Then, on April 30, he got another cable from the German War Office. Had he received the notice? Had he published it? In any case, the new message implied, the warning should be made public at once. Ambassador von Bernstorff thought it advisable to have the notice appear as a paid advertisement inserted in the regular shipping columns where people intending to travel would be most apt to read it.

Appearing at the last minute, so to speak, the notice did not have much immediate effect on the *Lusitania's* passenger list. A few people, taking the warning to heart, canceled their bookings. A few others decided they would transfer to an American Line ship—the illustrious old *New York*, scheduled to sail only a few hours later than the *Lusitania*, with Ellen Terry and Isadora Duncan among her passengers. But most of them stayed with plans made many months earlier; the wild notion that peaceable travelers might be "liable to destruction" added up to a very remote threat indeed.

One durable legend generated by the fame of the *Titanic* was the belief that first-class accommodations on Atlantic liners were reserved for human paragons—conspicuously philanthropic multimillionaires, gentle merchant princes, doughty dowagers from Denver, large-mannered men privy to the councils of state. Notions like this were still current when the *Lusitania* cast off her ropes and backed out into the North River on the first of May, 1915. But measured by the grandeur of *Titanic* standards, or even matched against almost any crack liner's passenger list, the crowd on the *Lusitania* comprised a fairly scruffy lot.

An exception was Alfred Gwynne Vanderbilt, thirty-seven years old and the scion of his family. His distinction, financially and socially, was absolute—a fact that not even a divorce and a second marriage had tarnished. In England, where he maintained a great house, Vanderbilt had a few years earlier done much to revive the sport of road-coaching by taking his famous drags "Viking" and "Venture" across the ocean to show them off as he was used to doing in clopping sweeps down the length of Fifth Avenue. "They knew him well on the Brighton Road," said a contemporary, "and children and their mothers were always sure of a salute and a smile as the coach rumbled past." While most of the voyagers were bent on business errands from which even the jeopardies of wartime could not dissuade them, Vanderbilt, accompanied only by his valet, was going over to England simply to talk to some men about a horse show.

Other famous and affluent individuals aboard were not so much representatives of American culture as they were purveyors of the commercial seam of it: Charles Klein, a playwright who had given the world "The Music Master," "The Lion and the Mouse" and "The Third Degree," was working on a new comedy to be entitled "Potash and Perlmutter in Society"; Charles Frohman, known as "The Colossus of the Theatre" because his influence straddled the show shops of Times Square and those of Shaftesbury Avenue, was going to London to see "Rosy Rapture," the new James M. Barrie play he had himself produced, and to look about for theatrical offerings he might import to Broadway; Elbert Hubbard, the yokel philosopher from East Aurora, New York, author of many books on the order of *Little Journeys to the Homes of Great Business Men* and of the inspirational "A Message to Garcia" (40 million copies sold, its words already bouncing off the auditorium walls of every high school in America), was determined to see the war close up. He wanted to make reports from on the spot, to store experience, he said, "in my bean," and in that way elude the censor and so be able to give it to his readers straight. He even had in mind to get to the Kaiser himself. "If," he said, chewing on an apple in his stateroom, "the Emperor won't see me in Berlin, I'll be patient a while and see him later in St. Helena."

The most notable Britons aboard were the Welsh coal magnate and politician, D. A. Thomas, and his daughter, Lady Mackworth, who was a militant suffragette. But most of the *Lusitania's* passengers belonged to the well-scrubbed lower middle-class—sober citizens whose lives had been changed or interrupted by the war and who had undertaken the voyage in a personal attempt to bring things back to normal. In the third class there were a number of returning emigrants, many Irish and English servant girls going home to see their families, and an excitable group of Persians from Chicago who were on their way to the scenes of Turkish massacres in the hope that they might learn something of the fate of missing relatives. The general run of passengers was British, well behaved, committed to the ordeal of pilgrimage and not the pleasures of holiday.

Everyone knew that the sinking of the *Titanic* had caused whole new systems of safety precautions to be installed in all the big ships, including the one they were on. It was presumed that the *Lusitania* now had lifeboats ample for all emergencies, watertight bulkheads that would not, should the ship go badly off keel, spill over one into the other. Unike other British ships, she had not been commandeered into military service. While she was under the close direction of the Admiralty, she sailed in the noncombatant status of a reserve ship. All this made for comforting assurances; and most people also knew that the *Lusitania* operated within the law of nations, even nations at war, which stated that a ship could not be sunk without warning and removal of its civilian passengers. And they knew that, in ten months of hostilities at sea, this humane policy had been observed. Safety considerations aside, who would want to travel on the superannuated *New York*, or any other little slowpoke of a liner when the grand *Lusitania* was available to him?

The voyage up the Great Circle was all but routine. There was fog off the Grand Banks. Some of the passengers who knew the ship's potential speed wondered why she was so sluggish. A few others, moved to action by considerable talk about submarines and discussions about the German Embassy's notice and whether or not it was merely a bluff, went to Captain William Thomas Turner to suggest that it might be advisable to hold a proper boat drill—one that would include passengers and a lowering of boats instead of the desultory assemblies on deck of a few crewmen that had been taking place. But the captain was not responsive to their suggestion. The safety of the *Lusitania*, he told them, lay wholly in her speed. After all, the best a U-boat could do was about 9 knots submerged, 15 on the surface. Nevertheless, he did on Thursday morning take the precaution of seeing that twenty-two lifeboats, eleven on each side of the ship, were swung out and their tarpaulin covers removed.

Passengers on the *Lusitania* did not know that twelve allied ships had been sunk by U-boats in the time it had taken their ship to get to its present position off the Irish coast, in sight of the famous Old Head of Kinsale. But the Admiralty did know. On the evening of May 6, a message bristling with concern was dispatched to the *Lusitania*: "Take Liverpool pilot at bar and avoid headlands. Pass harbors at full speed. Steer midchannel course. Submarines off Fastnet." As Captain Turner was reading this, Parry Jones the Welsh tenor and a group of his compatriots were holding their own *esteddfod* as an entertainment for first-class passengers in the grand saloon. Their task was not easy: the *Lusitania*'s travelers had much on their minds and "sociability . . . had been conspicuously absent during the past week of the voyage."

But lunch next day was uncommonly animated. New costumes to disembark in had been broken out; the buzz of imminent arrival was accompanied by a lilting rendition of "The Blue Danube." Everyone was relieved and delighted to have land actually in sight.

"I had just finished a run on deck," said James Brooks, a businessman from Bridgeport, Connecticut, "when I glanced out over the water. It was perfectly smooth. My eyes alighted on a white streak making its way with lightning-like rapidity towards the ship. I was so high in that position above the surface of the water that I could make out the outline of a torpedo. It appeared to be about twelve feet long, and came along possibly three feet below the surface, its sides white with bubbles of foam. I watched its passage, fascinated, until it passed out of sight behind the bridge, and in another moment came the explosion. The ship, recoiling under the force of the blow, was jarred and lifted, as if it had struck an immovable object. A column of water shot up to the bridge deck, carrying with it a lot of debris, and, despite the fact that I must have been twenty yards from the spot at which the torpedo struck, I was knocked off my feet. Before I could recover myself, the iron forepart of the ship was enveloped in a blinding cloud of steam, due, not, I think, to the explosion of a second torpedo, as some thought, but to the fact that the two forward boilers had been jammed close together and 'jacknifed' upwards. . . . We had been in sight of land for some time, and the head of the ship, which had already begun to settle, was turned toward the Old Head of Kinsale."

Oliver Bernard, a scenic artist returning to his job at London's Covent Garden Theatre after a period of residence with the Boston Opera House, also witnessed the attack. "I saw the periscope of a submarine about two hundred yards away," he said. "Then I noticed a long white streak of foam. A woman and two men came up to me and exclaimed 'Is that a torpedo?' I felt too sick to answer and turned away, knowing too well that it was a torpedo. When the torpedo came within a yard or two I covered my eyes and corked my ears as I did not want to hear the explosion. Almost immediately there was a violent impact followed by the explosion. Fragments of material, dust, and water shot up in a great column. A few moments after the explosion the vessel toppled over, and I was flung against the starboard rail. I then made for the funnel deck, and the last person I noticed particularly, because of his demeanour, was Mr. Alfred Vanderbilt. He looked quite happy and perfectly composed. He was chatting to a friend. In his right hand he held a purple leather jewel case."

"He stood there," said still another shipmate of Vanderbilt's, "the personification of sportsmanlike coolness. In my eyes he was the figure of a gentleman waiting for a train." In the view of his contemporaries, a rich man had once more demonstrated the superiority that was a kind of moral adjunct to the possession of hard cash. While Vanderbilt was the paragon, he was not alone. "Actuated by a less acute fear or by a higher degree of bravery which the high-bred man seems to feel in moments of danger," said an observer, "the men of wealth and position for the most part hung back while others rushed for the boats."

The suddenness of the attack had brought the *Lusitania's* company to a state described by Hanson Baldwin as not so much fear as "that mental and sensory narcosis which so often precedes the first sharp stab of pain or realization." A mere 290 pounds of an explosive called trotyl, packed into one torpedo, had blown open the ship's hull to a breadth of thirty or forty feet, a height of ten or fifteen feet. In barely twenty minutes, with a dip of her schooner bow that lifted her enormous black stern and her four propellors high in the air, with "a thunderous roar as of the collapse of a great building during a fire," the *Lusitania* plunged out of sight in 360 feet of water—a depth that was, curiously, less than half the length of her. Hundreds of passengers caught inside the ship were pulled down with her; hundreds of others were crushed or suffocated in the roiling waters where she disappeared. "Not only were the boats undermanned before being lowered," said an irate survivor, "but the equipment itself was faulty. The raft I was on leaked and the collapsible boats had rusty, unworkable hinges, a matter that could have been remedied by oiling once in a fortnight. If the members of the crew got their deserts the stewards would be praised to Heaven and the stokers would be damned to hell."

In moments, the whole watery area "was a boiling wilderness that rose up as if a volcanic disturbance had occurred beneath a placid sea." In some places pieces of wreckage were clotted so thickly together "as to form an undulating horrible mattress of deck chairs, oars, boxes and human heads." It would be months before a figure could be posted, but the number of persons lost would finally be fixed at 1,198. And for years, the almost instantaneous foundering of a ship equipped with watertight compartments and every ingenious device for remaining afloat would continue to puzzle seamen. "Why," asked one of them, "if struck in the after boiler-room and with the engine room flooded, did the ship sink by the head, and why, with her very complete subdivision, did she sink in 20 minutes—indeed, why did she sink at all?"

The overarching significance of the *Lusitania,* as it turned out, lay not merely in casualty figures but in the graphic demonstration of "Hunnish brutality," "Teutonic bestiality" and "Prussian barbarism" that her sinking provided. In the ferocity of the propaganda that ensued, the event itself tended to dwindle as a human catastrophe and to expand out of all proportion as an instance of criminal depravity. No matter what would be made of it, the event was a wartime encounter between ships and men of belligerent nations. Each in his own routine way was "honorably" following a course that had been assigned to him.

Kapitanleutnant Walther Schwieger, for instance—who was already well on his way toward the achievement of sinking the 190,000 tons of Allied shipping with which the record books would credit him. A well-educated man in his early thirties, unmarried, the Kapitanleutnant came from a cultured family of Berliners and was noted for having "in the highest degree the gifts of poise and urbane courtesy." As one of his naval colleagues described him, "he was tall, broad-shouldered, and of a distinguished bearing, with well-cut features, blue eyes and blond hair—a particularly fine-looking fellow. He was the soul of kindness toward the officers and men under him. His temperament was joyous and his talk full of gaiety and pointed wit."

As commander of the *Unterseeboot-20,* the Kapitanleutnant kept a meticulous log book. Entries for the first week of May, 1915, indicated that the hunting off the southeast coast of Ireland was good; three merchant freighters in a row had been torpedoed and sunk. Now, on the afternoon of May 7, he had still another success to record.

"2:20 P.M. Directly in front of us I sight four funnels and masts of a steamer at right angles to our course, coming from south-southwest and going toward Galley Head. It is recognized as a passenger steamer. 2:25 P.M. Have advanced 11 metres toward steamer, in hope it will change course. . . . 2:35 P.M. Steamer turns, takes direction to Queens-town. We proceed at high speed in order to reach correct position. 3:10 P.M. Torpedo shot at distance of 700 metres. Hits steering center aft of bridge. Unusually great detonation with large cloud of smoke and debris hot above funnels. In addition to torpedo, a second explosion must have taken place. (Boiler, coal, or powder?) The ship stops . . . leans to starboard, at the same time sinking at the bow. It looks as though she would capsize in a short time. There is great confusion on board. Boats are cleared and many of them lowered into the water bow-

or stern-first and capsize. At the bow of the ship can be seen the name *Lusitania. . . ."*

Years later, when Schwieger gave his own unofficial eyewitness account of what happened on that Friday afternoon in May, the mad-dog rapacities of more colorful accounts had already accomplished what they were intended for, and the long war was over. "We had started back for Wilhelmshaven," said Schwieger, "and were drawing near the Channel. There was a heavy sea and a thick fog, with small chance of sinking anything. At the same time, a destroyer steaming through the fog might stumble over us before we knew anything about it. So I submerged to twenty metres, below periscope depth. About an hour and a half later I heard the sound of powerful screws—not the propellers of a destroyer. I went up to ten metres and took a look through the periscope. I saw a big armored cruiser. It had passed right over us and was now disappearing at full speed.

"After I was through swearing, I noticed that the fog was lifting. Presently I could see blue sky. I brought the boat to the surface, and we continued our course above water. A few minutes after we emerged I sighted on the horizon a forest of masts and stacks. At first I thought they must belong to several ships. Then I saw it was a great steamer coming over the horizon. It was coming our way. I dived at once, hoping to get a shot at it.

"When the steamer was two miles away it changed its course. I had no hope now, even if we hurried at our best speed, of getting near enough to attack her. I called my pilot, an old-time captain of the merchant marine, to take a look at her through the periscope. At that instant, while he was coming in answer to my call, I saw the steamer change her course again. She was coming directly at us. She could not have steered a more perfect course if she had deliberately tried to give us a dead shot. A short fast run, and we waited.

"I had already shot away my best torpedoes and had left only two bronze ones—not so good. The steamer was four hundred yards away when I gave an order to fire. The torpedo hit, and there was rather a small detonation and instantly after a much heavier one. The pilot was beside me. I told him to have a look at close range. He put his eye to the periscope and after a brief scrutiny yelled: 'My God, it's the *Lusitania!*'

"I took my position at the periscope again. The ship was sinking with unbelievable rapidity. There was a terrible panic on her deck. Overcrowded lifeboats, fairly torn from their positions, dropped into the water. Desperate people ran helplessly up and down the decks. Men and women jumped into the water and tried to swim to empty, overturned lifeboats. It was the most terrible sight I have ever seen. It was impossible for me to give any help. I could have saved only a handful. And then the cruiser that had passed us was not very far away and must have picked up the distress signals. She would shortly appear, I thought. The scene was too horrible to watch, and I gave orders to dive to twenty metres, and away."

"To all of us in the Company," said a Cunard spokesman, "the moment we first learned of our loss will remain the most awful moment of our lives—the moment when God Himself seemed to forsake us." But once the details of the sinking had been absorbed and reduced to comprehensibility, individuals who regarded the event as merely another act of war, even as a predictable German answer to the British blockade of German ports, were shouted down. Those who emphasized the fact that the Germans had given the *Lusitania* a fair and widely public warning which, they thought, she was foolish to ignore, were excoriated. "There is, indeed, puerile talk of 'warning' having been given on the day the *Lusitania* sailed," said *The Saturday Evening Post*. "But so does the Black Hand send its warnings. So does Jack the Ripper write his defiant letters to the police. Nothing of this prevents us from regarding such miscreants as wild beasts, against whom society has to defend itself at all hazards."

According to the cartoons in the newspapers, civilization itself had been torpedoed. Its corpse—usually represented by the figure of a willowy and well-endowed young woman in wetly clinging garments— was shown as being either washed ashore, fished from the sea by trawlers, or grasped like an *hors d'oeuvre* in the brutish hand of a ravening giant wearing a spiked helmet. "Impartial as it was ruthless," one commentator wrote, "the slaughter claimed babe of the wealthy and babe of the poor. The child that reposed in the handsomely appointed suite of the first cabin and the little fellow who romped in the steerage became martyrs together . . . inarticulate innocents, snatched from their play." In Wales, one evening newspaper was already in the hands of newsboys and on the streets before its editors realized just what they had contributed to the history of wowsers: "GREAT NATIONAL DISASTER," read the headlines, "D. A. THOMAS SAVED."

Dresden, Hiroshima, Biafra, My Lai—after these and all the other names and instances of the murderous course of the middle years of the twentieth century, it is all but impossible to recapture, even to understand, the sense of outrage, "the universal shout of execration," generated by the sinking of the *Lusitania*. "To those of us who spent the Second World War at sea," wrote one veteran, "[it] makes strange, even astounding reading. The memory of merchant ship sinkings as a daily event is still green and the world now has some knowledge of the meaning of 'total war.' It seems inconceivable that in 1915 the faith in 'humane' war according to the rules was so great that a ship of such size and value voluntarily had her speed reduced for economic reasons; that in a danger zone speed was further reduced in order to pick up a pilot at a suitable time; that it was still further cut down by fog; that there was no zigzag and no escort of any sort to meet her and finally that in spite of warnings so many people should elect to risk their lives in her."

Within a couple of decades the event would pass as an incident in the web and exigency of war. In its own time it was regarded as an act of monstrous criminality which, unthinkably, caused even women and children to die by violence. "For a parallel to the *Lusitania* horror," said one witness, "the mind gropes hopelessly through the events of recorded history. The Cawnpore Massacre in India in the Mutiny days is perhaps the most horrid crime which ever preceded the destruction of the *Lusitania*; but it was perpetrated by a people with infinitely less pretence of civilization than the Germans. The Armenian and other unspeakable outrages in the Near East are likewise the work of a race impervious to Western standards. Of course catastrophes like the Halifax explosion or the Galveston flood, where the moral element is entirely absent, cannot be named in the same breath with the German attacks upon our mothers, our wives, our sisters and our young children."

Walter Hines Page, American Ambassador to the Court of St. James, cabled President Woodrow Wilson: "The United States must declare war or forfeit European respect." The thing that gave the torpedoing of the *Lusitania* "its awful preeminence among the world's tragedies," said an American Government official, was its "element of incomparable spiritual turpitude."

German commentators saw things from a different perspective. "The passengers who went down with the *Lusitania*," said a Berlin newspaper, "are, if we wish to call things by their right names, a sacrifice to Great Britain's frivolity and avarice." Germany regarded the incident as a legitimate act of war in which her hitherto gadfly U-boat campaign had at last moved into a major phase. But in the emotional heat of the day, most people outside the reach of Prussian persuasions tended to agree with a remark made by a Danish journalist. "When in future the Germans venture to speak of their culture the answer will be 'It does not exist: it committed suicide on May 7th, 1915.'"

As minor as they seemed to be, the *Lusitania* did carry munitions— 5,468 cases of cartridges and shrapnel shells, unloaded—and tons of other kinds of cargo earmarked for the feeding of the war machine: 200,000 pounds of sheet brass, 111,762 pounds of copper, beef, furs, lubricating oil, shell cases, fuses. The Frankfurt *Zeitung* went as far as to suggest that the *Lusitania*'s owners were so craven as to allow the ship's passengers to "form a protection for the contraband and the lucrative shipment of arms which were on board." Consequently the Germans had considered her fair game—at least in retrospect. (As his diary suggests, the U-boat commander, Schwieger, who caught her in his periscope and destroyed her, knew only that she was a big ship that had floated, almost by design, into the easy reach of his next-to-last torpedo.) In the German view, the one torpedo that sped into the *Lusitania*'s side merely wounded the ship and left her inoperable. The sudden destruction of the ship—and the fact that she sank before Kapitanleutnant Schwieger's astonished eyes in a mere eighteen min- utes—was caused by the 10 or 11 tons of explosives the passenger ship was foolish and "frivolous" enough to carry.

In the formal investigation that ensued, the British at least took the rumor of munitions into account. But when a report was made to Parliament, the possibility was pooh-poohed mainly, it would seem, because the man who tried to establish it did not, personally, come up to scratch. "One witness," ran the official report, "who described himself as a French subject from the vicinity of Switzerland, and who was in the second-class dining room at the time of the explosion, stated that the nature of the explosion was 'similar to the rattling of a Maxim gun for a short period,' and suggested that this noise disclosed the 'secret' existence of some ammunition. The sound, he said, came from under- neath the whole floor. I did not believe this gentleman. His demeanour was very unsatisfactory."

While the Government was trying to quash suspicions, the Cunard Line was trying to placate and pacify scores of irate survivors who felt they had been led down a garden path. The company quite reasonably assumed that the risk of wartime travel was something every passenger had knowledgeably taken; passengers countered that they had assumed nothing of the kind—assurances from Cunard personnel on land and at sea had over and again emphasized their safety.

In an attempt to win backing for his claims of compensation for lost money and clothing, one S. Abramovitz even went so far as to address himself to the Lord Mayor of London. "I did not insure myself," he said, "because the Kunar Line Co had shown me the list of so many women and children and men of high standing, such as Mr. Vanderbilt. This inspired me with confidence and the escort of English Torpedo boats was assured."

Mary Delaney of Shannow, County Cavan, also felt she had been misled. "I am a survivor of the *Lusitania* that left New York the first day of May," she wrote the company, "and was sunk on the seventh. After spending 11 years in America I was obliged to return to Ireland this spring. I did not like to venture owing to reports so I made enquiries about travelling on the *Lusitania*. I was told there was no danger and had to pay twelve shillings War-Tax, but on Friday afternoon I was plunged into the water to sink. I thought there was nothing else in store for me as I don't know how to swim and I had no time to get a life-belt. I don't know how long I was in the water. I was unconscious when brought to Queenstown where I had to remain until the following Monday. Then I left for Cavan and now when I realize my trunk gone, which was value at least 50 pounds. My furs alone cost over 12 pounds. In my state room I had my hat box and hats value 4 pounds. A new leather suit case and all it contained value 3 pounds, some jewellery value for 6 pounds. Also my handbag and travelling money to the amount of 3 pounds. I bring this claim to your notice as I am a poor girl earning my own living and would be very glad to get compensation in place of all that was so dear to me."

Scores of similar letters, asking compensation for loss of life, service and property, soon came pouring into the Cunard offices. Some were written by semiliterate individuals, some by solicitors who eloquently described the plight of widows and orphans they represented. "Personally," wrote one who was trying to persuade Cunard to put up the money for shipment of some badly decomposed remains from Queenstown to Scotland, "I would not like to think of a great company like the Cunard stumbling over an odd pound or two with a widow who has lost her all in your boat."

Except in those instances where survivors had bought clothing to replace their lost or soaked garments, or run up hotel bills while they recovered from the shock of immersion, Cunard was reluctant to assume any financial responsibility. The company's answer to every kind of claim was routine: "Whilst deeply sympathising with you in your bereavement, we regret that compensation is not payable by the Company under the circumstances, and we can only suggest, therefore, that you communicate with the Under Secretary of State for Foreign Affairs, London, with a view to receiving compensation from Germany at the termination of hostilities."

The American consul in Queenstown at this crucial time was Wesley Frost, and it fell upon him and his office to deal with many of the grisly events in the aftermath of the sinking, including searches for American bodies through the morgues that were set up, and then attendance at autopsies. Consul Frost did not know it then, but his firsthand experiences of the *Lusitania* disaster would lead to his becoming a sort of informal historian of German undersea warfare, and to his being employed as lecturer or, more strictly and honestly speaking, as a propagandist for the Allied cause. As soon as the United States had entered the war, his skills as a publicist were requisitioned by the Committee on Public Information (a precursor of the United States Information Service). With the backing of the Chamber of Commerce of the United States he was sent on speaking tours that took him across the American continent.

Consul Frost first heard of the attack on the *Lusitania* when a wildfire rumor reached his shabby office over a saloon in downtown Queenstown. When he phoned the local headquarters of the Admiralty and reported what was being said in the streets, the Rear-Admiral's secretary was succinct. "It's true, Mr. Frost," he said. "We fear she is gone." In the following days the Consul's good offices were concerned with embalmings, caskets, notifications of next of kin and claims for damages. All identified bodies from first class, he decided, should be embalmed; bodies from other classes "should be sealed into leaden caskets so that they could be returned to America when desired." But identifications that would entitle a corpse to first-class treatment were not easy to make. "There was a curious effacement of social and mental distinction by death," he confessed. "We often believed a corpse to be important when it turned out to be decidedly the opposite."

The matter of caskets was also a bit troublesome—not only to the Consul but also to the Cunard Line. In the case of Frost, the difficulty lay in finding any in the environs of Queenstown or Cork that would be "suitable" for the remains of American citizens. In the case of the Cunard Line the difficulty lay in getting rid of an overstock.

In good faith, the company had ordered hundreds of coffins to accommodate the *Lusitania* dead. But in one gruesome turn of circumstance, the dead refused to accommodate Cunard. More than nine hundred corpses floated away in the great fanning out of the Gulf Stream, never to be recovered. Consul Frost eventually found the coffins he needed for his Americans, but Cunard was still trying to peddle its unused and partially used coffins many months after the sinking.

"To get rid of our surplus stock," said the Cunard office in Queenstown to the Cunard office in Liverpool, "we must be prepared to make great sacrifices . . . in case they are left as a drug on our hands." (The original cost of the coffins averaged four pounds apiece.) Liverpool, unhappy with this report, urged Queenstown to persist. The demand for coffins, they hinted, was not after all a seasonal phenomenon. In reply, the Queenstown office begged to say "that the coffins in our possession are in fairly good condition, being stowed in a dry building, but are a very poor lot at best, and some of them have held bodies which were afterwards transferred to other coffins. When last we tried to dispose of them none of the Undertakers at Cork or Queenstown would make an offer, with the exception of Moynihan, whose bid of 25 pounds you would not accept." Liverpool was growing impatient. "The offer is ridiculously low—in fact absurd when we consider the price we paid for them. Is it possible to dispose of the property through any other source than Undertakers?"

No, replied Queenstown. "We think it is very unlikely that the property would be of greater value to any one in another line of business." When Liverpool continued to press for disposal of the caskets, going so far as to suggest that Queenstown bypass the undertakers and try to sell them on a man-to-man basis, the Irish office finally gave up.

They had failed, they admitted, completely; they had tapped all possibilities; every effort had proved fruitless. "There is no likelihood of individual private sales," they wrote back, "as even the very poorest people in this country are particularly sensitive regarding such matters, and would not accept one of these coffins for their dead even if offered for nothing."

In the line of duty, Consul Frost was for days and weeks making mental notes on his morbid task of identifying the bodies that might be American as they were washed ashore. Soon large audiences from New York to California would be privy to his eloquent recollections. Of some of the cadavers, he reported, "The rigidity relaxed into an inebriate flabbiness and the features broke down into a preposterously animal-like repulsiveness. I was present as official witness to an autopsy performed on one body seventy-two days dead, but other corpses equaled it in the ravages they displayed. The faces registered every shading of the grotesque and hideous. The lips and noses were eaten away by sea-birds, and the eyes gouged out into staring pools of blood. It was almost a relief when the faces became indistinguishable as such. Toward the last the flesh was wholly gone from the grinning skulls, the trunks were bloated and distended with gases, and the limbs were partially eaten away or bitten clean off by sea-creatures so that stumps of raw bone were left projecting."

One thing was certain: there would be no further British passenger service on the North Atlantic for the duration of the war. But this was the least of the consequences of the *Lusitania*'s fatal voyage. In the United States, "The *Lusitania!*" became a rallying cry in the Hearst newspaper tradition of "Remember the Maine!" The Huns had skewered Belgian babies and now their steel claws had reached out to drown or batter one hundred and nineteen American citizens. Whatever justice the Germans might claim in their interpretation of the rules of war made little register on the outraged sensibilities of many average Americans. "The greatest crime in maritime history" was one of the factors urging citizens with a natural disposition to neutrality to join those other Americans whose thirst for vengeance would not be slaked this side of Belleau Wood.

PART FOUR

THE
LONG WAKE
1920-1968

⚜ SECTION I ⚜

FINGERING the spoils of war, dealing out ships as if they were playing cards, the Allies shuffled the German merchant marine into oblivion. At the same time, ships worn and weary from their years at war were repaired, reconverted, refurbished and sent out with a brave show of business as usual. But business was terrible. Vessels that sailed out on new careers soon had to come back, to be laid up in silent flotillas in basins and backwaters, and left to rust.

The German and British mammoths that had arrived on the ocean scene just in time to be transformed from pleasure palaces into floating barracks or hospitals were transformed once more. Their interior fittings were carted back from warehouses; tarpaulins that had veiled their paintings and statues were removed, their potted palms replaced, their swimming baths swabbed out and refilled. Below decks, new installations changed them from behemoths that burned coal to behemoths that drank oil. The *Olympic* was the first of the great ones to be so readapted. When it became clear that the use of oil could allow for a reduction of the number of men working in the stokehold from, say, 350 to about 50, other ships queued up to get into dry dock. On the whole, the affairs of ships and the sea in the postwar world were dominated by two complementary ideas: rehabilitation and retribution.

Fattened by the absorption of three enormous German prizes of war, three companies—two British and one American—could still make an impressive showing on the long ferry run from Sandy Hook to Bishop's Light. To avoid outbidding one another, Cunard and White Star had joined up to buy the *Imperator* and the *Bismarck*. Rechristened *Berengaria*, the *Imperator* would sail for Cunard. The *Vaterland* went to the United States as the *Leviathan*. The White Star got the *Bismarck*, rechristened *Majestic*, the one ship that had been caught high and dry on the stocks when war broke out. Under a British crew, the *Bismarck*, on her way to becoming the White Star flagship, left her fitting-out station in Hamburg on March 28, 1922. Thousands of people in that port who had come to know her lined the river banks to watch her go as if she were being led into bondage.

Three other great ships surviving the war were the White Star *Olympic*, and Cunard's *Mauretania* and *Aquitania*. Across the Channel, the four-funneled *France* was still intact, and the French Line was finally able to complete an even more beautiful ship, named the *Paris*. She had actually been launched on September 13, 1916, but exigencies of war had caused her to sit empty and unemployed for years. Now she was ready to emerge as the first French ship in the modern dispensation in which languid flourishes of *art nouveau* had begun to soften the heavy classicism of *L'Ecole de Beaux Arts*. The Third Republic's notions of style had begun to seem impoverished even to decorators of steamships. The consequence was lots of fancy ironwork and Lalique, the latter here and there, the former in the main dining room of the *Paris*, in which not only was the staircase made of wrought iron, but the columns supporting the cupola, the balcony and the mezzanine.

Few in number, these ships of the immediate postwar years nevertheless had an enormous combined carrying capacity. But the factors of size and payload that had been essential to prewar success on the ocean were the very factors that suddenly changed the floating cities into echo chambers. The one crucial event that most effected the nature of ocean travel was the passing of the Emergency Quota Act of 1921, commonly known so "The Three Percent Act." When Congress voted to approve a restrictive system whereby only three percent of the nationals of each country, based on the 1903 census, might be admitted to the United States, passenger traffic on westbound ships fell precipitously. In 1922, for instance, 230,000 fewer passengers came westward from Europe than in 1921. In the five years preceding the war, immigrants to the United States had come at the rate of 700,000 every twelve months. Now their numbers were reduced to a mere stream that would soon become a trickle.

The wide wooden lounges of the steerage and its rows of dormitory-like cabins had suddenly become as quiet as a school in summer. And since the numbers of the rich who could afford to stroll the promenade decks of first class were also seriously depleted, it seemed as though the steamships that had survived years of military assault would fall victims to economic attrition. Facing up to the situation, the chairman of the White Star Line said that "the building of further steamships of the monster type in the near future is rendered problematical . . . special attention will be given to steamers of the cabin and third-class type— increasingly popular in these democratic days."

Things were even worse for the flimsy and disorganized American concern that was trying to make the reluctant *Leviathan* show a profit. The trouble was simple: the Volsted Act had been written into law. Travelers, given a choice, particularly if they were Americans, avoided "dry" ships as though they were plague ships. When foreign liners came into New York, their liquor closets had to be locked and padlocked at the twelve-mile limit as firmly as if they were vaults of gold.

Yet, like bankrupt opera companies stranded on the sea roads, one by one the great liners pulled themselves together and came back into the transatlantic arena. To travelers who knew only the prewar sunset of the "Golden Age," the attempt at rehabilitation was not a success. "Everything about an ocean voyage is now changed," said an American lady who had crossed for every one of many years. "The boats are not shipshape; the whole idea is to make them as much as possible like hotels; the dear, picturesque portholes are gone, and plate glass windows try to deceive people. I rejoice that all my sailing days, I crossed on boats fitted for the sea. The restlessness, also, is unceasing; no one can take the shortest nap, there is such universal 'doing something noise.' Games of all kinds are arranged each day to 'amuse' the passengers: 'Potato races for the children,' 'egg and spoon races for ladies and children,' 'international tug of war,' etc., etc. The real rest of a sea voyage is gone forever; every disturbance and disaster in the whole world is reported by wireless, and large announcements are posted up each day saying that 'passengers can communicate to-day with friends on steamers so and so.'

"The war has changed so many, many things; ladies (?) now hire safety boxes in the Purser's office, and the manner with which they open these boxes and take out large jewel cases and lock away what jewellery they wore the night before, is very amusing to people like ourselves who are carrying all they own in small underpockets! The drinking on the outgoing boats is another calamity. The men begin as soon as they cross the three mile limit, and never cease until they are nearly insane. They don't know nor care what they do, nor do the officers or stewards try to control them. The officials coolly answer all objections by: 'they will soon disappear,' which, of course, they do, but while they 'appear,' it is certainly terrible."

Still, there were other, well-upholstered little liners on which technological progress and changing social mores could not disturb the expectations of middle-class taste. On the Allan Line's *Victorian*, for one, soberly attired ladies and gentlemen would assemble in the lounge to hear concerts of gramophone records being broadcast over a radius of nearly eight hundred miles. Then, as one record after another squawked and scratched to a halt, they could take satisfaction in the thought that people just like themselves were digesting roast beef and Yorkshire pudding in Morris chairs and tapestried settees all around the ocean. Calls for encores, tapped in Morse code and brought down to the lounge by the ship's wireless man, were just what the *Victorian's* passengers themselves most wanted to hear: Kreisler's "Caprice Viennois," Alma Gluck's "O Sleep Why Dost Thou Leave Me?" Harry Lauder's "I Love a Lassie" and, rollicking over the deep, the flying fishes of Cobb's "On the Road to Mandalay."

At the very lowest ebb, when shipping fortunes had been reduced to a fraction of their prewar levels, necessity generated the means by which most of the companies were tided over their worst period. Wearily contemplating half-empty ships and falling revenues, a number of passenger agents seem to have come upon the same idea almost at once. Why not, they said, upgrade steerage to third class and soften the sound of it by calling it "tourist" third or "tourist" cabin? Why not pack students, teachers and the good old American middle class into ships catering just to them and send them racketing to Europe in fiestas of democratic *joie de vivre?* "Such a jolly idea," said one brochure, "coziness and friendliness more than compensate for any lack of the sumptuous." "Today," said another, "sub-debs, younger members of the smart set, college professors and students, men and women of the business world, definitely prefer to be debonair shipmates in the congenial atmosphere of Tourist Third Cabin when they travel to the edge of a new world and back again."

It was not a new idea; it was simply one that had found its place and its good time. As a consequence, the waterways out of New York and Montreal were soon jumping with the beat of Dixieland bands as girls in cloche hats danced with boys in plus fours, or one another, on the open decks. Embarkations came to have the air of class reunions. Posed in formal tiers at the stern or on the steps leading to the sports deck, bow-lipped girls in fur-trimmed coats, boys with slicked-down hair, brass-buttoned blazers and flannel pants, solemnly squinted for the inevitable sailing-day photograph. The one in the front row center always had his head stuck through a life preserver, on which was printed the name of the ship.

The age of mass travel, of "tourism"—that phenomenon that had begun with a few nineteenth-century clergymen, lovers of Old Masters and Roman ruins, diary-keeping bluestockings and a few families in the van of their possessions like sheikhs in the desert—had moved into an entirely new dispensation. Now, anyone who could scrape together eighty or ninety dollars for a round-trip steamship ticket and another few hundred dollars for a long summer in Europe, was ready to join the great exodus.

The success of tourist third led to a category called tourist cabin, then to the gradual abolishment of third class, and finally to a whole new type of ship. This was the one-class liner, a floating democracy where no one looked down on any one—neither socially nor from the elevations of a restricted deck. It was an American idea that found most of its support in American patronage and it threatened for a time to change permanently the whole character of ocean traffic.

The New York Times interpreted the development with precision and evident satisfaction. "For many years," said one of its editorial writers, "the ocean liner has served as an example of the working out of the caste system. Class distinctions were not more clearly drawn in Hindustan. On shipboard the lines were fixed and taut. Captain, staff and crew made up the bureaucracy, the first cabin the aristocracy, the second cabin the *bourgeoisie,* and the steerage the proletariat. Today this venerable tradition of the high seas faces extinction.

"On shore, revolutions begin at the top but this mutiny against things as they were started at the bottom, abolishing the steerage. In its place appeared the 'Third Cabin,' now patronized by students, teachers, artists and tourists. . . . But the development which seems to spell the doom of class distinction at sea is the 'one-cabin ship.' This type provides accommodations which are varied but not segregated according to cost. . . . It has long been an axiom with steamship companies that Americans would travel first-class or not at all. To them, economies practiced by the traveling European have always appeared somewhat unpleasant. But this year . . . 40,000 Americans from all grades of society booked round trips in the rejuvenated steerage. Sociologists may attribute this swift change to the growth of democratic ideals but the real explanation seems to lie in the need of the steamship companies to make both ends meet.

"There will always be luxurious suites and private decks for the people who want them and can afford them. But for a multitude of these there is now the 'one-cabin' ship. It is probable that in years to come the bulk of the ocean-going public will be akin to those now taking their initial trip in the third cabin—men and women of moderate means who believe they are entitled to a dollar's worth for every dollar that they spend."

One consequence of cheap and easy travel to Europe was a noticeable change in its general purpose. Before the 1920s, most Americans traveling abroad went to see the Botticellis in the Ufizzi and the El Grecos in the Prado, to compare one Palladian villa with another, to wander moodily through the labyrinthine ruins of Pompeii and to brave, like Daisy Miller, the mephitic dampness of the Colosseum by moonlight. To do this they had to put up with discomfort, diarrhea and the inscrutable authority of an alien culture. Travel, as the prophet said, was a little bit of hell; yet to most people the rewards of Europe were worth all the expense and trouble. But suddenly overseas travel lost its character as an adventure fraught with hazards and became an extended outing under the leadership, perhaps, of a professional guide from Atlanta or Minneapolis and, in any case, watched over by American Express. Instead of being regarded as the scene of new and challenging experience, Europe tended to become a place for fun—good and clean, if that were your taste, or ooh-la-la if you had heard about those dough-boys on leave in Paris. In other words, Americans began to go to Europe on the pleasure principle—for the chance to drink when, where and what they pleased, to live on a scale beyond anything they could imagine in Kansas City or Pittsburgh, to "have" the wealth of centuries and to have it without approaching it all with the holy expectations of pilgrims.

"Instead of an athletic exercise," wrote Daniel Boorstin, "travel became a spectator sport. . . . This change can be described in a word. It was the decline of the traveler and the rise of the tourist. There is a wonderful, but neglected, precision in these words. The old English noun 'travel' (in the sense of a journey) was originally the same as 'travail' (meaning 'trouble,' 'work' or 'torment'). The traveler was an active man at work. . . . The tourist is passive; he expects interesting things to happen to him. He goes 'sight-seeing,' he expects everything to be done to him and for him."

To captains who had presided like potentates at tables reserved for Lords of the Exchequer, captains of industry and coupon-clipping scions of old families, the new dispensation was anathema. The steam-ship companies might be making money on these crowds of cut-rate passengers without a shred of social nicety, but to commanders who had themselves taken on the coloration and tastes of those they had invited to their tables, the behavior of this new breed of voyager was abominable. "There is a limit to frivolity and I fancy it has nearly been reached," said one of them. "It would be a calamity to see the line of demarcation between a British ship and a Dance Club wiped out altogether." Another old salt, observing the scramble of a treasure hunt "in which many well-known society folk took part," merely shook his head at the care-less folly of the rich. "Starting on the boat-deck clad in furs," he said, "they were only too glad to shed everything but 'the irreducible min-imum' by the time they arrived at one of the smoking room coal-scuttles where the treasure was eventually discovered." The eyes of Edith Somerville, an aristocratic Irish bluestocking, were equally censorious as they fell upon "English parsons (two), all things to all men, even wearing lay twin caps; one stoops to a grey sweater, but it is corrected by a gold cross and the ritual collar. The usual undergrowth of fat-legged flappers, who squeal in companies, walking arm-in-arm. Occa-sionally harassed stewards, with thin intellectual faces, bringing trays of tea to long silent rows of mummies in chaises longues."

For a while, the restless hunger for luxury and the biggest of every-thing that had characterized the prewar era on the sea appeared to be something that had been utterly superseded. But as economic conditions on shore improved and indications of easy affluence, if not elegance, were again widely in evidence, passenger ships began to reflect the upswing. It was all right for Jazz Age youths and school teachers on a budget to travel in the chintzy austerities of tourist third, but financially solid citizens began to expect something more. The legend of the grand saloon was more lively than anyone had guessed.

When the young Mr. and Mrs. F. Scott Fitzgerald actually got their hands on a hefty sum of money from the first of Scott's novels to win a big audience, their thoughts turned, not to the classless congeniality of the new ocean ferries, but to the best available: first class, no less, on the *Aquitania*. "Lustily splashing their dreams in the dark pool of gratification," wrote Zelda, "their fifty thousand dollars bought a cardboard day-nurse for Bonnie, a second-hand Marmon, a Picasso etching, a white satin dress . . . a dress as green as fresh wet paint, two white knickerbocker suits exactly alike, a broker's suit and two first-class tickets to Europe."

When Sinclair Lewis' Sam Dodsworth went to Europe, he went in the style the old shipping tycoons had led him to expect. "Free!" was the first word he uttered when he found himself alone, four hours out of New York, on the fictitious 32,000-ton "S.S. *Ultima*." But as an exemplar of American know-how and honest open-mindedness, his deeper feeling was a kind of awe for the efficiency and sophistication of the ship itself. "He explored the steamer. It was to him, the mechanic, the most sure and impressive mechanism he had ever seen; more satisfying than a Rolls, a Delauney-Belleville, which to him had been the equivalent of a Velasquez. He marveled at the authoritative steadi-ness with which the bow mastered the waves; at the powerful sweep of the lines of the deck and the trim stowage of cordage. He admired the first officers, casually pacing the bridge. He wondered that in this craft which was, after all, but a floating iron egg-shell, there should be the roseate music room, the smoking-room with its Tudor fireplace—solid and terrestrial as a castle—and the swimming pool, green-lighted water washing beneath Roman pillars. He climbed to the boat deck, and some never realized desire for sea-faring was satisfied as he looked along the sweep of gangways, past the huge lifeboats, the ventilators like giant saxophones, past the lofty funnels serenely dribbling black wooly smoke, to the forward mast. The snow-gusts along the deck, the mysteriousness of this new world but half seen in the frosty lights, only stimulated him . . . 'I'm at sea!' "

By the middle of the 1920s it was obvious that "the foetid artificiality of status travel" was just exactly what an awful lot of Americans were anxious to locate and then to embrace. The emergence of tourist third, tourist cabin and the one-class ship had provided a sort of interregnum belonging to the man in the street. But the captains and the kings had not quite departed; they were just waiting for their stocks in American Can and General Motors to pay better dividends. Soon the steamship companies were openly courting them and, what's more, using them as bait by which to catch a whole new group of potential travelers who had the money for Europe, the hunger for Europe, but no other preparation of any kind. "Crossing the Atlantic has taken on a sort of social significance," said one of the more sophisticated captains. "Thousands of persons, of no great consequence, have the self-satisfying experience of importance thrust upon them. They walk over the first-class gang-plank, are greeted by a band, are waited upon, deferred to, bowed to, coddled, and the rest, and each evening sit in a huge dining hall, wearing formal dinner dress, five nights in succession. This sort of thing becomes an annual pilgrimage into a small world where the ego is magnified and set to music. The North Atlantic deserves full credit for its uplift work among our prosperous nonentities. . . ."

"Old" money, and those who had been socially secure from the time their parents had entered their names at Groton or Miss Porter's, had their own antediluvian codes of behavior; and these were perhaps more rigidly adhered to at sea than they were ashore. Now that great numbers of newly rich Americans were beginning—via the certificate of a first-class passage ticket—to buy their way into the presence, if not the company, of the socially elect, something was needed to equip the *nouveau riche* with the kinds of knowledge their easy-going betters had absorbed in the nurseries of Murray Hill and Tuxedo Park.

That need was supplied by Emily Post. Deportment in general was, of course, her topic; but she did not neglect words of advice and somber warning for those of the *arriviste* middle class who were so audacious as to plan a transatlantic voyage. She did not exactly discourage the Smiths, the Joneses and the Robinsons, but her first remarks quite clearly fixed the limits of their shipboard expectations. "It may be pretty accurately said," said Mrs. Post, "that the faster and bigger the ship, the less likely one is to speak to strangers, and yet—as always—circumstances alter cases. Because the Worldlys, the Oldnames, the Eminents—all those who are innately exclusive—never 'pick up' acquaintances on shipboard, it does not follow that no fashionable and well-born people ever drift into acquaintanceship on European-American steamers of to-day, but they are at least not apt to do so. Many in fact take the ocean-crossing as a rest-cure and stay in their cabins the whole voyage. The Worldlys always have their meals served in their own 'drawing-rooms' and have their deck chairs placed so that no one is very near them, and keep to themselves except when they have invited friends of their own to play bridge or take dinner or lunch with them.

"But because the Worldlys and the Eminents—and the Snobsnifts who copy them—stay in their cabins, sit in segregated chairs and speak to no one except the handful of personal friends or acquaintances who happen to be on board, it does not follow that the Smiths, the Joneses and the Robinsons are not enlarging their acquaintance with every revolution of the screw. And if you happen to like to be talked to by strangers, and if they in turn like to talk to you, it cannot be said that there is any rule of etiquette against it."

Encouraged thus far, the Joneses and their shaggy ilk had still to be reminded of what they might expect in the dining saloon. "Very fashionable people," pronounced Mrs. Post, "as a rule travel a great deal, which means that they are known very well to the head steward, who reserves a table. Mr. and Mrs. Gilding, for instance, if they know that friends of theirs are sailing on the same steamer, ask them to sit at their table and ask for a sufficiently large one on purpose. Or if they are traveling alone, they arrange to have one of the small tables for two, to themselves.

"People of wide acquaintance in big cities are sure to find friends on board with whom they can arrange, if they choose, to sit on deck or in the dining saloon, but most people, unless really intimate friends are on board, sit wherever the head steward puts them. After a meal or two people always speak to those sitting next to them. None but the rudest snob would sit through meal after meal without ever addressing a word to his table companions."

Mrs. Post appears to be somewhat winsomely sorry for the Joneses in their plight, yet she can understand them. The one she seems unable to figure out is the climber, whose operations she has obviously watched with a combination of contempt and fascination. Just imagine, she says, "there are certain constant travelers who count on a European voyage to increase their social acquaintances by just so much each trip! Richan Vulgar, for instance, has his same especial table each time he crosses, which is four times a year! Walking through a 'steamer train' he sees a 'celebrity,' a brilliant, let us say, but unworldly man. Vulgar annexes him by saying, casually, 'Have you a seat at table? Better sit with me, I always have the table by the door; it is easy to get in and out.' The celebrity accepts, since there is no evidence that he is to be 'featured,' and the chances are that he remains unconscious to the end of time that he served as a decoy. Boarding the steamer, Vulgar sees the Lovejoys, and pounces: 'You must sit at my table! Celebrity and I are crossing together—he is the most delightful man! I want you to sit next to him.'

"They think Celebrity sounds very interesting; so, not having engaged a table for themselves, they say they will be delighted. On the deck, the Smartlys appear and ask the Lovejoys to sit with them. Vulgar, who is standing by (he is always standing by) breaks in even without an introduction and says: 'Mr. and Mrs. Lovejoy and Celebrity are sitting at my table, won't you sit with me also?' If the Smartlys protest that they have a table, he is generally insistent and momentarily over-powering enough to make them join forces with him. As the Smartlys particularly want to sit next to the Lovejoys and also like the idea of meeting Celebrity, it ends in Vulgar's table being a collection of fashionables whom he could not possibly have gotten together without just such a maneuver.

"The question of what he gets out of it is puzzling since with each hour the really well-bred people dislike him more and more intensely, and at the end of a day or so, his table's company are all eating on deck to avoid him. Perhaps there is some recompense that does not appear on the surface, but to the casual observer the satisfaction of telling others that the Smartlys, the Lovejoys and the Wellborns sat at his table would scarcely seem worth the effort."

In the matter of shipboard dress, propriety in the '20s allowed for choice and nicety; whereas, fifty years earlier, propriety and necessity were one. "The first requirement," advised a nineteenth-century traveler, "is a suit of thick clothes, so old and valueless that one can lounge upon the deck in them, with no fear of damage. (Dandyism is at a discount at sea—a lesson quickly and surely learned.) Then as thick an overcoat and gloves as can well be procured—the use of which will become patent, either among the fogs and ice-bergs of the Banks of Newfoundland, or on the Irish coast. A thick blanket, or a rough buffalo robe, to make lounging upon the deck easier. . . ." In 1876, a magazine devoted to information for ocean travelers gave this advice: "Take thick clothing, and plenty of it. Old clothes that you would not wear anywhere else are just the thing. When you get to Glasgow or Liverpool, put these 'traps' into an old carpet bag, or even in a brown paper parcel, and leave them at your hotel, or at the steamship office, until you call or send for them."

In 1922, Mrs. Post's notions were rigid, her admonitions calculated to chill. "On the deluxe steamers," she says, "nearly every one dresses for dinner; some actually in ball dresses, which is in the worst possible taste, and, like overdressing in public places, indicates that they have no other place to show their finery. People of position never put on formal evening dress on a steamer, not even in the à-la-carte restaurant. In the dining saloon they wear afternoon house dresses—without hats— for dinner. In the restaurant they wear semi-dinner dresses. Some smart men on the ordinary steamers put on a dark sack suit for dinner after wearing country clothes all day, but in the deluxe restaurant they wear Tuxedo coats. No gentleman wears a tailcoat on shipboard under any circumstances whatsoever."

The fashion mentor for Vogue was entirely on Mrs. Post's side. "As for dinner-dresses," she admonished, "remember that the mistake made by the average American, whether crossing for the first time or the twenty-first time, is to resemble the lily of the field with whom Solomon in all his glory refused to compete. Especially is this true on the return trip, where many otherwise excellent ladies try to wear each Paris frock at least once, to cheat the customs. To put it frankly, however, it simply isn't considered smart to appear too opulent. It subjects one to the suspicion of having nowhere else to wear one's clothes."

Basil Woon, an authority of fewer credentials but notably wider countenance was also forthright. "Remember, then, this," he wrote, "the one essential garment for a man aboard a ship is a dinner-jacket. He can dispense with all else, but the dinner-jacket is as necessary to an ocean traveler as a tailcoat is to a waiter. Without it you may not, except on the first and last nights out, come down to dinner. Without it you will have to sneak out of the smoking-room at eight P.M. Without it you will have no dances and no Great Moments with the young thing in crêpe-marocain on the lee of the starboard ventilator." For the hours on deck, "the Plus-Four is now considered absolutely the only garment fit to wear for promenading during daylight hours." Nevertheless, flannels were also *de rigeur*, since "they look very doggy for deck quoits and croquet and shovelboard." Woon also warned his male readers against bringing their Panama hats.

When people like New York's Mayor Jimmy Walker went abroad, however, they were their own fashion arbiters. Mr. Walker took forty-four suits, twenty white piqué vests, twelve pairs of fancy striped white trousers, six topcoats, one hundred cravats, several dozen shirts and a bushelful of shoes. When he appeared on the deck of the *Berengaria* he was dressed in a single-breasted brass-buttoned blue flannel coat, blue-striped white trousers, blue shirt and collar and black and white low shoes and, *noblesse oblige*, a Panama hat.

Litanies of injunctions aimed at them, and close discriminations made for them, meant little to most people from west of Buffalo, and nothing at all to wide-eyed naïfs like Lorelei Lee from Little Rock, Arkansas. When, in the course of the adventures recounted in Anita Loos' *Gentlemen Prefer Blondes*, Miss Lee makes a trip to Paris with her friend Dorothy, she chooses the White Star Line's *Majestic*. "April 11th," she writes in her diary. "Well Dorothy and I are really on the ship sailing to Europe as anyone could tell by looking at the ocean. I always love the ocean. I mean I always love a ship and I really love the *Majestic* because it is just like being at the Ritz, and the steward says the ocean is not so obnoxious this month as it generally is.

"So now the steward tells me it is luncheon time, so I will go upstairs as the gentleman Dorothy met on the steps has invited us to luncheon in the Ritz, which is a special dining room on the ship where you can spend a lot of money because they really give away the food in the other dining room.

"April 15th: Last night there was quite a maskerade ball on the ship which was really all for the sake of charity because most of the sailors seem to have orphans which they get from going on the ocean when the sea is very rough." Lorelei Lee does not mention the swimming bath on her ship, but it was obviously a place of emancipated amusement. "The mixed bathing season opened on the *Majestic* just before the end of May," reported the *White Star Magazine*, "and the ship's swimming bath was a scene of gaiety and excitement. The bathing dresses of the ladies were intricate affairs" and "in most cases a skirt came almost to the knees and then there were frills. It was a wonder that the wearers were able to keep afloat."

Even in repose, with only the humming of dynamos to show they were still "alive," the great ships were invitations to pleasure. One night when the *Aquitania* was docked in Southampton, Captain Thelwell answered a knock at the door to his quarters. It was his master at arms, to say that a party of visitors was about to come aboard. "Send them away," said the Captain.

"I'm afraid I can't, Sir," said the master at arms, "it's the Prince of Wales with a party of naval officers, and some ladies as well."

The Captain dressed and went below. "I peeped into the garden lounge," he said. "A dozen negro musicians were already tuning up. The Prince had borrowed a baton and was flexing himself in readiness to conduct. The tall, immaculate figure of Prince Louis Mountbatten was crouched behind the drums with drum-sticks poised and I recognized the King of Greece and the two Greek Princesses Irene and Xenia, with fur coats thrown over their evening dresses. Yet for all the gaiety, the scene had a pale and ghostly setting. The stage, the ornate, half-lit garden lounge was too vast for a handful of people to fill and it seemed to me sad that a man who was to be monarch soon should be obliged to go to such lengths to get a little innocent amusement for himself and give a little to his friends."

The affluence of the '20s continued to expand, like bubble gum, to the point where it would blot out vision and then blow up. A messy conclusion was in store for everyone. But, before that arrived, hundreds of thousands of Americans found they had more money than they knew what to do with—at least in America. Buick cabriolets and two-car garages, striped silk shirts and raccoon coats, "His Master's Voice" and Saturday on the links were no longer viable consolations. Patriotic slogans admonished good citizens to "See America First," but it was surprising how many of them wanted only to see Europe.

In some cases this urge was prompted by a sober desire to broaden one's view of the world and to see the documentations of history. In others it was an undefined hankering somehow to come to terms with that vague yet overwhelming culture whose emissaries—Bernhardt,

Pavlova, Paderewski, Max Reinhardt, even voluble Queen Marie of Roumania—had made headlines from coast to coast. ("Any American with the cash and the ambition," said one forthright brochure, "may travel in the self-same suites occupied by these great people.") In most cases, however, Americans simply had an urge to seek fun in new surroundings and perhaps to enhance the playgrounds of the Continent with the flat sincerities of a Middle-Western accent. "If you talk with Europeans," advised Julian Street, "it is always nice to give them fresh impressions of just what's the matter with their country and with them."

What was wrong with Europe to many disappointed Americans was the fact that it insisted on entering the twentieth century—that celebrated preserve marked out by Thomas A. Edison, Henry Ford and the Wright brothers to which only the United States had clear title. "The American who, in his own country is in a feverish haste to improve conditions," said a social historian, "when he sets foot in Europe, becomes the fanatical foe of progress. The Old World, in his judgement, ought to look old. He longs to hear the clatter of wooden shoes. If he had his way he would have laws enacted forbidding peasant folk to change their ancient costumes. He would preserve every relic of feudalism. He bitterly laments the division of great estates. He is enchanted with thatched cottages which look damp and picturesque. He detests the model dwellings which are built with a too-obvious regard for sanitation. A heath ought to be lonely, and fens ought to be preserved from drainage."

In almost all cases, Americans were pushovers for an enfilade of glossy prose issued by the steamship companies. Competition among those companies with liners having vast first-class accommodation was at its keenest, simply because other kinds of accommodation had become so widely available for less money and less fuss. In an attempt to winnow out its own upper crust—and to leave the undifferentiated masses to the devices of tourist third and one-class ships—the Cunard Line went all out. The result was a masterpiece of hucksterism—"The New Art of Going Abroad"—in the form of a four-color brochure, thin as a first volume of lyrics and as rich in the fluidities of poesy as an afternoon with the Browning Society.

Ostensibly phrased for the *cognoscenti*, the enticements of this pamphlet were actually directed toward the well-heeled rube. Years before *Harper's Bazaar* and *Vogue* had brought the shadings of debutante prose to a refinement that made them indistinguishable from the parodies of S. J. Perelman, Cunard copy writers had thrown down a gauntlet of doeskin. The appeal was blatant, its object that substratum of American prosperity that still found its totems of high culture in whatever it was—castles or shaving cream—that could be imported. "A week of life as it should be lived," promised the brochure. "A week that will leave you feeling like a duchess or a millionaire, or a favourite of the gods . . . whether you are or not. . . . A week that is as much a work of art as a goblet of Cellini . . . or a portrait by Zuloaga. . . . A week that will deserve to be sealed in memory—intricately—as a thing precious—superlative—a thing to be treasured. . . . In short, a week in one of the big Cunarders."

Dipping his pen in *eau gazeuse,* the copy writer continued to outline all that was in store for the voyager rich enough to afford first class and staunch enough to withstand its injunctions upon his taste, character and ancestry. "Turmoil . . . hubbub .´. . flurry!" begins the pellucid spiel. "Taxis chugging . . . Rolls-Royces emitting Wall Street-y gentlemen . . . tall slim-hipped young men recently at the Racquet Club . . . hypothetical debutantes . . . and provable cinema stars. Orchids . . . gardenias . . . photographers . . . flash lights . . . Trunks . . . trunks . . . trunks. Packages from Dean's, from Sherry's . . . from ten thousand far-flung florists. . . . Prelude to a sailing . . . overture to a week that, to the initiate, will be a largish bit of heaven . . . in a box from Cartier. . . .

"*For the initiate is aware that to live pleasantly it is necessary to consult one's taste before, and not after, embarking on a given course, or a given steamer.* . . . The initiate takes pains to choose the ship that suits him or her as carefully as a prima-donna chooses a gown or an actress her background.

"Today, ocean travel has taken its proper place as a special aspect of the very special art of living pleasantly. . . . People who *know* . . . sophisticated travelers . . . are aware that the transatlantic week, from pier to pier, can be—should be—one of the gala weeks of life . . . one of those rare and preciously *perfect intervals,* snatched from the grudging gods . . . can be—and *is*—on the Cunarders. . . . You've probably noticed, in the Social Notes of the *Times* . . . or *Spur* . . . or *Town and Country* that when Mrs. So and So, of the Ritz Tower, or the Savoy-Plaza, or Tuxedo, or Grosse Pointe, or Burlingame, or Beacon Hill, goes abroad —it's almost always on a Cunarder. . . . You may not quite have realized why. . . . It's simply because, through long years of catering to people who have always made an art of living and who are accustomed to the ultimate best—the ultimate best, in the way of service, appointments, food, has been evolved—*evoked*, in the Cunarders. . . . When it is more or less assumed that a certain line customarily carries princes of the Blood Royal, and international bankers who deal casually in figures that to most of us remain farce or fantasy—that Line must, of course, be prepared to function according to their standards. The result is a constant . . . consistent enforcement (in the tiniest, minimum rate cabin, just as much as in the "Prince of Wales" suite)—of the superlative, as it is conceived, today, by the people who live superlatively."

People whose parents or grandparents had stood by the steerage rails watching their verminous mattresses being jettisoned as they huddled in shawls while the Statue of Liberty came in sight, were now being asked to choose between damask or silk for their coverlets, duchesses or diplomats for their dining companions. Choice, suggested the brochure, was not just a privilege, it was an imperative. "To hear anyone say, 'We're sailing on the *Hottentot*, because the children go to camp on the tenth,' is a source of anguish to all sophisticated travelers. It's like renting just *any* house that happens to be empty—like joining *any* club because it's near by . . . or choosing just *any* hotel that has rooms that are vacant. How do you know you will like the club, the hotel, the town house . . . or the *Hottentot?* As a matter of fact, there should enter into your choice of a ship just as much consultation of your personal tastes . . . as you put into the choice of a summer hotel, or a country club, or a school for your children. More: you can resign from the club and join another or move from the hotel—but you can't jump off the *Hottentot* with your Vuitton trunks and your Hermes bags, if you change your mind!"

The "Big Three" at this time were the *Berengaria,* the *Aquitania* and the *Mauretania*; and they were all venerable, war-scarred, famous and weighted with three or four funnels. They could not claim priority in speed as the new German ships began to assert themselves; and they had little of the Latin dash of the Italian *Rex* and the *Conte di Savoia,* none of the Gallic panache of the *Ile de France.* What they had was also what they attained to—something that most of the world, ashore as well as at sea, had already put aside forever.

"Sailing in the Big Three recently have been . . . the front-page personalities of the world," continued the advertisement, "among these a Reigning Queen and two Royal Princes, a Premier of England, eighteen ambassadors . . . every American Cardinal, the admitted leader of American Banking . . . and names from *Burke's and DeBrett's Peerages* and the *Almanach de Gotha* too numerous to record . . . with their cousins and in-laws from Southampton, Newport, Bar Harbor, Chicago, San Francisco. . . ."

It was probably inevitable that the *Mauretania*—now more than twenty years old, on her last legs and badly in need of business—should be characterized as the favorite of youth. "She attracts the 'Younger Set,' " said the pamphlet, because her personality is "very gay, always, very chic; her sailings are gala nights, with the Junior League at its most junior visible all over the lot. . . . You will find her decks populous with young girls and young men who more nearly than any other flesh-and-blood young girls and young men look like the drawings in *Vanity Fair* and *Vogue*. Girls just 'out,' sophomores on vacation, whole families of sons and daughters going abroad for the summer or for school. People you've seen on the beach at Southampton or Newport . . . on the trails at Hot Springs . . . or at the polo at Meadowbrook in the fall. Dancing at dinner in the restaurant," said the ad-writer with a lack of condescension to the rules of grammar, "the floor looks like the Ambassador Grill during Christmas vacation. Tea in the lounge, like a coming-out party at the Colony Club. And the crowd, after dinner, dancing in the lounge, looks like a cross-section of any one of the Assemblies—as young, and as gay." Finally, inscrutably, said her salesman, the old dowager of a ship "holds the passionate allegiance of whole families of America's highest type, who would rather miss Ascot, or the first day of grouse shooting, than cross in any other ship afloat, but the *Mauretania*."

Without quite coming out with it, the writer pegged the big Brunhildelike *Berengaria* as the vulgarian among the three sisters he was charged to promote. In this he shared the feeling of one of the ship's own officers, a man whose cynicism had not been mellowed by his social opportunities. "Everybody on the *Berengaria*, even the dogs," he said, "were 'socially prominent.' . . . The *Berengaria* was principally a gleaming and bejewelled ferry boat for the rich and titled: for the Sultan of Jahore, Lord Duveen, the Earl of Warwick and many Cortlands, Vanderbilts and Swopes."

"The Big B" was, after all, of foreign origin, a war orphan, and could perhaps be forgiven for her disposition toward the loud, the flashy and the kind of insistent bad taste that went under the rubric of the debonair. "The *Berengaria* is accustomed to move through the night brighter than the Milky Way with the clustered constellations aboard her. . . . The Queens who cross in the *Berengaria* are the more conspicuous Queens . . . the more debonair Mayors choose her. A *Berengaria* sailing is tempestuous with the exploding of flashlights, the pursuit of reporters. . . . Everything about the *Berengaria* is on the grand, the opulent, scale. She is sensational. Sensational people board her. . . . Her passenger lists are electric with great names. Great enterprises of finance, of the world worldly, are flung back and forth across her tables. And you may find yourself the day after sailing with your deck chair next to one that rings louder around the world than any rumour of peace or war. . . . No one who is amused by encounters with celebrities should deprive himself of the chance acquaintances of the *Berengaria*."

The social *ton* and spiritual aura of both the *Mauretania* and the *Berengaria* were, it is clear, comprehensible and communicable. But in the case of the *Aquitania*, an evanescent, almost subliminal, *soupçon* of distinctiveness defied the rude adequacy of words. The message lay between the lines . . . and the burden of it seemed to be that she was a ship of such quintessential sophistication that only life as it was lived in the stately homes of England could provide a serviceable metaphor.

"The *Aquitania*'s passenger lists tend slightly toward Burke and DeBrett," continued the agency man. "The county-family sort of atmosphere . . . predisposes in her favor people of social consequence, people of title, people who like their transatlantic crossings to taste of that rather formal sub-division into hierarchies—social, political, hereditary—which mark their lives. . . . If a ship may be like a house, the *Aquitania* is like some Georgian house of weathered brick that looks through the mist toward the fairy tale outlines of Windsor Castle. A house quiet and beautiful with age without, and inside as modern, as perfectly appointed, as some tower apartment on Park Avenue that has sprung up overnight to forty stories. . . . The people who cross in her are people you might meet at an important Thursday-to-Monday, where blood and achievement both count. If you like to pack your simplest jumper suits and your heaviest boots alongside of your most explicitly chic evening gowns and slippers and go down to Surrey or Berkshire or "Bucks" to weekend in some Elizabethan house that shows how beauty may multiply with the years . . . you will like . . . the six-day crossing in the *Aquitania*, the aristocrat of the sea. By day, Harris tweeds . . . Chanel jerseys . . . indolent conversation and energetic sport. By night a sudden increase of tempo . . . a blaze of jewels . . . the gleam of ivory shoulders . . . gowns, rose, gold, green. . . . Men and women both wearing formality, brilliance, with the perfect ease that is the distinction and delight of aristocratic English life. The same sharp contrast of the extremes of informality and ceremony that makes English country life so stimulating is part of the charm of life, day by day, night by night. . . ."

The earlier art-museum pretensions of the *Aquitania* now took second place to notions that would have her represent a sort of sea-going stately home. Yet the suites named for great painters and hung with reproductions of each of the masters' most famous works were still a prime feature of her luxury accommodations. One small consequence of the ship's role as a floating gallery of reproductions was the removal of a genuine British national treasure—Gainsborough's "Blue Boy"— from the walls of a regal house in London and its shipment to the home of a railroad tycoon in California.

The art dealer, Lord Duveen, traveling to England on the *Aquitania*, found himself in a suite next to that of his old acquaintances, H. E. and Arabella Huntington. The Huntingtons were, in fact, ensconced in the Gainsborough Suite, which had a private dining room dominated by a large reproduction of the "Blue Boy." Invited to dine with the Huntingtons one evening, Lord Duveen was pleased to accept. As the meal progressed, he noted that Mr. Huntington's eyes were lifted time and again to the figure on the wall. Finally, according to Duveen's biographer, S. N. Behrman, Huntington cautiously addressed his art-dealer friend.

"Joe, who's the boy in the blue suit?"

"That is a reproduction of the famous 'Blue Boy' . . . Gainsborough's finest and most famous painting."

"Where's the original?"

"It belongs to the Duke of Westminster and hangs in his collection at Grosvenor House, London."

"How much is it?"

"It can probably not be had at any price."

"It must be a very great painting."

"Indeed, it is the greatest work of England's greatest master and would be the crown in any collection of English paintings."

"What do you think would be the price if it *were* for sale?"

"Probably about six hundred thousand dollars."

"I might see my way clear to paying that much."

The Huntingtons disembarked at Cherbourg; Duveen went on to Southampton. Wasting no time (he had heard rumors that the Duke of Westminster was somewhat pressed for funds), Duveen at once went on to London and called at Grosvenor House. The Duke was unhesitatingly receptive: as far as he was concerned, "Blue Boy" could go—so could almost anything else in the place. Duveen bought three paintings, including "Blue Boy," which he then had carefully wrapped so that he could carry it to Paris himself and unveil it for the Huntingtons in person.

The first sight of the original excited but also troubled the Huntingtons: wasn't this "Blue Boy" a lot *greener* than the "Blue Boy" on the *Aquitania?* Green or blue, they made it clear to Duveen that they wanted it for their very own. Duveen had the painting cleaned in the hope that a bit more blue would begin to show, then took it to New York himself. The Metropolitan Museum wanted to make a special exhibit of the painting, but Duveen refused their request. Instead, he showed it for several weeks at his own gallery on Fifth Avenue, then carted it across the continent and delivered it to H. E. and Arabella.

❧ SECTION II ❧

*The New Germans / Bremen and Europa / Jack Meets the
Giant / Ella Wheeler Wilcox and the Street of Shops / The
Four-Day Boat / Thomas Wolfe and the Knife of Love*

I N THE WIDE, dismal and debris-filled wake of World War
I, the German merchant marine was down; but only for the
briefest of interims was it out. Decimated, their celebrated liners
parceled out among their old rivals on the Atlantic, the German companies were left with only a few vessels too small to meet either the
demands of vengeance or the satisfactions of greed.

But as early as 1920, an eager and obliging American company—the
American Ship and Commerce Corporation—entered into a mutually
"convenient" agreement reestablishing most of Hamburg-Amerika's
worldwide prewar operations. This agreement did not include the incomparable services of Albert Ballin. The genius of the German shipping empire had endured the war but was unable to stand up to the
peace. He took his own life just at a point when he might have seen the
chance of renewing it.

In 1922, the Hamburg company and its Bremen rival were once more
admitted to the Atlantic "club"—the North Atlantic Passenger Conference—which controlled routes, rates and services, as well as general
maritime behavior, and which alone was able to confer the status

that would enable a company to operate. Resuming service, their small ships seemed merely to dog-paddle in the water while fabulous German-built ships under new names, with new oil burners, raced past them en route to New York or Southampton. Nevertheless, these little vessels persisted until the moment when Germany would again rock the maritime world with ships as sensational in their time as were the *Kaiser Wilhelm der Grosse* and the *Deutschland* in the first years of the century.

In conceiving the *Bremen* and the *Europa*, the directors of Norddeutscher Lloyd were concerned first with speed—or, as they put it, "emphatic pronunciations of the principle of rapid speed"—then with size. Finally they wanted a kind of interior decor that would end the Wagnerian emblazonry of the Teutonic phase of La Belle Epoque and, at the same time, suggest a future already adumbrated on the drawing boards of Bauhaus. "The ostentatious luxury of former times," said F. A. Breuhaus, "which no longer appeals to the man of today, has been avoided in the interior decorations by laying stress on the purity of form, on the beauty of line and on the superior quality of the material. The architecture of the *Bremen* emancipates us from a time which is not our own and leads us into the grandeur of our present age, in which we desire to breathe and not to suffocate."

To some of the new designers, the century's vogue for the decorative imitation of historical periods had led to one good thing: by 1925 or so the past had been unloaded, all the royal junkyards and attics had been thoroughly looted, the only period left was now. To a man like Le Corbusier, the chance had finally come to narrow the depressing gap between advanced engineering and retrograde architecture. "The ship," he said, "is the first stage in the realization of a world organized according to the new spirit," and he seemed to imply that the true new aesthetic would be created by engineers unhampered by the maniacal eclecticism of decorators. Thus the new German ships were conceived in the climate of an emergent international aesthetic and its recognition of the beauty of functional objects.

As for speed, recovery of the Blue Riband from England was to be taken as a matter of course. The really crucial concern was for enough speed to guarantee that just two ships could initiate and carry on a week-by-week express service all the way from Bremerhaven to Ambrose Lightship. This meant that, within the space of seven days, each of the new ships would have to be able to cross the Atlantic, refuel, reprovision, reload passengers and be ready to cast off on a dovetailing schedule designed to work most of the year around. Previously, especially in the case of the British companies, such express service had called for the constant use of three, sometimes four, crack liners. With a tonnage of 50,000, the new ships were in a category just a bit below that of the old *Vaterland, Imperator* and *Bismarck*. But in terms of decor, they were in another class altogether. To get a new "German look" in marine interiors, the company's directors had gone to a rising generation of designers whose simple, flat, geometrical surfaces and absence of ornamentation had already begun to influence architecture around the world. The result was decor of a kind that made the superseded old liners seem as far in the past as a Junker hunting lodge would be from the Potsdam Tower.

The keel of the *Bremen* was laid in the Weser shipyards of her namesake city on June 18, 1927, at the same time that the keel of her sister ship and running mate was laid in the Blohm & Voss yards of Hamburg. Confident that they had picked winners, determined that the entrance of their new challengers would be dramatic, the North German Lloyd Company staged a sort of two-city launching festival. On consecutive days in August, 1928, before an audience of scores of thousands, including a press corps that numbered hundreds, the *Bremen* and the *Europa* slid down their respective ways. Their joint tonnage made a big splash, and the sister act might have gained even greater coverage if the original plan for simultaneous, record-breaking maiden voyages could have been carried out. But the *Europa* suffered serious damage by fire while she was being fitted out and had to hang back for a whole year before she was able to join her stable mate.

In the meantime the *Bremen* had proved herself a knockout—a passenger ship with the cut and audacity of a destroyer—and a potential giant-killer. Sadly enough, the giant she would kill was neither some craven sea raider nor some gimcrack fun house afloat, but the graciously aging *Mauretania*. The two ships first met, or were at least mutually sighted, quite by coincidence, in the English Channel in June, 1929. The *Mauretania*—mellow, rich and aristocratic—had just left Cherbourg en route to New York; the *Bremen*—raw, new, streamlined and characterless—was returning from a shakedown cruise in the open sea, coasting easily between the Casquets and Bishop's Rock. "It was a summer night," wrote Humfrey Jordan. "Many passengers would not disturb their rest or their amusement to gaze at the lighted shadow of a distant ship, but from the bridge, from the forecastle, from the port-holes, from the nearest spot they could reach from which to see, men and women of her crew did. To these men and women, for there were not a few stewardesses in the *Mauretania* who had proper pride in their ship, that passing of the *Bremen* in the night was a tremendous happening. They could not see much of her; they had to guess at much of what they only saw dimly; but there were many eyes straining to get some idea of her. She was there, actually steaming the seas, almost ready for the contest; that was the fact of tremendous importance."

Impervious to such sentiments or considerations, the *Bremen* had the brash coltishness of the new thing. To the strains of "Deutschland Über Alles," she was pulled away from Bremerhaven's Columbus Quay on July 16, 1929. Then, as all of Germany listened in to daily sea-to-shore broadcasts of the ship's progress—"an interesting experiment in wireless transmission"—she set her bows westward. In one swoop, crossing the Atlantic at a mere shade under 28 knots, she made the old ships seem just as obsolete and top-heavy as, in truth, they were. All by herself, she gave the long-settled quality of transatlantic travel a nudge and its sagging glamour a boost.

Even at a glance the *Bremen* communicated the excitement of something arrestingly novel and genuinely new. Her hull, constructed on an oval plan, had lines that gave her an air of graceful staunchness; her two massive funnels were stocky and short, getting away completely from the somewhat precarious stovepipe feeling that characterized the great prewar liners. They were in fact too short, almost stubby. Though they conveyed a sense of potency they also conveyed splashes of oil and smut that made her open decks aft a hazard for promenaders and passengers bundled in deck chairs. But even when these were replaced, the *Bremen*'s stacks were still notably shorter than those of any other big ship. Her two masts were also short, raked back like the funnels with military smartness. A suggestion of streamlining emanated from her rounded-off bridge. Her breadth of 102 feet made her the broadest ship on the ocean and, to one observer, gave her the appearance of "a vast sea-going cathedral of steel."

The most notable thing about the conception of the *Bremen*, however, was the fact that her interior designers had somehow recognized and acceded to the fact that she was a ship with a shape and a function. Instead of merely installing restaurants and ballrooms that might have been appropriate for any good Berlin hotel or club, her designers took care to follow the lines of her structure and to make their interiors conform to all its sweeps and nuances. Highly polished rosewood, ebony and brass; a main saloon with walls "pierced by rows of high, narrow, round-headed windows, outlined with rims of polished brass," gave the *Bremen* a marine look, a "shippiness" that ran directly counter to the cozy house-in-the-country look of British ships and the vacuously empty hotel-lobby atmosphere of the American liners.

Yet, in avoiding the "ostentatious luxury of former times," the decorators of the *Bremen* came to pitfalls that made their claims to "the grandeur of the present age" highly questionable. Replacing the overstuffed with the understated, they ended up with a ship that was in many ways as clinical as an emergency ward. When paintings and tapestries carrying out "cute" themes with a bold Hanoverian realism were hung on shiny bare walls, the effect was one of a cheapness earlier designers would not for a moment have countenanced. There was a sense of cleanliness and efficiency about the *Bremen* and her sister ship, qualities that made them seem a bit cold and dehumanized. In a way, the taste of an upholstered era had simply been replaced by the taste of one for which the word "functional" had overtones of magic. But the worst aspects of the new dispensation were its unprecedented allowances for large displays of kitsch. Mosaics and tapestries on the level of calendar art were bad enough; some of the most celebrated features of the *Bremen* were worse. In the middle of the dance floor— where, according to the ship's printed program, "Dancing with little surprises will enjoy the guests"—stood an illuminated fountain which changed colors as formally dressed couples turned to the rhythms of "Yes, Sir, That's My Baby." The wooden walls of the library and writing room were "adorned with tarsia-work," and enscrolled upon them were homiletic advices from Ella Wheeler Wilcox, Benjamin Franklin and, of all people, Aaron Burr. In the Street of Shops, a little fountain placed in a niche lined with mother of pearl sent up a spout of real, honest-to-God perfume.

The new Atlantic speed record clicked off by the *Bremen* was a passage time of 4 days, 17 hours, 42 minutes. The reign of the *Mauretania,* much longer than that of any other ship in the books, was finally over. The old Queen of the Seas was actually at her dock in the North River when the *Bremen* sailed up beside her, flaunting the Blue Riband. "Observing the niceties of a decent rivalry," her Captain McNeil boarded the German liner to tender his personal congratulations to Captain Ziegenbaum and to see for himself the nature of the ship that had bested his.

With one crossing, the era of the "four-day boat" was ushered in, as well as a minor interregnum—from the *Bremen's* record crossing in 1929 to that of the *United States* in 1952—when international attention to the whereabouts of the Blue Riband was at a greater intensity than at any time since the earlier Anglo-German contest had ended with victory for Great Britain in 1907. "No liner in modern times has so caught the imagination of the public," boasted the North German Lloyd. "Already she has become a legend and a classic. Her name gleams like a new planet." By the time that the *Europa*, just as steely, sleek and "new," had proved that she was as fast and, on some crossings, even faster than the *Bremen*, the two sisters from the north of Germany had quite captured the cash and kudos of the transatlantic business. Their success hastened the end of the old refurbished dowagers of England and France and quickened the plans—particularly those of the Cunard Line—to build ships that might match the express service the Germans had so efficiently begun.

Thomas Wolfe, returning from his first trip to Europe in August, 1925, had found Aline Bernstein, the love of his short life, on board the *Olympic*. Since Mrs. Bernstein was traveling first class and he was in third, they did not meet on the voyage until the next-to-last night, when she came down and he went up, to join a gala in second. "He turned," wrote Wolfe in the voice of his surrogate Eugene Gant, "and saw her then, and so finding her, was lost, and so losing self, was found, and so seeing her, saw for a fading moment only the pleasant image of the woman that perhaps she was, and that life saw. He never knew; he only knew that from that moment his spirit was impaled upon the knife of love."

On the last night, as the *Olympic* lay anchored in Quarantine off Staten Island, Wolfe and Mrs. Bernstein exchanged, in the words of biographer Andrew Turnbull, "their first endearments." Three years later, speaking for himself, Wolfe said, "My life has been a strange and miraculous thing. In a thousand places the miracle has happened to me.

Because I was penniless and took one ship instead of another, I met the great and beautiful friend who has stood by me through all the torture, struggle and madness of my nature."

When he came, almost inevitably, to write an epiphany to an ocean liner that might match his famous discourse on trains in *Look Homeward, Angel,* the ship he had in mind was partly the old Cunard stager and partly the spanking new *Europa,* on which he crossed in 1931. In this flight of poetic prose, he chose to picture the great ship as she rode at anchor, preparing to leave Cherbourg for New York, lying "in the water with the living stillness of all objects that were made to move."

Oddly enough, Wolfe saw this composite Anglo-German ship of his fancy as a "visitant from a new world." She was American, he felt, because her spirit was American, as well as "the impulse that communicated itself in each of her lines." She was alive, he felt, "with the supreme ecstasy of the modern world, which is the voyage to America." But beyond her symbolism, he clearly saw her as fabulous and beautiful. "In this soft, this somewhat languid air," he wrote, "the ship glowed like an immense and brilliant jewel. All of her lights were on; they burned row by row straight across her 900 feet of length, with the small, hard twinkle of cut gems; it was as if the vast, black cliff of her hull, which strangely suggested the glittering night-time cliff of the fabulous city that was her destination, had been sown with diamonds.

"And above this, her decks were ablaze with light. Her enormous super structure, with its magnificent frontal sweep, her proud breast which was so full of power and speed, her storied decks and promenades as wide as city streets . . . all of this, made to move upon the stormy seas, leaning against eternity and the grey welter of the Atlantic at twenty-seven knots an hour, tenanted by ghosts, impregnated by the subtle perfumes of thousands of beautiful and expensive women, alive with the memory of the silken undulence of their long backs, with the naked, living velvet of their shoulders as they paced down the decks at night—all of this, with the four great funnels that in the immense drive and energy of their slant were now cut sharp and dark against the evening sky, burned with a fierce, exultant vitality in the soft melancholy of this coast."

⚝ SECTION III ⚝

Ships in the Air / Shadows on the Sea Lanes / Walter Wellman and His Nondescript Balloon / The Spirit of St. Louis / Prophets in Goggles

VEHICLES, with or without wings, feathers and wax, that might be made to stay in the air had been thought about for centuries. Ideas about actual air-borne transportation were as old as Leonardo da Vinci. Among those who speculated on the subject long after Leonardo's time was the American inventor and jack-of-all-trades, Rufus Porter.

In the 1850s, Porter envisioned air travel across continents and oceans. When, as editor of the periodical *Scientific American*, Mr. Porter was in Washington trying to raise money to form a company, the journal reported: "The funds, when raised, are to be applied to the construction of an aerial ship capable of containing 150 passengers and which, Mr. Porter says, will easily carry them to California or London in three or four days. He proposed to call for an instalment of one dollar only per share, until after a machine has been built capable of carrying three persons and a journey has been made to Baltimore and back, thereby demonstrating the feasibility of the plan. He says that several hundreds of persons have already bespoken passage. Among

457

other advantages Mr. Porter includes that of transporting soldiers in time of war. Only think of the astonishment of an enemy quietly encamped in the soft moonlight, having, in the twinkling of an eye, a whole regiment of Uncle Sam's Invincibles dropped upon them from a squadron of Porter's ships. But, in process of time, our enemies will have them also, so that, hereafter, contending squadrons must meet in mid-air, while the peaceable portion of mankind can rest quietly below. Verily there are stirring times ahead."

Nothing came of Rufus Porter's madcap trip to Baltimore. But as early as 1910, another American, by the name of Walter Wellman, actually persuaded five grown men to join him in a dirigible flight that was supposed to take them from the minarets of Atlantic City to the steeples of Europe. Since the airship, christened *America*, was driven by gasoline motors, the first problem to be solved in planning an overseas crossing was the means of carrying sufficient fuel. Wellman thought he had solved it by attaching gasoline containers to ropes trailing from the after part of the dirigible in a way that would allow them also to function as ballast. At the start of the flight, these containers would float on the water, dragged along by the dirigible. Then, as fuel was needed, they would be pulled up one by one, emptied and jettisoned.

The craft took off—or was released from the tug of its ropes—on October 18, 1910. As soon as it got out over the Atlantic the trailing gasoline drums proved to be a terrific drag, bouncing from wave to wave with a vigor that threatened to twist and turn the *America* to pieces. By the time the shaken little party was four hundred miles southeast of Sandy Hook, the motors had begun to cough and sputter, a leak in the gas bag was discernible, and disaster waited.

Sagging and coughing to a grim conclusion, the expedition was all but over when, out of the blue—the sea, not the sky—the Royal Mail liner *Trent* appeared. The men in the air attracted the ship's attention with distress signals sent out by Morse lamp and wireless. Full steam, the *Trent* came on and was soon wallowing under the dirigible and maneuvering with difficulty to stay there. Along with everything else, the airship had a lifeboat suspended beneath her gondola. But Wellman was unable to figure out how to use this as long as his craft was high in the air. He proposed to Captain Down of the *Trent* that he guide his ship to a position directly underneath the aircraft, grapple the lines from the gondola, and hold onto them while he and his crew lowered themselves onto the liner's upper deck. The thought of a disabled airship bulging with hydrogen and drifting a few feet above his funnels did not thrill the Captain, yet he allowed himself to be persuaded. The airship-to-deck transfer was hardly begun, however, when it became obvious to him that the maneuver was going to be too delicate and too dangerous for everyone. Wellman and his men then proceeded to take their seats in the flying lifeboat, waited for the dirigible to stop swinging with every gust of wind, and eventually cut their ropes and let go. They tobogganed into the water with a jolt, but did not capsize. The dirigible soared away like a bird released from the hand, settled down on the sea and expired. The six men in a boat were lifted onto the *Trent* and brought into New York as thousands cheered—including President William Howard Taft, who sent a personal message to Captain Down, and an anonymous poet commending the ship's crew for "Saving Wellman and his crew/ Who were rescued, not too soon/ From their nondescript balloon."

On May 27, 1927, young Charles A. Lindbergh piloted a single-engine plane, the *Spirit of St. Louis,* from Mineola, Long Island, nonstop to Paris. During the thirty-three hours he spent above the ocean he passed just about all of the big liners of the decade except for the *Bremen* and the *Europa.* None of them heard it, but the sound of the engine of the *Spirit of St. Louis* had the impact of a tolling bell. Above the clamor in the shipyards and the clamor at pier sides, that death knell would ring for forty years. The great transatlantic ferry run would soon be reduced to a few summertime crossings aimed at skimming the cream of what was left of travelers who had money, leisure and a terror of airplanes. Then ships would be making pitiful efforts to survive by publicly announcing that they were *not* boring, or by pretending that they were floating resorts for handsome bachelors, or nice places to visit, or that they were gourmet restaurants that just happened to be leaving the Hudson River for Europe.

Long before Lindbergh's spectacular solo, the hint that planes might replace ships as Atlantic carriers had blossomed into possibility, then burgeoned into a likelihood that put the shadow of dread upon the whole shipping fraternity. When the famous Dutch designer of aircraft, Anthony Herman Gerard Fokker, boarded the *Berengaria* for a voyage to New York in 1925, his words to reporters seemed almost contemptuous. "In five years," he said as he gazed down the length of the liner's sun-swept boat deck, "I shall be able to fly to New York in a few hours."

But to most maritime men, statements like this belonged in the encyclopedia of human crankery. "People who amuse themselves with speculations as to the time when steamers will no longer plough the oceans," said one of them in 1925, "and when all our overseas transportation will be done by airmen in air machines, are in the happy company of those who still pursue the pleasures of alchemy, those who are always trying to square a circle, and that other cheerful companion of dreamers who have faith in the possibilities of perpetual motion."

In that same year an aeronautical designer, Jose G. Navarro, came out with a plan to make air travel between the United Kingdom and the United States "comparatively cheap and extremely expeditious." Navarro proposed to build planes with a wing spread of 185 feet, 9 engines, a crew of 38, with a saloon on each of several decks that would be 45 feet long and 9 feet high. There were to be dining rooms, sleeping compartments and electric kitchens. The capacity, at first, would be limited to 150 passengers who would be "whirled through space at the rate of 150 miles an hour, or just a full day's run from the aerodromes in Liverpool and London to those in New York and Boston." To make these crossings entirely feasible, stops would be made in Newfoundland and Ireland on the way over; Marseilles, Lisbon and the Azores on the way back.

This was all fine for readers of scientific fiction, but men who knew the sea could say precisely how and why transatlantic air travel simply would not work. Who in the world would choose to endure what was envisioned for the air traveler as early as 1926? "Given even a giant plane," said one prophet, "with accommodation for say fifty people. Everything is done in frantic, not to say delirious, haste, for the chief thought of the air voyager is to land safely on the other side. It is a rush from start to finish, and the traveler's greatest fear must be not how far he is from his destination, but how deep he will dive if he does not reach it. He is, and must be, cribbed, cabin'd and confined, and however spacious his accommodations may be it must inevitably fall far below that which is available on the smallest liner."

"We have long known that mechanically, the Atlantic flight is perfectly feasible," said another. "It is not any misgiving as to the machine which causes people to hold their breath when a man, or men, jump off into the blue, with no possibility of landing under at least a thousand leagues. It is doubts as to their ability to counter those factors, any of which may entirely neutralize the perfection of the machine. Chief amongst these are the weather and the problem of human endurance." Even should these somehow be overcome, he said, "the simple truth is that aerial transport can never be made to pay. It can only be run on a scale of charges, which, compared with stateroom fares, is simply preposterous. There will, probably, always be a very limited number of people prepared to pay these charges, just as there will always be people prepared to face the heavy irreducible risks of flying. The fundamental fact to bear in mind, in regarding the airplane as a commercial proposition is that four-fifths of her total power must always be expended in keeping her in the air, leaving her only one-fifth to exert on her payable load. . . . Flying has come to stay. But I cannot believe that the airway will ever replace the seaway. We can step aboard a Cunarder at either Southampton or Liverpool, with a feeling of assurance that we shall be in New York with time-table punctuality, travelling in luxury and safety. The aircraft can never hold such assurance."

✄ SECTION IV ✄

THE SHUTTING off of all but a trickle of emigrant traffic—and a conviction that the flow would never be resumed—had led the steamship lines to take ingenious steps to fill their thousands of berths. But this recurrence of adversity as the mother of necessity did not please them a bit. Distrustful of the new, supposedly democratic, boom in ocean-going, they were uncertain about which of the new categories might endure, reluctant to order new ships until they knew what kind of ship might be made to pay. The result was to prolong an already extended hiatus. No British ship of any size had been built since the prewar *Britannic*, no French ship since the *Paris* of 1916, no German ship since the *Majestic*, née *Bismarck*.

In the absence of new attractions, the sea lanes were busy with vessels which, in one way or the other, were "making do." Their decks had become bewilderingly transformed. First class was now cabin class; third class was tourist; steerage was tourist third. Without quite disguising origins, one kind of decor was imposed and superimposed upon another, so that Britannia ruled the waves with a glint of Prussia in her blue eyes. To confuse matters further, a middle-class clientele was suddenly demanding cabins *de luxe* and gladly paying exorbitant prices for them just when many of the sons and daughters of the rich were booking "poor."

"Miss Hope Iselin Livermore," reported a social editor, "daughter of Mr. and Mrs. Philip W. Livermore, of 1105 Park Avenue, New York, [is] making a trip in the tourist third class cabin section of the *Berengaria*, as a sort of society experiment which is becoming increasingly popular." The possibility that the Livermores were feeling the pinch, or that their darling daughter was lucky to be able to scare up a few century notes for a summer abroad, were not in the realm of the credible.

In the midst of reversals and confusions, there arose a notion that gave comfort to those who traveled "hard" either because they were thrifty or because they were destitute. This was the cozy belief that third cabin or tourist, or whatever the austerity accommodations were called, somehow attracted individuals free of the corruptions of status, money and power. It became the thing to say that ocean travel on the cheap was "more amusing." This belief, persisting through the rest of the steamship era, made the arid *longueurs* of third-class travel seem preferable to the cushioned *longueurs* of first. Individuals who, having survived the rigors of thrift, had the courage to say they were appalled to find the shipboard experience of the affluent different only in appointments and open spaces, were not able to weaken this conviction. Some of the steamship companies attempted to play it both ways. You did not dress for dinner in third class, suggested a brochure from Hamburg-Amerika, unless you simply could not bear the thought of slumming. "Dressing in Third Class?" asked the pamphlet, then answered its own question. "Many who are quite accustomed to putting on evening wear at home, take this class as a vacation from 'dressing up.' Dinner jackets are distinctly in the minority, although occasionally some dandy will slip on his 'smoking' through force of habit."

In any case, as business began noticeably to pick up, the Cunard Line, with a fine display of retrograde imagination, ordered several ships of moderate size and decked them out in ways that promised to bring back the *folie de grandeur* and operatic fancies of the prewar scene. The *Carinthia*, for instance, a sort of Iberian *capriccio* incongruously flying the Union Jack, boasted a smoking room with a scheme "based on certain elements in the Toledo house of the great Spanish painter, El Greco," along with copies of "Murillo's famous *Jeune Mendi-ant*, Velasquez' Philip IV and Ribera's satirical study of a philosopher." In this room a complete suit of Spanish armor stood beside a fireplace with a recess "formed by a typical arch, the inner curve being lined with intaglio tiles." Even the interstices of the recess were notable, fitted as they were with "a repeat of sixteen *motifs* representing abstract ideas."

Still, the new dispensation would not neglect the arts and crafts of Merrie England. In the *Franconia,* another Cunarder of modest tonnage, there was a saloon "typical of an old English Inn, oak-paneled, half-timbered and arranged with a striking brick ingle-nook."

A business that seemed always able to disguise its often depressing economic realities in the easy romance of the high seas no longer took the trouble. As far as steamships were concerned, the early years of the '20s were homogenized and dull—except for those liners operated by the Compagnie Générale Transatlantique. As soon after the war as it was possible to travel overseas, American intellectuals had begun a love affair with the French Line. The rehabilitated *France* and the new *Paris,* making much of the fact that their passengers were surrounded by all the totems and customs of *la belle France* as soon as they stepped aboard, became sea-going rendezvous for artists, writers, musicians and other Americans literate enough to know who Toulouse-Lautrec was, what *escargots* were and how to get to the Lapin Agile. For those who believed that "the most moving and pathetic fact in the social life of America today is emotional and aesthetic starvation," flight from Indi-ana to Greenwich Village was merely the first stage on their way out of bondage. The French Line pier adjoined the Hudson River side of the Village and there they could find, as the company advertised, "The Longest Gangplank in the World." Then, to capture expatriates and home-grown bohemians almost totally, came the beloved *Ile de France* —huge, black-funneled and proud in the water. No one would ever quite account for her matchless power to attract the talented and youth-ful, the stylish and the famous. No one could ever say why one ship, with appointments and dimensions neither better nor bigger than those of a dozen other ships, would win for herself devotion and affection that set her apart. In the course of her long life, she seemed to be always at the center of things—from the day she went careening like a bronco out of her fitting-out basin to the day, so many years later, when she was blown up, for fun, off the coast of Japan.

Constructed by French workers in the St. Nazaire yards of Chantier de Penhoët, decorated by more than thirty different French firms, the *Ile de France* managed to absorb and integrate all influences. The result was something uneven in particulars, yet, on the whole, quintessentially Gallic. Neither new nor old, she possessed a warmth, a palpable sense of aristocratic reserve, a sort of *laissez-faire* grace that hid her touches of ugliness and mellowed the strains of the *brut* and the stridently *moderne* that were evident throughout the length of her. Some things about her called forth the silly statistics and hyperbolic *soufflés* that new steamships had always evoked. Her "tremendous" main dining room was "twenty feet wider than the Church of the Madeleine"; the dance floor in the Salon de Conversation measured 516 square yards; the bar in the first-class lounge was "the longest afloat." Where other ships had their conventional garden lounges, she had a complete Parisian sidewalk café with awnings above, and saucers marked "6 francs" on the tables; in her children's playroom there was a real carousel with painted ponies and proper music to go around by.

"Wishing to show all the richness and all the imagination of French decorative art," said a journalist, "the Compagnie Générale Transatlantique decided to make the 439 cabins in first class different from each other and to add four apartments of great luxury and ten of luxury. Furthermore the ship was decorated with statues by Baudry and Dejean, bas-reliefs by Jeanniot, Bouchard and Saupique, enamel panels by Schmied, artistic iron-work by Subes and Szabo, paintings by Ducos de la Haille, Gernez, Balande, not forgetting, in the chapel, an admirable Stations of the Cross sculptured in wood by Le Bourgeois."

This fairly dubious litany of forgotten names can perhaps be explained—if not excused—by the fact that the great painters of "*le bateau lavoir*" and the age of Picasso and Matisse were still *avant-garde* artists and not figures of wide public concern. It would take another generation or two before a general public would covet versions of their works on matchboxes, towels, posters from Sears Roebuck—and the walls of staterooms. The *Ile de France* belonged largely to an older dispensation slightly desecrated by what were rapidly coming to be known as modern improvements.

To enter the *Ile*'s 700-seat dining room was to descend, under the *mal-de-tête* glare of high ceiling lights, into a vast mausoleum "done in three shades of grey marble from the Pyrenees" that was additionally illuminated by 112 motifs of electrified Lalique. Throughout the ship—prefiguring the high style of the 1930s—were great slabs of laminated wood polished to a clinical glossiness. In spite of such details, the scale and shape of the *Ile*'s public rooms were admirable; she was handsome without being grand, comfortable without being overstuffed, class-conscious without living by exclusions. The same ill-defined and curious streak of conservatism was evident in her outward appearance. With a coal-black hull and a solid white superstructure out of which rose three tall, red-and-black funnels only slightly raked, she was the picture of "imposing dignity and curiously old-fashioned grace."

The one indisputably new thing about the *Ile de France* was the clutter of a plane-launching catapult installed high on her afterdeck. This contraption was designed as a means of shortening the delivery time of transoceanic mail by a full twenty-four hours. It worked so well that the dramatic torpedo-like launching of a plane—one day out from New York or from Cherbourg—was part of the entertainment of an *Ile de France* crossing for more than two years. The maiden flight of this service took place on August 13, 1928. When the liner was still four hundred miles northeast of Sandy Hook, nearly all of her passengers gathered on the boat deck to witness the birth of a new era. In leather and goggles, Lieutenant Louis-Marie Demougeot and his radioman climbed into a Lioré & Oliver biplane and sat there waiting while every-one held his breath. Then with an ear-shattering detonation the thrust of the catapult sent them high out over the foaming wake of the *Ile*. As their 480-horsepower Gnome and Rhone Jupiter engine took hold, they dipped back, circled the ship to waving handkerchiefs and applause from all classes, and disappeared toward the American shore. Three hours and seven minutes later they splashed down near Quarantine in New York Harbor, delivered up their mailbags and went into Man-hattan to await the arrival of their shipmates on the following day.

One year later the *Bremen* was fitted with a similar plane-launching device. The next logical thing seemed to be landing spaces on liners that would save a day at each end of the voyage for passengers as well as for mails. "The fast mail liner of the future," went one prediction, "may well be built with an immense flight-deck, like that of an aircraft carrier, on which a swarm of her own planes will alight when the ship is clear of the Channel, to rise again when she is nearing New York, and carry important travelers to their destination."

On her very first day of sailing anywhere, the *Ile de France* barely avoided being decapitated, or beached, or both. At 1:30 P.M. on May 29, 1927, she was sitting in her fitting-out basin in St. Nazaire, steam up and straining at her hawsers, awaiting the scheduled two o'clock arrival of tugboats that would guide her through the narrow entrance of the basin. Over this entrance, presumably ready to spring open as she approached, was a drawbridge. With everything set to go, her captain had dipped into his cabin to make out some last-minute reports when he sensed that, incredibly, his ship was moving. She was—someone had jumped the gun in giving orders to cast off; the ship was swiftly pulling away from her berth; her mizzenmast was already heading directly into the boom of a shipyard crane.

The captain raced to the bridge and gave the signal "Reverse engines—full speed astern." At once his message was answered with: "Cannot reverse engines—controls jammed." He was now faced with two equally sickening alternatives: to smash through the drawbridge that lay immovably horizontal and unmanned at the basin's outlet, or to run the ship aground, so to speak, by plowing through a wooden pier on the basin's edge. His instant choice was the latter; the *Ile*'s hull could better sustain damage than her superstructure. His hand was actually on the helm and ready to send the liner veering into the pier when he saw the drawbridge miraculously beginning to rise. He changed his mind, let the ship have her head, and shot through the needle's-eye passage with a clearance of less than four feet on either side of her 43,000 tons. By the time she had gained open water, her controls had become unstuck. To slow her tremendous momentum, the captain ordered the anchor down and she was soon riding safe and easy. The hero of the afternoon turned out to be the Lieutenant of the Port. Divining that something was amiss when the ship had begun to move without her captain on the flying bridge, he had taken off like a rabbit for the drawbridge.

A month later, in a blast of whistles and fog horns, surrounded by private yachts, ferryboats, tugboats, splashed by spray from plumes of water sent up by fireboats, the *Ile de France* glided past the Statue of Liberty, gave a deep-throated cry of thanks to her escorts, and was warped into the French Line pier. Thus began her career as "The Boulevard of the Atlantic." In the twelve ensuing years before she would be sent off to war, the *Ile* would make 347 crossings of the Atlantic. Names that would appear, again and again, between the embossed and tasseled cover of her souvenir passenger lists made up a roster that perhaps begins to indicate her character as well as to fix her in time: Arturo Toscanini, Maurice Chevalier, Will Rogers, Maude Adams, John D. Rockefeller, Jascha Heifetz, Bernard Baruch, Argentina, Ivar Kreuger, Jeanette MacDonald, Tallulah Bankhead, Gloria Swanson, Barbara Hutton, Helen Morgan, Pola Negri, Chaliapin.

In those years to come, evenings on the *Ile de France* might be remembered for everything and anything—except that they were spent in the middle of the ocean. The ship as a *place* had become a reality; the ocean was as incidental as the street that runs by a hotel. On one of these evenings, young Ernest Hemingway, en route to Paris and traveling in cabin class because he was broke, was invited to dine in first class by a friend who was also able to provide him with a tuxedo. As the two men were beginning their meal, a "spectacle in white" appeared at the top of the grand staircase. As Hemingway said later, it was "The Kraut, of course." Marlene Dietrich, in a beaded creation that fitted her like kidskin, paused for a long count before her solo descent, then slowly made her way toward a table laid for twelve. As the men of the party rose to honor her arrival, she suddenly shook her head. No, she could not bear to be thirteenth at the table, she said, and turned to leave. At this point, Hemingway rushed into the breach. *He* would make *fourteen*, he said, and the dinner party reshuffled itself into order. "That was how we met," he told his friend A. E. Hotchner. "Pretty romantic, eh?"

ALMOST as if they worked hand in glove with the publicity departments of steamship lines, the American and English press gave endless coverage to the personalities who traveled first class on liners and to the life of glamour, scandal and money-to-burn they were supposed to represent. Cheesecake photographs of actresses, heiresses and divorcées had become obligatory features of the daily paper and the Sunday rotogravure. Ships' reporters' stories about Walter Hagen driving five hundred golf balls from the stern of the *Majestic*—or of Tom Mix leading Tony the "wonder horse" along the companionways of the *Aquitania*—added their mite to the vast literature of trivia for which the decade had an endless appetite. Beyond the froth and below decks, the serious business of transporting ordinary people trying to salvage old lives or to begin new ones continued.

The third-class passenger, especially if he were a European en route to America, was still identified with the unwashed hordes of the great migration. "It might well be argued," said one captain who could not disguise his contempt, "that he is entitled to neat counter-panes on his bed, Vinolia soap to wash with, serviettes at the dinner tables, and a few more modern 'thrills.' "

Like the whiskered old salts before them, the commodores and captains of the '20s had to oversee, as a matter of policy and profits, the meat-and-potatoes aspects of ship travel. But their deeper concern was reserved for the kingly role into which they had been cast by good seamanship, social finesse and years of *haute cuisine*. The grandest of all of these was probably Sir James Charles, Commodore of the Cunard Line, who quietly keeled over at the conclusion of his seven hundred and twenty-eighth voyage across the Atlantic. To social chronicler Lucius Beebe, this man's lordly ways and Lucullan tastes were a dazzlement and an enchantment. "Guests at Sir James' table lived by protocol," wrote Beebe. "It was an age when the dinner jacket was in universal acceptance among Englishmen as evening attire, and one's steward, on instructions from the bridge, laid out smoking or tails as the commodore might have decreed and left a note naming the dinner hour. You didn't dine at your convenience but the commodore's, and on evenings of the Captain's Dinner full evening dress was required with decorations, which put Americans, unless they were of military background, at a disadvantage in the matter of crosses, ribbons, and miniatures.

"Sir James' tastes at table were vaguely those of Emil Jannings playing Henry VIII. Stewards wheeled in carcasses of whole roasted oxen one night and the next evening small herds of grilled antelope surrounded a hilltop of Strasbourg *foie gras* surmounted with peacock fans. Electrically illuminated *pièces montées* representing the battle of Waterloo and other patriotic moments made an appearance while the ship's orchestra played Elgar. Chefs in two-foot-high hats emerged to make thrusts in tierce at turrets of Black Angus that towered above the arched eyebrows of the diners, and soufflés the size of the chefs' hats blossomed toward the end, like the final set pieces of a Paine's fireworks display on the Fourth of July. Through these flanking movements and skirmishes champagne circulated in jeroboams, Mumm's 1916, Irroy, and Perrier-Jouet, ditto.

"Sir James Charles, a grandee of the sea lanes so portly and full of honors that his mess jackets required structural bracing in their internal economy to support the weight of his decorations, died in line of duty, at sea, almost literally leading an assault on a citadel of pastry moated with diamond-back turtle stew *au Madeira*. When they took him ashore at Southampton it was necessary to open both wings of the *Aquitania*'s half-ports to accommodate his going. It was the exit of a nobleman and a warrior."

Sir James was no doubt the most lordly of lords of the sea and chairmen of the groaning boards, yet other captains shared, on a lesser scale, his tastes and his meticulous sense of the social proprieties. Consequently, it is little wonder that their first reactions to the encroachments of democracy on the sea lanes was one of barely subdued outrage. "Third Class passengers going eastward," observed one of them, "having tasted the fruits of what we call 'civilization,' have acquired a few of the virtues, and all the vices, of their new cult. They are more likely to grumble and to be aggressive, making many unreasonable demands. Girls who, a few years ago, were glad to wear one frock for the whole voyage, are now dressed in the latest styles, carry elegant suit-cases and silver-handled umbrellas, talk loudly, go to bed late at night, and otherwise give themselves all the airs and graces of 'society folks.'"

As for bona-fide emigrants, they had become even more uppity. "Whereas," said the captain, "medicine [once] had practically to be forced upon them, they now carry prescriptions, one for some tonic to help them eat, and one for some sedative to help them after they have eaten too much. They ask for gargles, mouth-washes and all the latest toilet requisites. If a filling comes out of a gold-capped tooth they want it replaced in record time. Why should they not have equal rights with the best in the land? No one disputes it; I am simply recording the transformation of a few years."

But to the man at the helm the really painful thing about the travelers of the '20s were signs of an erosion of moral standards. By the hundreds, men and women "with comfortable figures—showing years of devotion to the menu," were abandoning the Reading Room for the dance floor, there to join "flappers attired scantily, both above and below the equator" and Melachrino-smoking sheikhs. The decline of the Sunday service only reflected what had become obvious.

In the years before the war, attendance had dropped to about 20 percent of the passengers. Then the dangers of wartime at sea had brought them back in holy droves. But by 1924, the figures had slid to 15 percent and threatened to dip to 10. Instead of constituting a model sea-going society that knew how to behave, when to go to bed, and how to observe the Sabbath, first-class passengers in particular had become the profligates of the Atlantic. Instances of misbehavior recorded by one captain told the sad story: "*a*. Some young fellows in the ballroom dancing indecently with bobbed flappers; all hilarious with drink and making themselves a nuisance. *b*. A lady, drunk for the fourth day, locks herself into a gentleman's room and refuses to budge, declaring she has as much right there as some of his other lady friends whom she names. *c*. A man (old enough to know better) makes nasty advances to a young girl. The mother objects. *d*. An all-night orgy by a party of six ends in a general smashing up of the state-room. *e*. A girl accepts an invitation to a young man's room. She takes care that the door is not locked. At a given time her lady 'guardian' enters the room and accuses him of decoying the girl, but—after a scene—suggests that if he will pay her five hundred dollars she will say nothing more about it. Scared out of his life, the youth pays up. *f*. Using empty state-rooms and even boats during night hours for immoral purposes.

"Variations of such cases crop up from time to time. In the ballroom one sometimes sees dancing which is highly objectionable—dancing one would expect in some cabarets, but not amongst refined people. Young 'modern' men, perchance even college ones, are the chief offenders, ably supported by 'modern' flappers who also, I presume, boast of a high-school education. They hold each other familiarly, sometimes with heads together; charge all over the floor regardless of the comfort or even the safety of others, and are noisy and aggressive. I have been given to understand that both parties consider themselves 'smart.' "

On October 29, 1929, the *Ile de France* was midocean with a long list of passengers enjoying the feeling that Paris was still with them as they sailed westward, sitting down to the pleasures of a *cordon-bleu* table, dancing through evenings enlivened by *le jazz hot*. Just a few steps from "the longest bar afloat," the brokerage house—Compagnie de St. Phalle—had a shipboard office with a blackboard on which stock quotations, radioed from the Bourse and Wall Street, were constantly recorded, revised and erased. On this board, somberly, methodically, the company's clerks chalked those figures of the great stock market crash that changed the pleasures of the postsummer crossing to lugubrious *rites de passage*. The long galleries and the grand saloons were filled with "the funereal silence of ruined men." The great ship continued on her course; the bands played, the pastry cook, "encased in his cage like a candidate for the *prix de Rome*," bravely sculptured his centerpiece for the evening. But for many of her passengers, the *Ile de France* was suddenly on a voyage to nowhere. "Even the pastry," said one of them, "was flavored with tears."

❧ SECTION VI ❧

William Francis Gibbs Defines / Dinosaurs of the Deep / The Normandie! / U.S.S. Lafayette / Death in the Hudson River

M R. GIBBS, how would you define a superliner?"
William Francis Gibbs, who looked, someone said, "as though he had just stepped out of a coffin," was perhaps the one man in the world most qualified to answer this question. As a boy of nine, he had stood in a great crowd to watch Mrs. Grover Cleveland christen the *St. Louis*; as a man of sixty-five, he had capped a brilliant career by designing the S.S. *United States*.

"A superliner," said Mr. Gibbs, "is the equivalent of a large cantilever bridge covered with steel plates, containing a power plant that could light any of our larger cities, with a first-class luxury hotel on top."

The dinosaurs of the deep, bigger and more powerful than ever, had begun to move into that twilight from which they would never emerge. Their decks were broader and higher, their platings stronger and more tensile, their engines incomparable. Yet they were becoming rapidly superannuated, less and less useful to the societies which produced them. As they gathered in the antediluvian gloom, they would put on the grandest maritime show ever conceived. But pterodactyls, slicing

474

the air above them, would begin to send out the signals that would tell them they were extinct. In the irony of circumstance, ships within the next forty years would reach the zenith of technological sophistication, and almost at the very moment, become obsolete.

When the Great Depression sent its long cold shadow across the Western world, it fell simultaneously on St. Nazaire on the northwest coast of France and on Clydebank in the southwest corner of Scotland. The hull on the stocks of the Penhoët shipyards in the French port would take to the water as the *Normandie*. In Scotland, the massive structure rising in the yards of John Brown Ltd. was the hull, numbered 534, that would eventually go down the ways as the *Queen Mary*. Each was conceived to meet the still-unanswered challenge from Germany that the saucy careers of the *Bremen* and *Europa* had kept urgently alive.

In 1932, for instance, when the Cunard Line had to admit to an abysmal operating loss of nearly twenty million dollars, the Norddeutscher Lloyd Company quietly presented its stockholders with a hefty dividend. In their respective ways, each of the new ships was to be a national monument as explicit as the Arc de Triomphe and the Albert Memorial. In ways they shared, each (under the umbrella of a government subsidy) was to make money for an army of stockholders who were quite willing to tolerate the high-falutin' aesthetics of the thing as long as Aubusson tapestries and walls of marquetry were reflected in dividends. As one old-time economist had said, "Solvency is in the ideas and mechanism of an Englishman. The Crystal Palace is not considered honest until it pays."

In the album of vanished Atlantic liners, the *Normandie* figures as the ship without peer. In the large account of scientific enterprise in the twentieth century, she remains a profound embarrassment. Probably the greatest ship ever built anywhere, she was a lively and beloved legend while she lived; and when, after four brief years on the ocean, she died, she became a shameful reminder of the way in which blind, brutal carelessness allows men to kill the things they love. Afloat in her grand *ampleur*, when she slid easily into New York Harbor amid festoons and veils of water fountaining out of fire boats on June 2, 1935, she had broken all existing Atlantic records; a few days afterwards she would sail out to confirm her eminence by breaking them again. Seven years later, half submerged in the fecal ooze of the Hudson, rolled over like an elephant on its side, she lay mercilessly exposed to every eye in the high center of the city. "It requires an effort of the imagination," said *The New York Times*, "to realize that that great hulk of a once proud ship lying on her beam in the Hudson River at the foot of Forty-ninth Street is not suffering humiliation. The sight of her hurts the human eye and heart."

Before the Cunard Line had declared its intention to build a colossal ship, the Compagnie Générale Transatlantique had begun to put into action plans of its own for the biggest ship in the world. Thus the two liners had grown up together until, in the exigencies of hard times, work was altogether halted on Hull 534, while the French Government assisted the builders of the *Normandie* with a loan that would enable her to assume pride of place. Laid down in January, 1931, she was launched on October 29, 1932. When Mme. LeBrun, wife of the President of France, christened her with a bottle that was festooned with long streamers and which contained six quarts of sparkling champagne, the ship slid down the greased ways at a speed of seventeen miles an hour, and pulled a hundred spectators into the water after her. No one was killed; the mass dunking was merely another comic episode in the course of an establishment ritual.

The *Normandie* was ready to go to sea early in 1935—a whole year before the debut of the *Queen Mary*. A compact and graceful 80,000 tons plus, 1,029 feet long, she had two working funnels and one dummy. Squat to begin with, these funnels receded progressively in height, fore to aft. The high thrust of her great clipper bow made her unique among her kind—even though, to some old sailors, "a clipper bow without a bowsprit" was "a terrible sight to behold." The clean, swept look of her superstructure made the decks of almost any other ship seem cluttered and unnecessarily busy. Overall, she possessed an ineluctable air of authority—an authority that suggested innate ability rather than extraneous endowment.

As in the case of the *Bremen* and *Europa*, her interior designers tried to move away from the encyclopedic excesses of the pre-World War I liners still in service, and to offer something that was both identifiably Gallic and unquestionably new. "*Il semble que dans cette voie que côtoie l'anachronisme,*" said one bemused historian of art, "*il n'y ait pas lieu de s'arrêter. Allons-nous voir d'autres pastiches, le bar à cocktail Henry II, le salon de bridge assyrien, les salles de bains d'Isabelle la Catholique?*"

Like the German decorators, the French were determined to further *"l'élimination progressive des copies de style ancien par des meubles de conception et de dessins entièrement modernes."* While they wanted to avoid those earlier kinds of ship decoration that gave *"une impression de grande simplicité et de banalité,"* their slightly arrogant insistence that the new age, *their* new age, was a golden one, or at least one of oxidized steel, did not save them from lending themselves to acts of aesthetic atrocity. The decorating firm of Acon et Patout was mainly responsible for the *Normandie*'s interiors. The effects they achieved were richer than those of the *Bremen* and slightly more "marine," according to one architect, but lacking in the German ship's "disciplined elegance."

All in all, the result, to most Frenchmen, was overwhelming. To a question posed by one of the proudest of them—"What palace, what Triumphal Way, what memorial have we built to perpetuate our civilization, as the cathedrals perpetuate that of the Middle Ages, the castles of the Loire that of the Renaissance, and Versailles that of the age of Louis XIV?"—the only answer was "The *Normandie!*"

Berthed in New York when the Nazis invaded France, the *Normandie* had been instructed by orders from Paris to stay put. But when the United States entered the war, she was requisitioned by the American Navy. The idea was to convert her into a troop ship of a greater carrying capacity than anything else available to American forces. Renamed U.S.S. *Lafayette*, she was in the process of conversion on February 9, 1942, when sparks from the torch of a welder who was cutting away a stanchion in the grand saloon showered onto a bundle of kapok-filled life preservers. A blaze flared up, setting off a leaping chain of fire that had the entire ship ablaze in minutes. Two thousand terrified workers scuttled for the open decks and onto the pier; yet there was not one among them who thought of calling the fire department until fourteen minutes after the flames had broken out. When fire engines and fire boats finally reached the scene, "confusion and lack of coordination" led to a grotesque comedy of errors, a resounding, black, Keystone-cops joke, of which the incomparable ship was the victim. As if she were some obstreperous harbor scow that deserved a good wetting down, the men on the fire boats poured 3,500 tons of water into her and so, with good avuncular intentions—to put the best construction on it—made sure that she would die.

When she could take no more—literally and, one is tempted to say, humanly—the *Normandie* simply listed over until the portside cheeks of her big oval funnels were scraped by ice floating in the river. As she expired, a pall of smoke, like a last breath, drifted over the skyscrapers of midtown Manhattan.

The *Normandie*'s posthumous career was as sorry as her demise. For more than a year, she was worked on by pumps that sucked 15,000 tons of silt and 10,000 tons of water out of her huge compartments. Rising out of her own watery grave, she had gradually begun to right herself by August, 1943, and to reassume the shape by which she might be recognized. A few months later, her streamlined superstructure cut flat away by acetylene torches, she was towed to the Brooklyn Navy Yard. The Navy still had notions of making some wartime use of her, and there was even talk of converting her into an aircraft carrier. But the war had reduced working manpower and materials to such short supply that all such plans were put aside. Once more, a featureless rusting hulk, she was towed away, "a grim and silent spectacle," this time to Port Newark, New Jersey, to be broken up and, at long last, obliterated.

❧ SECTION VII ❧

THE BRITISH—in the slough of the same Great Slump that could not prevent the French from turning out a maritime masterpiece—had muddled through to the disposition of one wonder ship and the completion of another.

The first of these was a vision, a blueprint, a ghost ship—a liner as big and as grand as any other ever conceived. Her name was going to be *Oceanic*, to celebrate the viability of a company tradition that had brought the first superb ship of that name onto the Atlantic in 1871, the second by that name in 1899. Ordered by the White Star Line in 1928, she was to be built in the same Harland & Wolff yards that had not so long ago delivered the *Olympic* and the *Titanic*. The first ship to have a length of more than one thousand feet, the *Oceanic* had long, clean lines which, on the drawing boards at least, were meant to demonstrate that even a colossus might possess serenity and style. Her keel was laid and her hull was beginning to take shape when, sensing the economic catastrophe that awaited a ship launched into the muddy waters of the Slump, her owners called the whole thing off. Consequently, the

Oceanic would survive only as an illustration, an idea on paper—one of the loveliest ships never built.

The other British bid for first place seemed for a while to be equally feckless. Just as Hull 534 was about eighty percent completed, the gloom of the Depression rolled like an impenetrable fog over the industrial reaches of Clydeside. Like one of their own passengers, who said of a foggy day, "We see nothing, and we fear everything," the directors of the Cunard Line were stymied. They ordered work on the great ship to be stopped on December 11, 1931. More than 3,500 workers were laid off; more than 10,000 others dependent on the incomes of shipbuilders in the yards had nothing to do, or sell. Rooks and starlings, quarreling and skittering as they settled into the scaffoldings, replaced the clang of hammers and the sputter of welding torches. The great resoundings of steel upon steel that meant that the John Brown yards were alive were suddenly still. "Adversity—scorching, lasting—came upon these men in the midst of their great work," said a maritime writer. "A sudden silence fell upon the great yard. For two years and four months there was no sound, save the seeping mutter of the tides and the throaty cawing of the rooks resting in the cranes which brooded over the deserted hull." An embryo that looked like a skeleton, the unchristened ship sat in the empty yards while Clydeside, always teetering on the edge of poverty, sank into the desuetude of still another of the cycles of capitalist economics.

When, at last, salvation came, it was the consequence of much maneuvering behind the scenes. Facing up to the fact that England's two greatest shipping companies were equally helpless, the Government was minded to save both by showing its particular favor to neither. As the Prime Minister, Neville Chamberlain, recorded in his diary, "My own aim has always been to use the 534 as a lever for bringing about a merger between the Cunard and White Star Lines, thus establishing a strong British firm on the North Atlantic trade." It took little persuasion for the directors of both companies to agree to pooling their resources, especially when the Government's salvage operation was once more on the magnanimous scale that had rescued Cunard from the clutches of J. Pierpont Morgan in 1902. If, said His Majesty's Government, the two companies would place their resources under one rubric, the Cunard-White Star Line, the national exchequer would lend the new company 9,500,000 pounds: 3,000,000 of this would go toward the completion of Hull 534, 1,500,000 would be marked for working capital, a whopping 5,000,000 more pounds would be set aside for a future sister ship. The offer, tempting in almost any circumstance, was irresistible in the abyss of 1934.

"For more than two years," said the labor leader David Kirkwood, "the Clyde had been like a tomb—not a tomb newly made, but a tomb with a vast and inescapable skeleton brooding over its silence." In a skirl of bagpipes and Scottish nationalist songs, work was resumed on 534 in April, 1934. Half the income of Clydeside was restored at once. Miles from the building site and the huge black battlement that would be the Queen Mary, "little depressed towns perked up pluckily in the light of her requirements."

Just six months later, the ship was ready for launching. For the first time ever, the reigning King and Queen lent their presence to the launching rituals of a merchant ship. Before more than two hundred thousand spectators who had gathered, under umbrellas, like wet black-birds, King George V said he had "the happy task of sending on her way . . . the stateliest ship in the world." Queen Mary cut a ribbon releasing a bottle of Australian wine that served to baptize the ship Queen Mary. Then "this mass of metal" that "had become the symbol of a national self-respect," sat as though she were immovable for the one awful moment that seems always to occur before a ship begins its long parturitional slide, and finally started toward "the wan water of the Clyde." "There were yards of ermine and gold braid," said a Scottish observer, "and a long roster of resounding titles, behind the rain-flooded glass of the launching dais. A bottle smashed high upon the precipice that was the port bow of the ship—a curiously feeble sound in the rain-filled space of the yard. Heavy hammers thumped on blocks of wood. Thirty thousand tons of steel, painted white, were moving, nay, plunging toward the water. Chains whipped and lashed like snakes. There was a spurt of flame, dowsed in clouds of oily smoke, over the greased way. She seemed to move at a terrific speed. She was surely rushing to disaster. The army of spectators was silent. Then it liberated itself in a roar. For there was the Queen Mary, no longer a number in the books, riding high and light in the narrow river, and the tugs bearing down on her with the purposefulness of terriers after a rat."

The dimensions of the *Queen Mary* taxed every talent for hyperbole. To further "the elucidation of the lay mind," especially if that mind were familiar with Trafalgar Square and its environs, one illustration, meticulously drawn to scale, tried to imagine the scene should the great ship be set down there. "The Nelson Column is on her starboard beam," said the legend beneath, "the crown of Nelson's hat reaches to about the boat deck. Her stern has pushed in the walls of the Garrick Theatre in Charing Cross Road; her port side only just fits alongside St. Martin's Church and South Africa House; the National Gallery is severely damaged, and her stem has protruded into White Hall."

Statistics eventually got to be more ingenious than awesome. The *Queen Mary*'s power was calculated to be about equal to the muscle power of seven million galley slaves all rowing in unison. Cables carrying electric energy through the ship were, it was estimated, 4,000 miles long, or long enough to reach from New York to San Francisco and then 800 miles out into the Pacific. The torch in the hand of the Statue of Liberty would barely top the roof of the bridge. The head of the Sphinx would not even come up to main deck at the stern. The main dining room and foyer were big enough to house the *Britannia*, Cunard's first liner, and still have room to pack in beside her Columbus' *Nina*, *Pinta* and *Santa Maria*. The tonnage of the *Queen Mary* was 22,000 more than the tonnage of the whole Spanish Armada. In fact, said one man who had visited her while she was still on the stocks, the sight of her made him "feel like a fly crawling along the floor at the base of a hung carcass of Highland beef."

It took courage to build the "inevitable" ship at the very point of change in the way most people would travel the ocean—and that courage was not blind. "The crux of the matter," said Cunard's chairman Colonel Bates, "will lie in whether twenty-five years from now it would be the universal desire of mankind to travel like rockets at supersonic speeds in a closed metal container, probably without windows, or whether many would still prefer a more leisurely progression."

For more than a year and a half the new *Queen* remained in the fitting-out basin of the John Brown yards. Though Cunard, with a rare flip of imagination, sent a man over to France incognito to spy on the *Normandie* in the shipyard, and on a crossing to New York, in order to learn what her designers had been up to, his reports apparently had little effect on the complacent banality of his British colleagues. "The stateliest ship in being" (an epithet that was to win wide support from

maritime experts who studied her bearing and behavior) had to submit
to depredations of a brand of British taste that had progressed in two
decades only from a schizophrenic eclecticism to that misapprehension
of the modern that results in the *"moderne."*

The sensibilities of those governing the *Queen Mary* as a commercial
product were so far behind and below the sensibilities of those who
built and crafted her in the yards and sheds of John Brown's as to represent another order of conscience. A week before her maiden voyage,
the company gave a series of gala dinners to celebrities, newspaper
people, travel agents and old customers at London's famous old Edwardian hangout—the Trocadero. To disguise all vestiges of its passé
decor and to exorcise the waltzing shadows of Edward VII and Miss
Maxine Elliott, they attempted to make the restaurant look like the
Queen Mary herself. "The corridor entrance from Shaftesbury Avenue
had been pictorially arranged to represent Southampton Docks," wrote
the journalist team of Potter and Frost, "and a wall two feet thick had
been cut through so that guests could use a regulation gangway to 'go
aboard.' In the restaurant itself there was a captain's bridge and a five-
tier deck, built to scale. Searchlights, bells, navigation lights, house
flags of the company, and *Queen Mary* lifeboats completed the setting,
with the periodic roar of a whistle adding local colour. Guests sat in
deck-chairs and were served by waiters dressed as stewards. [Commodore]
Sir Edgar [Britten] had autographed all the menus. After a cabaret the
guests danced in the rays of a searchlight in a salon which took the
form of a raft moored to the ship, and the orchestra played from the
lifeboats." This tawdry idyll, according to the same writers, "was typical
of the spirit and age of the *Queen Mary*, for she had so captivated the
imagination of the nation."

Miles of linoleum that glistened like a low-grade fever, acres of
laminated surfaces—flooded with "indirect" lighting and machine-waxed
to the glow of a subaltern's shoes—gave the ship the atmosphere of an
enormous sanitarium. First-class staterooms, each with its electric grate
on the order of the shilling-in-the-slot gas heaters of the Earl's Court
"bed-sit," were paneled in flats of carefully split wood that put huge
Rorschach blots on every wall. There was a palpable sense of uplift and
grandeur in the high rectangle of the naturally lighted main lounge;
but pillars of a Theban sort of massiveness qualified any expectation
that this was a place where people of less than episcopal probity might

meet. J. Pierpont Morgan—particularly in the mood in which Edward Steichen's camera catches him—looked as though he quite belonged in the smoking room, but hardly any one else. High-backed wing chairs, upholstered in the sort of on-the-hoof leather associated with the Victorian sporting house and the cattleman's private pullman car, tended to make a man of ordinary girth and modest mien look like an elf on a toadstool.

Some Englishmen were charmed to learn from professionals that the *Queen Mary* was "as docile as a yacht," and took to heart a discrimination offered by a Danish observer: "The French built a beautiful hotel and put a ship around it. The British built a beautiful ship and put a hotel inside it." But others of His Majesty's subjects who had a chance to learn just what the hotel inside the *Queen Mary* looked like were appalled. To the art critic Clive Bell, the aesthetique of the interior of the ship could be described as "teddy bear." Bell praised Cunard's naval architects for having given the *Mary* lines that made for overall grace and cohesion. But, he said, "inside awaits disappointment . . . good wooden surfaces have been broken up and disfigured with what businessmen call 'art.' "

Yet another art critic, Raymond Mortimer, viewed the matter from much the same point of view as did Cunard's directors. "A super-luxury transatlantic liner," he said, "depends largely on the patronage of international film stars, financiers, and opera singers and their taste is presumably reflected in the international style of decoration which you find in the palatial hotels all over the world from Palm Beach to the Lido." Ugh! said an English columnist, "shiny rayon damask . . . engraved Dianas with streaming hair and big-eyed unicorns racing across mirrors. Hideously patterned carpets. Strip-lit Winter Gardens with rubber plants. Strip-lit dressing tables with beech-grained plastic laminates."

"The general effect," said the *Architect and Building News*, "is one of mild but expensive vulgarity." To a London columnist she was "outstandingly vulgar, overwhelmingly voluminous, and impressively voluptuous. Outwardly she is a very handsome lass, although a good deal too plump to be called an ocean greyhound. Inwardly she is a riot of ostentation carefully executed in the Leicester Square style. . . . The design and décor of her public rooms, her bars, and her restaurants seem to have been aimed at dollar millionaires from the Mid-west and their opposite numbers in England who claim that, 'Where there is muck, there is money.' The workmanship is magnificent, the materials used are splendid, the result is appalling."

But these impeachments did little to damp down the enthusiasms of Englishmen who tended to view the new maritime prodigy with pride touched with awe. In the mortal words of the Poet Laureate, John Masefield, they heard once more an echo that had sounded through centuries of sea-faring:

> a rampart of a ship,
> Long as a street and lofty as a tower,
> Ready to glide in thunder from the slip
> And shear the sea with majesty of power.
>
> I long to see you leaping to the urge
> Of the great engines, rolling as you go.

She rolled so much, as a matter of fact, that she broke crockery like an angry fishwife, trundled some astonished passengers out of their beds and bunks and made others wonder how anything so big could veer with the dizzying lean of a motorcycle sidecar cutting a corner, and still remain on keel. Stabilizers eventually corrected this proclivity of the *Mary's*. But in the years before these were installed she gave her passengers to understand that she was not the Trocadero, or a segment of Leicester Square, but a ship on the water.

❄ SECTION VIII ❧

Cruise Ships: From the Holy Land to Nowhere / "I Went to Havana, on One of Those Cruises, for Forty-nine Fifty. . . ." William Makepeace Thackeray on the Lady Mary Wood / *The Dream of Rob. M. Sloman / The* Nightingale, *from Portsmouth, New Hampshire / The* Great Eastern *Fiascoes / The Innocents Abroad, Mark Twain and the* Quaker City / Tyburnia *Defiant Albert Ballin: The Breakthrough / Laconia: The Route of Magellan / Troglodytes of the Seven Seas / The Captain as "Someone Royal" / The Desecration of the S.S.* Independence

RUE TO FORM and the traditions of a hundred years, the new French and English superships took to themselves most of the patronage that had once gone to the *Mauretania*, the *Olympic* and to the racers of the North German Lloyd. But the "load factor" (as it would soon be called) of the veteran ocean liners had already suffered a mortal decline. Americans who, a few summers earlier, had crowded the *Promenade des Anglais*, the Simplon-Orient Express and the links at St. Andrews, were now making day trips to Lake Onondaga, pitching tents in the Wisconsin woods and tapping balls across the dwarf landscapes of miniature golf courses.

In the absence of tourists bound for Europe, the hard-pressed steamship companies came up with a novel idea: instead of letting the behemoths lie at their moorings between voyages, eating up overhead in their gargantuan idleness, why not send them off on short trips to Nassau, Palm Beach, Miami, Havana?

Thus was born the "booze cruise," the cut-rate junket into the "Four Society Playgrounds," the frenetic weekend at sea of which the jilted stenographer would sing: "I went to Havana, on one of those cruises, for forty-nine fifty. . . ." Now, on English bank holiday cruises for three pounds per person, the Edwardian vastnesses of the *Olympic* echoed with the unaccustomed clatter of cockney multitudes. On a cruise for "$80.00 and up" the *Mauretania* now resounded with the nasal sonorities of the "Rudy Vallee Vagabonds" and the boop-boop-a-doop petulance of girls called "Marge." "THIS IS CERTAINLY GOING TO BE A GRAND VACATION!" said the girl in the one-piece bathing suit on the cover of the brochure. "I want a change. I'm tired of being an old stick-in-the-mud. One of the *Mauretania* sea-breeze vacation cruises to the West Indies and South America is the answer to a maiden's prayer. Marge took one of these Cunard cruises last summer and she says she met the nicest people on board . . . and you know she gets around a lot, too. There will be evenings under a velvet sky with a faint sickle moon and the twinkling stars dropping one by one as. . . . Well, let's not go into that. Say, by the way, why don't you come along?"

The particular nature of the sea-excursion occasioned by the tight-money days of the early '30s was something entirely new. But Atlantic liners diverted from their normal runs and cruising for pleasure had been a marginal part of the shipping business for nearly a hundred years.

No one can pinpoint the very first pleasure cruise; any one of a number of voyages on record might be granted the historical honor. The only thing certain about cruises as opposed to ocean passages is that they did not occur until the rigors of sea-going had been modified to the point where people of means would elect to endure them.

Equipped with eighteen shirts and "a sea stock of Russian ducks," William Makepeace Thackeray made a brief Mediterranean *giro* on the Peninsular & Oriental Company's steamship *Lady Mary Wood* in 1844. But since the trip was made on three different ships before it was over, and since Thackeray was a guest of the company, his cruise should perhaps be discounted—at least in the search for the pioneer. But because the reasons that sent him sailing were the same reasons that would be equally persuasive to other trippers for decades, they are noteworthy. "In the space of months," said the novelist, "as many men and cities were to be seen as Ulysses surveyed and noted in ten years. Malta, Athens, Smyrna, Constantinople, Jerusalem, Cairo, were to be visited, and everybody was to be back in London by Lord Mayor's Day." The idea of writing a presailing letter to his family, "stating that they were not to expect him to dinner on Saturday fortnight, as he would be at Jerusalem on that day" delighted him; and when a friend who had already made up his mind coaxed him with "Come—in all your life you will never probably have a chance again to see so much in so short a time," Thackeray was all but en route.

Early in 1845, a Hamburg shipping man who signed himself Rob. M. Sloman (he was later to have a brief fling with transatlantic steamships) dreamed up what might have been the first round-the-world pleasure cruise ever. Advertised plans for this voyage tended to emphasize edification rather more than accommodation, but this did not succeed in garnering a sufficient number of adventurers to make the voyage feasible. The advertisement Sloman placed in the *Leipziger Illustrierte Zeitung* was no magnet in 1845, but it may very well have been the touchstone, nearly fifty years later, for the first really successful cruise operation on a grand scale.

On his way up the gilded ladder of success, Albert Ballin had worked for Edward Carr, who had begun his shipping career with Sloman's steerage and freight business. Though offices changed hands, the obscure little newspaper notice, pigeon-holed for forty-five years, came to Ballin's attention just when its message was most timely—in 1890, as he was trying to come upon some way of easing the losses sustained by his passenger ships in the slack winter season. At once, the old vision of Rob. M. Sloman became his: excused from their duties as common carriers, ships would become pleasure pavilions; bound neither by purpose or exigency, voyages would become seminars in ancient history, exotic sojourns, rest cures and exercises in spiritual rejuvenation.

"An Opportunity for Taking Part in a Voyage Round the World," read Sloman's original advertisement. "The undersigned Hamburg shipowner proposes to equip one of his large sailing vessels for a cruise round the world, to start this summer, during which the passengers will be able to visit Lisbon, Madeira, Teneriffe, Cap Verde Islands, Rio de Janeiro, Rio de la Plata, Falkland Islands, Valparaiso, and all the intermediate ports of call on the Pacific coast of South America as far as Guayaquil (for Quito), the Marquesas Islands, Friendly Islands (Otaheite), and other island groups in the Pacific, China (Choosan, Hongkong, Canton, Macao, Whampoa), Manila, Singapore, Ceylon,

Ile de France or Madagascar, the Cape of Good Hope, St. Helena, Ascension Island, the Azores, and back to Hamburg.

"The cruise is not intended for business purposes of any kind; but the whole equipment and accommodations of the vessel, the time spent at the various ports of call, and the details of the whole cruise, are to be arranged with the solid object of promoting the safety, the comfort, the entertainment, and the instruction of the passengers.

"Admission will·be strictly confined to persons of unblemished repute and of good education, those possessing a scientific education receiving preference.

"The members of the expedition may confidently look forward to a pleasant and successful voyage. A first-class ship, an experienced and well-educated captain, a specially selected crew, and a qualified physician are sufficient guarantees to ensure a complete success.

"The fare for the whole voyage is so low that it only represents a very slight addition to the ordinary cost of living incurred on shore. In return, the passenger will have many opportunities of acquiring a first-hand knowledge of the wonders of the world, of the beautiful scenery of the remotest countries, and of the manners and customs of many different nations. During the whole voyage he will be surrounded by the utmost comfort, and will enjoy the company of numerous persons of culture and refinement. The sea air will be of immeasurable benefit to his health, and the experience which he is sure to gain will remain a source of pleasure to him for the rest of his life."

So grand and salubrious a program seems not to have occurred to any other shipowner, yet cruising for the sheer pleasure of it was an idea that had remained lively, if unfulfilled, for many years. When a group of Americans got hold of it, they enlarged upon it in terms of comfort and convenience while soft-pedaling its spiritual enhancements. Their concept was a "floating hotel" that would, on its very first voyage, be anchored in the river Thames. To make it easy for Americans to visit the Great Exhibition of 1851 in Hyde Park, they commissioned the clipper ship *Nightingale* to be built in Portsmouth, New Hampshire. "Transatlantic Excursion to the World's Fair," they advertised, "Rare Opportunity for a Cheap and Delightful Trip to London. Captain Miller, so favorably known to the public on both sides of the Atlantic as a Noble Navigator and Gentleman, goes out in command of the *Nightingale*. To sail from Boston on or about June 10th."

After this proposed trip to the Thames and back, they intended to dispatch her to places all over the world. On a luxurious yacht the rich would be allowed to indulge their endless idleness in such propitious new territories as Tahiti and Teneriffe. But as it developed, the expense of the new ship, even before she was ready to be launched, became so onerous that those who had commissioned her could not raise enough money to take possession of her. At this impasse, her builder took over, called his subcontractors together, and won their agreement to complete the *Nightingale* with the intention of putting her up for auction in Boston. There she was the object of "infinite attention as being one of the most beautiful ships that had ever been seen in that port," and found a buyer in the shipping firm of Sampson & Tappan. But this company was not interested in the frivolities of parasoled excursionists. The *Nightingale*'s maiden voyage was an arduous working run to Sydney, and on to Shanghai to pick up hundreds of chests of tea. She stayed in the China trade for about fifteen years. Then the lovely ship that had been designed to float the fashionable to the Crystal Palace in saloons of horsehair and plush was put into a trade that forced her to carry slaves packed like cattle into her damp wooden dungeons.

The *Great Eastern*—to capitalize upon the brouhaha of her debut in New York—made two bona-fide cruises: one to Cape May, another to Old Point Comfort and Norfolk. Both were disasters. On the first trip her owners sold two thousand excursion tickets in full knowledge that the ship had only six hundred available berths. Food ran out, or was quietly commandeered by a score of waiters hastily rounded up before sailing; water was in short supply. People who had tickets saying their stateroom was Number 32 skirmished in the companionways with people who flourished tickets saying the same thing. Piles of mattresses provided by the company for people without staterooms were hauled away by other passengers who suddenly turned into pitchmen and sold them at holdup prices. When someone carelessly left a stopcock open, the ice house and storeroom were flooded. The few passengers whom boredom and frustration had not driven to take part in the fracas on deck that lasted all night long, called an indignation meeting. The situation was irremediable, yet the irate and sober few passed a resolution stating that they had been "not only disappointed, but swindled." On her next cruise, the *Great Eastern*, "Our Big Visi-

37. Southampton: the crew comes home

38. The commodore personified:
Sir James Charles,
K.B.E., R.D., R.N.R.

39. First class: a fox-trot on the promenade

40. Tourist third: Dixieland on deck

41. Welcome aboard: the foyer of the *Majestic*

42. On to the Palm Court

43. S.S. *Leviathan*: all the comforts of home—if you lived in Newport,
Tuxedo Park or Oyster Bay

44. R.M.S. *Homeric*: a stately home of England puts to sea

45. The *Bremen*: "Her name gleams like a new planet."

46. Cunard's dream of fair women: going to dinner, R.M.S. *Queen Mary*

47. This bow sliced H.M.S. *Curaçao* in two

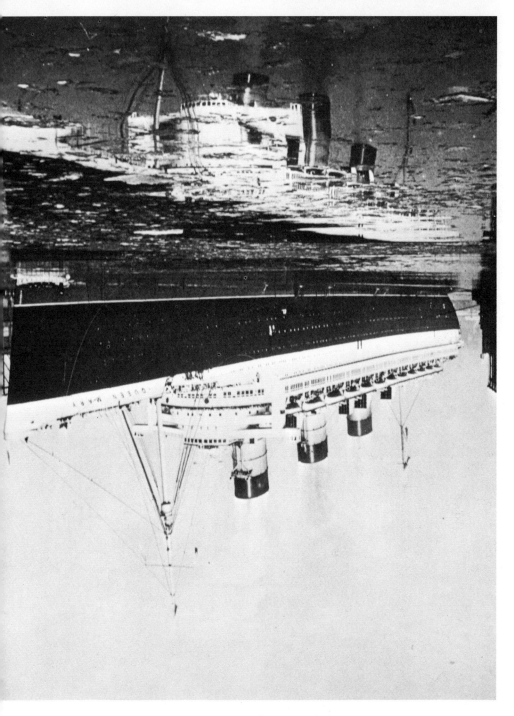

48. The *Mary*: glory and its reflection and vice versa

49. The era of *art deco*:
(TOP) The *Queen Mary*'s main lounge;
(BOTTOM) the forward cocktail lounge

50. The Bessemer saloon steamer: how it *should* have worked

51. The lovely *Independence*: degraded and despoiled

52. "Getting There is Half the Fun"

Garrett Price

54. S.S. *United States*: neglected artifact of American genius

55. Going nowhere: the great *Queen Elizabeth 2* ready for launching

tor," sailed away with just one hundred passengers wandering about saloons and galleys that would have been able to take care of Noah and all his animals twice over.

The first extensive cruise by an Atlantic liner (always excepting Cornelius Vanderbilt's family outing to St. Petersburg and around the Continent to Constantinople) remains to this day the most famous one, simply because its most unhappy member, Mark Twain, survived to tell about it in a book. *Quaker City* was the name of the paddle-wheeled liner; the book is *The Innocents Abroad*.

In spite of an eloquently morbid view of sea travel expressed in sermons that had once frozen whole congregations in their pews, Henry Ward Beecher of the Plymouth Church, Brooklyn, was the unlikely sponsor of the pioneer cruise. When he led a party of patriots to Charleston in 1865 to be present at the raising of the Union flag over Fort Sumter, Beecher was, in effect, blooded. Now, having it in mind to write a biography of Jesus Christ, he wanted to lead an equally fervent band of pilgrims to the Holy Land where, on the spot, he might check out certain points about his subject's living conditions. The man he had in mind to take care of the business end of things was by great luck also the man capable of serving as master of the ship. This was Captain Charles C. Duncan, one of the zealous superintendents of the Plymouth Church's Sunday School. His credentials seemed sterling, yet this was the man of whom Mark Twain would write: "I think I have good reason for believing him to be wholly without principle, without moral sense, without honor of any kind. . . . I know him to be a canting hypocrite, filled to the chin with sham godliness, and forever oozing and dripping false piety and pharasiacal prayers." In spite of this minimal recommendation, Captain Duncan would become the legitimate promoter, leader and social director of the prototype of the modern luxury cruise.

Not just anybody was *persona grata* in the saloons of the *Quaker City*. Prospective excursionists had to submit written applications to a committee in the hope that their credit and social stature were sound enough to gain them a place among the elect. Twain got by—but just. He had originally planned to go around the world, sailing westward from San Francisco and to write fifty letters about the trip for the *Daily Alta Californian*. But when he went East to St. Louis to say goodbye to his mother, he was, as he said, "bitten" by Captain Duncan's prospectus of the *Quaker City* cruise. The newspaper obligingly agreed to his change of plans, promised to publish his letters about the voyage at twenty dollars apiece, paid the expensive cost of his ticket, outlined his credentials and affirmed his professional standing. This was all put in jeopardy when Twain went for a personal interview with Captain Duncan. On this occasion, according to the Captain, Twain exuded "fumes of bad whisky." But since Twain had in the first place been introduced to him as a Baptist minister, Deacon Duncan extended a Christian's forbearance to this errant wearer of the cloth.

The *Quaker City*'s itinerary—reaching as far to the east as the Crimea—was in itself grand, and a proviso in the announcement contained at least the hint of flexibility en route: "The trip can be extended, and the route changed, by *unanimous* vote of the passengers." It was also useful to know that five dollars in gold would likely take care of all *per diem* traveling expenses ashore; heartening to hear that the "ship will at all times be a home, where the excursionists, if sick, will be surrounded by kind friends, and have all possible comfort and sympathy."

In the event, Twain himself never exacted such spiritual emollience, nor gave it. For him the cruise was "a funeral excursion without a corpse" in which days at sea repeated a routine of "solemnity, decorum, dinner, dominoes, prayers, slander." The Reverend Beecher did not, finally, choose to sail. But his sponsorship of the pilgrimage had given it a sort of apostolic sanction; everyone on board, Twain came to think, was a professed or latent divine. Except for his cabinmate, a "splendid, immoral, tobacco-smoking, wine-drinking, godless" man named Daniel Slote, Twain found them a saintly and suffocating lot. His distaste was no doubt sharpened by his disappointment in the failure of the cruise to realize the promises it had so handsomely held out.

"It was a novelty in the way of excursions," he wrote. "Its like had not been thought of before, and it compelled that interest which attractive novelties always command. It was to be a picnic on a gigantic scale. The participants . . . instead of freighting an ungainly steam ferry-boat with youth and beauty and pies and doughnuts, and paddling up some obscure creek to disembark upon a grassy lawn and wear themselves out with a long summer day's laborious frolicking . . . were to sail away in a great steamship with flags flying and cannon pealing, and take a royal holiday beyond the broad ocean. . . . They were to sail for months over the breezy Atlantic and the sunny Mediterranean; they were to scamper about the decks by day, filling the ship with shouts and laughter—or read novels and poetry in the shade of the smoke-stacks, or watch for the jelly-fish and the nautilus, over the side, and the shark, the whale, and other stranger monsters of the deep; and at night they were to dance in the open air, on the upper deck, in the midst of a ball-room that stretched from horizon to horizon, and was domed by the benign heavens and lighted by no meaner lamps than the stars . . . dance, and promenade, and smoke, and sing, and make love, and search the skies for constellations. . . ."

Instead, Twain found himself among a company of well-heeled, teetotaling, patriotic bigots who descended upon the shores of the Mediterranean with the cupidity of vandals and the naïveté of children *en travestie*. "The people stared at us everywhere," he wrote, "and we stared at them. We generally made them feel rather small, too, before we got done with them, because we bore down on them with America's greatness until we crushed them. And yet we took kindly to the manners and customs, and especially to the fashions of the various people we visited. When we left the Azores, we wore awful capotes and used fine tooth combs—successfully. When we came back from Tangier, in Africa, we were topped with fezzes of the bloodiest hue, hung with tassels like an Indian's scalp-hook. In France and Spain we attracted some attention in these costumes. In Italy they naturally took us for distempered Garibaldians, and sent a gunboat to look for anything significant in our changes of uniform. We made Rome howl. We could have made any place howl when we had all our clothes on. But at Constantinople, how we turned out! Turbans, scimitars, fezzes, horse-pistols, tunics, sashes, baggy trousers, yellow slippers— Oh, we were gorgeous!"

Homesickness aboard the *Quaker City* was, according to Twain, "epidemic," and one suspects that he himself was among the more serious cases. For five long months the little sea-going hagiocracy sent its emissaries into the tombs and temples of Christian and infidel alike. Some of the company had apparently backslid a bit under the weight of the experience. "At last," said Twain, "one pleasant morning, we steamed up the harbor of New York, all on deck, all dressed in Christian garb—by special order, for there was a latent disposition in some quarters to come out as Turks—and amid a waving of handkerchiefs from welcoming friends, the glad pilgrims noted the shiver of the decks that told that ship and pier had joined hands again and the long, strange cruise was over. Amen."

For most of the century, pleasure cruising was a small and marginal activity. A Peninsular & Orient vessel named *Ceylon*, "the first exclusive cruising yacht," made a number of trips for the Polytechnic Touring Association in the 1880s. In the same decade, the American Steam Ship Company of Philadelphia sent its 3,100-ton *Ohio* on "yachting cruises" to the West Indies. In 1884, a British sailing ship—the twenty-seven-year-old *Tyburnia*—made one of the more noteworthy cruises on record. After a quarter of a century of trading between Scotland and India, this little vessel was given a new role in life when she was taken on charter by an outfit calling itself the Pleasure Cruising Yacht Company. The *Tyburnia's* first cruise was to be a trip through the islands of the West Indies, and the big advertised attraction was the low cost: only one guinea per person per day. But while she was now devoted to the pleasures of the bounding main, this did not prevent her owners from sending her out with cement and other British products for which, it was hoped, she might find a market en route. When she anchored at Quarantine under the Loo Battery at Madeira, the Portuguese customs men demanded accounting and payment for goods in transit under the threat of seizure and confiscation. The *Tyburnia's* master, a Captain Kennaley, who had been a blockade runner in the American Civil War, let the customs officers know that he recognized extortion when he saw it and told them to keep hands off. Any official attempting to board his ship, he said, would be heaved into the drink.

The *Tyburnia* was riding at anchor in easy range of the Loo Battery; the Portuguese commander felt it was just a matter of time before Captain Kennaley would realize the hopelessness of his predicament. You make a move to slip moorings, they informed him, and we'll open fire. When the Captain explained to his passengers just what a fix they were in and told them what he intended to do, they supported him to a man. Next morning, the *Tyburnia* lifted anchor. The first two shots from the Battery were blanks, intended to show that the command meant what it said. Undeterred, full sail and flags flying, the *Tyburnia* began to drift out of range. A third shot was the real thing, as was the volley that followed it. Some cordage from the bowsprit was torn away; the sea around was punctured by little explosions.

All the cruise passengers, assembled in their bombazine and serge on the quarterdeck, cheered as Captain Kennaley, returning every shot with a defiant dip of his ensign, hurried his vessel beyond the reach of the guns and set her, barely scathed, on a course for "the Barbadoes."

The real breakthrough in pleasure cruising—at least as the twentieth century would come to know it—was pretty much the single-handed gesture of Hamburg-Amerika's Albert Ballin. When, in 1890, he was studying charts that predicted another almost inevitable dip in trans-ocean traffic during the oncoming winter months, Ballin took a new look at the plans Rob. M. Sloman had discarded and thought what a good idea it would be to send his company's 8,ooo-ton *Augusta Victoria*—normally in service on the Hamburg–New York run—on a sightseeing excursion around the Mediterranean. But when he presented this idea to his board of directors, he found them to be unenthusiastic and dubious. Germans were not sea-loving people, they said. Germans would travel in pursuit of profit, or out of family necessity, but they would surely not submit themselves to the hazards and discomforts of a long voyage just for the incidental fun of it.

Luckily, Ballin was in a position to overrule his colleagues. He put out advertisements for the cruise, enlisted a complement of 241 passengers and for good measure added his own name and that of his wife to the pioneer list. Starting from Hamburg on January 22, 1891, they called at Southampton, then went on to Gibraltar, Genoa, Alexandria (allowing for a shore trip to Cairo), Jaffa (for Jerusalem), Beirut (for Damascus), Constantinople, Athens, Malta, Naples and Lisbon. The outing was a social success, an educational adventure and a good time—such a good time that the two-month-long trip was again undertaken in 1892, revised to allow for a departure from New York in 1893, and repeated by the *Augusta Victoria* and her sister ships every year until the outbreak of World War I.

The German example was soon followed; cruise ships began to proliferate. Accenting the "sumptuous" aspects of a voyage meant only to divert the blasé and entertain the idle, the Orient Line sent their *Lusitania* to the West Indies, the Canaries and the Azores in 1895. Offering the ultimate—"*chambres de luxe* with private bathroom"—the French Line's *La Touraine* sailed from New York on a three-continent swing around the Mediterranean in February of the same year.

At the time of its debut, the cruise ship was the exclusive preserve of the seriously rich and those who had, or pretended to, social eminence. Within the space of thirty years the cruise ship would become an excursion boat available to almost anyone with ten days and a few hundred dollars to spare. Within sixty years, "packaged," hopped-up, democratized and air-conditioned, it would become the last "place" on earth where the rich *or* the socially eminent would allow themselves to be discovered.

Meanwhile, there would be "millionaire cruises" (only millionaires or those who acted liked them could manage to set aside the runs of time and bundles of money it took to join them); there would be round-the-world tours attracting the aged rich (below the sounds of the *bon voyage* party, one might hear the thud of coffins being loaded into the hold), and those of advanced age ready to blow a lifetime's savings on one grand caper in the footsteps of Phineas Fogg and Nelly Bly. But by the time it had become a permanent part of the shipping business, cruising had lost nearly all of its early cachet; the Edwardian "sojourn" in the Antilles had become the go-go cruise to "five swinging islands."

When it became evident that there was a great and largely untapped market for pleasure cruising, the steamship companies at first merely separated the lesser ships of their fleets from their normal schedules and gave them holiday itineraries in a warm climate. Then they began to order new ships designed exclusively for cruising, or to recondition older ones, giving them coats of white paint and erecting awnings on their afterdecks. The model of the new breed designed for tropical waters was Hamburg-Amerika's *Prinzessin Victoria Luise*. As regal in appearance as her name, she had the white hull of a yacht, a long clipper stem and bowsprit, buff-colored funnels. All of her passengers paid first-class rates and slept in brass beds. But fine feathers were no substitute for good seamanship. The *Prinzessin*, with all of her gilded company, was wrecked off Plum Point, Jamaica, in 1906. There was no loss of life, but the sea had claimed one of its prettiest prizes.

Of the great transatlantic record breakers, the first to be diverted to cruising was the 17,000-ton North German Lloyd liner *Deutschland*. Refitted, repainted, and renamed in honor of the princess whose namesake had cracked up, she became, simply, *Victoria Luise*.

The real expansion of cruising as a business did not occur until the general affluence of the '20s provided a potential market for cruise passengers who were as eager to sail overnight to the Bahamas as to spend a month in getting to the Seychelles. The first round-the-world cruises, inaugurated in the 1890s, were really sea-and-land tours. Canadian Pacific, for instance, would take a passenger in a ship from Liverpool eastward to Yokohama and on to San Francisco or Vancouver. But he would then have to cross Canada or the United States by rail and pick up another ship in Montreal or New York.

All cruising trips ended abruptly with the outbreak of World War I, but by 1922 the *Laconia*, a Cunard ship, chartered by the American Express Company just for the purpose, was ready to make the first bona-fide round-the-world cruise by an ocean liner. Tracking the route of Magellan, the *Laconia* opened up the world to pleasure travel with such resounding success that, for every ensuing year until the Depression, the company was able to offer anyone who could afford it the opportunity of circumnavigating the earth in a deck chair. The result was to open a new world, as well as the famous sites of the ancient one, to the investigations of people for whom the universe itself had been the corner store, the Presbyterian Church and the gas station across from the Elks' Lodge. On the way back to the ship from an excursion to Baalbek, one lady passenger was heard to say to another, "*How* does American Express *find* these places?"

Encouraged by this first venture, American Express went all out when, in 1923 they chartered the *Mauretania*—still the undisputed queen of the seas after fifteen years of service on the Great Circle—for a sunny little junket into the Mediterranean. "So fine a collection of men and women with money to waste," said an English shipping man, "had possibly never been assembled before in the hull of one ship." One Judge Gary, head of the Steel Trust, paid for the comforts of a whole suite to himself, and a place at the captain's table, to the tune of twenty-five thousand dollars. American Express, according to the same shipping man, had "arranged the prices so that no man or woman who could not lay their hands on considerable sums of cash could possibly go upon that cruise. They trailed not a luxury lure but one of real squandering upon a majestic scale. Passengers could say proudly—and one assumes that only people who could be made proud by such a claim were passengers—'I was in the *Mauretania* when she was the millionaire ship. We did splash it around.'"

Once the attention of the very rich had been caught by such extravagant boat rides, Cunard changed the tune and began to cater to what might be left of their good common sense. Why submit to all the fuss of managing your yacht? Why stay stuck in a mansion on an estate that goes nowhere when you might be living in a floating mansion that would, every other morning or so, sidle up to a mooring in Piraeus or Bombay? The ship designed especially for the plutocrat was the *Franconia*. "Handy as a big destroyer," said the brochure, "full of the very latest navigational engineering devices, with an electrical installation bigger than many towns, a swimming-bath and racquets court, and a thousand other intriguing features, the *Franconia* is one of those modern right-up-to-the-minute ships which make you wonder why people who can afford to live at sea ever bother about houses. There is scarcely a wealthy man nowadays who troubles about going into the seven seas in his steam yacht; he finds it easier, immeasurably cheaper, and altogether more satisfactory to travel in one of these Cunarders, with his private suite of rooms and all the facilities and resources of the best hotel thrown in. There is more deck space to get about, there are lifts to take him from even the boat deck to the gymnasium in the bowels of the ship, and the wireless enables him to keep in touch with the rest of the globe. What else can be desired?"

Enticements like these proved effective. For one of the *Franconia*'s first cruises all of fifty millionaires, or facsimiles thereof, assembled in New York to sail away. Within a few years there had developed a whole American subculture—a seam of society akin, in every way but in numbers and income, to the hundreds of thousands, eventually millions, of citizens who chose to live in trailers and trailer camps—made up mostly of widows and grandparent couples. Like the men on Melville's *Pequod*, these men and women lived for the greater part of every year at sea, "not so much bound to any havens ahead as rushing from all havens astern." These were the people who did not book accommodations merely for one cruise, but for cruises back to back, cruises that ended just in time to allow them to join other cruises, or even for a whole season of cruises on the same ship. They hired their main-deck suites as they would lease an apartment; and if they did not quite take to one circle of shipboard acquaintance, there was always a chance that on the next go round the passenger list would offer better pickings.

One of the most famous of these troglodytes of the ocean was an ancient spinster from New York City who chose to hole up in Cunard's

Caronia. Over the course of many years she became a fixture on that ship's cruises, a burden to the staff whose solicitude her money insured and a point of speculation to shipmates. To some of them she was a warning of a fall from grace, like the sight of a college classmate now selling shoelaces and pencils in a doorway. One such shipmate was John Hinsdale Thompson who first encountered this old lady of the sea as he was standing in a reception line waiting to shake hands with Captain Law. "My precedence was suddenly preempted by an officer begging my pardon," wrote Thompson, "followed by a steward, waltzing backward, leading with his stiff forearms and wrists a desiccated grande dame the height of a monkey and the thickness of a passport. *Danse macabre.* She made fairly good headway, considering that each step advanced her a two-inch shuffle forward. Her right-of-way took her in no time before the captain, who performed his obeisance before her, as he had (I heard later) uncountable times on this ship, which was home to her more often than to him.

"She will sail in any direction the *Caronia* has schedules for. Around the world, the North Cape, the Black Sea, anywhere. She has not *seen* anything for many years. She appears in public for the Captain's Reception the second night out, and for the rest of the cruise keeps to her stateroom, not even seeing the portholes, let alone seeing any shores or ships outside them. She resents that the *Caronia* is obliged to maroon her once a year while she (the ship) is anti-fouled. But, protest as she may, she is once a year obliged to try those thin stalks as landlegs for the six weeks that Mother Ship is having her bottom scraped and her Lido deck caulked."

Nearly all of the cruise ships eventually acquired their own ancient mariners; but these individuals—some of whom, given the chance, would have *bought* the vessels they wanted to live and die upon—provided but a trifling part of cruising income. On a lower economic, and perhaps social, scale, passengers in great numbers began to take advantage of the bargain "all-in" or "package" deals that cruise ships had begun to offer. More than any other single development since the advent of Thomas Cook's tours and their opportunities for men and women "to coalesce for mutual benefit," the cruise ship tended to reduce the vision of the expectant traveler to the egocentric purview of the tourist.

From the moment he stepped on board, the passenger had more or less arrived where he was going. The ship was not a means, but an end; a destination, not an avenue. (Once this had happened, the emergence, decades later, of the "cruise to nowhere"—the long weekend house party with its connotations of the sexual raffle—was inevitable.) He would of course visit a number of places on the map, but the "shore excursion" beginning and ending in the back seat of a closed car or bus, at the foot of a gangplank, would be designed to insulate him from the weird, grubby or outrageous reality of any one place in favor of exposing him to polite glimpses of its military establishments, its bazaars and the nightclubs where natives entertained him with show-biz parodies of themselves.

As one cruise passenger put it, "The blissful isolation of a cruise is not seriously interfered with when the ship stops at a port. The visits are too brief to allow local, contemporary reality to disturb our detachment." The only remotely human contact—outside of a quick visit to a waterfront crib house—open to most passengers would be a minor business exchange. Bargaining for an article and paying for it, he might for a moment be pleased to think that he had participated in the exotic, without losing control of his own prerogatives.

As the sea roads open to tourists became more and more the same roads, façades of commercial establishments began to replace, or to shield, open spaces in the same way that miles of gas stations, hamburger stands and shopping plazas homogenize the suburban margins of a city. The memories one might bring back from a cruise shifted from what one *saw* in Malta or Martinique to what one *did* at the Captain's Reception or on the night of the Crazy Hat Parade. The essential experience of a cruise lay not in the people you saw on land but the people you met on board. Instead of being judged on the basis of what they offered in the way of balanced itineraries, ships came to be distinguished on the basis of the kind of passenger they attracted, the kind of entertainer they hired, and the number of hours they allowed for shopping in the boutiques of St. Thomas and the diamonds and emeralds supermarkets in Curaçao.

Early on, cruise promoters had to face up to the fact that there were just so many ports of call that a pleasure ship could visit, or might want to. The itinerary of the *Quaker City* in 1867 anticipated those of thousands of similar trips during the ensuing one hundred years. Contemporary cruises to the West Indies vary only in length. The places where they stop are more or less the same places visited the very first time a ship cruised the Caribbean. Every now and then, an obscure port improves its dockage or anchorage facilities to the point where a big liner may risk a visit. But as early as the first years of the twentieth century there was hardly a place that might be added to give a fillip to the old round. Even the most inveterate sightseer would find that his third or fourth visit to the dusty squalor of Kingston, Jamaica or the rock-piled jewel marts and oil storage tanks of Curaçao, Netherlands West Indies, had begun to pall.

This paucity of islands led the shipping companies to search for novelties—not in points ashore, where native entrepreneurs have their own intractable ideas about public entertainment—but at sea, where they could put matters into the well-mannered hands of a cruise director. Before cruises began to feature days at sea devoted almost exclusively to bridge, or golf lessons, or dieting, or lectures by Hendrik Willem van Loon or John Ciardi, one of the most useful innovations was that made in 1927—mere months, actually, before Lindbergh's solo flight from New York to Paris. This was the installation—"with the objective of giving the passengers opportunity to enjoy from bird's view the scenic beauty of the countries visited"—on the North German Lloyd Cruise ship *Lützow* of a catapult capable of launching a seaplane for small flights around the Mediterranean. When passenger response to this proved to be enthusiastic, the company put a Junkers Globetrotter onto the upper deck of their ship *Columbus* and sent her off to the Antilles.

As for ships' captains, some of the more grand-mannered among them took to cruising in the same holiday spirit as did their passengers and were delighted to steer their Leviathans through the translucent waters of coral islands while natives, squinting in long silent rows, watched their festooned arrivals and departures. Some of them were not above the flatteries attendant upon their braided eminence, especially when these came from new passengers to whom the hierarchy of a ship was something of almost regal significance. "No doubt," said the English travel writer Cyril Dunn, "there was something faintly absurd about the larger ladies arriving for the Captain's reception in a full fig to which most of them had devoted months of happy preparation, and dropping the hint of a curtsey to their host, as if they had mistaken him—splendid in tropical white and gold—momentarily for someone royal. But it was also moving, when one considered how rarely the normal lives of most of us are enlivened by this kind of social glamour."

Other captains came to feel that, on cruise duty, their position was less that of commanders of great ships than of nursemaids watching over nurseries ringing with the shouts of dangerous children. Rigorous moralists among them had to learn to countenance kinds of behavior they would not tolerate ashore and to witness with stolidity, if not forbearance, the replacement of the gentleman in the white linen suit and Panama hat by the old boy in the baseball cap, Hawaiian sport shirt and sox that sagged beneath his droopy walking shorts. With the disappearance of the lady in shawls and draperies, nibbling at cucumber sandwiches over afternoon tea in the Verandah Garden, he had to suffer the affront of the enameled old babe at the end of the bar who clanked the fifty-five charms of her bracelet over a double Bull Shot-on-the-rocks. One of the more philosophically bent among the captains connected deportment—even ethics—with the compulsions of climate. "Specially does it apply to long voyages in tropical waters," he said. "There are plenty of cases on record of girls and women who under the spell of hot weather and starlit nights at sea in the tropics, have lost control of themselves and yielded to temptations which on shore they would have spurned. On the short, cold-weather voyages the climatic conditions are less exacting, and there is less time for romances to mature, so we have to look elsewhere for the causes of infidelity."

Short cruises by long ships in the Depression years were a stopgap— a sad and ultimately feckless attempt to keep alive liners that had quite played out the roles for which they had been cast. When business on the Atlantic began to pick up, the new travelers wanted to travel in the publicized new ships. One by one, the *Olympic*, the *Berengaria*, the *Aquitania*, even the ageless *Mauretania*—by then rusting in white cruise paint "like a wedding cake gone wrong"—were towed away, dismantled, and broken up. Smaller ships, meanwhile, carried on the cruise business, following old sea-tracks in the Caribbean and Mediterranean, arriving at Hammerfest, Norway, just in time to catch the full glory of the Midnight Sun, turning up in Rio to give their passengers a chance to join the ether-sniffing crowds of *carnivale*. Then, just as World War I had cleared the decks, World War II came down like a drop-scene; afterwards, everything would be different.

The difference was a consequence—of numbers, of affluence, of a shift in cruise advertising from an emphasis on elegance and leisure to an emphasis on home comforts afloat, native nightclubs on land, uninterrupted activity everywhere. These factors quite transformed the outlook of shipping men: the cruise as a stopgap—an employment of resources not to make money but to carry the overhead—was now a thing of the past. There was money in the air and, on the scent of it, shipowners tried to anticipate the demands of a new race of sea-goers to whom the old standards of travel afloat were unknown or meaningless.

Like the old McKinley era hotel that dispenses with its verandah and rocking chairs for a glass front of shops; dismantles its palm garden and puts away its wicker to replace them with a dim-lighted cave of leatherette and a Hammond organ; tears up its croquet court to make room for a swimming pool; paves over the rose garden to make a parking lot, then calls itself a Motor Inn—ships built in one image suddenly found themselves being revised to show another. With the exception of the Swedish *Stella Polaris*—that paragon of cruise ships which sailed summer and winter with the pride of a swan in a clamor of ducks—all ships either built for cruising or revised to meet its demands gradually surrendered to the contagion of pop culture and pop art and the kinds of furnishings that might be secured with a hundred books of Green Stamps. A process that continued for years— marked by a holding action there, a stubborn refusal here—it could only end, as it did, in the triumph of the abominable.

One bright morning in November, 1968, something no one had ever seen before—a real psychedelic "go-go" ocean liner—backed out of her mid-Manhattan berth and began to move down the Hudson. A knowledgeable eye, discerning the outlines of the tall, lovely "pearl of the American Merchant Marine," could only blink, then stare, then weep. Looking for all the world like a billboard advertising hair oil or breakfast food, the *Independence* was putting out to sea. Under the sponsorship of Fugazy Sales Corporation, a subsidiary of the Diners' Club, she was setting off on a cut-rate "experimental" cruise during which, for one thing, passengers would choose and pay for their meals in any one of four restaurants and, for another, drink and dance in public rooms festooned, like a gymnasium for a high school prom, with blown-up reminders of the Roaring '20s. Her once immaculate white sides painted with a huge globelike caricature with leering eyes, rakish eyebrows and a sunburst of black streaks that extended from the waterline to the boat deck, the *Independence* was bound for the Caribbean, utter failure and blessed retirement.

A matter of ease and cultural curiosity at first—as well as a boon to an industry that had overreached itself—cruising finally became a sort of European charter service for Americans hungry for five meals a day and bourbon at duty-free prices. Only twelve years after the *Independence* had made her embarrassed exit, every Atlantic passenger ship owned in the United States had followed her. Cruise business had brought prosperity to European shipping companies, yet its sensational growth had served only to shunt American companies into a series of squabbles between management and labor ending in mutual paralysis. By that time, spanking new vessels flying the flags of Yugoslavia, Poland and the Soviet Union were crisscrossing the Caribbean from Hispaniola to the very least of the Lesser Antilles. As these were joined by other smart white ships from Norway, Greece and Germany, the great American liners lay idle in coastal backwaters. They were still comparatively new-minted, loaded with power and pretty as pictures, yet the *United States, Constitution, Independence, Argentina, Brasil, Santa Rosa* and *Santa Paula,* abandoned to rust and the weather, were being allowed to waste away. The prophecy voiced one hundred and twenty-three years earlier, when the S.S. *Washington* had gone bungling onto the Atlantic, was as true as ever: Americans could build ships but they could not manage them.

ℳ SECTION IX ℳ

A *Nazi in the Sky* / *Dr. Eckener's Gamble* / *The Flaming*
Hindenburg / *R.M.S.* Queen Elizabeth: "*The Ultimate Ship*"
Escape of "*An Empress Incognito*" / *The Dash of the* Bremen

ENGAGED in their game of tag on the wastes of the Atlantic,
the *Normandie* and the *Queen Mary* were hardly aware that
another big rotund vessel was sailing serenely above them or
of the fact that she was bettering, almost by half, the best crossing
time either of them had ever made. Their new rival overhead was
the *Graf Zeppelin*, the first airship to be put on the transatlantic run
by the Deutsche Zeppelin-Reederei, for whom, significantly, the agents
were Hamburg-Amerika and North German Lloyd. "Seeing the world
from above," said a brochure, "from an airship gliding calmly through
the circumambient ether is an event with which nought else is fully
comparable."

Beside a photograph of the *Graf Zeppelin*, a big, new-minted swastika
on her fin, large type announced: "2½ Days to Europe—Travel to
Europe by Zeppelin!" Accommodations for passengers on the *Graf*,
without stressing the luxurious, were nevertheless remarkable. Fifty
passengers could be carried in two-berth staterooms, each equipped with
washstands providing hot and cold running water. They could spend

air-borne days in a reading and writing room, a lounge and bar, and dine at one sitting in a gallery. They could stroll on promenade decks placed on either side of the airship and they had access to shower baths. Yet the *Graf*'s fittings were coldly practical and without grace; in attracting customers the main emphasis was placed on the dependability of the airship.

This had been established on the *Graf*'s first flight to New York, in 1928, and was the consequence of a midocean accident publicized by wireless almost from the moment it had occurred. By an ironic twist in the way people reacted to it, the incident served the *Graf Zeppelin*'s career in the same way that the dashing steamer *Arizona* was served when she became celebrated for safety only after she had plowed head-on into an iceberg. With more than sixty people aboard, the silvery smooth *Graf* was nosing westward when, a morning beyond the Azores, she was caught by a gust of wind that knocked coffee cups from the breakfast table, dumped Lady Drummond Hay into the lap of a surprised German gentleman and caused the airship herself to roll like a fifty-cent cigar. As the man at the helm was trying to parry the sudden onslaught of wind and bring the *Graf* back on course, bad news came skittering along the catwalk. The lower covering on the stabilizer had been torn away, the chief machinist reported; shreds of fabric were snapping in the wind: more of it would surely be ripped away. Commander Hugo Eckener ordered the engines stopped and called for volunteers to act as an emergency repair crew. Seven men responded, including the Commander's son Knud, who was a helmsman engineer. Held by ropes, some of these men climbed inside the damaged fin, tore off the streamers of ragged fabric, put a patchwork of blankets over the exposed portions of the stabilizer and tied the whole thing together with cord. Meanwhile, without engine power, the *Graf Zeppelin* was sinking perilously close to the surface of the ocean. Dr. Eckener and the men in the control car knew that a sudden movement caused by resumption of power might sweep the volunteers off the tail of the ship. Yet this risk had to be taken. Just as the *Graf* was about to settle onto the water and melt like a snowflake, Dr. Eckener gave the order: "Start engines!" Nobody was blown off, the homemade patchwork held, and the zeppelin proceeded to her New Jersey mooring. Instead of registering the danger implicit in the mishap—or the absurdity of a great technological monster being saved by bedclothes and parcel wrapping—Americans tended to applaud the ingenuity of it all and place a confidence in the zeppelin that was, subsequently, almost justified.

By the end of 1935, it was pointed out, the *Graf Zeppelin* had made 437 round trips, including 194 ocean crossings and a voyage around the world, adding up to a total mileage of over 650,000. Twenty-eight thousand passengers had been carried; nearly six million pieces of mail. For a ticket priced at only four hundred dollars—as against three thousand dollars in 1928—you could be wafted from Lakehurst, New Jersey, to Frankfurt am Main, "free from unpleasant motion, such as rolling and pitching."

The day of the dependable Atlantic airlift was closer than anyone suspected—and so was the sudden, total demise of the ocean-going zeppelin. But in the brief meantime, the success of the experimental *Graf Zeppelin* had led to the construction of the bigger and far more handsomely appointed *Hindenburg*. Since this was the airship that was finally going to give ocean liners a run for their money, her passenger quarters were designed to emulate, in comfort if not in scale, those on the crack North German Lloyd ships. For the first time an airship had a smoking room (thanks to the replacement of hydrogen by helium) as well as a spacious promenade deck and a lounge in which stood a Blüthner piano, made of light metal, that weighed only 112 pounds. "To me," said the *Hindenburg*'s interior designer Breuhaus, "a piano is an earthbound instrument which does not rightfully belong in an airship." But American passengers had an ear for live music en route, and he gave in.

Some travelers had begun to take zeppelin crossings for granted: you lived in the air more or less as you did on water, but for only half as many days. For her first eastward crossing in the late spring of 1937, the *Hindenburg* was fully booked, with a waiting list of Americans hoping to be on hand for the coronation of George VI in Westminster Abbey. She flew over from Germany smoothly and on schedule. But when she got to Lakehurst and was being eased out of the sky on ropes pulled by a large ground crew, she burst into flames, reared back, then came to earth like a falling pillar of fire. The last hope that ships in the sky might replace or seriously rival ships on the sea was cremated, like the *Hindenburg* herself, in a matter of seconds.

Two months later, the schedule of transoceanic crossings haltingly attempted by the *Hindenburg* and the *Graf Zeppelin* was given a new, revolutionary and permanent step forward: on July 4, 1937, Pan American's *Clipper III* and Imperial Airways' *Caledonia* lifted themselves into the skies from opposite shores of the Atlantic. The trails in the sky they blazed were swift, untrammeled and, as time would tell, apocalyptic.

In the very cradle and shadow of the *Queen Mary*, meanwhile, the biggest passenger liner that would ever be built was slowly rising to her ultimate grandeur above the red brick sheds of John Brown's shipyard.

The new ship was the *Queen Elizabeth*. When she was ready to sail, it would be possible, for the first time in history, to maintain a British express service between Southampton and New York with just two liners. Long hoped for and planned for, a schedule of once a week from each side of the Atlantic was the whole reason for the gargantuan dimensions of the new ships, and for their unprecedented speed. "The speed is dictated by the time necessary to perform the journey at all seasons of the year," said Director Sir Percy Bates, "the size is dictated by the necessity to make money . . . to pay for the speed. To go beyond these conditions would be extravagant; to fall below them would be incompetent."

In the summer of 1935, for the first time in five depression-ridden years, traffic on the ocean had shown an upswing. The *Queen Elizabeth* was laid down in 1936, just when it began to seem likely that her sister would become a money maker. Much the same sort of ship as the *Mary* in a general way, the *Elizabeth* had one less funnel, a few more cabins, just as many touches of misguided decoration and just as odd an assortment of *objets d'art* from the counties. "Strength, solidity, safety," was a sort of unwritten motto for the new supership. It seemed to indicate that Britain's maritime architects and designers were having none of the streamlined litheness of the new ships from the Continent. Instead, they were trying somehow to unite the "official" awesomeness of a Russian or Polish Palace of Culture with the overstuffed banality of a suburban drawing room. Throughout the ship, bleached wood with a coffee-and-cream-colored veneer continued the gloss-and-polish tradition of the *Queen Mary*. The keystone work of art, a bas-relief entitled—with perhaps a bow to Sibelius—"Oceanides," was placed at the top of the stairs on Promenade Deck Square. Its centerpiece was composed "of the nude figures of a man and a woman in eurythmic attitudes." But the big decorative feature of the *Elizabeth* was wood—wood of all kinds, including wych elm, bog oak, Australian bean wood, padauk, primavera, coromandel, thuya, red sanders, zebrano, Rio rosewood, colo bolo, almond and camphor.

Nothing since Noah's Ark had probably carried so much deciduous stuff. In fact, as the *Elizabeth* was being riveted together a certain hard-shelled Scotsman became newly aware of her biblical predecessor. Henry Robb, a shipping man from Leith, pointed out how cleverly the *Elizabeth*'s builders were following Noah, in that the patriarch had himself found the "correct principles of stability" long before modern science had determined just what these might be. According to Mr. Robb, the Ark was 450 feet long, 75 feet in the beam, with a depth of 45 feet—dimensions similar to those of a modern vessel of about 12,000 tons. She had three decks—or stories, as the Bible called them—and took a live cargo (humans and beasts) and water. These were the two most dangerous cargoes a ship could handle, and yet the Ark had endured "the most terrific storm the world had ever experienced" and survived it.

Unaware, most likely, of the scriptural orthodoxy of their procedures, the marine architects employed by Cunard in Clydeside continued with their plans for "the ultimate ship." They determined that, just where the designers of the *Normandie* had put a full-sized tennis court, the *Elizabeth* would have a big, partially enclosed deck square for the use of tourist-class passengers. This caused some trouble, simply because it made it possible for travelers domiciled in the rabbit warrens of tourist to rise, by fast elevators, to the point where they could actually look *down* upon any first-class passenger who happened to be strolling the boat deck. According to an old and sacrosanct tradition of the sea, first could look down at third, but for third to be allowed to look down on first was to scramble all the guidelines. Fortunately, not many passengers enjoyed walking on the windy boat deck of the *Queen Elizabeth*; and those first-class passengers who happened to catch the offending gaze of tourist-class passengers above them could always make their way aft and, for compensation, stare down on cabin.

The new queen of the seas was supposed to set off on her maiden voyage on April 24, 1940. But on that very day, instead of sailing out of Southampton in a flutter of pennants, she found herself, hospital gray from stem to stern, sitting in exile at the foot of West Forty-ninth Street, New York City.

When World War II broke out in September, 1939, the *Elizabeth*—one year after she had been launched by the Queen whose name she bore—was quietly berthed in the fitting-out basin at Clydeside. But since she was a sitting duck for German bombers, she was moved just as soon as she could be got ready to put to sea under her own power. A directive from Winston Churchill himself told her to get out of the British Isles and stay out, "just as long as this order is in force." Almost empty, untried and unfinished, she was eased out of her basin on February 26, 1940. A week later, under secret orders and a broadcast barrage of propaganda meant to divert both German and British attention from her real plans, she began a zigzag crossing to New York. Five days and nineteen hours later, "like an Empress incognito, grey-veiled for her desperate exploit," she turned up in the Narrows. The *Queen Mary*, berthed next to the still-upright *Normandie*, was waiting for her at Pier 90. Soon the two great sister ships were trooping the seas like military workhorses. The *Elizabeth* would not take up the career she was meant to follow for another six years. By that time, all the competition she had been designed to overshadow and engineered to outrun had disappeared.

The outbreak of World War II had disrupted not only the *Elizabeth*'s plans, but the *Bremen*'s as well. The German ship was supposed to carry a late-summer crowd of Germans and Americans to Bremerhaven. Instead, she had to cancel everything in order to make a dash for it—but not before she was detained by the United States Treasury Department.

Arriving in New York on August 29, 1939—a peculiarly unpropitious date for a Nazi ship to be so far from home—she was searched from her keel to her funnels to make sure that she was no threat to the city or, indeed, to the nation. "There will be no repetition of the situation in 1917," said U.S. Attorney General Frank Murphy, "when a democracy was unprepared to meet the espionage problem." When she was allowed to depart on the night of August 30, even *The New York Times* dropped a nostalgic tear. "As twilight fell," said an editorial writer, "the liner *Bremen*, her long reaches of deck empty, save for an occasional white-jacketed steward or blue-clad officer, slipped away from her West Forty-sixth Street dock with a band playing German airs. Unlike many other occasions of the past, when the two immense buff-colored stacks were illuminated by piercing floodlights and the cabins filled with passengers eagerly looking forward to whatever lay before them in European resorts, the great liner slipped away almost furtively down the river, with every light extinguished except the running lights required for navigation."

Her quadruple screws churning to the limit of their power, the *Bremen* pounded across the ocean on an arc far north of that made by the Great Circle and thereby confounded Allied search parties on the lookout for her in the air and on the water. En route across the Atlantic—just as the *Lusitania* had once, for safety's sake, run up the Stars and Stripes—she hoisted the Hammer and Sickle of the U.S.S.R. Hugging the coastlines of Arctic islands, her decks piled high with barrels of gasoline that were to be instantly set ablaze should she be intercepted, the most destroyerlike of all ocean liners eventually steamed into Murmansk and the protection of her Russian hosts. After a brief stay here, she started south, kept close to the mouths of Norwegian fjords, and got to her home port—only to be bombed and set afire so badly that she was good for nothing but scrap. Fed piecemeal to the munitions factories of the Ruhr, the remains of the most stunning ship of an era were melted down, to reappear like scatter shot in some theater of war.

⚝ SECTION X ⚝

Mal de Mer: *"The Nauseate Sublime"* / Baltimore: *The End of the Scourge* / General Ballou: *Ship of Mercy* / *Mothersill's and Others* / *Grouches and Lyricists* / *The Bessemer Saloon Ship* / *Diagnoses and Treatments*

O F ALL the scourges visited upon the traveler by sea—piracy, boredom, satyriasis, nymphomania, mildew, impressment into a foreign navy, scurvy, gluttony, claustrophobia, agora-phobia, hi-jacking, shanghaiing, sun stroke, malaria, paranoia, diarrhea, shipwreck, fire, ice, fog and St. Elmo's fire—the one claiming the greatest number of victims and responsible for the deepest suffering was, by all odds, seasickness. "Gods! What a retrospect!" said one just back from its living grave. "It seems like an eternity of spasmodic suf-fering—talk of amputation! Mental anxiety—chronic disease—why what is the whole catalogue of human ills compared to this attic salt— this bilious dissolution—this sea-emetic?"

In spite of the witches' brews of preventives and curatives they carried on board with them, travelers escaped neither its green orchida-ceous fever nor the warm soupiness of its bilious embrace. In spite of prayers they offered day and night toward that end, very few travelers died of it. When seasickness overtook people who had survived amputa-tion without anesthesia, suppuration without analgesia, asthmatic suf-focation, gastric convulsions and torture by the exquisite devices of imaginative aborigines, they recalled such miseries with the nostalgia and longing of old men remembering their youth. Anyone who has ever been seasick—classically seasick, as opposed to those mild forms of the malaise in which one is said to be "peaky," "squeamish" or "off his feed"—knows that it is the only and ultimate sickness: the one living death of faculty and will that involves the whole man, individually and ontologically.

The end of this scourge of centuries of sea-going came abruptly and by accident, long after men had given up seriously looking for it. The place where the cure was discovered was the city of Baltimore; the actual scene was the Allergy Clinic of the Johns Hopkins University and Hospital, on whose staff were Dr. Leslie N. Gay and Dr. Paul E. Carliner. Working as a team, these two physicians were investigating the possible uses of a number of drugs in the relief of allergic conditions like rhinitis, urticaria and hay fever. Among their drugs was a synthetic antihistamine, $C_{17}H_{22}No.C_7H_6ClN_4O_2$, called dimenhydrinate, and they had been giving it to a pregnant woman patient afflicted with hives. This patient, who had also suffered all of her life from carsickness, nevertheless had to make her visits to the clinic by streetcar. When it became evident that dimenhydrinate—or Dramamine, as it would soon be generally known—was curing her of hives, it also became evident that, if she took a capsule of the drug before setting out on her crosstown journey, she got complete relief from the nausea that had always made her trolley rides a misery.

Alerted by her off-hand report, the two doctors made their finding known to the United States Army—with the result that, first, the U.S.S. *America* and then a troop transport engaged in ferrying military personnel and their families between Bremerhaven and New York were put at their disposal to carry out "Operation Seasickness." This ship was the 13,000-ton U.S.A.T. *General Ballou*, with a capacity of 1,376 passengers in austerity accommodations, and scheduled to make a trip to Germany in November, when, for the purposes of the Doctors Gay and Carliner, the weather would be obligingly rough. To test the drug for both preventive and curative properties, the physicians divided the 485 men chosen to submit to their experiment into two groups. The first group was then subdivided and given a Dramamine capsule of 100 milligrams as the ship sailed out of New York Harbor.

The second part of the subdivided group got a capsule containing only sugar. With the doctors alone in possession of the knowledge of who got what, similar capsules were administered six hours later, then once before each meal and before bedtime. One hundred and thirty-four men got Dramamine, and not one of them complained of nausea or vomiting while taking it. One hundred and twenty-three men got sugar capsules; of these, thirty-five became seasick within twelve hours of sailing. "The corridors," reported Doctors Gay and Carliner, "were congested by sick men, so ill that they were unable to reach the latrines. The men who reached these areas were unable to return to their compartments and remained stretched out in semi-conscious condition on the floors until more seaworthy individuals managed to drag them to the sick bay or back to their hammocks. The latrines became temporarily indescribably repulsive." Yet, with only one exception, all of these men were brought back to normal by Dramamine within three hours.

None of those in the curative trial group got any Dramamine at the beginning of the voyage. Fifteen of these became seasick; twelve got better at once when Dramamine was administered. In a whole crisscross schedule of tests and countertests on this voyage and a return voyage in December, on which a great number of the trial subjects were women, the doctors found that less than two percent of the passengers who got Dramamine as a preventive measure were vulnerable to seasickness.

Drab in her Army gray, the U.S.A.T. *General Ballou* came back to New York bearing no visible sign that she was a ship of historical import, that she was worthy of a medal to be hung beside those memorializing the *Argo*, the *Golden Hind* and the *Robert E. Lee*, or that the still-secret burden she carried was, to generations yet unborn, salvation on earth and a hope of heaven. Had Army regulations allowed it, the *General Ballou* should have run up a pennant imprinted with one word: Eureka!

A little pellet worth its weight in pitchblende had suddenly made obsolete remedies for the prevention, cure or endurance of *mal de mer* that included the following: bismuth; soda; salol; opium; valerian; a combination of Beltafoline and soluble camphor; chloral; chloreton; "a little soup with cayenne"; morphine with atropine; a slice of fat pork fried with garlic; "patience and a good walk on shore"; hyoscin hydrobromide; a pint of sea water "in one gulp"; phenacetin with caffein; arrowroot and wine; sodium amytal; tomato sauce; mustard leaf; animal magnetism; trinitrin and cocaine; veronal; a spinal ice bag; luminal; small doses of tincture of iodine; mustard pickles; lemon and ginger; toasting the ear canals; caviar; *cannabis indica*; Worcestershire sauce; sodium nitrate; chewing gum; musk pills; dry toast; a belladonna plaster on the stomach; vinegar and water in sips; capsules of sodium phenobarbital.

"How pure and sweet the air would be at sea," said one lyrical observer, "if it were not for the repeated vomiting of bile, whose effluvia are extremely volatile and settle down at once in the curtains, floor, ceiling, paint, sofa and beds of the cabins." To cope with the effects of ship's motion and "ship's smell" and that disposition to immediate surrender they all but guaranteed, many people after 1908 depended upon a little pill that came, without much likelihood, from Detroit. This was Mothersill's Seasick Remedy, certified "not to contain cocaine, morphine, opium, chloral, or any coal-tar products." Mothersill's, according to its makers, had received unqualified endorsement from such people as Bishop Taylor Smith, Lord Northcliffe and hosts of "doctors, bankers and professional men, as well as leading clubwomen," all of whom had presumably been uplifted and straightened out by the pill while "sailing the English Channel, Irish Sea and the Baltic." The cost of a box that would last the transatlantic voyage was one dollar. In World War I, the company's promotion reached out particularly to mothers. "To prevent seasickness," read the advertisements, "and insure him a pleasant voyage, be sure to remember to put in his bag a package of Mothersill's Seasick Remedy." "Him" was, of course, a doughboy.

Like every other remedy, Mothersill's for the most part worked only for those who thought it did. These were not apt to be among the more advanced cases, and many a box of the stuff lay barely touched beside the pale hands of the stricken.

Although later investigations would show decisively that psychogenic factors were of small account, the most time-honored method of treating seasickness was entirely verbal: you simply told the victim—in a tone of voice implying that some slackening of moral fiber was involved—that it was all in his mind. Sympathy for the man or woman who is intractably supine and viridescent, is—like gratitude—an emotion noted for its short term. Sometimes it has no term at all. Mark Twain, observing anguish all about him, handsomely states the case for those who not only are unsusceptible to the malaise, but also lack any shred of human feeling. "I knew what was the matter with them," said Twain of his shipmates. "They were seasick. And I was glad of it. We all like to see people seasick when we are not, ourselves. Playing whist by the cabin lamps, when it is storming outside, is pleasant; walking the quarterdeck in the moonlight is pleasant; smoking in the breezy foretop is pleasant, when one is not afraid to go up there; but these are all feeble and commonplace compared with the joy of seeing people suffering the miseries of seasickness."

On the other hand, Irvin S. Cobb's bout with seasickness made him philosophical. "As in the case of drowning persons," he noted, "there passed in review before my eyes several of the more recent events of my past life—meals mostly." To old Judge Haliburton, rejuvenated by a voyage on the *Great Western*, seasickness was a frustration. "How I should like to make love," he said, "if it was only for the fun of the thing just to keep one's hand in; but alas! all the young girls are sick— devilish sick, and I trust I need not tell you that a love-sick girl is one thing, and a sea-sick girl another. I like to have my love returned, but not my dinner."

The distress of another early steamship passenger is expressed with sincerity and erudition. "I felt, rather than saw my enemy approach," he said. "He came upon a tall wave, with a white ensign, and a sparkling lance. His first blow was aimed at the very point of the system where the Ancients seated courage." When his ship—Cunard's paddle-wheeled *Asia*—came within sight of icebergs, his companions urged him to come see. "But if each iceberg had been as radiant with gold and orange, green and violet," he said, "and prismatic generally as Trinity Church windows, with a Polar bear surmounting each glittering pinnacle, the scene would not have aroused my sense of the beautiful. If there is to be found beauty or sublimity upon the ocean, the mental tentacula must reach out and find it. But when they are paralyzed and shrunken by this everlasting sea-sickness—where is the sub—— I beg pardon. Eureka! It is the sublimity Burke discovered in Spencer's Cave of Error—the *nauseate sublime!* Its monosyllabic expression is simply—Ugh!"

The most drastic and expensive measure ever taken to deal with sea-sickness was that by Henry Bessemer, inventor of the process, bearing his name, by which steel is produced by the action of a blast of air forced through molten iron. On a crosschannel trip from Calais to Dover in 1868, Sir Henry was overcome by seasickness of such an intensity that he suffered not only throughout the voyage but also for the duration of the train ride up to London and into the day following his arrival home. His personal physician, alarmed, sat with him through the length of a night and eventually brought him around by administering small doses of prussic acid. The experience turned Bessemer's inventive mind "to the causes of this painful malady" which—as did almost everyone else—he mistakenly attributed "to the diaphragm being subjected to the sudden motions of the ship." The upshot was that famous contribution to the catacombs of pretentious curiosities known as the Bessemer Saloon.

In conception, nothing could have been simpler: to isolate a part of the passenger deck of a ship "to prevent it from partaking of the general rolling and pitching motion." Bessemer built a model in which was installed a suspended cabin, supported on separate axes placed at right angles to each other. Pleased by the success of backyard experiments under contrived conditions that he somehow thought were duplicates of conditions on the English Channel, he organized the Bessemer Saloon Ship Company and proceeded to build a pioneer vessel.

Patented in 1869, the finished product came out in 1873—a cabin of such proportion and appointments as had never before been seen on "the silver streak." Seventy feet long and thirty feet wide, with a ceiling twenty feet from the floor, the *salon de Bessemer* was furnished with seats covered in morocco placed among carved-oak divisions and spiral columns. Its wall panels, on which were hand-painted cartoons, were prettily touched up with gilt. It gave, said Bessemer, "an idea of luxury to the future Channel passage which all seemed to appreciate."

But nothing worked. The saloon refused to swing in a compensating direction, and sometimes not at all. To the assaults on equilibrium made by normal rolling and pitching, it added the wild disorientation of a carnival ride. The first actual open-sea tests were disastrous, yet Bessemer was convinced that, once he had got the bugs out and his device was working at sea as it had worked on land, the new era of salubrious water travel would begin. But, in the ironic fact that the vessel in which the saloon was contained was more eccentric than the saloon itself, Bessemer was robbed of his chance to prove his invention.

At some crucial point in its docking maneuvers, the mechanism of the Bessemer Saloon ship would apparently refuse to respond to orders. After banging into the pier at Calais on her first trip, the ship was repaired and made ready for a second chance. On this occasion in May, 1873, Bessemer was himself aboard.

"We had arrived," he wrote in his diary, "very slowly, it must be admitted—at the entrance of Calais Harbour. I, knowing what had occurred on a previous occasion, held my breath while the veteran Captain Pittock gave his orders to the man at the helm. But the ship did not obey him, and crash she went along the pier sides, knocking down the huge timbers like so many ninepins! I knew what it all meant to me. That five minutes had made me a poorer man by thirty-four thousand pounds; it had deprived me of one of the greatest triumphs of a long professional life, and had wrought the loss of the dearly-cherished hope that buoyed me up and helped to carry me through my personal labours. I had fondly hoped to remove for ever from thousands yet unborn the bitter pangs of the Channel passage, and thus by intercourse, and a greater appreciation of each other, to strengthen the bonds of mutual respect and esteem between two great nations. . . . All this had gone forever. It will be readily understood that this second catastrophe at Calais finally determined the fate of the Bessemer Saloon Steamboat Company, which had thus become hopelessly discredited." Bessemer died still believing that his invention had not failed—simply because it had never really been properly tried. Over the smirks and laughter (an oscillating ballroom had slammed into France like a battering ram!) no champion arose to prove him right, no investor willing to let him make another try.

Except by accident, or do-it-yourself voodoo, no one had yet been able to cure himself of seasickness. But the actual cause of it had been discerned, and means of dealing with it devised, as early as 1870. In that year, an unknown writer defined the trouble succinctly. "The sickness is not occasioned, as is quite often supposed, by the mechanical effect of the motion of the ship on the digestive organs. The derangement of the system by the motion of the sea is primarily an affection of the brain, the affects upon the other organs being secondary and symptomatic; and the function of the brain through the disturbance of which the morbid action begins is what is called the 'instinct of equilibrium'—that is, the instinct by which the mind, through some hidden action of the brain, takes cognizance of the relation of the body to the perpendicular."

Among the random and gratuitous kinds of advice for the victim were a number of ideas based on this diagnosis. "If qualms persist," said one authority, "pack the ears with gauze until a firm pressure on the tympanic membrane can be felt." When therapy by electric device was possible, someone invented a "seasick collar," by which to warm the neck and the base of the brain; and there was a related device by which the ear canals could be "toasted." The closest thing to Dramamine in its effects was probably the therapy offered by the medical staffs of the *Bremen* and *Europa* in the early '30s—the Dammert Inhalation Treatment. For fifty cents a go, this could be administered to those in need of it twice every day. "The patient who takes it," said an advocate, "lies down and breathes, through a nose-and-mouth cap, a mixture of oxygen and atropine. Atropine acts specifically to soothe the balancing system of the body which lies in the vestibulary apparatus of the inner ear, and once these centers are calmed, even a tottering great-aunt may become a trapeze performer."

To such instances of ingenuity, old salts remained impervious and unconvinced. "The cure for seasickness," said a commodore of the Cunard fleet, "is to separate the passenger from the ship." Yet one of the most remarkable things about the ocean was its power to maintain high romance in the teeth of its tendency to reduce even ardent sea-lovers to comatose bundles of bile. At its boisterous worst, the sea for many people was a manifestation of divine grandeur not to be denied by so trivial a thing as a man's organic disfunction. "The solitude of a stormy night upon the ocean!" wrote one of these. "What pen can describe! And yet who can be insensible to the luxury of that solitude —to its melancholy sublimity! And now as I write, our ship plunges and rolls in the heavy sea, and a death-like nausea comes over me. Our ship rises and plunges over these vast waves with much grandeur. It is majestically sickening, sublimely nauseating."

❧ SECTION XI ❧

Interval of War / *New Silhouettes on the North Atlantic* / *The* Queen Mary *and the* Curaçao / *Resurgence in "Steamship Row"* / S.S. United States: Prima Ballerina Assoluta / *The Luck of Captain Manning* / *Maiden Voyage: "Just Like a Destroyer"* *Good Sports in Southampton* / Andrea Doria *Inbound*, Stockholm *Out* / Ile de France *on the Scene* / *Settlement and Aftermath*

1940. Tethered to Manhattan like circus animals with no place to go, the great liners—*Ile de France, Normandie, Queen Mary, Queen Elizabeth, Aquitania, Rex*—lightly rose and fell with the tides of the Hudson. Then, one by one, refitted and reduced to anonymous shades of military gray, they were sent off on missions of war. In a sense, they would never come back again. The *concours d'élégance* was over; the golden rosettes and silver loving cups had all been awarded. Sailing out as sovereigns, ultimate embodiments of man's quest for locomotive power, speed and creature comfort, they would sail back as revenants, Leviathans out of epoch and, before long, out of work.

In the interval of a war, speed in the air had reduced their own grand Atlantic preserve to the dimensions of a lake, the arc of their Great Circle to the brevity of a nonstop hop. Their celebrated virtues, the amusing charm of their theatrical pretensions, were moribund. They would move ponderously about for a few years, fight among themselves as they grew weaker, watch with consternation the emergence of a few monsters almost, but not quite, like themselves. Finally they would succumb to the pressures of a new age that had no place or role for them except as big inter-island barges for travelers going nowhere.

When the war was over, there was still a great number of serious travelers who, to the surprise of the shipping industry and its agents, chose ships over planes. This preference gave new life to the prewar veterans that had come back into service and even encouraged shipping companies to order new ships. When these arrived, a number of them—at least to the unbiased and unsentimental—were handsomer, more comfortable and decidedly more tasteful than the famous liners of the early part of the century. But to most of the public, now air-minded if not yet air-borne, they were simply efficient ocean carriers, no doubt punctual and trustworthy, yet altogether lacking in the power to charm that had caught their fathers and grandfathers.

Among the new silhouettes about to be sighted on the Great Circle was the *America*. Groomed to signify "the reawakening of American ambitions," this new standard bearer was launched on a day—August 31, 1939—so inauspicious as to suggest a breakdown in the operations of national intelligence. Since she could not cross the ocean without risking everything, she was sent, like a child ordered to go out and play, into the cruising business until she might be needed for the war. Then she was rechristened *West Point* and, under that name, sailed as a trooper for half a million miles.

The big British *Queens*, once they were quit of their obligations as transports for returning GIs and relieved of ferrying war brides and the thousands of infants born out of an access of wartime conviviality, were once more civilian vessels. Lower decks where, not long before "the atmosphere had a ripe, zoo quality," and as many as fifteen thousand soldiers "stood in line for hours to get skimpy rations of dehydrated potatoes, some sort of smashed meat substitute and an unidentifiable juice," were disinfected of the last remaining spoor of war. The general removal and dismantling included: the jackknife carvings of Kilroy and his buddies on every millimeter of wood around the promenade decks; big liquor cabinets that had been installed in the main-deck suite occupied on three separate occasions by Winston Churchill; the *Queen Mary*'s badly smashed forefoot.

Though not easily visible, the new cutwater installed on the *Mary* was a reminder of the saddest and most excruciating moment of the ship's military career. That moment had come when, plowing through the far North Atlantic in convoy, the *Queen Mary* and her escorting British cruiser *Curaçao* got their signals mixed. The lapse was brief but catastrophic: the great liner butted the little warship in the stern with a force that sent her spinning around at an angle of 90 degrees, then simply ran over her, slicing her in two like an apple. As 338 men suffocated in their bunks and hammocks, or drowned in the open water into which they were catapulted, the *Queen Mary*—under Admiralty orders never to put herself and her huge complement of men and materiel in jeopardy—plunged on without a backward glance. The only damage she herself sustained was a ragged gash in the bow.

Refurbished in the shining geometry of the emergent style that would eventually be known as *art deco,* the *Elizabeth* and the *Mary* were at last sent shuttling back and forth in the ocean ferry service for which Cunard had built them. Their weekly transatlantic *pas de deux* was so successful that, for each of three years in a row, the *Queens* between them racked up a profit of fifty million dollars.

The *Elizabeth*'s Southampton-to-New York voyage in October, 1946, was in fact her maiden voyage as a commercial liner. "She performed beautifully," said her Captain Bissett, "just like a sewing machine." The food served in her bedighted first-class restaurant—nearly all of it imported from Canada in the hold of the fading old *Aquitania*—was absurdly modest by prewar standards; but to the ration-weary British, as well as to the Soviet emissaries to the United Nations, Molotov and Vishinsky, the length and variety of the *Elizabeth*'s menu was Lucullan. For one full year the new flagship of the Cunard Line ran the Great Circle route alone. Then, one day in August, 1947, the *Mary*'s resonant siren—pitched two octaves below Middle A and said to be audible for ten miles—boomed out across Southampton Water. Sliding into the Channel, the *Queen Mary* was ready to reassume her majority as the most beloved ship of the Atlantic twilight.

As the war receded, new shipping activity became lively almost everywhere. One by one, new ships carrying unmistakable national images and bewildering new company flags filed past the torch of the Statue of Liberty and into the oily slips along Manhattan's "Steamship Row." The race was to the swiftest and grandest, yet small ships, flying the Cunard ensign and continuing the staid Cunard tradition, supported the superliners in giving the company a greater share of transatlantic custom than any other single line. For veteran travelers unimpressed with the overblown claims of the Olympians, a ship like the Cunard White Star *Britannic* was just the ticket. "A dark, pink-shaded bar," said a devotee, "it had fake baronial chairs. Fake tapestry upholstery. Pub-like tables. Panelled walls. Toby jugs, heavy curtains in dried-blood brownish red. An enormous Victorian-esque mahogany bar. And a real fireplace, burning real logs. It was square and old-fashioned. But it was so friendly that even the non-drinkers queued to get in. So animal-loving British and endearingly inefficient that even my dogs were allowed in and, moreover, were allowed to hog the hearth-rug."

Maritime history tends to grant almost every decade its one supreme ship, its one *prima ballerina assoluta*. For the 1950s that ship is the S.S. *United States*. In some ways she is the most mechanically advanced and structurally elegant of all passenger liners; in other ways she is a kind of eagle among birds of paradise—a ship of war that could never quite disguise her military origins or the fact that she was enjoined always to be ready to strip away her veneer of civilian opulence and reveal her naked steel.

Laid down in a special dry dock at Newport News, Virginia, in February, 1950, the *United States* was constructed, in secrecy, to blueprints approved by the United States Navy and under the surveillance of Navy personnel. A number of her "defense" features were similar to those of full-scale warships, including an abnormally large fuel capacity, subdivisions of watertight compartments and distributions of machinery that would allow for operation of the ship even though part of her might be demolished. Her capacity was great enough to house fourteen thousand troops; if necessary she could carry these troops ten thousand miles without even one stop for fuel and water. More aluminum was built into her than in any other single structure ashore or at sea. She in fact heralded the age of aluminum on the waterways of the world; her funnels were made of it, her lifeboats, davits, deck rails, even the twelve hundred vases she carried as receptacles for *bon voyage* flowers. Aluminum also held her together; into her hull were driven 1,200,000 rivets which were "prepared by first heating them to 1,040 degrees to blend the alloys, then stored in deep freeze and finally driven quick-frozen instead of red hot, in order to guarantee maximum strength."

At 53,000 tons, the *United States* was only two thirds the size of Cunard's *Queens*, yet she could carry as many passengers as either of them. Nine hundred and seventeen feet long, one hundred and two feet wide, she was slim enough to squeeze, if she had to, through the Panama Canal. Except for the pianos in her lounges (Theodore Steinway had absolutely refused to supply aluminum ones) and the butchers' blocks in her kitchen galleys, nothing on the *United States* was inflammable; even her bedspreads and draperies were made of glass. The first big ship to be fireproof, she was also the first to be air-conditioned throughout.

The least "decorated" of all liners in her class, she had the functional grace and minimal trappings of a clipper; huge tear-shaped funnels sampan-topped; a cleanness of line and a cool shine of surface that set her apart. Americans took to her because she was sleek and fast, comfortable in the antiseptic way of an air-conditioned hotel in the Arizona desert, and full of Americans. But in the lively memory of the old floating palaces, cowed by the avalanche of mind-taxing statistics under which the new *Queens* arrived upon the ocean scene, Americans on the whole never granted their own ship her title to excellence or gave her a place among the artifacts of Yankee genius. Perhaps in no other vessel did all the silvery articulations of a dynamo and its agents of power so visibly obtrude. "Well, why not?" said designer Gibbs. "The *United States* is a ship, not an ancient inn with oaken beams and plaster walls." For all its visibility, the functional engineering of the *United States* was of a level of craft so exquisite that it threatened to dissolve the barriers separating practical art from the graphic. To sail in her was not to be cradled and cosseted in superogatory comfort, but to be an involved witness to the workings of a superb machine that made quite clear its disdain for petulant human preferences and venial human habits.

Command of the first American superliner was given to Captain Harry Manning, a seaman who was already a celebrity. Manning was at the helm on an Atlantic crossing in 1929 when his ship was summoned to the assistance of a small Italian freighter named *Florida*. Arriving at the scene as the freighter was in a condition in which she might sink at any moment, he personally directed the lifeboat operation, braving wild seas to save every member of a thirty-two-man crew. The story of this midocean rescue so thrilled New York that when he came into port Manning was given a civic welcome. Sitting in an open car, he was driven up Broadway in showers of ticker tape and confetti over the same route taken, only a little while before, by Charles A. Lindbergh.

Captain Manning was also himself a pilot, as well as a navigator and radio operator for Amelia Earhart when, in 1937, she had first attempted to fly around the world. He had accompanied Miss Earhart as far as Hawaii, but when their plane was grounded for repairs that necessitated a long delay, he had to return to New York because the United States Lines refused to extend his leave of absence. Consequently, unable to join Miss Earhart on her second world flight, he was back on the bridge of a ship when she disappeared forever in the Pacific.

Among the two thousand passengers—and the thirteen thousand visitors who came to bid them *bon voyage* on July 3, 1952—there was probably not one who doubted that the *United States* would crack every ocean record on her maiden voyage. To keep them in suspense, her Captain saw to it that she would start sedately. But on her second day out, at a speed of 35.6 knots, "just like a destroyer," she covered 801 miles—a greater distance than any other ship had ever made in a twenty-four-hour period; and on the third day her speed was upped to 36.17 knots, or about 41 land miles per hour. Except for Navy personnel and a few men involved in building her, nobody knew —and would not know for sixteen years—that the *United States* could, all out, do 48 land miles per hour on a horsepower of 240,000—nearly 100,000 horsepower greater than any other ship—and that on her maiden voyage, as well as on every succeeding one, she was deeply under wraps. Most of the passengers stayed up all night to be in on the historic occasion when the record would be bested. At 6:16 A.M. on July 7, when the *United States* was 3 days, 10 hours, 40 minutes out from Sandy Hook, Margaret Truman, standing at Captain Manning's side, figuratively pulled the whistle. Her gesture signaled the news everyone awaited: the *Queen Mary*'s fourteen-year-old record had been sliced by an amazing 10 hours, 2 minutes. As the siren of the new champion pierced gale winds to claim the Blue Riband, hundreds of passengers in conga lines went shaking and snaking through the labyrinth of public rooms. Once again, the honor of the seas had come to the Land of the Free and the Home of the Brave.

Le Havre gave her a bright morning's welcome. A few hours later, as thousands of Frenchmen cheered from the quay, she started across the Channel serenaded by the Royal Marine Band of the H.M.S. *Indomitable*. An American destroyer and a flotilla of launches from the Royal Navy kept her company into Southampton Water. She had vanquished that port's proudest ship, yet Southampton produced a welcome that surprised her officers and abashed some of the more jubilant American boosters among her passengers. The cheers and waving hands that hailed the *United States* were, in fact, so clearly joyous and so unexpectedly generous that the ship's passengers gathered along deck rails found themselves choked with emotion. One young woman, like many others who stood beside her, tended to read into the welcome that spirit of World War II which, for Americans, had made England that great good place behind the White Cliffs of Dover. "These wonderful people," she kept saying, "these wonderful people." William Francis Gibbs, who had made the voyage from New York, responded to British good sportsmanship with an equal display of grace. "We honor you," he said, "for your achievement in ships. We have tried to emulate you." The English came aboard in vast numbers to file through her aluminum companionways and walk decks that were not of holystoned wood but of a rubber substance that could be washed like a kitchen floor. They made full appraisals of those aspects of the ship that bespoke a military sort of austerity, yet in the spirit of this first visit they were nice about it all. *The Times* of London commented only that "it would be unreasonable to think that the dual purposes of the ship have been achieved without effect on the passenger accommodation." More gracious, and funnier, *Punch* confessed that "after the loud and fantastic claims made in advance for the liner *United States* it comes as something of a disappointment to find them all true."

Turning around in a trice, the *United States* then sailed out, and, for the clincher, broke the record going westward as well. She arrived back in New York flying a royal blue banner forty feet long and twenty feet wide. A notion that had always seemed purely symbolic was suddenly tangible. The legendary Blue Riband was real and it was hers; she would never relinquish it.

So great was the margin of victory achieved by the *United States* that, with no rival to offer a challenge or even to contemplate one, she maintained absolute priority for the rest of her career. But by the mid-'50s, neither her record, her still-untested potential for speed, nor all the honors she had brought America mattered for very much. While she had made the Atlantic a skip, airplanes had made it a hop; the confounding main had been domesticated, utterly. Instead of her speed, her owners were reduced to advertising her food. "You're just fifteen gourmet meals from Europe on the world's fastest ship," claimed the United States Lines. "Caviar from Iran, pheasant from Scotland . . . you can choose superfood from all over the world, another rewarding experience in gracious living. . . . There's a pool, gym, 2 theatres, 3 Meyer Davis orchestras. It's a 5-day adventure in the lost art of leisure."

The Atlantic had been domesticated—but not to the point where it was not capable of will-o'-wisp whimsicality and murderous surprise. Physically tranquilized by Dramamine and stabilizers, socially homogenized by the ascendancy of the tourist over the traveler, tightly organized in to-the-minute timetables a year or more in advance, ocean travel was no longer an adventure but the most routine of routines. Then, one hazy hot morning in July, 1956, one of the newest and most exquisite ships ever built, a joyful sign and symbol of Italy's postwar renaissance, simply buckled over in the shallow waters of the continental shelf and sank out of sight.

It was a night on the high curve of summer: July 25, 1956. Two ships —one chalk white in hull and superstructure, the other with a carbon-black hull and an enormous single white funnel banded at the top with the green, red and white of the Italian flag—each intermittently washed by floods of moonlight, were riding calm seas at that point in the Great Circle where its western arc begins to dissolve in the seaward glow of Manhattan Island. The *Andrea Doria* was inbound, two hours late, but still hoping to arrive on schedule at her North River dock by morning. The *Stockholm* was outward bound, having left New York that afternoon. Thick, wadding blankets of fog, then soft scarves of haze, would alternately drift into the space separating the two ships; these vapors would thin "like an over-watered *pernod*" and lift, or drift off altogether, clearing the surface of the sea as far as the eye could reach. Fair skies or foul, the two ships were bent on a fatal interview, racing toward one another at a combined speed of nearly 40 knots.

As they were approaching the appointed spot, they saw each other—but only in glimpses and for moments. When they actually met, it was in an envelope of fog enclosing them both. The *Stockholm*, the smallest liner in the North Atlantic passenger service, yet "a picture of Scandinavian efficiency and cleanness," had a clipper bow constructed of two rows of inch-thick steel plating separated by an air space two feet wide, designed to be capable of following in the path of an icebreaker as it cut its way through pack ice. This extraordinary forward strength provided her with a measure of safety and—in the right circumstances—a hint of menace. On this occasion, the circumstance was "right," the menace explicit. "With the force of a battering ram of more than one million tons," wrote Alvin Moscow, "the *Stockholm* plunged into the speeding Italian ship, crumpling her like a thin sheet of tin, until her energy was spent. With the *Stockholm* pinioned in her, the *Andrea Doria*, twice her size, pivoted sharply under the impact, dragging the *Stockholm* along as the giant propellers of the Italian liner churned the black sea violently to white."

As the two ships wrenched apart, the *Andrea* listed over to 18 degrees —a figure denoting that, already beginning to sink, she was very likely beyond redemption. Seven of her eleven decks had been penetrated by the *Stockholm*—from upper deck all the way down to the fuel oil tanks in her bottom. The Swedish ship drifted into the dark, carrying in the ragged metal of her prow the body of a woman who had been caught in her stateroom, and a bruised, dazed, girl of fourteen. Linda Morgan—daughter of the American radio commentator Edward P. Morgan—had been lifted from the bed where she slept and catapulted to a point eighty feet behind the *Stockholm*'s prow. Her sister, asleep in the same cabin, had been instantly killed.

Radio calls for help had meanwhile started a marine rescue operation unprecedented in peacetime history. Among a small swarm of ships responding was the dowager *Ile de France*, en route to Le Havre with nearly a thousand passengers and a crew of 826. Forty-four miles away when the call came through, the *Ile*, with her thirty-year-old engines, came pounding through the checkered sea, now fogged-in, now moonlit. By this time the *Stockholm*'s Captain Gunnar Nordensen had been able to assess the damage to his ship. When he concluded that she was out of danger and would remain afloat, he ordered her boats to be lowered and sent to the *Andrea*, now leaning over at a precipitous 25, 28, then 30 degrees.

As the first survivors were ferried across and helped aboard, a feeling of chagrin not much short of disgust overwhelmed many of the *Stockholm*'s crew and passengers. Setting up tables of food, piling up blankets and first-aid supplies, they had already transformed the public rooms of the ship into a sort of Red Cross disaster encampment. But instead of giving comfort to the frightened women and children they were prepared to receive, they found themselves handing out roast beef sandwiches and Scotch highballs to a hundred men in stewards' jackets and a hundred others wearing the gray kapok life jackets issued only to crew members.

This apparent reversal of the old tradition of the sea—from women and children first to deck hands and stewards first—was well published in the following weeks and months, and its justification widely debated. In the nineteenth century there would have been no point at issue: the behavior of crew members involved would have been declared blackguard and criminal. In the twentieth century, those who defended their behavior or, at least, countenanced it, took the position that any man has a right to save himself—especially a man whose role is that of an underpaid, overworked slave in the lower-deck galleys of a palace of pleasure. Had it not been for the fact that, of the *Andrea*'s 1,134 passengers, all who had not been killed in the actual collision were rescued, these men would likely have become so many J. Bruce Ismays—survivors in truth, but otherwise, living reminders of an action and a circumstance no one on earth could forgive.

Lights ablaze the length of her, the *Ile de France* got to the humped-over ship at two A.M. Two hours later, all of the sinking vessel's passengers had been taken off and hoisted, chilled and blinking, into the fading chic of the *Café de Paris* and the *Salon de Conversation*. At this point the *Andrea*'s Captain Piero Calamai ordered his crew—at least that part of it that was not already taking its ease in the crowded lounges of the *Stockholm*—to abandon ship. At the same time, he asked for volunteers to stay aboard to await the assistance of United States Coast Guard tugboats. These rescue ships were hurrying from Cape Cod to the collision scene in the last hope of towing the *Andrea* to shallow water on Davis Shoal, off Nantucket, twenty-two miles to the north. Forty men said they would remain; but as the ship's list soon increased to an imminently mortal forty degrees, the Captain gradually relieved their numbers until only twelve of them, mostly officers, were left. Proud in his anguish, Captain Calamai was determined to stay with his ship until the ocean overwhelmed her. When the urgings of his officers could not dissuade him from committing this time-honored form of hara-kiri, they said, in effect, "All right, we won't leave either." At this the Captain gave in. The first light of dawn began to put streaks on a calm, flat sea when, at last, the *Andrea Doria* was abandoned. Immersed—lying on her face as though she had suffered some intolerable embarrassment—the handsome black and white ship continued imperceptibly to fill. At ten that morning, while newspapermen in tiny planes were buzzing around her like gnats over a carcass, the pride of the Italian merchant marine turned over and, in one wallowing ripple, went under.

Down with the *Andrea Doria* went the bodies of forty-three people unlucky enough to have been at those precise points where the *Stockholm's* bow came harpooning through. The one body carried off by the Swedish ship brought the number of dead to forty-four; the number rescued came to 1,662 out of a combined crew and passenger complement of 1,706.

The Italian Line sued the Swedish Line for thirty million dollars; the Swedish Line sued the Italian Line for two million. The claimants went to court in New York, painfully and tediously rehearsed the events of that night, and agreed finally to settle matters out of the spotlight, on terms of their own. The extra-legal disposition was based on a mutual promise to halt damage suits, to end all legal tactics, to place blame on neither the *Stockholm* nor the *Andrea Doria,* and to keep their mouths shut about the whole thing. Yet when the evidence was sifted and every circumstance of time and place was recreated on charts and drawings, one grand and irreducible fact took precedence over a plethora of little ones: because she was improperly ballasted, the *Andrea Doria,* losing stability almost at the moment of impact, could not regain balance in time to keep her watertight compartments from spilling over, one into the other, until the sudden weight of a cargo of sea water dragged her under.

❊ SECTION XII ❊

ONCE MORE the *Ile de France*, "a robust old girl" in the affectionate eyes of her Captain Raoul de Beaudéan, found herself in the limelight. She carried only two of her three original funnels now; efficiency had somewhat qualified her grace. Yet her serenity and dignity were as commanding as ever before. She had survived eight months of wartime incarceration in the limbo of Tompkinsville, Staten Island. She had served as a troop ship on assignments as far away as Fremantle and Bombay. When her sister ships, the older *Paris* and the younger *Normandie*, had burned and capsized, one in Le Havre and the other in New York, she was the only great French ship left to carry on. Facing up to that circumstance, she proceeded quite calmly to lay claim and take title to all the international chic and glamour for which, in comparison, the British *Queens* and the *United States* still went begging.

How she maintained this hold on the worlds of art, fashion and "old" money remains a mystery. "Honor," according to a French writer, "had come to the *Ile de France* for having started the series of ships decorated according to contemporary ideas and tastes, consisting of

531

columns and simple lines, a search for straight line and bare surface and the choice of rich materials and exotic refinements." But even when she was refurbished to the nines, the *Ile de France* was almost as distressingly homely inside as she was handsome out. Her dining tables and the food on them were discolored by the sickly light of horizontal neon strips, some of them with a tendency to pulsate. Her *Café de Paris*, which should have been soigné beyond reproach, was so full of leatherette, tubular chairs and *art moderne* as to suggest a midtown cocktail lounge with Parnassian ambitions. Her staterooms, except for a slight expansiveness in the deluxe suites were, in first class, mostly suffocating, padded little sewing boxes. In cabin class they were barracks with exposed plumbing and pock-marked portholes; in tourist, something close to wooden cattle stalls. Compared with almost all of her new rivals, she offered a sort of *declassé* tattiness in first and an air, in other classes, of "reduced circumstances" slightly mollified by *sauce Bernaise* and free table wine. Her passenger lists nevertheless continued to exude a *cachet* that made the complements of other ships seem like boatloads of raffle winners.

Yet the days of the *Ile* were numbered; not only because she was fast becoming the oldest liner in service, but also because the once-charmed circle of the cultured or fashionable, or both, was beginning visibly to shrink. Her two-story cabin-class lounge with its broad swirl of a staircase was still a gathering place for young intellectuals, musicians, writers and undifferentiated Francophiles. But the character of her first class began to reflect the incursion into what was left of Society by those who belonged more strictly to Café Society, along with pashas of the expense account and tycoons of the credit card. Instead of carrying fastidious women to the Paris openings, the *Ile* was more apt to carry the hawk-eyed entrepreneurs of Seventh Avenue. Instead of individuals bound, guidebook in hand, for Mont-Saint-Michel and the châteaux of the Loire, she carried business people with an eye out for something French, or "French-y," on which to slap their company labels. The dining habits of these new passengers were so fixed and unadventuresome that the expert chefs and *sommeliers* serving them suffered erosions of spirit. Prepared to serve up exquisitely subtle dishes in commemoration of Auguste Escoffier, wines preserved in rows as hushed as the vaults of Cartier, they found themselves responding to endless requests for planked steaks, mashed potatoes and double J & B's on the rocks.

In 1959 the *Ile*—dear and old, but no longer a paying proposition—was sold for scrapping to a firm in Osaka. As a band played "The Marseillaise" and a few hundred of her faithful friends blew kisses and hesitantly waved their hands, she sailed out of Le Havre, her Tricolor aloft, and started the long voyage to her graveyard. When she was out of sight, the French flag was lowered and the ensign of the Rising Sun run up. She became at once the *Furanzu Maru*, bound for the Orient—and a humiliation at the hands of Japanese junk dealers matched only by the desecration visited upon the *Independence* by hucksters of the American travel market.

When she got to Japan early in April, the sorry story was already out: a Hollywood movie producer had arranged with Okada Gumi, the owners of the Osaka scrapyard, to "hire" the *Ile de France*, for four thousand dollars per day, with the intention of blowing her up at sea in the interests, *faute de mieux*, of "dramatic realism." "We do everything for real," said the producer. "When a boiler explodes—a boiler explodes. When a funnel collapses, bashing in the front deck, a funnel collapses and bashes in the front deck. Bulkheads really explode." The ship would not be actually sunk midocean, he added, but in coastal shallows where she could be raised and given back to the scrapping firm more or less intact.

The French Line, a bit late in the day, purported to be displeased with all of this, and so did the French Government. Meanwhile, in an ineluctably clever display of Nipponese finesse, the scrapping firm made plans for a holy ceremonial of decommission. Invitations were sent out to the diplomatic corps of Western nations in Tokyo, to leading figures in the shipping world, to naval attachés and to individuals of high social standing whose presence might be palliative. A Shinto altar was erected in the *Ile*'s first-class dining room and, on the appointed day, food for the gods was laid out not far from a board of delicacies for the thousand people who had turned up. When speeches had been listened to, and the assembled company had done its freeloading, a Shinto priest in full ceremonial garb emerged to perform the rites of purification. Cleansed, spiritually immaculate, the beloved old *Ile de France*—

denuded, dispossessed and far from home—was then declared officially "dead."

Dead or alive, she was ignominiously dragged out to sea so that Dorothy Malone and Robert Stack might have the advantage of utter realism in the backgrounds of a cinematic turkey entitled *The Last Voyage*. The ritual declaration of the *Ile*'s demise had in the meantime done nothing to placate the anguish of ship lovers, even those who knew the old liner only by distant sight and reports in the papers. Expressions of outrage from all over the world prompted the French Line, backed up by the Government, to demand that the name *Ile de France* not be visible in any movie shot of the liner, under threat of banning the producer's pictures, now and forever, from French cinema theaters. The name was removed under this pressure, but the cameras were not prevented from rolling. Brutally wrecked, burned, exploded, vandalized and half sunk, the old ship had suffered ultimate depredation. Then, partially pumped out again, she was towed back to Osaka and, in the last reach of mercy, obliterated.

ꙮ SECTION XIII ꙮ

Last Chances / Lively Sea Lanes of the 1950s / Light on the
Liberté / *"The Flounder" / The Dutch Experiment / Vapor*
Trails: The Handwriting on the Wall / The France / *The Ships*
from Genoa / Queens in Desuetude / On the Auction Block
"The Queens Are Dead! Long Live the Queen!" / Disparities:
Makers and Users / The Long Wake: September 25, 1967

A S LONG as travelers by air had to endure flights of twelve
and fourteen hours, shuffling down ramps in the middle of
the night at Shannon, Ireland, or dragging themselves across
snow-swept concrete toward the shanty barracks of Gander, Newfoundland, steamships were able to hold their own. Americans in greater
numbers than ever were going to Europe and most of them were
going by sea. As airline schedules expanded in the early part of the 1950s
there was a decrease in the percentage of steamship customers, but this
was no more than a nibble into a big apple and no cause for alarm.

The old business of scheduled Atlantic liners was moving on toward
its one hundred and fiftieth anniversary in a last burst of economic prosperity and social gaiety. Cunard's superships were each making millions
of pounds each year. In New York, the rafters of the breezy piers of the
North River were still hung with big childish alphabets for customs
examinations; waterside ledges were still dusted with confetti left over
from gala departures. In England, schoolchildren continued to gather
by the hundreds on the terrace of the Ocean Terminal to wave the big

ships in or boarded ancient paddle-wheelers with fuming smokestacks to go careening alongside them through Southampton Water. Crossing the Atlantic by steamship was even still something of a social event. Summoned to Hobe Sound for the season or to Paris for the couturier openings, individuals of eminence and affluence showed their determination to keep up the side. The Duke and Duchess of Windsor, for instance, were constant travelers on the *United States*—in Main Deck suites not very far from the staterooms of Mr. and Mrs. Philip Rhinelander, "of New York society," as well as those inhabited by Mr. and Mrs. J. R. Donnell of Findlay, Ohio (he was an oil company vice president) and Mr. and Mrs. Charles H. Hornberg, Jr. (he was the West Coast distributor for Jaguar). Instead of climbing onto a Constellation and flying five abreast with forty-four-pounds of drip-dry shirts and wash-and-wear skirts squashed into a featherweight bag, these were the people who spaciously sailed, with steamer trunks covered with exotic labels, cartloads of matched luggage and bright little dogs on leashes. Ships were still being met by reporters; male celebrities belted into polo coats said "cheese" for photographers from *The Tatler*; hyperthyroid starlets and sloe-eyed movie queens showed cheesecake for photographers from the *Daily News*. The merriment spelled profits and generated competition. Italians, Greeks and Scandinavians began to put whole new fleets of passenger liners onto sea lanes that had once belonged almost exclusively to the British, French and Germans.

The aging *Ile de France* continued to show the best of France afloat. Then, dredged up from the ooze of Le Havre, came the *Liberté*. Exhumed, glossed over with anything and everything Gallic that might disguise her Teutonic origins, this mighty ship was the old North German Lloyd *Europa*. Raised and refurbished at a cost of twenty million dollars, she came to New York in 1950 looking like a band wagon from Montparnasse and began a posthumous career that lasted for twelve years. When she was piloted up the Narrows flying the Tricolor and heralded by publicity that gave her an aura of Bollinger Brut, *pâté-de-foie-gras* and let-em-eat-cake snobbishness, few people guessed what a miracle of reclamation she was. Taken over by the United States Navy as a trooper at the time of the German occupation, she had made two voyages returning GIs to New York. Then, in 1946, she was awarded to France by the International Reparations Commission. That same year she was sent to St. Nazaire to receive fittings that might transform her from a sleek, fiercely modern Hanseatic racer of the '20s to a Parisian soubrette of the '50s. Lying at her refitting dock, she was ripped from her moorings by a wild gale off the Atlantic that sent her careening into the submerged hull of the old French Line flagship *Paris*. The collision tore a hole in her side so big that she filled at once and foundered.

There were many determinedly "new" features installed on the *Liberté* and one of these, borrowed from the night spots of Pigalle, was neon strip-lighting. The illumination it gave was comparatively cheap and it was supposed to be efficient. But what it did to diners and what they dined upon was unspeakable: rare steaks turned a liverish purple on the plate, women's faces took on the character of *Fauves* paintings. Technicians were called in, adjustments made, complexions and *filets mignons* tested. The result was still another peculiarly nasty glow of infra-red the company chose to call "cocktail rose" and which it stubbornly kept. Otherwise, stuffed with needlepoint, Aubussons and roseate draperies, the rehabilitated liner had much the feel of an older dispensation. Yet the *Liberté* was still basically German; against the lambencies of scrolled gilt and curving tulipwood in *Le Grand Salon* and *La Salle à Manger* the geometry both of Biedermeier and of Bauhaus made irreparable claims.

A less makeshift representative of France at sea was the *Flandre*, the first Atlantic carrier out of a French shipyard after World War II. At first glance she was staunch and sturdy, water-worthy as a duck. While she looked the very model and prototype of the small ocean liner, looks were deceiving. She had neither grace nor power, *joie de vivre* nor efficiency. When she was barely out of the English Channel on her maiden voyage, her oil filter became clogged, starting up a long chain reaction of failures that made the crossing a sort of tragicomedy. When her boiler fires died down and her steam pressure dropped, she was without power to drive her or even to light her. Emergency generators eventually brought her back to life; until then the *Flandre* drifted about the ocean in total darkness, as much at the whim and mercy of the waves as a waterlogged egg crate. Some of her passengers were tranquilized and placated by an endless flow of Mumm's Cordon Rouge provided gratis by her captain; other, more sober, travelers were incredulous and scared to death. Approaching New York eighteen full hours off schedule, she dropped her anchor at Quarantine, then discovered there was no power to pull it up again. Rescued by tugboats, the mortified liner was pushed up the river as flotillas of small water craft saluted her Manhattan arrival with whistles and horns and sprays of water. When she tried to respond to these greetings, her own whistle made a few mournfully wispy sounds, began to lisp as steam pressure sank, then disappeared. The embarrassment was too much for the *Flandre* to outlive. Cruelly rechristened "the Flounder," she plied the North Atlantic without distinction for a few years, then was transferred to warmer climates and territories where her ignominy was not a matter of public record.

Dutch ships, always known for their spic-and-span hominess, began to move away from the sustaining virtue of comfort toward those transient forms of luxury on which competition turned. With Katharine Hepburn and Spencer Tracy privately, though not secretly, aboard in adjoining staterooms, where the tables were perpetually set for sessions of gin rummy, the *Nieuw Amsterdam* arrived on her maiden voyage to New York in 1948. Caught by the outbreak of hostilities while she was somnolently cruising between La Guaira and Porto Cabello on a tour of the West Indies, she had at once headed for haven in New York. Employed as a troop ship for six long years, she was finally able to go home to Holland on the seventh anniversary of her launching. A handsome gray ship with a light-foot air of plushy ease hardly expected from the Dutch, she was an immediate winner. Retaining three classes, two funnels, old manners and comforts, she satisfied the postwar hunger of thousands of travelers who wanted something close to what they had once enjoyed and of the thousands who had merely read about ships just as elegantly appointed and big-proportioned.

Then, just when the *Nieuw Amsterdam* was most profitably launched onto the Great Circle, her owners took the lead in an experiment that was to be the last major change in the class system of the North Atlantic. When the sister ships *Maasdam* and *Ryndam* made their bow, they provided run-of-the-ship accommodations for eight hundred tourist-class passengers and space on a small upper deck for only forty first-class passengers—a ratio of 1 to 20. In a single stroke, travelers in first class became the underprivileged. Their cabins were a bit bigger, but that was about all: their dining room was not much larger than that in a modest private house, their deck space limited to the dimensions of a dog run, their main lounge an almost untrammeled little den of a library-cum-card room in the fore part of the ship. Travelers of the old school—those who believed that, at sea, class barriers were even more sacrosanct than on land—found themselves enisled in their topside quarters while, only one deck below, their less affluent shipmates tossed back snorts of Genever at ten cents a glass and turned the length of the ship into a *kermess* lasting for seven days. This reversal of the privileges of first and tourist was so successful that nearly every other line but those running to Italy soon followed suit. By the time the gracious, largely one-class *Statendam* was joined by the huge *Rotterdam*, it was no longer possible to tell—at least by the decor of public rooms—which class was first and which was tourist. A quiet revolution on the Atlantic had occurred: democratic numbers had overwhelmed the devotees of the class system and driven them into top-deck enclaves from which the only thing they could finally look down upon was the sea.

In the late '50s, pure jets—as distinguished from jet-assisted planes like the Britannia—began to streak through the troposphere from New York to London in six and a half hours. The message they wrote in vapor trails was clear: the age of the passenger liner on the North Atlantic was ended. Sea travel did not so much decline or diminish as plummet—almost out of sight. The uneasy balance between sea and air, maintained for a few transitional years, went wildly out of kilter. Hawks in for the kill, the jet planes took over—to such an extent that, by the late '60s, for every twenty-four passengers who went to Europe, only one of them went by sea. This one recidivist and his antiquarian shipmates were not exactly a pitiful minority. Frightened—by the cattle-count logistics of airlines and airports as much as by the danger of flying—they were not afraid to spend unconscionable sums of money to travel quite as they wanted to. The steamship era's holdovers and late-comers, they were prepared for a last stand, if only they could find where to make it.

On the *Queen Elizabeth*, for instance, the Captain's Reception had become both an occasion of uneasy gaiety and an index to despair. The ladies and gentlemen of the first class would, by custom, dress up for the second-night-out assembly that signified the social beginning of the voyage. By the time they had lifted their third curl of smoked salmon and their fourth dry martini from the salvers held out to them, Commodore Geoffrey Thrippleton Marr himself would mount a dais and tap his glass for attention. In a set speech that regular voyagers were soon used to, he would congratulate them—first for having chosen the sea over the sky, then for the charming carelessness about money that had brought them entrée into the great Lounge that evening, finally for the good taste that had led them to prefer Cunard. There would always be at least a few people like them, he suggested, lovers of life on the ocean wave and devotees of Beluga caviar, who would resist being hurried into metal cylinders and sent soaring across the Atlantic night just for the sake of "saving" a few days. At these brave words the assembled company would clap their hands and cheer. As cries of "Bravo!" and "Hear! Hear!" rose among the great pillars, one could hear the echoes of gladiators in the Colosseum: *Morituri*, said the blue-haired ladies and balding gentlemen, *te salutamus*. Then, as stewards began to brush away crumbs and to bring in balloons and streamers for the Get-Together Dance later on, they would all disperse. Weaving slightly under the influence of Beefeater Gin, some would go down to the ice sculptures and cornucopian fruit baskets of the restaurant, others up to the shaded lamps and flambéed chafing dishes of the Verandah Grill. A few years later, packed even more closely together than their forebears had been packed into steerage, most of them would go to Europe in Boeing 747s. Commodore Marr, meanwhile, part curator, part caretaker, would be spending the long Florida days watching over his empty ship in the limbo of Port Everglades.

With a boldness that would ultimately prove the lesser part of valor, the French Line undertook to build and launch the biggest ship of the postwar world. With a tonnage of more than 66,000 and measurements that made her the longest ocean liner ever, the *France*, everyone supposed, would be the successor to the *Normandie*, a phoenix rising in splendor from the flaming debris and steaming sewage of the North River. As words about her size, cost and sumptuousness were released to news media, everything about her promised that she would call a halt to the fading of grandeur on the ocean and give new life to a tradition that had become mainly a subject for nostalgia. The promise was not kept. Once the confetti was swept away and the machinery of advertising and public relations had spoken its introductions, the *France* was revealed as one of the most resounding disappointments in the history of shipping.

The fault lay not with her designers and builders but with her decorators. Her exterior lines and bearing were handsome and proud;

her two great funnels with their swept-back wings were comforting, even a bit chic; her black hull and immaculate white superstructure were familiarly grand. Inside, however, she was a kind of floating *marché aux puces* exhibiting the taste of still another generation stamped with the imprimatur of the bourgeoisie. Somehow, the country that had in the twentieth century produced the delicate simplicities of the Matisse chapel at Vence and the murals and stained glass of Assy, the same nation that had cherished and nurtured Picasso, Juan Gris and Brancusi, was now represented by a ship with decorative features so boldly and inexplicably ugly as to appall the veteran traveler, puzzle the initiate, and send everyone else back to the Folies Bergère. There are a few moments in the interior clutter of the *France*, but these only point to cross-purposes and extend irony. Except for inviting vistas of royal blue and red carpeting throughout and for the golden circle of an elegantly muted main dining room, these moments are provided by advertisers: little grottoes, devised by the high-camp mentors of the Rue St. Honoré and placed here and there along companionways, show nuances of color, texture and design elsewhere absent throughout the ship. Retrograde, misconceived, stridently inelegant or absurd, almost all of the interior aspects of the *France* defy explanation. Passengers accommodated in some of the sun-deck cabins, for instance, look out upon a bleak Spanish patio replete with a tile overhang, iron grillwork tipped with gilt affixed to windows, wall-plaque ceramics depicting matadors, señoritas and cute Disney bulls. In the view of the poet Turner Cassity, the shadow of the *Normandie* still overwhelms her progeny:

> The Channel clouds; the ships merge utterly;
> Our faith now is in the *France*, for good or ill.
> But when the bored foresake the guarding rail,
> The life preserver, spotlit, still reads *Normandie*.

Dogged from the first by expectations she could not fulfil, the *France* nevertheless came quickly into her heyday. The mere vastness and bravado of a vessel so new and so expensive was enough to provide an illusion of glamour in a dying industry and to impress a sufficient number of customers to make her—dollar for dollar and franc for franc —the most successful Atlantic carrier of the decade.

Glamour on the ocean, dwindling for years, was nevertheless still a selling point. The *France* faked glamour and got away with it, but most of what was left of the idea, or even of the real thing, belonged securely to the ships of the Italian Line. The flagship *Cristoforo Colombo*, first of the postwar fleet, had quickly achieved a reputation for excellence that not even the notoriety attending the affair of the *Andrea Doria* could crimp. Then came the *Leonardo da Vinci* followed by the *Michelangelo* and *Raffaello*, sister ships with spindly smokestacks caged in cubist-inspired constructions that had the look of wire wastebaskets overturned. Decorated in the *alta moda* of the Italian aesthetic revival after World War II, these glistening white liners sailed with an almost visible Genovesian and Florentine panache. Yet an uncoordinated and unfocussed sense of taste kept their appointments from assuming the assurance of the first rate. In some respects, the ships from Genoa were floating museums of Italian history; in other respects they continued the melodrama of earlier ships under the same flag in whose public rooms kitsch had been brought to its purest Sicilian refinement. Yet their engaging boldness and their hundreds of tons of marble and mosaics made them spirited emblems of national pride, the very cut and trim of *bella figura* on the sunniest lanes of the Atlantic.

For the growing numbers of southern-route travelers, the distinctive feature of life on Italian liners was the bemused demeanor of well-trained crews and the pervasive sense of domestic intimacy this assured. Zest for a good table and the white-linen amenities of the nineteenth century gave the ships a combined air of opulence and hominess; and a characteristic open curiosity about everything human on the part of their staffs inevitably checked the pretensions to aristocratic elegance the Italian Line's advertising encouraged. Unlike workers on vessels conceived in northern weather and Lutheran sobriety, the Neapolitans and Genovese who accepted the disciplines necessary to the workings of a great liner were not repressed by them. The ageless stewardesses of the Cunard ships, with their flat shoes and flat faces, often looked as though they might have been in the Crimea with Florence Nightingale. On an Italian ship, a passenger pressing his call button would likely be greeted in a few moments by a stand-in for Sophia Loren. As she stood poised on the threshold of his cabin, costumed in black skin-tight poplin and frills of a sort once associated only with postcards depicting the raunchier side of domestic life in Paris, his signorina would address him with one enormously self-assured stare. "Sir," she would ask, "what can I do for you?"

If there were any lingering doubts about Italian seamanship in the aftermath of the *Andrea Doria*, any skepticism about the way in which an Italian crew might stand up to emergency, these were dispelled at once in 1966. On an April voyage from Genoa to New York, the *Michelangelo* encountered one of those almost inexplicable mountainous crests of water which, every ten years or so in the history of steamships, have rolled like a rumble of doom upon even the greatest of liners. Often, in calm seas, they have come out of nowhere; sometimes they have come, like a *coup de grâce*, as a ship is battling the worst gale force of the Atlantic. In the *Michelangelo*'s case, it was the latter. Moving through wild seas, the 900-foot length of her seemed to those aboard to be actually whipping back and forth, as though she were swiveling and might at any moment snap in two. As terrified passengers tossed in their beds and bunks or clung together in tortuous movements along companionways that forced them to "cling together like a cluster of grapes," a few others still tried to carry on the normal life of a ship at sea. Among these was the German novelist Günter Grass. He was chatting with some shipboard acquaintances in a smoking room when one of them, a man from Chicago, said he wanted to watch the storm from the big window of his upper-deck stateroom. Grass and the others, invited to join him, decided they would stay where they were. Their friend went to his cabin, U-19, and was killed, perhaps instantly, when the big wave battered down the forward wall and with one overwhelming blow wrecked the bridge, the officers' quarters and twenty first-class staterooms. A second passenger and a member of the crew also died under its impact; and a woman, wedged into debris in her cabin, was saved by crewmen who cut a hole in the door with axes, only after water had poured into the room up to her waist. The *Michelangelo* came into New York like a ship of mourning. Her flag flew at half-mast and over the ruined front of her was stretched, like a bandage, an enormous tarpaulin.

On the ascendancy, nonetheless, when nearly every other company was in decline, the Italian Line was in a position to absorb much of the passenger traffic that once belonged to the New York–Southampton run, and it did. Italian liners in the '60s became the busiest of those of any European nation. Awaiting the gong announcing their departures from Naples or New York, passengers became used to a warning by stewards whose syllables have been precisely documented by the novelist Shirley Hazzard. "*La nave é in partenza*," they would cry. "The sheep is living!"

But late in 1970, indicating that even a comparative monopoly of Atlantic sea travel was bringing them insufficient rewards, their owners announced plans for the phasing out of their whole passenger fleet. The penultimate had succumbed to the ultimate; the last best hope of those who still looked forward to going abroad in the old way had vanished.

To Americans who remembered the salad days of the great British *Queens*, all the crazy outsize grandeur that would make a voyager feel that the Radio City Music Hall had somehow got loose from Sixth Avenue and Fiftieth Street and taken him to sea, the '60s were years of deepening nostalgia. The fabulous dimensions were still there, the awesome power and technological might. But a sort of creeping venality in the management of the peerless ships had reduced them to austere shadows of themselves.

The new ocean traveler—the man, perhaps, who felt he had achieved a life-long dream as he walked through the canvas tunnel of Cunard's Pier 90 gangplank—was in for consternation and shock. The famous Main Deck Square, the ship's old Rialto and plaza where, once upon a time, big men with big cigars dawdled among duchesses, was now preempted: a British sports car, flanked by tall panels of advertising matter, stood plunk in the middle, demanding all of his attention. Seeking out his first drink of the voyage, he might make his way to the Observation Lounge with its two levels and spray-splashed windows where, years before, he could have watched the plunging bow from a height. He would find that the lounge was now converted into a characterless pub in which the glittery surfaces of the original *art deco* had been touched up with shamrocks, fluted paperboard and other decorative whimsies of bartenders. He would find the old ballroom aft of the main lounge gone altogether. In its place, there was the Midships Bar, designed by a director's wife—a woman of enterprise whose taste ran to jalousies meant to give the illusion of windows where there were none, to furniture of a sort familiar to Americans from the modestly banal foyers of apartment hotels. Decline, as usual, was most clearly written in trivia.

Voyagers in the twilight of the Cunard tradition would feel, perhaps, how even the wide wooden decks of the *Queens*, with their unhinged benches, rusted joinings and oil-smutted railings, recalled the years of Ellis Island. Should they have embarked at Cherbourg or Cobh, they would find, as their tender sidled toward the towering hull, rust in long leaks from maindeck to the waterline, bulbous rivets flaking black paint, circles of porthole brass no longer shining Bristol-fashion but oxidized and eaten by decades of weather. The distance from the days of the *Great Eastern* would suddenly seem negligible.

As their final decade drew toward its end, the *Queens*, more often than not, were the ghost ships of the Great Circle. It was then possible for a single solitary passenger to turn up for tea in the dim depths of the grand saloon and sit, magnificently alone, while a dozen white-jacketed stewards stood about like sentries, alert to his command. As he chose his sandwiches and scones and cakes from portable caddies, as all the pyramidal napkins on all the white tables in the gloaming multiplied his sense of isolation, he might notice that a shadowy figure at the furthest end of the room was seating himself at the Wurlitzer. Then, as the great ship creaked and rolled, the intruder would shiver the air with selections from "Rose Marie" and "The Desert Song." Not even the dining room in *Citizen Kane* was emptier.

Yet the penultimate voyager would not be altogether disillusioned. There remained a few old-school stewards—men of the long-standing Southampton tradition of masterly servants who took care of their passengers totally and almost invisibly. These men, however, increasingly few, found themselves increasingly disheartened: the services they were prepared to render were often awkwardly dismissed or openly rejected by travelers, used only to motels and self-service, who did not quite know how to accept them.

There also began to appear a new order of British serving man who worked his hours on duty in a mood of barely controlled insolence. He suspected, often correctly, that he was financially better off than many of his first-class passengers, and knew that he was more literate and far wiser in the ways of the world. He was not disposed to cater to those who flashed bankrolls from their barstools or dragged sables across the floor of the Verandah Grill or to those who, attempting to impress him and take him in with back-slapping American egalitarianism, blithely advertised their provincialism.

The last days of the *Queens* only reflected what was happening on land: Society, in the sense of a well-mannered elite had all but disappeared or gone underground; Democracy, in the sense of the all-powerful common man, was still trying to find a means of grace somehow to temper its implacable demands for everything that was efficient, average and anonymous.

In less than thirty years the two *Queens* had recapitulated the whole story of passenger liners on the Atlantic. Starting out as necessary adjuncts to the life of nations, they had become nothing more than expensive alternatives to a night in the air, long holiday weekends for those who believed that "Getting There is Half the Fun." As the tradition they could not extend entered its final phase, they themselves became obsolescent. When this happened, Cunard's directors decided to put them up for sale to the highest bidder. The imaginary price tag affixed to each of them represented a paltry fraction of what they had cost yet, sadly, reflected precisely what they had come to be worth.

The sea-loving British shook their heads when this astonishing news was out, wrote saucy or impassioned letters to *The Times*, proposed hundreds of ingenious countermeasures aimed at keeping the *Queens* in home waters or, at least, guaranteeing them a dignified demise even if that meant scuttling and sea burial. But nothing would stay the wrinkled, supposedly empty, but still high, hand of Cunard. The two most formidable ships of the century, encrusted with brine, history and the affection of millions of people who had never even seen them, were hauled away—the *Mary* to the alien corn of Long Beach, California, the *Elizabeth* to that of Fort Lauderdale, Florida, and, early in 1971, to the Orient and, presumably, a career as a floating university. As they witnessed the wheeling and dealing attending these developments, hundreds of thousands of Britons were ashamed and stunned. It was as though, in America, the lawns of George Washington's lovely Mount Vernon had suddenly acquired the bright abomination of a Holiday Inn sign, as though the Statue of Liberty had been sold to some Latin American amusement park to be used as a parachute drop. In itself, the disposal of the *Queens* was a sad, mean, yet understandable action; when it was made to seem inevitable it became heinous.

Yet for champions of Britain on the ocean there was still hope. At the very same time that the *Queens* were being sold down the river, Cunard was building that paragon of ships eventually to be known as *Queen Elizabeth 2*. Something entirely new in British ship design, she would not so much extend the tradition of Samuel Cunard as she would represent its postlude and aftermath. The man brought in to oversee her construction and launch her onto the narrowing sea lanes of the late '60s was one whose previous associations had been with airliners and air travel. His name was Sir Basil Smallpiece, and he took his assignment with a sense of mission. "Cunard, like so many British businesses, like Britain herself," he said, "had become ossified in patterns set by past success. They had been living precariously on their fat until suddenly the supply ran out."

Presiding over the sorry scene when the two great Cunarders were put on the auction block, Sir Basil was just as unsullied by sentiment as habitués of the board rooms in Liverpool had always been. His attitude reflected an old and useful ambiguity. Like most other government-subsidized steamship lines, Cunard had over the years played the game two ways: when bankruptcy threatened, its ships were held to be wards of the state, mascots of the sentimental public, ambassadors of national honor deserving every kind of support—especially money; when a chance for unexpected profit loomed, its ships were suddenly private property to be dealt with privately and without regard for the noisome claims of the heirs of Nelson, the pathetic tears of flag-waving children or the outrage of Empire widows. To sell the *Queens*, as though they were so many tons of junkyard steel, was of course regrettable, said Sir Basil, "but we cannot allow our affection or our sense of history to divert us from the aim of making Cunard a thriving company, and no other decision will make commercial sense."

As the new Cunard ship grew in the foggy cradle of Cunarders on the banks of the Clyde, hopes and expectations began to generate legend: she would be the miracle ship, the only one to outshine the heretofore peerless *Queens*, the one to recoup the glory of Britain on the seas. "The *Queens* are dead! Long live the *Queen!*" echoed fervently through the millions of words written about the ship even while she was still years away from the ceremonies that would launch her. Everyone got into the act, from pedlars of beer, gum, razor blades, whiskey-flavored cake, sweat shirts, dolls and ball-points printed with "Q4" (the "working" name of the ship) to the reigning monarch herself. Lord Snowdon turned up in the workrooms of designer Dennis Lennon to run an informed eye over a mock-up of one section of the first-class restaurant. Down from Balmoral with Her Majesty for the Clydeside christening came Prince Philip; Princess Margaret flew up from London to join them. Standing on a platform under the bulbous forefoot of the graceful monster, they all lifted their eyes as the great thrust of the bow was urged backward by gravity (assisted by 9 tons of tallow, 70 tons of sperm oil, 14 hundredweight of black soap, 7 gallons of spindle oil). "There are always too many people ready to knock and slam our country," the Princess said later, "and too many people wringing their hands over poor old Britain. But this new Cunarder will show that design in Britain is not only exciting and full of vigorous common sense but is always out in front, leading the field. A great ship like the *Queen Elizabeth* 2 must inevitably be looked upon as a sort of flagship for the nation. It just might have turned out to be a grandmotherly, chintzy hotel."

Chintzy the *Queen Elizabeth* 2 is not: computerized, articulated with the silvery precision of a Rolls Royce, designed and decorated in a mood of controlled bravura, she conspicuously emphasizes efficiency over raw power, lively good taste over the thudding opulence of generations past. Her interior style—a matter of bold shapes, textures and surfaces—is high, moderately eclectic and cheerfully theatrical. The take-it-or-leave-it John Bullish parochialism that was once generally felt to be a virtue—like the royal family on a soup plate—is absent. Her crisp and shining appointments are in fact so appealing that even the workmen who fitted her out were moved to acquire some of them. When an electrician in the shipyard was caught in the act of pilfering, constables did not wait upon invitation to visit him at home. There they found thirty yards of carpeting, three bookcases, two chests of drawers, five lampshades, table settings for six, a radiator, three hundred and fifty feet of cable and a toilet seat. The ship on which rode so much private and public money and so many hopes was otherwise plagued—by internecine squabbles among craft unions that led to strikes, by rising costs and by the scudding shadows of a thousand jet planes. But when, at last, she was ready to leave the Clyde and make her way through the Irish Sea to Southampton, she was living proof that Cunard had somehow transcended its reputation for cold mutton stolidity and come up with something startlingly in advance of all of its promises.

About two thirds of the tonnage of the *Mary* and the old *Elizabeth*, her length is surprisingly little less than theirs, her height a little more. She is able to carry almost as many passengers as either of them—an advantage made possible by developments in structural materials, especially in aluminum, since the 1930s. Steam turbines capable of 110,000 shaft horsepower drive her two 6-bladed propellers. Her service speed of 28½ knots and almost everything inside her is regulated and controlled by a computer no bigger than a bedside radio. She generates more power on less fuel and with more overall economy than any other passenger ship. Conceived not so much as an Atlantic runner than as a cruise ship, she is able to go anywhere—through the Panama and Suez Canals, under the bridges of Sydney and Bilbao. She does not have to depend on tides, either in New York or in Southampton.

For all that, she is in every essential way just another ship, subject to the vagaries of those who serve her and those who handle her. The first unpromising evidence of this is the fact that the imagination and talents of the men who brought the dream ship into port have already been superseded by notions of "practicality." The hucksterism that served to advertise the desuetude of the old *Queens* has been carried over into the new one. James Gardner was the man responsible for realizing the general "idea" and end-to-end coherence of the ship. His philosophy of design was essentially humanist: to find the point of human engagement, to make people want to be where they are, and "give the passenger a sense of being in a special place; of pleasure and of dignity." Gardner had once contemplated keynoting the central foyer with a piece of abstract sculpture by, say, Barbara Hepworth, or a series of Ben Nicholson's "pure" paintings. But doubts about the suitability of these led him to think of something more pictorially obvious and programmatic, something that would not discomfit passengers of unsophisticated tastes. What he finally had to settle for was not proper graphic art of any kind, but the art of persuasion: the main entrance to the *Queen Elizabeth 2* is an elaborate pavilion of commercialism in which various kinds of Schweppes fizzwater importune the embarking passenger even before he has had a chance to locate his stateroom.

Inch by inch, inside and out, the *Queen Elizabeth 2* is probably the most beautiful, powerful and efficient passenger ship of all time. Men of genius and masterly craftsmanship have given her an aesthetic and technological character *sans pareil*. Ordinary men and women have still to give her the subtly human character of the kind that has allowed ships like the *Mauretania*, the *Ile de France* and the *Queen Mary* to live in history like personages. In her first year of service, the disparity between the dreams of those who made the *Queen Elizabeth 2* and those who, as patrons or as employees, made use of her, was abysmal. British travelers who crossed on her maiden voyage deplored the ever-present dust of cigarette ash on her dramatic ink-black carpetings, the scuffs and scars that already marked her molded plastics, the depositories for waste and random trash that visibly spilled over, the dispiriting bank holiday shuffle of a British Railways Channel boat—and wearily ascribed it all to the callousness and rough manners of those Americans on whom, alas, the ship's prosperity would so largely depend. A few months later, when she made her first cruises into the Caribbean, the shoe was on the other foot. Surveying deckscapes variously strewn with damp towels, T-shirts, hair nets, drying bikinis; transistor radios mingling island calypso with country rock; the pulpy dregs of a hundred Planters Punches and Whiskey Sours with straws crumpled into them; paper cups, cigar butts, orange rinds and balled-up napkins sliding in runnels along the scuppers—American passengers sighed to heaven and ascribed it all to socialism, Carnaby Street and the decline of the British working orders. Surprised and dismayed, both Briton and Yankee had perhaps felt an intimation of the awful truth: the visionaries of the *Queen Elizabeth 2*, laboring for years, had brought forth settings for instant squalor.

The nature of this last great Cunarder, even some of her aspirations, only confirm what had become obvious: ships are drifting resorts or, for a summer season, Atlantic carriers almost as confining and impersonal as airplanes. When the builders of the *Queen Elizabeth 2* agreed to abolish the Promenade Deck, travelers who love the sea, delight in studying its moods, and like to walk in the sight and smell of it, were left with almost no place to go. The publicized idea of afterdecks as "a series of steps—windbreaks—trays for offering passengers to the sun" serves those who move most congenially *en masse*; the contemplative, driven indoors, are confined there. This transformation of a ship from a thing *of* the sea to a buttress *against* the sea merely continued a trend. As early as the first years of the '60s, passengers could sail across the ocean as impervious to its calms and storms as if they wore space suits. Instead of looking through "magic casements, opening on the foam of perilous seas," they could check it all out just by turning on their weather-scanning TV sets. Instead of hearing the sough and slosh of waves against the moving hull, they could, just by turning up the volume, listen to the homogenized music that came, as if from a faucet, into their cabins all day long. Bit by bit, steamships had become their antithesis: when crossing by water finally approximated the hermetic insulation of crossing by air, travel by sea threatened to become antique, joyless and redundant.

Early in 1968, the *Queen Elizabeth* 2 sailed into what was modestly termed "an uncertain future." But in the long view of history and the ways of man, the ships she was meant to succeed had already taken the future with them.

12:10 A.M. September 25, 1967. The *Queen Elizabeth*, largest ship in the world, twenty-seven years old, is bound westward; at some point in the early morning she will meet and pass the *Queen Mary*, the next-largest ship in the world, thirty-one years old, bound east. This will be their final meeting, their last sight of one another, ever. For more than two decades they have been the proudest sisters on the ocean, deferential to one another, secure in the knowledge that they are the most celebrated things on water since rafts went floating down the Tigris and Euphrates.

Notices of this encounter have been broadcast and posted throughout the ship. But as usual at this hour most passengers have gone to bed, leaving only a few individuals strolling and dawdling on the Promenade Deck. Most of these have chosen to be alone; and they are a bit sheepish, a bit embarrassed, as though ashamed to be seen in the thrall of sentiment, even by others equally enthralled.

As the appointed moment draws near, they begin to disappear from the Promenade Deck, only to reappear in the darkness of the broad glassed-in observation area on Boat Deck forward. They stand apart from one another and do not speak, their eyes fixed on the visible horizon to the east as the vibration of the ship gives a slightly stroboscopic blur to everything they see. The mid-Atlantic sky is windless, a dome of hard stars; the ocean glows, an immense conjunction of inseparable water and air. Entranced, the late watchers try to pick out some dot of light that will not turn out to be a star. Hushed, the minutes pass. These ten or twelve of the faithful in their shadowy stances might be postulants on a Vermont hillside, waiting in their gowns for the end of the world. Then the light of certainty: almost as if she were climbing the watery slopes of the globe, the oncoming *Queen* shows one wink at her topmost mast, then two.

Spotted, she grows quickly in size and brightness. In the dim silence of the enclosure there are mutters, the click of binoculars against plate glass, an almost reverential sense of breath withheld. On she comes, the *Mary*, with a swiftness that takes everyone by surprise: together the great ships, more than 160,000 tons of steel, are closing the gap that separates them at a speed of nearly 60 miles an hour. Cutting the water deeply, pushing it aside in great crested arrowheads, they veer toward one another almost as if to embrace, and all the lights blaze out, scattering the dark. The huge funnels glow in their Cunard red, the basso-profundo horns belt out a sound that has less the quality of a salute than of one long mortal cry. Standing at attention on the portside wing of his flying bridge, the *Elizabeth*'s captain doffs his hat; on the starboard wing of the *Mary* her captain does the same. As though they had not walked and climbed there but had been somehow instantly transported to the topmost deck, the few passengers who have watched the *Mary* come out of the night now watch her go. All through the episode, mere minutes long, have come giggles and petulant whimpers from sequestered corners of the top deck. Indifferent to the moment, untouched by the claims of history, youngsters not yet born when the two *Queens* were the newest wonders of the world cling together in adolescent parodies of passion and do not bother even to look up. As the darkness closes over and the long wakes are joined, the sentimentalists stand for a while watching the ocean recover its seamless immensity. Then, one by one, like people dispersing downhill after a burial, they find their way to their cabins and close their doors.

BIBLIOGRAPHY
INDEX

❦ BIBLIOGRAPHY ❧

ABBOTT, WILLIS J., *The Story of Our Merchant Marine*. New York, 1919.

ANDERSON, ROY, *White Star*. Prescot, Lancashire, 1964.

ALBION, ROBERT G., *The Rise of New York Port, 1815–1860*. New York, 1939.

———— *Square-riggers on Schedule*. Princeton, 1938.

ALLOTT, KENNETH, *Jules Verne*. London, 1940.

AMORY, CLEVELAND, *Who Killed Society?* New York, 1960.

ANGAS, W. MACK, *Rivalry on the Atlantic, 1833–1939*. New York, 1939.

ANNAN, WILLIAM, ed., *The Speeches and Public Letters of the Hon. Joseph Howe*. Boston, 1858.

APPLEYARD, ROLLO, *Charles Parsons*. London, 1933.

ARCHIBALD, E. H. H., *Travellers By Sea*. London, 1962.

ARMSTRONG, WARREN, *Atlantic Bridge*. London, 1956.

———— *The Collins Story*. London, 1957.

ARVIN, NEWTON, ed., *The Selected Letters of Henry Adams*. New York, 1951.

AYLMER, GERALD, *R.M.S. Mauretania: The Ship and Her Record*. London, 1935.

BAARSLAG, KARL, *S.O.S.* London, 1937.

BABCOCK, F. LAWRENCE, *Spanning the Atlantic*. New York, 1931.

BALDWIN, HANSON W., *Sea Fights and Ship Wrecks*. New York, 1938.

BEAUDÉAN, RAOUL DE, *Captain of the Ile*. New York, 1960.

BEAUMONT, J. C. H., *Ships and People*. New York, 1930.

BEAVER, PATRICK, *The Big Ship*. London, 1969.

BEEBE, LUCIUS, *The Big Spenders*. New York, 1966.

BEHRMAN, S. N., *Duveen*. New York, 1952.

BELL, MALCOLM, JR., *Savannah, Ahoy!* Savannah, 1959.

BENEDICT, CLARE, *The Benedicts Abroad*. London, n.d.

BENSTEAD, C. R., *Atlantic Ferry*. London, 1926.

BERNARD, OLIVER P., *Cock Sparrow*. London, 1936.

BESSEMER, HENRY B., *Autobiography*. London, 1905.

BILLINGS, HENRY, *Superliner S.S. United States*. New York, 1954.

BISSET, JAMES, *Tramps and Ladies*. New York, 1959.

BLAKE, GEORGE, *British Ships and Shipbuilders*. London, 1946.

—— *Down to the Sea*. London, 1937.

BOER, M. G. DE, *The Holland-America Line 1873–1923*. Rotterdam, 1923.

BONSOR, N. R. P., *North Atlantic Seaway*. Prescot, Lancashire, 1955.

BOORSTIN, DANIEL J., *The Image: A Guide to Pseudo-Events in America*. New York, 1964.

BOWEN, FRANK C., *A Century of Atlantic Travel*. London, 1935.

BOWEN, FRANK C. and PARKER, H., *Mail and Passenger Steamships of the Nineteenth Century*. Philadelphia, 1928.

BRAYNARD, FRANK O., *Lives of the Liners*. New York, 1947.

—— *S. S. Savannah: the Elegant Steamship*. Atlanta, 1963.

BREUHAUS, F. A., *The Ocean Express "Bremen."* Munich, 1930.

BRIGGS, ASA, *Victorian People*. Chicago, 1955.

BROADLEY, A. M., *The Ship Beautiful: Art and the Aquitania*. Liverpool and London, 1914.

BROOKS, VAN WYCK, *The Dream of Arcadia*. New York, 1958.

—— *New England: Indian Summer, 1865–1915*. New York, 1940.

BROWN, ALEXANDER CROSBY, *Women and Children Last*. London, 1962.

BRUNEL, ISAMBARD, *Life of Isambard Kingdom Brunel*. London, 1870.

BUCHANAN, LAMONT, *Ships of Steam*. New York, 1956.

BUCKLEY, M. B., *Diary of a Tour in America*. Dublin, 1886.

BUSHELL, T. A., *"Royal Mail": A Centenary History of the Royal Mail Line, 1830–1939*. London, 1940.

CANGARDEL, HENRI, *De J. B. Colbert au Paquebot Normandie*. Paris, 1957.

CARSE, ROBERT, *The Twilight of Sailing Ships*. New York, 1965.

CECIL, LAMAR, *Albert Ballin*. Princeton, 1967.

CHADWICK, F. E., *The Development of the Steamship*. New York, 1887.

CHADWICK, F. E., et al, *Ocean Steamships*. New York, 1891.

CHAPIN, HENRY, and SMITH, W. F. G., *The Ocean River*. New York, 1952.

CHATTERTON, E. KEBLE, *Steamships and Their Story*. London, 1910.

—— *The Mercantile Marine*. London, 1923.

CHISHOLM, JOSEPH A., *Speeches and Public Letters of Joseph Howe*. Halifax, 1909.

CHOULES, JOHN OVERTON, *The Cruise of the Steam Yacht "North Star."* Boston, 1854.

CLARK, ARTHUR H., *The Clipper Ship Era*. New York, 1910.

CLAXTON, CHRISTOPHER, *Log of the First Voyage of the Great Western*. Bristol, 1838.

—— *History and Description of the Steam-Ship Great Britain, etc.* New York, 1845.

COBB, IRVIN S., *Europe Revised*. New York, 1914.

COBURN, SILAS R., *Across the Ferry*. Lowell, Mass., 1866.

COOPER, JAMES FENIMORE, *Homeward Bound*. New York, 1838.

COREY, LEWIS, *The House of Morgan*. New York, 1930.

CORSON, F. REID, *The Atlantic Ferry in the 20th Century*. London, 1931.

CROIL, JAMES, *Steam Navigation*. Toronto, 1898.

CROWTHERS, SAMUEL M., *Humanly Speaking*. Boston and New York, 1912.

CUTLER, CARL C., *Greyhounds of the Sea*. Annapolis, 1930.

———— *Queens of the Western Ocean*. Annapolis, 1961.

DANA, R. H., *A Transatlantic Tour*. Philadelphia, 1845.

"DEAN, JULIA," *The Wonderful Narrative of Miss Julia Dean, the Only Survivor of the Steamship "City of Boston" Lost at Sea in 1870*. Philadelphia, 1880.

DEISS, JOSEPH J., *The Roman Years of Margaret Fuller*. New York, 1970.

DERBY, ELIAS HASKET, *Two Months Abroad*. Boston, 1844.

DEW, WALTER, *I Caught Crippen*. London and Glasgow, 1938.

DIGGLE, E. G., *The Romance of a Modern Liner*. London, n.d.

DOLLAR, ROBERT, *One Hundred Thirty Years of Steam Navigation*. San Francisco, 1931.

DREISER, THEODORE, *A Traveller at Forty*. New York, 1913.

DUGAN, JAMES, *The Great Iron Ship*. London, 1953.

DUNLAP, ORRIN E., *Marconi, The Man and His Wireless*. New York, 1937.

DUNN, LAURENCE, *North Atlantic Liners 1899–1913*. London, 1961.

———— *Passenger Liners*. London, 1961.

DUPEE, F. W., and STADE, GEORGE, eds., *Selected Letters of E. E. Cummings*. New York, 1969.

EDDY, DANIEL C., *Europa*. Boston, 1860.

EMERSON, RALPH WALDO, *English Traits*. Boston, 1856.

ESKEW, GARNETT L., *The Pageant of the Packets*. New York, 1929.

FARR, GRAHAME, *The Steamship Great Britain*. Bristol, 1970.

———— *The Steamship Great Western*. Bristol, 1963.

FEARON, HENRY BRADSHAW, *Narrative of a Journey*. London, 1818.

FLETCHER, R. A., *Steamships and Their Story*. London, 1910.

———— *Travelling Palaces*. London, 1913.

FORWOOD, WILLIAM B., *Reminiscences of a Liverpool Shipowner*. Liverpool, 1920.

FOWLER, GENE, *Beau James*. New York, 1949.

FRERE-COOK, GERVIS, ed., *The Decorative Arts of the Mariner*. Boston, 1966.

FROST, WESLEY, *German Submarine Warfare*. New York, 1918.

FULLER, HECTOR, *Abroad with Mayor Walker*. New York, 1928.

GIBBS, C. R. VERNON, *Passenger Liners of the Western Ocean*. London, 1952.

GRACIE, COL. ARCHIBALD, *The Truth About the Titanic*. New York, 1913.

GRANT, KAY, *Samuel Cunard*. London and New York, 1967.

GREELEY, HORACE, *Glances at Europe*. New York, 1851.

GREENWOOD, GRACE, *Haps and Mishaps of a Tour in Europe*. Boston, 1854.

GUILLOT, E. C., *The Great Migration*. New York, 1937.

HAESSLER, C. H., *Across the Atlantic*. Philadelphia, 1868.

HALIBURTON, THOMAS C., *The Letter-Bag of the Great Western*. London, 1840.

———— *Life in a Steamer*. London, 1858.

HALL, BASIL, *Travels in North America*. Edinburgh, 1829.

HANCOCK, H. E., *Wireless at Sea*. Chelmsford, England, 1950.

HANDLIN, OSCAR, *The Uprooted*. New York, 1951.

HARDING, ADDIE CLARK, *America Rides the Liners*. New York, 1956.

HATCH, ALDEN, *American Express*. New York, 1950.

HAWKES, ELLISON, *The Romance of the Merchant Ship*. New York, 1932.

HAYES, BERTRAM, *Hull Down*. New York, 1925.

HILL, CHARLES S., *History of American Shipping*. New York, 1883.

HILL, RALPH NADING, *Sidewheeler Saga*. New York, 1953.

HODDER, EDWIN, *Life of Sir George Burns*. London, 1890.

HODGINS, ERIC, *Ocean Express*. New York, 1932.

HOEHLING, A. A. and MARY, *The Last Voyage of the Lusitania*. New York, 1956.

HOLMES, GEORGE C. V., *Ancient and Modern Ships*. London, 1910.

HOLT, EMILY, *Encyclopedia of Etiquette*. New York, 1901.

HONE, PHILIP, *The Diary of Philip Hone 1828–1851*. New York, 1889.

HOPKINS, ALBERT A., ed., *The Scientific American Handbook of Travel*. New York, 1911.

HOPPIN, AUGUSTUS, *Crossing the Atlantic*. Boston, 1872.

HOVEY, CARL, *The Life Story of Pierpont Morgan*. New York, 1911.

HOYT, EDWIN P., JR., *The House of Morgan*. New York, 1966.

HUBBARD, ELBERT, *Hollyhocks and Goldenglow*. East Aurora, New York, 1912.

HULDERMANN, BERNHARD, *Albert Ballin*. London, 1922.

HURD, A. S., *Merchant Fleet at War*. London, 1920.

ISHERWOOD, J. H., *Steamers of the Past*. Liverpool, 1966.

JACKSON, C. G., *The Story of the Liner*. London, 1931.

JAMES, HENRY, *A Small Boy and Others*. New York, 1913.

———— *The Art of Travel*, Zabel, Morton Dauwen, ed. New York, 1958.

JOHNSON, EDGAR, *Charles Dickens, His Tragedy and Triumph*. New York, 1952.

JONES, CLEMENT, *Pioneer Ship Owners*. Liverpool, 1934.

JORDAN, HUMFREY, *Mauretania*. London, 1936.

JULIAN, PHILIPPE, *Oscar Wilde*. London, 1969.

KAPLAN, JUSTIN, *Mr. Clemens and Mark Twain*. New York, 1966.

KAVALER, LUCY, *The Astors*. New York, 1966.

KELLEY, J. D. JERROLD, *The Ship's Company and Other Sea People*. New York, 1897.

KEMBLE, FRANCES ANN, *Record of a Girlhood*. London, 1878.

KENNEDY, JOHN, *History of Steam Navigation*. Liverpool, 1903.

KNOX, THOMAS W., *The Life of Robert Fulton*. New York, 1886.

LAING, ALEXANDER, *Clipper Ship Men*. New York, 1944.

LAING, SAMUEL, *Observations on the Social and Political States of the European People*. New York, 1850.

LANE, WHEATON J., *Commodore Vanderbilt: an Epic of the Steam Age*. New York, 1942.

LAURIAT, CHARLES E., *The Lusitania's Last Voyage*. Boston, 1915.

LEE, CHARLES E., *The Blue Riband*. London, 1930.

LE FLEMING, H. M., *Cunard White Star Liners of the 1930's*. London, n.d.

LEHMANN, ERNEST A., *Zeppelin*. London and New York, 1937.

LEWIS, LLOYD, and SMITH, HENRY JUSTIN, *Oscar Wilde Discovers America*. New York, 1936.

LEWIS, SINCLAIR, *Dodsworth*. New York, 1929.

LIGHTOLLER, C. H., *Titanic and Other Ships*. London, 1935.

LINDSAY, W. S., *A History of Merchant Shipping*. London, 1876.

LLOYD, CHRISTOPHER, *Lord Cochrane*. London, 1947.

LOCKHART, J. G., *The Sea, Our Heritage*. London, 1940.

LONGFORD, ELIZABETH, *Queen Victoria: Born to Succeed*. New York, 1965.

LORD, WALTER, *A Night to Remember*. London, 1956.

LUBBOCK, BASIL, *The Western Ocean Packets*. Glasgow, 1925.

LYELL, CHARLES, *A Second Visit to North America*. London, 1855.

MacDONALD, A. FRASER, *Our Ocean Railways*. London, 1893.

MACKINNON, CAPTAIN R. N., *Atlantic and Transatlantic*. New York, 1852.

MAGINNIS, A. J., *The Atlantic Ferry*. London, 1892.

MARCUS, GEOFFREY, *The Maiden Voyage*. London, 1969.

MARIE, JEAN, and HAFFNER, LEON, *L'Art et La Mer*. Paris, 1952.

MARTINEAU, HARRIET, *Retrospect of Western Travel*. London, 1838.

MARVIN, W. L., *The American Merchant Marine*. New York, 1910.

MAURY, SARAH MYTTON, *An Englishwoman in America*. Liverpool, 1848.

McKAY, R. C., *Some Famous Sailing Ships and Their Builder, Donald McKay*. New York, 1928.

McNEIL, S. G. S., *In Great Waters*. London, 1932.

MENCKEN, AUGUST, ed., *First Class Passenger*. New York, 1938.

MILES, PLINY, *Ocean Steam Navigation*. Boston, 1957.

———— *Steam Communication between Europe and America via Galway*. Boston, 1859.

MILLAR, W. J., *The Clyde*. London, 1888.

MORFORD, HENRY, *Over-Sea, or England, France and Scotland as Seen by a Live American*. New York, 1867.

MORISON, SAMUEL E., *The Maritime History of Massachusetts, 1783–1860*. Boston, 1921.

———— *"Old Bruin."* Boston, 1967.

MORRIS, JAMES, *Pax Britannica*. London, 1968.

MOSCOW, ALVIN, *Collision Course*. New York, 1959.

NAPIER, CHARLES, *An Account of the War in Portugal Between Don Pedro and Don Miguel*. London, 1836.

NAPIER, JAMES, *Life of Robert Napier*. Edinburgh and London, 1904.

NEVINS, ALLAN, *Sail On: The story of the American Merchant Marine*. New York, 1946.

NEWELL, GORDON, *Ocean Liners of the 20th Century*. Seattle, 1963.

NOBLE, CELIA B., *The Brunels, Father and Son*. London, 1938.

OGILVIE, F. W., *The Tourist Movement*. London, 1933.

OLDHAM, WILTON J., *The Ismay Line*. Liverpool, 1961.

O'LEARY, JOHN G., ed., *Struggles and Triumphs of P. T. Barnum*. London, 1967.

OUTHWAITE, LEONARD, *The Atlantic*. New York, 1957.

PADFIELD, PETER, *An Agony of Collisions*. London, 1966.

—— *The Titanic and the Californian*. London, 1965.

PARRY, E., *Memoir of Rear Admiral W. E. Parry*. London, 1857.

PEABODY, MARIAN LAWRENCE, *To Be Young Was Very Heaven*. Boston, 1967.

POND, E. LEROY, *Junius Smith*. New York, 1927.

POST, EMILY, *Etiquette*. New York, 1922.

POTTER, NEIL and FROST, JACK, *The Elizabeth*. London, 1965.

—— *The Mary*. London, 1961.

POWER, TYRONE, *Impressions of America*. Philadelphia, 1836.

PRAY, ISAAC CLARK, *Memoirs of James Gordon Bennett and His Times*. New York, 1855.

PREBLE, G. H., *History of Steam Navigation*. Philadelphia, 1882.

PUDNEY, JOHN, *The Thomas Cook Story*. London, 1953.

RADDALL, THOMAS H., *Halifax, Warden of the North*. New York, 1965.

RAINEY, THOMAS, *Ocean Steam Navigation and the Ocean Post*. New York, 1857.

REGAN, JOHN, *The Emigrants' Guide*. Edinburgh, n.d.

RIESENBERG, FELIX, *Early Steamships*. London, 1933.

—— *Living Again*. New York, 1937.

—— *Vignettes of the Sea*. New York, 1926.

ROLT, L. T. C., *Isambard Kingdom Brunel*. London, 1957.

ROY, JAMES, A. *Joseph Howe: A Study in Achievement and Frustration*. Toronto, 1935.

RUTHERFORD, WILFRID, *The Man Who Built the "Mauretania."* London, n.d.

SATTERLEE, HERBERT L., *J. Pierpont Morgan*. New York, 1939.

SAWTELL, CLEMENT CLEVELAND, *Captain Nash De Cost and the Liverpool Packets*. Mystic, Conn., 1955.

SIGOURNEY, L. H., *Pleasant Memories of Pleasant Lands*. Boston, 1842.

SILLIMAN, BENJAMIN, *A Visit to Europe in 1851*. New York, 1853.

SMITH, A. D. HOWDEN, *Commodore Vanderbilt*. New York, 1927.

SMITH, J. JAY, *A Summer's Jaunt Across the Water*. Philadelphia, 1846.

SMITH, JUNIUS, *Letters upon Atlantic Navigation*. London, 1841.

SMITH, RUSSELL J., *The Ocean Carrier*. New York, 1908.

SMITH, T. T. VERNON, *The Past, Present and Future of Atlantic Ocean Steam Navigation*. Fredericton, New Brunswick, 1857.

SNYDER, LOUIS L., *The Military History of the Lusitania*. New York, 1965.

SPEARS, JOHN R., *The Story of the American Merchant Marine*. New York, 1915.

SPEDDING, CHARLES T., *Reminiscences of Trans-Atlantic Travellers*. London, 1926.

SPRATT, H. P., *Outline History of Transatlantic Paddle Steamers*. Glasgow, 1951.

STAFF, FRANK, *The Transatlantic Mail*. New York, 1937.

STANFORD, DON, *Ile de France*. London, 1960.

STANTON, SAMUEL W., *American Steam Vessels*. New York, 1895.

STEVENSON, ROBERT LOUIS, *The Amateur Immigrant*. Chicago, 1895.

STOKES, FREDERICK A., *College Tramps*. New York, 1880.

STOKES, I. N. PHELPS, *The Iconography of Manhattan Island 1498–1909*. New York, 1909.

STREET, JULIAN, *Ship-Bored*. New York, 1914.

STUART, CHARLES B., *The Naval and Mail Steamers of the United States*. New York, 1853.

SWANBERG, W. A., *Dreiser*. New York, 1965.

TALBOT, FREDERICK A., *Steamship Conquest of the World*. London, 1912.

THAYER, JOHN B., *The Sinking of the S.S. Titanic*. Philadelphia, 1940.

TOLAND, JOHN, *Ships in the Sky*. New York, 1957.

TOWN, ITHIEL, *Navigating the Atlantic Ocean*. New York, 1838.

TOWNSHEND, CHARLES HERVEY, *Self-Portrait of an American Packet Ship Sailor*. Mystic, Conn., 1940.

TRAFTON, ADELINE, *An American Girl Abroad*. Boston, 1872.

TULLY, JIM, *Beggars Abroad*. New York, 1930.

TUTE, WARREN, *Atlantic Conquest*. Boston, 1962.

TWAIN, MARK, *The Innocents Abroad*. Hartford, 1871.

TYLER, DAVID B., *Steam Conquers the Atlantic*. New York, 1939.

VERCEL, ROGER, ed., *Histoire de la Compagnie Générale Transatlantique*. Paris, 1955.

VERNE, JULES, *A Floating City and the Blockade Runners*. New York, 1874.

VILLIERS, ALAN, *Wild Ocean*. New York, 1957.

WADE, MASON, *Margaret Fuller*. New York, 1940.

WALKER, JAMES, *The First Trans-Atlantic Steamer*. London, 1898.

WATKINS, J. ELFRETH, *The Log of the "Savannah."* Washington, 1890.

WHALL, W. B., *The Romance of Navigation*. London, 1926.

WHIDDEN, JOHN D., *Old Sailing Ship Days*. London, 1925.

WHITE, RUTH, *Yankee from Sweden*. New York, 1960.

WILKES, GEORGE, *Europe in a Hurry*. New York, 1852.

WILLIS, N. P., *Letters from Under a Bridge*. New York, 1840.

WILLITTS, A. A., *Journal of the First Voyage of the Steamship "Atlantic."* Philadelphia, 1871.

WINOCOUR, JACK, ed., *The Story of the Titanic*. New York, 1960.

WINSOR, JUSTIN, ed., *Memorial History of Boston*. Boston, 1881.

WITMER, THEODORE B., *Wild Oats, Sown Abroad*. Philadelphia, 1853.

WOODHAM–SMITH, CECIL, *The Great Hunger*. London, 1962.

WOON, BASIL, *The Frantic Atlantic*. New York, 1927.

WRIGHT, C. P., *The Origins and Early Years of the Transatlantic Packet Ships of New York 1817–1835*, doctoral dissertation. Harvard, 1932.

WYLLIE, W. L., and WREN, R. F., *Sea Fights of the Great War*. London, 1918.

YOUNG, FILSON, ed., *The Trial of Hawley Harvey Crippen*. Edinburgh and London, 1920.

❧ INDEX ❧

THIS BOOK WAS SET IN

ATF BASKERVILLE AND ELECTRA TYPES

PRINTED AND BOUND BY

THE HADDON CRAFTSMEN.

TYPOGRAPHY AND DESIGN ARE BY

LARRY KAMP AND BARBARA COHEN